FIX-IT
and
FORGET-IT
COOKBOOK

FIX-IT and FORGET-IT COOKBOOK

Feasting with your slow cooker

Dawn J. Ranck
Phyllis Pellman Good

Good Books
Intercourse, PA 17534
800/762-7171 • www.goodbks.com

Cover design and illustrations by Cheryl Benner
Design by Dawn J. Ranck

Fix-It and Forget-It Cookbook: Feasting with Your Slow Cooker
Copyright © 2000 by Good Books, Intercourse, PA 17534
International Standard Book Number: 1-56148-317-6
Library of Congress Catalog Card Number: 00-052110

Library of Congress Cataloging-in-Publication Data
Ranck, Dawn J.
    Fix-it and forget-it cookbook : feasting with your slow
        cooker / Dawn J. Ranck, Phyllis Pellman Good.
    p.cm.
    Includes index.
    ISBN 1-56148-317-6
    1. Electric cookery, Slow. I. Good, Phyllis Pellman II. Title.
TX827.R35 2000
641.5'884--dc21   00-052110

Table of Contents

About This Cookbook

Slow Cookers have long ago proven to be the efficient friend of those cooks who are gone all day, but want to offer substantial home-cooked food to their households.

Slow Cookers have aged, but they haven't faded. Instead, they've shown themselves to be first-rate adaptable appliances. They handle dried beans famously well, pleasing the growing numbers of vegetarians. They do their job whatever their size—1-quart, 3-quart, 6-quart, or in between. Little ones work well for singles or doubles—or cook the vegetables while the beef stew burbles away in a bigger Cooker, sharing the counter-space.

And Slow Cookers are mobile tools. You can prepare a dish one evening, store the filled "lift-out" vessel in the frig overnight, and then place it into its electric holder in the morning as you do your dash to the door. Or you can tote the whole works to a buffet or carry-in meal, doing no damage to the quality of its contents.

Slow Cookers prefer cheap cuts of meat. Tell that to your favorite graduate student, or newly independent young adult, or to the parents of a growing brood.

The recipes in this collection are tried and true favorites from heavy-duty Cooker-users. We've weeded out a lot of duplicates and still have 800 plus for you to try. There's tempting variety among the recipes, and many that differ only by a tantalizing ingredient or two.

What's more, you'll find helpful Tips spread among the recipes—the kind of pointers that you usually learn only after a long acquaintance with a Slow Cooker. These Tips tell you how to maximize the usefulness of your Cooker, plus how to realize top flavor from the food you prepare in it.

May the *Fix-It and Forget-It Cookbook* help make your meal preparations less harried and your dinners more satisfying!

— *Dawn J. Ranck and Phyllis Pellman Good*

Appetizers, Snacks, and Spreads

Quick and Easy Nacho Dip

Kristina Shull
Timberville, VA

Makes 10-15 servings

1 lb. ground beef
dash of salt
dash of pepper
dash of onion powder
2 garlic cloves, minced,
    optional
2 16-oz. jars salsa (as hot
    or mild as you like)
15-oz. can refried beans
1½ cups sour cream
3 cups shredded cheddar
    cheese, divided
tortilla chips

1. Brown ground beef.
Drain. Add salt, pepper,
onion powder, and minced
garlic.
2. Combine beef, salsa,
beans, sour cream, and 2
cups cheese in slow cooker.

3. Cover. Heat on Low 2
hours. Just before serving
sprinkle with 1 cup cheese.
4. Serve with tortilla chips.

Southwest Hot Chip Dip

Annabelle Unternahrer
Shipshewana, IN

Makes 15-20 servings

1 lb. ground beef,
    browned, crumbled fine,
    and drained
2 15-oz. cans refried beans
2 10-oz. cans diced
    tomatoes and chilies
1 pkg. taco seasoning
1 lb. Velveeta cheese,
    cubed
tortilla chips

1. Combine ground beef,
beans, tomatoes, and taco seasoning in slow cooker.

2. Cover. Cook on Low 3-4
hours, or on High 1½ hours.
3. Add cheese. Stir occa-
sionally. Heat until cheese is
melted.
4. Serve with tortilla chips.

Note:
Serve as a main dish alongside a soup.

Hot Refried Bean Dip

Sharon Anders
Alburtis, PA

*Makes 1½ quarts,
or 12-20 servings*

15-oz. can refried beans,
  drained and mashed
½ lb. ground beef
3 Tbsp. bacon drippings
1 lb. American cheese,
  cubed
1-3 Tbsp. taco sauce
1 Tbsp. taco seasoning
dash garlic salt
tortilla chips

1. In skillet, brown beans
and ground beef in bacon
drippings. Pour into slow
cooker.
2. Stir in cheese, taco
sauce, taco seasoning, and
garlic salt.
3. Cover. Cook on High 45
minutes, or until cheese is
melted, stirring occasionally.
Turn to Low until ready to
serve, up to 6 hours.

Chili-Cheese Taco Dip

Kim Stoltzfus
New Holland, PA

Makes 10-12 servings

1 lb. ground beef
1 can chili, without beans
1 lb. mild Mexican
  Velveeta cheese, cubed
taco *or* tortilla chips

1. Brown beef, crumble
into small pieces, and drain.
2. Combine beef, chili, and
cheese in slow cooker.
3. Cover. Cook on Low 1-
1½ hours, or until cheese is
melted, stirring occasionally
to blend ingredients.
4. Serve warm with taco or
tortilla chips.

Hamburger Cheese Dip

Julia Lapp
New Holland, PA

Makes 8-10 servings

1 lb. ground beef, browned
  and crumbled into small
  pieces
½ tsp. salt
½ cup chopped green
  peppers
¾ cup chopped onion
8-oz. can tomato sauce
4-oz. can green chilies,
  chopped
1 Tbsp. Worcestershire
  sauce
1 Tbsp. brown sugar
1 lb. Velveeta cheese,
  cubed
1 Tbsp. paprika
red pepper to taste
tortilla chips

1. Combine beef, salt,
green peppers, onion, tomato
sauce, green chilies,
Worcestershire sauce, and
brown sugar in slow cooker.
2. Cover. Cook on Low 2-3
hours. During the last hour
stir in cheese, paprika, and
red pepper.
3. Serve with tortilla chips.

Variation:
Prepare recipe using only
⅓-½ lb. ground beef.

Leave the lid on while the slow cooker cooks. The steam
that condenses on the lid helps cook the food from the top.
Every time you take the lid off, the cooker loses steam. After
you put the lid back on, it takes one to 20 minutes to regain
the lost steam and temperature. That means it takes longer
for the food to cook.

Pam Hochstedler
Kalona, IA

Chili-Cheese Dip

Ruth Hofstetter
Versailles, Missouri
Paula King
Harrisonburg, VA

Makes 10 servings

1 lb. ground beef,
  browned, crumbled fine,
  and drained.
2 lbs. Velveeta cheese,
  cubed
10-oz. can tomatoes with
  chilies
1 tsp. Worcestershire sauce
½ tsp. chili powder
tortilla *or* corn chips

1. Combine all ingredients
except chips in slow cooker.
Mix well.
2. Cover. Cook on High 1
hour, stirring occasionally
until cheese is fully melted.
3. Serve immediately, or
turn to Low for serving up to
6 hours later.
4. Serve with tortilla or
corn chips.

Variation:
For a thicker dip, make a
smooth paste of 2 Tbsp. flour
mixed with 3 Tbsp. cold
water. Stir into hot dip.

Michelle's Taco Dip

Michelle Strite
Harrisonburg, VA

Makes 6-8 servings

1½ lbs. ground beef,
  browned, crumbled fine,
  and drained
1 pkg. taco seasoning mix
10-oz. jar salsa
1 lb. Velveeta cheese,
  cubed
¼ cup chopped onion
tortilla chips

1. Combine all ingredients
except chips in slow cooker.
2. Cover. Heat on Low for
2-3 hours.
3. Serve with tortilla chips.

Variation:
The recipe can be made
with half the amount of meat
called for, if you prefer.

Karen's Nacho Dip

Karen Stoltzfus
Alto, MI

Makes 10-12 servings

1 lb. ground beef
2 lbs. American cheese,
  cubed
16-oz. jar salsa (mild,
  medium, *or* hot,
  whichever you prefer)
1 Tbsp. Worcestershire
  sauce
tortilla *or* corn chips

1. Brown beef, crumble
into small pieces, and drain.
2. Combine beef, cheese,
salsa, and Worcestershire
sauce in slow cooker.
3. Cover. Cook on High 1
hour, stirring occasionally
until cheese is fully melted.
4. Serve immediately, or
turn to Low for serving up to
6 hours later.

Mexican Chip Dip Ole'

Joy Sutter
Iowa City, IA

Makes 10-12 servings

2 lbs. ground turkey
1 large onion, chopped
15-oz. can tomato sauce
4-oz. can green chilies, chopped
3-oz. can jalapeno peppers, chopped
2 lbs. Velveeta cheese, cubed
tortilla chips

1. Brown turkey and onion. Drain.
2. Add tomato sauce, chilies, jalapeno peppers, and cheese. Pour into slow cooker.
3. Cover. Cook on Low 4 hours, or High 2 hours.
4. Serve warm with tortilla chips.

Barbara's Chili Cheese Dip

Barbara Shie
Colorado Springs, CO

Makes 8-10 servings

1 lb. ground beef
1 lb. Velveeta cheese, cubed
8-oz. can green chilies and tomato sauce
2 tsp. Worcestershire sauce
1/2 tsp., or more, chili powder
1/4 cup salsa with jalapeno peppers
tortilla *or* corn chips

1. Brown ground beef, crumble fine, and drain.
2. Combine all ingredients except chips in slow cooker. Stir well.
3. Cover. Cook on High 1 hour, stirring until cheese is melted. Serve immediately, or turn on Low for serving up to 6 hours later.
4. Serve with tortilla or corn chips.

Note:
Serve over rice, noodles, or baked potatoes as a main dish, making 4-5 servings.

Pizza Fondue

Lisa Warren
Parkesburg, PA

Makes 8-12 servings

1 lb. ground beef
2 cans pizza sauce with cheese
8 oz. grated cheddar cheese
8 oz. grated mozzarella cheese
1 tsp. dried oregano
1/2 tsp. fennel seed, optional
1 Tbsp. cornstarch
tortilla chips

1. Brown beef, crumble fine, and drain.
2. Combine all ingredients except tortilla chips in slow cooker.
3. Cover. Heat on Low 2-3 hours.
4. Serve with tortilla chips.

Super Bowl Super Dip

Colleen Heatwole
Burton, MI

*Makes 4-5 cups,
or approximately 12 servings*

1 lb. ground beef
1 lb. Mexican Velveeta
cheese spread
8-oz. salsa (mild, medium,
or hot)
tortilla chips

1. Brown ground beef,
crumble into fine pieces, and
drain. Place in slow cooker.
Add cheese.
2. Cover. Cook on High for
45 minutes, stirring occasionally until cheese melts.
3. Add salsa. Reduce heat
to Low and cook until heated
through.
4. Serve warm with tortilla
chips.

Hamburger Hot Dip

Janice Martins
Fairbank, IA

Makes 6 cups dip

1 lb. ground beef
1 medium onion, chopped
fine
1/2 tsp. salt
1/4 tsp. pepper
8-oz. jar salsa
14-oz. can nacho cheese
soup
8 slices Velveeta cheese
nacho chips

1. Brown ground beef and
onions in saucepan. Drain.
Season with salt and pepper.
2. Combine all ingredients
in slow cooker.
3. Cover. Cook on Low 4
hours. Stir occasionally.
4. Serve with nacho chips.

Chili Con Queso Cheese Dip

Melanie Thrower
McPherson, KS

Makes 8 servings

1 lb. ground beef
1/2 cup chopped onion
1 cup Velveeta cheese,
cubed
10-oz. can diced tomatoes
and green chilies
1 can evaporated milk
2 Tbsp. chili powder
tortilla chips

1. Brown ground beef and
onion. Crumble beef into fine
pieces. Drain.
2. Combine all ingredients
except tortilla chips in slow
cookers.
3. Cover. Heat on Low 1-2
hours, until cheese is melted.
4. Serve with tortilla chips.

Good 'n' Hot Dip

Joyce B. Suiter
Garysburg, NC

Makes 30-50 servings

1 lb. ground beef
1 lb. bulk sausage
10¾-oz. can cream of
 chicken soup
10¾-oz. can cream of
 celery soup
24-oz. jar salsa (use hot for
 some zing)
1 lb. Velveeta cheese,
 cubed
chips

1. Brown beef and
sausage, crumbling into small
pieces. Drain.
2. Combine meat, soups,
salsa, and cheese in slow
cooker.
3. Cover. Cook on High 1
hour. Stir. Cook on Low until
ready to serve.
4. Serve with chips.

Cheese Queso Dip

Janie Steele
Moore, OK

Makes about 2 quarts dip

2-lbs. Velveeta cheese,
 cubed
10-oz. can diced tomatoes
 and chilies
1 lb. bulk sausage,
 browned, crumbled fine,
 and drained
tortilla chips

1. Combine cheese, toma-
toes, and sausage in slow
cooker.
2. Cover. Heat on Low 1-2
hours.
3. Serve with tortilla chips.

Hot Cheese and Bacon Dip

Lee Ann Hazlett
Freeport, IL

Makes 6-8 servings

16 slices bacon, diced
2 8-oz. pkgs. cream cheese,
 cubed and softened
4 cups shredded mild
 cheddar cheese
1 cup half-and-half
2 tsp. Worcestershire sauce
1 tsp. dried minced onion
½ tsp. dry mustard
½ tsp. salt
2-3 drops Tabasco

1. Brown and drain bacon.
Set aside.
2. Mix remaining ingredi-
ents in slow cooker.
3. Cover. Cook on Low 1
hour, stirring occasionally
until cheese melts.
4. Stir in bacon.
5. Serve with fruit slices or
French bread slices. (Dip fruit
in lemon juice to prevent
browning.)

Championship Bean Dip

Renee Shirk
Mt. Joy, PA
Ada Miller
Sugarcreek, OH

Makes 4½ cups dip

15-oz. can refried beans
1 cup picante sauce
1 cup (4 oz.) shredded
    Monterey Jack cheese
1 cup (4 oz.) shredded
    cheddar cheese
3/4 cup sour cream
3-oz. pkg. cream cheese,
    softened
1 Tbsp. chili powder
1/4 tsp. ground cumin
tortilla chips
salsa

1. In a bowl, combine all ingredients except chips and salsa. Transfer to slow cooker.
2. Cover. Cook on High 2 hours, or until heated through, stirring once or twice.
3. Serve with tortilla chips and salsa.

Refried Bean Dip

Maryann Markano
Wilmington, DE

Makes 6 servings

20-oz. can refried beans
1 cup shredded cheddar
    cheese
1/2 cup chopped green
    onions
1/4 tsp. salt
2-4 Tbsp. bottled taco
    sauce (depending upon
    how spicy a dip you
    like)
tortilla chips

1. Combine beans, cheese, onions, salt, and taco sauce in slow cooker.
2. Cover. Cook on Low 2-2½ hours, or cook on High 30 minutes and then on Low 30 minutes.
3. Serve with tortilla chips.

Jeanne's Chile Con Queso

Jeanne Allen
Rye, CO

Makes 15-20 servings

40-oz. can chili without
    beans
2-lbs. Velveeta cheese,
    cubed
16-oz. jar picante sauce
    (mild, medium, *or* hot,
    whichever you prefer)
tortilla chips

1. Combine all ingredients except chips in slow cooker.
2. Cover. Cook on Low 1-2 hours, until cheese is melted. Stir.
3. Serve with tortilla chips.

A slow cooker is great for taking food to a potluck supper, even if you didn't prepare it in the cooker.
Irma H. Schoen
Windsor, CT

Maryann's Chili Cheese Dip

Maryann Westerberg
Rosamond, CA

Makes about 10 servings

2 lbs. Velveeta cheese,
  cubed
16-oz. can chili without
  beans
10-oz. can diced tomatoes
  with chilies, drained
10¾-oz. can cream of
  mushroom soup
tortilla chips

1. Combine cheese and chili in slow cooker. Heat on Low until cheese melts, stirring occasionally.
2. Add tomatoes and soup.
3. Cover. Cook on Low 2 hours. Stir before serving.
4. Serve with tortilla chips.

Tina's Cheese Dip

Tina Houk
Clinton, MO

Makes 12 servings

2 8-oz. pkgs. cream cheese,
  softened
3 15½-oz. cans chili
2 cups shredded cheddar
  or mozzarella cheese
tortilla chips

1. Spread cream cheese in bottom of slow cooker.
2. Spread chili on top of cream cheese.
3. Top with shredded cheese.
4. Cover. Cook on Low 1-1½ hours, until shredded cheese is melted. Stir.
5. Serve with tortilla chips.

Cheese Spread

Barbara Kuhns
Millersburg, OH

*Makes approximately
12-15 servings*

1 lb. white American
  cheese, cubed
1½ cups milk
crackers

1. Combine cheese and milk in slow cooker.
2. Cover. Cook on Low about 2 hours, or until cheese is melted, stirring occasionally.
3. Serve on crackers.

Mexicana Dip

Julia B. Boyd
Memphis, TN
Sue Williams
Gulfport, MS

Makes 10-12 servings

2 lbs. American, *or*
  Velveeta cheese, cubed
10-oz. can tomatoes with
  green chilies
tortilla chips, corn chips,
  or potato chips

1. Combine cheese and tomatoes in slow cooker.
2. Cover. Cook on Low 2-3 hours, stirring until cheese is melted. If mixture is too thick, add a little milk.
3. Serve as a dip, or pour over platter of favorite chips.

Variation:
Stir in ½ lb. browned bulk sausage, crumbled into small pieces.

Jane Steele
Moore, OK

Marilyn's Chili Con Queso

Marilyn Mowry
Irving, TX

Makes 2 cups dip

1 Tbsp. chopped green peppers
1 Tbsp. chopped celery
1 Tbsp. chopped onions
2 Tbsp. diced tomatoes
2 tsp. chopped jalapeno pepper
1/2 cup water
3/4 cup heavy cream
8 oz. Velveeta cheese, cubed
2 oz. cheddar cheese, shredded
tortilla chips

1. Place first 5 ingredients in slow cooker. Add water.
2. Cover. Cook on High 1 hour, or until vegetables are tender.
3. Stir in cream and cheeses.
4. Reduce heat to Low. Cook until cheese is melted. Serve immediately, or keep warm on Low for hours.
5. Serve with tortilla chips.

Chili Con Queso Dip

Jenny R. Unternahrer
Wayland, IA

Makes approximately 12 servings

1 lb. Velveeta cheese, cubed
1 cup salsa (mild, medium, *or* hot, whichever you prefer)
1 cup sour cream
tortilla chips

1. Combine cheese, salsa, and sour cream in slow cooker.
2. Cover. Heat on Low, stirring occasionally until cheese melts and dip is well blended, about 1-1½ hours.
3. Serve with tortilla chips.

Short-Cut Fondue Dip

Jean Butzer
Batavia, NY

Makes 8-10 servings

2 10¾-oz. cans condensed cheese soup
2 cups grated sharp cheddar cheese
1 Tbsp. Worcestershire sauce
1 tsp. lemon juice
2 Tbsp. dried chopped chives
celery sticks
cauliflower florets
corn chips

1. Combine soup, cheese, Worcestershire sauce, lemon juice, and chives in slow cooker.
2. Cover. Heat on Low 2-2½ hours. Stir until smooth and well blended.
3. Serve warm dip with celery sticks, cauliflower, and corn chips.

Chili Verde con Queso Dip

Bonita Ensenberger
Albuquerque, NM

Makes 1 quart (8-10 servings)

2 10¾-oz. cans cheddar
  cheese soup
7-oz. can chopped green
  chilies
1 garlic clove, minced
½ tsp. dried cilantro leaves
½ tsp. ground cumin
corn chips

1. Mix together all ingredients except corn chips in slow cooker.
2. Cover. Cook on Low 1-1½ hours. Stir well. Cook an additional 1½ hours.
3. Serve with corn chips.

Variation:
Make this a main dish by serving over baked potatoes.

Lilli's Nacho Dip

Lilli Peters
Dodge City, KS

Makes 10 servings

3-lbs. Velveeta cheese,
  cubed
10¾-oz. can cream of
  chicken soup
2 4-oz. cans chopped green
  chilies and juice
tortilla chips

1. Place cheese in slow cooker. Cook on Low until cheese melts, stirring occasionally.
2. Add soup and chilies. Stir. Heat on Low 1 hour.
3. Pour over tortilla chips just before serving.

Note:
If you want to speed up the process, melt the cheese in the microwave. Heat on High for 1½ minutes, stir, and continue heating at 1½-minute intervals as long as needed.

Variations:
1. Instead of using 2 4-oz. cans chilies, use 10-oz. can tomatoes and chilies.
2. For a heartier dip, add ½-1 lb. bulk sausage, browned, crumbled into small pieces, and drained.

Reuben Spread

Clarice Williams
Fairbank, IA
Julie McKenzie
Punxsutawney, PA

Makes 5 cups spread

½ lb. corned beef,
  shredded *or* chopped
16-oz. can sauerkraut, well
  drained
1-2 cups shredded Swiss
  cheese
1-2 cups shredded cheddar
  cheese
1 cup mayonnaise
snack rye bread
Thousand Island dressing,
  optional

1. Combine all ingredients except bread and Thousnd Island dressing in slow cooker. Mix well.
2. Cover. Cook on High 1-2 hours until heated through, stirring occasionally.
3. Turn to Low and keep warm in cooker while serving. Put spread on bread slices. Top individual servings with Thousand Island dressing, if desired.

Note:
Low-fat cheese and mayonnaise are not recommended for this spread.

Variation:
Use dried beef instead of corned beef.

Cheesy New Orleans Shrimp Dip

Kelly Evenson
Pittsboro, NC

Makes 3-4 cups dip

1 slice bacon
3 medium onions, chopped
1 garlic clove, minced
4 jumbo shrimp, peeled and deveined
1 medium tomato, peeled and chopped
3 cups Monterey Jack cheese, shredded
4 drops Tabasco sauce
1/8 tsp. cayenne pepper
dash of black pepper
chips

1. Cook bacon until crisp. Drain on paper towel. Crumble.
2. Saute onion and garlic in bacon drippings. Drain on paper towel.
3. Coarsely chop shrimp.
4. Combine all ingredients except chips in slow cooker.
5. Cover. Cook on Low 1 hour, or until cheese is melted. Thin with milk if too thick. Serve with chips.

Broccoli Cheese Dip

Carla Koslowsky
Hillsboro, KS

Makes 6 cups dip

1 cup chopped celery
1/2 cup chopped onion
10-oz. pkg. frozen chopped broccoli, cooked
1 cup cooked rice
10 3/4-oz. can cream of mushroom soup
16-oz. jar cheese spread, *or* 15 slices American cheese, melted and mixed with 2/3 cup milk
snack breads or crackers

1. Combine all ingredients in slow cooker.
2. Cover. Heat on Low 2 hours.
3. Serve with snack breads or crackers.

Roasted Pepper and Artichoke Spread

Sherril Bieberly
Salina, KS

Makes 3 cups, or about 12 servings

1 cup grated Parmesan cheese
1/2 cup mayonnaise
8-oz. pkg. cream cheese, softened
1 garlic clove, minced
14-oz. can artichoke hearts, drained and chopped finely
1/3 cup finely chopped roasted red bell peppers (from 7 1/4-oz. jar)
crackers, cut-up fresh vegetables, *or* snack-bread slices

1. Combine Parmesan cheese, mayonnaise, cream cheese, and garlic in food processor. Process until smooth. Place mixture in slow cooker.
2. Add artichoke hearts and red bell pepper. Stir well.
3. Cover. Cook on Low 1 hour. Stir again.
4. Use as spread for crackers, cut-up fresh vegetables, or snack-bread slices.

The great thing about using a slow cooker in hot weather is that it doesn't heat up your kitchen like an oven does.
Carol Peachey
Lancaster, PA

Baked Brie with Cranberry Chutney

Amymarlene Jensen
Fountain, CO

Makes 8-10 servings

1 cup fresh, *or* dried, cranberries
1/2 cup brown sugar
1/3 cup cider vinegar
2 Tbsp. water, *or* orange juice
2 tsp. minced crystallized ginger
1/4 tsp. cinnamon
1/8 tsp. ground cloves
oil
8-oz. round of Brie cheese
1 Tbsp. sliced almonds, toasted
crackers

1. Mix together cranberries, brown sugar, vinegar, water or juice, ginger, cinnamon, and cloves in slow cooker.
2. Cover. Cook on Low 4 hours. Stir once near the end to see if it is thickening. If not, remove top, turn heat to High and cook 30 minutes without lid.
3. Put cranberry chutney in covered container and chill for up to 2 weeks. When ready to serve, bring to room temperature.
4. Brush ovenproof plate with vegetable oil, place unpeeled Brie on plate, and bake uncovered at 350° for 9 minutes, until cheese is soft and partially melted. Remove from oven.

5. Top with at least half the chutney and garnish with almonds. Serve with crackers.

Artichokes

Susan Yoder Graber
Eureka, IL

Makes 4 servings

4 artichokes
1 tsp. salt
2 Tbsp. lemon juice
melted butter

1. Wash and trim artichokes by cutting off the stems flush with the bottoms of the artichokes and by cutting 3/4-1 inch off the tops. Stand upright in slow cooker.
2. Mix together salt and lemon juice and pour over artichokes. Pour in water to cover 3/4 of artichokes.
3. Cover. Cook on Low 8-10 hours, or High 2-4 hours.
4. Serve with melted butter. Pull off individual leaves and dip bottom of each into butter. Using your teeth, strip the individual leaf of the meaty portion at the bottom of each leaf.

Curried Almonds

Barbara Aston
Ashdown, AR

Makes 4 cups nuts

2 Tbsp. melted butter
1 Tbsp. curry powder
1/2 tsp. seasoned salt
1 lb. blanched almonds

1. Combine butter with curry powder and seasoned salt.
2. Pour over almonds in slow cooker. Mix to coat well.
3. Cover. Cook on Low 2-3 hours. Turn to High. Uncover cooker and cook 1-1 1/2 hours.
4. Serve hot or cold.

Chili Nuts

Barbara Aston
Ashdown, AR

Makes 5 cups nuts

1/4 cup melted butter
2 12-oz. cans cocktail peanuts
1 5/8-oz. pkg. chili seasoning mix

1. Pour butter over nuts in slow cooker. Sprinkle in dry chili mix. Toss together.
2. Cover. Heat on Low 2-2 1/2 hours. Turn to High. Remove lid and cook 10-15 minutes.
3. Serve warm or cool.

All-American Snack

Doris M. Coyle-Zipp
South Ozone Park, NY
Melissa Raber, Millersburg, OH
Ada Miller, Sugarcreek, OH
Nanci Keatley, Salem, OR

Makes 3 quarts snack mix

3 cups thin pretzel sticks
4 cups Wheat Chex
4 cups Cheerios
12-oz. can salted peanuts
1/4 cup melted butter, *or* margarine
1 tsp. garlic powder
1 tsp. celery salt
1/2 tsp. seasoned salt
2 Tbsp. grated Parmesan cheese

1. Combine pretzels, cereal, and peanuts in large bowl.
2. Melt butter. Stir in garlic powder, celery salt, seasoned salt, and Parmesan cheese. Pour over pretzels and cereal. Toss until well mixed.
3. Pour into large slow cooker. Cover. Cook on Low 2½ hours, stirring every 30 minutes. Remove lid and cook another 30 minutes on Low.
4. Serve warm or at room temperature. Store in tightly covered container.

Variations:
1. Use 3 cups Wheat Chex (instead of 4 cups) and 3 cups Cheerios (instead of 4 cups). Add 3 cups Corn Chex.
Marcia S. Myer
Manheim, PA

2. Alter the amounts of pretzels, cereal, and peanuts to reflect your preferences.

Hot Caramel Dip

Marilyn Yoder
Archbold, OH

Makes about 3 cups dip

1/2 cup butter
1/2 cup light corn syrup
1 cup brown sugar
1 can sweetened condensed milk
apple slices

1. Mix together all ingredients except apples in saucepan. Bring to boil.
2. Pour into crockpot. Set on Low.
3. Dip fresh apple slices into hot caramel.

Variation:
Add 1/2 cup peanut butter to dip.

Rhonda's Apple Butter

Rhonda Burgoon
Collingswood, NJ

Makes about 2 pints apple butter

4 lbs. apples
2 tsp. cinnamon
1/2 tsp. ground cloves

1. Peel, core, and slice apples. Place in slow cooker.
2. Cover. Cook on High 2-3 hours. Reduce to Low and cook 8 hours. Apples should be a rich brown and be cooked down by half.
3. Stir in spices. Cook on High 2-3 hours with lid off. Stir until smooth.
4. Pour into freezer containers and freeze, or into sterilized jars and seal.

Shirley's Apple Butter

Shirley Sears
Tiskilwa, IL

Makes 6-10 pints apple butter

4 qts. finely chopped tart
  apples
2¾ cups sugar
2¾ tsp. cinnamon
¼ tsp. ground cloves
⅛ tsp. salt

1. Pour apples into slow cooker.
2. Combine remaining ingredients. Drizzle over apples.
3. Cover. Cook on High 3 hours, stirring well with a large spoon every hour. Reduce heat to Low and cook 10-12 hours, until butter becomes thick and dark in color. Stir occasionally with strong wire whisk for smooth butter.
4. Freeze or pour into sterilized jars and seal.

Kelly's Apple Butter

Kelly Evenson
Pittsboro, NC

Makes 4-5 pints apple butter

4 lbs. cooking apples
2 cups cider
3 cups sugar
2 tsp. cinnamon
1 tsp. ground cloves,
  optional
⅛ tsp. allspice

1. Stem, core, and quarter apples. Do not peel.
2. Combine apples and cider in large slow cooker.
3. Cover. Cook on Low 10 hours.
4. Stir in sugar and spices. Continue cooking 1 hour. Remove from heat and cool thoroughly. Blend to mix in skins.
5. Freeze in pint containers, or pour into hot sterilized jars and seal.

Charlotte's Apple Butter

Charlotte Fry
St. Charles, MO

Makes 5 pints apple butter

3 quarts Jonathan, *or*
  Winesap, apples
2 cups apple cider
2½ cups sugar
1 tsp. star anise, optional
2 Tbsp. lemon juice
2 sticks cinnamon

1. Peel, core, and chop apples. Combine with apple cider in large slow cooker.
2. Cover. Cook on Low 10-12 hours.
3. Stir in sugar, star anise, lemon juice, and stick cinnamon.
4. Cover. Cook on High 2 hours. Stir. Remove lid and cook on High 2-4 hours more, until thickened.
5. Pour into sterilized jars and seal.

Dolores' Apple Butter

Dolores Metzler
Mechanicsburg, PA

Makes 3 quarts apple butter

3 quarts unsweetened
    applesauce
3 cups sugar (or sweeten to
    taste)
2 tsp. cinnamon
1 tsp., *or* less, ground
    cloves

1. Combine all ingredients
in large slow cooker.
2. Cover. Cook on High 8-
10 hours. Remove lid during
last 4 hours. Stir occasionally.

Ann's Apple Butter

Ann Bender
Ft. Defiance, VA

Makes 2 pints apple butter

7 cups unsweetened
    applesauce
2-3 cups sugar, depending
    upon the sweetness of
    the applesauce and your
    own preference
2 tsp. cinnamon
1 tsp. ground nutmeg
1/4 tsp. allspice

1. Combine all ingredients in
slow cooker.
2. Put a layer of paper
towels under lid to prevent
condensation from dripping
into apple butter. Cook on
High 8-10 hours. Remove lid
during last hour. Stir occasionally.

Variation:
Use canned peaches,
pears, or apricots in place of
applesauce.

Anna's Slow-Cooker Apple Butter

Anna Musser
Manheim, PA

Makes 6 pints apple butter

1 cup cider, *or* apple juice
2 1/2 quarts unsweetened
    applesauce
2-3 cups sugar, depending
    upon the sweetness of
    the applesauce and your
    own preference
1 tsp. vinegar
1 tsp. cinnamon
1/2 tsp. allspice

1. Boil cider until 1/2 cup
remains.
2. Combine all ingredients
in slow cooker.
3. Cover. Cook on High 12-
16 hours, until apple butter
has cooked down to half the
original amount. Put in containers and freeze.

Marilyn's Slow-Cooker Apple Butter

Marilyn Yoder
Archbold, OH

Makes 80 servings

2 qts. unsweetened
    applesauce
2-4 cups sugar, depending
    upon sweetness of
    applesauce and your
    preference
1/2 tsp. ground cloves
2 Tbsp. lemon juice
1/4 heaping cup red hot
    candies

1. Combine all ingredients
in slow cooker.
2. Vent lid. Cook on Low
8-10 hours, stirring about
every hour. Apple butter
thickens as it cooks, so cook
longer to make it thicker.

Dianna's Apple Butter

Dianna Milhizer
Springfield, VA

Makes 6 pints apple butter

**1 bushel red tart apples
(Winesap, Rome, *or*
Macintosh)
1 quart "raw" honey *or*
least-processed honey
available
1/2 cup cinnamon sticks
1 Tbsp. salt**

1. Peel, core, and slice apples.
2. Combine all ingredients in large slow cooker. If apples don't fit, continue to add them as butter cooks down.
3. Cover. Cook on High 8 hours. Stir. Remove lid and let butter cook down on Low 8 additional hours. Consistency should be thick and creamy.
4. Freeze, or pack into sterilized jars and seal.

Lilli's Apple Butter

Lilli Peters
Dodge City, KS

Makes about 2 pints apple butter

**7 cups unsweetened
applesauce
2 cups apple cider
1 1/2 cups honey
1 tsp. cinnamon
1/2 tsp. ground cloves
1/2 tsp. allspice**

1. Combine all ingredients in slow cooker. Mix well with whisk.
2. Cook on Low 14-15 hours.

Peach or Apricot Butter

Charlotte Shaffer
East Earl, PA

Makes 6 8-oz. jars butter

**4 1-lb. 13-oz. cans peaches,
or apricots
2 3/4-3 cups sugar
2 tsp. cinnamon
1 tsp. ground cloves**

1. Drain fruit. Remove pits. Puree in blender. Pour into slow cooker.
2. Stir in remaining ingredients.

3. Cover. Cook on High 8-10 hours. Remove cover during last half of cooking. Stir occasionally.

Note:
Spread on bread, or use as a topping for ice cream or toasted pound cake.

Pear Butter

Dorothy Miller
Gulfport, MI

Makes 6 pints pear butter

**8 cups pear sauce
3 cups brown sugar
1 Tbsp. lemon juice
1 Tbsp. cinnamon**

1. Combine all ingredients in slow cooker.
2. Cover. Cook on High 10-12 hours.

Note:
To make pear sauce, peel, core, and slice 12 large pears. Place in slow cooker with 3/4 cup water. Cover and cook on Low 8-10 hours, or until very soft. Stir to blend.

Breakfast Foods

Welsh Rarebit

Sharon Timpe
Mequon, WI

Makes 6-8 servings

12-oz. can beer
1 Tbsp. dry mustard
1 tsp. Worcestershire sauce
1/2 tsp. salt
1/8 tsp. black, *or* white, pepper
1 lb. American cheese, cubed
1 lb. sharp cheddar cheese, cubed
English muffins, or toast
bacon, cooked until crisp
tomato slices

1. In slow cooker, combine beer, mustard, Worcestershire sauce, salt, and pepper.
2. Cover and cook on High 1-2 hours, until mixture boils.
3. Add cheese, a little at a time, stirring constantly until all the cheese melts.
4. Heat on High 20-30 minutes with cover off, stirring frequently.
5. Serve hot over toasted English muffins or over toasted bread cut into triangles. Garnish with strips of crisp bacon and tomato slices.

Note:
This is a good dish for brunch with fresh fruit, juice, and coffee. Also makes a great lunch or late-night light supper. Serve with a tossed green salad, especially fresh spinach and orange slices with a vinaigrette dressing.

One hour on High equals about 2 to 2½ hours on Low.
Rachel Kauffman
Alto, MI

Cheese Souffle Casserole

Iva Schmidt
Fergus Falls, MN

Makes 6 servings

8 slices bread (crusts removed), cubed *or* torn into squares
2 cups (8 oz.) grated cheddar, Swiss, *or* American, cheese
1 cup cooked, chopped ham
4 eggs
1 cup light cream, *or* milk
1 cup evaporated milk
1/4 tsp. salt
1 Tbsp. parsley
paprika

1. Lightly grease slow cooker. Alternate layers of bread and cheese and ham.
2. Beat together eggs, milk, salt, and parsley. Pour over bread in slow cooker.
3. Sprinkle with paprika.
4. Cover and cook on Low 3-4 hours. (The longer cooking time yields a firmer, dryer dish.)

Breakfast Casserole

Shirley Hinh
Wayland, IA

Makes 8-10 servings

6 eggs, beaten
1 lb. little smokies (cocktail wieners), *or* 1 1/2 lbs. bulk sausage, browned and drained
1 1/2 cups milk
1 cup shredded cheddar cheese
8 slices bread, torn into pieces
1 tsp. salt
1/2 tsp. dry mustard
1 cup shredded mozzarella cheese

1. Mix together all ingredients except cheese. Pour into greased slow cooker.
2. Sprinkle mozzarella cheese over top.
3. Cover and cook 2 hours on High, and then 1 hour on Low.

Egg and Cheese Bake

Evie Hershey
Atglen, PA

Makes 6 servings

3 cups toasted bread cubes
1 1/2 cups shredded cheese
fried, crumbled bacon, *or* ham chunks, optional
6 eggs, beaten
3 cups milk
3/4 tsp. salt
1/4 tsp. pepper

1. Combine bread cubes, cheese, and meat in greased slow cooker.
2. Mix together eggs, milk, salt, and pepper. Pour over bread.
3. Cook on Low 4-6 hours.

Egg and Broccoli Casserole

Joette Droz
Kalona, IA

Makes 6 servings

24-oz. carton small-curd cottage cheese
10-oz. pkg. frozen chopped broccoli, thawed and drained
2 cups (8 oz.) shredded cheddar cheese
6 eggs, beaten
1/3 cup flour
1/4 cup melted butter, *or* margarine
3 Tbsp. finely chopped onion
1/2 tsp. salt
shredded cheese, optional

1. Combine first 8 ingredients. Pour into greased slow cooker.
2. Cover and cook on High 1 hour. Stir. Reduce heat to Low. Cover and cook 2 1/2-3 hours, or until temperature reaches 160° and eggs are set.
3. Sprinkle with cheese and serve.

Creamy Old-Fashioned Oatmeal

Mary Wheatley
Mashpee, MA

Makes 4 servings

1 1/3 cups dry old-fashioned rolled oats
2 1/2 cups, plus 1 Tbsp., water
dash of salt

1. Mix together cereal, water, and salt in slow cooker.
2. Cook on Low 6 hours.

Note:
The formula is this: for one serving, use 1/3 cup dry oats and 2/3 cup water, plus a few grains salt. Multiply by the number of servings you need.

Variation:
Before cooking, stir in a few chopped dates or raisins for each serving, if you wish.
Cathy Boshart
Lebanon, PA

Baked Oatmeal

Ellen Ranck
Gap, PA

Makes 4-6 servings

1/3 cup oil
1/2 cup sugar
1 large egg, beaten
2 cups dry quick oats
1 1/2 tsp. baking powder
1/2 tsp. salt
3/4 cup milk

1. Pour the oil into the slow cooker to grease bottom and sides.
2. Add remaining ingredients. Mix well.
3. Bake on Low 2 1/2-3 hours.

Apple Oatmeal

Frances B. Musser
Newmanstown, PA

Makes 4-5 servings

2 cups milk
2 Tbsp. honey
1 Tbsp. butter (no
  substitute!)
1/4 tsp. salt
1/2 tsp. cinnamon
1 cup dry old-fashioned
  oats
1 cup chopped apples
1/2 cup chopped walnuts
2 Tbsp. brown sugar

1. Mix together all ingredients in greased slow cooker.
2. Cover. Cook on Low 5-6 hours.
3. Serve with milk or ice cream.

Variation:
Add 1/2 cup light or dark raisins to mixture.
  Jeanette Oberholtzer
    Manheim, PA

Don't peek. It takes 15-20 minutes for the cooker to regain lost steam and return to the right temperature.
Janet V. Yocum
Elizabethtown, PA

Breads

Healthy Whole Wheat Bread

Esther Becker
Gordonville, PA

Makes 8 servings

**2 cups warm reconstituted
    powdered milk**
2 Tbsp. vegetable oil
**1/4 cup honey, *or* brown
    sugar**
3/4 tsp. salt
1 pkg. yeast
**2 1/2 cups whole wheat
    flour**
1 1/4 cups white flour

1. Mix together milk, oil,
honey or brown sugar, salt,
yeast, and half the flour in
electric mixer bowl. Beat
with mixer for 2 minutes.
Add remaining flour. Mix
well.

2. Place dough in well-
greased bread or cake pan
that will fit into your cooker.

Cover with greased tin foil.
Let stand for 5 minutes. Place
in slow cooker.

3. Cover cooker and bake
on High 2 1/2-3 hours. Remove
pan and uncover. Let stand
for 5 minutes. Serve warm.

Corn Bread From Scratch

Dorothy M. Van Deest
Memphis, TN

Makes 6 servings

1 1/4 cups flour
3/4 cup yellow cornmeal
1/4 cup sugar
4 1/2 tsp. baking powder
1 tsp. salt
1 egg, slightly beaten
1 cup milk
1/3 cup melted butter, *or* oil

1. In mixing bowl sift
together flour, cornmeal,
sugar, baking powder, and
salt. Make a well in the center.

2. Pour egg, milk, and butter into well. Mix into the dry
mixture until just moistened.

3. Pour mixture into a
greased 2-quart mold. Cover
with a plate. Place on a trivet
or rack in the bottom of slow
cooker.

4. Cover. Cook on High 2-3
hours.

Broccoli Corn Bread

Winifred Ewy
Newton, KS

Makes 8 servings

1 stick margarine, melted
10-oz. pkg. chopped
    broccoli, cooked and
    drained
1 onion, chopped
1 box corn bread mix
4 eggs, well beaten
8 oz. cottage cheese
1¼ tsp. salt

1. Combine all ingredients. Mix well.

2. Pour into greased slow cooker. Cook on Low 6 hours, or until toothpick inserted in center comes out clean.

3. Serve like spoon bread, or invert the pot, remove bread, and cut into wedges.

Lemon Bread

Ruth Ann Gingrich
New Holland, PA

Makes 6 servings

½ cup shortening
¾ cup sugar
2 eggs, beaten
1⅔ cups flour
1⅔ tsp. baking powder
½ tsp. salt
½ cup milk
½ cup chopped nuts
grated peel from 1 lemon

Glaze:
¼ cup powdered sugar
juice of 1 lemon

1. Cream together shortening and sugar. Add eggs. Mix well.

2. Sift together flour, baking powder, and salt. Add flour mixture and milk alternately to shortening mixture.

3. Stir in nuts and lemon peel.

4. Spoon batter into well-greased 2-pound coffee can and cover with well-greased tin foil. Place in cooker set on High for 2-2¼ hours, or until done. Remove bread from coffee can.

5. Mix together powdered sugar and lemon juice. Pour over loaf.

6. Serve plain or with cream cheese.

Old-Fashioned Gingerbread

Mary Ann Westerberg
Rosamond, CA

Makes 6-8 servings

½ cup butter, softened
½ cup sugar
1 egg
1 cup light molasses
2½ cups flour
1½ tsp. baking soda
1 tsp. ground cinnamon
2 tsp. ground ginger
½ tsp. ground cloves
½ tsp. salt
1 cup hot water
warm applesauce, optional
whipped cream, optional
nutmeg, optional

1. Cream together butter and sugar. Add egg and molasses. Mix well.

2. Stir in flour, baking soda, cinnamon, ginger, cloves, and salt. Mix well.

3. Add hot water. Beat well.

4. Pour batter into greased and floured 2-pound coffee can.

5. Place can in cooker. Cover top of can with 8 paper towels. Cover cooker and bake on High 2½-3 hours.

6. Serve with applesauce. Top with whipped cream and sprinkle with nutmeg.

A slow cooker provides enough warmth to a raise dough.
Donna Barnitz
Jenks, OK

Soups, Stews, and Chilis

Nancy's Vegetable Beef Soup

Nancy Graves
Manhattan, KS

Makes 6-8 servings

2-lb. roast cut into bite-
sized pieces, *or* 2 lbs.
stewing meat
15-oz. can corn
15-oz. can green beans
1-lb. bag frozen peas
40-oz. can stewed tomatoes
5 beef bouillon cubes
Tabasco to taste
? tsp. salt

1. Combine all ingredients
in slow cooker. Do not drain
vegetables.
2. Add water to fill slow
cooker to within 3 inches of
top
3. Cover. Cook on Low 8
hours, or until meat is tender
and vegetables are soft.

Variation:
Add 1 large onion, sliced,
2 cups sliced carrots, and ¾
cup pearl barley to mixture
before cooking.

Frances' Hearty Vegetable Soup

Frances Schrag
Newton, KS

Makes 10 servings

1 lb. round steak, cut into
½-inch pieces
14½-oz. can diced
tomatoes
3 cups water
2 potatoes, peeled and
cubed
2 onions, sliced
3 celery ribs, sliced
2 carrots, sliced
3 beef bouillon cubes
½ tsp. dried basil
½ tsp. dried oregano

1 tsp. salt
¼ tsp. pepper
1½ cups frozen mixed
vegetables, *or* your
choice of frozen
vegetables

1. Combine first 3 ingredients in slow cooker.
2. Cover. Cook on High 6
hours.
3. Add remaining ingredi-
ents. Cover and cook on High
2 hours more, or until meat
and vegetables are tender.

Variation:
Cut salt back to ½ tsp.
Increase dried basil to 1 tsp.
and dried oregano to 1 tsp.
Tracy Clark
Mt. Crawford, VA

Anona's Beef Vegetable Soup

Anona M. Teel
Bangor, PA

Makes 6 servings

1-1½-lb. soup bone
1 lb. stewing beef cubes
1½ qts. cold water
1 Tbsp. salt
¾ cup diced celery
¾ cup diced carrots
¾ cup diced potatoes
¾ cup diced onion
1 cup frozen mixed
　vegetables of your
　choice
1-lb. can tomatoes
⅛ tsp. pepper
1 Tbsp. chopped dried
　parsley

1. Put all ingredients in slow cooker.
2. Cover. Cook on Low 8-10 hours. Remove bone before serving.

"Absent Cook" Stew

Kathy Hertzler
Lancaster, PA

Makes 5-6 servings

2 lbs. stewing beef, cubed
2-3 carrots, sliced
1 onion, chopped
3 large potatoes, cubed
3 ribs celery, sliced
10¾-oz. can tomato soup
1 soup can water
1 tsp. salt
dash of pepper
2 Tbsp. vinegar

1. Combine all ingredients in slow cooker.
2. Cover. Cook on Low 10-12 hours.

Kim's Vegetable Beef Soup

Kim McEuen
Lincoln University, PA

Makes 8-10 servings

1-2 lbs. beef shanks, *or*
　short ribs
1-lb. can tomatoes
2 carrots, sliced
3 ribs celery, sliced
2 medium onions, chopped
2 medium potatoes,
　chopped
3 cups water
1 tsp. salt
4-6 whole peppercorns
5 beef bouillon cubes
10-oz. pkg. frozen mixed
　vegetables, *or* its
　equivalent of your
　favorite frozen, fresh, *or*
　canned vegetables

1. Combine all ingredients in slow cooker. Mix well.
2. Cover. Cook on Low 12-14 hours, or High 4-6 hours.

Note:
　I have a scrap vegetable container which I keep in the freezer. When I have too much of a fresh vegetable I throw it in this container and freeze it. When the container gets full, I make soup.

Variation:
　To increase the proportion of vegetables, add another 10-oz. pkg. of vegetables.

　You may want to revise herb amounts when using a slow cooker. Whole herb and spices increase their flavoring power, while ground spices tend to lose some flavor. It's a good idea to season to taste before serving.
Irma H. Schoen
Windsor, CT

Lilli's Vegetable Beef Soup

Lilli Peters
Dodge City, KS

Makes 10-12 servings

3 lbs. stewing meat, cut in
  1-inch pieces
2 Tbsp. oil
4 potatoes, cubed
4 carrots, sliced
3 ribs celery, sliced
14-oz. can diced tomatoes
14-oz. can Italian
  tomatoes, crushed
2 medium onions, chopped
2 wedges cabbage, sliced
  thinly
2 beef bouillon cubes
2 Tbsp. fresh parsley
1 tsp. seasoned salt
1 tsp. garlic salt
1/2 tsp. pepper
water

1. Brown meat in oil in skillet. Drain.
2. Combine all ingredients except water in large slow cooker. Cover with water.
3. Cover. Cook on Low 8-10 hours.

Ruby's Vegetable Beef Soup

Ruby Stoltzfus
Mount Joy, PA

Makes 8-10 servings

1 lb. beef cubes
1 cup beef broth
1 1/2 cups chopped cabbage
1 1/2 cups stewed tomatoes,
  undrained
1 1/2 cups frozen, *or* canned,
  corn
1 1/2 cups frozen peas
1 1/2 cups frozen green
  beans
1 1/2 cups sliced carrots
3/4 tsp. salt
1/4-1/2 tsp. pepper

1. Combine all ingredients in slow cooker.
2. Cover. Cook on Low 6-8 hours, or High 3-4 hours.

Jeanne's Vegetable Beef Borscht

Jeanne Heyerly
Chenoa, IL

Makes 8 servings

1 lb. beef roast, cooked
  and cubed
half a head of cabbage,
  sliced thin
3 medium potatoes, diced
4 carrots, sliced
1 large onion, diced
1 cup tomatoes, diced
1 cup corn
1 cup green beans
2 cups beef broth
2 cups tomato juice
1/4 tsp. garlic powder
1/4 tsp. dill seed
2 tsp. salt
1/2 tsp. pepper
water
sour cream

1. Mix together all ingredients except water and sour cream. Add water to fill slow cooker three-quarters full.
2. Cover. Cook on Low 8-10 hours.
3. Top individual servings with sour cream.

Variation:
Add 1 cup diced cooked red beets during the last half hour of cooking.

Sharon's Vegetable Soup

Sharon Wantland
Menomonee Falls, WI

Makes 6-8 servings

46-oz. can tomato juice
5 beef bouillon cubes
4 celery ribs, sliced
4 large carrots, sliced
1 onion, chopped
one-quarter head of
   cabbage, chopped
1-lb. can green beans
2 cups water
1 lb. beef stewing meat,
   browned
4-oz. can sliced
   mushrooms

1. Combine all ingredients in slow cooker.
2. Cover. Cook on Low 8 hours, or until meat and vegetables are tender.

Winter's Night Beef Soup

Kimberly Jensen
Bailey, CO

Makes 8-12 servings

1 lb. boneless chuck, cut in
   1/2-inch cubes
1-2 Tbsp. oil
28-oz. can tomatoes
2 tsp. garlic powder
2 carrots, sliced
2 ribs celery, sliced
4 cups water
1/2 cup red wine
1 small onion, coarsely
   chopped
4 beef bouillon cubes
1 tsp. pepper
1 tsp. dry oregano
1/2 tsp. dry thyme
1 bay leaf
1/4-1/2 cup couscous

1. Brown beef cubes in oil in skillet.
2. Place vegetables in bottom of slow cooker. Add beef.
3. Combine all other ingredients in separate bowl except couscous. Pour over ingredients in slow cooker.
4. Cover. Cook on Low 6 hours. Stir in couscous. Cover and cook 30 minutes.

Variation:
Add zucchini or mushrooms to the rest of the vegetables before cooking.

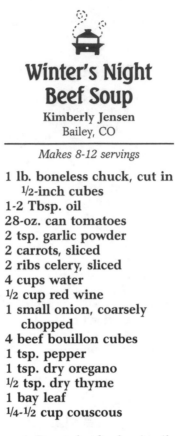

Old-Fashioned Vegetable Beef Soup

Pam Hochstedler
Kalona, IA

Makes 8-10 servings

1-2 lbs. beef short ribs
2 qts. water
1 tsp. salt
1 tsp. celery salt
1 small onion, chopped
1 cup diced carrots
1/2 cup diced celery
2 cups diced potatoes
1-lb. can whole kernel
   corn, undrained
1-lb. can diced tomatoes
   and juice

1. Combine meat, water, salt, celery salt, onion, carrots, and celery in slow cooker.
2. Cover. Cook on Low 4-6 hours.
3. Debone meat, cut into bite-sized pieces, and return to pot.
4. Add potatoes, corn, and tomatoes.
5. Cover and cook on High 2-3 hours.

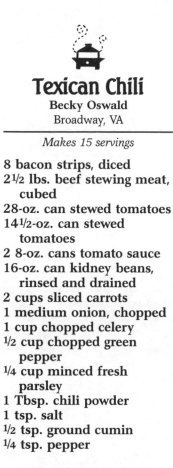

Texican Chili

Becky Oswald
Broadway, VA

Makes 15 servings

8 bacon strips, diced
2 1/2 lbs. beef stewing meat,
  cubed
28-oz. can stewed tomatoes
14 1/2-oz. can stewed
  tomatoes
2 8-oz. cans tomato sauce
16-oz. can kidney beans,
  rinsed and drained
2 cups sliced carrots
1 medium onion, chopped
1 cup chopped celery
1/2 cup chopped green
  pepper
1/4 cup minced fresh
  parsley
1 Tbsp. chili powder
1 tsp. salt
1/2 tsp. ground cumin
1/4 tsp. pepper

1. Cook bacon in skillet
until crisp. Drain on paper
towel.
2. Brown beef in bacon
drippings in skillet.
3. Combine all ingredients
in slow cooker.
4. Cover. Cook on Low 9-
10 hours, or until meat is tender. Stir occasionally.

Forgotten Minestrone

Phyllis Attig
Reynolds, IL

Makes 8 servings

1 lb. beef stewing meat
6 cups water
28-oz. can tomatoes, diced,
  undrained
1 beef bouillon cube
1 medium onion, chopped
2 Tbsp. minced dried
  parsley
1 1/2 tsp. salt
1 1/2 tsp. dried thyme
1/2 tsp. pepper
1 medium zucchini, thinly
  sliced
2 cups finely chopped
  cabbage
16-oz. can garbanzo beans,
  drained
1 cup uncooked small
  elbow, *or* shell,
  macaroni
1/4 cup grated Parmesan
  cheese

1. Combine beef, water,
tomatoes, bouillon, onion,
parsley, salt, thyme, and pepper.
2. Cover. Cook on Low 7-9
hours, or until meat is tender.
3. Stir in zucchini, cab-
bage, beans, and macaroni.
Cover and cook on High 30-
45 minutes, or until vegetables are tender.
4. Sprinkle individual servings with Parmesan cheese.

Slow-Cooker Minestrone

Dorothy Shank
Sterling, IL

Makes 8 servings

3 cups water
1 1/2 lbs. stewing meat, cut
  into bite-sized pieces
1 medium onion, diced
4 carrots, diced
14 1/2-oz. can tomatoes
2 tsp. salt
10-oz. pkg. frozen mixed
  vegetables, *or* your
  choice of frozen
  vegetables
1 Tbsp. dried basil
1/2 cup dry vermicelli
1 tsp. dried oregano
grated Parmesan cheese

1. Combine all ingredients
except cheese in slow cooker.
Stir well.
2. Cover. Cook on Low 10-
12 hours, or on High 4-5
hours.
3. Top individual servings
with Parmesan cheese.

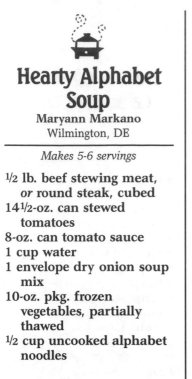

Hearty Alphabet Soup

Maryann Markano
Wilmington, DE

Makes 5-6 servings

½ lb. beef stewing meat,
   or round steak, cubed
14½-oz. can stewed
   tomatoes
8-oz. can tomato sauce
1 cup water
1 envelope dry onion soup
   mix
10-oz. pkg. frozen
   vegetables, partially
   thawed
½ cup uncooked alphabet
   noodles

1. Combine meat, tomatoes, tomato sauce, water, and soup mix in slow cooker.
2. Cover. Cook on Low 6-8 hours. Turn to High.
3. Stir in vegetables and noodles. Add more water if mixture is too dry and thick.
4. Cover. Cook on High 30 minutes, or until vegetables are tender.

Hamburger Vegetable Soup

Donna Conto
Saylorsburg, PA

Makes 6-8 servings

½ lb. ground beef,
   browned
6 beef bouillon cubes,
   crushed
16-oz. can tomatoes
1 large onion, diced
¾ cup sliced celery
1 medium carrot, diced
1 garlic clove, minced
1 bay leaf
½ tsp. salt
⅛ tsp. pepper
10-oz. pkg. frozen peas
3 Tbsp. chopped parsley

1. Combine all ingredients except peas and parsley in slow cooker.
2. Cover. Cook on Low 5 hours.
3. Stir in peas during last hour.
4. Garnish with parsley before serving.

Vegetable Beef Soup

Ruth Ann Swartzendruber
Hydro, OK

Makes 4-5 servings

1 lb. ground beef, browned
   and drained
2 cups tomato juice
2 cups beef broth
1 lb. frozen mixed
   vegetables, *or* your
   choice of vegetables

1. Combine all ingredients in slow cooker.
2. Cover. Cook on High 3 hours, and then on Low 3-4 hours.

Quick and Easy Italian Vegetable Beef Soup

Lisa Warren
Parkesburg, PA

Makes 8-10 servings

1 lb. ground beef, *or* turkey, browned and drained
3 carrots, sliced
4 potatoes, peeled and cubed
1 small onion, diced
1 tsp. garlic powder
1 tsp. Italian seasoning
3/4 tsp. salt
1/4 tsp. pepper
15-oz. can diced Italian tomatoes, *or* 2 fresh tomatoes, chopped
6-oz. can Italian-flavored tomato paste
4 1/2 cups water
1 quart beef broth

1. Combine all ingredients in slow cooker.
2. Cover. Cook on High 6-8 hours, or until potatoes and carrots are tender.

Spicy Beef Vegetable Stew

Melissa Raber
Millersburg, OH

Makes 12 servings

1 lb. ground beef
1 cup chopped onions
30-oz. jar meatless spaghetti sauce
3 1/2 cups water
1 lb. frozen mixed vegetables
10-oz. can diced tomatoes with green chilies
1 cup sliced celery
1 tsp. beef bouillon granules
1 tsp. pepper

1. Cook beef and onion in skillet until meat is no longer pink. Drain. Transfer to slow cooker.
2. Stir in remaining ingredients.
3. Cover. Cook on Low 8 hours.

Hearty Beef and Cabbage Soup

Carolyn Mathias
Williamsville, NY

Makes 8 servings

1 lb. ground beef
1 medium onion, chopped
40-oz. can tomatoes
2 cups water
15-oz. can kidney beans
1 tsp. salt
1/2 tsp. pepper
1 Tbsp. chili powder
1/2 cup chopped celery
2 cups thinly sliced cabbage

1. Saute beef in skillet. Drain.
2. Combine all ingredients except cabbage in slow cooker.
3. Cover. Cook on Low 3 hours. Add cabbage. Cook on High 30-60 minutes longer.

I find that adding 1/4-1/2 cup of a burgundy or Chablis wine to most soup and stew recipes brings out the flavor of the other seasonings.

Joyce Kant
Rochester, NY

Hamburger Soup with Barley

Becky Oswald
Broadway, VA

Makes 10 servings

1 lb. ground beef
1 medium onion, chopped
3 14½-oz. cans beef consomme
28-oz. can diced, *or* crushed, tomatoes
3 carrots, sliced
3 celery ribs, sliced
8 Tbsp. barley
1 bay leaf
1 tsp. dried thyme
1 Tbsp. dried parsley
1 tsp. salt
½ tsp. pepper

1. Brown beef and onion in skillet. Drain.
2. Combine all ingredients in slow cooker.
3. Cover. Cook on High 3 hours, or Low 6-8 hours.

Vegetable Soup with Potatoes

Annabelle Unternahrer
Shipshewana, IN

Makes 6-8 servings

1 lb. hamburger, browned and drained
2 15-oz. cans diced tomatoes
2 carrots, sliced *or* cubed
2 onions, sliced *or* cubed
2 potatoes, diced
1-2 garlic cloves, minced
12-oz. can V-8 vegetable juice
1½-2 cups sliced celery
2 tsp. beef stock concentrate, *or* 2 beef bouillon cubes
2-3 cups vegetables (cauliflower, peas, corn, limas, *or* your choice of leftovers from your freezer)

1. Combine all ingredients in slow cooker.
2. Cover. Cook on Low 12 hours, or High 4-6 hours.

Note:
If using leftover vegetables that are precooked, add during last hour if cooking on Low, or during last half hour if cooking on High.

Variation:
Use 3 cups pre-cooked dried beans or lentils instead of hamburger.

Vegetable Potato Beef Soup

Beth Shank
Wellman, IA

Makes 6-8 servings

1½ cups sliced carrots
1½ cups cubed potatoes
1 cup sliced celery
½ cup chopped onion
2 cups water
1¼ lbs. ground beef, browned and drained
2 tsp. salt
5 cups tomato juice
1 Tbsp. brown sugar

1. Combine vegetables and water in microwave-safe container. Cover and microwave on High 18-20 minutes. Do not drain. Place vegetables in slow cooker.
2. Combine all ingredients in slow cooker.
3. Cover. Cook on Low 6-8 hours, or until vegetables are done.

Variation:
Add 15-oz. can green beans, drained, *or* 15-oz. can lima beans, drained.

Hamburger Lentil Soup

Juanita Marner
Shipshewana, IN

Makes 8 servings

1 lb. ground beef
1/2 cup chopped onions
4 carrots, diced
3 ribs celery, diced
1 garlic clove, minced, *or* 1
   tsp. garlic powder
1 qt. tomato juice
1 Tbsp. salt
2 cups dry lentils, washed
   with stones removed
1 qt. water
1/2 tsp. dried marjoram
1 Tbsp. brown sugar

1. Brown ground beef and onion in skillet. Drain.
2. Combine all ingredients in slow cooker.
3. Cover. Cook on Low 8-10 hours, or High 4-6 hours.

Vegetable Soup with Noodles

Glenda S. Weaver
New Holland, PA

Makes 6 servings

1 pint water
2 beef bouillon cubes
1 onion, chopped
1 lb. ground beef
1/4 cup ketchup
1 tsp. salt
1/8 tsp. celery salt
1/2 cup uncooked noodles
12-16 oz. pkg. frozen
   mixed vegetables, *or*
   vegetables of your
   choice
1 pint tomato juice

1. Dissolve bouillon cubes in water.
2. Brown onion and beef in skillet. Drain.
3. Combine all ingredients in slow cooker.
4. Cover. Cook on Low 6 hours, or on High 2-3 hours, until vegetables are tender.

Steak Soup

Ilene Bontrager
Arlington, KS
Deb Unternahrer
Wayland, IA

Makes 10-12 servings

2 lbs. coarsely ground
   chuck, browned and
   drained
5 cups water
1 large onion, chopped
4 ribs celery, chopped
3 carrots, sliced
2 14 1/2-oz. cans diced
   tomatoes
10-oz. pkg. frozen mixed
   vegetables
5 Tbsp. beef-based
   granules, *or* 5 beef
   bouillon cubes
1/2 tsp. pepper
1/2 cup melted butter
1/2 cup flour
2 tsp. salt

1. Combine chuck, water, onion, celery, carrots, tomatoes, mixed vegetables, beef granules, and pepper in slow cooker.
2. Cover. Cook on Low 8-12 hours, or High 4-6 hours.
3. One hour before serving, turn to High. Make a paste of melted butter and flour. Stir until smooth. Pour into slow cooker and stir until well blended. Add salt.
4. Cover. Continue cooking on High until thickened.

Dottie's Creamy Steak Soup

Debbie Zeida
Mashpee, MA

Makes 4-6 servings

1 lb. ground beef
half a large onion, chopped
12-oz. can V-8 vegetable
  juice
2-3 medium potatoes,
  diced
10¾-oz. can cream of
  mushroom soup
10¾-oz. can cream of
  celery soup
16-oz. pkg. frozen mixed
  vegetables, *or* your
  choice of frozen
  vegetables
2 tsp. salt
½-¾ tsp. pepper

1. Saute beef and onions in skillet. Drain.
2. Combine all ingredients in slow cooker.
3. Cover. Cook on Low 8-10 hours.

Taco Soup with Black Beans

Alexa Slonin
Harrisonburg, VA

Makes 6-8 servings

1 lb. ground beef, browned
  and drained
28-oz. can crushed
  tomatoes
15¼-oz. can corn,
  undrained
15-oz. can black beans,
  undrained
15½-oz. can red kidney
  beans, undrained
1 envelope dry Hidden
  Valley Ranch Dressing
  mix
1 envelope dry taco
  seasoning
1 small onion, chopped
tortilla, *or* corn, chips
shredded cheese
sour cream

1. Combine all ingredients except chips, shredded cheese, and sour cream in slow cooker.
2. Cover. Cook on Low 4-6 hours.
3. Garnish individual servings with chips, cheese, and sour cream.

Taco Soup with Pinto Beans

Janie Steele
Moore, OK

Makes 10-12 servings

1 lb. ground beef
1 large onion, chopped
3 14-oz. cans pinto beans
14-oz. can tomatoes with
  chilies
14½-oz. can chopped
  tomatoes
15-oz. can tomato sauce
1 pkg. dry Hidden Valley
  Ranch Dressing mix
1 pkg. dry taco seasoning
15¼-oz. can corn, drained

1. Brown beef and onions in skillet. Drain.
2. Combine all ingredients in slow cooker.
3. Cover. Cook on Low 4 hours, or until ingredients are heated through.

Sante Fe Soup with Melted Cheese

Carla Koslowsky
Hillsboro, KS

Makes 8 servings

1 lb. Velveeta cheese, cubed
1 lb. ground beef, browned and drained
15¼-oz. can corn, undrained
15-oz. can kidney beans, undrained
14½-oz. can diced tomatoes with green chilies
14½-oz. can stewed tomatoes
2 Tbsp. dry taco seasoning
corn chips, *or* soft tortillas

1. Combine all ingredients except chips or tortillas in slow cooker.
2. Cover. Cook on High 3 hours.
3. Serve with corn chips as a side, or dip soft tortillas in individual servings in soup bowls.

Taco Soup with Whole Tomatoes

Marla Folkerts
Holland, OH

Makes 6-8 servings

1 lb. ground beef
½ cup chopped onions
28-oz. can whole tomatoes with juice
14-oz. can kidney beans with juice
17-oz. can corn with juice
8-oz. can tomato sauce
1 pkg. dry taco seasoning
1-2 cups water
salt to taste
pepper to taste
1 cup grated cheddar cheese
taco, *or* corn, chips

1. Brown beef and onions in skillet. Drain.
2. Combine all ingredients except cheese and chips in slow cooker.
3. Cover. Cook on Low 4-6 hours.
4. Ladle into bowls. Top with cheese and serve with chips.

Taco Soup with Pork and Beans

Beth Shank
Wellman, IA

Makes 6 servings

1 lb. ground beef
half a small onion, finely diced
1 envelope dry taco seasoning
2 Tbsp. brown sugar
⅛ tsp. red cayenne pepper
15-oz. can kidney beans, drained
15-oz. can whole kernel corn, drained
15-oz. can pork and beans
46-oz. can tomato juice
taco chips, crushed
shredded cheese
sour cream

1. Brown beef and onion in skillet. Drain. Place in slow cooker.
2. Stir in taco seasoning, brown sugar, and pepper. Add beans, corn, pork and beans, and tomato juice. Mix well.
3. Cover. Cook on Low 4-6 hours.
4. Garnish individual servings with taco chips, cheese, and dollop of sour cream.

Taco Soup with Pizza Sauce

Barbara Kuhns
Millersburg, OH

Makes 8-10 servings

2 lbs. ground beef,
  browned
1 small onion, chopped
  and sauteed in ground
  beef drippings
3/4 tsp. salt
1/2 tsp. pepper
1 1/2 pkgs. dry taco
  seasoning
1 qt. pizza sauce
1 qt. water
tortilla chips
shredded mozzarella
  cheese
sour cream

1. Combine ground beef,
onion, salt, pepper, taco seasoning, pizza sauce, and
water in 5-quart, or larger,
slow cooker.
2. Cover. Cook on Low 3-4
hours.
3. Top individual servings
with tortilla chips, cheese,
and sour cream.

Variation:
  Add 15-oz. can black beans
and 4-oz. can chilies to mixture before cooking. (Be sure
to use one very large cooker,
or two medium-sized cook-
ers.)

Easy Chili

Sheryl Shenk
Harrisonburg, VA

Makes 10-12 servings

1 lb. ground beef
1 onion, chopped
1 green pepper, chopped
1 1/2 tsp. salt
1 Tbsp. chili powder
2 tsp. Worcestershire sauce
29-oz. can tomato sauce
3 16-oz. cans kidney beans,
  drained
14 1/2-oz. can crushed, *or*
  stewed, tomatoes
6-oz. can tomato paste
2 cups grated cheddar
  cheese

1. Brown meat in skillet.
Add onion and green pepper
halfway through browning
process. Drain. Pour into slow
cooker.
2. Stir in remaining ingredients except cheese.
3. Cover. Cook on High 3
hours, or Low 7-8 hours.
4. Serve in bowls topped
with cheddar cheese.

Note:
  This chili can be served
over cooked rice.

Berenice's Favorite Chili

Berenice M. Wagner
Dodge City, KS

Makes 6 servings

2 16-oz. cans red kidney
  beans, drained
2 14 1/2-oz. cans diced
  tomatoes
2 lbs. coarsely ground beef,
  browned and drained
2 medium onions, coarsely
  chopped
1 green pepper, coarsely
  chopped
2 garlic cloves, minced
2-3 Tbsp. chili powder
1 tsp. pepper
2 1/2 tsp. salt

1. Combine all ingredients
in slow cooker in order listed.
Stir once.
2. Cover. Cook on Low 10-
12 hours, or High 5-6 hours.

Variations:
  1. Top individual servings
with green onion, sour
cream, and cheese.
    Judy Govotsus
    Monrovia, MD

  2. Increase proportion of
tomatoes in chili by adding
8-oz. can tomato sauce before
cooking.
    Bernice A. Esau
    North Newton, KS

Slow-Cooker Chili

Wanda S. Curtin
Bradenton, FL
Ann Sunday McDowell
Newtown, PA

Makes 10 servings

2 lbs. ground beef,
  browned and drained
2 16-oz. cans red kidney
  beans, drained
2 14½-oz. cans diced
  tomatoes, drained
2 medium onions, chopped
2 garlic cloves, crushed
2-3 Tbsp. chili powder
1 tsp. ground cumin
1 tsp. black pepper
1 tsp. salt

1. Combine all ingredients
in slow cooker.
2. Cover. Cook on Low 8-
10 hours.

Note:
Use leftovers over lettuce
and other fresh garden vegetables to make a taco salad.

Variations:
1. For more flavor, add
cayenne pepper or a jalapeno
pepper before cooking.
Dorothy Shank
Sterling, IL

2. Add 1 cup chopped
green peppers before cooking.
Mary V. Warye
West Liberty, OH

Trail Chili

Jeanne Allen
Rye, CO

Makes 8-10 servings

2 lbs. ground beef
1 large onion, diced
28-oz. can diced tomatoes
2 8-oz. cans tomato puree
1, *or* 2, 16-oz. cans kidney
  beans, undrained
4-oz. can diced green
  chilies
1 cup water
2 garlic cloves, minced
2 Tbsp. mild chili powder
2 tsp. salt
2 tsp. ground cumin
1 tsp. pepper

1. Brown beef and onion
in skillet. Drain. Place in
slow cooker on High.
2. Stir in remaining ingredients. Cook on High 30 minutes.
3. Reduce heat to Low.
Cook 4-6 hours.

Note:
Top individual servings
with shredded cheese. Serve
with taco chips.

Judy's Chili Soup

Judy Buller
Bluffton, OH

Makes 6 servings

1 lb. ground beef
1 onion, chopped
10¾-oz. can condensed
  tomato soup
16-oz. can kidney beans,
  drained
1 qt. tomato juice
⅛ tsp. garlic powder
1 Tbsp. chili powder
½ tsp. pepper
½ tsp. ground cumin
½ tsp. salt

1. Brown hamburger and
onion in skillet. Drain.
2. Combine all ingredients
in slow cooker. Mix well.
3. Cover. Cook on Low 7-8
hours.

Variation:
Use ground venison
instead of ground beef.

Colleen's Favorite Chili

Colleen Heatwole
Burton, MI

Makes 6-8 servings

2 medium onions, coarsely
 chopped
1-1½ lbs. ground beef,
 browned and drained
2 garlic cloves, minced
 fine, *or* ½ tsp. garlic
 powder
¾ cup finely diced green
 peppers
2 14½-oz. cans diced
 tomatoes, *or* 1 quart
 home-canned tomatoes
30-32 oz. beans—kidney, *or*
 pinto, *or* mixture of the
 two
8-oz. can tomato sauce
¼ tsp. beaumonde spice,
 optional
1 tsp. ground cumin
½ tsp. pepper
1 tsp. seasoned salt
1 Tbsp., or more, chili
 powder
1 tsp. dried basil

1. Combine all ingredients
in slow cooker.
2. Cover. Cook on Low 8-
12 hours, or High 5-6 hours.

Variations:
 1. Add 1 Tbsp. brown
sugar to mixture before cooking.
 2. Put in another 1 lb.
beans and then decrease
ground beef to 1 lb.

Chili Con Carne

Donna Conto
Saylorsburg, PA

Makes 8 servings

1 lb. ground beef
1 cup chopped onions
¾ cup chopped green
 peppers
1 garlic clove, minced
14½-oz. can tomatoes, cut
 up
16-oz. can kidney beans,
 drained
8-oz. can tomato sauce
2 tsp. chili powder
½ tsp. dried basil

1. Brown beef, onion,
green pepper, and garlic in
saucepan. Drain.
2. Combine all ingredients
in slow cooker.
3. Cover. Cook on Low 5-6
hours.
4. Serve in bread bowl.

Variation:
 Add 16-oz. can pinto
beans, ¼ tsp. salt, and ¼ tsp.
pepper in Step 2.
 Alexa Slonin
 Harrisonburg, VA

Quick and Easy Chili

Nan Decker
Albuquerque, NM

Makes 4 servings

1 lb. ground beef
1 onion, chopped
16-oz. can stewed tomatoes
11½-oz. can Hot V-8 juice
2 15-oz. cans pinto beans
¼ tsp. cayenne pepper
½ tsp. salt
1 Tbsp. chili powder
sour cream
chopped green onions
grated cheese
sliced ripe olives

1. Crumble ground beef in
microwave-safe casserole.
Add onion. Microwave, covered, on High 15 minutes.
Drain. Break meat into
pieces.
2. Combine all ingredients
in slow cooker.
3. Cook on Low 4-5 hours.
4. Garnish with sour
cream, chopped green onions,
grated cheese, and sliced ripe
olives.

Cindy's Chili
Cindy Krestynick
Glen Lyon, PA

Makes 4-6 servings

1 lb. ground beef, browned
  and drained
3 15½-oz. cans chili beans
  (hot *or* mild)
28-oz. can stewed
  tomatoes, chopped
1 rib celery, chopped
4 cups tomato juice
½ tsp. garlic salt
½ tsp. chili powder
¼ tsp. pepper
¼ tsp. Tabasco sauce

1. Combine all ingredients
in large slow cooker.
2. Cover. Cook on Low 4-6
hours.

Ed's Chili
Marie Miller
Scotia, NY

Makes 4-6 servings

1 lb. ground beef
1 pkg. dry taco seasoning
  mix
half a 12-oz. jar salsa
16-oz. can kidney beans,
  undrained
15-oz. can black beans,
  undrained
14½-oz. can diced
  tomatoes, undrained
pinch of sugar
shredded cheese
chopped onions
sour cream
diced fresh tomatoes
guacamole
sliced black olives

1. Brown ground beef in
skillet. Drain.
2. Combine first 7 ingredients in slow cooker.
3. Cover. Heat on High
until mixture comes to boil.
Reduce heat to Low. Simmer
1½ hours.
4. To reduce liquids, continue cooking uncovered.
5. Top individual servings
with choice of shredded
cheese, onions, a dollop of
sour cream, fresh diced tomatoes, guacamole, and sliced
olives.

Pirate Stew
Nancy Graves
Manhattan, KS

Makes 4-6 servings

¾ cup sliced onion
1 lb. ground beef
¼ cup uncooked, long
  grain rice
3 cups diced raw potatoes
1 cup diced celery
2 cups canned kidney
  beans, drained
1 tsp. salt
⅛ tsp. pepper
¼ tsp. chili powder
¼ tsp. Worcestershire
  sauce
1 cup tomato sauce
½ cup water

1. Brown onions and
ground beef in skillet. Drain.
2. Layer ingredients in
slow cooker in order given.
3. Cover. Cook on Low 6
hours, or until potatoes and
rice are cooked.

Variation:
Add a layer of 2 cups
sliced carrots between potatoes and celery.
                Katrine Rose
                Woodbridge, VA

Corn Chili

Gladys Longacre
Susquehanna, PA

Makes 4-6 servings

1 lb. ground beef
1/2 cup chopped onions
1/2 cup chopped green
   peppers
1/2 tsp. salt
1/8 tsp. pepper
1/4 tsp. dried thyme
14 1/2-oz. can diced
   tomatoes with Italian
   herbs
6-oz. can tomato paste,
   diluted with 1 can water
2 cups frozen whole kernel
   corn
16-oz. can kidney beans
1 Tbsp. chili powder
sour cream
shredded cheese

1. Saute ground beef,
onions, and green peppers in
deep saucepan. Drain and
season with salt, pepper, and
thyme.
2. Stir in tomatoes, tomato
paste, and corn. Heat until
corn is thawed. Add kidney
beans and chili powder. Pour
into slow cooker.
3. Cover. Cook on Low 5-6
hours.
4. Top individual servings
with dollops of sour cream,
or sprinkle with shredded
cheese.

White Bean Chili

Tracey Stenger
Gretna, LA

Makes 10-12 servings

1 lb. ground beef, browned
   and drained
1 lb. ground turkey,
   browned and drained
3 bell peppers, chopped
2 onions, chopped
4 garlic cloves, minced
2 14 1/2-oz. cans chicken, *or*
   vegetable, broth
15 1/2-oz. can butter beans,
   rinsed and drained
15-oz. can black-eyed peas,
   rinsed and drained
15-oz. can garbanzo beans,
   rinsed and drained
15-oz. can navy beans,
   rinsed and drained
4-oz. can chopped green
   chilies
2 Tbsp. chili powder
3 tsp. ground cumin
2 tsp. dried oregano
2 tsp. paprika
1 1/2-2 tsp. salt
1/2 tsp. pepper

1. Combine all ingredients
in slow cooker.
2. Cover. Cook on Low 8-
10 hours.

Lotsa-Beans Chili

Jean Weller
State College, PA

Makes 12-15 servings

1 lb. ground beef
1 lb. bacon, diced
1/2 cup chopped onions
1/2 cup brown sugar
1/2 cup sugar
1/2 cup ketchup
2 tsp. dry mustard
1 tsp. salt
1/2 tsp. pepper
2 15-oz. cans green beans,
   drained
2 14 1/2-oz. cans baked
   beans
2 15-oz. cans butter beans,
   drained
2 16-oz. cans kidney beans,
   rinsed and drained

1. Brown ground beef and
bacon in slow cooker. Drain.
2. Combine all ingredients
in slow cooker.
3. Cover. Cook on High 1
hour. Reduce heat to Low
and cook 7-8 hours.

Dorothea's Slow-Cooker Chili
Dorothea K. Ladd
Ballston Lake, NY

Makes 6-8 servings

1 lb. ground beef
1 lb. bulk pork sausage
1 large onion, chopped
1 large green pepper, chopped
2-3 ribs celery, chopped
2 15½-oz. cans kidney beans
29-oz. can tomato puree
6-oz. can tomato paste
2 cloves garlic, minced
2 Tbsp. chili powder
2 tsp. salt

1. Brown ground beef and sausage in skillet. Drain.
2. Combine all ingredients in slow cooker.
3. Cover. Cook on Low 8-10 hours.

Variations:
1. For extra flavor, add 1 tsp. cayenne pepper.
2. For more zest, use mild or hot Italian sausage instead of regular pork sausage.
3. Top individual servings with shredded sharp cheddar cheese.

Chili for Twenty
Janie Steele
Moore, OK

Makes 15-20 servings

4 lbs. ground beef
3 onions, finely chopped
3 green peppers, finely chopped
2 garlic cloves, minced
4 16-oz. cans Italian-style tomatoes
4 16-oz. cans kidney beans, drained
10-oz. can diced tomatoes and chilies
2 6-oz. cans tomato paste
1 cup water
1 Tbsp. salt
1 tsp. pepper
3 whole cloves
2 bay leaves
2 Tbsp. chili powder

1. Brown meat, onions, and peppers in soup pot on top of stove. Drain.
2. Combine all ingredients in large bowl. Divide among several medium-sized slow cookers.
3. Cover. Cook on Low 3-4 hours.

Crab Soup
Susan Alexander
Baltimore, MD

Makes 10 servings

1 lb. carrots, sliced
½ bunch celery, sliced
1 large onion, diced
2 10-oz. bags frozen mixed vegetables, *or* your choice of frozen vegetables
12-oz. can tomato juice
1 lb. ham, cubed
1 lb. beef, cubed
6 slices bacon, chopped
1 tsp. salt
¼ tsp. pepper
1 Tbsp. Old Bay seasoning
1 lb. claw crabmeat

1. Combine all ingredients except seasonings and crabmeat in large slow cooker. Pour in water until cooker is half-full.
2. Add spices. Stir in thoroughly. Put crab on top.
3. Cover. Cook on Low 8-10 hours.
4. Stir well and serve.

Special Seafood Chowder

Dorothea K. Ladd
Ballston Lake, NY

Makes 8-10 servings

1/2 cup chopped onions
2 Tbsp. butter
1 lb. fresh *or* frozen cod, *or* haddock
4 cups diced potatoes
15-oz. can creamed corn
1/2 tsp. salt
dash pepper
2 cups water
1 pint half-and-half

1. Saute onions in butter in skillet until transparent but not brown.
2. Cut fish into 3/4-inch cubes. Combine fish, onions, potatoes, corn, seasonings, and water in slow cooker.
3. Cover. Cook on Low 6 hours, until potatoes are tender.
4. Add half-and-half during last hour.

Variation:
To cut milk fat, use 1 cup half-and-half and 1 cup skim milk, instead of 1 pint half-and-half.

Manhattan Clam Chowder

Joyce Slaymaker
Strasburg, PA
Louise Stackhouse
Benton, PA

Makes 8 servings

1/4 lb. salt pork, *or* bacon, diced and fried
1 large onion, chopped
2 carrots, thinly sliced
3 ribs celery, sliced
1 Tbsp. dried parsley flakes
1-lb. 12-oz. can tomatoes
1/2 tsp. salt
2, *or* 3, 8-oz. cans clams with liquid
2 whole peppercorns
1 bay leaf
1 1/2 tsp. dried crushed thyme
3 medium potatoes, cubed

1. Combine all ingredients in slow cooker.
2. Cover. Cook on Low 8-10 hours.

Rich and Easy Clam Chowder

Rhonda Burgoon
Collingswood, NJ

Makes 4-5 servings

3 10 3/4-oz. cans cream of potato soup
2 10 3/4-oz. cans New England clam chowder
1/2 cup butter
1 small onion, diced
1 pint half-and-half
2 6 1/2-oz. cans clams, chopped

1. Combine all ingredients in slow cooker.
2. Cover. Cook on Low 2-4 hours.

Chicken Clam Chowder

Irene Klaeger
Inverness, Fl

Makes 10-12 servings

1 lb. bacon, diced
1/4 lb. ham, cubed
2 cups chopped onions
2 cups diced celery
1/2 tsp. salt
1/4 tsp. pepper
2 cups diced potatoes
2 cups cooked, diced
  chicken
4 cups chicken broth
2 bottles clam juice, *or*
  2 cans clams with juice
1-lb. can whole kernel corn
  with liquid
3/4 cup flour
4 cups milk
4 cups shredded cheddar,
  or Jack, cheese
1/2 cup whipping cream
  (not whipped)
2 Tbsp. fresh parsley

1. Saute bacon, ham,
onions, and celery in skillet
until bacon is crisp and
onions and celery are limp.
Add salt and pepper.
2. Combine all ingredients
in slow cooker except flour,
milk, cheese, cream, and
parsley.
3. Cover. Cook on Low 6-8
hours, or on High 3-4 hours.
4. Whisk flour into milk.
Stir into soup, along with
cheese, whipping cream, and
parsley. Cook one more hour
on High.

Chicken Broth

Ruth Conrad Liechty
Goshen IN

Makes about 6 cups broth

bony chicken pieces from 2
  chickens
1 onion, quartered
3 whole cloves, optional
3 ribs celery, cut up
1 carrot, quartered
1 1/2 tsp. salt
1/4 tsp. pepper
4 cups water

1. Place chicken in slow
cooker.
2. Stud onion with cloves.
Add to slow cooker with
other ingredients.
3. Cover. Cook on High 4-5
hours.
4. Remove chicken and
vegetables. Discard vegetables. Debone chicken. Cut up
meat and add to broth. Use
as stock for soups.

Chicken Noodle Soup

Beth Shank
Wellman, IA

Makes 6-8 servings

5 cups hot water
2 Tbsp. chicken bouillon
  granules, *or* 2 chicken
  bouillon cubes
46-oz. can chicken broth
2 cups cooked chicken
1 tsp. salt
4 cups "homestyle"
  noodles, uncooked
1/3 cup thinly sliced celery,
  lightly pre-cooked in
  microwave
1/3 cup shredded, *or*
  chopped, carrots

1. Dissolve bouillon in
water. Pour into slow cooker.
2. Add remaining ingredi-
ents. Mix well.
3. Cover. Cook on Low 4-6
hours.

Brown Jug Soup

Dorothy Shank
Sterling, IL

Makes 10-12 servings

10½-oz. can chicken broth
4 chicken bouillon cubes
1 qt. water
2 cups (3-4 ribs) diced
  celery
2 cups (2 medium-sized)
  diced onions
4 cups (4 large) diced
  potatoes
3 cups (8 medium-sized)
  diced carrots
10-oz. pkg. frozen whole
  kernel corn
2 10¾-oz. cans cream of
  chicken soup
½ lb. Velveeta cheese,
  cubed

1. Combine all ingredients
except cheese in slow cooker.
2. Cover. Cook on Low
10-12 hours, or until vegetables are tender.
3. Just before serving, add
cheese. Stir until cheese is
melted. Serve.

Chicken Corn Soup

Eleanor Larson
Glen Lyon, PA

Makes 4-6 servings

2 whole boneless skinless
  chicken breasts, cubed
1 onion, chopped
1 garlic clove, minced
2 carrots, sliced
2 ribs celery, chopped
2 medium potatoes, cubed
1 tsp. mixed dried herbs
⅓ cup tomato sauce
12-oz. can cream-style corn
14-oz. can whole kernel
  corn
3 cups chicken stock
¼ cup chopped Italian
  parsley
1 tsp. salt
¼ tsp. pepper

1. Combine all ingredients
except parsley, salt, and pepper in slow cooker.
2. Cover. Cook on Low 8-9
hours, or until chicken is tender.
3. Add parsley and seasonings 30 minutes before serving.

Chili, Chicken, Corn Chowder

Jeanne Allen
Rye, CO

Makes 6-8 servings

¼ cup oil
1 large onion, diced
1 garlic clove, minced
1 rib celery, finely chopped
2 cups frozen, *or* canned,
  corn
2 cups cooked, deboned,
  diced chicken
4-oz. can diced green
  chilies
½ tsp. black pepper
2 cups chicken broth
salt to taste
1 cup half-and-half

1. In saucepan, saute
onion, garlic, and celery in oil
until limp.
2. Stir in corn, chicken,
and chilies. Saute for 2-3 minutes.
3. Combine all ingredients
except half-and-half in slow
cooker.
4. Cover. Heat on Low 4
hours.
5. Stir in half-and-half
before serving. Do not boil,
but be sure cream is heated
through.

Slow cookers come in a variety of sizes, from 2- to 8-
quarts. The best size for a family of four or five is a 5-6
quart-size.
Dorothy M. Van Deest
Memphis, TN

White Chili

Esther Martin
Ephrata, PA

Makes 8 servings

3 15-oz. cans Great
  Northern beans, drained
8 oz. cooked and shredded
  chicken breasts
1 cup chopped onions
1½ cups chopped yellow,
  red, *or* green bell
  peppers
2 jalapeno chili peppers,
  stemmed, seeded, and
  chopped (optional)
2 garlic cloves, minced
2 tsp. ground cumin
½ tsp. salt
½ tsp. dried oregano
3½ cups chicken broth
sour cream
shredded cheddar cheese
tortilla chips

1. Combine all ingredients
except sour cream, cheddar
cheese, and chips in slow
cooker.
2. Cover. Cook on Low 8-
10 hours, or High 4-5 hours.
3. Ladle into bowls and
top individual servings with
sour cream, cheddar cheese,
and chips.

White Chili Speciality

Barbara McGinnis
Jupiter, FL

Makes 8-10 servings

1 lb. large Great Northern
  beans, soaked overnight
2 lbs. boneless, skinless
  chicken breasts, cut up
1 medium onion, chopped
2 4½-oz. cans chopped
  green chilies
2 tsp. cumin
½ tsp. salt
14½-oz. can chicken broth
1 cup water

1. Put soaked beans in
medium-sized saucepan and
cover with water. Bring to
boil and simmer 20 minutes.
Discard water.
2. Brown chicken, if
desired, in 1-2 Tbsp. oil in
skillet.
3. Combine pre-cooked
and drained beans, chicken,
and all remaining ingredients
in slow cooker.
4. Cover. Cook on Low 10-
12 hours, or High 5-6 hours.

Chicken Tortilla Soup

Becky Harder
Monument, CO

Makes 6-8 servings

4 chicken breast halves
2 15-oz. cans black beans,
  undrained
2 15-oz. cans Mexican
  stewed tomatoes, *or*
  Rotel tomatoes
1 cup salsa (mild, medium,
  or hot, whichever you
  prefer)
4-oz. can chopped green
  chilies
14½-oz. can tomato sauce
tortilla chips
2 cups grated cheese

1. Combine all ingredients
except chips and cheese in
large slow cooker.
2. Cover. Cook on Low 8
hours.
3. Just before serving,
remove chicken breasts and
slice into bite-sized pieces.
Stir into soup.
4. To serve, put a handful
of chips in each individual
soup bowl. Ladle soup over
chips. Top with cheese.

Tortilla Soup

Joy Mintzer
Newark, DE

Makes 6 servings

4 chicken breast halves
1 garlic clove, minced
2 Tbsp. margarine
2 14½-oz. cans chicken broth
2 14½-oz. cans chopped stewed tomatoes
1 cup salsa (mild, medium, *or* hot, whichever you prefer)
½ cup chopped cilantro
1 Tbsp., *or* more, ground cumin
8-oz. Monterey Jack cheese, cubed
sour cream
tortilla chips

1. Cook, debone, and shred chicken.
2. Add minced garlic to margarine in slow cooker. Saute.
3. Combine all ingredients except cheese, sour cream, and chips.
4. Cover. Cook on Low 8-10 hours.
5. Divide cubed cheese among 6 individual soup bowls. Ladle soup over cheese. Sprinkle with chips and top each bowl with a dollop of sour cream.

Tex-Mex Chicken Chowder

Janie Steele
Moore, OK

Makes 8-10 servings

1 cup chopped onions
1 cup thinly sliced celery
2 garlic cloves, minced
1 Tbsp. oil
1½ lbs. boneless, skinless chicken breasts, cubed
32-oz. can chicken broth
1 pkg. country gravy mix
2 cups milk
16-oz. jar chunky salsa
32-oz. bag frozen hash brown potatoes
4½-oz. can chopped green chilies
8 oz. Velveeta cheese, cubed

1. Combine onions, celery, garlic, oil, chicken, and broth in 5-quart or larger slow cooker.
2. Cover. Cook on Low 2½ hours, until chicken is no longer pink.
3. In separate bowl, dissolve gravy mix in milk. Stir into chicken mixture. Add salsa, potatoes, chilies, and cheese and combine well. Cook on Low 2-4 hours, or until potatoes are fully cooked.

Chicken and Ham Gumbo

Barbara Tenney
Delta, PA

Makes 4 servings

1½ lbs. boneless, skinless chicken thighs
1 Tbsp. oil
10-oz. pkg. frozen okra
½ lb. smoked ham, cut into small chunks
1½ cups coarsely chopped onions
1½ cups coarsely chopped green peppers
2 or 3 10-oz. cans cannellini beans, drained
6 cups chicken broth
2 10-oz. cans diced tomatoes with green chilies
2 Tbsp. chopped fresh cilantro

1. Cut chicken into bite-sized pieces. Cook in oil in skillet until no longer pink.
2. Run hot water over okra until pieces separate easily.
3. Combine all ingredients but cilantro in slow cooker.
4. Cover. Cook on Low 6-8 hours. Stir in cilantro before serving.

Variations:
1. Stir in ½ cup long grain, dry rice with rest of ingredients.
2. Add ¾ tsp. salt and ¼ tsp. pepper with other ingredients.

Easy Southern Brunswick Stew

Barbara Sparks
Glen Burnie, MD

Makes 10-12 servings

2-3 lbs. pork butt
17-oz. can white corn
14-oz. bottle ketchup
2 cups diced, cooked poatotes
10-oz. pkg. frozen peas
2 10³/4-oz. cans tomato soup
hot sauce to taste
salt to taste
pepper to taste

1. Place pork in slow cooker.
2. Cover. Cook on Low 6-8 hours. Remove meat from bone and shred.
3. Combine all ingredients in slow cooker.
4. Cover. Bring to boil on High. Reduce heat to Low and simmer 30 minutes.

Joy's Brunswick Stew

Joy Sutter
Iowa City, IA

Makes 8 servings

1 lb. skinless, boneless chicken breasts, cut into bite-sized pieces
2 potatoes, thinly sliced
10³/4-oz. can tomato soup
16-oz. can stewed tomatoes
10-oz. pkg. frozen corn
10-oz. pkg. frozen lima beans
3 Tbsp. onion flakes
1/4 tsp. salt
1/8 tsp. pepper

1. Combine all ingredients in slow cooker.
2. Cover. Cook on High 2 hours. Reduce to Low and cook 2 hours.

Variation:
For more flavor, add 1, *or 2*, bay leaves during cooking.

Brunswick Soup Mix

Joyce B. Suiter
Garysburg, NC

Makes 14 servings

1 large onion, chopped
4 cups frozen, cubed, hash browns, thawed
4 cups chopped cooked chicken, *or* 2 20-oz. cans canned chicken
14¹/2-oz. can diced tomatoes
15-oz. can tomato sauce
15¹/4-oz. can corn
15¹/4-oz. can lima beans, drained
2 cups chicken broth
1/2 tsp. salt
1/2 tsp. pepper
1/4 tsp. Worcestershire sauce
1/4 cup sugar

1. Combine all ingredients in large slow cooker.
2. Cover. Cook on High 7 hours.
3. Cool and freeze in 2-cup portions.
4. To use, empty 1 frozen portion into saucepan with small amount of liquid: tomato juice, V-8 juice, or broth. Cook slowly until soup mixture thaws. Stir frequently, adding more liquid until of desired consistency.

Oriental Turkey Chili

Kimberly Jensen
Bailey, CO

Makes 6 servings

2 cups yellow onions, diced
1 small red bell pepper,
   diced
1 lb. ground turkey,
   browned
2 Tbsp. minced gingerroot
3 cloves garlic, minced
1/4 cup dry sherry
1/4 cup hoisin sauce
2 Tbsp. chili powder
1 Tbsp. corn oil
2 Tbsp. soy sauce
1 tsp. sugar
2 cups canned whole
   tomatoes
16 oz. can dark red kidney
   beans, undrained

1. Combine all ingredients
in slow cooker.
2. Cover. Cook on Low 6
hours.
3. Serve topped with chow
mein noodles or over cooked
white rice.

Note:
If you serve this chili over
rice, this recipe will yield 10-
12 servings.

Joyce's Slow-Cooked Chili

Joyce Slaymaker
Strasburg, PA

Makes 10 servings

2 lbs. ground turkey
2 16-oz. cans kidney beans,
   rinsed and drained
2 14½-oz. cans diced
   tomatoes, undrained
8-oz. can tomato sauce
2 medium onions, chopped
1 green pepper, chopped
2 cloves garlic, minced
2 Tbsp. chili powder
2 tsp. salt, optional
1 tsp. pepper
shredded cheddar cheese,
   optional

1. Brown ground turkey in
skillet. Drain. Transfer to
slow cooker.
2. Stir in remaining ingredients except cheese.
3. Cover. Cook on Low 8-
10 hours, or on High 4 hours.
4. Garnish individual servings with cheese.

Turkey Chili

Dawn Day
Westminster, CA

Makes 6-8 servings

1 large chopped onion
2-3 Tbsp. oil
1 lb. ground turkey
½ tsp. salt
3 Tbsp. chili powder
6-oz. can tomato paste
3 1-lb. cans small red
   beans with liquid
1 cup frozen corn

1. Saute onion in oil in
skillet until transparent. Add
turkey and salt and brown
lightly in skillet.
2. Combine all ingredients
in slow cooker. Mix well.
3. Cover. Cook on Low 8-9
hours.

Note:
Ground beef can be used
in place of turkey.

Variation:
Serve over rice, topped
with shredded cheddar
cheese and sour cream.

Chili Sans Cholesterol

Dolores S. Kratz
Souderton, PA

Makes 4 servings

1 lb. ground turkey
1/2 cup chopped celery
1/2 cup chopped onions
8-oz. can tomatoes
14-oz. can pinto beans
14 1/2-oz. can diced
   tomatoes
1/2 tsp., *or more*, chili
   powder
1/2 tsp. salt
dash pepper

1. Saute turkey in skillet until browned. Drain.
2. Combine all ingredients in slow cooker.
3. Cover. Cook on Low 6 hours.

Leftover Turkey Soup

Janie Steele
Moore, OK

Makes 8-10 servings

1 small onion, chopped
1 cup chopped celery
1 Tbsp. oil
2-3 cups diced turkey
1 cup cooked rice
leftover gravy, *or*
   combination of leftover
   gravy and chicken broth

1. Saute onion and celery in oil in saucepan until translucent.
2. Combine all ingredients in slow cooker, adding gravy and/or broth until of the consistency you want.
3. Cover. Cook on Low for at least 2-3 hours, or until heated through.

Italian Vegetable Soup

Patti Boston
Newark, OH

Makes 4-6 servings

3 small carrots, sliced
1 small onion, chopped
2 small potatoes, diced
2 Tbsp. chopped parsley
1 garlic clove, minced
3 tsp. beef bouillon
   granules, *or* 3 beef
   bouillon cubes
1 1/4 tsp. dried basil
1/2 tsp. salt
1/4 tsp. pepper
16-oz. can red kidney
   beans, undrained
3 cups water
14 1/2-oz. can stewed
   tomatoes, with juice
1 cup diced, cooked ham

1. Layer carrots, onions, potatoes, parsley, garlic, beef bouillon, basil, salt, pepper, and kidney beans in slow cooker. Do not stir. Add water.
2. Cover. Cook on Low 8-9 hours, or on High 4 1/2-5 1/2 hours, until vegetables are tender.
3. Stir in tomatoes and ham. Cover and cook on High 10-15 minutes.

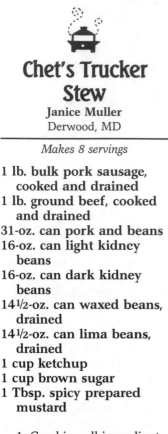

Chet's Trucker Stew

Janice Muller
Derwood, MD

Makes 8 servings

1 lb. bulk pork sausage,
   cooked and drained
1 lb. ground beef, cooked
   and drained
31-oz. can pork and beans
16-oz. can light kidney
   beans
16-oz. can dark kidney
   beans
14 1/2-oz. can waxed beans,
   drained
14 1/2-oz. can lima beans,
   drained
1 cup ketchup
1 cup brown sugar
1 Tbsp. spicy prepared
   mustard

1. Combine all ingredients
in slow cooker.
2. Cover. Simmer on High
2-3 hours.

Spicy Potato Soup

Sharon Kauffman
Harrisonburg, VA

Makes 6-8 servings

1 lb. ground beef, *or* bulk
   sausage, browned
4 cups cubed peeled
   potatoes
1 small onion, chopped
3 8-oz. cans tomato sauce
2 tsp. salt
1 1/2 tsp. pepper
1/2-1 tsp. hot pepper sauce
water

1. Combine all ingredients
except water in slow cooker.
Add enough water to cover
ingredients.
2. Cover. Cook on Low 8-
10 hours, or High 5 hours,
until potatoes are tender.

Hearty Potato Sauerkraut Soup

Kathy Hertzler
Lancaster, PA

Makes 6-8 servings

4 cups chicken broth
10 3/4-oz. can cream of
   mushroom soup
16-oz. can sauerkraut,
   rinsed and drained
8 oz. fresh mushrooms,
   sliced
1 medium potato, cubed
2 medium carrots, peeled
   and sliced
2 ribs celery, chopped
2 lbs. Polish kielbasa
   (smoked), cubed
2 1/2 cups chopped cooked
   chicken
2 Tbsp. vinegar
2 tsp. dried dillweed
1 1/2 tsp. pepper

1. Combine all ingredients
in large slow cooker.
2. Cover. Cook on Low 10-
12 hours.
3. If necessary, skim fat
before serving.

Sauerkraut Soup

Barbara Tenny
Delta, PA

Makes 8 servings

1 lb. smoked Polish
    sausage, cut into 1/2-inch
    pieces
5 medium potatoes, cubed
2 large onions, chopped
2 large carrots, cut into
    1/4-inch slices
42-45-oz. can chicken
    broth
32-oz. can *or* bag
    sauerkraut, rinsed and
    drained
6-oz. can tomato paste

1. Combine all ingredients
in large slow cooker. Stir to
combine.
2. Cover. Cook on High 2
hours, and then on Low 6-8
hours.
3. Serve with rye bread.

Kielbasa Soup

Bernice M. Gnidovec
Streator, IL

Makes 8 servings

16-oz. pkg. frozen mixed
    vegetables, *or* your
    choice of vegetables
6-oz. can tomato paste
1 medium onion, chopped
3 medium potatoes, diced
1 1/2 lbs. kielbasa, cut into
    1/4-inch pieces
4 qts. water
fresh parsley

1. Combine all ingredients
except parsley in large slow
cooker.
2. Cover. Cook on Low 12
hours.
3. Garnish individual servings with fresh parsley.

Curried Pork and Pea Soup

Kathy Hertzler
Lancaster, PA

Makes 6-8 servings

1 1/2-lb. boneless pork
    shoulder roast
1 cup yellow, *or* green, split
    peas, rinsed and drained
1/2 cup finely chopped
    carrots
1/2 cup finely chopped
    celery
1/2 cup finely chopped
    onions
49 1/2-oz. can
    (approximately 6 cups)
    chicken broth
2 tsp. curry powder
1/2 tsp. paprika
1/4 tsp. ground cumin
1/4 tsp. pepper
2 cups torn fresh spinach

1. Trim fat from pork and
cut pork into 1/2-inch pieces.
2. Combine split peas, carrots, celery, and onions in
slow cooker.
3. Stir in broth, curry powder, paprika, cumin, and pepper. Stir in pork.
4. Cover. Cook on Low 10-
12 hours, or on High 4 hours.
5. Stir in spinach. Serve
immediately.

Ruth's Split Pea Soup

Ruth Conrad Liechty
Goshen, IN

Makes 6-8 servings

1 lb. bulk sausage,
   browned and drained
6 cups water
1 bag (2¼ cups) dry split
   peas
2 medium potatoes, diced
1 onion, chopped
½ tsp. dried marjoram, *or*
   thyme
½ tsp. pepper

1. Wash and sort dried
peas, removing any stones.
Then combine all ingredients
in slow cooker.
2. Cover. Cook on Low 12
hours.

Kelly's Split Pea Soup

Kelly Evenson
Pittsboro, NC

Makes 8 servings

2 cups dry split peas
2 quarts water
2 onions, chopped
2 carrots, peeled and sliced
4 slices Canadian bacon,
   chopped
2 Tbsp. chicken bouillon
   granules, *or* 2 chicken
   bouillon cubes
1 tsp. salt
¼-½ tsp. pepper

1. Combine all ingredients
in slow cooker.
2. Cover. Cook on Low 8-9
hours.

Variation:
   For a creamier soup,
remove half of soup when
done and puree. Stir back
into rest of soup.

Karen's Split Pea Soup

Karen Stoltzfus
Alto, MI

Makes 6 servings

2 carrots
2 ribs celery
1 onion
1 parsnip
1 leek (keep 3 inches of
   green)
1 ripe tomato
1 ham hock
1¾ cups (1 lb.) dried split
   peas, washed, with
   stones removed
2 Tbsp. olive oil
1 bay leaf
1 tsp. dried thyme
4 cups chicken broth
4 cups water
1 tsp. salt
¼ tsp. pepper
2 tsp. chopped fresh
   parsley

1. Cut all vegetables into
¼-inch pieces and place in
slow cooker. Add remaining
ingredients except salt, pepper, and parsley.
2. Cover. Cook on High 7
hours.
3. Remove ham hock.
Shred meat from bone and
return meat to pot.
4. Season soup with salt
and pepper. Stir in parsley.
Serve immediately.

Sally's Split Pea Soup

Sally Holzem
Schofield, WI

Makes 8 servings

1-lb. pkg. split peas
1 ham hock
1 carrot, diced
1 onion, diced
1 rib celery, diced
2 qts. water
1/4 tsp. pepper
1 bay leaf
2 whole allspice
3 potatoes, diced
1 tsp. sugar

1. Wash and sort split peas, removing any stones. Then combine ingredients in slow cooker.
2. Cover. Cook on Low 8-10 hours.
3. Remove ham bone. Cut meat off and dice. Return meat to soup. Stir through.
4. Remove bay leaf before serving.

Dorothy's Split Pea Soup

Dorothy M. Van Deest
Memphis, TN

Makes 6-8 servings

2 Tbsp. butter, *or* margarine
1 cup minced onions
8 cups water
2 cups (1 lb.) green split peas, washed and stones removed
4 whole cloves
1 bay leaf
1/4 tsp. pepper
1 ham hock
1 cup finely minced celery
1 cup diced carrots
1/8 tsp. dried marjoram
1 Tbsp. salt
1/8 tsp. dried savory

1. Combine all ingredients in slow cooker.
2. Cover. Cook on Low 8-10 hours.
3. Remove ham bone and bay leaf before serving. Debone meat, cut into bite-sized pieces, and return to soup. Stir in and serve.

Variation:
For a thick soup, uncover soup after 8-10 hours and turn heat to High. Simmer, stirring occasionally, until the desired consistency is reached.

Rosemarie's Pea Soup

Rosemarie Fitzgerald
Gibsonia, PA
Shirley Sears
Tiskilwa, IL

Makes 4-6 servings

2 cups dried split peas
4 cups water
1 rib celery, chopped
1 cup chopped potatoes
1 large carrot, chopped
1 medium onion, chopped
1/4 tsp. dried thyme, *or* marjoram
1 bay leaf
1/2 tsp. salt
1 garlic clove
1/2 tsp. dried basil

1. Combine all ingredients in slow cooker.
2. Cover. Cook on Low 8-12 hours, or on High 6 hours, until peas are tender.

Variations:
For increased flavor, use chicken broth instead of water. Stir in curry powder, coriander, or red pepper flakes to taste.

French Market Soup

Ethel Mumaw
Berlin, OH

Makes 2½ quarts soup

2 cups dry bean mix,
  washed with stones
  removed
2 quarts water
1 ham hock
1 tsp. salt
¼ tsp. pepper
16-oz. can tomatoes
1 large onion, chopped
1 garlic clove, minced
1 chili pepper, chopped, *or*
  1 tsp. chili powder
¼ cup lemon juice

1. Combine all ingredients
in slow cooker.
2. Cover. Cook on Low 8
hours. Turn to High and cook
an additional 2 hours, or until
beans are tender.
3. Debone ham, cut meat
into bite-sized pieces, and stir
back into soup.

Nine Bean Soup with Tomatoes

Violette Harris Denney
Carrollton, GA

Makes 8-10 servings

2 cups dry nine-bean soup
  mix
1 lb. ham, diced
1 large onion, chopped
1 garlic clove, minced
½-¾ tsp. salt
2 qts. water
16-oz. can tomatoes,
  undrained and chopped
10-oz. can tomatoes with
  green chilies, undrained

1. Sort and wash bean
mix. Place in slow cooker.
Cover with water 2 inches
above beans. Let soak
overnight. Drain.
2. Add ham, onion, garlic,
salt, and 2 quarts fresh water.
3. Cover. Cook on Low 7
hours.
4. Add remaining ingredi-
ents and continue cooking on
Low another hour. Stir occasionally.

Note:
Bean Soup mix is a mix of
barley pearls, black beans,
red beans, pinto beans, navy
beans, Great Northern beans,
lentils, split peas, and black-
eyed peas.

Calico Ham and Bean Soup

Esther Martin
Ephrata, PA

Makes 6-8 servings

1 lb. dry bean mix, rinsed
  and drained, with
  stones removed
6 cups water
2 cups cubed cooked ham
1 cup chopped onions
1 cup chopped carrots
1 tsp. dried basil
1 tsp. dried oregano
¾ tsp. salt
¼ tsp. pepper
2 bay leaves
6 cups water
1 tsp. liquid smoke,
  optional

1. Combine beans and 6
cups water in large saucepan.
Bring to boil, reduce heat,
and simmer uncovered for 10
minutes. Drain, discarding
cooking water, and rinse
beans.
2. Combine all ingredients
in slow cooker.
3. Cover. Cook on Low 8-
10 hours, or High 4-5 hours.
Discard bay leaves before
serving.

Bean and Herb Soup

LaVerne A. Olson
Willow Street, PA

Makes 6-8 servings

1½ cups dry mixed beans
5 cups water
1 ham hock
1 cup chopped onions
1 cup chopped celery
1 cup chopped carrots
2-3 cups water
1 tsp. salt
¼-½ tsp. pepper
1-2 tsp. fresh basil, *or*
    ½ tsp. dried basil
1-2 tsp. fresh oregano, *or*
    ½ tsp. dried oregano
1-2 tsp. fresh thyme, *or*
    ½ tsp. dried thyme
2 cups fresh tomatoes,
    crushed, *or* 14½-oz. can
    crushed tomatoes

1. Combine beans, water, and ham in saucepan. Bring to boil. Turn off heat and let stand 1 hour.
2. Combine onions, celery, and carrots in 2-3 cups water in another saucepan. Cook until soft. Mash slightly.
3. Combine all ingredients in slow cooker.
4. Cover. Cook on High 2 hours, and then on Low 2 hours.

Northern Bean Soup

Patricia Howard
Albuquerque, NM

Makes 6-8 servings

1 lb. dry Northern beans
1 lb. ham
2 medium onions, chopped
half a green pepper,
    chopped
1 cup chopped celery
16-oz. can diced tomatoes
4 carrots, peeled and
    chopped
4-oz. can green chili
    peppers
1 tsp. garlic powder
1-2 qts. water
2-3 tsp. salt

1. Wash beans. Cover with water and soak overnight. Drain. Pour into slow cooker.
2. Dice ham into 1-inch pieces. Add to beans.
3. Stir in remaining ingredients.
4. Cover. Cook on High 2 hours, then on Low 10-12 hours, or until beans are tender.

Easy Lima Bean Soup

Barbara Tenney
Delta, PA

Makes 8-10 servings

1 lb. bag large dry lima
    beans
1 large onion, chopped
6 ribs celery, chopped
3 large potatoes, cut in
    ½-inch cubes
2 large carrots, cut in
    ¼-inch rounds
2 cups ham, sausage, *or*
    kielbasa
1 Tbsp. salt
1 tsp. pepper
2 bay leaves
3 quarts water, *or*
    combination water and
    beef broth

1. Sort beans. Soak overnight. Drain.
2. Combine all ingredients in slow cooker.
3. Cover. Cook on Low 8-10 hours.

Variation:
For extra flavor, add 1 tsp. dried oregano before cooking.

Most slow cookers perform best when more than half full.
Dorothy M. Van Deest
Memphis, TN

Slow Cooked Navy Beans with Ham

Julia Lapp
New Holland, PA

Makes 8-10 servings

1 lb. dry navy beans (2½ cups)
5 cups water
1 garlic clove, minced
1 ham hock
1 tsp. salt

1. Soak beans in water at least 4 hours in slow cooker.
2. Add garlic and ham hock.
3. Cover. Cook on Low 7-8 hours, or High 4 hours. Add salt during last hour of cooking time.
4. Remove ham hock from cooker. Allow to cool. Cut ham from hock and stir back into bean mixture. Correct seasonings and serve in soup bowls with hot corn bread.

Variation:
For added flavor, stir 1 chopped onion, 2-3 chopped celery stalks, 2-3 sliced carrots, and 3-4 cups canned tomatoes into cooker with garlic and ham hock.

Navy Bean Soup

Joyce Bowman
Lady Lake, FL

Makes 8 servings

1 lb. dry navy beans
8 cups water
1 onion, finely chopped
2 bay leaves
½ tsp. ground thyme
½ tsp. nutmeg
2 tsp. salt
½ tsp. lemon pepper
3 garlic cloves, minced
one ham hock, *or* 1-lb. ham pieces

1. Soak beans in water overnight. Strain out stones but reserve liquid.
2. Combine all ingredients in slow cooker.
3. Cover. Cook on Low 8-10 hours. Debone meat and cut into bite-sized pieces. Set ham aside.
4. Puree three-fourths of soup in blender in small batches. When finished blending, stir in meat.

Variation:
Add small chunks of cooked potatoes when stirring in ham pieces after blending.

Overnight Bean Soup

Marie Morucci
Glen Lyon, PA

Makes 6-8 servings

1 lb. dry small white beans
6 cups water
2 cups boiling water
2 large carrots, diced
3 ribs celery, diced
2 tsp. chicken bouillon granules, *or* 2 chicken bouillon cubes
1 bay leaf
½ tsp. dried thyme
½ tsp. salt
¼ tsp. pepper
¼ cup chopped fresh parsley
1 envelope dry onion soup mix
crispy, crumbled bacon, optional

1. Rinse beans. Combine beans and 6 cups water in saucepan. Bring to boil. Reduce heat to low and simmer 2 minutes. Remove from heat. Cover and let stand 1 hour or overnight.
2. Place beans and soaking water in slow cooker. Add 2 cups boiling water, carrots, celery, bouillon, bay leaf, thyme, salt, and pepper.
3. Cover. Cook on High 5-5½ hours, or on Low 10-11 hours, until beans are tender.
4. Stir in parsley and soup mix. Cover. Cook on High 10-15 minutes.

5. Remove bay leaf. Garnish individual servings with bacon.

Old-Fashioned Bean Soup

Gladys M. High
Ephrata, PA

Makes 6 servings

1 lb. dry navy beans, *or* dry green split peas
1-lb. meaty ham bone, *or* 1 lb. ham pieces
1-2 tsp. salt
¼ tsp. ground pepper
½ cup chopped celery leaves
2 qts. water
1 medium onion, chopped
1 bay leaf, optional

1. Soak beans or peas overnight. Drain, discarding soaking water.
2. Combine all ingredients in slow cooker.
3. Cover. Cook on High 8-9 hours.
4. Debone ham bone, cut meat into bite-sized pieces, and stir back into soup.

Caribbean-Style Black Bean Soup

Sheryl Shenk
Harrisonburg, VA

Makes 8-10 servings

1 lb. dried black beans, washed and stones removed
3 onions, chopped
1 green pepper, chopped
4 cloves garlic, minced
1 ham hock, *or* ¾ cup cubed ham
1 Tbsp. oil
1 Tbsp. ground cumin
2 tsp. dried oregano
1 tsp. dried thyme
1 Tbsp. salt
½ tsp. pepper
3 cups water
2 Tbsp. vinegar
sour cream
fresh chopped cilantro

1. Soak beans overnight in 4 quarts water. Drain.
2. Combine beans, onions, green pepper, garlic, ham, oil, cumin, oregano, thyme, salt, pepper, and 3 cups fresh water. Stir well.
3. Cover. Cook on Low 8-10 hours, or on High 4-5 hours.
4. For a thick soup, remove half of cooked bean mixture and puree until smooth in blender or mash with potato masher. Return to cooker. If you like a soup-ier soup, leave as is.
5. Add vinegar and stir well. Debone ham, cut into bite-sized pieces, and return to soup.
6. Serve in soup bowls with a dollop of sour cream in the middle of each individual serving, topped with fresh cilantro.

Vegetable Bean Soup

Kathi Rogge
Alexandria, IN

Makes 6-8 servings

6 cups cooked beans: navy, pinto, Great Northern, etc.
1 meaty ham bone
1 cup cooked ham, diced
¼ tsp. garlic powder
1 small bay leaf
1 cup cubed potatoes
1 cup chopped onions
1 cup chopped celery
1 cup chopped carrots
water

1. Combine all ingredients except water in 3½-quart slow cooker. Add water to about 1 inch from top.
2. Cover. Cook on Low 5-8 hours.
3. Remove bay leaf before serving.

Slow-Cooker Black Bean Chili

Mary Seielstad
Sparks, NV

Makes 8 servings

1 lb. pork tenderloin, cut into 1-inch chunks
16-oz. jar thick chunky salsa
3 15-oz. cans black beans, rinsed and drained
1/2 cup chicken broth
1 medium red bell pepper, chopped
1 medium onion, chopped
1 tsp. ground cumin
2-3 tsp. chili powder
1-1 1/2 tsp. dried oregano
1/4 cup sour cream

1. Combine all ingredients except sour cream in slow cooker.
2. Cover. Cook on Low 6-8 hours, or until pork is tender.
3. Garnish individual servings with sour cream.

Note:
This is good served over brown rice.

Katelyn's Black Bean Soup

Katelyn Bailey
Mechanicsburg, PA

Makes 4-6 servings

1/3 cup chopped onions
1 garlic clove, minced
1-2 Tbsp. oil
2 15 1/2-oz. cans black beans, undrained
1 cup water
1 chicken bouillon cube
1/2 cup diced, cooked, smoked ham
1/2 cup diced carrots
1 dash, *or more*, cayenne pepper
1-2 drops, *or more*, Tabasco sauce
sour cream

1. Saute onion and garlic in oil in saucepan.
2. Puree or mash contents of one can of black beans. Add to sauteed ingredients.
3. Combine all ingredients except sour cream in slow cooker.
4. Cover. Cook on Low 6-8 hours.
5. Add dollop of sour cream to each individual bowl before serving.

Baked Bean Soup

Maryann Markano
Wilmington, DE

Makes 5-6 servings

1-lb. 12-oz. can baked beans
6 slices browned bacon, chopped
2 Tbsp. bacon drippings
2 Tbsp. finely chopped onions
14 1/2-oz. can stewed tomatoes
1 Tbsp. brown sugar
1 Tbsp. vinegar
1 tsp. seasoning salt

1. Combine all ingredients in slow cooker.
2. Cover. Cook on Low 4-6 hours.

Mjeodrah or Esau's Lentil Soup

Dianna Milhizer
Springfield, VA

Makes 8 servings

1 cup chopped carrots
1 cup diced celery
2 cups chopped onions
1 Tbsp. olive oil, *or* butter
2 cups brown rice
1 Tbsp. olive oil, *or* butter
6 cups water
1 lb. lentils, washed and
   drained
garden salad
vinaigrette

1. Saute carrots, celery, and onions in 1 Tbsp. oil in skillet. When soft and translucent place in slow cooker.
2. Brown rice in 1 Tbsp. oil until dry. Add to slow cooker.
3. Stir in water and lentils.
4. Cover. Cook on High 6-8 hours.
5. When thoroughly cooked, serve 1 cup each in individual soup bowls. Cover each with a serving of fresh garden salad (lettuce, spinach leaves, chopped tomatoes, minced onions, chopped bell peppers, sliced olives, sliced radishes). Pour favorite vinaigrette over all.

French Onion Soup

Jenny R. Unternahrer
Wayland, IA
Janice Yoskovich
Carmichaels, PA

Makes 10 servings

8-10 large onions, sliced
1/2 cup butter *or* margarine
6 10 1/2-oz. cans condensed
   beef broth
1 1/2 tsp. Worcestershire
   sauce
3 bay leaves
10 slices French bread,
   toasted
grated Parmesan and/or
   shredded mozzarella
   cheese

1. Saute onions in butter until crisp-tender. Transfer to slow cooker.
2. Add broth, Worcestershire sauce, and bay leaves.
3. Cover. Cook on Low 5-7 hours, or until onions are tender. Discard bay leaves.
4. Ladle into bowls. Top each with a slice of bread and some cheese.

Note:
For a more intense beef flavor, add one beef bouillon cube, or use home-cooked beef broth instead of canned broth.

Potato Soup

Jeanne Hertzog, Bethlehem, PA
Marcia S. Myer, Manheim, PA
Rhonda Lee Schmidt
Scranton, PA
Mitzi McGlynchey
Downingtown, PA
Vera Schmucker, Goshen, IN
Kaye Schnell, Falmouth, MA
Elizabeth Yoder
Millersburg, OH

Makes 8-10 servings

6 potatoes, peeled and
   cubed
2 leeks, chopped
2 onions, chopped
1 rib celery, sliced
4 chicken bouillon cubes
1 Tbsp. dried parsley
   flakes
5 cups water
1 Tbsp. salt
pepper to taste
1/3 cup butter
13-oz. can evaporated milk
chopped chives

1. Combine all ingredients except milk and chives in slow cooker.
2. Cover. Cook on Low 10-12 hours, or High 3-4 hours. Stir in milk during last hour.
3. If desired, mash potatoes before serving.
4. Garnish with chives.

Variations:
1. Add one carrot, sliced, to vegetables before cooking.
2. Instead of water and bouillon cubes, use 4-5 cups chicken stock.

No-Fuss Potato Soup

Lucille Amos
Greensboro, NC
Lavina Hochstedler
Grand Blanc, MI
Betty Moore
Plano, IL

Makes 8-10 servings

6 cups diced, peeled
  potatoes
5 cups water
2 cups diced onions
1/2 cup diced celery
1/2 cup chopped carrots
1/4 cup margarine, *or*
  butter
4 tsp. chicken bouillon
  granules
2 tsp. salt
1/4 tsp. pepper
12-oz. can evaporated milk
3 Tbsp. chopped fresh
  parsley
8 oz. cheddar, *or* Colby,
  cheese, shredded

1. Combine all ingredients
except milk, parsley, and
cheese in slow cooker.
2. Cover. Cook on High 7-8
hours, or until vegetables are
tender.
3. Stir in milk and parsley.
Stir in cheese until it melts.
Heat thoroughly.

Variations:
1. For added flavor, stir in
3 slices bacon, browned until
crisp, and crumbled.
2. Top individual servings
with chopped chives.

Baked Potato Soup

Kristina Shull
Timberville, VA

Makes 6-8 servings

4 large baked potatoes
2/3 cup butter
2/3 cup flour
6 cups milk, whole *or* 2%
3/4 tsp. salt
1/2 tsp. pepper
4 green onions, chopped
12 slices bacon, fried and
  crumbled
2 cups shredded cheddar
  cheese
1 cup (8 oz.) sour cream

1. Cut potatoes in half.
Scoop out pulp and put in
small bowl.
2. Melt butter in large kettle. Add flour. Gradually stir
in milk. Continue to stir until
smooth, thickened, and bubbly.
3. Stir in potato pulp, salt,
pepper, and three-quarters of
the onions, bacon, and
cheese. Cook until heated.
Stir in sour cream.
4. Transfer to slow cooker
set on Low. Top with remaining onions, bacon, and
cheese. Take to a potluck, or
serve on a buffet table,
straight from the cooker.

Variation:
Add several slices of
Velveeta cheese to make soup
extra cheesy and creamy.

Sandy's Potato Soup

Sandra D. Thony
Jenks, OK

Makes 8-10 servings

8 large potatoes, cubed
2 medium onions, chopped
3 Tbsp. butter, *or*
  margarine
1/2-1 lb. bacon, cooked
  crisp, drained, and
  crumbled
3 chicken bouillon cubes
2 Tbsp. dried parsley
6 cups water
2 cups milk
1/2 cup flour
1/4 cup water
1 tsp. salt
1/4-1/2 tsp. pepper

1. Combine all ingredients
except flour, 1/4 cup water,
salt, and pepper in large slow
cooker.
2. Cover. Cook on High 6
hours, and then on Low 3
hours.
3. Make paste out of flour
and water. Stir into soup one
hour before serving. Season
with salt and pepper.

Variations:
1. Make Cheesy Potato
Soup by adding 1/4 lb. cubed
Velveeta, or your choice of
cheese, during last hour of
cooking.
2. For added richness, use
1 cup whole milk and 1 cup
evaporated milk.

German Potato Soup

Lee Ann Hazlett
Freeport, IL

Makes 6-8 servings

1 onion, chopped
1 leek, trimmed and diced
2 carrots, diced
1 cup chopped cabbage
1/4 cup chopped fresh
  parsley
4 cups beef broth
1 lb. potatoes, diced
1 bay leaf
1-2 tsp. black pepper
1 tsp. salt, optional
1/2 tsp. caraway seeds,
  optional
1/4 tsp. nutmeg
1 lb. bacon, cooked and
  crumbled
1/2 cup sour cream

1. Combine all ingredients
except bacon and sour cream.
2. Cover. Cook on Low 8-
10 hours, or High 4-5 hours.
3. Remove bay leaf. Use a
slotted spoon to remove potatoes. Mash potatoes and mix
with sour cream. Return to
slow cooker. Stir in. Add
bacon and mix together thoroughly.

Potato Comfort Soup

Charlotte Bull
Cassville, MO

Makes 8 servings

6 cups cubed, peeled
  potatoes
2 cups chopped onions
1/2 cup chopped celery
1 cup chopped carrots
5 cups water
1/4 cup butter, *or*
  margarine
1-2 tsp. salt, optional
1/4-1/2 tsp. pepper
2 cups milk
2 eggs
flour
1-2 Tbsp. dried parsley
butter, *or* margarine

1. Combine vegetables,
water, 1/4 cup butter or margarine, salt, and pepper in
slow cooker.
2. Cover. Cook on High 7-8
hours, or until vegetables are
tender.
3. Add milk. Stir in.
4. Make "drop noodles" by
beating eggs in a small bowl.
Add enough flour to make a
very soft, almost runny, batter. Dribble spoonfuls into
hot soup in cooker. (You may
find it easiest to use two
spoons to do this: one spoon
to dip up the "noodles"; the
other to push them into the
cooker. "Noodles" should not
be big clumps, yet they need
to be big enough to hold
together.)
5. Cover. Cook on Low
one more hour.
6. When ready to serve,
add parsley and a block of
butter or margarine to each
individual bowl.

Milk products such as cream, milk, and sour cream can
curdle and separate when cooked for a long period. Add
them during the last 10 minutes if cooking on High, or dur-
ing the last 20-30 minutes if cooking on Low.
Mrs. J.E. Barthold
Bethlehem, PA
Marilyn Yoder
Archbold, OH

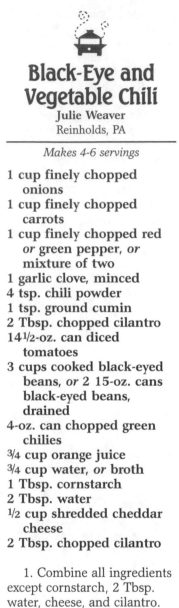

Black-Eye and Vegetable Chili

Julie Weaver
Reinholds, PA

Makes 4-6 servings

1 cup finely chopped
  onions
1 cup finely chopped
  carrots
1 cup finely chopped red
  or green pepper, *or*
  mixture of two
1 garlic clove, minced
4 tsp. chili powder
1 tsp. ground cumin
2 Tbsp. chopped cilantro
14½-oz. can diced
  tomatoes
3 cups cooked black-eyed
  beans, *or* 2 15-oz. cans
  black-eyed beans,
  drained
4-oz. can chopped green
  chilies
¾ cup orange juice
¾ cup water, *or* broth
1 Tbsp. cornstarch
2 Tbsp. water
½ cup shredded cheddar
  cheese
2 Tbsp. chopped cilantro

1. Combine all ingredients
except cornstarch, 2 Tbsp.
water, cheese, and cilantro.
2. Cover. Cook on Low 6-8
hours, or High 4 hours.
3. Dissolve cornstarch in
water. Stir into soup mixture
30 minutes before serving.
4. Garnish individual servings with cheese and cilantro.

Veggie Chili

Wanda Roth
Napoleon, OH

Makes 6 servings

2 qts. whole *or* diced
  tomatoes, undrained
6-oz. can tomato paste
½ cup chopped onions
½ cup chopped celery
½ cup chopped green
  peppers
2 garlic cloves, minced
1 tsp. salt
1½ tsp. ground cumin
1 tsp. dried oregano
¼ tsp. cayenne pepper
3 Tbsp. brown sugar
15-oz. can garbanzo beans

1. Combine all ingredients
except beans in slow cooker.
2. Cook on Low 6-8 hours,
or High 3-4 hours. Add beans
one hour before serving.

Variation:
If you prefer a less toma-
toey taste, substitute 2 vegetable bouillon cubes and 1
cup water for tomato paste.

Beans and Tomato Chili

Becky Harder
Monument, CO

Makes 6-8 servings

15-oz. can black beans,
  undrained
15-oz. can pinto beans,
  undrained
16-oz. can kidney beans,
  undrained
15-oz. can garbanzo beans,
  undrained
2 14½-oz. cans stewed
  tomatoes and juice
1 pkg. prepared chili
  seasoning

1. Pour beans, including
their liquid, into slow cooker.
2. Stir in tomatoes and
chili seasoning.
3. Cover. Cook on Low
4-8 hours.
4. Serve with crackers, and
topped with grated cheddar
cheese, sliced green onions,
and sour cream, if desired.

Variation:
Add additional cans of
white beans or 1 tsp. dried
onion.

VEGETARIAN SOUPS

Vegetarian Chili
Connie Johnson
Loudon, NH

Makes 6 servings

3 garlic cloves, minced
2 onions, chopped
1 cup textured vegetable protein (T.V.P.)
1-lb. can beans of your choice, drained
1 green bell pepper, chopped
1 jalapeno pepper, seeds removed, chopped
28-oz. can diced Italian tomatoes
1 bay leaf
1 Tbsp. dried oregano
1/2-1 tsp. salt
1/4 tsp. pepper

1. Combine all ingredients in slow cooker.
2. Cover. Cook on Low 6-8 hours.

Hearty Black Bean Soup
Della Yoder
Kalona, IA

Makes 6-8 servings

3 medium carrots, halved and thinly sliced
2 celery ribs, thinly sliced
1 medium onion, chopped
4 cloves garlic, minced
20-oz. can black beans, drained and rinsed
2 14 1/2-oz. cans chicken broth
15-oz. can crushed tomatoes
1 1/2 tsp. dried basil
1/2 tsp. dried oregano
1/2 tsp. ground cumin
1/2 tsp. chili powder
1/2 tsp. hot pepper sauce

1. Combine all ingredients in slow cooker.
2. Cover. Cook on Low 9-10 hours.

Note:
May be served over cooked rice.

Variation:
If you prefer a thicker soup, use only 1 can chicken broth.

Black Bean and Corn Soup
Joy Sutter
Iowa City, IA

Makes 6-8 servings

2 15-oz. cans black beans, drained and rinsed
14 1/2-oz. can Mexican stewed tomatoes, undrained
14 1/2-oz. can diced tomatoes, undrained
11-oz. can whole kernel corn, drained
4 green onions, sliced
2-3 Tbsp. chili powder
1 tsp. ground cumin
1/2 tsp. dried minced garlic

1. Combine all ingredients in slow cooker.
2. Cover. Cook on High 5-6 hours.

Variations:
1. Use 2 cloves fresh garlic, minced, instead of dried garlic.
2. Add 1 large rib celery, sliced thinly, and 1 small green pepper, chopped.

Tuscan Garlicky Bean Soup

Sara Harter Fredette
Williamsburg, MA

Makes 8-10 servings

1 lb. dry Great Northern,
  or other dry white,
  beans
1 qt. water
1 qt. beef broth
3 Tbsp. olive oil
2 garlic cloves, minced
4 Tbsp. chopped parsley
olive oil
2 tsp. salt
1/2 tsp. pepper

1. Place beans in large soup pot. Cover with water and bring to boil. Cook 2 minutes. Remove from heat. Cover pot and allow to stand for 1 hour. Drain, discarding water.

2. Combine beans, 1 quart fresh water, and beef broth in slow cooker.

3. Saute garlic and parsley in olive oil in skillet. Stir into slow cooker. Add salt and pepper.

4. Cover. Cook on Low 8-10 hours, or until beans are tender.

Bean Soup

Joyce Cox
Port Angeles, WA

Makes 10-12 servings

1 cup dry Great Northern
  beans
1 cup dry red beans, *or*
  pinto beans
4 cups water
28-oz. can diced tomatoes
1 medium onion, chopped
2 Tbsp. vegetable bouillon
  granules, *or* 4 bouillon
  cubes
2 garlic cloves, minced
2 tsp. Italian seasoning,
  crushed
9-oz. pkg. frozen green
  beans, thawed

1. Soak and rinse dried beans.

2. Combine all ingredients except green beans in slow cooker.

3. Cover. Cook on High 5 1/2-6 1/2 hours, or on Low 11-13 hours.

4. Stir green beans into soup during last 2 hours.

Veggie Stew

Ernestine Schrepfer
Trenton, MO

Makes 10-15 servings

5-6 potatoes, cubed
3 carrots, cubed
1 onion, chopped
1/2 cup chopped celery
2 cups canned diced *or*
  stewed tomatoes
3 chicken bouillon cubes
  dissolved in 3 cups
  water
1 1/2 tsp. dried thyme
1/2 tsp. dried parsley
1/2 cup brown rice,
  uncooked
1 lb. frozen green beans
1 lb. frozen corn
15-oz. can butter beans
46-oz. can V-8 juice

1. Combine potatoes, carrots, onion, celery, tomatoes, chicken stock, thyme, parsley, and rice in 5-quart cooker, or two medium-sized cookers.

2. Cover. Cook on High 2 hours. Puree one cup of mixture and add back to slow cooker to thicken the soup.

3. Stir in beans, corn, butter beans, and juice.

4. Cover. Cook on High 1 more hour, then reduce to Low and cook 6-8 more hours.

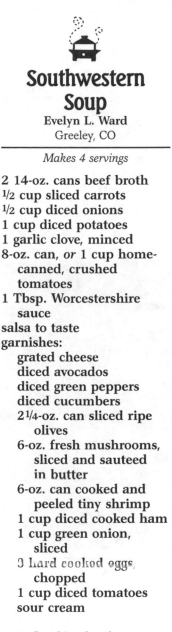

Southwestern Soup

Evelyn L. Ward
Greeley, CO

Makes 4 servings

2 14-oz. cans beef broth
1/2 cup sliced carrots
1/2 cup diced onions
1 cup diced potatoes
1 garlic clove, minced
8-oz. can, *or* 1 cup home-
    canned, crushed
    tomatoes
1 Tbsp. Worcestershire
    sauce
salsa to taste
garnishes:
    grated cheese
    diced avocados
    diced green peppers
    diced cucumbers
    2 1/4-oz. can sliced ripe
      olives
    6-oz. fresh mushrooms,
      sliced and sauteed
      in butter
    6-oz. can cooked and
      peeled tiny shrimp
    1 cup diced cooked ham
    1 cup green onion,
      sliced
    3 hard cooked eggs,
      chopped
    1 cup diced tomatoes
    sour cream

1. Combine broth, carrots, onions, potatoes, garlic, tomatoes, and Worcestershire sauce in slow cooker. Cook on Low 6-8 hours.
2. Before serving, stir in salsa, sampling as you go to get the right balance of flavors.
3. Serve the soup in bowls, allowing guests to add garnishes of their choice.

Heart Happy Tomato Soup

Anne Townsend
Albuquerque, NM

Makes 6 servings

46-oz. can tomato juice
8-oz. can tomato sauce
1/2 cup water
1 Tbsp. bouillon granules
1 sprig celery leaves,
    chopped
half an onion, thinly sliced
1/2 tsp. dried basil
2 Tbsp. sugar
1 bay leaf
1/2 tsp. whole cloves

1. Combine all ingredients in greased slow cooker. Stir well.
2. Cover. Cook on Low 5-8 hours. Remove bay leaf and cloves before serving.

Note:
    If you prefer a thicker soup, add 1/4 cup instant potato flakes. Stir well and cook 5 minutes longer.

Vegetarian Minestrone Soup

Connie Johnson
Loudon, NH

Makes 6 servings

6 cups vegetable broth
2 carrots, chopped
2 large onions, chopped
3 ribs celery, chopped
2 garlic cloves, minced
1 small zucchini, cubed
1 handful fresh kale,
    chopped
1/2 cup dry barley
1 can chickpeas, *or* white
    kidney beans, drained
1 Tbsp. parsley
1/2 tsp. dried thyme
1 tsp. dried oregano
28-oz. can crushed Italian
    tomatoes
1 tsp. salt
1/4 tsp. pepper
grated cheese

1. Combine all ingredients except cheese in slow cooker.
2. Cover. Cook on Low 6-8 hours, or until vegetables are tender.
3. Sprinkle individual servings with grated cheese.

Joyce's Minestrone

Joyce Shackelford
Green Bay, Wisconsin

Makes 6 servings

3½ cups beef broth
28-oz. can crushed
   tomatoes
2 medium carrots, thinly
   sliced
½ cup chopped onion
½ cup chopped celery
2 medium potatoes, thinly
   sliced
1-2 garlic cloves, minced
16-oz. can red kidney
   beans, drained
2 oz. thin spaghetti,
   broken into 2-inch
   pieces
2 Tbsp. parsley flakes
2-3 tsp. dried basil
1-2 tsp. dried oregano
1 bay leaf

1. Combine all ingredients
in slow cooker.
2. Cover. Cook on Low 10-
16 hours, or on High 4-6
hours.
3. Remove bay leaf. Serve.

Grace's Minestrone Soup

Grace Ketcham
Marietta, GA

Makes 8 servings

¾ cup dry elbow macaroni
2 qts. chicken stock
2 large onions, diced
2 carrots, sliced
half a head of cabbage,
   shredded
½ cup celery, diced
1-lb. can tomatoes
½ tsp. salt
½ tsp. dried oregano
1 Tbsp. minced parsley
¼ cup each frozen corn,
   peas, and lima beans
¼ tsp. pepper
grated Parmesan, *or*
   Romano, cheese

1. Cook macaroni accord-
ing to package directions. Set
aside.
2. Combine all ingredients
except macaroni and cheese
in large slow cooker.
3. Cover. Cook on Low 8
hours. Add macaroni during
last 30 minutes of cooking
time.
4. Garnish individual servings with cheese.

Cabbage Soup

Margaret Jarrett
Anderson, IN

Makes 8 servings

half a head of cabbage,
   sliced thin
2 ribs celery, sliced thin
2-3 carrots, sliced thin
1 onion, chopped
2 chicken bouillon cubes
2 garlic cloves, minced
1 qt. tomato juice
1 tsp. salt
¼ tsp. pepper
water

1. Combine all ingredients
except water in slow cooker.
Add water to within 3 inches
of top of slow cooker.
2. Cover. Cook on High
3½-4 hours, or until vegetables are tender.

Salsa Soup

Sue Hamilton
Minooka, IL

Makes 6 servings

3 cups (26 oz.) corn-black
   bean mild salsa
6 cups beef broth
¼ cup white long grain
   rice, uncooked

1. Combine all ingredients
in slow cooker.

2. Cover. Cook on Low 4-6 hours, or until rice is tender.

Winter Squash and White Bean Stew

Mary E. Herr
Three Rivers, MI

Makes 6 servings

1 cup chopped onions
1 Tbsp. olive oil
1/2 tsp. ground cumin
1/4 tsp. salt
1/4 tsp. cinnamon
1 garlic clove, minced
3 cups peeled, butternut squash, cut into 3/4-inch cubes
11/2 cups chicken broth
19-oz. can cannellini beans, drained
141/2-oz. can diced tomatoes, undrained
1 Tbsp. chopped fresh cilantro

1. Combine all ingredients in slow cooker.
2. Cover. Cook on High 1 hour. Reduce heat to Low and heat 2-3 hours.

Variations:
1. Beans can be pureed in blender and added during the last hour.
2. Eight ounces dried beans can be soaked overnight, cooked until soft, and used in place of canned beans.

Corn Chowder

Charlotte Fry
St. Charles, MO
Jeanette Oberholtzer
Manheim, PA

Makes 4 servings

6 slices bacon, diced
1/2 cup chopped onions
2 cups diced peeled potatoes
2 10-oz. pkgs. frozen corn
16-oz. can cream-style corn
1 Tbsp. sugar
1 tsp. Worcestershire sauce
1 tsp. seasoned salt
1/4 tsp. pepper
1 cup water

1. In skillet, brown bacon until crisp. Remove bacon, reserving drippings.
2. Add onions and potatoes to skillet and saute for 5 minutes. Drain.
3. Combine all ingredients in slow cooker. Mix well.
4. Cover. Cook on Low 6-7 hours.

Variations:
1. To make Clam Corn Chowder, drain and add 2 cans minced clams during last hour of cooking.
2. Substitute 1 quart home-frozen corn for the store-bought frozen and canned corn.

Cheese and Corn Chowder

Loretta Krahn
Mt. Lake, MN

Makes 8 servings

3/4 cup water
1/2 cup chopped onions
11/2 cups sliced carrots
11/2 cups chopped celery
1 tsp. salt
1/2 tsp. pepper
151/4-oz. can whole kernel corn, drained
15-oz. can cream-style corn
3 cups milk
11/2 cup grated cheddar cheese

1. Combine water, onions, carrots, celery, salt, and pepper in slow cooker.
2. Cover. Cook on High 4-6 hours.
3. Add corn, milk, and cheese. Heat on High 1 hour, and then turn to Low until you are ready to eat.

Cream of Broccoli Soup

Barb Yoder
Angola, IN

Makes 6-8 servings

1 small onion, chopped
oil
20-oz. pkg. frozen broccoli
2 10¾-oz. cans cream of
   celery soup
10¾-oz. can cream of
   mushroom soup
1 cup grated American
   cheese
2 soup cans milk

1. Saute onion in oil in skillet until soft.
2. Combine all ingredients in slow cooker.
3. Cover. Cook on Low 3-4 hours.

Broccoli-Cheese Soup

Darla Sathre
Baxter, MN

Makes 8 servings

2 16-oz. pkgs. frozen
   chopped broccoli
2 10¾-oz. cans cheddar
   cheese soup
2 12-oz. cans evaporated
   milk
¼ cup finely chopped onions

½ tsp. seasoned salt
¼ tsp. pepper
sunflower seeds, optional
crumbled bacon, optional

1. Combine all ingredients except sunflower seeds and bacon in slow cooker.
2. Cover. Cook on Low 8-10 hours.
3. Garnish with sunflower seeds and bacon.

Broccoli-Cheese with Noodles Soup

Carol Sherwood
Batavia, NY

Makes 8 servings

2 cups cooked noodles
10-oz. pkg. frozen chopped
   broccoli, thawed
3 Tbsp. chopped onions
2 Tbsp. butter
1 Tbsp. flour
2 cups cubed processed
   cheese
½ tsp. salt
5½ cups milk

1. Cook noodles just until soft in saucepan while combining rest of ingredients in slow cooker. Mix well.
2. Drain cooked noodles and stir into slow cooker.
3. Cover. Cook on Low 4 hours.

Double Cheese Cauliflower Soup

Zona Mae Bontrager
Kokomo, IN

Makes 6 servings

4 cups (1 small head)
   cauliflower pieces
2 cups water
8-oz. pkg. cream cheese,
   cubed
5 oz. American cheese
   spread
¼ lb. dried beef, torn into
   strips *or* shredded
½ cup potato flakes *or*
   buds

1. Combine cauliflower and water in saucepan. Bring to boil. Set aside.
2. Heat slow cooker on Low. Add cream cheese and cheese spread. Pour in cauliflower and water. Stir to be sure the cheese is dissolved and mixed through the cauliflower.
3. Add dried beef and potato flakes. Mix well.
4. Cover. Cook on Low 2-3 hours.

Main Dishes

Beef Stew

Wanda S. Curtin, Bradenton, FL
Paula King, Harrisonburg, VA
Miriam Nolt, New Holland, PA
Jean Shaner, York, PA
Mary W. Stauffer, Ephrata, PA
Alma Z. Weaver, Ephrata, PA

Makes 6 servings

2 lbs. beef chuck, cubed
1 tsp. Worcestershire sauce
1/4-1/2 cup flour
1 1/2 tsp. salt
1/2 tsp. pepper
1 tsp. paprika
1 1/2 cups beef broth
half garlic clove, minced
1 bay leaf
4 carrots, sliced
2 onions, chopped
1 rib celery, sliced
3 potatoes, diced

1. Place meat in slow cooker.

2. Combine flour, salt, pepper, and paprika. Stir into meat until coated thoroughly.

3. Add remaining ingredients. Mix well.

4. Cover. Cook on Low 10-12 hours, or High 4-6 hours. Stir before serving.

Audrey's Beef Stew

Audrey Romonosky
Austin, TX

Makes 4-6 servings

3 carrots, sliced
3 potatoes, cubed
2 lbs. beef chuck, cubed
2 cups water
2 beef bouillon cubes
1 tsp. Worcestershire sauce
1/2 tsp. garlic powder
1 bay leaf
1/4 tsp. salt
1/2 tsp. pepper
1 tsp. paprika
3 onions, chopped
1 rib celery, sliced
1/4 cup flour
1/3 cup cold water

1. Combine all ingredients except flour and 1/3 cup cold water in slow cooker. Mix well.

2. Cover. Cook on Low 8 hours.

3. Dissolve flour in 1/3 cup water. Stir into meat mixture. Cook on High until thickened, about 10 minutes.

Herbed Beef Stew

Carol Findling
Princeton, IL

Makes 6-8 servings

1 lb. beef round, cubed
4 Tbsp. seasoned flour *
1½ cups beef broth
1 tsp. Worcestershire sauce
1 garlic clove
1 bay leaf
4 carrots, sliced
3 potatoes, cubed
2 onions, diced
1 rounded tsp. fresh thyme, *or* ½ tsp. dried thyme
1 rounded tsp. chopped fresh basil, *or* ½ tsp. dried basil
1 Tbsp. fresh parsley, *or* 1 tsp. dried parsley
1 rounded tsp. fresh marjoram, *or* 1 tsp. dried marjoram

1. Put meat in slow cooker. Add seasoned flour. Toss with meat. Stir in remaining ingredients. Mix well.
2. Cover. Cook on High 4-6 hours, or Low 10-12 hours.

* **Seasoned Flour**
1 cup flour
1 tsp. salt
1 tsp. paprika
¼ tsp. pepper

Beef Stew Olé

Andrea O'Neil
Fairfield, CT

Makes 6-8 servings

4 carrots, cubed
4 potatoes, peeled and cubed
1 onion, quartered
1½ lbs. beef stewing meat, cubed
8-oz. can tomato sauce
1 pkg. dry taco seasoning mix
2 cups water, divided
1½ Tbsp. cornstarch
2 tsp. salt
¼ tsp. pepper

1. Layer first four ingredients in slow cooker. Add tomato sauce.
2. Combine taco seasoning with 1½ cups water. Stir cornstarch into remaining ½ cup water until smooth. Stir into rest of water with taco seasoning. Pour over ingredients in slow cooker.
3. Sprinkle with salt and pepper.
4. Cover. Cook on Low 7-8 hours.
5. Serve over rice.

Variation:
If those eating at your table are cautious about spicy food, choose a "mild" taco seasoning mix and add 1 tsp. sugar to the seasonings.

Pot Roast

Carole Whaling
New Tripoli, PA

Makes 8 servings

4 medium potatoes, cubed
4 carrots, sliced
1 onion, sliced
3-4-lb. rump roast, *or* pot roast, cut into serving-size pieces
1 tsp. salt
½ tsp. pepper
1 bouillon cube
½ cup boiling water

1. Put vegetables and meat in slow cooker. Stir in salt and pepper.
2. Dissolve bouillon cube in water, then pour over other ingredients.
3. Cover. Cook on Low 10-12 hours.

Swiss Steak

Marilyn Mowry
Irving, TX

Makes 4-6 servings

3-4 Tbsp. flour
½ tsp. salt
¼ tsp. pepper
1½ tsp. dry mustard
1½-2 lbs. round steak
oil
1 cup sliced onions
1 lb. carrots

14 1/2-oz. can whole
  tomatoes
1 Tbsp. brown sugar
1 1/2 Tbsp. Worcestershire
  sauce

1. Combine flour, salt, pepper, and dry mustard.
2. Cut steak into serving pieces. Dredge in flour mixture. Brown on both sides in oil in saucepan. Place in slow cooker.
3. Add onions and carrots.
4. Combine tomatoes, brown sugar, and Worcestershire sauce. Pour into slow cooker.
5. Cover. Cook on Low 8-10 hours, or High 3-5 hours.

Round Steak Casserole

Gladys High
Ephrata, PA

Makes 6 servings

2 lbs. round steak, cut
  1/2-inch thick
1 tsp. salt
1/4 tsp. pepper
1 onion, thinly sliced
3-4 potatoes, pared and
  quartered
16-oz. can French-style
  green beans, drained
1 clove garlic, minced
10 3/4-oz. can tomato soup
14 1/2-oz. can tomatoes

1. Season roast with salt and pepper. Cut into serving pieces and place in slow cooker.

2. Add onion, potatoes, green beans, and garlic. Top with soup and tomatoes.
3. Cover and cook on Low 8-10 hours, or High 4-5 hours. Remove cover during last half hour if too much liquid has collected.

Hearty Beef Stew

Charlotte Shaffer
East Earl, PA

Makes 4-5 servings

2 lbs. stewing beef, cubed
5 carrots, sliced
1 large onion, cut in
  chunks
3 ribs celery, sliced
22-oz. can stewed tomatoes
1/2 tsp. ground cloves
2 bay leaves
1 1/2 tsp. salt
1/4-1/2 tsp. pepper

1. Combine all ingredients in slow cooker.
2. Cover. Cook on High 5-6 hours.

Variations:
1. Substitute 1 whole clove for the 1/2 tsp. ground cloves. Remove before serving.
2. Use venison instead of beef.
3. Cut back the salt to 1 tsp. and use 1 tsp. soy sauce.
  Betty B. Dennison
  Grove City, PA

Judy's Beef Stew

Judy Koczo
Plano, IL

Makes 4-6 servings

2 lbs. stewing meat, cubed
5 carrots, sliced
1 onion, diced
3 ribs celery, diced
5 potatoes, cubed
28-oz. can tomatoes
1/3-1/2 cup quick-cooking
  tapioca
2 tsp. salt
1/2 tsp. pepper

1. Combine all ingredients in slow cooker.
2. Cover. Cook on Low 10-12 hours, or High 5-6 hours.

Variation:
Add 1 whole clove and 2 bay leaves to stew before cooking.
  L. Jean Moore
  Pendleton, IN

Slow-Cooker Stew
Trudy Kutter
Corfu, NY

Makes 6-8 servings

2 lbs. boneless beef, cubed
4-6 celery ribs, sliced
6-8 carrots, sliced
6 potatoes, cubed
2 onions, sliced
28-oz. can tomatoes
1/4 cup minute tapioca
1 tsp. salt
1/4 tsp. pepper
1/2 tsp. dried basil,
   or oregano
1 garlic clove, pressed *or*
   minced

1. Combine all ingredients in slow cooker.
2. Cover. Cook on Low 8-10 hours.

Variation:
Add 2 10 1/2-oz. cans beef gravy and 1/2 cup water in place of the tomatoes. Reduce tapioca to 2 Tbsp.

Italian Stew
Ann Gouinlock
Alexander, NY

Makes 6 servings

1 1/2 lbs. beef cubes
2-3 carrots, cut in 1-inch chunks
3-4 ribs celery, cut in 3/4-1-inch pieces
1-1 1/2 cups coarsely chopped onions
14 1/2-oz. can stewed, *or* diced, tomatoes
1/3 cup minute tapioca
1 1/2 tsp. salt
1/4 tsp. pepper
1/4 tsp. Worcestershire sauce
1/2 tsp. Italian seasoning

1. Combine all ingredients in slow cooker.
2. Cover. Cook on Low 8-10 hours.

Herby Beef Stew
Tracy Supcoe
Barclay, MD

Makes 6 servings

1-2 lbs. stewing meat, cubed
2/3 cup flour
1 1/2 tsp. salt
1/4 tsp. pepper
oil
14 1/2-oz. can diced tomatoes
8-oz. can tomato sauce
14 1/2-oz. can beef broth
2 Tbsp. Worcestershire sauce
1 bay leaf
2 tsp. kitchen bouquet
2 Tbsp. dried parsley
1 tsp. Hungarian sweet paprika
4 celery heart ribs, chopped
5 mushrooms, sliced
3 potatoes, cubed
3 cloves garlic, minced
1 large onion, chopped

1. Combine flour, salt, and pepper in bowl. Dredge meat in seasoned flour, then brown in oil in saucepan. Place meat in slow cooker.
2. Combine remaining ingredients in bowl. Pour over meat and mix well.
3. Cover. Cook on High 5-6 hours, or Low 10-12 hours. Stir before serving.

Liquids don't boil down in a slow cooker. At the end of the cooking time, remove the cover, set dial on High and allow the liquid to evaporate, if the dish is soup-ier than you want.
John D. Allen
Rye, CO

Venison or Beef Stew

Frances B. Musser
Newmanstown, PA

Makes 6 servings

1½ lbs. venison *or* beef cubes
2 Tbsp. oil
1 medium onion, chopped
4 carrots, peeled and cut into 1-inch pieces
1 rib celery, cut into 1-inch pieces
4 medium potatoes, peeled and quartered
12-oz. can whole tomatoes, undrained
10½-oz. can beef broth
1 Tbsp. Worcestershire sauce
1 Tbsp. parsley flakes
1 bay leaf
2½ tsp. salt
¼ tsp. pepper
2 Tbsp. quick-cooking tapioca

1. Brown meat cubes in skillet in oil over medium heat. Transfer to slow cooker.
2. Add remaining ingredients. Mix well.
3. Cover. Cook on Low 8-9 hours.

Variations:

1. Substitute 1½ tsp. garlic salt and 1 tsp. salt for 2½ tsp. salt.
2. For added color and flavor, add 1 cup frozen peas 5 minutes before end of cooking time.

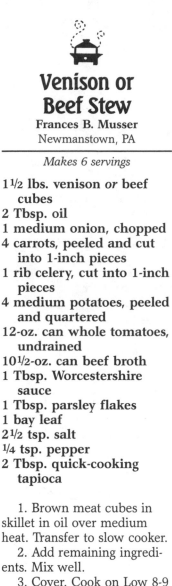

Layered Herby Stew

Elizabeth L. Richards
Rapid City, SD

Makes 8 servings

2½ lbs. lean beef chuck, cubed
1 medium to large onion, cut in 1-inch pieces
8-12 small red potatoes *or* potato chunks
4-6 carrots, cut in 1-inch pieces
2 large ribs celery, cut in 1-inch pieces
2 Tbsp. Worcestershire sauce
¼ cup red wine, *or* water
3 Tbsp. brown sugar
1 tsp. salt
½ tsp. pepper
⅛ tsp. allspice
¼ tsp. dried marjoram
¼ tsp. dried thyme
2 bay leaves
6 Tbsp. minute tapioca (use only 5 Tbsp. if using water instead of red wine)
28-oz. can diced tomatoes
½ cup chopped fresh parsley

1. Layer all ingredients except parsley in slow cooker in order given.
2. Cover. Cook on High 6 hours.
3. Immediately before serving, garnish with parsley.

Waldorf Astoria Stew

Mary V. Warye
West Liberty, OH

Makes 6-8 servings

3 lbs. beef stewing meat, cubed
1 medium onion, chopped
1 cup celery, sliced
2 cups carrots, sliced
4 medium potatoes, cubed
3 Tbsp. minute tapioca
1 Tbsp. sugar
1 Tbsp. salt
½ tsp. pepper
10¾-oz. can tomato soup
⅓ cup water

1. Layer meat, onion, celery, carrots, and potatoes in slow cooker. Sprinkle with seasonings and tapioca. Add soup and water.
2. Cover. Cook on Low 7-9 hours.

Busy Day Beef Stew

Dale Peterson
Rapid City, SC

Makes 6-8 servings

2 lbs. stewing meat, cubed
2 medium onions, diced
1 cup chopped celery
2 cups sliced carrots
4 medium potatoes, diced
2½ Tbsp. quick-cooking
   tapioca
1 Tbsp. sugar
1 tsp. salt
½ tsp. pepper
10¾-oz. can tomato soup
1½ soup cans water

1. Layer meat and vegetables in slow cooker. Sprinkle with tapioca, sugar, salt, and pepper. Combine soup and water and pour into slow cooker. Do not stir.
2. Cover. Cook on Low 6-8 hours.

Pungent Beef Stew

Grace Ketcham
Marietta, GA

Makes 4-6 servings

2 lbs. beef chuck, cubed
1 tsp. Worcestershire sauce
1 garlic clove, minced
1 medium onion, chopped
2 bay leaves
½ tsp. salt
½ tsp. paprika
¼ tsp. pepper
dash of ground cloves, *or*
   allspice
6 carrots, quartered
4 potatoes, quartered
2 ribs celery, chopped
10¾-oz. can tomato soup
½ cup water

1. Combine all ingredients in slow cooker.
2. Cover. Cook on Low 10-12 hours.

Donna's Beef Stew

Donna Treloar
Gaston, IN

Makes 6 servings

2 lbs. beef, cubed
4-5 potatoes, cubed
4-5 carrots, sliced
3 ribs celery, sliced
2 onions, chopped
1 Tbsp. sugar
2 tsp. salt
¼-½ tsp. pepper
2 Tbsp. instant tapioca
3 cups V-8, *or* tomato,
   juice

1. Place meat and vegetables in slow cooker. Sprinkle with sugar, salt, pepper, and tapioca. Toss lightly. Pour juice over the top.
2. Cover. Cook on Low 8-10 hours.

Variation:
   Add 10-oz. pkg. frozen succotash or green beans.

When I want to warm rolls to go with a slow-cooker stew, I wrap them in foil and lay them on top of the stew until they're warm.
Donna Barnitz
Jenks, OK

Venison Swiss Steak

Dede Peterson
Rapid City, SD

Makes 6 servings

2 lbs. round venison steak
flour
2 tsp. salt
1/2 tsp. pepper
oil
2 onions, sliced
2 ribs celery, diced
1 cup carrots, diced
2 cups fresh, *or* stewed,
    tomatoes
1 Tbsp. Worcestershire
    sauce

1. Combine flour, salt, and pepper. Dredge steak in flour mixture. Brown in oil in skillet. Place in slow cooker.
2. Add remaining ingredients.
3. Cover. Cook on Low 7 1/2-8 1/2 hours.

Swiss Steak

Wanda S. Curtin
Bradenton, FL
Jeanne Hertzog
Bethlehem, PA

Makes 6 servings

1 1/2 lbs. round steak, about
    3/4" thick
2-4 tsp. flour
1/2-1 tsp. salt
1/4 tsp. pepper
1 medium onion, sliced
1 carrot, chopped
1 rib celery, chopped
14 1/2-oz. can diced
    tomatoes, *or* 15-oz. can
    tomato sauce

1. Cut steak into serving pieces.
2. Combine flour, salt, and pepper. Dredge meat in seasoned flour.
3. Place onions in bottom of slow cooker. Add meat. Top with carrots and celery and cover with tomatoes.
4. Cover. Cook on Low 8-10 hours, or High 3-5 hours.
5. Serve over noodles or rice.

Jacqueline's Swiss Steak

Jacqueline Stafl
East Bethany, NY

Makes 4 servings

1 1/2 lbs. round steak
2-4 Tbsp. flour
1/2 lb. sliced carrots, *or*
    1 lb. baby carrots
1 pkg. dry onion soup mix
8-oz. can tomato sauce
1/2 cup water

1. Cut steak into serving-size pieces. Dredge in flour.
2. Place carrots in bottom of slow cooker. Top with steak.
3. Combine soup mix, tomato sauce, and water. Pour over all.
4. Cover. Cook on Low 8-10 hours.
5. Serve over mashed potatoes.

Margaret's Swiss Steak

Margaret Rich
North Newton, KS

Makes 6 servings

1 cup chopped onions
½ cup chopped celery
2-lb. ½-inch thick round
   steak
¼ cup flour
3 Tbsp. oil
1 tsp. salt
¼ tsp. pepper
16-oz. can diced tomatoes
¼ cup flour
½ cup water

1. Place onions and celery in bottom of slow cooker.
2. Cut steak in serving-size pieces. Dredge in ¼ cup flour. Brown on both sides in oil in saucepan. Place in slow cooker.
3. Sprinkle with salt and pepper. Pour on tomatoes.
4. Cover. Cook on Low 9 hours. Remove meat from cooker and keep warm.
5. Turn heat to High. Blend together ¼ cup flour and water. Stir into sauce in slow cooker. Cover and cook 15 minutes. Serve with steak.

Nadine & Hazel's Swiss Steak

Nadine Martinitz, Salina, KS
Hazel L. Propst, Oxford, PA

Makes 6-8 servings

3-lb. round steak
⅓ cup flour
2 tsp. salt
½ tsp. pepper
3 Tbsp. shortening
1 large onion, *or more*,
   sliced
1 large pepper, *or more*,
   sliced
14½-oz. can stewed
   tomatoes, *or* 3-4 fresh
   tomatoes, chopped
water

1. Sprinkle meat with flour, salt, and pepper. Pound both sides. Cut into 6 or 8 pieces. Brown meat in shortening over medium heat on top of stove, about 15 minutes. Transfer to slow cooker.
2. Brown onion and pepper. Add tomatoes and bring to boil. Pour over steak. Add water to completely cover steak.
3. Cover. Cook on Low 6-8 hours.

Variation:
To add some flavor, stir in your favorite dried herbs when beginning to cook the steak, or add fresh herbs in the last hour of cooking.

Beef, Tomatoes, & Noodles

Janice Martins
Fairbank, IA

Makes 8 servings

1½ lbs. stewing beef,
   cubed
¼ cup flour
2 cups stewed tomatoes (if
   you like tomato chunks),
   or 2 cups crushed
   tomatoes (if you prefer a
   smoother gravy
1 tsp. salt
¼-½ tsp. pepper
1 medium onion, chopped
water
12-oz. bag noodles

1. Combine meat and flour until cubes are coated. Place in slow cooker.
2. Add tomatoes, salt, pepper, and onion. Add water to cover.
3. Cover. Simmer on Low 6-8 hours.
4. Serve over cooked noodles.

Big Beef Stew

Margaret H. Moffitt
Bartlett, TN

Makes 6-8 servings

3-lb. beef roast, cubed
1 large onion, sliced
1 tsp. dried parsley flakes
1 green pepper, sliced
3 ribs celery, sliced
4 carrots, sliced
28-oz. can tomatoes with
  juice, undrained
1 garlic clove, minced
2 cups water

1. Combine all ingredients.
2. Cover. Cook on High 1 hour. Reduce heat to Low and cook 8 hours.
3. Serve on rice or noodles.

Note:
This is a low-salt recipe. For more zest, add 2 tsp. salt and ¾ tsp. black pepper.

Spanish Round Steak

Shari Jensen
Fountain, CO

Makes 4-6 servings

1 small onion, sliced
1 rib celery, chopped
1 green bell pepper, sliced
  in rings
2 lbs. round steak
2 Tbsp. chopped fresh
  parsley, *or* 2 tsp. dried
  parsley
1 Tbsp. Worcestershire
  sauce
1 Tbsp. dry mustard
1 Tbsp. chili powder
2 cups canned tomatoes
2 tsp. dry minced garlic
½ tsp. salt
¼ tsp. pepper

1. Put half of onion, green pepper, and celery in slow cooker.
2. Cut steak into serving-size pieces. Place steak pieces in slow cooker.
3. Put remaining onion, green pepper, and celery over steak.
4. Combine remaining ingredients. Pour over meat.
5. Cover. Cook on Low 8 hours.
6. Serve over noodles or rice.

Slow-Cooked Pepper Steak

Carolyn Baer, Conrath, WI
Ann Driscoll
Albuquerque, NM

Makes 6-8 servings

1½-2 lbs. beef round
  steak, cut in 3" x 1"
  strips
2 Tbsp. oil
¼ cup soy sauce
1 garlic clove, minced
1 cup chopped onions
1 tsp. sugar
½ tsp. salt
¼ tsp. pepper
¼ tsp. ground ginger
2 large green peppers, cut
  in strips
4 tomatoes cut into
  eighths, *or* 16-oz. can
  diced tomatoes
½ cup cold water
1 Tbsp. cornstarch

1. Brown beef in oil in saucepan. Transfer to slow cooker.
2. Combine soy sauce, garlic, onions, sugar, salt, pepper, and ginger. Pour over meat.
3. Cover. Cook on Low 5-6 hours.
4. Add green peppers and tomatoes. Cook 1 hour longer.
5. Combine water and cornstarch to make paste. Stir into slow cooker. Cook on High until thickened, about 10 minutes.
6. Serve over rice or noodles.

Pepper Steak Oriental

Donna Lantgen
Rapid City, SD

Makes 6 servings

1 lb. round steak, sliced
    thin
3 Tbsp. soy sauce
1/2 tsp. ground ginger
1 garlic clove, minced
1 green pepper, thinly
    sliced
4-oz. can mushrooms,
    drained, *or* 1 cup fresh
    mushrooms
1 onion, thinly sliced
1/2 tsp. crushed red pepper

1. Combine all ingredients
in slow cooker.
2. Cover. Cook on Low 6-8
hours.
3. Serve as steak sand-
wiches topped with pro-
volone cheese, or over rice.

Note:
Round steak is easier to
slice into thin strips if it is
partially frozen when cut.

Powerhouse Beef Roast with Tomatoes, Onions, and Peppers

Donna Treloar
Gaston, IN

Makes 5-6 servings

3-lb. boneless chuck roast
1 garlic clove, minced
1 Tbsp. oil
2-3 onions, sliced
2-3 sweet green and red
    peppers, sliced
16-oz. jar salsa
2 14 1/2-oz. cans Mexican-
    style stewed tomatoes

1. Brown roast and garlic
in oil in skillet. Place in slow
cooker.
2. Add onions and pep-
pers.
3. Combine salsa and
tomatoes and pour over ingredients in slow cooker.
4. Cover. Cook on Low 8-
10 hours.
5. Slice meat to serve.

Variation:
Make Beef Burritos with
the leftovers. Shred the beef
and heat with remaining peppers, onions, and 1/2 cup of
the broth. Add 1 Tbsp. chili
powder, 2 tsp. cumin, and
salt to taste. Heat thoroughly.
Fill warm flour tortillas with
mixture and serve with sour
cream, salsa, and guacamole.

Steak San Morco

Susan Tjon
Austin, TX

Makes 4-6 servings

2 lbs. stewing meat, cubed
1 envelope dry onion soup
    mix
29-oz. can peeled, *or*
    crushed, tomatoes
1 tsp. dried oregano
garlic powder to taste
2 Tbsp. oil
2 Tbsp. wine vinegar

1. Layer meat evenly in
bottom of slow cooker.
2. Combine soup mix,
tomatoes, spices, oil, and
vinegar in bowl. Blend with
spoon. Pour over meat.
3. Cover. Cook on High 6
hours, or Low 8-10 hours.

Pat's Meat Stew

Pat Bishop
Bedminster, PA

Makes 4-5 servings

1-2 lbs. beef roast, cubed
2 tsp. salt
1/4 tsp. pepper
2 cups water
2 carrots, sliced
2 small onions, sliced
4-6 small potatoes, cut up
   in chunks, if desired
1/4 cup quick-cooking
   tapioca
1 bay leaf
10-oz. pkg. frozen peas, *or*
   mixed vegetables

1. Brown beef in saucepan. Place in slow cooker.

2. Sprinkle with salt and pepper. Add remaining ingredients except frozen vegetables. Mix well.

3. Cover. Cook on Low 8-10 hours, or on High 4-5 hours. Add vegetables during last 1-2 hours of cooking.

Ernestine's Beef Stew

Ernestine Schrepfer
Trenton, MO

Makes 5-6 servings

1 1/2 lbs. stewing meat,
   cubed
2 1/4 cups tomato juice
10 1/2-oz. can consomme
1 cup chopped celery
2 cups sliced carrots
4 Tbsp. quick-cooking tapioca
1 medium onion, chopped
3/4 tsp. salt
1/4 tsp. pepper

1. Combine all ingredients in slow cooker.

2. Cover. Cook on Low 7-8 hours. (Do not peek.)

Beef Stew with Vegetables

Joyce B. Suiter
Garysburg, NC

Makes 8 servings

3 lbs. stewing beef, cubed
1 cup water
1 cup red wine
1.2-oz. envelope beef-
   mushroom soup mix
2 cups diced potatoes
1 cup thinly sliced carrots
10-oz. pkg. frozen peas and
   onions

1. Layer all ingredients in order in slow cooker.

2. Cover. Cook on Low 8-10 hours.

Note:
You may increase all vegetable quantities with good results!

Becky's Beef Stew

Becky Harder
Monument, CO

Makes 6-8 servings

1 1/2 lbs. beef stewing meat,
   cubed
2 10-oz. pkgs. frozen
   vegetables—carrots,
   corn, peas
4 large potatoes, cubed
1 bay leaf
1 onion, chopped
15-oz. can stewing
   tomatoes of your
   choice—Italian,
   Mexican, *or* regular
8-oz. can tomato sauce
2 Tbsp. Worcestershire
   sauce
1 tsp. salt
1/4 tsp. pepper

1. Put meat on bottom of slow cooker. Layer frozen vegetables and potatoes over meat.

2. Mix remaining ingredients together in large bowl and pour over other ingredients.

3. Cover. Cook on Low 6-8 hours.

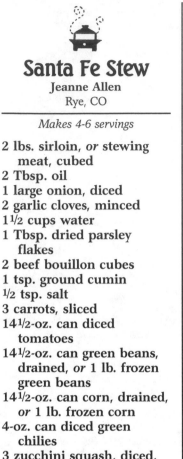

Santa Fe Stew

Jeanne Allen
Rye, CO

Makes 4-6 servings

2 lbs. sirloin, *or* stewing
  meat, cubed
2 Tbsp. oil
1 large onion, diced
2 garlic cloves, minced
1 1/2 cups water
1 Tbsp. dried parsley
  flakes
2 beef bouillon cubes
1 tsp. ground cumin
1/2 tsp. salt
3 carrots, sliced
14 1/2-oz. can diced
  tomatoes
14 1/2-oz. can green beans,
  drained, *or* 1 lb. frozen
  green beans
14 1/2-oz. can corn, drained,
  or 1 lb. frozen corn
4-oz. can diced green
  chilies
3 zucchini squash, diced,
  optional

1. Brown meat, onion, and garlic in oil in saucepan until meat is no longer pink. Place in slow cooker.
2. Stir in remaining ingredients.
3. Cover. Cook on High 30 minutes. Reduce heat to Low and cook 4-6 hours.

Gone All-Day Casserole

Beatrice Orgish
Richardson, TX

Makes 12 servings

1 cup uncooked wild rice,
  rinsed and drained
1 cup chopped celery
1 cup chopped carrots
2 4-oz. cans mushrooms,
  stems and pieces,
  drained
1 large onion, chopped
1 clove garlic, minced
1/2 cup slivered almonds
3 beef bouillon cubes
2 1/2 tsp. seasoned salt
2-lb. boneless round steak,
  cut into 1-inch cubes
3 cups water

1. Please ingredients in order listed in slow cooker.
2. Cover. Cook on Low 6-8 hours or until rice is tender. Stir before serving.

Variations:
1. Brown beef in saucepan in 2 Tbsp. oil before putting in slow cooker for deeper flavor.
2. Add a bay leaf and 4-6 whole peppercorns to mixture before cooking. Remove before serving.
3. Substitute chicken legs and thighs (skin removed) for beef.

Sweet-Sour Beef and Vegetables

Jo Haberkamp
Fairbank, IA

Makes 6 servings

2 lbs. round steak, cut in
  1-inch cubes
2 Tbsp. oil
2 8-oz. cans tomato sauce
2 tsp. chili powder
2 cups sliced carrots
2 cups small white onions
1 tsp. paprika
1/4 cup sugar
1 tsp. salt
1/3 cup vinegar
1/2 cup light molasses
1 large green pepper, cut in
  1-inch pieces

1. Brown steak in oil in saucepan.
2. Combine all ingredients in slow cooker.
3. Cover. Cook on High 4-6 hours.

Irish Beef Stew

Teena Wagner
Waterloo, ON

Makes 4-6 servings

2 lbs. stewing beef, cubed
1 envelope dry onion soup mix
2 10¾-oz. cans tomato soup
1 soup can water
1 tsp. salt
½ tsp. pepper
2 cups diced carrots
2 cups diced potatoes
1-lb. package frozen peas
¼ cup water

1. Place beef, onion soup, tomato soup, soup can of water, salt, pepper, carrots, and potatoes in slow cooker.
2. Cover. Cook on Low 8 hours.
3. Add peas and ¼ cup water. Cover. Cook on Low 1 more hour.

Slow Cooker Stew

Ruth Shank
Gridley, IL

Makes 8-10 servings

3-4-lb. beef round steak, *or* beef roast, cubed
⅓ cup flour
1 tsp. salt
½ tsp. pepper
3 carrots, sliced
1-2 medium onions, cut into wedges
4-6 medium potatoes, cubed
4-oz. can sliced mushrooms, drained
10-oz. pkg. frozen mixed vegetables
10½-oz. can condensed beef broth
½ cup water
2 tsp. brown sugar
14½-oz. can, *or* 1 pint, tomato wedges with juice
¼ cup flour
¼ cup water

1. Toss beef cubes with ⅓ cup flour, salt, and pepper in slow cooker.
2. Combine all vegetables except tomatoes. Add to meat.
3. Combine beef broth, ½ cup water, and brown sugar. Pour over meat and vegetables. Add tomatoes and stir carefully.
4. Cover. Cook on Low 10-14 hours, or on High 4-5½ hours.
5. One hour before serving, mix together ¼ cup flour and ¼ cup water. Stir into slow cooker. Turn to High. Cover and cook remaining time.

Note:
    For better color add half of the frozen vegetables (partly thawed) during the last hour.

Full-Flavored Beef Stew

Stacy Petersheim
Mechanicsburg, PA

Makes 6 servings

2-lb. beef roast, cubed
2 cups sliced carrots
2 cups diced potatoes
1 medium onion, sliced
1½ cups peas
2 tsp. quick-cooking tapioca
1 Tbsp. salt
½ tsp. pepper
8-oz. can tomato sauce
1 cup water
1 Tbsp. brown sugar

1. Combine beef and vegetables in slow cooker. Sprinkle with tapioca, salt, and pepper.
2. Combine tomato sauce and water. Pour over ingredients in slow cooker. Sprinkle with brown sugar.
3. Cover. Cook on Low 8 hours.

Variation:
    Add peas one hour before cooking time ends to keep their color and flavor.

Lazy Day Stew

Ruth Ann Gingrich
New Holland, PA

Makes 8 servings

2 lbs. stewing beef, cubed
2 cups diced carrots
2 cups diced potatoes
2 medium onions, chopped
1 cup chopped celery
10-oz. pkg. lima beans
2 tsp. quick-cooking
    tapioca
1 tsp. salt
1/2 tsp. pepper
8-oz. can tomato sauce
1 cup water
1 Tbsp. brown sugar

1. Place beef in bottom of slow cooker. Add vegetables.
2. Sprinkle tapioca, salt, and pepper over ingredients.
3. Mix together tomato sauce and water. Pour over top.
4. Sprinkle brown sugar over all.
5. Cover. Cook on Low 8 hours.

Variation:
Instead of lima beans, use 1 1/2 cups green beans.
    Rose M. Hoffman
    Schuylkill Haven, PA

Beef with Mushrooms

Doris Perkins
Mashpee, MA

Makes 4-6 servings

1 1/2 lbs. stewing beef,
    cubed
4-oz. can mushroom
    pieces, drained (save
    liquid)
half a garlic clove, minced
3/4 cup sliced onions
3 Tbsp. shortening
1 beef bouillon cube
1 cup hot water
8-oz. can tomato sauce
2 tsp. sugar
2 tsp. Worcestershire sauce
1 tsp. dried basil
1 tsp. dried oregano
1/2 tsp. salt
1/8 tsp. pepper

1. Brown meat, mushrooms, garlic, and onions in shortening in skillet.
2. Dissolve bouillon cube in hot water. Add to meat mixture.
3. Stir in mushroom liquid and rest of ingredients. Mix well. Pour into slow cooker.
4. Cover. Cook on High 3 hours, or until meat is tender.
5. Serve over cooked noodles, spaghetti, or rice.

Easy Company Beef

Joyce B. Suiter
Garysburg, NC

Makes 8 servings

3 lbs. stewing beef, cubed
10 3/4-oz. can cream of
    mushroom soup
7-oz. jar mushrooms,
    undrained
1/2 cup red wine
1 envelope dry onion soup
    mix

1. Combine all ingredients in slow cooker.
2. Cover. Cook on Low 10 hours.
3. Serve over noodles, rice, or pasta.

To get the best flavor, saute vegetables or brown meat before placing in cooker to cook.
Connie Johnson
Loudon, NH

Beef Pot Roast

Alexa Slonin
Harrisonburg, VA

Makes 8-10 servings

12 oz. whole tiny new
   potatoes, *or* 2 medium
   potatoes, cubed, *or*
   2 medium sweet
   potatoes, cubed
8 small carrots, cut in
   small chunks
2 small onions, cut in
   wedges
2 ribs celery, cut up
2½-3 lb. beef chuck, *or* pot
   roast
2 Tbsp. cooking oil
¾ cup water, dry wine, *or*
   tomato juice
1 Tbsp. Worcestershire
   sauce
1 tsp. instant beef bouillon
   granules
1 tsp. dried basil

1. Place vegetables in bottom of slow cooker.
2. Brown roast in oil in skillet. Place on top of vegetables.
3. Combine water, Worcestershire sauce, bouillon, and basil. Pour over meat and vegetables.
4. Cover. Cook on Low 10-12 hours.

Easy Pot Roast and Veggies

Tina Houk, Clinton, MO
Arlene Wiens, Newton, KS

Makes 6 servings

3-4-lb. chuck roast
4 medium-sized potatoes,
   cubed
4 medium-sized carrots,
   sliced, *or* 1 lb. baby
   carrots
2 celery ribs, sliced thin,
   optional
1 envelope dry onion soup
   mix
3 cups water

1. Put roast, potatoes, carrots, and celery in slow cooker.
2. Add onion soup mix and water.
3. Cover. Cook on Low 6-8 hours.

Variations:

1. To add flavor to the broth, stir 1 tsp. kitchen bouquet, ½ tsp. salt, ½ tsp. black pepper, and ½ tsp. garlic powder into water before pouring over meat and vegetables.
   Bonita Ensenberger
   Albuquerque, NM

2. Before putting roast in cooker, sprinkle it with the dry soup mix, patting it on so it adheres.
   Betty Lahman
   Elkton, VA

3. Add one bay leaf and 2 cloves minced garlic to Step 2.
   Susan Tjon
   Austin, TX

Pot Roast

Janet L. Roggie
Linville, NY

Makes 6-8 servings

3 potatoes, thinly sliced
2 large carrots, thinly
   sliced
1 onion, thinly sliced
1 tsp. salt
½ tsp. pepper
3-4-lb. pot roast
½ cup water

1. Put vegetables in bottom of slow cooker. Stir in salt and pepper. Add roast. Pour in water.
2. Cover. Cook on Low 10-12 hours.

Variations:

1. Add ½ tsp. dried dill, a bay leaf, and ½ tsp. dried rosemary for more flavor.

2. Brown roast on all sides in saucepan in 2 Tbsp. oil before placing in cooker.
   Debbie Zeida
   Mashpee, MA

Easy Roast
Lisa Warren
Parkesburg, PA

Makes 6-8 servings

3-4-lb. beef roast
1 envelope dry onion soup mix
14½-oz. can stewed tomatoes, *or* seasoned tomatoes

1. Place roast in slow cooker. Cover with onion soup and tomatoes.
2. Cover. Cook on Low 8 hours.

Hearty Beef Stew
Lovina Baer
Conrath, WI

Makes 4-6 servings

2-lb. round steak
4 large potatoes, cubed
2 large carrots, sliced
2 ribs celery, sliced
1 medium onion, chopped
1 qt. tomato juice
1 Tbsp. Worcestershire sauce
2 tsp. salt
½ tsp. pepper
¼ cup sugar
1 Tbsp. clear jel

1. Combine meat, potatoes, carrots, celery, and onion in slow cooker.
2. Combine tomato juice, Worcestershire sauce, salt, and pepper. Pour into slow cooker.
3. Mix together sugar and clear jel. Add to remaining ingredients, stirring well.
4. Cover. Cook on High 6-7 hours.

Variation:
Instead of clear jel, use ¼ cup instant tapioca.

Virginia's Beef Stew
Virginia Bender
Dover, DE

Makes 6 servings

3 lbs. boneless beef
1 envelope dry onion soup
28-oz. can diced tomatoes, undrained
1 Tbsp. minute tapioca
4-5 potatoes, cubed
1 onion, chopped
6 carrots, sliced
1 tsp. sugar
1 Tbsp. salt
½ tsp. pepper

1. Combine all ingredients in slow cooker.
2. Cover. Bake on High 5 hours.

Variation:
Add 2 cups frozen peas during last 10 minutes of cooking.

Rump Roast and Vegetables
Kimberlee Greenawalt
Harrisonburg, VA

Makes 6-8 servings

1½ lbs. small potatoes (about 10), *or* medium potatoes (about 4), halved
2 medium carrots, cubed
1 small onion, sliced
10-oz. pkg. frozen lima beans
1 bay leaf
2 Tbsp. quick-cooking tapioca
2-2½-lb. boneless beef round rump, round tip, *or* pot roast
2 Tbsp. oil
10¾-oz. can condensed vegetable beef soup
¼ cup water
¼ tsp. pepper

1. Place potatoes, carrots, and onion in slow cooker. Add frozen beans and bay leaf. Sprinkle with tapioca.
2. Brown roast on all sides in oil in skillet. Place over vegetables in slow cooker.
3. Combine soup, water, and pepper. Pour over roast.
4. Cover. Cook on Low 10-12 hours, or High 5-6 hours.
5. Discard bay leaf before serving.

Hearty New England Dinner

Joette Droz
Kalona, IA

Makes 6-8 servings

2 medium carrots, sliced
1 medium onion, sliced
1 celery rib, sliced
3-lb. boneless chuck roast
1/2 tsp. salt
1/4 tsp. pepper
1 envelope dry onion soup
  mix
2 cups water
1 Tbsp. vinegar
1 bay leaf
half a small head of
  cabbage, cut in wedges
3 Tbsp. melted margarine,
  or butter
2 Tbsp. flour
1 Tbsp. dried minced
  onion
2 Tbsp. prepared
  horseradish
1/2 tsp. salt

1. Place carrots, onion, and celery in slow cooker. Place roast on top. Sprinkle with 1/2 tsp. salt and pepper. Add soup mix, water, vinegar, and bay leaf.

2. Cover. Cook on Low 7-9 hours. Remove beef and keep warm. Just before serving, cut into pieces or thin slices.

3. Discard bay leaf. Add cabbage to juice in slow cooker.

4. Cover. Cook on High 1 hour, or until cabbage is tender.

5. Melt margarine in saucepan. Stir in flour and onion. Add 1 1/2 cups liquid from slow cooker. Stir in horseradish and 1/2 tsp. salt. Bring to boil. Cook over low heat until thick and smooth, about 2 minutes. Return to cooker and blend with remaining sauce in cooker. When blended, serve over or alongside meat and vegetables.

Easy Beef Stew

Connie Johnson
Loudon, NH

Makes 6 servings

1 lb. stewing beef
1 cup cubed turnip
2 medium potatoes, cubed
1 large onion, sliced
1 garlic clove, minced
2 large carrots, sliced
1/2 cup green beans, cut up
1/2 cup peas
1 bay leaf
1/2 tsp. dried thyme
1 tsp. chopped parsley
2 Tbsp. tomato paste
2 Tbsp. celery leaves
1/2 tsp. salt
1/4 tsp. pepper
1 qt., *or* 2 14 1/2-oz. cans,
  beef broth

1. Place meat, vegetables, and seasonings in slow cooker. Pour broth over all.

2. Cover. Cook on Low 6-8 hours.

Pot Roast

Julie McKenzie
Punxsutawney, PA

Makes 8 servings

3-lb. rump roast
1/2 envelope dry onion
  soup mix
1 small onion, sliced
4-oz. can mushrooms with
  liquid
1/3 cup dry red wine
1/3 cup water
1 garlic clove, minced
1 bay leaf
1/2 tsp. dried thyme
2 Tbsp. chopped fresh
  basil, *or* 1 tsp. dried
  basil

1. Combine all ingredients in slow cooker.

2. Cover. Cook on Low 10-12 hours.

Variations:

1. Add 1/2 tsp. salt, if desired.

2. Mix 3 Tbsp. cornstarch into 1/2 cup cold water. At the end of the cooking time remove bay leaf and discard. Remove meat to serving platter and keep warm. Stir dissolved cornstarch into hot liquid in slow cooker. Stir until absorbed. Cover and cook on High 10 minutes, until sauce thickens. Serve over top or alongside sliced meat.

Pot Roast with Gravy and Vegetables

Irene Klaeger, Inverness, FL
Jan Pembleton, Arlington, TX

Makes 4-6 servings

3-4-lb. bottom round, rump, *or* arm roast
2-3 tsp. salt
1/2 tsp. pepper
2 Tbsp. flour
1/4 cup cold water
1 tsp. kitchen bouquet, *or* gravy browning seasoning sauce
1 garlic clove, minced
2 medium onions, cut in wedges
4-6 medium potatoes, cubed
2-4 carrots, quartered
1 green pepper, sliced

1. Place roast in slow cooker. Sprinkle with salt and pepper.
2. Make paste of flour and cold water. Stir in kitchen bouquet and spread over roast.
3. Add garlic, onions, potatoes, carrots, and green pepper.
4. Cover. Cook on Low 8-10 hours, or High 4-5 hours.
5. Taste and adjust seasonings before serving.

Round Steak Casserole

Cheryl Bartel, Hillsboro, KS
Barbara Walker, Sturgis, SD

Makes 4-6 servings

2-lb. 1/2"-thick round steak
1/2 tsp. garlic salt
1 tsp. salt
1/4-1/2 tsp. pepper
1 onion, thinly sliced
3-4 potatoes, quartered
3-4 carrots, sliced
14 1/2-oz. can French-style green beans, drained, *or* 1 lb. frozen green beans
10 3/4-oz. can tomato soup
14 1/2-oz. can stewed tomatoes

1. Cut meat into serving-size pieces, place in slow cooker, stir in seasonings, and mix well.
2. Add potatoes, carrots, and green beans. Top with soup and tomatoes.
3. Cover. Cook on High 1 hour. Reduce heat to Low and cook 8 hours, or until done. Remove cover during last half hour if there is too much liquid.

"Smothered" Steak

Susan Yoder Graber
Eureka, IL

Makes 6 servings

1 1/2-lb. chuck, *or* round, steak, cut into strips
1/3 cup flour
1/2 tsp. salt
1/4 tsp. pepper
1 large onion, sliced
1-2 green peppers, sliced
14 1/2-oz. can stewed tomatoes
4-oz. can mushrooms, drained
2 Tbsp. soy sauce
10-oz. pkg. frozen French-style green beans

1. Layer steak in bottom of slow cooker. Sprinkle with flour, salt, and pepper. Stir well to coat steak.
2. Add remaining ingredients. Mix together gently.
3. Cover. Cook on Low 8 hours.
4. Serve over rice.

Variations:
1. Use 8-oz. can tomato sauce instead of stewed tomatoes.
2. Substitute 1 Tbsp. Worcestershire sauce in place of soy sauce.
Mary E. Martin
Goshen, IN

Veal and Peppers

Irma H. Schoen
Windsor, CT

Makes 4 servings

1 1/2 lbs. boneless veal, cubed
3 green peppers, quartered
2 onions, thinly sliced
1/2 lb. fresh mushrooms, sliced
1 tsp. salt
1/2 tsp. dried basil
2 cloves garlic, minced
28-oz. can tomatoes

1. Combine all ingredients in slow cooker.
2. Cover. Cook on Low 7 hours, or on High 4 hours.
3. Serve over rice or noodles.

Variation:

Use boneless, skinless chicken breast, cut into chunks, instead of veal.

Beef and Beans

Robin Schrock
Millersburg, OH

Makes 8 servings

1 Tbsp. prepared mustard
1 Tbsp. chili powder
1/2 tsp. salt
1/4 tsp. pepper
1 1/2-lb. boneless round steak, cut into thin slices
2 14 1/2-oz. cans diced tomatoes, undrained
1 medium onion, chopped
1 beef bouillon cube, crushed
16-oz. can kidney beans, rinsed and drained

1. Combine mustard, chili powder, salt, and pepper. Add beef slices and toss to coat. Place meat in slow cooker.
2. Add tomatoes, onion, and bouillon.
3. Cover. Cook on Low 6-8 hours.
4. Stir in beans. Cook 30 minutes longer.
5. Serve over rice.

Roast with Veggies

Arlene Wengerd
Millersburg, OH

Makes 6 servings

2-lb. roast, partially thawed
1 medium onion, sliced
1 pint tomato juice
1 tsp. salt
1 tsp. black pepper
1 tsp. dried marjoram
4-5 medium potatoes, cut in thick slices
4-5 carrots, sliced
dash of white vinegar
10 3/4-oz. can golden cream of mushroom soup

1. Place roast in slow cooker. Arrange onions on top.
2. Carefully pour tomato juice over top. Sprinkle with spices.
3. Cover. Cook on High 5 hours.
4. Drain juice from roast into bowl. Pull roast apart into bite-sized pieces. Return meat to slow cooker.
5. Partially cook potatoes and carrots in saucepan in boiling water with a dash of white vinegar. (The white vinegar gives vegetables a bright color.) Layer veggies on top of roast.
6. Pour soup over all. Cover and cook on High 1 more hour.

Fresh vegetables take longer to cook than meats, because, in a slow cooker, liquid simmers rather than boils. Remember this if you've adapted range-top recipes to slow cooking.

Beatrice Orgish
Richardson, TX

Round Steak

Janet V. Yocum
Elizabethtown, PA

Makes 4 servings

2-lb. round steak, cut into
serving-size chunks
1 onion, chopped
4 ribs celery, chopped
4 carrots, chopped
4 potatoes, cut into bite-
sized pieces
2 tsp. salt
1 tsp. seasoning salt
1/2 tsp. pepper
10 3/4-oz. can cream of
celery, *or* cream of
mushroom, soup
water

1. Put steak in bottom of
slow cooker.
2. Stir vegetables, seasonings, and soup together in
large bowl. Pour over meat.
3. Add water if needed to
cover meat and vegetables.
4. Cover. Cook on Low 8
hours.

Forget It Pot Roast

Mary Mitchell
Battle Creek, MI

Makes 6 servings

6 potatoes, quartered
6 carrots, sliced
3-3 1/2-lb. chuck roast
1 envelope dry onion soup
mix
10 3/4-oz. can cream of
mushroom soup
2-3 Tbsp. flour
1/4 cup cold water

1. Place potatoes and carrots in slow cooker. Add
meat. Top with soups.
2. Cover. Cook on Low 8-9
hours.
3. To make gravy, remove
meat and vegetables to serving platter and keep warm.
Pour juices into saucepan and
bring to boil. Mix 2-3 Tbsp.
flour with 1/4 cup cold water
until smooth. Stir into juices
in pan until thickened. Serve
over meat and vegetables, or
alongside as a gravy.

Beef Stew Bourguignonne

Jo Haberkamp
Fairbank, IA

Makes 6 servings

2 lbs. stewing beef, cut in
1-inch cubes
2 Tbsp. cooking oil
10 3/4-oz. can condensed
golden cream of
mushroom soup
1 tsp. Worcestershire sauce
1/3 cup dry red wine
1/2 tsp. dried oregano
2 tsp. salt
1/2 tsp. pepper
1/2 cup chopped onions
1/2 cup chopped carrots
4-oz. can mushroom
pieces, drained
1/2 cup cold water
1/4 cup flour
noodles, cooked

1. Brown meat in oil in
saucepan. Transfer to slow
cooker.
2. Mix together soup,
Worcestershire sauce, wine,
oregano, salt and pepper,
onions, carrots, and mushrooms. Pour over meat.
3. Cover. Cook on Low 10-
12 hours.
4. Combine water and
flour. Stir into beef mixture.
Turn cooker to High.
5. Cook and stir until
thickened and bubbly.
6. Serve over noodles.

A slow cooker is perfect for less tender meats such as a
round steak. Because the meat is cooked in liquid for hours,
it turns out tender and juicy.

Carolyn Baer
Conrath, WI
Barbara Sparks
Glen Burnie, MD

Baked Steak

Shirley Thieszen
Lakin, KS

Makes 6 servings

2½ lbs. round steak, cut into 10 pieces
1 Tbsp. salt
½ tsp. pepper
oil
½ cup chopped onions
½ cup chopped green peppers
1 cup cream of mushroom soup
½ cup water

1. Season the steak with salt and pepper. Brown on both sides in oil in saucepan. Place in slow cooker.
2. Stir in onions, green peppers, mushroom soup, and water.
3. Cover. Cook on High 1 hour, and then on Low 3-4 hours.

Creamy Swiss Steak

Jo Ellen Moore
Pendleton, IN

Makes 6 servings

1½-lb. ¾-inch thick round steak
2 Tbsp. flour
1 tsp. salt
¼ tsp. pepper
1 medium onion, sliced
10¾-oz. can cream of mushroom soup
1 carrot, chopped
1 small celery rib, chopped

1. Cut steak into serving-size pieces.
2. Combine flour, salt, and pepper. Dredge meat in flour.
3. Place onions in bottom of slow cooker. Add meat.
4. Spread cream of mushroom soup over meat. Top with carrots and celery.
5. Cover. Cook on Low 8-10 hours, or High 3-5 hours.

Saucy Round Steak Supper

Shirley Sears
Tiskilwa, IL

Makes 6-8 servings

2 lbs. round steak, sliced diagonally into ⅛-inch strips (reserve meat bone)
½ cup chopped onions
½ cup chopped celery
8-oz. can mushrooms, stems and pieces, drained (reserve liquid)
⅓ cup French dressing
2½-oz. pkg. sour cream sauce mix
⅓ cup water
1 tsp. Worcestershire sauce

1. Place steak and bone in slow cooker. Add onions, celery, and mushrooms.
2. Combine dressing, sour cream sauce mix, water, Worcestershire sauce, and mushroom liquid. Pour over mixture in slow cooker.
3. Cover. Cook on Low 8-9 hours.
4. Serve over noodles.

Variation:

Instead of using the sour cream sauce mix, remove meat from cooker at end of cooking time and keep warm. Stir 1 cup sour cream into gravy, cover, and cook on High 10 minutes. Serve over steak.

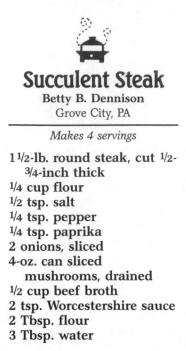

Succulent Steak

Betty B. Dennison
Grove City, PA

Makes 4 servings

1 1/2-lb. round steak, cut 1/2-
3/4-inch thick
1/4 cup flour
1/2 tsp. salt
1/4 tsp. pepper
1/4 tsp. paprika
2 onions, sliced
4-oz. can sliced
    mushrooms, drained
1/2 cup beef broth
2 tsp. Worcestershire sauce
2 Tbsp. flour
3 Tbsp. water

1. Mix together 1/4 cup flour, salt, pepper, and paprika.

2. Cut steak into 5-6 pieces. Dredge steak pieces in seasoned flour until lightly coated.

3. Layer half of onions, half of steak, and half of mushrooms into cooker. Repeat.

4. Combine beef broth and Worcestershire sauce. Pour over mixture in slow cooker.

5. Cover. Cook on Low 8-10 hours.

6. Remove steak to serving platter and keep warm. Mix together 2 Tbsp. flour and water. Stir into drippings and cook on High until thickened, about 10 minutes. Pour over steak and serve.

Steak Hi-Hat

Bonita Ensenberger
Albuquerque, NM

Makes 8-10 servings

10 3/4-oz. can cream of
    chicken soup
10 3/4-oz. can cream of
    mushroom soup
1 1/2 Tbsp. Worcestershire
    sauce
1/2 tsp. black pepper
1 tsp. paprika
2 cups onion, chopped
1 garlic clove, minced
1 cup fresh, small button
    mushrooms, quartered
2 lbs. round steak, cubed
1 cup sour cream
cooked noodles with
    poppy seeds
crisp bacon bits, optional

1. Combine chicken soup, mushroom soup, Worcestershire sauce, pepper, paprika, onion, garlic, and mushrooms in slow cooker.

2. Stir in steak.

3. Cover. Cook on Low 8-9 hours.

4. Stir in sour cream during the last 20-30 minutes.

5. Serve on hot buttered noodles sprinkled with poppy seeds. Garnish with bacon bits.

Variation:
Add 1 tsp. salt with seasonings in Step 1.

Steak Stroganoff

Marie Morucci
Glen Lyon, PA

Makes 6 servings

2 Tbsp. flour
1/2 tsp. garlic powder
1/2 tsp. pepper
1/4 tsp. paprika
1 3/4-lb. boneless beef round
    steak
10 3/4-oz. can cream of
    mushroom soup
1/2 cup water
1 envelope dried onion
    soup mix
9-oz. jar sliced mushrooms,
    drained
1/2 cup sour cream
1 Tbsp. minced fresh
    parsley

1. Combine flour, garlic powder, pepper, and paprika in slow cooker.

2. Cut meat into 1 1/2 x 1/2-inch strips. Place in flour mixture and toss until meat is well coated.

3. Add mushroom soup, water, and soup mix. Stir until well blended.

4. Cover. Cook on High 3-3 1/2 hours, or Low 6-7 hours.

5. Stir in mushrooms, sour cream, and parsley. Cover and cook on High 10-15 minutes, or until heated through.

6. Serve with rice.

Scrumptious Beef
Julia Lapp
New Holland, PA

Makes 4-8 servings (depending upon amount of beef used)

1-2 lbs. beef, cubed
1/2 lb. mushrooms, sliced
10 1/2-oz. can beef broth, *or*
    1 cup water and
    1 cube beef bouillon
1 onion, chopped
10 3/4-oz. can cream of
    mushroom soup
3 Tbsp. dry onion soup mix

1. Combine all ingredients in slow cooker.
2. Cover. Cook on High 3-4 hours, or on Low 7-8 hours.
3. Serve over hot cooked rice.

Beef Stew with Mushrooms
Dorothy M. Pittman
Pickens, SC

Makes 6 servings

2 lbs. stewing beef, cubed
10 3/4-oz. can cream of
    mushroom soup
4-oz. can mushrooms
1 envelope dry onion soup
    mix
1/2 tsp. salt
1/4 tsp. pepper
half a soup can of water

1. Sprinkle bottom of greased slow cooker with one-fourth of dry soup mix. Layer in meat, mushroom soup, canned mushrooms, and remaining dry onion soup mix. Pour water over.
2. Cover. Cook on Low 8 hours, or High 4 hours.
3. Serve over potatoes, rice, or noodles.

Good 'n Easy Beef 'n Gravy
Janice Crist
Quinter, KS

Makes 8 servings

3-lb. beef roast, cubed
1 envelope dry onion soup
    mix
1/2 cup beef broth
10 3/4-oz. can cream of
    mushroom, *or* cream of
    celery, soup
4-oz. can sliced
    mushrooms, drained

1. Combine all ingredients in slow cooker.
2. Cover. Cook on Low 10-12 hours.

Variation:
Use 1/2 cup sauterne instead of beef broth.
Joyce Shackelford
Green Bay, WI

Elaine's Beef Stroganoff
Elaine Unruh
Minneapolis, MN

Makes 4 servings

1-lb. round steak, cubed
1 Tbsp. shortening
1/2 cup chopped onions
1/2 cup chopped celery
10 3/4-oz. can cream of
    celery soup
4-oz. can mushroom
    pieces, drained
1 cup sour cream
1/4 tsp. garlic salt

1. Brown meat in shortening in saucepan. Add onions and celery and saute until just tender.
2. Combine all ingredients in slow cooker.
3. Cover. Cook on Low 6-8 hours.
4. Serve over hot cooked noodles.

Easy Dinner Surprise

Nancy Graves
Manhattan, KS

Makes 4-5 servings

1-1½ lbs. stewing meat,
  cubed
10¾-oz. can cream of
  mushroom soup
10¾-oz. can cream of
  celery soup
1 pkg. dry onion soup mix
4-oz. can mushroom pieces

1. Combine all ingredients in slow cooker.
2. Cover. Cook on Low 8-10 hours.
3. Serve over rice or baked potatoes.

Variation:
  Add ¼ cup finely chopped celery for color and texture.

Delicious, Easy Chuck Roast

Mary Jane Musser
Manheim, PA

Makes 4-8 servings

2-4-lb. chuck roast
salt to taste
pepper to taste
1 onion, sliced
10¾-oz. can cream of
  mushroom soup

1. Season roast with salt and pepper and place in slow cooker.
2. Add onion. Pour soup over all.
3. Cover. Cook on Low 8-10 hours, or on High 6 hours.

Creamy Swiss Steak

Connie B. Weaver
Bethlehem, PA

Makes 4-6 servings

2 lbs. round, *or* Swiss
  steak, cut ¾-inch thick
salt to taste
pepper to taste
1 large onion, thinly sliced
10¾-oz. can cream of
  mushroom soup
½ cup water

1. Cut steak into serving-size pieces. Season with salt and pepper. Place in slow cooker. Layer onion over steak.
2. Combine soup and water. Pour into slow cooker.
3. Cover. Cook on Low 8-10 hours.
4. Serve over noodles or rice.

Dale & Shari's Beef Stroganoff

Dale and Shari Mast
Harrisonburg, VA

Makes 4 servings

4 cups beef cubes
10¾-oz. can cream of
  mushroom soup
1 cup sour cream

1. Place beef in slow cooker. Cover with mushroom soup.
2. Cover. Cook on Low 8 hours, or High 4-5 hours.
3. Before serving stir in sour cream.
4. Serve over cooked rice, pasta, or baked potatoes.

Round Steak

Dorothy Hess, Willow Street, PA
Betty A. Holt, St. Charles, MO
Betty Moore, Plano, IL
Michelle Strite,
Harrisonburg, VA
Barbara Tenney, Delta, PA
Sharon Timpe, Mequon, WI

Makes 4-5 servings

2-lb. boneless round steak
oil
1 envelope dry onion soup
   mix
10³/4-oz. can cream of
   mushroom soup
¹/2 cup water

1. Cut steak into serving-size pieces. Brown in oil in saucepan. Place in slow cooker. Sprinkle with soup mix.
2. Combine soup and water. Pour over meat.
3. Cover. Cook on Low 7-8 hours.

Variation:

To make a dish lower in sodium, replace the onion soup mix and mushroom soup with 1 cup diced onions, ¹/2 lb. sliced mushrooms, 1 Tbsp. fresh parsley, ¹/4 tsp. pepper, ¹/2 tsp. dried basil, all stirred gently together. Place on top of meat in cooker. Dissolve 2 Tbsp. flour in ³/4 cup cold water. Pour over vegetables and meat. Mix together. Cover and cook according to directions above.
Della Yoder
Kalona, IA

Pot Roast with Creamy Mushroom Sauce

Colleen Konetzni
Rio Rancho, NM
Janet V. Yocum
Elizabethtown, PA

Makes 6-8 servings

2-2¹/2-lb. boneless beef
   chuck roast
1 envelope dry onion soup
   mix
10³/4-oz. can condensed
   cream of mushroom
   soup

1. Place roast in slow cooker. Sprinkle with dry soup mix. Top with mushroom soup.
2. Cover. Cook on High 1 hour, and then on Low 8 hours, or until meat is tender.
3. Slice. Serve with mashed potatoes or cooked noodles.

Variation:

Add cubed potatoes and sliced carrots to beef. Proceed with directions above.
Marla Folkert
Holland, OH

Slow Cooker Beef

Sara Harter Fredette
Williamsburg, MA

Makes 4-6 servings

¹/2 cup flour
2 tsp. salt
¹/4 tsp. pepper
2-3 lbs. stewing beef,
   cubed
2 Tbsp. oil
10³/4-oz. can cream of
   mushroom soup
1 envelope dry onion soup
   mix
¹/2 cup sour cream

1. Combine flour, salt, and pepper in plastic bag. Add beef in small batches. Shake to coat beef. Saute beef in oil in saucepan. Place browned beef in slow cooker.
2. Stir in mushroom soup and onion soup mix.
3. Cover. Cook on Low 6-8 hours.
4. Stir in sour cream before serving. Heat for a few minutes.
5. Serve with noodles or mashed potatoes.

For a juicy beef roast to be ready by noon, put a roast in the slow cooker in the evening and let it on all night on Low.
Ruth Hershey
Paradise, PA

Paul's Beef Bourguignon

Janice Muller
Derwood, MD

Makes 4 servings

3-lb. chuck roast, cubed
2 Tbsp. oil
2 10¾-oz. cans golden cream of mushroom soup
1 envelope dry onion soup mix
1 cup cooking sherry

1. Brown meat in oil in skillet. Drain. Place in slow cooker. Add remaining ingredients and cover.
2. Refrigerate 6-8 hours, or up to 14 hours, to marinate.
3. Remove from refrigerator, cover, and cook on Low 8-10 hours.
4. Serve over cooked egg noodles or rice.

Beef Pot Roast

Julia B. Boyd
Memphis, TN

Makes 6-8 servings

3-4-lb. chuck, *or* English-cut, beef roast
1 envelope dry onion-mushroom soup mix
10¾-oz. can cream of celery soup
1 soup can water
2-3 Tbsp. flour
2-3 beef bouillon cubes
1 medium onion, chopped

1. Combine all ingredients in slow cooker.
2. Cover. Cook on Low 10-12 hours.

Variations:
Use leftover meat to make soup. Add one large can tomatoes and any leftover vegetables you have on hand. Add spices such as minced onion, garlic powder, basil, bay leaf, celery seed. To increase the liquid, use V-8 juice and season with 1-2 tablespoons butter for a richer soup base. Cook on Low 6-12 hours. If you wish, stir in cooked macaroni or rice just before serving.

Chuck Roast

Hazel L. Propst
Oxford, PA

Makes 6-8 servings

4-5-lb. boneless chuck roast
⅓ cup flour
3 Tbsp. oil
1 envelope dry onion soup mix
water
¼ cup flour
⅓ cup cold water

1. Rub roast with flour on both sides. Brown in oil in saucepan. Place in slow cooker (cutting to fit if necessary).
2. Sprinkle dry soup mix over roast. Add water to cover roast.
3. Cover. Cook on Low 8 hours.
4. Stir flour into ⅓ cup cold water until smooth. Remove roast to serving platter and keep warm. Stir paste into hot sauce and stir until dissolved. Cover and cook on High until sauce is thickened.

For more flavorful gravy, first brown the meat in a skillet. Scrape all browned bits from the bottom of the skillet and add to the slow cooker along with the meat.
Carolyn Baer
Conrath, WI

Roast Beef

Judy Buller
Bluffton, OH

Makes 6 servings

2 1/2-3-lb. bottom round
 roast
2 cups water
2 beef bouillon cubes
1/2 tsp. cracked pepper
1/4 cup flour
1/2 tsp. salt
3/4 cup cold water

1. Cut roast into 6-8 pieces
and place in slow cooker. Add
water and bouillon cubes.
Sprinkle with pepper.
2. Cover. Cook on High 2
hours. Reduce heat to Low
and cook 4-5 hours, or until
meat is tender.
3. Dissolve flour and salt
in cold water. Remove roast
from cooker and keep warm.
Stir flour paste into hot broth
in cooker until smooth. Cover
and cook on High for 5 minutes. Serve gravy with sliced
roast beef.

Roast

Tracey Yohn
Harrisburg, PA

Makes 6 servings

2-3-lb. shoulder roast
1 tsp. salt
1 tsp. pepper
1 tsp. garlic salt
1 small onion, sliced in
 rings
1 cup boiling water
1 beef bouillon cube

1. Place roast in slow
cooker. Sprinkle with salt,
pepper, and garlic salt. Place
onion rings on top.
2. Dissolve bouillon cube
in water. Pour over roast.
3. Cover. Cook on Low 10-
12 hours, or on High 5-6
hours.

Savory Sweet Roast

Martha Ann Auker
Landisburg, PA

Makes 6-8 servings

3-4-lb. blade, *or* chuck,
 roast
oil
1 onion, chopped
10 3/4-oz. can cream of
 mushroom soup
1/2 cup water
1/4 cup sugar
1/4 cup vinegar
2 tsp. salt
1 tsp. prepared mustard
1 tsp. Worcestershire sauce

1. Brown meat in oil on
both sides in saucepan. Put in
slow cooker.
2. Blend together remain-
ing ingredients. Pour over
meat.
3. Cover. Cook on Low 12-
16 hours.

Hungarian Goulash

Kim Stoltzfus
New Holland, PA

Makes 8 servings

2-lb. round steak, cubed
½ tsp. onion powder
½ tsp. garlic powder
2 Tbsp. flour
½ tsp. salt
½ tsp. pepper
1½ tsp. paprika
10¾-oz. can tomato soup
½ soup can water
1 cup sour cream

1. Mix meat, onion powder, garlic powder, and flour together in slow cooker until meat is well coated.
2. Add remaining ingredients, except sour cream. Stir well.
3. Cover. Cook on Low 8-10 hours, or High 4-5 hours.
4. Add sour cream 30 minutes before serving.
5. Serve over hot noodles.

Dilled Pot Roast

C.J. Slagle
Roann, IN

Makes 6 servings

3-3½-lb. beef pot roast
1 tsp. salt
¼ tsp. pepper
2 tsp. dried dillweed, divided
¼ cup water
1 Tbsp. vinegar
3 Tbsp. flour
½ cup water
1 cup sour cream

1. Sprinkle both sides of meat with salt, pepper, and 1 tsp. dill. Place in slow cooker. Add water and vinegar.
2. Cover. Cook on Low 7-9 hours, or until tender. Remove meat from pot. Turn to High.
3. Dissolve flour in water. Stir into meat drippings. Stir in additional 1 tsp. dill. Cook on High 5 minutes. Stir in sour cream. Cook on High another 5 minutes.
4. Slice meat and serve with sour cream sauce over top.

Herbed Roast with Gravy

Sue Williams
Gulfport, MS

Makes 8-10 servings

4-lb. roast
2 tsp. salt
½ tsp. pepper
2 medium onions, sliced
half a can (10¾-oz.) condensed cheddar cheese soup
8-oz. can tomato sauce
4-oz. can mushroom pieces and stems, drained
¼ tsp. dried basil
¼ tsp. dried oregano

1. Season roast with salt and pepper. Place in slow cooker.
2. Combine remaining ingredients and pour over meat.
3. Cover. Cook on Low 8-10 hours, or on High 4-5 hours.
4. Serve with gravy.

Beef Burgundy
Jacqueline Stefl
East Bethany, NY

Makes 6 servings

5 medium onions, thinly
  sliced
2 lbs. stewing meat, cubed
1½ Tbsp. flour
½ lb. fresh mushrooms,
  sliced
1 tsp. salt
¼ tsp. dried marjoram
¼ tsp. dried thyme
⅛ tsp. pepper
¾ cup beef broth
1½ cups burgundy wine

1. Place onions in slow
cooker.
2. Dredge meat in flour.
Put in slow cooker.
3. Add mushrooms, salt,
marjoram, thyme, and pep-
per.
4. Pour in broth and wine.
5. Cover. Cook 8-10 hours
on Low.
6. Serve over cooked noo-
dles.

Goodtime Beef Brisket
AmyMarlene Jensen
Fountain, CO

Makes 6-8 servings

3½-4-lb. beef brisket
1 can beer
2 cups tomato sauce
2 tsp. prepared mustard
2 Tbsp. balsamic vinegar
2 Tbsp. Worcestershire
  sauce
1 tsp. garlic powder
½ tsp. ground allspice
2 Tbsp. brown sugar
1 small green, *or* red, bell
  pepper, chopped
1 medium onion, chopped
1 tsp. salt
½ tsp. pepper

1. Place brisket in slow
cooker.
2. Combine remaining
ingredients. Pour over meat.
3. Cover. Cook on Low 8-
10 hours.
4. Remove meat from
sauce. Slice very thin.
5. Serve on rolls or over
couscous.

Pot Roast
Judi Manos
West Islip, NY

Makes 8 servings

4-lb. chuck roast *or* stewing
  meat, cubed
1 Tbsp. oil
¾ can beer
½ cup, plus 1 Tbsp.,
  ketchup
1 onion, sliced
½ cup cold water
1½ Tbsp. flour

1. Brown meat in oil in
saucepan.
2. Combine beer and
ketchup in slow cooker. Stir
in onion and browned meat.
3. Cover. Cook on Low 8
hours.
4. Remove meat and keep
warm. Blend flour into cold
water until dissolved. Stir into
hot gravy until smooth.
5. Serve gravy and meat
together.

Less tender, less expensive cuts of meat are better suited for
slow cooking than expensive cuts of meat. If desired, you can
brown meat on top of the stove first, for additional flavor.
Beatrice Orgish
Richardson, TX

Italian Beef

Joyce Bowman
Lady Lake, FL

Makes 10-12 servings

3-4-lb. beef roast
1 pkg. dry Italian dressing
mix
12-oz. can beer

1. Place roast in slow
cooker. Sprinkle with dry
Italian dressing mix. Pour
beer over roast.
2. Cover. Cook on Low 8-
10 hours, or High 3-4 hours.
3. When beef is done,
shred and serve with juice on
crusty rolls.

Variations:
In place of beef, use pork
chops or chicken legs and
thighs (skin removed).

Slow-Cooker Roast Beef

Ernestine Schrepfer
Trenton, MO

Makes 6 servings

3-lb. sirloin tip roast
1/2 cup flour
1 envelope dry onion soup
mix
1 envelope brown gravy
mix
2 cups ginger ale

1. Coat roast with flour
(reserve remaining flour).
Place in slow cooker.
2. Combine soup mix,
gravy mix, remaining flour,
and ginger ale in bowl. Mix
well. Pour over roast.
3. Cover. Cook on Low 8-
10 hours.

Pepsi Pot Roast

Mrs. Don Martins
Fairbank, IA

Makes 6-8 servings

3-4-lb. pot roast
10¾-oz. can cream of
mushroom soup
1 envelope dry onion soup
mix
16-oz. bottle Pepsi, *or*
other cola

1. Place meat in slow
cooker.
2. Top with mushroom
soup and onion soup mix.
Pour in Pepsi.
3. Cover. Cook on High 6
hours.

Cola Roast

Janice Yoskovich
Carmichaels, PA

Makes 8-10 servings

3-lb. beef roast
1 envelope dry onion soup
mix
2 cans cola

1. Place roast in slow
cooker. Sprinkle with soup
mix. Pour soda over all.
2. Cover. Cook on Low 7-8
hours.

Note:
Diet cola does not work
with this recipe.

Zippy Beef Tips

Maryann Westerberg
Rosamond, CA

Makes 6-8 servings

2 lbs. stewing meat, cubed
2 cups sliced fresh
mushrooms
10¾-oz. can cream of
mushroom soup
1 envelope dry onion soup
mix
1 cup 7-Up, *or* other
lemon-lime carbonated
drink

1. Place meat and mush-
rooms in slow cooker.

2. Combine mushroom soup, soup mix, and soda. Pour over meat.

3. Cover. Cook on Low 8 hours.

4. Serve over rice.

Hungarian Goulash

Audrey Romonosky
Austin, TX

Makes 5-6 servings

2 lbs. beef chuck, cubed
1 onion, sliced
1/2 tsp. garlic powder
1/2 cup ketchup
2 Tbsp. Worcestershire
sauce
1 Tbsp. brown sugar
1/2 tsp. salt
2 tsp. paprika
1/2 tsp. dry mustard
1 cup cold water
1/4 cup flour

1. Place meat in slow cooker. Add onion.

2. Combine garlic powder, ketchup, Worcestershire sauce, brown sugar, salt, paprika, and mustard. Pour over meat.

3. Cover. Cook on Low 8 hours.

4. Dissolve flour in water. Stir into meat mixture. Cook on High until thickened, about 10 minutes.

5. Serve over noodles.

Horseradish Beef

Barbara Nolan
Pleasant Valley, NY

Makes 6-8 servings

3-4-lb. pot roast
2 Tbsp. oil
1/2 tsp. salt
1/2 tsp. pepper
1 onion, chopped
6-oz. can tomato paste
1/3 cup horseradish sauce

1. Brown roast on all sides in oil in skillet. Place in slow cooker. Add remaining ingredients.

2. Cover. Cook on Low 8-10 hours.

Spicy Pot Roast

Jane Talso
Albuquerque, NM

Makes 6-8 servings

3-4-lb. beef pot roast
salt to taste
pepper to taste
3/4-oz. pkg. brown gravy
mix
1/4 cup ketchup
2 tsp. Dijon mustard
1 tsp. Worcestershire sauce
1/8 tsp. garlic powder
1 cup water

1. Sprinkle meat with salt and pepper. Place in slow cooker.

2. Combine remaining ingredients. Pour over meat.

3. Cover. Cook on Low 8-10 hours, or High 4-5 hours.

Chinese Pot Roast

Marsha Sabus
Fallbrook, CA

Makes 6 servings

3-lb. boneless beef pot
roast
2 Tbsp. flour
1 Tbsp. oil
2 large onions, chopped
salt to taste
pepper to taste
1/2 cup soy sauce
1 cup water
1/2 tsp. ground ginger

1. Dip roast in flour and brown on both sides in oil in sauccpan. Place in slow cooker.

2. Top with onions, salt and pepper.

3. Combine soy sauce, water, and ginger. Pour over meat.

4. Cover. Cook on High 10 minutes. Reduce heat to Low and cook 8-10 hours.

5. Slice and serve with rice.

Peppery Roast

Lovina Baer
Conrath, WI

Makes 8-10 servings

4-lb. beef, *or* venison, roast
1 tsp. garlic salt
1 tsp. onion salt
2 tsp. celery salt
1 1/2 tsp. salt
2 tsp. Worcestershire sauce
2 tsp. pepper
1/2 cup ketchup
1 Tbsp. liquid smoke
3 Tbsp. brown sugar
1 Tbsp. dry mustard
dash of nutmeg
1 Tbsp. soy sauce
1 Tbsp. lemon juice
3 drops hot pepper sauce

1. Place roast in slow cooker.
2. Combine remaining ingredients and pour over roast.
3. Cover. Cook on High 6-8 hours.

Mexican Pot Roast

Bernice A. Esau
North Newton, KS

Makes 6-8 servings

3 lbs. beef brisket, cubed
2 Tbsp. oil
1/2 cup slivered almonds
2 cups mild picante sauce,
   or hot, if you prefer
2 Tbsp. vinegar
1 tsp. garlic powder
1/2 tsp. salt
1/4 tsp. cinnamon
1/4 tsp. dried thyme
1/4 tsp. dried oregano
1/8 tsp. ground cloves
1/8 tsp. pepper
1/2-3/4 cup water, as needed

1. Brown beef in oil in skillet. Place in slow cooker.
2. Combine remaining ingredients. Pour over meat.
3. Cover. Cook on Low 10-12 hours. Add water as needed.
4. Serve with potatoes, noodles, or rice.

Chuck Wagon Beef

Charlotte Bull
Cassville, MO

Makes 8 servings

4-lb. boneless chuck roast
1 tsp. garlic salt
1/4 tsp. black pepper
2 Tbsp. oil
6-8 garlic cloves, minced
1 large onion, sliced
1 cup water
1 bouillon cube
2-3 tsp. instant coffee
1 bay leaf, *or* 1 Tbsp.
   mixed Italian herbs
3 Tbsp. cold water
2 Tbsp. cornstarch

1. Sprinkle roast with garlic salt and pepper. Brown on all sides in oil in saucepan. Place in slow cooker.
2. Saute garlic and onion in meat drippings in saucepan. Add water, bouillon cube, and coffee. Cook over low heat for several minutes, stirring until drippings loosen. Pour over meat in cooker.
3. Add bay leaf or herbs.
4. Cover. Cook on Low 8-10 hours, or until very tender. Remove bay leaf and discard. Remove meat to serving platter and keep warm.
5. Mix water and cornstarch together until paste forms. Stir into hot liquid and onions in cooker. Cover. Cook 10 minutes on High, or until thickened.
6. Slice meat and serve with gravy over top or on the side.

French Dip
Barbara Walker
Sturgis, SD

Makes 6-8 servings

3-lb. rump roast
1/2 cup soy sauce
1 beef bouillon cube
1 bay leaf
1 tsp. dried thyme
3-4 peppercorns
1 tsp. garlic powder

1. Combine all ingredients in slow cooker. Add water to almost cover meat.
2. Cover. Cook on Low 10-12 hours.

French Dip Roast
Patti Boston
Newark, OH

Makes 8-10 servings

1 large onion, sliced
3-lb. beef bottom roast
1/2 cup dry white wine, *or* water
1 pkg. dry au jus gravy mix
2 cups beef broth

1. Place onion in slow cooker. Add roast.
2. Combine wine and gravy mix. Pour over roast.
3. Add enough broth to cover roast.

4. Cover. Cook on High 5-6 hours, or Low 10-12 hours.
5. Remove meat from liquid. Let stand 5 minutes before slicing thinly across grain.

Beef Au Jus
Jean Weller
State College, PA

Makes 6-8 servings

3-lb. eye, *or* rump, roast
1 pkg. dry au jus gravy mix
1 tsp. garlic powder
1 tsp. onion powder
1/2 tsp. salt
1/4-1/2 tsp. pepper

1. Place roast in slow cooker.
2. Prepare gravy according to package directions. Pour over roast.
3. Sprinkle with garlic powder, onion powder, salt, and pepper.
4. Cover. Cook on Low 6 hours. After 6 hours, remove meat and trim fat. Shred meat and return to slow cooker, cooking until desired tenderness. Add more water if roast isn't covered with liquid when returning it to cooker.

Dripped Beef
Mitzi McGlynchey
Downingtown, PA

Makes 8 servings

3-4-lb. chuck roast
1 tsp. salt
1 tsp. seasoned salt
1 tsp. white pepper
1 Tbsp. rosemary
1 Tbsp. dried oregano
1 Tbsp. garlic powder
1 cup water

1. Combine all ingredients in slow cooker.
2. Cover. Cook on Low 6-7 hours.
3. Shred meat using two forks. Strain liquid and return liquid and meat to slow cooker. Serve meat and au jus over mashed potatoes, noodles, or rice.

If you use ground herbs and spices, add them during the last hour of cooking.
Darlene Raber
Wellman, IA

Deep Pit Beef
Kristina Shull
Timberville, VA

Makes 6-8 servings

1 tsp. garlic salt, *or* powder
1 tsp. celery salt
1 tsp. lemon pepper
1½ Tbsp. liquid smoke
2 Tbsp. Worcestershire
  sauce
3-4-lb. beef roast

1. Combine seasonings in small bowl. Spread over roast as a marinade. Cover tightly with foil. Refrigerate for at least 8 hours.
2. Place roast in slow cooker. Cover with marinade sauce.
3. Cover. Cook on Low 6-7 hours. Save juice for gravy and serve with roast.

Note:
  This is also good served cold, along with picnic foods.

Barbecued Roast Beef
Kim Stoltzfus
New Holland, PA

Makes 10-12 servings

4-lb. chuck roast
1 cup ketchup
1 cup barbecue sauce
2 cups chopped celery
2 cups water
1 cup chopped onions
4 Tbsp. vinegar
2 Tbsp. brown sugar
2 Tbsp. Worcestershire
  sauce
1 tsp. chili powder
1 tsp. garlic powder
1 tsp. salt

1. Combine all ingredients in large bowl. Spoon into 5-quart cooker, or 2 3½-quart cookers.
2. Cover. Cook on Low 6-8 hours, or High 3-4 hours.
3. Slice meat into thin slices and serve in barbecue sauce over mashed potatoes or rice.

Italian Roast Beef
Elsie Russett
Fairbank, IA

Makes 6-8 servings

4-lb. beef rump roast
flour
1 onion
2 garlic cloves
1 large rib celery
2-oz. salt pork, *or* bacon
1 onion, sliced

1. Lightly flour roast.
2. In blender, grind onion, garlic, celery, and salt pork together. Rub ground mixture into roast.
3. Place sliced onion in slow cooker. Place roast on top of onion.
4. Cover. Cook on Low 8-10 hours.

Diane's Gutbuster
Joyce Cox
Port Angeles, WA

Makes 10-15 servings

5-lb. chuck roast
1 large onion, sliced
2 tsp. salt
¾ tsp. pepper
28-oz. can stewed tomatoes
1 Tbsp. brown sugar
1 cup water
half a bottle barbecue sauce
1 Tbsp. Worcestershire sauce

1. Combine all ingredients except barbecue sauce and Worcestershire sauce in slow cooker.

2. Cover. Cook on Low 6-7 hours. Refrigerate for at least 8 hours.

3. Shred meat and place in slow cooker. Add barbecue sauce and Worcestershire sauce.

4. Cover. Cook on Low 4-5 hours.

5. Serve as main dish or in hamburger buns.

Barbecue Brisket

Patricia Howard
Albuquerque, NM

Makes 8-10 servings

4-5-lb. beef brisket
1/8 tsp. celery salt
1/4 tsp. garlic salt
1/4 tsp. onion salt
1/4 tsp. salt
1.5-oz. bottle liquid smoke
1 1/2 cups barbecue sauce

1. Place brisket in slow cooker.

2. Sprinkle with celery salt, garlic salt, onion salt, and salt.

3. Pour liquid smoke over brisket. Cover. Refrigerate for 8 hours.

4. Cook on Low 8-10 hours, or until tender. During last hour pour barbecue sauce over brisket.

Beef Ribs

Maryann Westerberg
Rosamond, CA

Makes 8-10 servings

3-4-lb. boneless beef, *or* short ribs
1 1/2 cups barbecue sauce, divided
1/2 cup apricot, *or* pineapple, jam
1 Tbsp. soy sauce

1. Place ribs in baking pan.

2. Combine 3/4 cup barbecue sauce, jam, and soy sauce. Pour over ribs. Bake at 450° for 30 minutes to brown.

3. Take out of oven. Layer beef and sauce used in oven in slow cooker.

4. Cover. Cook on Low 8 hours.

5. Mix remaining 3/4 cup barbecue sauce with sauce from slow cooker. Pour over ribs and serve.

Reuben Sandwiches

Maryann Markano
Wilmington, DE

Makes 3-4 servings

1-lb. can sauerkraut
1 lb. sliced corned beef brisket
1/4-lb. Swiss cheese, sliced
sliced rye bread
sandwich spread, *or* Thousand Island Dressing

1. Drain sauerkraut in sieve, then on paper towels until very day. Place in bottom of slow cooker.

2. Arrange layer of corned beef slices over sauerkraut. Top with cheese slices.

3. Cover. Cook on Low 3-4 hours.

4. Toast bread. Spread generously with sandwich spread or dressing. Spoon ingredients from slow cooker onto toasted bread, maintaining layers of sauerkraut, meat, and cheese.

If I want to have a hot dish at noon time on Sunday, I bake a casserole on Saturday. Then on Sunday morning I put it into a slow cooker, turn it on High for 30 minutes, then on Low while I'm at church.

Ruth Hershey
Paradise, PA

Smoky Brisket

Angeline Lang
Greeley, CO

Makes 8-10 servings

2 medium onions, sliced
3-4-lb. beef brisket
1 Tbsp. smoke-flavored salt
1 tsp. celery seed
1 Tbsp. mustard seed
1/2 tsp. pepper
12-oz. bottle chili sauce

1. Arrange onions in bottom of slow cooker.
2. Sprinkle both sides of meat with smoke-flavored salt.
3. Combine celery seed, mustard seed, pepper, and chili sauce. Pour over meat.
4. Cover. Cook on Low 10-12 hours.

Easy Barbecued Venison

Tracey B. Stenger
Gretna, LA

Makes 6 servings

2-3-lb. venison, *or* beef, roast, cubed
2 large onions, sliced in rings
1-2 18-oz. bottles barbecue sauce

1. Put layer of meat and layer of onion rings in slow cooker. Drizzle generously with barbecue sauce. Repeat layers until meat and onion rings are all in place.
2. Cover. Cook on Low 8-10 hours.
3. Eat with au gratin potatoes and a vegetable, or slice thin and pile into steak rolls, drizzled with juice.

Note:
To be sure venison cooks tender, marinate overnight in 1 cup vinegar and 2 Tbsp. dried rosemary. In the morning, discard marinade, cut venison into cubes, and proceed with recipe.

Sour Beef

Rosanne Hankins
Stevensville, MD

Makes 6-8 servings

3-4-lb. pot roast
1/3 cup cider vinegar
1 large onion, sliced
3 bay leaves
1/2 tsp. salt
1/4 tsp. ground cloves
1/4 tsp. garlic powder

1. Place roast in slow cooker. Add remaining ingredients.
2. Cover. Cook on Low 8-10 hours.

Old World Sauerbraten

C.J. Slagle
Roann, IN
Angeline Lang
Greeley, CO

Makes 8 servings

3 1/2-4-lb. beef rump roast
1 cup water
1 cup vinegar
1 lemon, sliced but unpeeled
10 whole cloves
1 large onion, sliced
4 bay leaves
6 whole peppercorns
2 Tbsp. salt
2 Tbsp. sugar
12 gingersnaps, crumbled

1. Place meat in deep ceramic or glass bowl.
2. Combine water, vinegar, lemon, cloves, onion, bay leaves, peppercorns, salt, and sugar. Pour over meat. Cover and refrigerate 24-36 hours. Turn meat several times during marinating.
3. Place beef in slow cooker. Pour 1 cup marinade over meat.
4. Cover. Cook on Low 6-8 hours. Remove meat.
5. Strain meat juices and return to pot. Turn to High. Stir in gingersnaps. Cover and cook on High 10-14 minutes. Slice meat. Pour finished sauce over meat.

Meatloaf Dinner

Esther Lehman
Croghan, NY

Makes 4 servings

6 potatoes, cubed
4 carrots, thinly sliced
1/4 tsp. salt
1 egg, slightly beaten
1 large shredded wheat
 biscuit, crushed
1/4 cup chili sauce
1/4 cup finely chopped
 onion
1/2 tsp. salt
1/4 tsp. dried marjoram
1/8 tsp. pepper
1 lb. ground beef

1. Place potatoes and carrots in slow cooker. Season with salt.
2. Combine egg, shredded wheat, chili sauce, onion, salt, marjoram, and pepper. Add ground beef. Mix well. Shape into loaf, slightly smaller in diameter than the cooker. Place on top of vegetables, not touching sides of cooker.
3. Cover. Cook on Low 9-10 hours.

Variation:
 Substitute 1/2 cup bread crumbs or dry oatmeal for crushed shredded wheat biscuit.

Easy, All-Day Meatloaf and Vegetables

Ann Sunday McDowell
Newtown, PA

Makes 6 servings

4 large, *or* 6 medium,
 potatoes, sliced
6 carrots, sliced
1/4 tsp. salt
1 1/2 lbs. ground beef
2 eggs, beaten
3/4 cup cracker crumbs
1/3 cup ketchup
1/3 cup finely chopped
 onions
3/4 tsp. salt
1/4 tsp. dried marjoram
1/4 tsp. black pepper

1. Place potatoes and carrots in slow cooker. Sprinkle with 1/4 tsp. salt.
2. Combine remaining ingredients. Mix well and shape into loaf. Place loaf on top of vegetables, making sure that it doesn't touch sides of slow cooker.
3. Cover. Cook on Low 8-10 hours.

Ruth Ann's Meatloaf

Ruth Ann Hoover
New Holland, PA

Makes 4 servings

1 egg
1/4 cup milk
2 slices day-old bread,
 cubed
1/4 cup chopped onions
2 Tbsp. chopped green
 peppers
1 tsp. salt
1/4 tsp. pepper
1 1/2 lbs. ground beef
1/4 cup ketchup
8 small red potatoes
4-6 medium carrots, cut in
 1-inch chunks

1. Beat together eggs and milk.
2. Stir in bread cubes, onions, green peppers, salt, and pepper. Add beef and mix well.
3. Shape into loaf that is about an inch smaller in circumference than the inside of the slow cooker. Place loaf into slow cooker.
4. Spread top with ketchup.
5. Peel strip around the center of each potato. Place carrots and potatoes around Meatloaf.
6. Cover. Cook on High 1 hour. Reduce heat to Low. Cook 7-8 hours longer.

Don't peek. It takes 15-20 minutes for the cooker to regain lost steam and return to the right temperature.
Janet V. Yocum
Elizabethtown, PA

Betty's Meatloaf

Betty B. Dennison
Grove City, PA

Makes 4-6 servings

2 lbs. ground beef
1/2 cup chopped green
 peppers
1/2 cup chopped onions
1/2 tsp. salt
1 cup cracker crumbs
1 egg
7/8-oz. envelope brown
 gravy mix
1 cup milk
4-6 small potatoes, cut up,
 optional

1. Combine all ingredients
except potatoes in large bowl.
Shape into loaf. Place in slow
cooker.
2. Place potatoes alongside
meatloaf.
3. Cover. Cook on Low 8-
10 hours, or High 4-5 hours.

Tracey's Italian Meatloaf

Tracey Yohn
Harrisburg, PA

Makes 8 servings

2 lbs. ground beef
2 cups soft bread crumbs
1/2 cup spaghetti sauce
1 large egg
2 Tbsp. dried onion
1/4 tsp. pepper
1 1/4 tsp. salt
1 tsp. garlic salt
1/2 tsp. dried Italian herbs
1/4 tsp. garlic powder
2 Tbsp. spaghetti sauce

1. Fold a 30"-long piece of
foil in half lengthwise. Place in
bottom of slow cooker with
both ends hanging over the
edge of cooker. Grease foil.
2. Combine beef, bread
crumbs, 1/2 cup spaghetti
sauce, egg, onion, and seasonings. Shape into loaf. Place on
top of foil in slow cooker.
Spread 2 Tbsp. spaghetti
sauce over top.
3. Cover. Cook on High
2 1/2-3 hours, or Low 5-6
hours.

Mary Ann's Italian Meatloaf

Mary Ann Wasick
West Allis, WI

Makes 8-10 servings

2 lbs. ground beef
2 eggs, beaten
2/3 cup quick-cooking oats
1 envelope dry onion soup
 mix
1/2 cup pasta sauce (your
 favorite)
1 tsp. garlic powder
onion slices

1. Combine ground beef,
eggs, oats, soup mix, pasta
sauce, and garlic powder.
Shape into a loaf. Place in
slow cooker. Garnish top of
loaf with onion slices.
2. Cover. Cook on Low 8
hours.
3. Serve with pasta and
more of the sauce that you
mixed into the meatloaf.

To remove meatloaf or other meats from your cooker,
make foil handles to lift the food out. Use double strips of
heavy foil to make 3 strips, each about 20" x 3". Crisscross
them in the bottom of the pot and bring them up the sides in
a spoke design before putting in the food.
John D. Allen
Rye, CO
Esther Lehman
Croghan, NY

Meatloaf Sensation

Andrea O'Neil
Fairfield, CT

Makes 8 servings

2½ lbs. ground beef
half of an 8-oz. jar salsa
1 pkg. dry taco seasoning, divided
1 egg, slightly beaten
1 cup bread crumbs
12-oz. pkg. shredded Mexican-mix cheese
2 tsp. salt
½ tsp. pepper

1. Combine all ingredients, except half of taco seasoning. Mix well. Shape into loaf and place in slow cooker. Sprinkle with remaining taco seasoning.
2. Cover. Cook on Low 8-10 hours.

Barbecue Hamburger Steaks

Jeanette Oberholtzer
Manheim, PA

Makes 4 servings

1 lb. ground beef
1 tsp. salt
1 tsp. pepper
½ cup milk
1 cup soft bread crumbs
2 Tbsp. brown sugar
2 Tbsp. vinegar
3 Tbsp. Worcestershire sauce
1 cup ketchup

1. Combine beef, salt, pepper, milk, and bread crumbs. Mix well. Form into patties. Brown in saucepan and drain.
2. Combine brown sugar, vinegar, Worcestershire sauce, and ketchup in slow cooker. Add ground beef patties, pushing them down into the sauce, so that each one is well covered.
3. Cover. Cook on Low 4-6 hours.

Nutritious Meatloaf

Elsie Russett
Fairbank, IA

Makes 6 servings

1 lb. ground beef
2 cups finely shredded cabbage
1 medium green pepper, diced
1 Tbsp. dried onion flakes
½ tsp. caraway seeds
1 tsp. salt

1. Combine all ingredients. Shape into loaf and place on rack in slow cooker.
2. Cover. Cook on High 3-4 hours.

Poor Man's Steak

Elsie Schlabach
Millersburg, OH

Makes 8-10 servings

1½ lbs. ground beef
1 cup milk
¼ tsp. pepper
1 tsp. salt
1 small onion, finely
    chopped
1 cup cracker crumbs
1 tsp. brown sugar
10¾-oz. can cream of
    mushroom soup
1 soup can water

1. Mix together all ingredients except soup and water. Shape into narrow loaf. Refrigerate for at least 8 hours.
2. Slice and fry until brown in skillet.
3. Mix soup and water together until smooth. Spread diluted soup on each piece. Place slices into cooker. Pour any remaining soup over slices in cooker.
4. Cover. Cook on Low 2-3 hours.

Beef Stroganoff

Julette Leaman
Harrisonburg, VA

Makes 6 servings

2 lbs. ground beef
2 medium onions, chopped
2 garlic cloves, minced
6½-oz. can mushrooms
1½ cups sour cream
4 Tbsp. flour
2½ tsp. salt
¼ tsp. pepper
1 cup bouillon
3 Tbsp. tomato paste

1. In skillet, brown beef, onions, garlic, and mushrooms until meat and onions are brown. Drain. Pour into slow cooker.
2. Combine sour cream and flour. Add to mixture in slow cooker. Stir in remaining ingredients.
3. Cover. Cook on Low 6-8 hours.
4. Serve over hot buttered noodles.

Chili and Cheese on Rice

Dale and Shari Mast
Harrisonburg, VA

Makes 6 servings

1 lb. ground beef
1 onion, diced
1 tsp. dried basil
1 tsp. dried oregano
16-oz. can light red kidney
    beans
15½-oz. can chili beans
1 pint stewed tomatoes,
    drained
cooked rice
grated cheddar cheese

1. Brown ground beef and onion in skillet. Season with basil and oregano.
2. Combine all ingredients except rice and cheese in slow cooker.
3. Cover. Cook on Low 4 hours.
4. Serve over cooked rice. Top with cheese.

Roasting bags work well in the slow cooker. Simply fill with meat and vegetables and cook as directed in slow cooker recipes. Follow manufacturer's directions for filling and sealing bags.

Charlotte Shaffer
East Earl, PA

Loretta's Spanish Rice

Loretta Krahn
Mt. Lake, MN

Makes 8 servings

2 lbs. ground beef, browned
2 medium onions, chopped
2 green peppers, chopped
28-oz. can tomatoes
8-oz. can tomato sauce
1½ cups water
2½ tsp. chili powder
2 tsp. salt
2 tsp. Worcestershire sauce
1½ cups rice, uncooked

1. Combine all ingredients in slow cooker.
2. Cover. Cook on Low 8-10 hours, or High 6 hours.

Evie's Spanish Rice

Evie Hershey
Atglen, PA

Makes 10-12 servings

2 lbs. lean ground beef
2 onions, chopped
2 green peppers, chopped
1 qt. canned tomatoes
8-oz. can tomato sauce
1 cup water
2½ tsp. chili powder
2 tsp. salt

2 tsp. Worcestershire sauce
1 cup converted rice, uncooked

1. Brown beef in skillet. Drain.
2. Combine all ingredients in slow cooker. Stir.
3. Cover. Cook on Low 7-9 hours.

A Hearty Western Casserole

Karen Ashworth
Duenweg, MO

Makes 5 servings

1 lb. ground beef, browned
16-oz. can whole corn, drained
16-oz. can red kidney beans, drained
10¾-oz. can condensed tomato soup
1 cup (4 oz.) Colby cheese
¼ cup milk
1 tsp. minced dry onion flakes
½ tsp. chili powder

1. Combine beef, corn, beans, soup, cheese, milk, onion, and chili powder in slow cooker.
2. Cover. Cook on Low 1 hour.

Variation:
1 pkg. (of 10) refrigerator biscuits
2 Tbsp. margarine
¼ cup yellow cornmeal

Dip biscuits in margarine and then in cornmeal. Bake 20 minutes or until brown. Top beef mixture with biscuits before serving.

Green Chili Stew

Jeanne Allen
Rye, CO

Makes 6-8 servings

3 Tbsp. oil
2 garlic cloves, minced
1 large onion, diced
1 lb. ground sirloin
½ lb. ground pork
3 cups chicken broth
2 cups water
2 4-oz. cans diced green chilies
4 large potatoes, diced
10-oz. pkg. frozen corn
1 tsp. black pepper
1 tsp. crushed dried oregano
½ tsp. ground cumin
1 tsp. salt

1. Brown onion, garlic, sirloin, and pork in oil in skillet. Cook until meat is no longer pink.
2. Combine all ingredients in slow cooker.
3. Cover. Cook on Low 4-6 hours, or until potatoes are soft.

Note:
Excellent served with warm tortillas or corn bread.

Cowboy Casserole

Lori Berezovsky
Salina, KS

Makes 4-6 servings

1 onion, chopped
1 1/2 lbs. ground beef,
    browned and drained
6 medium potatoes, sliced
1 clove garlic, minced
16-oz. can kidney beans
15-oz. can diced tomatoes
    mixed with 2 Tbsp.
    flour, *or* 10 3/4-oz. can
    tomato soup
1 tsp. salt
1/4 tsp. pepper

1. Layer onions, ground
beef, potatoes, garlic, and
beans in slow cooker.
2. Spread tomatoes or soup
over all. Sprinkle with salt
and pepper.
3. Cover. Cook on Low 5-6
hours, or until potatoes are
tender.

10-Layer Slow-Cooker Dish

Norma Saltzman
Shickley, NE

Makes 6-8 servings

6 medium potatoes, thinly
    sliced
1 medium onion, thinly
    sliced
salt to taste
pepper to taste
15-oz. can corn
15-oz. can peas
1/4 cup water
1 1/2 lbs. ground beef,
    browned
10 3/4-oz. can cream of
    mushroom soup

1. Layer 1: 1/4 of potatoes,
1/2 of onion, salt, and pepper
2. Layer 2: 1/2 can of corn
3. Layer 3: 1/4 of potatoes
4. Layer 4: 1/2 can of peas
5. Layer 5: 1/4 of potatoes,
1/2 of onion, salt, and pepper
6. Layer 6: remaining corn
7. Layer 7: remaining potatoes
8. Layer 8: remaining peas
and water
9. Layer 9: ground beef
10. Layer 10: soup
11. Cover. Cook on High 4
hours.

Hamburger Potatoes

Juanita Marner
Shipshewana, IN

Makes 3-4 servings

3 medium potatoes, sliced
3 carrots, sliced
1 small onion, sliced
2 Tbsp. dry rice
1 tsp. salt
1/2 tsp. pepper
1 lb. ground beef, browned
    and drained
1 1/2-2 cups tomato juice, as
    needed to keep dish
    from getting too dry

1. Combine all ingredients
in slow cooker.
2. Cover. Cook on Low 6-8
hours.

When cooking meats and vegetables together, especially
when cooking on Low, place the vegetables on the bottom
where they will be kept moist.
Roseann Wilson
Albuquerque, NM

Shipwreck

Betty Lahman
Elkton, VA

Makes 8 servings

1 lb. ground beef, browned
4-5 potatoes, cut in French-
   fry-like strips
1-2 onions, chopped
16-oz. can light red kidney
   beans, drained
1/4-lb. Velveeta cheese,
   cubed
10³/4-oz. can tomato soup
1 1/2 tsp. salt
1/4 tsp. pepper
butter

1. Layer in slow cooker in
this order: ground beef, potatoes, onions, kidney beans,
and cheese. Pour soup over
top. Season with salt and pepper. Dot with butter.
2. Cover. Cook on Low 6-8
hours.

Note:
   This is particularly good
served with Parmesan cheese
sprinkled on top at the table.

Beef and Lentils

Esther Porter
Minneapolis, MN

Makes 12 servings

1 medium onion
3 whole cloves
5 cups water
1 lb. lentils
1 tsp. salt
1 bay leaf
1 lb. (or less) ground beef,
   browned and drained
1/2 cup ketchup
1/4 cup molasses
2 Tbsp. brown sugar
1 tsp. dry mustard
1/4 tsp. Worcestershire
   sauce
1 onion, finely chopped

1. Stick cloves into whole
onion. Set aside.
2. In large saucepan, combine water, lentils, salt, bay
leaf, and whole onion with
cloves. Simmer 30 minutes.
3. Meanwhile, combine all
remaining ingredients in slow
cooker. Stir in simmered
ingredients from saucepan.
Add additional water if mixture seems dry.
4. Cover. Cook on Low 6-8
hours (check to see if lentils
are tender).

Note:
   Freezes well.

Variation:
   Top with sour cream
and/or salsa when serving.

Judy's Hamburger Stew

Judy Koczo
Plano, IL

Makes 6-8 servings

3 large potatoes, sliced
3 carrots, sliced
1 lb. frozen peas
1 onion, diced
2 ribs celery, sliced thin
salt to taste
pepper to taste
1 1/2 lbs. ground beef,
   browned and drained
10³/4-oz. can tomato soup
1 soup can water

1. Put vegetables in slow
cooker in layers as listed.
Season each layer with salt
and pepper.
2. Layer beef on top of celery. Mix together soup and
water. Pour over ground beef.
3. Cover. Cook on Low 6-8
hours, or High 2-4 hours, stirring occasionally.

Variation:
   Substitute 28-oz. can
whole or diced tomatoes in
place of tomato soup and
water.

Ann Bender
Fort Defiance, VA

Taters n' Beef

Maryland Massey
Millington, MD

Makes 6-8 servings

2 lbs. ground beef,
  browned
1 tsp. salt
1/2 tsp. pepper
1/4 cup chopped onions
1 cup canned tomato soup
6 potatoes, sliced
1 cup milk

1. Combined beef, salt,
pepper, onions, and soup.
2. Place a layer of potatoes
in bottom of slow cooker.
Cover with a portion of the
meat mixture. Repeat layers
until ingredients are used.
3. Cover. Cook on Low 4-6
hours. Add milk and cook on
High 15-20 minutes.

Variations:
1. Use home-canned
spaghetti sauce instead of
tomato soup.
2. Add a layer of chopped
raw cabbage after each layer
of sliced potatoes to add to
the flavor, texture, and nutri-
tional value of the meal.

Jeanne's Hamburger Stew

Jeanne Heyerly
Chenoa, IL

Makes 8 servings

2 lbs. ground beef
1 medium onion, chopped
1 garlic clove, minced
2 cups tomato juice
2-3 carrots, sliced
2-3 ribs celery, sliced
half a green pepper,
  chopped
2 cups green beans
2 medium potatoes, cubed
2 cups water
1 Tbsp. Worcestershire
  sauce
1/4 tsp. dried oregano
1/4 tsp. dried basil
1/4 tsp. dried thyme
dash of hot pepper sauce
2 Tbsp. dry onion soup
  mix, *or* 1 beef bouillon
  cube
1 tsp. salt
1/4 tsp. pepper

1. Brown meat and onion
in saucepan. Drain. Stir in
garlic and tomato juice. Heat
to boiling.
2. Combine all ingredients
in slow cooker.
3. Cover. Cook on Low 8-
10 hours.

Variation:
Use 1 cup barley in place
of potatoes.

Supper-in-a-Dish

Martha Hershey
Ronks, PA

Makes 8 servings

1 lb. ground beef, browned
  and drained
1 1/2 cups sliced raw
  potatoes
1 cup sliced carrots
1 cup peas
1/2 cup chopped onions
1/2 cup chopped celery
1/4 cup chopped green
  peppers
1 tsp. salt
1/4 tsp. pepper
10 3/4 -oz. can cream of
  chicken, *or* mushroom,
  soup
1/4 cup milk
2/3 cup grated sharp cheese

1. Layer ground beef, potatoes, carrots, peas, onions,
celery, green peppers, salt,
and pepper in slow cooker.
2. Combine soup and milk.
Pour over layered ingredients.
Sprinkle with cheese.
3. Cover. Cook on High 4
hours.

Working-Woman Favorite

Martha Ann Auker
Landisburg, PA

Makes 6-8 servings

2 lbs. ground beef,
　browned and drained
4 ribs celery, chopped
1 small green pepper,
　chopped
1 onion, chopped
2 tsp. sugar
1/2 tsp. salt
dash of pepper
10 3/4-oz. can cream of
　mushroom soup

1. Combine all ingredients in slow cooker.
2. Cover. Cook on Low 8-10 hours.
3. Serve over warm biscuits.

Note:
Sprinkle individual servings with shredded cheddar cheese.

Ground Beef Casserole

Lois J. Cassidy
Willow Street, PA

Makes 6-8 servings

1 1/2 lbs. ground beef
6-8 potatoes, sliced
1 medium onion, sliced
14 1/2-oz. can cut green
　beans with juice
1/2 tsp. salt
dash of pepper
10 3/4-oz. can cream of
　mushroom soup

1. Crumble uncooked ground beef in bottom of slow cooker. Add potatoes, onion, salt, and pepper. Pour beans over all. Spread can of mushroom soup over beans.
2. Cover. Cook on Low 6-8 hours.

Variation:
Brown the beef before putting in the slow cooker. Mix half a soup can of water with the mushroom soup before placing over beans.

Chinese Hamburger

Esther J. Yoder
Hartville, OH

Makes 8 servings

1 lb. ground beef, browned
　and drained
1 onion, diced
2 ribs celery, diced
10 3/4-oz. can chicken
　noodle soup
10 3/4-oz. can cream of
　mushroom soup
12-oz. can Chinese
　vegetables
salt to taste, about 1/4-1/2
　tsp.
pepper to taste, about 1/4
　tsp.
1 green pepper, diced
1 tsp. soy sauce

1. Combine all ingredients in slow cooker.
2. Cover. Cook on High 3-4 hours.
3. Serve over rice.

You may want to revise herb amounts when using a slow cooker. Whole herbs and spices increase their flavoring power, while ground spices tend to lose some flavor. It's a good idea to season to taste before serving.
Irma H. Schoen
Windsor, CT

115

Tater Tot Casserole

Shirley Hinh
Wayland, IA

Makes 6-8 servings

32-oz. bag frozen tater tots
1 lb. ground beef, browned
1/2 tsp. salt
1/4 tsp. pepper
2 14 1/2-oz. cans green
　beans, drained
10 3/4-oz. can cream of
　mushroom soup
1 Tbsp. dried onions
1/4 cup milk

1. Line slow cooker with frozen tater tots.
2. Combine remaining ingredients. Pour over potatoes.
3. Cover. Cook on High 3 hours.

Note:
　Sprinkle individual servings with your choice of grated cheese.

Bean Tator Tot Casserole

Marjora Miller
Archbold, OH

Makes 6 servings

1 lb. ground beef
1/2 tsp. salt
1/4 tsp. pepper
1 onion, chopped
1-lb. bag frozen string
　beans
10 3/4-oz. can cream of
　mushroom soup
1 cup shredded cheese
21-oz. bag. frozen tator tots

1. Crumble raw ground beef in bottom of slow cooker. Sprinkle with salt and pepper.
2. Layer remaining ingredients on beef in order listed.
3. Cover. Cook on High 1 hour. Reduce heat to Low and cook 3 hours.

Variation:
　In order to reduce the calorie content of this dish, use raw shredded potatoes instead of tater tots.

Meal-in-One-Casserole

Elizabeth Yoder
Millersburg, OH
Marcella Stalter
Flanagan, IL

Makes 4-6 servings

1 lb. ground beef
1 medium onion, chopped
1 medium green pepper,
　chopped
15 1/4-oz. can whole kernel
　corn, drained
4-oz. can mushrooms,
　drained
1 tsp. salt
1/4 tsp. pepper
11-oz. jar salsa
5 cups uncooked medium
　egg noodles
28-oz. can diced tomatoes,
　undrained
1 cup shredded cheddar
　cheese

1. Cook beef and onion in saucepan over medium heat until meat is no longer pink. Drain. Transfer to slow cooker.
2. Top with green pepper, corn, and mushrooms. Sprinkle with salt and pepper. Pour salsa over mushrooms. Cover and cook on Low 3 hours.
3. Cook noodles according to package in separate pan. Drain and add to slow cooker after mixture in cooker has cooked for 3 hours. Top with tomatoes. Sprinkle with cheese.

4. Cover. Cook on Low 1 more hour.

Variation:

Add uncooked noodles after salsa. Pour tomatoes and 1 cup water over all. Sprinkle with cheese. Cover and cook on Low 4 hours, or until noodles are tender.

Nadine Martinitz
Salina, KS

Noodle Hamburger Dish

Esther J. Yoder
Hartville, OH

Makes 10 servings

1 1/2 lbs. ground beef, browned and drained
1 green pepper, diced
1 qt. whole tomatoes
10 3/4-oz. can cream of mushroom soup
1 large onion, diced
1 1/2 Tbsp. Worcestershire sauce
8-oz. pkg. noodles, uncooked
1 tsp. salt
1/4 tsp. pepper
1 cup shredded cheese

1. Combine all ingredients except cheese in slow cooker.
2. Cover. Cook on High 3-4 hours.
3. Sprinkle with cheese before serving.

Yum-e-setti

Elsie Schlabach
Millersburg, OH

Makes 6-8 servings

1 1/2 lbs. ground beef, browned and drained
10 3/4-oz. can tomato soup
8-oz. pkg. wide noodles, cooked
10 3/4-oz. can cream of chicken soup
1 cup chopped celery, cooked tender
2 tsp. salt
1 lb. frozen mixed vegetables
1/2 lb. Velveeta cheese, cubed

1. Combine ground beef and tomato soup.
2. Combine chicken soup, noodles, and celery.
3. Layer beef mixture, chicken mixture, and vegetables. Sprinkle with salt. Lay cheese over top.
4. Cover. Cook on Low 2-3 hours.

Variation:

For more "bite," use shredded cheddar cheese instead of cubed Velveeta.

Shell Casserole

Jean Butzer
Batavia, NY

Makes 4-5 servings

1 lb. ground beef
1 small onion, chopped
3/4 tsp. salt
1/4 tsp. garlic powder
1 tsp. Worcestershire sauce
1/4 cup flour
1 1/4 cups hot water
2 tsp. beef bouillon granules
2 Tbsp. red wine
6 oz. medium-sized shell pasta, uncooked
4-oz. can sliced mushrooms, drained
1 cup sour cream

1. Brown ground beef and onion in saucepan. Drain. Place in slow cooker.
2. Stir in salt, garlic powder, Worcestershire sauce, and flour.
3. Add water, bouillon, and wine. Mix well.
4. Cover. Cook on Low 2-3 hours.
5. Cook pasta in separate pan according to package directions. Stir cooked pasta, mushrooms, and sour cream into slow cooker. Cover. Cook on High 10-15 minutes.

Family Favorite Casserole

Lizzie Weaver
Ephrata, PA

Makes 6-8 servings

1½ lbs. ground beef
1 onion, chopped
1½ cups diced potatoes
1½ cups sliced carrots
1½ cups peas
1½ cups macaroni, cooked
10¾-oz. can cream of
celery soup
½ lb. cheddar cheese,
grated
2 cups milk
1½ tsp. salt

1. Fry beef and onion in saucepan until brown. Drain.
2. Cook vegetables just until soft.
3. Combine all ingredients in slow cooker.
4. Cover. Cook on High 2 hours, or Low 4-5 hours.

Variation:
Skip pre-cooking the vegetables; add them raw to the slow cooker. Increase cooking time to 4 hours on High, or 8-10 hours on Low. Add the cooked macaroni and the milk during the last 15 minutes if cooking on High, or during the last 30 minutes if cooking on Low.

Tastes-Like-Turkey

Lizzie Weaver
Ephrata, PA

Makes 6 servings

2 lbs. hamburger, browned
1 tsp. salt
½ tsp. pepper
2 10¾-oz. cans cream of
chicken soup
10¾-oz. can cream of
celery soup
4 scant cups milk
1 large pkg. bread stuffing,
or large loaf of bread,
torn in pieces

1. Combine all ingredients in large buttered slow cooker.
2. Cover. Cook on High 3 hours, or Low 6-8 hours.

Meatball Stew

Nanci Keatley, Salem, OR
Ada Miller, Sugarcreek, OH

Makes 8 servings

2 lbs. ground beef
½ tsp. salt
½ tsp. pepper
6 medium potatoes, cubed
1 large onion, sliced
6 medium carrots, sliced
1 cup ketchup
1 cup water
1½ tsp. balsamic vinegar
1 tsp. dried basil
1 tsp. dried oregano
½ tsp. salt
½ tsp. pepper

1. Combine beef, ½ tsp. salt, and ½ tsp. pepper. Mix well. Shape into 1-inch balls. Brown meatballs in saucepan over medium heat. Drain.
2. Place potatoes, onion, and carrots in slow cooker. Top with meatballs.
3. Combine ketchup, water, vinegar, basil, oregano, ½ tsp. salt, and ½ tsp. pepper. Pour over meatballs.
4. Cover. Cook on High 4-5 hours, or until vegetables are tender.

Here's a real time-saver from our house: Brown large quantities (10 lbs.) of ground beef, seasoned with onion, basil, and oregano to taste. Drain and cool. Freeze in pint freezer containers. The meat is readily available with no prep time or cleanup need when preparing a slow cooker recipe or casserole that calls for browned ground beef.
Dale and Shari Mast
Harrisonburg, VA

Sweet and Sour Meatballs

Barbara Katrine Rose
Woodbridge, VA

Makes 4-6 servings

4 tsp. Worcestershire sauce
2 tsp. vinegar
1 tsp. dried Italian
  seasoning
1/4 tsp. garlic powder
1/4 tsp. cinnamon
1/4 tsp. pepper
2 4-oz. cans sliced
  mushrooms, undrained
2 cups sliced carrots
3 cups tomato juice
4 tsp. instant minced
  onion
4 Tbsp. minced green
  peppers
1 recipe Meatballs (see
  next recipe)

1. Combine all ingredients
in slow cooker.
2. Cover. Cook on High 3-4
hours.
3. Serve over rice.

Meatballs

Makes 24 small meatballs

1 lb. ground beef
1 cup drained,
  unsweetened crushed
  pineapple
2 slices crumbled whole
  wheat bread
2 tsp. instant minced
  onion
2 tsp. Worcestershire sauce
1/4 tsp. garlic powder
1/4 tsp. dry mustard
1/4 tsp. pepper

1. Combine all ingredients.
Shape into meatballs, using 1
heaping tablespoon mixture
for each. Place on rack in
baking pan.
2. Bake at 350° for 30 minutes, or until done.

BBQ Meatballs

Kathryn Yoder
Minot, ND

*Makes 12-15 main-dish servings,
or 20-25 appetizer servings*

Meatballs:
3 lbs. ground beef
5-oz. can evaporated milk
1 cup dry oatmeal (rolled
  or instant)
1 cup cracker crumbs
2 eggs
1/2 cup chopped onions
1/2 tsp. garlic powder
2 tsp. salt
1/2 tsp. pepper
2 tsp. chili powder

Sauce:
2 cups ketchup
1 cup brown sugar
1 1/2 tsp. liquid smoke
1/2 tsp. garlic powder
1/4 cup chopped onions

1. Combine all meatball
ingredients. Shape into wal-
nut-sized balls. Place on
waxed paper-lined cookie
sheets. Freeze. When fully
frozen, place in plastic bag
and store in freezer until
needed.
2. When ready to use,
place frozen meatballs in
slow cooker. Cover. Cook on
High as you mix up sauce.
3. Pour combined sauce
ingredients over meatballs.
Stir.
4. Cover. Continue cooking
on High 1 hour. Stir. Turn to
Low and cook 6-9 hours.

Variation:
Instead of using barbecue
sauce, cook meatballs with
spaghetti sauce or cream of
mushroom soup.

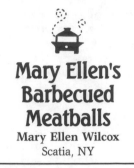

Mary Ellen's Barbecued Meatballs

Mary Ellen Wilcox
Scatia, NY

Makes about 60 small meatballs

Meatballs:
3/4-lb. ground beef
3/4 cup bread crumbs
1 1/2 Tbsp. minced onion
1/2 tsp. horseradish
3 drops Tabasco sauce
2 eggs, beaten
3/4 tsp. salt
1/2 tsp. pepper
butter

Sauce:
3/4 cup ketchup
1/2 cup water
1/4 cup cider vinegar
2 Tbsp. brown sugar
1 Tbsp. minced onion
2 tsp. horseradish
1 tsp. salt
1 tsp. dry mustard
3 drops Tabasco
dash pepper

1. Combine all meatball ingredients except butter. Shape into 3/4-inch balls. Brown in butter in skillet. Place in slow cooker.
2. Combine all sauce ingredients. Pour over meatballs.
3. Cover. Cook on Low 5 hours.

Cocktail Meatballs

Irene Klaeger
Inverness, FL

Makes 6 main-dish servings, or 12 appetizer servings

2 lbs. ground beef
1/3 cup ketchup
3 tsp. dry bread crumbs
1 egg, beaten
2 tsp. onion flakes
3/4 tsp. garlic salt
1/2 tsp. pepper
1 cup ketchup
1 cup packed brown sugar
6-oz. can tomato paste
1/4 cup soy sauce
1/4 cup cider vinegar
1-1 1/2 tsp. hot pepper sauce

1. Combine ground beef, 1/3 cup ketchup, bread crumbs, egg, onion flakes, garlic salt, and pepper. Mix well. Shape into 1-inch meatballs. Place on jelly roll pan. Bake at 350° for 18 minutes, or until brown. Place in slow cooker.
2. Combine 1 cup ketchup, brown sugar, tomato paste, soy sauce, vinegar, and hot pepper sauce. Pour over meatballs.
3. Cover. Cook on Low 4 hours.

Sweet and Sour Meatballs

Elaine Unruh
Minneapolis, MN

Makes 6-8 main-dish servings, or 20-30 appetizer servings

Meatballs:
2 lbs. ground beef
1 1/4 cups bread crumbs
1 1/2 tsp. salt
1 tsp. pepper
2-3 Tbsp. Worcestershire sauce
1 egg
1/2 tsp. garlic salt
1/4 cup finely chopped onions

Sauce:
1 can pineapple chunks, juice reserved
3 Tbsp. cornstarch
1/4 cup cold water
1-1 1/4 cups ketchup
1/4 cup Worcestershire sauce
1/4 tsp. salt
1/4 tsp. pepper
1/4 tsp. garlic salt
1/2 cup chopped green peppers

1. Combine all meatball ingredients. Shape into 60-80 meatballs. Brown in skillet, rolling so all sides are browned. Place meatballs in slow cooker.
2. Pour juice from pineapples into skillet. Stir into drippings.
3. Combine cornstarch and cold water. Add to skillet and

stir until thickened.

4. Stir in ketchup and Worcestershire sauce. Season with salt, pepper, and garlic salt. Add green peppers and pineapples. Pour over meatballs.

5. Cover. Cook on Low 6 hours.

Festive Cocktail Meatballs

Sharon Timpe
Mequon, WI

Makes about 4 dozen meatballs

Sauce:
2 cups ketchup
1 cup brown sugar
2 Tbsp. Worcestershire
   sauce

Meatballs:
2 lbs. ground beef
1 envelope dry onion soup
   mix
1/2 cup milk

1. Mix together ketchup, brown sugar, and Worcestershire sauce in slow cooker. Turn on High while mixing up meatballs.

2. Combine ground beef, soup mix, and milk. Mix well. Shape into 1-inch balls. Bake at 325° for 20 minutes. Drain. Add to slow cooker.

3. Cover. Cook on Low 2-2½ hours, stirring gently, twice throughout the cooking time.

Barbecued Meatballs

Esther Becker
Gordonville, Pa
Ruth Shank, Gridley, IL

Makes 30 small meatballs

1½ cups chili sauce
1 cup grape, *or* apple, jelly
3 tsp. brown spicy
   mustard
1 lb. ground beef
1 egg
3 Tbsp. dry bread crumbs
1/2 tsp. salt

1. Combine chili sauce, jelly, and mustard in slow cooker. Mix well.

2. Cover. Cook on High while preparing meatballs.

3. Mix together remaining ingredients. Shape into 30 balls. Place in baking pan and bake at 400° for 15-20 minutes. Drain well. Spoon into slow cooker. Stir gently to coat well.

4. Cover. Cook on Low 6-10 hours.

Variations:
1. To increase flavor, add 1/4 tsp. pepper, 1/4 tsp. Italian spice, and a dash of garlic powder to the meatball mixture.

Sandra Thom
Jenks, OK

2. Use Italian or seasoned bread crumbs in meatball mixture. Add 1 tsp. Worcestershire sauce and 1½ Tbsp.

fresh parsley to meatball mixture.

Barbara Sparks
Glen Burnie, MD

3. Make meatballs larger and serve with rice or noodles.

Great Meatballs
Judy Denney
Lawrenceville, GA

Makes 12-16 main dish-size servings, or 24 appetizer-size servings

4 lbs. ground beef
2 eggs
4 slices fresh bread, torn
   into bread crumbs
1½ tsp. salt
1/2 tsp. pepper
1 cup tomato juice
2 10-oz. jars chili sauce
2 cans whole cranberry
   sauce

1. Mix together beef, eggs, bread crumbs, seasonings, and tomato juice. Form into small meatballs. Place in slow cooker.

2. Pour chili sauce and cranberry sauce on top of meatballs. Stir lightly.

3. Cover. Cook on High 2 hours. Reduce heat to Low and cook 3 more hours.

Nancy's Meatballs

Betty Richards
Rapid City, SD

Makes 8 main-dish servings

3-4-lb. bag prepared
  meatballs (or make your
  own, using recipe for
  meatballs with BBQ
  Meatballs, page 119)
3 10¾-oz. cans cream of
  mushroom, *or* cream of
  celery, soup
4-oz. can button mushrooms
16-oz. jar Cheese Whiz
1 medium onion, diced

1. Combine all ingredients
in slow cooker.
2. Cover. Cook on Low 6-8
hours.
3. Use as an appetizer, or
as a main dish served over
noodles or rice.

Party Meatballs

Marie Miller
Scotia, NY

Makes 8-10 main-dish servings

16-oz. jar salsa
16-oz. can jellied cranberry
  sauce
2 lbs. frozen meatballs (see
  recipe for making BBQ
  Meatballs on page 119)

1. Melt cranberry sauce in
saucepan. Stir in salsa and
meatballs. Bring to boil. Stir.
Pour into slow cooker.
2. Cover. Cook on Low 2-4
hours.

Swedish Cabbage Rolls

Jean Butzer, Batavia, NY
Pam Hochstedler, Kalona, IA

Makes 6 servings

12 large cabbage leaves
1 egg, beaten
¼ cup milk
¼ cup finely chopped onions
1 tsp. salt
¼ tsp. pepper
1 lb. ground beef, browned
  and drained
1 cup cooked rice
8-oz. can tomato sauce
1 Tbsp. brown sugar
1 Tbsp. lemon juice
1 tsp. Worcestershire sauce

1. Immerse cabbage leaves
in boiling water for about 3
minutes or until limp. Drain.
2. Combine egg, milk,
onions, salt, pepper, beef, and
rice. Place about ¼ cup meat
mixture in center of each leaf.
Fold in sides and roll ends over
meat. Place in slow cooker.
3. Combine tomato sauce,
brown sugar, lemon juice,
and Worcestershire sauce.
Pour over cabbage rolls.
4. Cover. Cook on Low 7-9
hours.

Cabbage Dinner

Kathi Rogge
Alexandria, IN

Makes 6-8 servings

medium head of cabbage
6-8 medium-sized potatoes
2 lbs. smoked sausage, *or*
  turkey sausage
salt to taste
1 qt. water

1. Cut cabbage into 1-2
inch-wide wedges. Place in
slow cooker.
2. Wash and quarter pota-
toes. Do not peel. Add to cabbage in slow cooker.
3. Cut sausage into bite-
sized pieces. Add to slow
cooker. Add salt and mix
well.
4. Pour water into slow
cooker.
5. Cover. Cook on High
2 hours, and then on Low 6-8
hours, or until vegetables are
tender.

Stuffed Cabbage
Barbara Nolan
Pleasant Valley, NY

Makes 6 servings

4 cups water
12 large cabbage leaves
1 lb. ground beef, lamb, *or* turkey
1/2 cup cooked rice
1/2 tsp. salt
1/8 tsp. pepper
1/4 tsp. dried thyme
1/4 tsp. nutmeg
1/4 tsp. cinnamon
6-oz. can tomato paste
3/4 cup water

1. Boil 4 cups water in deep kettle. Remove kettle from heat. Soak cabbage leaves in hot water 5 minutes, or just until softened. Remove. Drain. Cool.
2. Combine ground beef, rice, salt, pepper, thyme, nutmeg, cinnamon, and tomato paste. Place 2 Tbsp. of mixture on each leaf. Roll up firmly. Stack stuffed leaves in slow cooker.
3. Combine tomato paste and 3/4 cup water until smooth. Pour over cabbage rolls.
4. Cover. Cook on Low 6-8 hours.

Stuffed Green Peppers
Lois Stoltzfus
Honey Brook, PA

Makes 6 servings

6 large green peppers
1 lb. ground beef, browned
2 Tbsp. minced onion
1 tsp. salt
1/8 tsp. garlic powder
2 cups cooked rice
15-oz. can tomato sauce
3/4 cup shredded mozzarella cheese

1. Cut peppers in half and remove seeds.
2. Combine all ingredients except peppers and cheese.
3. Stuff peppers with ground beef mixture. Place in slow cooker.
4. Cover. Cook on Low 6-8 hours, or High 3-4 hours. Sprinkle with cheese during last 30 minutes.

Stuffed Bell Peppers
Mary Puterbaugh
Elwood, IN

Makes 8 servings

8 large bell peppers
2 lbs. ground beef, lightly browned
1 large onion, chopped
1 cup cooked rice
2 eggs, beaten
1/2 cup milk
1/2 cup ketchup
dash hot pepper sauce
2 tsp. salt
1/2 tsp. pepper

1. Combine all ingredients except peppers. Gently pack mixture into peppers which have been capped and seeded. Place in greased slow cooker.
2. Cover. Cook on Low 9-11 hours, or High 5-6 hours.

I often start the slow cooker on High until I'm ready for work, then switch it to Low as I go out the door. It may only be 45 minutes to 1 hour on High, but I feel it starts the cooking process faster, thus preserving flavor.
Evie Hershey
Atglen, PA

123

Stuffed Peppers

Eleanor J. Ferreira
N. Chelmsford, MA

Makes 6-8 servings

6-8 green peppers
1-2 lbs. ground beef
1 onion, chopped
¼ tsp. salt
¼ tsp. pepper
1 egg
1 slice white bread
28-oz. can whole, *or*
   stewed, tomatoes

1. Cut peppers in half and remove seeds.
2. Combine ground beef, onion, salt, pepper, and egg. Tear bread into small pieces. Add to ground beef mixture. Stuff into peppers.
3. Form remaining meat into oblong shape. Place meatloaf and peppers into slow cooker. Pour in tomatoes.
4. Cover. Cook on Low 6-12 hours, or High 4-5 hours.

Helen's Lasagna

Helen King, Fairbank, IA
Clarice Williams,
Fairbank, IA
Nancy Zimmerman
Loysville, PA

Makes 6-8 servings

1 lb. ground beef
1 medium onion, chopped
2 cloves garlic, minced
29-oz. can tomato sauce
1 cup water
6-oz. can tomato paste
1 tsp. salt
1 tsp. dried oregano
8-oz. pkg. lasagna noodles,
   uncooked
4 cups (16 oz.) shredded
   mozzarella cheese
1½ cups (12 oz.) small-
   curd cottage cheese
½ cup grated Parmesan
   cheese

1. Cook beef, onion, and garlic together in saucepan until browned. Drain.
2. Stir in tomato sauce, water, tomato paste, salt, and oregano. Mix well.
3. Spread one-fourth of meat sauce in ungreased slow cooker. Arrange one third of noodles over sauce.
4. Combine the cheeses. Spoon one-third of mixture over noodles. Repeat layers twice. Top with remaining meat sauce.
5. Cover. Cook on Low 4-5 hours.

Variation:
For a fuller flavor, use 24-oz. can tomato sauce instead of 6-oz. can tomato paste and water. Add ½ tsp. garlic powder, 1 tsp. dried basil, and ¼ tsp. pepper.
Dolores S. Kratz
Souderton, PA

Spicy Lasagna

Kathy Hertzler, Lancaster, PA
L. Jean Moore, Pendleton, IN
Mary Ellen Musser
Reinholds, PA

Makes 6 servings

10-oz. pkg. lasagna
   noodles, broken into
   bite-sized pieces, cooked
1 lb. ground beef, browned
½ lb. Italian sausage,
   sliced and browned
1 onion, chopped
1 clove garlic, minced
12 oz. mozzarella cheese,
   shredded
12 oz. cottage, *or* ricotta,
   cheese
16-oz. can tomato sauce
1 tsp. dried basil
½ tsp. dried oregano
1½ Tbsp. dried parsley
   flakes
½ tsp. pepper
1½ tsp. salt

1. Combine all ingredients in greased slow cooker.
2. Cover. Cook on Low 7-9 hours, or High 3-5 hours.

Variation:

Replace mix of ground beef and sausage with 1½ lbs. ground beef.

Violette's Lasagna

Violette Harris Denney
Carrollton, GA

Makes 8 servings

8 lasagna noodles, uncooked
1 lb. ground beef
1 tsp. Italian seasoning
28-oz. jar spaghetti sauce
⅓ cup water
4-oz. can sliced mushrooms
15 oz. ricotta cheese
2 cups shredded mozzarella cheese

1. Break noodles. Place half in bottom of greased slow cooker.
2. Brown ground beef in saucepan. Drain. Stir in Italian seasoning. Spread half over noodles in slow cooker.
3. Layer half of sauce and water, half of mushrooms, half of ricotta cheese, and half of mozzarella cheese over beef. Repeat layers.
4. Cover. Cook on Low 5 hours.

Rigatoni

Susan Alexander
Baltimore, MD

Makes 10 servings

28-oz. jar spaghetti sauce
12 oz. rigatoni, cooked
1-1½ lbs. ground beef, browned
3 cups shredded mozzarella cheese
½ lb. pepperoni slices
sliced mushrooms, optional
sliced onions, optional

1. In 4-quart slow cooker, layer half of each ingredient in order listed. Repeat.
2. Cover. Cook on Low 4-5 hours.

Variation:

Use 1 lb. ground beef and 1 lb. sausage.

Beef Enchiladas

Jane Talso
Albuquerque, NM

Makes 12-16 servings

4-lb. boneless chuck roast
2 Tbsp. oil
4 cups sliced onions
2 tsp. salt
2 tsp. black pepper
2 tsp. cumin seeds
2 4½-oz. cans peeled, diced green chilies
14½-oz. can peeled, diced tomatoes
8 large tortillas (10-12 inch size)
1 lb. cheddar cheese, shredded
4 cups green, or red, enchilada sauce

1. Brown roast on all sides in oil in saucepan. Place roast in slow cooker.
2. Add remaining ingredients except tortillas, cheese, and sauce.
3. Cover. Cook on High 4-5 hours.
4. Shred meat with fork and return to slow cooker.
5. Warm tortillas in oven. Heat enchilada sauce. Fill each tortilla with ¾ cup beef mixture and ½ cup cheese. Roll up and serve with sauce.

Variation:

Use 2 lbs. ground beef instead of chuck roast. Brown without oil in saucepan, along with chopped onions.

Slow Cooker Enchiladas

Lori Berezovsky, Salina, KS
Tracy Clark,
Mt. Crawford, VA
Mary E. Herr and Michelle Reineck, Three Rivers, MI
Marcia S. Myer, Manheim, PA
Renee Shirk, Mt. Joy, PA
Janice Showalter, Flint, MI

Makes 4 servings

1 lb. ground beef
1 cup chopped onions
1/2 cup chopped green peppers
16-oz. can red kidney beans, rinsed and drained
15-oz. can black beans, rinsed and drained
10-oz. can diced tomatoes with green chilies, undrained
1/3 cup water
1 1/2 tsp. chili powder
1/2 tsp. ground cumin
1/2 tsp. salt
1/4 tsp. pepper
1 cup (4 ozs.) shredded sharp cheddar cheese
1 cup (4 ozs.) shredded Monterey Jack, *or* pepper Monterey Jack, cheese
6 flour tortillas (6-7 inches in diameter)

1. Cook beef, onions, and green peppers in skillet until beef is browned and vegetables are tender. Drain.
2. Add next 8 ingredients and bring to boil. Reduce heat. Cover and simmer 10 minutes.
3. Combine cheeses.
4. In slow cooker, layer about 3/4 cup beef mixture, one tortilla, and about 1/3 cup cheese. Repeat layers.
5. Cover. Cook on Low 5-7 hours or until heated through.
6. To serve, reach to bottom with each spoonful to get all the layers, or carefully invert onto large platter and cut into wedges. Serve with sour cream and/or guacamole.

Shredded Beef for Tacos

Dawn Day
Westminster, CA

Makes 6-8 servings

2-3-lb. round roast, cut into large chunks
1 large onion, chopped
3 Tbsp. oil
2 serrano chilies, chopped
3 garlic cloves, minced
1 tsp. salt
1 cup water

1. Brown meat and onion in oil. Transfer to slow cooker.
2. Add chilies, garlic, salt, and water.

3. Cover. Cook on High 6-8 hours.
4. Pull meat apart with two forks until shredded.
5. Serve with fresh tortillas, lettuce, tomatoes, cheese, and guacamole.

Southwestern Flair

Phyllis Attig
Reynolds, IL

Makes 8-12 servings

3-4-lb. chuck roast, *or* flank steak
1 envelope dry taco seasoning
1 cup chopped onions
1 Tbsp. white vinegar
1 1/4 cup green chilies
flour tortillas
grated cheese
refried beans
shredded lettuce
chopped tomatoes
salsa
sour cream
guacamole

1. Combine meat, taco seasoning, onions, vinegar, and chilies in slow cooker.
2. Cover. Cook on Low 9 hours.
3. Shred meat with fork.
4. Serve with tortillas and your choice of the remaining ingredients.

Tostadas

Elizabeth L. Richards
Rapid City, SD

Makes 6-10 servings

1 lb. ground beef, browned
2 cans refried beans
1 envelope dry taco
　seasoning mix
8-oz. can tomato sauce
1/2 cup water
10 tostada shells
1 1/2 cups shredded lettuce
2 tomatoes, diced
1/2 lb. shredded cheddar
　cheese
1 can sliced black olives
1 pint sour cream
guacamole
salsa

1. Combine ground beef, refried beans, taco seasoning mix, tomato sauce, and water in slow cooker.
2. Cover. Cook on Low 6 hours.
3. Crisp tostada shells.
4. Spread hot mixture on tostada shells. Top with remaining ingredients.

Pecos River Red Frito Pie

Donna Barnitz
Jerks, OK

Makes 6 servings

1 large onion, chopped
　coarsely
3 lbs. coarsely ground
　hamburger
2 garlic cloves, minced
3 Tbsp. ground hot red
　chili peppers
2 Tbsp. ground mild red
　chili peppers
1 1/2 cups water
corn chips
shredded Monterey Jack
　cheese
shredded cheddar cheese

1. Combine onion, hamburger, garlic, chilies, and water in slow cooker.
2. Cover. Cook on Low 8-10 hours. Drain.
3. Serve over corn chips. Top with mixture of Monterey Jack and cheddar cheeses.

Nachos

Arlene Miller
Hutchinson, KS

Makes 8 servings

1 lb. ground beef
1/4 cup diced onions
1/4 cup diced green peppers
1 pint taco sauce
1 can refried beans
10 3/4-oz. can cream of
　mushroom soup
1 envelope dry taco
　seasoning
salt to taste
2 cups Velveeta, *or*
　cheddar, cheese
tortilla chips
lettuce
chopped tomatoes
sour cream

1. Brown ground beef, onions, and green peppers in saucepan. Drain.
2. Combine all ingredients except tortilla chips, lettuce, tomatoes, and sour cream in slow cooker.
3. Cover. Cook on High 1 hour, stirring occasionally until cheese is fully melted.
4. Pour into serving bowl and serve immediately with chips, lettuce, tomatoes, and sour cream, or turn to Low to keep warm and serve from cooker.

If a recipe calls for cooked noodles, macaroni, etc., cook them before adding to the cooker. Don't overcook; instead, cook just till slightly tender.

If cooked rice is called for, stir in raw rice with the other ingredients. Add 1 cup extra liquid per cup of raw rice. Use long grain converted rice for best results in all-day cooking.

Mrs. Don Martins
Fairbank, IA

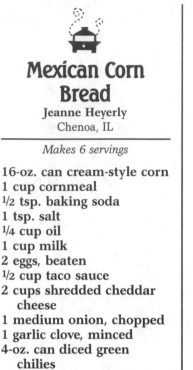

Mexican Corn Bread

Jeanne Heyerly
Chenoa, IL

Makes 6 servings

16-oz. can cream-style corn
1 cup cornmeal
1/2 tsp. baking soda
1 tsp. salt
1/4 cup oil
1 cup milk
2 eggs, beaten
1/2 cup taco sauce
2 cups shredded cheddar
  cheese
1 medium onion, chopped
1 garlic clove, minced
4-oz. can diced green
  chilies
1 lb. ground beef, lightly
  cooked and drained

1. Combine corn, corn-meal, baking soda, salt, oil, milk, eggs, and taco sauce. Pour half of mixture into slow cooker.
2. Layer cheese, onion, garlic, green chilies, and ground beef on top of corn-meal mixture. Cover with remaining cornmeal mixture.
3. Cover. Cook on High 1 hour and on Low 3 1/2-4 hours, or only on Low 6 hours.

Tamale Pie

Jeannine Janzen
Elbing, KS

Makes 8 servings

3/4 cup cornmeal
1 1/2 cups milk
1 egg, beaten
1 lb. ground beef, browned
  and drained
1 envelope dry chili
  seasoning mix
16-oz. can diced tomatoes
16-oz. can corn, drained
1 cup grated cheddar
  cheese

1. Combine cornmeal, milk, and egg.
2. Stir in meat, chili sea-soning mix, tomatoes, and corn until well blended. Pour into slow cooker.
3. Cover. Cook on High 1 hour, then on Low 3 hours.
4. Sprinkle with cheese. Cook another 5 minutes until cheese is melted.

Piquant French Dip

Marcella Stalter
Flanagan, IL

Makes 8 servings

3-lb. chuck roast
2 cups water
1/2 cup soy sauce
1 tsp. dried rosemary
1 tsp. dried thyme
1 tsp. garlic powder
1 bay leaf
3-4 whole peppercorns
8 French rolls

1. Place roast in slow cooker. Add water, soy sauce, and seasonings.
2. Cover. Cook on High 5-6 hours, or until beef is tender.
3. Remove beef from broth. Shred with fork. Keep warm.
4. Strain broth. Skim fat. Pour broth into small cups for dipping. Serve beef on rolls.

Note:
If you have leftover broth, freeze it to use later for gravy or as a soup base.

Carol's Italian Beef

Carol Findling
Princeton, IL

Makes 6-8 servings

3-4-lb. lean rump roast
2 tsp. salt, divided
4 garlic cloves
2 tsp. Romano, *or*
　Parmesan, cheese,
　divided
12-oz. can beef broth
1 tsp. dried oregano

1. Place roast in slow cooker. Cut 4 slits in top of roast. Fill each slit with ½ tsp. salt, 1 garlic clove, and ½ tsp. cheese.
2. Pour broth over meat. Sprinkle with oregano.
3. Cover. Cook on Low 10-12 hours, or High 4-6 hours.
4. Remove meat and slice or shred. Serve on buns with meat juices on the side.

Lauren's Italian Beef

Lauren Eberhard
Seneca, IL

Makes 16 servings

4-5-lb. boneless roast,
　cubed
1 medium onion, chopped
1-2 garlic cloves, minced
2-3 pkgs. dry Good Seasons
　Italian dressing mix
½ cup water
16 steak rolls
mozzarella cheese,
　shredded

1. Combine first five ingredients in slow cooker.
2. Cover. Cook on Low 10 hours. Stir occasionally.
3. Slice meat into thin slices. Pile on rolls, top with cheese, and serve immediately.

Tangy Barbecue Sandwiches

Lavina Hochstedler
Grand Blanc, MI
Lois M. Martin, Lititz, PA

Makes 14-18 sandwiches

3 cups chopped celery
1 cup chopped onions
1 cup ketchup
1 cup barbecue sauce
1 cup water
2 Tbsp. vinegar
2 Tbsp. Worcestershire
　sauce
2 Tbsp. brown sugar
1 tsp. chili powder
1 tsp. salt
½ tsp. pepper
½ tsp. garlic powder
3-4-lb. boneless chuck
　roast
14-18 hamburger buns

1. Combine all ingredients except roast and buns in slow cooker. When well mixed, add roast.
2. Cover. Cook on High 6-7 hours.
3. Remove roast. Cool and shred meat. Return to sauce. Heat well.
4. Serve on buns.

Always defrost meat or poultry before putting it into the slow cooker, or cook recipes containing frozen meats an additional 4-6 hours on Low, or 2 hours on High.
Rachel Kauffman
Alto, MI

129

Mile-High Shredded Beef Sandwiches

Miriam Christophel
Battle Creek, MI
Mary Seielstad, Sparks, NV

Makes 8 servings

3-lb. chuck roast, *or* round
    steak
2 Tbsp. oil
1 cup chopped onions
1/2 cup sliced celery
2 cups beef broth, *or*
    bouillon
1 garlic clove
1 tsp. salt
3/4 cup ketchup
4 Tbsp. brown sugar
2 Tbsp. vinegar
1 tsp. dry mustard
1/2 tsp. chili powder
3 drops Tabasco sauce
1 bay leaf
1/4 tsp. paprika
1/4 tsp. garlic powder
1 tsp. Worcestershire sauce

1. In skillet brown both sides of meat in oil. Add onions and celery and saute briefly. Transfer to slow cooker. Add broth or bouillon.

2. Cover. Cook on Low 6-8 hours, or until tender. Remove meat from cooker and cool. Shred beef.

3. Remove vegetables from cooler and drain, reserving 1 1/2 cups broth. Combine vegetables and meat.

4. Return shredded meat and vegetables to cooker. Add broth and remaining ingredients and combine well.

5. Cover. Cook on High 1 hour. Remove bay leaf.

6. Pile into 8 sandwich rolls and serve.

Slow-Cooker Beef Sandwiches

Elaine Unruh
Minneapolis, MN
Winifred Ewy, Newton, KS

Makes 6-8 servings

2-3-lb. chuck roast, cubed
1 pkg. dry onion soup mix
12-oz. can cola

1. Place meat in slow cooker.

2. Sprinkle soup mix over meat. Pour cola over all.

3. Cover. Cook on Low 8-10 hours.

4. Serve as roast or shred the beef, mix with sauce, and serve on buns.

Variation:

Layer 4 medium potatoes, sliced, and 4 carrots, sliced, in bottom of pot. Place meat and rest of ingredients on top, and follow recipe for cooking.

Barbecue Beef

Elizabeth Yoder
Millersburg, OH

Makes 12 servings

3-lb. boneless chuck roast
1 cup barbecue sauce
1/2 cup apricot preserves
1/3 cup chopped green
    peppers
1 small onion, chopped
1 Tbsp. Dijon mustard
2 tsp. brown sugar
12 sandwich rolls

1. Cut roast into quarters. Place in greased slow cooker.

2. Combine barbecue sauce, preserves, green peppers, onion, mustard, and brown sugar. Pour over roast.

3. Cover. Cook on Low 6-8 hours. Remove roast and slice thinly. Return to slow cooker. Stir gently.

4. Cover. Cook 20-30 minutes.

5. Serve beef and sauce on rolls.

Fill the cooker no more than 2/3 full and no less than half-full.

Rachel Kauffman
Alto, MI

Barbecue Beef Sandwiches

Eleanor Larson
Glen Lyon, PA

Makes 18-20 sandwiches

3 1/2-4-lb. beef round steak,
  cubed
1 cup finely chopped
  onions
1/2 cup firmly packed
  brown sugar
1 Tbsp. chili powder
1/2 cup ketchup
1/3 cup cider vinegar
12-oz. can beer
6-oz. can tomato paste
buns

1. Combine all ingredients except buns in slow cooker.
2. Cover. Cook on Low 10-12 hours.
3. Remove beef from sauce with slotted spoon. Place in large bowl. Shred with 2 forks.
4. Add 2 cups sauce from slow cooker to shredded beef. Mix well.
5. Pile into buns and serve immediately.
6. Reserve any remaining sauce for serving over pasta, rice, or potatoes.

Hearty Italian Sandwiches

Rhonda Lee Schmidt
Scranton, PA
Robin Schrock
Millersburg, OH

Makes 8 servings

1 1/2 lbs. ground beef
1 1/2 lbs. bulk Italian
  sausage
2 large onions, chopped
2 large green peppers,
  chopped
2 large sweet red peppers,
  chopped
1 tsp. salt
1 tsp. pepper
shredded Monterey Jack
  cheese
8 sandwich rolls

1. In skillet brown beef and sausage. Drain.
2. Place one-third onions and peppers in slow cooker. Top with half of meat mixture. Repeat layers. Sprinkle with salt and pepper.
3. Cover. Cook on Low 6 hours, or until vegetables are tender.
4. With a slotted spoon, serve about 1 cup mixture on each roll. Top with cheese.

Note:
For some extra flavor, add a spoonful of salsa to each roll before topping with cheese.

Barbecued Spoonburgers

Mrs. Paul Gray
Beatrice, NE

Makes 8-10 servings

2 Tbsp. oil
1 1/2 lbs. ground beef
1/2 cup chopped onions
1/2 cup diced celery
half a green pepper,
  chopped
1 Tbsp. Worcestershire
  sauce
1/2 cup ketchup
1 garlic clove, minced
1 tsp. salt
3/4 cup water
1/8 tsp. pepper
1/2 tsp. paprika
6-oz. can tomato paste
2 Tbsp. vinegar
2 tsp. brown sugar
1 tsp. dry mustard

1. Brown beef in oil in saucepan. Drain.
2. Combine all ingredients in slow cooker.
3. Cover. Cook on Low 6-8 hours, or High 3-4 hours.
4. Serve on buns or over mashed potatoes, pasta, or rice.

Jean & Tammy's Sloppy Joes

Jean Shaner, York, PA
Tammy Smoker
Cochranville, PA

Makes 12 servings

3 lbs. ground beef,
  browned and drained
1 onion, finely chopped
1 green pepper, chopped
2 8-oz. cans tomato sauce
3/4 cup ketchup
1 Tbsp. Worcestershire
  sauce
1 tsp. chili powder
1/4 tsp. pepper
1/4 tsp. garlic powder
sandwich rolls

1. Combine all ingredients
except rolls in slow cooker.
2. Cover. Cook on Low 8-
10 hours, or High 3-4 hours.
3. Serve in sandwich rolls.

Penny's Sloppy Joes

Penny Blosser
Beavercreek, OH

Makes 6 servings

1 lb. ground beef, browned
  and drained
10 3/4-oz. can cream of
  mushroom soup
1/4 cup ketchup
1 small onion, diced

1. Combine all ingredients
in slow cooker.
2. Cover. Cook on Low 1-2
hours.
3. Serve on rolls or over
baked potatoes.

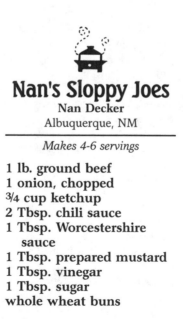

Nan's Sloppy Joes

Nan Decker
Albuquerque, NM

Makes 4-6 servings

1 lb. ground beef
1 onion, chopped
3/4 cup ketchup
2 Tbsp. chili sauce
1 Tbsp. Worcestershire
  sauce
1 Tbsp. prepared mustard
1 Tbsp. vinegar
1 Tbsp. sugar
whole wheat buns

1. Brown beef and onion
in saucepan. Drain.

2. Combine all ingredients
in slow cooker.
3. Cover. Cook on Low 4-5
hours.
4. Serve on buns.

Corned Beef

Margaret Jarrett
Anderson, IN

Makes 6-7 servings

2-3-lb. cut of marinated
  corned beef
2-3 garlic cloves, minced
10-12 peppercorns

1. Place meat in bottom of
cooker. Top with garlic and
peppercorns. Cover with
water.
2. Cover. Cook on High 4-5
hours, or until tender.
3. Cool meat, slice thin,
and use to make Reuben
sandwiches along with sliced
Swiss cheese, sauerkraut, and
Thousand Island dressing on
toasted pumpernickel bread.

Corned Beef and Cabbage

Rhoda Burgoon
Collingswood, NJ
Jo Ellen Moore, Pendleton, IN

Makes 6-8 servings

3 carrots, cut in 3" pieces
3-4-lb. corned beef brisket
2-3 medium onions,
    quartered
3/4-1 1/4 cups water
half a small head of
    cabbage, cut in wedges

1. Layer all ingredients except cabbage in slow cooker.
2. Cover. Cook on Low 8-10 hours, or High 5-6 hours.
3. Add cabbage wedges to liquid, pushing down to moisten. Turn to High and cook an additional 2-3 hours.

Note:
    To cook more cabbage than slow cooker will hold, cook separately in skillet. Remove 1 cup broth from slow cooker during last hour of cooking. Pour over cabbage wedges in skillet. Cover and cook slowly for 20-30 minutes.

Variations:
    1. Add 4 medium potatoes, halved, with the onions.
    2. Top individual servings with mixture of sour cream and horseradish.
        Kathi Rogge
        Alexandria, IN

Eleanor's Corned Beef and Cabbage

Eleanor J. Ferreira
N. Chelmsford, MA

Makes 6 servings

2 medium onions, sliced
2 1/2-3-lb. corned beef
    brisket
1 cup apple juice
1/4 cup brown sugar,
    packed
2 tsp. finely shredded
    orange peel
6 whole cloves
2 tsp. prepared mustard
6 cabbage wedges

1. Place onions in slow cooker. Place beef on top of onions.
2. Combine apple juice, brown sugar, orange peel, cloves, and mustard. Pour over meat.
3. Place cabbage on top.
4. Cover. Cook on Low 10-12 hours, or High 5-6 hours.

Cranberry Pork Roast

Barbara Aston
Ashdown, AR

Makes 6-8 servings

3-4-lb. pork roast
salt to taste
pepper to taste
1 cup ground, *or* finely
    chopped, cranberries
1/4 cup honey
1 tsp. grated orange peel
1/8 tsp. ground cloves
1/8 tsp. ground nutmeg

1. Sprinkle roast with salt and pepper. Place in slow cooker.
2. Combine remaining ingredients. Pour over roast.
3. Cover. Cook on Low 8-10 hours.

Use your slow cooker to cook a hen, turkey, or roast beef for use in salads or casseroles. The meat can even be frozen when you put it in the slow cooker. Set the cooker on Low, and let the meat cook all night while you sleep.
Julia B. Boyd
Memphis, TN

133

Cranberry Pork Roast

Phyllis Attig, Reynolds, IL
Mrs. J.E. Barthold
Bethlehem, PA
Kelly Bailey
Mechanicsburg, PA
Joyce Kaut, Rochester, NY

Makes 4-6 servings

2½-3-lb. boneless rolled
  pork loin roast
16-oz. can jellied cranberry
  sauce
½ cup sugar
½ cup cranberry juice
1 tsp. dry mustard
¼ tsp. ground cloves
2 Tbsp. cornstarch
2 Tbsp. cold water
1 tsp. salt

1. Place roast in slow cooker.
2. Combine cranberry sauce, sugar, cranberry juice, mustard, and cloves. Pour over roast.
3. Cover. Cook on Low 6-8 hours, or until meat is tender.
4. Remove roast and keep warm.
5. Skim fat from juices. Measure 2 cups, adding water if necessary. Pour into saucepan. Bring to boil over medium heat. Combine the cornstarch and cold water to make a paste. Stir into gravy. Cook and stir until thickened. Season with salt.
6. Serve with sliced pork.

Savory Pork Roast

Betty A. Holt
St. Charles, MO

Makes 8-10 servings

4-5-lb. pork loin roast
large onion, sliced
1 bay leaf
2 Tbsp. soy sauce
1 Tbsp. garlic powder

1. Place roast and onion in slow cooker. Add bay leaf, soy sauce, and garlic powder.
2. Cover. Cook on High 1 hour and then on Low 6 hours.
3. Slice and serve.

Teriyaki Pork Roast

Janice Yoskovich
Carmichaels, PA

Makes 8 servings

¾ cup unsweetened apple
  juice
2 Tbsp. sugar
2 Tbsp. soy sauce
1 Tbsp. vinegar
1 tsp. ground ginger
¼ tsp. garlic powder
⅛ tsp. pepper
3-lb. boneless pork loin
  roast, halved
2½ Tbsp. cornstarch
3 Tbsp. cold water

1. Combine apple juice, sugar, soy sauce, vinegar, ginger, garlic powder, and pepper in greased slow cooker.
2. Add roast. Turn to coat.
3. Cover. Cook on Low 7-8 hours. Remove roast and keep warm.
4. In saucepan, combine cornstarch and cold water until smooth. Stir in juices from roast. Bring to boil. Cook and stir for 2 minutes, or until thickened. Serve with roast.

> Since I work full-time, I often put my dinner into the slow cooker to cook until I get home. My three teenagers and umpire/referee husband can all get a hot nutritious meal no matter what time they get home.
> **Rhonda Burgoon**
> Collingswood, NJ

134

Pork Roast with Potatoes and Onions

Trudy Kutter
Corfu, NY

Makes 6-8 servings

2 1/2-3-lb. boneless pork
 loin roast
1 large garlic clove, slivered
5-6 potatoes, cubed
1 large onion, sliced
3/4 cup broth, tomato juice,
 or water
1 1/2 Tbsp. soy sauce
1 Tbsp. cornstarch
1 Tbsp. cold water

1. Make slits in roast and insert slivers of garlic. Put under broiler to brown.
2. Put potatoes in slow cooker. Add half of onions. Place roast on onions and potatoes. Cover with remaining onions.
3. Combine broth and soy sauce. Pour over roast.
4. Cover. Cook on Low 8 hours. Remove roast and vegetables from liquid.
5. Combine cornstarch and water. Add to liquid in slow cooker. Turn to High until thickened. Serve over sliced meat and vegetables.

Variation:
 Use sweet potatoes instead of white potatoes.

Chalupa

Jeannine Janzen
Elbing, KS

Makes 12-16 servings

3-lb. pork roast
1 lb. dry pinto beans
2 garlic cloves, minced
1 Tbsp. ground cumin
1 Tbsp. dried oregano
2 Tbsp. chili powder
1 Tbsp. salt
4-oz. can chopped green
 chilies
water

1. Cover beans with water and soak overnight in slow cooker.
2. In the morning, remove beans (reserve soaking water), and put roast in bottom of cooker. Add remaining ingredients (including the beans and their soaking water) and more water if needed to cover all the ingredients.
3. Cook on High 1 hour, and then on Low 6 hours. Remove meat and shred with two forks. Return meat to slow cooker.
4. Cook on High 1 more hour.
5. Serve over a bed of lettuce. Top with grated cheese and chopped onions and tomatoes.

Tangy Pork Chops

Tracy Clark, Mt. Crawford, VA
Lois M. Martin, Lititz, PA
Becky Oswald, Broadway, PA

Makes 4 servings

4 1/2-inch thick pork chops
1/2 tsp. salt
1/8 tsp. pepper
2 medium onions, chopped
2 celery ribs, chopped
1 large green pepper, sliced
14 1/2-oz. can stewed
 tomatoes
1/2 cup ketchup
2 Tbsp. cider vinegar
2 Tbsp. brown sugar
2 Tbsp. Worcestershire sauce
1 Tbsp. lemon juice
1 beef bouillon cube
2 Tbsp. cornstarch
2 Tbsp. water

1. Place chops in slow cooker. Sprinkle with salt and pepper.
2. Add onions, celery, pepper, and tomatoes.
3. Combine ketchup, vinegar, brown sugar, Worcestershire sauce, lemon juice, and bouillon. Pour over vegetables.
4. Cover. Cook on Low 5-6 hours.
5. Combine cornstarch and water until smooth. Stir into slow cooker.
6. Cover. Cook on High 30 minutes, or until thickened.
7. Serve over rice.

Variation:
 Use chunks of beef or chicken legs and thighs instead of pork.

Spicy Pork Chops

Mary Puskar
Forest Hill, MD

Makes 5 servings

5-6 center-cut loin pork
  chops
3 Tbsp. oil
1 onion, sliced
1 green pepper, cut in
  strips
8-oz. can tomato sauce
3-4 Tbsp. brown sugar
1 Tbsp. vinegar
1½ tsp. salt
1-2 tsp. Worcestershire
  sauce

1. Brown chops in oil in
skillet. Transfer to slow
cooker.
2. Add remaining ingredi-
ents to cooker.
3. Cover. Cook on Low 6-8
hours.
4. Serve over rice.

Saucy Pork Chops

Bonita Ensenberger
Albuquerque, NM

Makes 4 servings

4 pork chops
salt to taste
pepper to taste
1 tsp. garlic powder
1 Tbsp. oil
2-2½ cups ketchup
½ cup brown sugar
1 Tbsp. hickory-flavored
  liquid smoke
1 cup onions, chopped

1. Season chops with salt,
pepper, and garlic powder.
Brown on both sides in oil in
skillet. Drain.
2. Combine ketchup,
brown sugar, and liquid
smoke in bowl.
3. Place onions in slow
cooker. Dip browned pork
chops in sauce mixture and
place on onions. Pour remaining sauce over chops.
4. Cover. Cook on Low 7-9
hours, or High 4-5 hours.
5. Makes a great meal
served with cole slaw and
oven-roasted, cut-up root vegetables.

Barbecue Pork Chops

Annabelle Unternahrer
Shipshewana, IN
Evelyn L. Ward
Greeley, CO

Makes 8 servings

8 pork chops
1 cup (or more) barbecue,
  or sweet-sour, sauce

1. Brush each pork chop
generously with sauce, then
place in slow cooker.
2. Cover. Cook on Low 7-8
hours.

Trim as much visible fat from meat as possible before
placing it in the slow cooker in order to avoid greasy gravy.
Carolyn Baer
Conrath, WI

Pork Chops in Bean Sauce

Shirley Sears
Tiskilwa, IL

Makes 6 servings

6 pork chops
⅓ cup chopped onions
½ tsp. salt
⅓ tsp. garlic salt
⅛ tsp. pepper
28-oz. can vegetarian, *or* baked, beans
¼ tsp. hot pepper sauce
13½-oz. can crushed pineapple, undrained
⅓ cup chili sauce

1. Brown pork chops in skillet five minutes per side. Place in slow cooker.
2. Saute onion in skillet in meat juices. Spread over pork chops.
3. Sprinkle with salt, garlic salt, and pepper.
4. Combine beans and hot sauce. Pour over chops.
5. Combine pineapple and chili sauce. Spread evenly over beans.
6. Cover. Cook on Low 7-8 hours.

Chops and Beans

Mary L. Casey
Scranton, PA

Makes 4-6 servings

2 1-lb. cans pork and beans
½ cup ketchup
2 slices bacon, browned and crumbled
½ cup chopped onions, sauteed
1 Tbsp. Worcestershire sauce
¼ cup firmly packed brown sugar
4-6 pork chops
2 tsp. prepared mustard
1 Tbsp. brown sugar
¼ cup ketchup
one lemon

1. Combine beans, ½ cup ketchup, bacon, onions, Worcestershire sauce, and ¼ cup brown sugar in slow cooker.
2. Brown chops in skillet. In separate bowl, mix together 2 tsp. mustard, 1 Tbsp. brown sugar, and ¼ cup ketchup. Brush each chop with sauce, then carefully stack into cooker, placing a slice of lemon on each chop. Submerge in bean/bacon mixture.
3. Cover. Cook on Low 4-6 hours.

Italian Chops

Jan Moore
Wellsville, KS

Makes 2-4 servings

16-oz. bottle Italian salad dressing (use less if cooking only 2 chops)
2-4 pork chops

1. Place pork chops in slow cooker. Pour salad dressing over chops.
2. Cover. Cook on High 6-8 hours.

Variation:

Add cubed potatoes and thinly sliced carrots and onions to meat before pouring dressing over top.

Cooker Chops

Lucille Metzler
Wellsboro, PA

Makes 4 servings

4 pork chops
10³/4-oz. can cream of
   mushroom soup
1/4 cup ketchup
2 tsp. Worcestershire sauce

1. Put chops in slow cooker.
2. Combine remaining ingredients. Pour over chops.
3. Cover. Cook on High 3-4 hours, or Low 8-10 hours.

Variation:
   Add one sliced onion to mixture.
   Maryland Massey
   Mellington, MD

Easy Sweet and Sour Pork Chops

Jeanne Hertzog
Bethlehem, PA

Makes 6 servings

16-oz. bag frozen Oriental
   vegetables
6 pork chops
12-oz. bottle sweet and
   sour sauce
1/2 cup water
1 cup frozen pea pods

1. Place partially thawed Oriental vegetables in slow cooker. Arrange chops on top.
2. Combine sauce and water. Pour over chops
3. Cover. Cook on Low 7-8 hours.
4. Turn to High and add pea pods.
5. Cover. Cook on High 5 minutes.

Chicken-Fried Pork Chops

Martha Ann Auker
Landisburg, PA

Makes 6 servings

1/2 cup flour
3/4 tsp. salt
1 1/2 tsp. dry mustard
3/4 tsp. garlic powder
6 pork chops
2 Tbsp. oil
10³/4-oz. can cream of
   chicken soup
1 soup can water

1. Combine flour, salt, dry mustard, and garlic powder. Dredge pork chops in flour mixture. Brown in oil in skillet. Place in slow cooker.
2. Combine soup and water. Pour over meat.
3. Cover. Cook on High 6-8 hours.

Golden Glow Pork Chops

Pam Hochstedler
Kalona, IA

Makes 5-6 servings

5-6 pork chops
salt to taste
pepper to taste
29-oz. can cling peach
   halves, drained (reserve
   juice)
1/4 cup brown sugar
1/2 tsp. ground cinnamon
1/4 tsp. ground cloves
8-oz. can tomato sauce
1/4 cup vinegar

1. Lightly brown pork chops on both sides in saucepan. Drain. Arrange in slow cooker. Sprinkle with salt and pepper.
2. Place drained peach halves on top of pork chops.
3. Combine brown sugar, cinnamon, cloves, tomato sauce, 1/4 cup peach syrup, and vinegar. Pour over peaches and pork chops.
4. Cover. Cook on Low 3-4 hours.

Perfect Pork Chops

Brenda Pope
Dundee, OH

Makes 2 servings

2 small onions
2 ¾-inch thick, boneless, center loin pork chops, frozen
fresh ground pepper to taste
1 chicken bouillon cube
¼ cup hot water
2 Tbsp. prepared mustard with white wine
fresh parsley sprigs, *or* lemon slices, optional

1. Cut off ends of onions and peel. Cut onions in half crosswise to make 4 thick "wheels." Place in bottom of slow cooker.
2. Sear both sides of frozen chops in heavy skillet. Place in cooker on top of onions. Sprinkle with pepper.
3. Dissolve bouillon cube in hot water. Stir in mustard. Pour into slow cooker.
4. Cover. Cook on High 3-4 hours.
5. Serve topped with fresh parsley sprigs or lemon slices, if desired.

Pork Chops and Gravy

Sharon Wantland
Menomonee Falls, WI

Makes 8 servings

8 pork chops
salt to taste
pepper to taste
2 Tbsp. oil
2 10¾-oz. cans cream of mushroom soup
1 large onion, sliced
12-oz. can evaporated milk

1. Season pork chops with salt and pepper. Brown in oil. Drain. Transfer to slow cooker.
2. In separate bowl, whisk together mushroom soup, onion, and evaporated milk until smooth. Pour over chops.
3. Cook on High 3-4 hours, or Low 6-8 hours.

Variations:
To increase flavor, stir ½-1 cup sour cream, or ¼ cup sherry, into mixture during last 30 minutes of cooking time.

Pork Chops and Mushrooms

Michele Ruvola
Selden, NY

Makes 4 servings

4 boneless pork chops, ½-inch thick
2 medium onions, sliced
4-oz. can sliced mushrooms, drained
1 envelope dry onion soup mix
¼ cup water
10¾-oz. can golden cream of mushroom soup

1. Place pork chops in greased slow cooker. Top with onions and mushrooms.
2. Combine soup mix, water, and mushroom soup. Pour over mushrooms.
3. Cover. Cook on Low 6-8 hours.

Lightly grease your slow cooker before adding casserole ingredients.
Sara Wilson
Blainstown, MO

Pork Chops with Mushroom Sauce

Jennifer J. Gehman
Harrisburg, PA

Makes 4-6 servings

4-6 boneless thin or thick
   pork chops
10¾-oz. can cream of
   mushroom soup
¾ cup white wine
4-oz. can sliced
   mushrooms
2 Tbsp. quick cooking
   tapioca
2 tsp. Worcestershire sauce
1 tsp. beef bouillon
   granules, *or* 1 beef
   bouillon cube
¼ tsp. minced garlic
¾ tsp. dried thyme,
   optional

1. Place pork chops in
slow cooker.
2. Combine remaining
ingredients and pour over
pork chops.
3. Cook on Low 8-10
hours, or on High 4½-5
hours.
4. Serve over rice.

Pork Chops and Gravy

Barbara J. Fabel
Wausau, WI

Makes 3-4 servings

3 large onions, quartered
   or sliced
3 ribs of celery, chunked *or*
   sliced
3-4 pork chops
10¾-oz. can cream of
   mushroom, *or* cream of
   celery, soup

1. Place onions and celery
in slow cooker. Wash pork
chops and place on top of
onions and celery. Pour soup
over all.
2. Cover. Cook on High 1
hour. Reduce heat to Low
and cook 3-4 hours, or until
chops are tender.

Pork Chop Surprise

Jan Moore
Wellsville, KS

Makes 4 servings

4 pork chops
6 potatoes, sliced
10¾-oz. can cream of
   mushroom soup
water

1. Brown pork chops on
both sides in skillet. Transfer
to slow cooker.
2. Add potatoes. Pour soup
over top. Add enough water
to cover all ingredients.
3. Cover. Cook on High 6-8
hours.

Variation:
   Combine 1 envelope dry
onion soup mix with mush-
room soup before pouring
over chops and potatoes.
Trudy Kutter
Corfu, NY

Pork Chop Casserole

Doris Bachman
Putnam, IL

Makes 4-6 servings

4-6 pork chops
3 cups water
1 cup rice, uncooked
10¾-oz. can cream of
   mushroom soup
1 tsp. salt
1 tsp. dried parsley
¼ tsp. pepper

1. Saute pork chops in skillet until brown. Transfer to
slow cooker.
2. Mix remaining ingredi-
ents and pour over chops in
cooker.
3. Cover. Cook on Low 6-8
hours, or High 3-4 hours.

Jean's Pork Chops

Jean Weller
State College, PA

Makes 6 servings

1/2 cup flour
1 Tbsp. salt
1 1/2 tsp. dry mustard
1/2 tsp. garlic powder
6-8 1-inch thick pork
  chops
2 Tbsp. oil
15 1/2-oz. can chicken and
  rice soup

1. Combine flour, salt, dry mustard, and garlic powder. Dredge pork chops in flour mixture. Brown in oil in skillet. Transfer to slow cooker. Add soup.
2. Cover. Cook on Low 6-8 hours, or on High 3 1/2 hours.

Variation:
For increased flavor, step up the dry mustard to 1 Tbsp. and add 1 tsp. pepper.
Mary Puskar
Forest Hill, MD

Tender Pork Chops

Dawn M. Propst
Levittown, PA
Kim McEuen
Lincoln University, PA

Makes 6 servings

6 pork chops
1/2 cup flour
1 tsp. salt
1/2 tsp. garlic powder
1 1/2 tsp dry mustard
2 Tbsp. oil
15-oz. can chicken gumbo
  soup

1. Coat chops with a combination of flour, salt, garlic powder, and mustard. Brown chops in skillet. Place in slow cooker. Drain drippings from skillet.
2. Add soup to skillet. Stir to loosen brown bits from pan. Pour over pork chops.
3. Cover. Cook on Low 6-8 hours.

Pork and Cabbage Dinner

Mrs. Paul Gray
Beatrice, NE

Makes 8 servings

2 lbs. pork steaks, *or*
  chops, *or* shoulder
3/4 cup chopped onions
1/4 cup chopped fresh
  parsley, *or* 2 Tbsp. dried
  parsley
4 cups shredded cabbage
1 tsp. salt
1/8 tsp. pepper
1/2 tsp. caraway seeds
1/8 tsp. allspice
1/2 cup beef broth
2 cooking apples, cored
  and sliced 1/4-inch thick

1. Place pork in slow cooker. Layer onions, parsley, and cabbage over pork.
2. Combine salt, pepper, caraway seeds, and allspice. Sprinkle over cabbage. Pour broth over cabbage.
3. Cover. Cook on Low 5-6 hours.
4. Add apple slices 30 minutes before serving.

Put your cooker meal together the night before you want to cook it. The following moring put the mixture in the slow cooker, cover, and cook.
Sara Wilson
Blairstown, MO

Ham and Cabbage Supper

Louise Stackhouse
Benten, PA

Makes 4 servings

1 medium-size cabbage
head, cut into quarters
4-lb. smoked picnic ham
1/4 cup water

1. Place cabbage quarters in bottom of slow cooker. Place ham on top. Pour in water.
2. Cover. Cook on Low 8-10 hours.

Variation:
To cabbage quarters, add 2 sliced carrots, 1 sliced onion, 2 potatoes cut into cubes, and 2 bay leaves for additional flavor and nutrition.

Ham and Scalloped Potatoes

Penny Blosser
Beavercreek, OH
Jo Haberkamp, Fairbank, IA
Ruth Hofstetter
Versailles, Missouri
Rachel Kauffman, Alto, MI
Mary E. Martin, Goshen, IN
Brenda Pope, Dundee, OH
Joyce Slaymaker
Strasburg, PA

Makes 6-8 servings

6-8 slices ham
8-10 medium potatoes,
thinly sliced
2 onions, thinly sliced
salt to taste
pepper to taste
1 cup grated cheddar, *or*
American, cheese
10¾-oz. can cream of
celery, *or* mushroom,
soup
paprika

1. Put half of ham, potatoes, and onions in slow cooker. Sprinkle with salt, pepper, and cheese. Repeat layers.
2. Spoon soup over top. Sprinkle with paprika.
3. Cover. Cook on Low 8-10 hours, or High 4 hours.

Variation:
If you like a lot of creamy sauce with your ham and potatoes, stir ¾ soup can of milk into the soup before pouring it over the layers.
Alma Z. Weaver
Ephrata, PA

Miriam's Scalloped Potatoes with Ham

Miriam Christophel
Battle Creek, MI

Makes 6 servings

6 cups raw potatoes, cut
into small cubes
1 medium onion, minced
1 tsp. salt
½ lb. cooked ham, cubed
4 Tbsp. butter
4 Tbsp. flour
1 tsp. salt
2 cups milk
1½ cups shredded cheddar
cheese

1. Layer potatoes, onion, 1 tsp. salt, and ham into slow cooker.
2. Melt butter in saucepan. Stir in flour and 1 tsp. salt. Cook until bubbly. Gradually add milk. Cook until smooth and thickened. Add cheese and stir until melted. Pour over potato-ham mixture, stirring lightly.
3. Cover. Cook on Low 6-7 hours, or High 3-4 hours.

Michelle's Scalloped Potatoes and Ham
Michelle Strite
Harrisonburg, VA

Makes 6-8 servings

6 cups cooked, shredded
  potatoes
4 cups diced ham
dash pepper, if desired
10³/4-oz. can cream of
  mushroom soup
10³/4-oz. can cream of
  celery soup
1 cup milk

1. Combine all ingredients in slow cooker.
2. Cover. Cook on Low 3-4 hours.

Potatoes and Ham
Janice Martins
Fairbank, IA

Makes 8 serving

5 potatoes, sliced
1/2 lb. ham, diced
1/4-lb. Velveeta cheese,
  cubed
half a small onion, diced
10³/4-oz. can cream of
  chicken soup

1. Layer potatoes, ham, cheese, and onion in slow cooker. Top with soup.
2. Cover. Cook on Low 6 hours.

Barbara's Scalloped Potatoes with Ham
Barbara Katrine Rose
Woodbridge, VA

Makes 10-12 servings

4-lb. potatoes, sliced
1¹/2 lbs. cooked ham, cut
  into 1/4-inch strips
3 Tbsp. minced dried
  onions
1 cup water
2 11-oz. cans condensed
  cheddar cheese soup

1. Layer potatoes, ham, and onions in very large slow cooker.
2. Combine soup and water. Pour over layers in pot.
3. Cover. Cook on Low 6-8 hours.

Country Scalloped Potatoes and Ham
Deb Unternahrer
Wayland, IA

Makes 10 servings

8 potatoes, thinly sliced
1 onion, chopped
1 lb. fully-cooked ham,
  cubed
1-oz. pkg. dry country-style
  gravy mix
10³/4-oz. can cream of
  mushroom soup
2 cups water
2 cups shredded cheddar
  cheese

1. Combine potatoes, onion, and ham in lightly greased slow cooker.
2. Combine gravy mix, mushroom soup, and water. Whisk until combined. Pour over potaotes.
3. Cover. Cook on Low 7-9 hours, or High 3-4 hours.
4. Top with cheese during last 30 minutes of cooking.

Variation:
Put half the potatoes, onion, and ham in cooker. Top with half the grated cheese. Repeat layers. Spoon undiluted soup over top. Cover and cook on Low 7-9 hours, or High 3-4 hours. Sprinkle individual servings with paprika.
Doris Bachman
Putnam, IL

Au Gratin Potatoes and Ham

Donna Lantgen
Rapid City, SD

Makes 6-8 servings

10 potatoes, thinly sliced
1 onion, chopped
2 Tbsp. flour
1/4 tsp. pepper, optional
1/2 lb. Velveeta cheese, cubed
1/2 cup milk
1/2-1 cup fully cooked ham, *or* sliced hot dogs

1. Combine all ingredients in slow cooker.
2. Cover. Cook on Low 7-8 hours.

Ham and Potatoes

Ruth Shank
Gridley, IL

Makes 6-8 servings

6-8 medium red, *or* russet, potatoes, cut into chunks
2-3-lb. boneless ham
1/2 cup brown sugar
1 tsp. dry mustard

1. Prick potato pieces with fork. Place in slow cooker.
2. Place ham on top of potatoes. Crumble brown sugar over ham. Sprinkle with dry mustard.
3. Cover. Cook on Low 10 or more hours, until potatoes are tender.
4. Pour juices over ham and potatoes to serve.

Ham 'n Cola

Carol Peachey
Lancaster, PA

Makes 8-10 servings

1/2 cup brown sugar
1 tsp. dry mustard
1 tsp. prepared horseradish
1/4 cup cola-flavored soda
3-4-lb. precooked ham

1. Combine brown sugar, mustard, and horseradish. Moisten with just enough

cola to make a smooth paste. Reserve remaining cola.
2. Rub entire ham with mixture. Place ham in slow cooker and add remaining cola.
3. Cover. Cook on Low 6-10 hours, or High 2-3 hours.

Ham in Cider

Dorothy M. Van Deest
Memphis, TN

Makes 6-8 servings

3-lb. ham (or larger; whatever fits your slow cooker)
4 cups sweet cider, *or* apple juice
1 cup brown sugar
2 tsp. dry mustard
1 tsp. ground cloves
2 cups white seedless raisins

1. Place ham and cider in slow cooker.
2. Cover. Cook on Low 8-10 hours.
3. Remove ham from cider and place in baking pan.
4. Make a paste of sugar, mustard, cloves, and a little hot cider. Brush over ham. Pour a cup of juice from slow cooker into baking pan. Stir in raisins.
5. Bake at 375° for 30 minutes, until the paste has turned into a glaze.

Sweet-Sour Pork

Mary W. Stauffer
Ephrata, PA

Makes 4-6 servings

2 lbs. pork shoulder, cut in
  strips
1 green pepper, cut in
  strips
half a medium onion,
  thinly sliced
¾ cup shredded carrots
2 Tbsp. coarsely chopped
  sweet pickles
¼ cup brown sugar,
  packed
2 Tbsp. cornstarch
¼ cup water
1 cup pineapple syrup
  (reserved from
  pineapple chunks)
¼ cup cider vinegar
1 Tbsp. soy sauce
2 cups pineapple chunks

1. Place pork strips in slow
cooker.
2. Add green pepper,
onion, carrots, and pickles.
3. In bowl, mix together
brown sugar and cornstarch.
Add water, pineapple syrup,
vinegar, and soy sauce. Stir
until smooth.
4. Pour over ingredients in
slow cooker.
5. Cover. Cook on Low 5-7
hours. One hour before serving, add pineapple chunks.
Stir.
6. Serve over buttered noodles with an additional dash
of vinegar or garlic to taste.

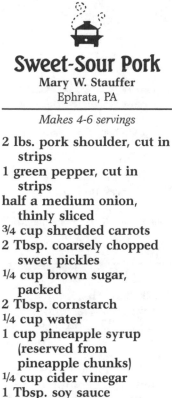

Barbecued Spareribs

Mrs. Paul Gray
Beatrice, NE

Makes 4 servings

4-lb. country-style
  spareribs, cut into
  serving-size pieces
10¾-oz. can tomato soup
½ cup cider vinegar
½ cup brown sugar
1 Tbsp. soy sauce
1 tsp. celery seed
1 tsp. salt
1 tsp. chili powder
dash cayenne pepper

1. Place ribs in slow
cooker.
2. Combine remaining
ingredients and pour over
ribs.
3. Cover. Cook on Low 6-8
hours.
4. Skim fat from juices
before serving.

Tender and Tangy Ribs

Betty Moore, Plano, IL
Renee Shirk, Mount Joy, PA

Makes 2-3 servings

¾-1 cup vinegar
½ cup ketchup
2 Tbsp. sugar
2 Tbsp. Worcestershire
  sauce
1 garlic clove, minced
1 tsp. dry mustard
1 tsp. paprika
½ tsp. salt
⅛ tsp. pepper
2 lbs. pork spareribs
1 Tbsp. oil

1. Combine all ingredients
except spareribs and oil in
slow cooker.
2. Brown ribs in oil in skillet. Transfer to slow cooker.
3. Cover. Cook on Low 4-6
hours.

"High" on most slow cookers is approximately 300°F.
"Low" is approximately 200°F.
Annabelle Unternahrer
Shipshewana, IN

Michele's Barbecued Ribs

Michele Ruvola
Selden, NY

Makes 8 servings

3 lbs. pork loin back ribs, cut into serving-size pieces
2 Tbsp. instant minced onion
1 tsp. crushed red pepper
1/2 tsp. ground cinnamon
1/2 tsp. garlic powder
1 medium onion, sliced
1/2 cup water
1 1/2 cups barbecue sauce

1. Combine onion, red pepper, cinnamon, and garlic powder. Rub mixture into ribs. Layer ribs and onion in slow cooker. Pour water around ribs.
2. Cover. Cook on Low 8-9 hours.
3. Remove ribs from slow cooker. Drain and discard liquid. Pour barbecue sauce in bowl and dip ribs in sauce. Return ribs to slow cooker. Pour remaining sauce over ribs.
4. Cover. Cook on Low 1 hour.

Sharon's Barbecued Ribs

Sharon Easter
Yuba City, CA

Makes 4-6 servings

3-4-lb. boneless pork ribs, cut into serving-size pieces
1 cup barbecue sauce
1 cup Catalina salad dressing

1. Place ribs in slow cooker.
2. Combine barbecue sauce and salad dressing. Pour over ribs.
3. Cover. Cook on Low 8 hours.

Variation:
Add 1 garlic clove sliced thin to top of sauce before cooking.

Awfully Easy Barbecued Ribs

Sara Harter Fredette,
Williamsburg, MA
Colleen Konetzni,
Rio Rancho, NM
Mary Mitchell,
Battle Creek, MI
Audrey Romonosky
Austin, TX
Iva Schmidt, Fergus Falls, MN
Susan Tjon
Austin, TX

Makes 4-6 servings

3-4-lb. baby back, *or* country-style, spareribs
1/2 tsp. salt, optional
1/2 tsp. pepper, optional
2 onions, sliced
16-24-oz. bottle barbecue sauce (depending upon how saucy you like your chops)

1. Brown ribs under broiler. Slice into serving-size pieces, season, and place in slow cooker.
2. Add onions and barbecue sauce.
3. Cover. Cook on Low 6 hours. These are good served with baked beans and corn on the cob.

Variation:
Instead of broiling the ribs, place them in slow cooker with other ingredients and cook on High 1 hour. Turn to Low and cook 8 more hours.

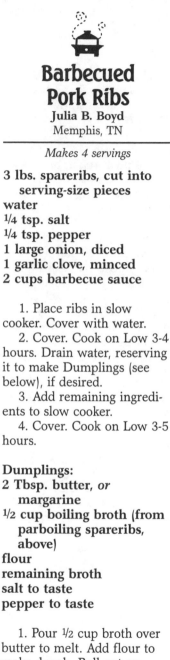

Barbecued Pork Ribs

Julia B. Boyd
Memphis, TN

Makes 4 servings

3 lbs. spareribs, cut into
    serving-size pieces
water
1/4 tsp. salt
1/4 tsp. pepper
1 large onion, diced
1 garlic clove, minced
2 cups barbecue sauce

1. Place ribs in slow cooker. Cover with water.
2. Cover. Cook on Low 3-4 hours. Drain water, reserving it to make Dumplings (see below), if desired.
3. Add remaining ingredients to slow cooker.
4. Cover. Cook on Low 3-5 hours.

Dumplings:
2 Tbsp. butter, *or*
    margarine
1/2 cup boiling broth (from
    parboiling spareribs,
    above)
flour
remaining broth
salt to taste
pepper to taste

1. Pour 1/2 cup broth over butter to melt. Add flour to make dough. Roll out on floured board until pastry-thin.
2. Pour remaining reserved broth into soup pot and add

salt and pepper to taste. Bring to boil.
3. Slice dough into 1 1/2" strips and drop into boiling broth in soup pot. Cover, but watch carefully that the broth does not boil over. The dumplings will rise to the surface and be done within 5-10 minutes. Serve with barbecued ribs.

Just Peachy Ribs

Amymarlene Jensen
Fountain, CO

Makes 4-6 servings

4-lb. boneless pork
    spareribs
1/2 cup brown sugar
1/4 cup ketchup
1/4 cup white vinegar
1 garlic clove, minced
1 tsp. salt
1 tsp. pepper
2 Tbsp. soy sauce
15-oz. can spiced cling
    peaches, cubed, with
    juice

1. Cut ribs in serving-size pieces and brown in broiler or in saucepan in oil. Drain. Place in slow cooker.
2. Combine remaining ingredients. Pour over ribs.
3. Cover. Cook on Low 8-10 hours.

Sesame Pork Ribs

Joette Droz
Kalona, IA

Makes 6 servings

1 medium onion, sliced
3/4 cup packed brown
    sugar
1/4 cup soy sauce
1/2 cup ketchup
1/4 cup honey
2 Tbsp. cider, *or* white
    vinegar
3 garlic cloves, minced
1 tsp. ground ginger
1/4-1/2 tsp. crushed red
    pepper flakes
5 lbs. country-style pork
    ribs
2 Tbsp. sesame seeds,
    toasted
2 Tbsp. chopped green
    onions

1. Place onions in bottom of slow cooker.
2. Combine brown sugar, soy sauce, ketchup, honey, vinegar, garlic, ginger, and red pepper flakes in large bowl. Add ribs and turn to coat. Place on top of onions in slow cooker. Pour sauce over meat.
3. Cover. Cook on Low 5-6 hours.
4. Place ribs on serving platter. Sprinkle with sesame seeds and green onions. Serve sauce on the side.

Barbecued Pork
Grace Ketcham, Marietta, GA
Mary Seielstad, Sparks, NV

Makes 6 servings

3 lbs. pork, cubed
2 cups chopped onions
3 green peppers, chopped
½ cup brown sugar
¼ cup vinegar
6-oz. can tomato paste
1½ Tbsp. chili powder
1 tsp. dry mustard
2 tsp. Worcestershire sauce
2 tsp. salt

1. Combine all ingredients in slow cooker.
2. Cover. Cook on High 8 hours.
3. Shred meat with fork. Mix into sauce and heat through.
4. Serve on hamburger buns wtih grated cheese and cole slaw on top.

Variation:
Substitute cubed chuck roast or stewing beef for the pork, or use half beef, half pork.

Barbecued Pork in the Slow Cooker
Dawn Day
Westminster, CA

Makes 6-8 servings

2-3-lb. boneless pork roast, cubed
2 onions, chopped
12-oz. bottle barbecue sauce
¼ cup honey
sandwich rolls

1. Place meat in slow cooker. Add onions, barbecue sauce, and honey.
2. Cover. Cook on Low 6-8 hours.
3. Use 2 forks to shred meat.
4. Serve on rolls with sauce.

Pork Barbecue
Mary Sommerfeld
Lancaster, PA

Makes 8-12 sandwiches

2 onions, sliced
4-5-lb. pork roast, *or* fresh picnic ham
5-6 whole cloves
2 cups water

Sauce:
1 large onion, chopped
16-oz. bottle barbecue sauce

1. Put half of sliced onions in bottom of slow cooker. Add meat, cloves, and water. Cover with remaining sliced onions.
2. Cover. Cook on Low 8-12 hours.
3. Remove bone from meat. Cut up meat. Drain liquid.
4. Return meat to slow cooker. Add chopped onion and barbecue sauce.
5. Cover. Cook on High 1-3 hours, or Low 4-8 hours, stirring two or three times.
6. Serve on buns.

Note:
This freezes well.

A word of caution—it is a common mistake to add too much liquid.
Mrs. J.E. Barthold
Bethlehem, PA

Shredded Pork

Sharon Easter
Yuba City, CA

Makes 4-6 servings

2-3-lb. pork butt roast, *or*
**boneless country-style
spareribs**
1/2-1 cup water
**1 pkg. dry taco seasoning
mix**

1. Place meat in slow cooker. Add water and seasoning mix.
2. Cover. Cook on Low 24 hours. Shred meat with two forks.
3. Use in tacos or in rolls, or use the sauce as gravy and serve over rice.

Melt-in-Your-Mouth Sausages

Ruth Ann Gingrich,
New Holland, PA
Ruth Hershey, Paradise, PA
Carol Sherwood, Batavia, NY
Nancy Zimmerman
Loysville, PA

Makes 6-8 servings

**2 lbs. sweet Italian
sausage, cut into 5-inch
lengths**
48-oz. jar spaghetti sauce
6-oz. can tomato paste
**1 large green pepper,
thinly sliced**
1 large onion, thinly sliced
**1 Tbsp. grated Parmesan
cheese**
1 tsp. dried parsley, *or*
**1 Tbsp. chopped fresh
parsley**
1 cup water

1. Place sausage in skillet. Cover with water. Simmer 10 minutes. Drain.
2. Combine remaining ingredients in slow cooker. Add sausage.
3. Cover. Cook on Low 6 hours.
4. Serve in buns, or cut sausage into bite-sized pieces and serve over cooked spaghetti. Sprinkle with more Parmesan cheese.

Sauerkraut & Trail Bologna

Carol Sommers
Millersburg, OH

Makes 10 servings

**32-oz. bag sauerkraut,
rinsed**
1/4-1/2 cup brown sugar
1 ring Trail Bologna

1. Combine sauerkraut and brown sugar in slow cooker.
2. Remove casing from bologna and cut into 1/4-inch slices. Add to sauerkraut. Stir.
3. Cover. Cook on Low 6-8 hours.

Note:
If you don't have access to Holmes County, Ohio's specialty Trail Bologna, use 1 large ring bologna.

Kraut and Sausage

Kathi Rogge
Alexandria, IN

Makes 4 servings

2 16-oz. cans sauerkraut,
   drained and rinsed
2 Tbsp. dark brown sugar
1 large onion, chopped
2 strips bacon, diced
1 lb. fully-cooked sausage,
   sliced

1. Combine sauerkraut
and brown sugar. Place in
slow cooker. Add layers of
onion, bacon, and sausage.
Add enough water to cover
half of sausage.
2. Cover. Cook on Low 5-6
hours, or on High 3 hours.

Sauerkraut and Kielbasa

Mary Ellen Wilcox
Scotia, NY

Makes 4-6 servings

64-oz. can sauerkraut
1 medium onion, chopped
1 large bay leaf
1 lb. kielbasa, cut into
   serving-sized pieces

1. Combine all ingredients
in slow cooker. Add enough
water to cover all ingredients.

2. Cover. Cook on High 30
minutes, and then on Low 6
hours. Remove bay leaf
before serving.

Polish Kraut 'n Apples

Lori Berezovsky, Salina, KS
Marie Morucci,
Glen Lyon, PA

Makes 4 servings

1 lb. fresh, *or* canned,
   sauerkraut
1 lb. lean smoked Polish
   sausage
3 tart cooking apples,
   thinly sliced
1/2 cup packed brown
   sugar
3/4 tsp. salt
1/8 tsp. pepper
1/2 tsp. caraway seeds,
   optional
3/4 cup apple juice, *or* cider

1. Rinse sauerkraut and
squeeze dry. Place half in
slow cooker.
2. Cut sausage into 2-inch
lengths and add to cooker.
3. Continue to layer
remaining ingredients in slow
cooker in order given. Top
with remaining sauerkraut.
Do not stir.
4. Cover. Cook on High
3-3 1/2 hours, or Low 6-7
hours. Stir before serving.

Old World Sauerkraut Supper

Josie Bollman, Maumee, OH
Joyce Bowman, Lady Lake, FL
Vera Schmucker, Goshen, IN

Makes 8 servings

3 strips bacon, cut into
   small pieces
2 Tbsp. flour
2 15-oz. cans sauerkraut
2 small potatoes, cubed
2 small apples, cubed
3 Tbsp. brown sugar
1 1/2 tsp. caraway seeds
3 lbs. Polish sausage, cut
   into 3-inch pieces
1/2 cup water

1. Fry bacon until crisp.
Drain, reserving drippings.
2. Add flour to bacon drippings. Blend well. Stir in
sauerkraut and bacon.
Transfer to slow cooker.
3. Add remaining ingredi-
ents.
4. Cover. Cook on Low 6-8
hours, or High 3-4 hours.

Polish Sausage Stew

Jeanne Heyerly, Chenoa, IL
Joyce Kaut, Rochester, NY
Joyce B. Suiter,
Garysburg, NC

Makes 6-8 servings

10³/4-oz. can cream of
celery soup
1/3 cup packed brown
sugar
27-oz. can sauerkraut,
drained
1 1/2 lbs. Polish sausage, cut
into 2-inch pieces and
browned
4 medium potatoes, cubed
1 cup chopped onions
1 cup (4 oz.) shredded
Monterey Jack cheese

1. Combine soup, sugar,
and sauerkraut. Stir in
sausage, potatoes, and onions.
2. Cover. Cook on Low 8
hours, or on High 4 hours.
3. Stir in cheese and serve.

Sausage Sauerkraut Supper

Ruth Ann Hoover,
New Holland, PA
Robin Schrock,
Millersburg, OH

Makes 10-12 servings

4 cups cubed carrots
4 cups cubed red potatoes
2 14-oz. cans sauerkraut,
rinsed and drained
2 1/2 lbs. fresh Polish
sausage, cut into 3-inch
pieces
1 medium onion, thinly
sliced
3 garlic cloves, minced
1 1/2 cups dry white wine,
or chicken broth
1/2 tsp. pepper
1 tsp. caraway seeds

1. Layer carrots, potatoes,
and sauerkraut in slow
cooker.
2. Brown sausage in skil-
let. Transfer to slow cooker.
Reserve 1 Tbsp. drippings in
skillet.
3. Saute onion and garlic
in drippings until tender. Stir
in wine. Bring to boil. Stir to
loosen brown bits. Stir in pepper and caraway seeds. Pour
over sausage.
4. Cover. Cook on Low 8-9
hours.

Kielbasa and Cabbage

Barbara McGinnis
Jupiter, FL

Makes 6 servings

1 1/2 lb.-head green cabbage,
shredded
2 medium onions, chopped
3 medium red potatoes,
peeled and cubed
1 red bell pepper, chopped
2 garlic cloves, minced
2/3 cup dry white wine
1 1/2 lbs. Polish kielbasa,
cut into 3-inch long
links
28-oz. can cut-up tomatoes
with juice
1 Tbsp. Dijon mustard
3/4 tsp. caraway seeds
1/2 tsp. pepper
3/4 tsp. salt

1. Combine all ingredients
in slow cooker.
2. Cover. Cook on Low 7-8
hours, or until cabbage is tender.

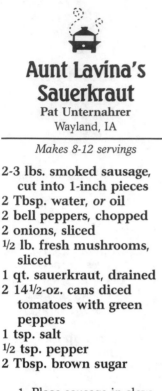

Aunt Lavina's Sauerkraut

Pat Unternahrer
Wayland, IA

Makes 8-12 servings

2-3 lbs. smoked sausage, cut into 1-inch pieces
2 Tbsp. water, *or* oil
2 bell peppers, chopped
2 onions, sliced
1/2 lb. fresh mushrooms, sliced
1 qt. sauerkraut, drained
2 14 1/2-oz. cans diced tomatoes with green peppers
1 tsp. salt
1/2 tsp. pepper
2 Tbsp. brown sugar

1. Place sausage in slow cooker. Heat on Low while you prepare other ingredients.
2. Saute peppers, onions, and mushrooms in small amount of water or oil in saucepan.
3. Combine all ingredients in slow cooker.
4. Cover. Cook on Low 5-6 hours, or High 3-4 hours.
5. Serve with mashed potatoes.

Pork and Kraut

Joyce B. Suiter
Garysburg, NC

Makes 6 servings

4-lb. pork loin
29-oz. can sauerkraut
1/4 cup water
1 onion, sliced
1 large white potato, sliced
10 3/4-oz. can cheddar cheese soup
1 Tbsp. caraway seeds
1 large Granny Smith apple, peeled and sliced
salt to taste
pepper to taste

1. Brown roast on all sides in skillet. Place in slow cooker.
2. Rinse sauerkraut and drain well. Combine sauerkraut, water, onion, potato, soup, caraway seeds, and apple. Pour over roast.
3. Cover. Cook on Low 10 hours.
4. Season with salt and pepper before serving.

Note:
Apple and potato disappear into the cheese soup as they cook, making a good sauce.

Pork Roast with Sauerkraut

Gail Bush
Landenberg, PA

Makes 8 servings

2 3-lb. pork shoulder roasts
1 large can sweet Bavarian sauerkraut with caraway seeds
1/4 cup brown sugar
1 envelope dry onion soup mix
1/2 cup water

1. Place roasts in slow cooker.
2. Rinse and drain sauerkraut. Combine sauerkraut, brown sugar, and onion soup mix. Layer over roasts. Pour water over all.
3. Cover. Cook on Low 7 hours.

Note:
If you can't find Bavarian sauerkraut with caraway seeds, substitute with a 27-oz. can regular sauerkraut and 1/2 tsp. caraway seeds.

Browning the meat, onions, and vegetables before putting them in the cooker improves their flavor, but this extra step can be skipped in most recipes. The flavor will still be good.
Dorothy M. Van Deest
Memphis, TN

Pork and Sauerkraut

Carole Whaling
New Tripoli, PA

Makes 6 servings

4 large potatoes, cubed
32-oz. bag sauerkraut, drained
1 large onion, chopped
1 large tart apple, chopped
2 Tbsp. packed brown sugar
1 tsp. caraway seeds
1 tsp. minced garlic
1/2 tsp. pepper
2 1/2-lb. boneless pork loin roast

1. Put potatoes in slow cooker.
2. Combine remaining ingredients, except pork, in slow cooker. Place half of the sauerkraut mixture on top of the potatoes. Add roast. Top with remaining sauerkraut mixture.
3. Cover. Cook on High 3-4 hours.

Country Ribs and Sauerkraut

Andrea O'Neil
Fairfield, CT

Makes 4-6 servings

2 27-oz. cans sauerkraut, drained and rinsed
2-3 lbs. country-style pork ribs, cut into serving-size pieces
6 slices bacon, browned
3-4 Tbsp. caraway seeds
2 cups water

1. Place alternating layers of sauerkraut and ribs in slow cooker, starting and ending with sauerkraut.
2. Crumble bacon and mix gently into top layer of sauerkraut. Sprinkle with caraway seeds. Pour water over all.
3. Cover. Cook on Low 7-8 hours.

Sauerkraut and Ribs

Margaret H. Moffitt
Bartlett, TN

Makes 6 servings

27-oz. can sauerkraut with juice
1 small onion, chopped
2 lbs. pork, *or* beef, ribs, cut into serving-size pieces
1 tsp. salt
1/4 tsp. pepper
half a sauerkraut can of water

1. Pour sauerkraut and juice into slow cooker. Add onion.
2. Season ribs with salt and pepper. Place on top of kraut. Add water.
3. Cover. Cook on High until mixture boils. Reduce heat to Low and cook 4 hours.
4. Serve with mashed potatoes.

Pork Spareribs with Sauerkraut

Char Hagner
Montague, MI

Makes 4-6 servings

2 small cooking apples,
  sliced in rings
1½-2 lbs. spareribs, cut
  into serving-size pieces
  and browned
1 qt. sauerkraut
½ cup apple cider, *or* juice
½ tsp. caraway seeds,
  optional

1. Layer apples, ribs, and
sauerkraut into slow cooker.
Pour on juice. Sprinkle with
caraway seeds.
2. Cover. Cook on Low 8
hours, or High 4 hours.

Pork Rib and Kraut Dinner

Betty A. Holt
St. Charles, MO

Makes 6-8 servings

3-4 lbs. country-style ribs
4 Tbsp. brown rice
1 Tbsp. caraway seeds
28-oz. can sauerkraut,
  rinsed
12-oz. can V-8 juice

1. Place ingredients in
slow cooker in order listed.
2. Cover. Cook on Low 6-8
hours, or High 3-4 hours.

Variation:
  To take the edge off the
sour flavor of sauerkraut, stir
in 3 Tbsp. mild molasses or
honey before cooking.

Ham Hock and Sauerkraut

Bernice M. Gnidovec
Streator, IL

Makes 2 servings

2 small ham hocks, *or*
  pork chops
14-oz. can sauerkraut,
  rinsed
1 large potato, cubed
1 Tbsp. butter
half a small onion, diced
1 Tbsp. flour
2 Tbsp. cold water

1. Place ham hocks or
chops in slow cooker. Top
with sauerkraut. Add enough
water to cover meat and
sauerkraut.
2. Cover. Cook on High
4 hours, or Low 6 ° hours.
3. Saute onions in butter in
saucepan until transparent.
Stir in flour and brown. Add
2 Tbsp. cold water, stirring
until thickened. Pour over
ingredients in slow cooker.
Cover and cook on High 5-10
minutes.

In recipes calling for rice, don't use minute or quick-cooking rice.

Mary Puskar
Forest Hill, MD

Simply Pork and Sauerkraut

Gladys Longacre
Susquehanna, PA

Makes 2-4 servings

2-4 pork chops
14-oz. can sauerkraut, *or* **more if you like sauerkraut**

1. Place pork chops in slow cooker. Cover with sauerkraut.
2. Cover. Cook on Low 7-8 hours.

Variations:
1. Brown pork chops before placing in slow cooker.
2. Substitute spareribs for pork chops.

Chops and Kraut

Willard E. Roth
Elkhart, IN

Makes 6 servings

1-lb. bag fresh sauerkraut
2 large Vidalia onions, sliced
6 pork chops

1. Make 3 layers in well-greased cooker: kraut, onions, and chops.
2. Cover. Cook on Low 6 hours.
3. Serve with mashed potatoes and applesauce or cranberry sauce.

Sauerkraut and Pork

Ethel Mumaw
Berlin, OH

Makes 6-8 servings

2 lbs. pork cutlets
2 14-oz. cans sauerkraut
2 apples, chopped
2 Tbsp. brown sugar

1. Cut pork into serving-size pieces. Brown under broiler or in 2 Tbsp. oil in skillet. Place in slow cooker.
2. Add remaining ingredients.
3. Cover. Cook on Low 24 hours.

Smothered Lentils

Tracey B. Stenger
Gretna, LA

Makes 6 servings

2 cups dry lentils, rinsed and sorted
1 medium onion, chopped
1/2 cup chopped celery
2 garlic cloves, minced
1 cup ham, cooked and chopped
1/2 cup chopped carrots
1 cup diced tomatoes
1 tsp. dried marjoram
1 tsp. ground coriander
salt to taste
pepper to taste
3 cups water

1. Combine all ingredients in slow cooker.
2. Cover. Cook on Low 8 hours. (Check lentils after 5 hours of cooking. If they've absorbed all the water, stir in 1 more cup water.)

Green Beans and Sausage

Alma Weaver
Ephrata, PA

Makes 4-6 servings

1 qt. green beans, cut into 2-inch pieces
1 carrot, chopped
1 small green pepper, chopped
8-oz. can tomato sauce
1/4 tsp. dried thyme
1/2 tsp. salt
1 lb. bulk pork sausage, *or* link sausage cut into 1-inch pieces

1. Combine all ingredients except sausage in slow cooker.
2. Cover. Cook on High 3-4 hours. Add sausage and cook another 2 hours on Low.

Sausage Supreme

Jan Moore
Wellsville, KS

Makes 4 servings

1 lb. fresh sausage, cut into 1-inch pieces and browned
2 10¾-oz. cans cream of mushroom soup
1 onion, chopped
4 potatoes, cubed

1. Combine all ingredients in slow cooker.
2. Cover. Cook on Low 8 hours. If mixture becomes too dry, stir in half a soup can or more of water.

Variation:
Substitute 1 can cheese soup for 1 can cream of mushroom soup.

Sausage and Apples

Evelyn L. Ward
Greeley, CO

Makes 4 servings

20-oz. can apple pie filling
1/4 cup water
ground nutmeg
10-oz. pkg. fully cooked and browned sausage patties

1. Spoon pie filling into slow cooker. Stir in water. Sprinkle with nutmeg. Top with sausage.
2. Cover. Cook on Low 4-6 hours.

Kielbasa and Cheese Casserole

Dolores S. Kratz
Souderton, PA

Makes 4-5 servings

3 cups uncooked noodles
oil
2 beef bouillon cubes
1 cup boiling water
1/4 cup flour
2 Tbsp. butter, melted
4 oz. cheese, shredded
1 lb. kielbasa, sliced
1 small onion, chopped
2 ribs celery, diced
2 carrots, grated
2-oz. jar pimentos

1. Cook noodles until barely tender. Drain. Toss with small amount of oil.
2. Dissolve bouillon in boiling water.
3. Combine all ingredients in slow cooker.
4. Cover. Cook on Low 8 hours.

Variation:
Instead of noodles, use gnocchi.

Supreme Sausage Dish

Shirley Thieszen
Lakin, KS

Makes 6 servings

1 lb. smoky wieners, cut in 1-inch pieces
2 cups cooked macaroni
1 cup frozen peas, *or* corn
1/2 cup chopped onions
1 tsp. dry parsley
1 small jar chopped pimentos (about 3 Tbsp.)
3/4 cup shredded American, *or* Velveeta, cheese
3 Tbsp. flour
3/4 tsp. salt
1/4 tsp. pepper
1 cup milk
1 cup water
1/2 Tbsp. vinegar

1. Combine wieners, macaroni, peas, onions, parsley, and pimentos in greased slow cooker.
2. In saucepan, combine cheese, flour, salt, pepper, milk, water, and vinegar. Cook until smooth and thickened. Pour into slow cooker. Mix well.
3. Cover. Cook on High 1 hour, and then on Low 3-4 hours.

Variation:
Use smoked sausage instead of smoky wieners.

Barbecued Sausage Pieces

Elizabeth Yutzy
Wauseon, OH

Makes 4-5 main-dish servings, or 8-10 snack-sized servings

1 lb. smoked sausage
1 cup hickory-flavored barbecue sauce
1/4 cup honey
2 Tbsp. brown sugar

1. Cut sausage in 1/2-inch pieces. Brown in skillet. Place in slow cooker.
2. Combine remaining ingredients. Pour over sausage.
3. Cover. Cook on Low 2 hours.
4. Serve over rice or noodles as a main dish or with toothpicks as a party snack.

Perfection Hot Dogs

Audrey L. Kneer
Williamsfield, IL

Makes 12 servings

12 hot dogs, bratwurst, *or* Polish sausage links

1. Place hot dogs or sausages in slow cooker.
2. Cover. Cook on High 1-2 hours.

Beer Brats

Mary Ann Wasick
West Allis, WI

Makes 6 servings

6 fresh bratwurst
2 garlic cloves, minced
2 Tbsp. olive oil
12-oz. can beer

1. Brown sausages and garlic in olive oil in skillet. Pierce sausage casings and cook 5 more minutes. Transfer to slow cooker.
2. Pour beer into cooker to cover sausages.
3. Cover. Cook on Low 6-7 hours.

Spiced Hot Dogs

Tracey Yohn
Harrisburg, PA

Makes 3-4 servings

1 lb. hot dogs, cut in pieces
2 Tbsp. brown sugar
3 Tbsp. vinegar
1/2 cup ketchup
2 tsp. prepared mustard
1/2 cup water
1/2 cup chopped onions

1. Place hot dogs in slow cooker.
2. Combine all ingredients except hot dogs in saucepan. Simmer. Pour over hot dogs.
3. Cover. Cook on Low 2 hours.

Barbecued Hot Dogs

Jeanette Oberholtzer
Manheim, PA

Makes 8 servings

1 cup apricot preserves
4 oz. tomato sauce
1/3 cup vinegar
2 Tbsp. soy sauce
2 Tbsp. honey
1 Tbsp. oil
1 tsp. salt
1/4 tsp. ground ginger
2 lbs. hot dogs, cut into
   1-inch pieces

1. Combine all ingredients except hot dogs in slow cooker.
2. Cover. Cook on High 30 minutes. Add hot dog pieces. Cook on Low 4 hours.
3. Serve over rice as a main dish, or as an appetizer.

Bits and Bites

Betty Richards
Rapid City, SD

Makes 12 servings

12-oz. can beer
1 cup ketchup
1 cup light brown sugar
1/2-1 cup barbecue sauce
1 lb. all-beef hot dogs,
   sliced 1 1/2-inches thick
2 lbs. cocktail sausages

1. Combine beer, ketchup, brown sugar, and barbecue sauce. Pour into slow cooker.
2. Add hot dogs and sausages. Mix well.
3. Cover. Cook on Low 3-4 hours.

Barbecued Mini-Franks

Zona Mae Bontrager
Kokomo, IN

*Makes 8-10 full-sized servings, or
16-20 appetizer-sized servings*

1 cup finely chopped
   onions
1 cup ketchup
1/3 cup Worcestershire
   sauce
1/4 cup sugar
1/4 cup vinegar
4 tsp. prepared mustard
1 tsp. pepper
4-lbs. miniature hot dogs

1. Combine all ingredients except hot dogs in slow cooker.
2. Cover. Heat on High 1 1/2 hours, or until hot. Add hot dogs.
3. Reduce heat to Low and simmer 4 hours.

Variations:
1. Add 1 Tbsp. finely chopped green pepper and 2 garlic cloves, pressed.
2. Use miniature smoked sausages instead of mini-hot dogs.

Spicy Franks

Char Hagner
Montague, MI

*Makes 4-6 full-sized servings, or
32 appetizer-sized servings*

2 1-lb. pkgs. cocktail
  wieners
1 cup chili sauce
1 cup bottled barbecue
  sauce
8-oz. can jellied cranberry
  sauce

1. Place wieners in slow
cooker.
2. In separate bowl, com-
bine chili sauce, barbecue
sauce, and cranberry sauce.
Pour over wieners.
3. Cover. Cook on Low 3-4
hours, or High 1½-2 hours.

Little Smokies

Sharon Kauffman
Harrisonburg, VA

*Makes 6-8 full-sized servings, or
12-15 appetizer-sized servings*

2 pkgs. Li'l Smokies
1 bottle chili sauce
1 small jar grape jelly

1. Combine all ingredients
in slow cooker.
2. Cover. Cook on Low 1-2
hours, or until heated
through.

Sweet and Sour Vienna Sausages

Judy Denney
Lawrenceville, GA

*Makes 10 full-sized servings, or
20 appetizer-sized servings*

8 cans Vienna sausages,
  drained
2 cups grape jelly
2 cups ketchup

1. Put sausages in slow
cooker.
2. Combine jelly and
ketchup. Pour over sausages.
Stir lightly. (Add more jelly
and ketchup if sausages are
not covered.)
3. Cover. Cook on High 1
hour, then turn to Low for 5
hours.

Variations:
Instead of Vienna
sausages, use smoky links.
Add 1 can pineapple chunks
and juice to jelly and
ketchup.

Barbecued Ham Sandwiches

Jane Steiner
Orrville, OH

Makes 4-6 full-sized servings

1 lb. turkey ham chipped,
  or chipped honey-glazed
  ham
1 small onion, finely diced
½ cup ketchup
1 Tbsp. vinegar
3 Tbsp. brown sugar
buns

1. Place half of meat in
greased slow cooker.
2. Combine other ingredi-
ents. Pour half of mixture
over meat. Repeat layers.
3. Cover. Cook on Low 5
hours.
4. Fill buns and serve.

A slow cooker set on Low does not burn food and will not
spoil a meal if cooked beyond the designated time.
Eleanor J. Ferreira
North Chelmsford, MA

Ham Barbecue

Janet V. Yocum
Elizabethtown, PA

Makes 6-8 servings

1 lb. boiled ham, cut into
  cubes
1 cup cola-flavored soda
1 cup ketchup

1. Place ham in slow
cooker. Pour cola and ketchup
over ham.
2. Cover. Cook on Low 8
hours.
3. Serve in hamburger
rolls.

Spaghetti Sauce

Doris Perkins
Mashpee, MA

Makes 18-24 servings

1/4-lb. bacon, diced
1 1/4-lb. ground beef
1/2 lb. ground pork
1 cup chopped onions
1/2 cup chopped green
  peppers
3 garlic cloves, minced
2 2-lb., 3-oz. cans Italian
  tomaoes
2 6-oz. cans tomao paste
1 cup dry red wine, *or*
  water
2 1/2 tsp. dried oregano
2 1/2 tsp. dried basil
1 bay leaf, crumbled
3/4 cup water
1/4 cup chopped fresh
  parsley
1 tsp. dried thyme
1 Tbsp. salt
1/4 tsp. pepper
1/4 cup dry red wine, *or*
  water

1. Brown bacon in skillet
until crisp. Remove. Add
ground beef and pork.
Crumble and cook until
brown. Stir in onions, green
peppers, and garlic. Cook 10
minutes.
2. Pour tomatoes into slow
cooker and crush with back
of spoon.
3. Add all other ingredi-
ents, except 1/4 cup wine, in
slow cooker.
4. Cover. Bring to boil on
High. Reduce heat to Low for
3-4 hours.

5. During last 30 minutes,
stir in 1/4 cup red wine *or*
water.

Italian
Spaghetti Sauce

Michele Ruvola
Selden, NY

Makes 8-10 servings

2 lbs. sausage, *or* ground
  beef
3 medium onions, chopped
  (about 2 1/4 cups)
2 cups sliced mushrooms
6 garlic cloves, minced
2 14 1/2-oz. cans diced
  tomatoes, undrained
29-oz. can tomato sauce
12-oz. can tomato paste
2 Tbsp. dried basil
1 Tbsp. dried oregano
1 Tbsp. sugar
1 tsp. salt
1/2 tsp. crushed red pepper
  flakes

1. Cook sausage, onions,
mushrooms, and garlic in
skillet over medium heat for
10 minutes. Drain. Transfer
to slow cooker
2. Stir in remaining ingredients.
3. Cover. Cook on Low 8-9
hours.

Note:
  This is also a good sauce to
use in lasagna.

Chunky Spaghetti Sauce

Patti Boston
Newark, OH

Makes 6 cups

1 lb. ground beef, browned
  and drained
1/2 lb. bulk sausage,
  browned and drained
14 1/2-oz. can Italian
  tomatoes with basil
15-oz. can Italian tomato
  sauce
1 medium onion, chopped
1 green pepper, chopped
8-oz. can sliced
  mushrooms
1/2 cup dry red wine
2 tsp. sugar
1 tsp. minced garlic

1. Combine all ingredients
in slow cooker.
2. Cover. Cook on High
3 1/2-4 hours, or Low 7-8
hours.

Variations:
1. For added texture and
zest, add 3 fresh, medium-
sized tomatoes, chopped, and
4 large fresh basil leaves,
torn. Stir in 1 tsp. salt and 1/2
tsp. pepper.
2. To any leftover sauce,
add chickpeas or kidney
beans and serve chili!

Sausage-Beef Spaghetti Sauce

Jeannine Janzen
Elbing, KS

Makes 16-20 servings

1 lb. ground beef
1 lb. Italian sausage, sliced
2 28-oz. cans crushed
  tomatoes
3/4 can (28-oz. tomato can)
  water
2 tsp. garlic powder
1 tsp. pepper
2 Tbsp. or more parsley
2 Tbsp. dried oregano
2 12-oz. cans tomato paste
2 12-oz. cans tomato puree

1. Brown ground beef and
sausage in skillet. Drain.
Transfer to large slow cooker.
2. Add crushed tomatoes,
water, garlic powder, pepper,
parsley, and oregano.
3. Cover. Cook on High 30
minutes. Add tomato paste
and tomato puree. Cook on
Low 6 hours.

Note:
Leftovers freeze well.

Italian Sausage Spaghetti

Eleanor Larson
Glen Lyon, PA

Makes 12 servings

6 Italian turkey sausage
  links (1 1/2 lbs.), cut into
  1 1/2-inch pieces
1 cup diced onions
3 Tbsp. sugar
1 tsp. dried oregano
1/2 tsp. salt
2 garlic cloves, minced
28-oz. can crushed
  tomatoes, undrained
15-oz. can tomato sauce
12-oz. can tomato paste
1 1/2 lbs. dry spaghetti

1. Combine all ingredients
except spaghetti in slow
cooker.
2. Cover. Cook on Low 8-
10 hours.
3. Cook spaghetti in large
soup pot. Drain and top with
sauce.

Cooked pasta and rice should be added during the last 1-1 1/2
hours of cooking time to prevent them from disintegrating.
John D. Allen
Rye, CO

Easy-Does-It Spaghetti

Rachel Kauffman, Alto, MI
Lois Stoltzfus, Honey Brook, PA
Deb Unternahrer, Wayland, IA

Makes 8 servings

2 lbs. ground chuck,
    browned and drained
1 cup chopped onions
2 cloves garlic, minced
2 15-oz. cans tomato sauce
2-3 tsp. Italian seasoning
1½ tsp. salt
¼ tsp. pepper
2 4-oz. cans sliced
    mushrooms, drained
6 cups tomato juice
16-oz. dry spaghetti,
    broken into 4-5-inch
    pieces
grated Parmesan cheese

1. Combine all ingredients
except spaghetti and cheese
in 4-quart (or larger) slow
cooker.
2. Cover. Cook on Low 6-8
hours, or High 3-5 hours.
Turn to High during last 30
minutes and stir in dry
spaghetti. (If spaghetti is not
fully cooked, continue cooking another 10 minutes,
checking to make sure it is
not becoming over-cooked.)
3. Sprinkle individual servings with Parmesan cheese.

Variation:
    Add 1 tsp. dry mustard
and ½ tsp. allspice in Step 1.
    Kathy Hertzler
    Lancaster, PA

Mom's Spaghetti and Meatballs

Mary C. Casey
Scranton, PA

Makes 8-10 servings

Sauce:
2 Tbsp. oil
¼-½ cup chopped onions
3 garlic cloves, minced
29-oz. can tomato puree
29-oz. can water
12-oz. can tomato paste
12-oz. can water
1 tsp. salt
1 Tbsp. sugar
2 tsp. dried oregano
¼ tsp. Italian seasoning
½ tsp. dried basil
⅛ tsp. pepper
¼ cup diced green peppers

Meatballs:
1 lb. ground beef
1 egg
2 Tbsp. water
¾ cup Italian bread
    crumbs
⅛ tsp. black pepper
½ tsp. salt
2 Tbsp. oil

1. Saute onions and garlic
in oil in saucepan.
2. Combine all sauce ingredients in slow cooker.
3. Cover. Cook on Low.
4. Mix together all meat-
ball ingredients except oil.
Form into small meatballs,
then brown on all sides in oil
in saucepan. Drain on paper
towels. Add to sauce.
5. Cover. Cook on Low 4-5
hours.

Spaghetti with Meat Sauce

Esther Lehman
Croghan, NY

Makes 8-10 servings

1 lb. ground beef, browned
2 28-oz. cans tomatoes
2 medium onions, quartered
2 medium carrots, cut into
    chunks
2 garlic cloves, minced
6-oz. can tomato paste
2 Tbsp. chopped fresh
    parsley
1 bay leaf
1 Tbsp. sugar
1 tsp. dried basil
¾ tsp. salt
½ tsp. dried oregano
dash pepper
2 Tbsp. cold water
2 Tbsp. cornstarch
hot cooked spaghetti
grated Parmesan cheese

1. Place meat in slow
cooker.
2. In blender, combine 1
can tomatoes, onions, carrots,
and garlic. Cover and blend
until finely chopped. Stir into
meat.
3. Cut up the remaining can
of tomatoes. Stir into meat mixture. Add tomato paste, parsley,
bay leaf, sugar, basil, salt,
oregano, and pepper. Mix well.
4. Cover. Cook on Low 8-10
hours.
5. To serve, turn to High.
Remove bay leaf. Cover and
heat until bubbly, about 10
minutes.

6. Combine water and cornstarch. Stir into tomato mixture. Cook 10 minutes longer.

7. Serve with spaghetti and cheese.

Slow Cooker Spaghetti Sauce

Lucille Amos, Greensboro, NC
Julia Lapp, New Holland, PA

Makes 6-8 servings

1 lb. ground beef
1 medium onion, chopped
2 14-oz. cans diced
   tomatoes, with juice
6-oz. can tomato paste
8-oz. can tomato sauce
1 bay leaf
4 garlic cloves, minced
2 tsp. dried oregano
1 tsp. salt
2 tsp. dried basil
1 Tbsp. brown sugar
1/2-1 tsp. dried thyme

1. Brown meat and onion in saucepan. Drain well. Transfer to slow cooker.

2. Add remaining ingredients.

3. Cover. Cook on Low 7 hours. If the sauce seems too runny, remove lid during last hour of cooking.

Nancy's Spaghetti Sauce

Nancy Graves
Manhattan, KS

Makes 4-6 servings

1/4 cup minced onion
garlic powder to taste
3 cups chopped fresh
   tomatoes, *or* 1-lb., 12-oz.
   can diced tomatoes with
   juice
6-oz. can tomato paste
3 1/2 tsp. salt
dash of pepper
1 basil leaf
1 chopped green pepper
1 lb. ground beef, browned
   and drained
4-oz. can sliced
   mushrooms

1. Combine all ingredients in slow cooker.

2. Cover. Cook on Low 3 hours.

Pasta Sauce with Meat and Veggies

Marla Folkerts
Holland, OH

Makes 6 servings

1/2 lb. ground turkey
1/2 lb. ground beef
1 rib celery, chopped
2 medium carrots,
   chopped
1 garlic clove, minced
1 medium onion, chopped
28-oz. can diced tomatoes
   with juice
1/2 tsp. salt
1/4 tsp. dried thyme
6-oz. can tomato paste
1/8 tsp. pepper

1. Combine turkey, beef, celery, carrots, garlic, and onion in slow cooker.

2. Add remaining ingredients. Mix well.

3. Cover. Cook on Low 7-8 hours.

4. Serve over pasta or rice.

Katelyn's Spaghetti Sauce
Katelyn Bailey
Mechanicsburg, PA

Makes 10-12 servings

1 lb. ground beef, browned
  and drained
3/4 cup chopped onions
1 garlic clove, minced
3 Tbsp. oil
2 6-oz. cans tomato paste
1 Tbsp. sugar
1 1/2 tsp. salt
1-1 1/2 tsp. dried oregano
1/2 tsp. pepper
1 bay leaf
2 qts. tomatoes, *or* tomato
  sauce

1. Combine all ingredients in slow cooker.
2. Cover. Cook on Low 8-10 hours. Remove bay leaf before serving.

Note:
This sauce freezes well.

Char's Spaghetti Sauce
Char Hagner
Montague, MI

Makes 16-20 servings

4 lbs. ground beef
2 large onions, chopped
1/4-lb. bacon, cut into small
  squares
5 garlic cloves, minced
1 Tbsp. salt
1/4 tsp. celery salt
4 10 3/4-oz. cans tomato
  soup
2 6-oz. cans tomato paste
8-oz. can mushrooms
3 green peppers, chopped

1. Brown ground beef, onions, bacon, and garlic in saucepan. Drain.
2. Combine all ingredients in large slow cooker.
3. Cover. Cook on Low 6 hours.

So-Easy Spaghetti
Ruth Ann Swartzendruber
Hydro, OK

Makes 4-6 servings

1 lb. ground beef
1/2 cup diced onions
1 pkg. dry spaghetti sauce
  mix
8-oz. can tomato sauce
3 cups tomato juice
4 oz. dry spaghetti, broken
  into 4-inch pieces

1. Brown meat and onions in skillet. Drain. Transfer to greased slow cooker.
2. Add remaining ingredients, except spaghetti.
3. Cover. Cook on Low 6-8 hours, or High 3 1/2 hours.
4. During last hour, turn to High and add spaghetti. Stir frequently to keep spaghetti from clumping together.

Try to have vegetable and meat pieces all cut about the same size and thickness.
Mary Puskar
Forest Hill, MD

Creamy Spaghetti

Dale Peterson
Rapid City, SD

Makes 6 servings

1 cup chopped onions
1 cup chopped green
  peppers
1 Tbsp. butter, *or*
  margarine
28-oz. can tomatoes with
  juice
4-oz. can mushrooms,
  chopped and drained
2 1/4-oz. can sliced ripe
  olives, drained
2 tsp. dried oregano
1 lb. ground beef, browned
  and drained
12 oz. spaghetti, cooked
  and drained
10 3/4-oz. can cream of
  mushroom soup
1/2 cup water
2 cups (8 oz.) shredded
  cheddar cheese
1/4 cup grated Parmesan
  cheese

1. Saute onions and green
peppers in butter in skillet
until tender. Add tomatoes,
mushrooms, olives, oregano,
and beef. Simmer for 10 minutes. Transfer to slow cooker.
2. Add spaghetti. Mix well.
3. Combine soup and
water. Pour over casserole.
Sprinkle with cheeses.
4. Cover. Cook on Low 4-6
hours.

Tomato Spaghetti Sauce

Jean Butzer
Batavia, NY

Makes 6 servings

1 cup finely chopped
  onions
2 garlic cloves, minced
2 lbs. fresh tomatoes,
  peeled and chopped, *or*
  28-oz. can tomatoes, cut
  up, with juice
6-oz. can tomato paste
1 Tbsp. sugar
2 tsp. instant beef bouillon
  granules
1 tsp. dried oregano
1/2 tsp. dried basil
1 large bay leaf
salt to taste
pepper to taste
4-oz. can sliced
  mushrooms
2 Tbsp. cornstarch
2 Tbsp. cold water

1. Combine all ingredients
except mushrooms, corn-
starch, and water in slow
cooker.
2. Cover. Cook on Low 10-
12 hours.
3. Remove bay leaf. Stir in
mushrooms.
4. Combine cornstarch and
water. Stir into sauce.
5. Cover. Cook on High
until thickened and bubbly,
about 25 minutes.

Italian Vegetable Pasta Sauce

Sherril Bieberly
Salina, KS

Makes 2 1/2 quarts sauce

3 Tbsp. olive oil
1 cup packed chopped
  fresh parsley
3 ribs celery, chopped
1 medium onion, chopped
2 garlic cloves, minced
2-inch sprig fresh
  rosemary, *or* 1/2 tsp.
  dried rosemary
2 small fresh sage leaves,
  or 1/2 tsp. dried sage
32-oz. can tomato sauce
32-oz. can chopped
  tomatoes
1 small dried hot chili
  pepper
1/4 lb. fresh mushrooms,
  sliced, *or* 8-oz. can sliced
  mushrooms, drained
1 1/2 tsp. salt

1. Heat oil in skillet. Add
parsley, celery, onion, garlic,
rosemary, and sage. Saute
until vegetables are tender.
Place in slow cooker.
2. Add tomatoes, chili pepper, mushrooms, and salt.
3. Cover. Cook on Low 12-
18 hours, or on High 5-6
hours.

Variation:
Add 2 lbs. browned
ground beef to olive oil and
sauted vegetables. Continue
with recipe.

Louise's Vegetable Spaghetti Sauce

Louise Stackhouse
Benton, PA

Makes 4-6 servings

6-7 fresh tomatoes, peeled
  and crushed
1 medium onion, chopped
2 green peppers, chopped
2 cloves garlic, minced
1/2 tsp. dried basil
1/2 tsp. dried oregano
1/4 tsp. salt
1/4 cup sugar
6-oz. can tomato paste,
  optional

1. Combine all ingredients in slow cooker.
2. Cover. Cook on Low 8-10 hours. If the sauce is too watery for your liking, stir in a 6-oz. can of tomato paste during the last hour of cooking.
3. Serve over cooked spaghetti or other pasta.

Pizza in a Pot

Marianne J. Troyer
Millersburg, OH

Makes 6-8 servings

1 lb. bulk Italian sausage,
  browned and drained
28-oz. can crushed
  tomatoes
15 1/2-oz. can chili beans
2 1/4-oz. can sliced black
  olives, drained
1 medium onion, chopped
1 small green pepper,
  chopped
2 garlic cloves, minced
1/4 cup grated Parmesan
  cheese
1 Tbsp. quick-cooking
  tapioca
1 Tbsp. dried basil
1 bay leaf
1 tsp. salt
hot cooked pasta
shredded mozzarella
  cheese

1. Combine all ingredients in slow cooker except pasta and mozzarella cheese.
2. Cover. Cook on Low 8-9 hours.
3. Discard bay leaf. Stir well.
4. Serve over pasta. Top with mozzarella cheese.

Slow-Cooker Pizza

Marla Folkerts, Holland, OH
Ruth Ann Swartzendruber
Hydro, OK
Arlene Wiens, Newton, KS

Makes 6-8 servings

1 1/2 lbs. ground beef, *or*
  bulk Italian sausage
1 medium onion, chopped
1 green pepper, chopped
half a box rigatoni, cooked
7-oz. jar sliced mushrooms,
  drained
3 oz. sliced pepperoni
16-oz. jar pizza sauce
10 oz. mozzarella cheese,
  shredded
10 oz. cheddar cheese,
  shredded

1. Brown ground beef and onions in saucepan. Drain.
2. Layer half of each of the following, in the order given, in slow cooker: ground beef and onions, green pepper, noodles, mushrooms, pepperoni, pizza sauce, cheddar cheese, and mozzarella cheese. Repeat layers.
3. Cover. Cook on Low 3-4 hours.

Note:
Keep rigatoni covered with sauce so they don't become dry and crunchy.

Variation:
Add a 10 3/4-oz. can cream of mushroom soup to the mix, putting half of it in as a layer after the first time the noodles appear, and the other

half after the second layer of noodles.

Dorothy Horst
Tiskilwa, IL

Pizza Rice

Sue Hamilton
Minooka, IL

Makes 6 servings

2 cups rice, uncooked
3 cups chunky pizza sauce
2½ cups water
7-oz. can mushrooms, undrained
4 oz. pepperoni, sliced
1 cup grated cheese

1. Combine rice, sauce, water, mushrooms, and pepperoni. Stir.
2. Cover. Cook on Low 10 hours, or on High 6 hours. Sprinkle with cheese before serving.

Wild Rice Hot Dish

Barbara Tenney
Delta, PA

Makes 8-10 servings

2 cups wild rice, uncooked
½ cup slivered almonds
½ cup chopped onions
½ cup chopped celery
8-12-oz. can mushrooms, drained
2 cups cut-up chicken
6 cups chicken broth
¼-½ tsp. salt
¼ tsp. pepper
¼ tsp. garlic powder
1 Tbsp. parsley

1. Wash and drain rice.
2. Combine all ingredients in slow cooker. Mix well.
3. Cover. Cook on Low 4-6 hours, or until rice is finished. Do not remove lid before rice has cooked 4 hours.

Frances' Roast Chicken

Frances Schrag
Newton, KS

Makes 6 servings

3-4-lb. whole frying chicken
half an onion, chopped
1 rib celery, chopped
salt to taste
pepper to taste
½ tsp. poultry seasoning
¼ tsp. dried basil

1. Sprinkle chicken cavity with salt, pepper, and poultry seasoning. Put onion and celery inside cavity. Put chicken in slow cooker. Sprinkle with basil.
2. Cover. Cook on Low 8-10 hours, or High 4-6 hours.

When adapting range-top recipes to slow cooking, reduce the amount of onion you normally use because the onion flavor gets stronger during slow cooking.
Beatrice Orgish
Richardson, TX

167

Donna's Cooked Chicken

Donna Treloar
Gaston, IN

Makes 1 chicken

chicken (boneless, skinless
    breasts are the easiest,
    but any chicken pieces
    will do)
1 onion, sliced
seasoned salt
pepper
minced garlic, *or* garlic
    powder

1. Layer onion in bottom
of slow cooker. Add chicken
and sprinke with seasoned
salt, pepper, minced garlic, or
garlic powder.
2. Cook on Low 4 hours or
until done but not dry. (Time
will vary according to
amount of chicken and size of
pieces.)
3. Use in stir-frys, chicken
salads, or casseroles, slice for
sandwiches, shred for enchi-
ladas, or cut up and freeze for
later use.

Variation:
Splash chicken with
2 Tbsp. soy sauce before
cooking.

Valerie's & Stacy's Roast Chicken

Valerie Hertzler
Weyers Cave, VA
Stacy Petersheim
Mechanicsburg, PA

Makes 4-6 servings

3-4-lb. chicken
salt to taste
pepper to taste
butter
basil to taste

1. Wash chicken thor-
oughly. Pat dry. Sprinkle cavity
with salt and pepper. Place in
slow cooker. Dot with butter.
Sprinkle with basil.
2. Cover. Cook on High
1 hour, and then on Low 8-10
hours.

Chicken-at-the-Ready

Mary Mitchell
Battle Creek, MI

Makes 2-3 pints cooked chicken

1 large whole chicken,
    skinned
1 cup water

1. Place chicken in greased
slow cooker. Add water.
2. Cover. Cook on Low 6-8
hours.

3. Remove meat from
bones, pack cooked meat into
plastic boxes, and store in
freezer to use in recipes that
call for cooked chicken.

Note:
I frequently put this on
late at night so that it is done
when I wake up in the morning.

Chicken in a Pot

Carolyn Baer, Conrath, WI
Evie Hershey, Atglen, PA
Judy Koczo, Plano, IL
Mary Puskar, Forest Hill, MD
Mary Wheatley, Mashpee, MA

Makes 6 servings

2 carrots, sliced
2 onions, sliced
2 celery ribs, cut in 1-inch
    pieces
3 lb. chicken, whole *or*
    cut up
2 tsp. salt
1/2 tsp. dried coarse black
    pepper
1 tsp. dried basil
1/2 cup water, chicken
    broth, *or* white cooking
    wine

1. Place vegetables in bottom of slow cooker. Place
chicken on top of vegetables.
Add seasonings and water.
2. Cover. Cook on Low 8-
10 hours, or High 3 1/2-5 hours
(use 1 cup liquid if cooking
on High).
3. This is a great founda-

tion for soups—chicken vegetable, chicken noodle . . .

Note:
To make this a full meal, add 2 medium-sized potatoes, quartered, to vegetables before cooking.

Another Chicken in a Pot
Jennifer J. Gehman
Harrisburg, PA

Makes 4-6 servings

1-lb. bag baby carrots
1 small onion, diced
14½-oz. can green beans
3-lb. whole chicken, cut
 into serving-size pieces
2 tsp. salt
½ tsp. black pepper
½ cup chicken broth
¼ cup white wine
½-1 tsp. dried basil

1. Put carrots, onion, and beans on bottom of slow cooker. Add chicken. Top with salt, pepper, broth, and wine. Sprinkle with basil.
2. Cover. Cook on Low 8-10 hours, or High 3½-5 hours.

Savory Slow-Cooker Chicken
Sara Harter Fredette
Williamsburg, MA

Makes 4 servings

2½ lbs. chicken pieces,
 skinned
1 lb. fresh tomatoes,
 chopped, *or* 15-oz. can
 stewed tomatoes
2 Tbsp. white wine
1 bay leaf
¼ tsp. pepper
2 garlic cloves, minced
1 onion, chopped
½ cup chicken broth
1 tsp. dried thyme
1½ tsp. salt
2 cups broccoli, cut into
 bite-sized pieces

1. Combine all ingredients except broccoli in slow cooker.
2. Cover. Cook on Low 8-10 hours.
3. Add broccoli 30 minutes before serving.

Chicken and Vegetables
Rosanne Hankins
Stevensville, MD

Makes 6 servings

1 chicken, cut up
salt to taste
pepper to taste
1 bay leaf
2 tsp. lemon juice
¼ cup diced onions
¼ cup diced celery
1 lb. frozen mixed
 vegetables

1. Sprinkle salt and pepper over chicken and place chicken in slow cooker. Add bay leaf and lemon juice.
2. Cover. Cook on Low 6-8 hours, or High 3-5 hours. Remove chicken from bones. Reserve liquid, skimming fat if desired.
3. Cook ½ cup liquid, celery and onions in microwave on High for 2 minutes. Add frozen vegetables and microwave until cooked through.
4. Return all ingredients to slow cooker and cook on High 30 minutes.
5. Serve over cooked rice.

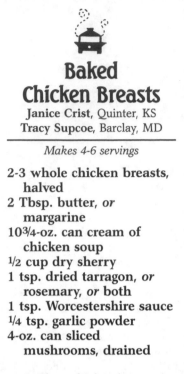

Baked Chicken Breasts

Janice Crist, Quinter, KS
Tracy Supcoe, Barclay, MD

Makes 4-6 servings

2-3 whole chicken breasts, halved
2 Tbsp. butter, *or* margarine
10¾-oz. can cream of chicken soup
½ cup dry sherry
1 tsp. dried tarragon, *or* rosemary, *or* both
1 tsp. Worcestershire sauce
¼ tsp. garlic powder
4-oz. can sliced mushrooms, drained

1. Place chicken breasts in slow cooker.
2. In saucepan, combine remaining ingredients. Heat until smooth and hot. Pour over chicken.
3. Cover. Cook on Low 8-10 hours.

Chicken Delicious

Janice Crist
Quinter, KS

Makes 8-12 servings

4-6 whole skinless chicken breasts, boned and halved
lemon juice
salt to taste
pepper to taste
celery salt to taste
paprika to taste
10¾-oz. can cream of mushroom soup
10¾-oz. can cream of celery soup
⅓ cup dry sherry, *or* white wine
grated Parmesan cheese

1. Season chicken with lemon juice, salt, pepper, celery salt, and paprika. Place in slow cooker.
2. Combine soups with sherry. Pour over chicken. Sprinkle with cheese.
3. Cover. Cook on Low 8-10 hours.
4. Serve with rice.

Chicken in Wine

Mary Seielstad
Sparks, NV

Makes 4-6 servings

2-3 lbs. chicken breasts, *or* pieces
10¾-oz. can cream of mushroom soup
10¾-oz. can French onion soup
1 cup dry white wine, *or* chicken broth

1. Put chicken in slow cooker.
2. Combine soups and wine. Pour over chicken.
3. Cover. Cook on Low 6-8 hours.
4. Serve over rice, pasta, or potatoes.

In place of ground meat in a recipe, use vegetarian burgers. Cut them up, and you won't need to brown the meat.
Sue Hamilton
Minooka, IL

Chicken in Mushroom Gravy

Rosemarie Fitzgerald
Gibsonia, PA
Audrey L. Kneer
Williamsfield, IL

Makes 6 servings

6 boneless, skinless
  chicken-breast halves
salt to taste
pepper to taste
1/4 cup dry white wine, *or*
  chicken broth
10 3/4-oz. can cream of
  mushroom soup
4-oz. can sliced
  mushrooms, drained

1. Place chicken in slow cooker. Season with salt and pepper.
2. Combine wine and soup. Pour over chicken. Top with mushrooms.
3. Cover. Cook on Low 7-9 hours.

Ruth's Slow-Cooker Chicken

Sara Harter Fredette
Williamsburg, MA

Makes 6 servings

6 boneless chicken-breast
  halves
10 3/4-oz. can cream of
  mushroom soup
1 pkg. dry mushroom soup
  mix
1/4-1/2 cup sour cream
4-oz. can mushrooms,
  drained

1. Combine chicken and soups in slow cooker.
2. Cover. Cook on Low 6-8 hours.
3. Just before serving, stir in sour cream and mushrooms. Reheat briefly.
4. Serve on noodles.

Note:
Leftover sauce makes a flavorful topping for grilled hamburgers.

Creamy Cooker Chicken

Violette Harris Denney
Carrollton, GA

Makes 6 servings

1 envelope dry onion soup
  mix
2 cups sour cream
10 3/4-oz. can cream of
  mushroom soup
6 boneless, skinless
  chicken-breast halves

1. Combine soup mix, sour cream, and cream of mushroom soup in slow cooker. Add chicken, pushing it down so it is submerged in the sauce.
2. Cover. Cook on Low 8 hours.
3. Serve over rice or noodles.

Mushroom Chicken

Brenda Pope
Dundee, OH

Makes 4 servings

1 lb. boneless, skinless chicken breast
1 pkg. dry chicken gravy mix
10¾-oz. can cream of mushroom, *or* chicken, soup
1 cup white wine
8-oz. pkg. cream cheese, softened

1. Put chicken in slow cooker. Sprinkle gravy mix on top. In separate bowl, combine soup and wine and pour over gravy mix.
2. Cover. Cook on Low 8 hours.
3. During last 30 minutes of cooking time, stir in cream cheese. Before serving, remove chicken (keeping it warm) and whisk the sauce until smooth.
4. Serve chicken and sauce over noodles or rice.

Creamy Mushroom Chicken

Patricia Howard
Albuquerque, NM

Makes 4-5 servings

2-3 lbs. chicken parts, skinned
4-oz. can mushrooms
2 10¾-oz. cans cream of chicken soup
1 envelope dry onion soup mix
½-1 cup chicken broth

1. Place chicken in slow cooker.
2. Combine remaining ingredients and pour over chicken.
3. Cover. Cook on Low 5-6 hours.

So You Forgot to Defrost!

Mary Seielstad
Sparks, NV

Makes 6 servings

6 boneless, skinless frozen chicken-breast halves
2 10¾-oz. cans cream of chicken soup
4-oz. can sliced mushrooms, *or* ½ cup sliced fresh mushrooms
¾ tsp. salt
¼ tsp. pepper

1. Place frozen chicken in slow cooker.
2. Mix together soup, mushrooms, salt, and pepper and pour over chicken.
3. Cover. Cook on Low 10-12 hours.
4. Serve over rice.

Continental Chicken

Jennifer J. Gehman, Harrisburg, PA
Gladys M. High, Ephrata, PA
L. Jean Moore, Pendleton, IN

Makes 4-6 servings

2¼-oz. pkg. dried beef
3-4 whole chicken breasts, halved, skinned, and boned
6-8 slices bacon
10¾-oz. can cream of mushroom soup, undiluted
¼ cup sour cream
¼ cup flour

1. Arrange dried beef in bottom of slow cooker.
2. Wrap each piece of chicken with a strip of bacon. Place on top of dried beef.
3. Combine soup, sour cream, and flour. Pour over chicken.
4. Cover. Cook on Low 7-9 hours, or High 3-4 hours.
5. Serve over hot buttered noodles.

Wanda's Chicken and Rice Casserole

Wanda Roth
Napoleon, OH

Makes 6-8 servings

1 cup long-grain rice, uncooked
3 cups water
2 tsp. chicken bouillon granules
10¾-oz can cream of chicken soup
16-oz. bag frozen broccoli
2 cups chopped, cooked chicken
¼ tsp. garlic powder
1 tsp. onion salt
1 cup grated cheddar cheese

1. Combine all ingredients in slow cooker.
2. Cook on High 3-4 hours.

Note:
If casserole is too runny, remove lid from slow cooker for 15 minutes while continuing to cook on High.

Chicken Rice Dish

Esther Porter
Minneapolis, MN

Makes 4 servings

1 cup cooked rice
10¾-oz. can cream of chicken soup
1 cup chicken broth
4 chicken thighs, partially cooked
10-oz. pkg. broccoli, frozen

1. Combine rice, soup, chicken broth, and chicken thighs. Place mixture in slow cooker.
2. Cover. Cook on Low 4 hours.
3. During last hour of cooking time, stir in broccoli.

Sharon's Chicken and Rice Casserole

Sharon Anders
Alburtis, PA

Makes 2 servings

10¾-oz. can cream of celery soup
2-oz. can sliced mushrooms, undrained
½ cup raw long grain rice
2 chicken-breast halves, skinned and boned
1 Tbsp. dry onion soup mix

1. Combine soup, mushrooms, and rice in greased slow cooker. Mix well.
2. Layer chicken breasts on top of mixture. Sprinkle with onion soup mix.
3. Cover. Cook on Low 4-6 hours.

Barbara's Chicken Rice Casserole

Barbara A. Yoder
Goshen, IN

Makes 6-8 servings

2 chicken bouillon cubes
2 cups hot water
½ cup margarine, melted
6-oz. box Uncle Ben's Long Grain and Wild Rice (Original Recipe), uncooked
4½-oz. jar sliced mushrooms
10-oz. can cooked chicken

1. Dissolve bouillon in hot water.
2. Combine all ingredients, including rice seasoning packet, in slow cooker.
3. Cover. Cook on High 2 hours, or until rice is tender.

Note:
To reduce salt in recipe, use 2 cups low- or no-sodium chicken broth instead of 2 chicken bouillon cubes and water.

Scalloped Potatoes and Chicken

Carol Sommers
Millersburg, OH

Makes 6-8 servings

¼ cup chopped green
   peppers
½ cup chopped onions
1½ cups diced Velveeta
   cheese
7-8 medium potatoes,
   sliced
salt to taste
10¾-oz. can cream of
   celery soup
1 soup can milk
3-4 whole boneless,
   skinless chicken breasts
salt to taste

1. Place layers of green peppers, onions, cheese, and potatoes and a sprinkling of salt in slow cooker.

2. Sprinkle salt over chicken breasts and lay on top of potatoes.

3. Combine soup and milk and pour into slow cooker, pushing meat down into liquid.

4. Cover. Cook on High 1½ hours. Reduce temperature to Low and cook 3-4 hours. Test that potatoes are soft. If not, continue cooking on Low another hour and test again, continuing to cook until potatoes are finished.

Scalloped Chicken

Carolyn W. Carmichael
Berkeley Heights, NJ

Makes 4 servings

5-oz. pkg. scalloped
   potatoes
scalloped potatoes dry
   seasoning pack
4 chicken-breast halves, *or*
   8 legs
10-oz. pkg. frozen peas
2 cups water

1. Put potatoes, seasoning pack, chicken, and peas in slow cooker. Pour water over all.

2. Cover. Cook on Low 8-10 hours, or High 4 hours.

Chicken-Vegetable Dish

Cheri Jantzen
Houston, TX

Makes 4 servings

4 skinless chicken-breast
   halves, with bone in
15-oz. can crushed
   tomatoes
10-oz. pkg. frozen green
   beans
2 cups water, *or* chicken
   broth
1 cup brown rice,
   uncooked
1 cup sliced mushrooms

2 carrots, chopped
1 onion, chopped
½ tsp. minced garlic
½ tsp. herb-blend
   seasoning
¼ tsp. dried tarragon

1. Combine all ingredients in slow cooker.

2. Cover. Cook on High 2 hours, and then on Low 3-5 hours.

Chicken and Vegetables

Jeanne Heyerly
Chenoa, IL

Makes 2 servings

2 medium potatoes,
   quartered
2-3 carrots, sliced
2 frozen chicken breasts, *or*
   2 frozen drumstick/thigh
   pieces
salt to taste
pepper to taste
1 medium onion, chopped
2 garlic cloves, minced
1-2 cups shredded cabbage
16-oz. can chicken broth

1. Place potatoes and carrots in slow cooker. Layer chicken on top. Sprinkle with salt, pepper, onion, and garlic. Top with cabbage. Carefully pour chicken broth around edges.

2. Cover. Cook on Low 8-9 hours.

California Chicken

Shirley Sears
Tiskilwa, IL

Makes 4-6 servings

3-lb. chicken, quartered
1 cup orange juice
1/3 cup chili sauce
2 Tbsp. soy sauce
1 Tbsp. molasses
1 tsp. dry mustard
1 tsp. garlic salt
2 Tbsp. chopped green
 peppers
3 medium oranges, peeled
 and separated into
 slices, *or* 13 1/2-oz. can
 mandarin oranges

1. Arrange chicken in slow cooker.
2. In separate bowl, combine juice, chili sauce, soy sauce, molasses, dry mustard, and garlic salt. Pour over chicken.
3. Cover. Cook on Low 8-9 hours.
4. Stir in green peppers and oranges. Heat 30 minutes longer.

Variation:

Stir 1 tsp. curry powder in with sauces and seasonings. Stir 1 small can pineapple chunks and juice in with green peppers and oranges.

Orange Chicken Leg Quarters

Kimberly Jensen
Bailey, CO

Makes 4-5 servings

4 chicken drumsticks
4 chicken thighs
1 cup strips of green and
 red bell peppers
1/2 cup canned chicken
 broth
1/2 cup prepared orange
 juice
1/2 cup ketchup
2 Tbsp. soy sauce
1 Tbsp. light molasses
1 Tbsp. prepared mustard
1/2 tsp. garlic salt
11-oz. can mandarin
 oranges
2 tsp. cornstarch
1 cup frozen peas
2 green onions, sliced

1. Place chicken in slow cooker. Top with pepper strips.
2. Combine broth, juice, ketchup, soy sauce, molasses, mustard, and garlic salt. Pour over chicken.
3. Cover. Cook on Low 6-7 hours.
4. Remove chicken and vegetables from slow cooker. Keep warm.
5. Measure out 1 cup of cooking sauce. Put in saucepan and bring to boil.
6. Drain oranges, reserving 1 Tbsp. juice. Stir cornstarch into reserved juice. Add to boiling sauce in pan.

7. Add peas to sauce and cook, stirring for 2-3 minutes until sauce thickens and peas are warm. Stir in oranges.
8. Arrange chicken pieces on platter of cooked white rice, fried cellophane noodles, or lo mein noodles. Pour orange sauce over chicken and rice or noodles. Top with sliced green onions.

Cranberry Chicken

Teena Wagner
Waterloo, ON

Makes 6-8 servings

3-4-lb. chicken pieces
1/2 tsp. salt
1/4 tsp. pepper
1/2 cup diced celery
1/2 cup diced onions
16-oz. can whole berry
 cranberry sauce
1 cup barbecue sauce

1. Combine all ingredients in slow cooker.
2. Cover. Bake on High for 4 hours, or on Low 6-8 hours.

175

Chicken Sweet and Sour

Willard E. Roth
Elkhart, IN

Makes 8 servings

4 medium potatoes, sliced
8 boneless, skinless
  chicken-breast halves
2 Tbsp. cider vinegar
1/4 tsp. ground nutmeg
1 tsp. dry basil, *or* 1 Tbsp.
  chopped fresh basil
2 Tbsp. brown sugar
1 cup orange juice
dried parsley flakes
17-oz. can waterpack
  sliced peaches, drained
fresh parsley
fresh orange slices

1. Place potatoes in greased slow cooker. Arrange chicken on top.
2. In separate bowl, combine vinegar, nutmeg, basil, brown sugar, and orange juice. Pour over chicken. Sprinkle with parsley.
3. Cover. Cook on Low 6 hours.
4. Remove chicken and potatoes from sauce and arrange on warm platter.
5. Turn cooker to High. Add peaches. When warm, spoon peaches and sauce over chicken and potatoes. Garnish with fresh parsley and orange slices.

Chicken with Tropical Barbecue Sauce

Lois Stoltzfus
Honey Brook, PA

Makes 6 servings

1/4 cup molasses
2 Tbsp. cider vinegar
2 Tbsp. Worcestershire
  sauce
2 tsp. prepared mustard
1/8-1/4 tsp. hot pepper sauce
2 Tbsp. orange juice
3 whole chicken breasts,
  halved

1. Combine molasses, vinegar, Worcestershire sauce, mustard, hot pepper sauce, and orange juice. Brush over chicken.
2. Place chicken in slow cooker.
3. Cover. Cook on Low 7-9 hours, or High 3-4 hours.

Fruited Barbecue Chicken

Barbara Katrine Rose
Woodbridge, VA

Makes 4-6 servings

29-oz. can tomato sauce
20-oz. can unsweetened
  crushed pineapple,
  undrained
2 Tbsp. brown sugar
3 Tbsp. vinegar
1 Tbsp. instant minced
  onion
1 tsp. paprika
2 tsp. Worcestershire sauce
1/4 tsp. garlic powder
1/8 tsp. pepper
3 lbs. chicken, skinned and
  cubed
11-oz. can mandarin
  oranges, drained

1. Combine all ingredients except chicken and oranges. Add chicken pieces.
2. Cover. Cook on High 4 hours.
3. Just before serving, stir in oranges. Serve over hot rice.

When I use mushrooms or green peppers in the slow cooker, I usually stir them in during the last hour so they don't get too mushy.

Trudy Kutter
Corfu, NY

Orange Chicken and Sweet Potatoes

Kimberlee Greenawalt
Harrisonburg, VA

Makes 6 servings

2-3 sweet potatoes, peeled and sliced
3 whole chicken breasts, halved
2/3 cup flour
1 tsp. salt
1 tsp. nutmeg
1/2 tsp. cinnamon
dash pepper
dash garlic powder
10³/4-oz. can cream of celery, *or* cream of chicken, soup
4-oz. can sliced mushrooms, drained
1/2 cup orange juice
1/2 tsp. grated orange rind
2 tsp. brown sugar
3 Tbsp. flour

1. Place sweet potatoes in bottom of slow cooker.
2. Rinse chicken breasts and pat dry. Combine flour, salt, nutmeg, cinnamon, pepper, and garlic powder. Thoroughly coat chicken in flour mixture. Place on top of sweet potatoes.
3. Combine soup with remaining ingredients. Stir well. Pour over chicken breasts.
4. Cover. Cook on Low 8-10 hours, or High 3-4 hours.
5. Serve over rice.

Orange-Glazed Chicken Breasts

Leona Miller
Millersburg, OH

Makes 6 servings

6-oz. can frozen orange juice concentrate, thawed
1/2 tsp. dried marjoram
6 boneless, skinless chicken-breast halves
1/4 cup cold water
2 Tbsp. cornstarch

1. Combine orange juice and marjoram in shallow dish. Dip each breast in orange-juice mixture and place in slow cooker. Pour remaining sauce over breasts.
2. Cover. Cook on Low 7-9 hours, or High 3¹/2-4 hours.
3. Remove chicken from slow cooker. Turn cooker to High and cover.
4. Combine water and cornstarch. Stir into liquid in slow cooker. Place cover slightly ajar on slow cooker. Cook until sauce is thick and bubbly, about 15-20 minutes. Serve over chicken.

Variation:
To increase "spice" in dish, add 1/2-1 tsp. Worcestershire sauce to orange juice-marjoram glaze.

Sweet and Sour Chicken

Bernice A. Esau
North Newton, KS

Makes 6 servings

1¹/2 cups sliced carrots
1 large green pepper, chopped
1 medium onion, chopped
2 Tbsp. quick-cooking tapioca
2¹/2-3 lb. chicken, cut into serving-size pieces
8-oz. can pineapple chunks in juice
1/3 cup brown sugar
1/3 cup vinegar
1 Tbsp. soy sauce
1/2 tsp. instant chicken bouillon
1/4 tsp. garlic powder
1/4 tsp. ground ginger, *or* 1/2 tsp. freshly grated ginger
1 tsp. salt

1. Place vegetables in bottom of slow cooker. Sprinkle with tapioca. Add chicken.
2. In separate bowl, combine pineapple, brown sugar, vinegar, soy sauce, bouillon, garlic powder, ginger, and salt. Pour over chicken.
3. Cover. Cook on Low 8-10 hours.
4. Serve over cooked rice.

Easy Teriyaki Chicken

Barbara Shie
Colorado Springs, CO

Makes 5-6 servings

2-3 lbs. skinless chicken pieces
20-oz. can pineapple chunks
dash of ground ginger
1 cup teriyaki sauce

1. Place chicken in slow cooker. Pour remaining ingredients over chicken.
2. Cover. Cook on Low 6-8 hours, or High 4-6 hours.

Creamy Chicken Italiano

Sharon Easter, Yuba City, CA
Rebecca Meyerkorth, Wamego, KS
Bonnie Milller, Cochranville, PA

Makes 4 servings

4 boneless, skinless chicken-breast halves
1 envelope dry Italian salad dressing mix
1/4 cup water
8-oz. pkg. cream cheese, softened
10 3/4-oz. can cream of chicken soup
4-oz. can mushroom stems and pieces, drained

1. Place chicken in slow cooker.
2. Combine salad dressing mix and water. Pour over chicken.
3. Cover. Cook on Low 3 hours.
4. Combine cheese and soup until blended. Stir in mushrooms. Pour over chicken.
5. Cover. Cook on Low 1 hour, or until chicken juices run clear.
6. Serve over noodles or rice.

Creamy Mushroom Chicken

Barbara Shie
Colorado Springs, CO

Makes 4-6 servings

4-6 boneless, skinless chicken-breast halves
12-oz. jar mushroom gravy
1 cup milk
8-oz. pkg. cream cheese, cubed
4 1/2-oz. can chopped green chilies
1 pkg. dry Italian salad dressing

1. Combine all ingredients in slow cooker.
2. Cover. Cook on Low 6 hours.
3. Serve over noodles or rice.

Super Easy Chicken

Mary Seielstad
Sparks, NV

Makes 4 servings

4 frozen chicken-breast halves
1 pkg. dry Italian dressing mix
1 cup warm water, *or* chicken stock

1. Place chicken in slow cooker. Sprinkle with dressing mix. Pour water over chicken.
2. Cover. Cook on Low 8-10 hours.

Ann's Chicken Cacciatore

Ann Driscoll
Albuquerque, NM

Makes 6-8 servings

1 large onion, thinly sliced
2 1/2-3 lb. chicken, cut up
2 6-oz. cans tomato paste
4-oz. can sliced mushrooms, drained
1 tsp. salt
1/4 cup dry white wine
1/4 tsp. pepper
1-2 garlic cloves, minced
1-2 tsp. dried oregano
1/2 tsp. dried basil

½ tsp. celery seed,
    optional
1 bay leaf

1. Place onion in slow cooker. Add chicken.
2. Combine remaining ingredients. Pour over chicken.
3. Cover. Cook on Low 7-9 hours, or High 3-4 hours.
4. Serve over spaghetti.

Darla's Chicken Cacciatore

Darla Sathre
Baxter, MN

Makes 6 servings

2 onions, thinly sliced
4 boneless chicken breasts,
    cubed
3 garlic cloves, minced
¼ tsp. pepper
2 tsp. dried oregano
1 tsp. dried basil
1 bay leaf
2 15-oz. cans diced
    tomatoes
8-oz. can tomato sauce
4-oz. can sliced
    mushrooms

1. Place onions in bottom of slow cooker. Add remaining ingredients.
2. Cover. Cook on Low 8 hours.
3. Serve over hot spaghetti.

Dorothea's Chicken Cacciatore

Dorothea K. Ladd
Ballston Lake, NY

Makes 4-6 servings

1 frying chicken, cut into
    serving-size pieces
¼ cup flour
2 Tbsp. oil
1 garlic clove, minced
46-oz. can tomato juice, *or*
    V-8 juice
12-oz. can tomato paste
2 Tbsp. dried parsley
2 Tbsp. sugar
2 tsp. salt
1 Tbsp. dried oregano
½ tsp. dried thyme
1 bay leaf

1. Put flour and chicken pieces in bag and shake to coat. Brown chicken and garlic in oil in skillet. Transfer chicken pieces and garlic to slow cooker.
2. Mix together tomato juice, tomato paste, parsley, sugar, salt, oregano, thyme, and bay leaf. Pour over chicken and garlic.
3. Cover. Cook on Low 8-10 hours.
4. Serve over spaghetti or rice.

Dale & Shari's Chicken Cacciatore

Dale and Shari Mast
Harrisonburg, VA

Makes 4 servings

4 chicken quarters, *or*
    4 boneless, skinless
    chicken-breast halves
15-oz. can tomato, *or*
    spaghetti, sauce
4-oz. can sliced
    mushrooms, drained
½ cup water
1 tsp. dry chicken broth
    granules
½ tsp. Italian seasoning

1. Place chicken in slow cooker. Pour on sauce, mushrooms, and water. Sprinkle with granules and seasoning.
2. Cover. Cook on High 3-4 hours, or Low 6-8 hours.
3. Serve over rice.

Chicken Parmigiana
Brenda Pope
Dundee, OH

Makes 6 servings

1 egg
1 tsp. salt
1/4 tsp. pepper
6 boneless, skinless
    chicken-breast halves
1 cup Italian bread crumbs
2-4 Tbsp. butter
14-oz. jar pizza sauce
6 slices mozzarella cheese
grated Parmesan cheese

1. Beat egg, salt, and pepper together. Dip chicken into egg and coat with bread crumbs. Saute chicken in butter in skillet. Arrange chicken in slow cooker.

2. Pour pizza sauce over chicken.

3. Cover. Cook on Low 6-8 hours.

4. Layer mozzarella cheese over top and sprinkle with Parmesan cheese. Cook an additional 15 minutes.

Easy Chicken A la King
Jenny R. Unternahrer
Wayland, IA

Makes 4 servings

1 1/2 lbs. boneless, skinless
    chicken breasts
10 3/4-oz. can cream of
    chicken soup
3 Tbsp. flour
1/4 tsp. pepper
9-oz. pkg. frozen peas and
    onions, thawed and
    drained
2 Tbsp. chopped pimentos
1/2 tsp. paprika

1. Cut chicken into bite-sized pieces and place in slow cooker.

2. Combine soup, flour, and pepper. Pour over chicken. Do not stir.

3. Cover. Cook on High 2 1/2 hours, or Low 5-5 1/2 hours.

4. Stir in peas and onions, pimentos, and paprika.

5. Cover. Cook on High 20-30 minutes.

Variation:
Add 1/4-1/2 cup chopped green peppers to Step 2.
Sharon Brubaker
Myerstown, PA

Coq au Vin
Kimberlee Greenawalt
Harrisonburg, VA

Makes 6 servings

2 cups frozen pearl onions,
    thawed
4 thick slices bacon, fried
    and crumbled
1 cup sliced button
    mushrooms
1 garlic clove, minced
1 tsp. dried thyme leaves
1/8 tsp. black pepper
6 boneless, skinless
    chicken-breast halves
1/2 cup dry red wine
3/4 cup chicken broth
1/4 cup tomato paste
3 Tbsp. flour

1. Layer ingredients in slow cooker in the following order: onions, bacon, mushrooms, garlic, thyme, pepper, chicken, wine, broth.

2. Cover. Cook on Low 6-8 hours.

3. Remove chicken and vegetables. Cover and keep warm.

4. Ladle 1/2 cup cooking liquid into small bowl. Cool slightly. Turn slow cooker to High. Cover. Mix reserved liquid, tomato paste, and flour until smooth. Return mixture to slow cooker, cover, and cook 15 minutes, or until thickened.

5. Serve chicken, vegetables, and sauce over noodles.

> When using raw meat, begin by cooking it for 1-2 hours on High to avoid cooking it too slowly.
> **Joy Sutter**
> Iowa City, IA

Lemon Garlic Chicken

Cindy Krestynick
Glen Lyon, PA

Makes 4 servings

1 tsp. dried oregano
1/2 tsp. seasoned salt
1/4 tsp. pepper
2 lbs. chicken-breast halves, skinned and rinsed
2 Tbsp. butter, *or* margarine
1/4 cup water
3 Tbsp. lemon juice
2 garlic cloves, minced
1 tsp. chicken bouillon granules
1 tsp. minced fresh parsley

1. Combine oregano, salt, and pepper. Rub all of mixture into chicken. Brown chicken in butter or margarine in skillet. Transfer to slow cooker.

2. Place water, lemon juice, garlic, and bouillon cubes in skillet. Bring to boil, loosening browned bits from skillet. Pour over chicken.

3. Cover. Cook on High 2-2 1/2 hours, or Low 4-5 hours.

4. Add parsley and baste chicken. Cover. Cook on High 15-30 minutes, until chicken is tender.

Lemon Honey Chicken

Carolyn W. Carmichael
Berkeley Heights, NJ

Makes 4-6 servings

1 lemon
1 whole roasting chicken, rinsed
1/2 cup orange juice
1/2 cup honey

1. Pierce lemon with fork. Place in chicken cavity. Place chicken in slow cooker.

2. Combine orange juice and honey. Pour over chicken.

3. Cover. Cook on Low 8 hours. Remove lemon and squeeze over chicken.

4. Carve chicken and serve.

Melanie's Chicken Cordon Bleu

Melanie Thrower
McPherson, KS

Makes 6 servings

3 whole chicken breasts, split and deboned
6 pieces thinly sliced ham
6 slices Swiss cheese
salt to taste
pepper to taste
6 slices bacon
1/4 cup water
1 tsp. chicken bouillon granules
1/2 cup white cooking wine
1 tsp. cornstarch
1/4 cup cold water

1. Flatten chicken to 1/8-1/4-inch thickness. Place a slice of ham and a slice of cheese on top of each flattened breast. Sprinkle with salt and pepper. Roll up and wrap with strip of bacon. Secure with toothpick. Place in slow cooker.

2. Combine 1/4 cup water, granules, and wine. Pour into slow cooker.

3. Cover. Cook on High 4 hours.

4. Combine cornstarch and 1/4 cup cold water. Add to slow cooker. Cook until sauce thickens.

Chicken Cordon Bleu

Barbara Nolan
Pleasant Valley, NY
Jenny R. Unternahrer,
Wayland, IA

Makes 6 servings

3 whole boneless, skinless chicken breasts
3 large Swiss cheese slices, halved
3 large, thin ham slices, halved
2 Tbsp. margarine
10³/4-oz. can cream of mushroom soup, *or* cream of chicken soup
3 Tbsp. milk
3 Tbsp. sherry, optional
¼ tsp. pepper

1. Cut whole breasts in half. Flatten each half with wooden mallet. Cover each half breast with half slice of cheese and ham. Roll up and secure with toothpicks. Brown each chicken roll in margarine in skillet. Transfer to slow cooker.
2. Combine remaining ingredients. Pour over chicken, making sure chicken pieces are fully covered.
3. Cover. Cook on Low 4-5 hours.

Stuffed Chicken Rolls

Lois M. Martin, Lititz, PA
Renee Shirk, Mount Joy, PA

Makes 6 servings

6 large boneless, skinless chicken-breast halves
6 slices fully cooked ham
6 slices Swiss cheese
¼ cup flour
¼ cup grated Parmesan cheese
½ tsp. rubbed sage
¼ tsp. paprika
¼ tsp. pepper
¼ cup oil
10³/4-oz. can cream of chicken soup
½ cup chicken broth
chopped fresh parsley, optional

1. Flatten chicken to ⅛-inch thickness. Place ham and cheese slices on each breast. Roll up and tuck in ends. Secure with toothpick.
2. Combine flour, Parmesan cheese, sage, paprika, and pepper. Coat chicken on all sides. Cover and refrigerate for 1 hour.
3. Brown chicken in oil in skillet. Transfer to slow cooker.
4. Combine soup and broth. Pour over chicken.
5. Cover. Cook on Low 4-5 hours.
6. Remove toothpicks. Garnish with parsley.

Ham and Swiss Chicken

Nanci Keatley, Salem, OR
Janice Yoskovich
Carmichaels, PA

Makes 6 servings

2 eggs, beaten
1½ cups milk
2 Tbsp. butter, melted
½ cup chopped celery
¼ cup diced onion
10 slices bread, cubed
12 thin slices deli ham, rolled up
2 cups grated Swiss cheese
2½ cups cubed cooked chicken
10³/4-oz. can cream of chicken soup
½ cup milk

1. Combine eggs and milk. Add butter, celery, and onion. Stir in bread cubes. Place half of mixture in greased slow cooker. Top with half the ham, cheese, and chicken.
2. Combine soup and milk. Pour half over chicken. Repeat layers.
3. Cover. Cook on Low 4-5 hours.

Dawn's Barbecued Chicken

Dawn M. Propst
Levittown, PA

Makes 6 servings

3 whole boneless, skinless chicken breasts, cut in half
¼ cup flour
¼ cup oil
1 medium onion, sliced
1 green, *or* yellow, pepper, sliced
½ cup chopped celery
2 Tbsp. Worcestershire sauce
1 cup ketchup
2 cups water
¼ tsp. salt
¼ tsp. paprika

1. Roll chicken breasts in flour. Brown in oil in skillet. Transfer chicken to slow cooker.
2. Saute onion, peppers, and celery in skillet, also, cooking until tender. Add remaining ingredients and bring to boil. Pour over chicken.
3. Cover. Cook on Low 8 hours.
4. Serve over noodles or rice.

Marcy's Barbecued Chicken

Marcy Engle
Harrisonburg, VA

Makes 6 servings

2 lbs. chicken pieces
¼ cup flour
1 cup ketchup
2 cups water
⅓ cup Worcestershire sauce
1 tsp. chili powder
½ tsp. salt
½ tsp. pepper
2 drops Tabasco sauce
¼ tsp. garlic salt
¼ tsp. onion salt

1. Dust chicken with flour. Transfer to slow cooker.
2. Combine remaining ingredients. Pour over chicken.
3. Cover. Cook on Low 5 hours.

Oriental Chicken

Marcia S. Myer
Manheim, PA

Makes 6 servings

2 2½-3 lb. broiler/fryer chickens, cut up
¼ cup flour
1½ tsp. salt
2 Tbsp. oil
6-oz. can lemonade concentrate, thawed
2 Tbsp. brown sugar
3 Tbsp. ketchup
1 Tbsp. vinegar
2 Tbsp. cold water
2 Tbsp. cornstarch

1. Combine flour with salt. Coat chicken. Brown chicken in oil in skillet. Transfer to slow cooker.
2. Combine lemonade concentrate, brown sugar, ketchup, and vinegar. Pour over chicken.
3. Cover. Cook on High 3-4 hours.
4. Remove chicken. Pour liquid into saucepan. Return chicken to cooker and cover to keep warm. Skim fat from liquid.
5. Combine water and cornstarch. Stir into hot liquid. Cook and stir until thick and bubbly.
6. Serve chicken and sauce over rice.

Awfully Easy Chicken

Martha Hershey
Ronks, PA

Makes 8 servings

1/2 cup water
4-lb. chicken legs and
  thighs
14-oz. bottle barbecue
  sauce

1. Place water in bottom of
slow cooker. Add chicken.
Pour barbecue sauce over
top.
2. Cover. Cook on Low 8
hours.

Note:
Serve any additional sauce
over mashed potatoes.
Judy Denney
Lawrenceville, GA

Variation:
Place 3 large onions, quartered or sliced, in bottom of
slow cooker. Then add
chicken and sauce.
Barbara J. Fabel
Wausau, WI

Tracy's Barbecued Chicken Wings

Tracy Supcoe
Barclay, MD

Makes 8 full-sized servings

4-lb. chicken wings
2 large onions, chopped
2 6-oz. cans tomato paste
2 large garlic cloves,
  minced
1/4 cup Worcestershire
  sauce
1/4 cup cider vinegar
1/2 cup brown sugar
1/2 cup sweet pickle relish
1/2 cup red, *or* white, wine
2 tsp. salt
2 tsp. dry mustard

1. Cut off wing tips. Cut
wings at joint. Place in slow
cooker.
2. Combine remaining
ingredients. Add to slow
cooker. Stir.
3. Cover. Cook on Low 5-6
hours.

Mary's Chicken Wings

Mary Casey
Scranton, PA

Makes 8-12 full-sized servings

3-6 lbs. chicken wings
1-3 Tbsp. oil
3/4-1 cup vinegar
1/2 cup ketchup
2 Tbsp. sugar
2 Tbsp. Worcestershire
  sauce
3 garlic cloves, minced
1 Tbsp. dry mustard
1 tsp. paprika
1/2-1 tsp. salt
1/8 tsp. pepper

1. Brown wings in oil in
skillet, or brush wings with
oil and broil, watching carefully so they do not burn.
2. Combine remaining
ingredients in 5-6 1/2-quart
slow cooker. Add wings. Stir
gently so that they are all
well covered with sauce.
3. Cover. Cook on Low 4-6
hours, or until tender.

Don't have enough time? A lot of dishes can be made in
less time by increasing the temperature to High and cooking
the dish for about half the time as is necessary on Low.
Jenny R. Unternahrer
Wayland, IA

Rosemarie's Barbecued Chicken Wings

Rosemarie Fitzgerald
Gibsonia, PA

Makes 10 full-sized servings

5 lbs. chicken wings, tips
  cut off
12-oz. bottle chili sauce
1/3 cup lemon juice
1 Tbsp. Worcestershire
  sauce
2 Tbsp. molasses
1 tsp. salt
2 tsp. chili powder
1/4 tsp. hot pepper sauce
dash garlic powder

1. Place wings in cooker.
2. Combine remaining ingredients and pour over chicken.
3. Cover. Cook on Low 6-8 hours, or High 2-3 hours.

Note:
These wings are also a great appetizer, yielding about 15 appetizer-size servings.

Take any leftover chicken off the bone and combine with leftover sauce. Serve over cooked pasta for a second meal.

Donna's Chicken Wings

Donna Conto
Saylorsburg, PA

Makes 10 full-sized servings

5 lbs. chicken wings
28-oz. jar spaghetti sauce
1 Tbsp. Worcestershire
  sauce
1 Tbsp. molasses
1 Tbsp. prepared mustard
1 tsp. salt
1/2 tsp. pepper

1. Place wings in slow cooker.
2. Combine remaining ingredients. Pour over wings and stir them gently, making sure all are covered with sauce.
3. Cover. Cook on High 3-4 hours.

Sweet Aromatic Chicken

Anne Townsend
Albuquerque, NM

Makes 4 servings

1/2 cup coconut milk
1/2 cup water
8 chicken thighs, skinned
1/2 cup brown sugar
2 Tbsp. soy sauce
1/8 tsp. ground cloves
2 garlic cloves, minced

1. Combine coconut milk and water. Pour into greased slow cooker.
2. Add remaining ingredients in order listed.
3. Cover. Cook on Low 5-6 hours.

Note:
What to do with leftover coconut milk?
1. Two or three spoonfuls over vanilla ice cream, topped with a cherry, makes a flavorful, quick dessert.
2. Family Pina Coladas are good. Pour the coconut milk into a pitcher and add one large can pineapple juice, along with some ice cubes. Decorate with pineapple chunks and cherries.

185

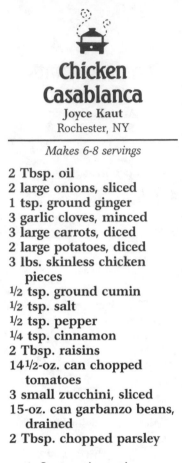

Chicken Casablanca

Joyce Kaut
Rochester, NY

Makes 6-8 servings

2 Tbsp. oil
2 large onions, sliced
1 tsp. ground ginger
3 garlic cloves, minced
3 large carrots, diced
2 large potatoes, diced
3 lbs. skinless chicken
  pieces
1/2 tsp. ground cumin
1/2 tsp. salt
1/2 tsp. pepper
1/4 tsp. cinnamon
2 Tbsp. raisins
14 1/2-oz. can chopped
  tomatoes
3 small zucchini, sliced
15-oz. can garbanzo beans,
  drained
2 Tbsp. chopped parsley

1. Saute onions, ginger, and garlic in oil in skillet. (Reserve oil.) Transfer to slow cooker. Add carrots and potatoes.
2. Brown chicken over medium heat in reserved oil. Transfer to slow cooker. Mix gently with vegetables.
3. Combine seasonings in separate bowl. Sprinkle over chicken and vegetables. Add raisins and tomatoes.
4. Cover. Cook on High 4-6 hours.
5. Add sliced zucchini, beans, and parsley 30 minutes before serving.

6. Serve over cooked rice or couscous.

Variation:
Add 1/2 tsp. turmeric and 1/4 tsp. cayenne pepper to Step 3.
Michelle Mann
Mt. Joy, PA

Chicken Kapaman

Judy Govotsus
Monrovia, MD

Makes 4-6 servings

4-6 potatoes, quartered
4-6 carrots, sliced
2-3-lbs. chicken pieces
2 onions, chopped
1 whole garlic bulb,
  minced
2 Tbsp. tomato paste
1 1/2 cups water
1 cinnamon stick
1/2 tsp. salt
1/4 tsp. pepper

1. Layer potatoes and carrots in slow cooker. Add chicken.
2. In separate bowl, mix remaining ingredients together and pour over vegetables and chicken in cooker.
3. Cover. Cook on High 4 hours. Remove lid and cook on Low an additional 1-1 1/2 hours.

Greek Chicken

Judy Govotsus
Monrovia, MD

Makes 4-6 servings

4-6 potatoes, quartered
2-3 lbs. chicken pieces
2 large onions, quartered
1 whole bulb garlic,
  minced
3 tsp. dried oregano
1 tsp. salt
1/2 tsp. pepper
1 Tbsp. olive oil

1. Place potatoes in bottom of slow cooker. Add chicken, onions, and garlic. Sprinkle with seasonings. Top with oil.
2. Cover. Cook on High 5-6 hours, or on Low 9-10 hours.

Cathy's Chicken Creole

Cathy Boshart
Lebanon, PA

Makes 6 servings

2 Tbsp. butter
half a medium green pepper, chopped
2 medium onions, chopped
1/2 cup chopped celery
1 lb. 4 oz.-can tomatoes
1/2 tsp. pepper, *or* your choice of dried herbs
1 1/2 tsp. salt, *or* your choice of dried herbs
1/8 tsp. red pepper
1 cup water
2 Tbsp. cornstarch
1 tsp. sugar
1 1/2 Tbsp. cold water
2 cups cooked and cubed chicken
6 green, *or* black, olives, sliced
1/2 cup sliced mushrooms

1. Melt butter in slow cooker. Add green pepper, onions, and celery. Heat.
2. Add tomatoes, pepper, salt and 1 cup water.
3. Cover. Cook on High while preparing remaining ingredients.
4. Combine cornstarch and sugar. Add 1 1/2 Tbsp. cold water and make a smooth paste. Stir into mixture in slow cooker. Add chicken, olives, and mushrooms.
5. Cover. Cook on Low 2-3 hours.

Barbara's Creole Chicken

Barbara McGinnis
Jupiter, FL

Makes 4 servings

2 (.9-oz.) pkgs. dry bearnaise sauce mix
1/2 cup dry white wine
1 lb. boneless, skinless chicken breasts, cut into bite-sized cubes
9-oz. pkg. frozen mixed vegetables
1 lb. cooked ham, cubed
1 lb. red potatoes, cubed
1 red bell pepper, chopped
1 green bell pepper, chopped
3 shallots, minced
1/2 tsp. garlic powder
1/2 tsp. turmeric powder
1/2 tsp. dried tarragon

1. Combine all ingredients in slow cooker.
2. Cover. Cook on Low 6 hours.

Chicken Curry

Maricarol Magill
Freehold, NJ

Makes 4 servings

4 boneless, skinless chicken-breast halves
1 small onion, chopped
2 sweet potatoes (about 1 1/2 lbs.), cubed
2/3 cup orange juice
1 garlic clove, minced
1 tsp. chicken bouillon granules
1 tsp. salt
1/4 tsp. pepper
4 tsp. curry powder
2 Tbsp. cornstarch
2 Tbsp. cold water
rice

Toppings:
sliced green onions
shredded coconut
peanuts
raisins

1. Place chicken in slow cooker. Cover with onions and sweet potatoes.
2. Combine orange juice, garlic, chicken bouillon granules, salt, pepper, and curry powder. Pour over vegetables.
3. Cover. Cook on Low 5-6 hours.
4. Remove chicken and vegetables and keep warm.
5. Turn slow cooker to High. Dissolve cornstarch in cold water. Stir into sauce in slow cooker. Cover. Cook on High 15-20 minutes.
6. Serve chicken and sauce over rice. Sprinkle with your choice of toppings.

Groundnut Stew

Cathy Boshart
Lebanon, PA

Makes 8 servings

2 green peppers, cut into
   rings
1 medium onion, cut into
   rings
2 Tbsp. shortening
6-oz. can tomato paste
3/4 cup peanut butter
3 cups chicken broth
1 1/2 tsp. salt
1 tsp. chili powder
1 tsp. sugar
1/2 tsp. ground nutmeg
4 cups cubed, cooked
   chicken
6 cups hot cooked rice

Toppings:
coconut
peanuts
raisins
hard-boiled eggs, chopped
bananas, chopped
oranges, cut up
eggplant, chopped
apples, chopped
tomatoes, chopped
carrots, shredded
green pepper, chopped
onion, chopped
pineapple, crushed

1. Cook and stir green pepper and onion rings in shortening in hot slow cooker.
2. Combine tomato paste and peanut butter. Stir into slow cooker.
3. Add broth and seasonings. Stir in chicken.
4. Cover. Cook on Low 3 hours.

5. Serve over hot rice with your choice of toppings.

Mulligan Stew

Carol Ambrose
Ripon, CA

Makes 8-10 servings

3-lb. stewing hen, cut up,
   or 4 lbs. chicken legs
   and thighs
1 1/2 tsp. salt
1/4-lb. salt pork, *or* bacon,
   cut in 1-inch squares
4 cups tomatoes, peeled
   and sliced
2 cups fresh corn, *or* 1-lb.
   pkg. frozen corn
1 cup coarsely chopped
   potatoes
10-oz. pkg. lima beans,
   frozen
1/2 cup chopped onions
1 tsp. salt
1/4 tsp. pepper
dash of cayenne pepper

1. Place chicken in very large slow cooker. Add water to cover. Add 1 1/2 tsp. salt.
2. Cover. Cook on Low 2 hours. Add more water if needed.
3. Add remaining ingredients. (If you don't have a large cooker, divide the stew between 2 average-sized ones.) Simmer on Low 5 hours longer.

Notes:
1. Flavor improves if stew is refrigerated and reheated

the next day. May also be made in advance and frozen.
2. You can debone the chicken after the first cooking for 2 hours. Stir chicken pieces back into cooker with other ingredients and continue with directions above.

African
Chicken Treat

Anne Townsend
Albuquerque, NM

Makes 4 servings

1 1/2 cups water
2 tsp. chicken bouillon
   granules
2 ribs celery, thinly sliced
2 onions, thinly sliced
1 red bell pepper, sliced
1 green bell pepper, sliced
8 chicken thighs, skinned
1/2 cup extra crunchy
   peanut butter
crushed chili pepper of
   your choice

1. Combine water, chicken bouillon granules, celery, onions, and peppers in slow cooker.
2. Spread peanut butter over both sides of chicken pieces. Sprinkle with chili pepper. Place on top of ingredients in slow cooker.
3. Cover. Cook on Low 5-6 hours.

Gran's Big Potluck
Carol Ambrose
Ripon, CA

Makes 10-15 servings

2½-3 lb. stewing hen, cut
    into pieces
½ lb. stewing beef, cubed
½-lb. veal shoulder, *or* roast,
    cubed
1½ qts. water
½ lb. small red potatoes,
    cubed
½ lb. small onions, cut in
    half
1 cup sliced carrots
1 cup chopped celery
1 green pepper, chopped
1-lb. pkg. frozen lima beans
1 cup okra, whole *or* diced,
    fresh *or* frozen
1 cup whole kernel corn
8-oz. can whole tomatoes
    with juice
15-oz. can tomato puree
1 tsp. salt
¼-½ tsp. pepper
1 tsp. dry mustard
½ tsp. chili powder
¼ cup chopped fresh
    parsley

1. Combine all ingredients
except last 5 seasonings in one
very large slow cooker, or
divide between two medium-
sized ones.
    2. Cover. Cook on Low 10-
12 hours. Add seasonings during last hour of cooking.

Note:
    You may want to debone the
chicken and mix it back into
the cooker before serving the
meal.

Marsha's Chicken Enchilada Casserole
Marsha Sabus
Fallbrook, CA

Makes 4-6 servings

1 onion, chopped
1 garlic clove, minced
1 Tbsp. oil
10-oz. can enchilada sauce
8-oz. can tomato sauce
salt to taste
pepper to taste
8 corn tortillas
3 boneless chicken-breast
    halves, cooked and cubed
15-oz. can ranch-style beans,
    drained
11-oz. can Mexicorn, drained
¾-lb. cheddar cheese, grated
2¼-oz. can sliced black
    olives, drained

1. Saute onion and garlic in
oil in saucepan. Stir in enchilada sauce and tomato sauce.
Season with salt and pepper.
    2. Place two tortillas in bot-
tom of slow cooker. Layer one-
third chicken on top. Top with
one-third sauce mixture, one-
third beans, one-third corn,
one-third cheese, and one-third
black olives. Repeat layers 2
more times. Top with 2 tortillas.
    3. Cover. Cook on Low 6-8
hours.

Variation:
    Substitute 1 lb. cooked and
drained hamburger for the
chicken.

Chicken Olé
Barb Yoder
Angola, IN

Makes 8 servings

10¾-oz. can cream of
    mushroom soup
10¾-oz. can cream of
    chicken soup
1 cup sour cream
2 Tbsp. grated onion
1½ cups grated cheddar
    cheese
12 flour tortillas, each torn
    into 6-8 pieces
3-4 cups cubed, cooked
    chicken
7-oz. jar salsa
½ cup grated cheddar
    cheese

1. In separate bowl, com-
bine soups, sour cream,
onion, and 1½ cups cheese.
    2. Place one-third of each
of the following in layers in
slow cooker: torn tortillas,
soup mixture, chicken, and
salsa. Repeat layers 2 more
times.
    3. Cover. Cook on Low 4-5
hours. (This recipe does not
respond well to cooking on
High.)
    4. Gently stir. Sprinkle
with remaining ½ cup
cheese. Cover. Cook on Low
another 15-30 minutes.
    5. Serve with tortilla chips
and lettuce.

Chicken Enchilada Casserole

Jane Talso
Albuquerque, NM

Makes 6-8 servings

3-4-lb. chicken
1 medium onion, finely chopped
1 Tbsp. oil
10¾-oz. can cream of mushroom soup
10¾-oz. can cream of chicken soup
1 cup sour cream
10-oz. can green enchilada sauce
4.5-oz. can peeled, diced green chilies
20 corn tortillas
3 cups shredded cheddar cheese

1. Boil chicken. Shred meat and discard bones and skin.
2. Saute onion in oil in saucepan until translucent. Stir in soups, sour cream, green enchilada sauce, and chilies. Heat until warm.
3. Tear tortillas into bite-sized pieces.
4. Layer half of sauce, chicken, tortillas, and cheese in slow cooker, alternating layers. Repeat, ending with cheese and sauce.
5. Cover. Cook on Low 5-6 hours, or High 2-3 hours.

Chicken Tortillas

Julette Leaman
Harrisonburg, VA

Makes 4 servings

1 fryer chicken, cooked and cubed
10¾-oz. can cream of chicken soup
½ cup (can) tomatoes with chilies
2 Tbsp. quick-cooking tapioca
6-8 tortillas, torn into pieces
1 medium onion, chopped
2 cups grated cheddar cheese

1. Combine chicken, soup, tomatoes with chilies, and tapioca.
2. Line bottom of slow cooker with one-third tortilla pieces. Add one-third chicken mixture. Sprinkle with one-third onion and cheese. Repeat layers.
3. Cover. Cook on Low 6-8 hours. (This recipe does not respond well to being cooked on High.)

Note:
Serve, if you wish, with shredded lettuce, chopped fresh tomatoes, diced raw onions, sour cream, and salsa.

Chicken at a Whim

Colleen Heatwole
Burton, MI

Makes 6-8 servings

6 medium-sized, boneless, skinless chicken-breast halves
1 small onion, sliced
1 cup dry white wine, chicken broth, *or* water
15-oz. can chicken broth
2 cups water
6-oz. can sliced black olives, with juice
1 small can artichoke hearts, with juice
5 garlic cloves, minced
1 cup dry elbow macaroni, *or* small shells
1 envelope dry savory garlic soup

1. Place chicken in slow cooker. Spread onion over chicken.
2. Combine remaining ingredients, except dry soup mix, and pour over chicken. Sprinkle with dry soup.
3. Cover. Cook on Low 4½ hours.

Browning meat in another pan means an extra step, but it adds a lot to a recipe's appearance and flavor.
Mary Puskar
Forest Hill, MD

Joyce's Chicken Tetrazzini

Joyce Slaymaker
Strasburg, PA

Makes 4 servings

2-3 cups diced cooked
    chicken
2 cups chicken broth
1 small onion, chopped
1/4 cup sauterne, white
    wine, *or* milk
1/2 cup slivered almonds
2 4-oz. cans sliced
    mushrooms, drained
10 3/4-oz. can cream of
    mushroom soup
1 lb. cooked spaghetti
grated Parmesan cheese

1. Combine all ingredients
except spaghetti and cheese
in slow cooker.
2. Cover. Cook on Low 6-8
hours.
3. Serve over buttered
spaghetti. Sprinkle with
Parmesan cheese.

Variations:
1. Place spaghetti in large
baking dish. Pour sauce in
center. Sprinkle with
Parmesan cheese. Broil until
lightly browned.
2. Add 10-oz. pkg. frozen
peas to Step 1.
    Darlene Raber
    Wellman, IA

Dorothy's Chicken Tetrazzini

Dorothy Shank
Sterling, IL

Makes 6 servings

3-4 cups diced, cooked
    chicken
2 cups chicken broth
10 3/4-oz. can cream of
    mushroom soup
1/2 lb. fresh mushrooms,
    sliced
1 cup half-and-half
1 lb. cooked spaghetti

1. Combine chicken,
broth, and soup in slow
cooker.
2. Cover. Cook on Low 4-6
hours.
3. During last hour of
cooking, stir in half-and-half.
4. Serve chicken and sauce
over cooked spaghetti.

Chickenetti

Miriam Nolt, New Holland, PA
Ruth Hershey, Paradise, PA

Makes 10 servings

1 cup chicken broth
16-oz. pkg. spaghetti,
    cooked
4-6 cups cubed and cooked
    chicken, *or* turkey,
    breast
10 3/4-oz. can cream of
    mushroom soup, *or*
    cream of celery soup
1 cup water
1/4 cup green peppers,
    chopped
1/2 cup diced celery
1/2 tsp. pepper
1 medium onion, grated
1/2 lb. white, *or* yellow,
    American cheese, cubed

1. Put cup of chicken
broth into very large slow
cooker. Add spaghetti and
meat.
2. In large bowl, combine
soup and water until smooth.
Stir in remaining ingredients,
then pour into slow cooker.
3. Cover. Cook on Low 2-3
hours.

Variations:
1. For a creamier dish, add
a 10 3/4-oz. can cream of
chicken soup to Step 2.
    Arlene Miller
    Hutchinson, KS

2. Add 4 1/2-oz. can
chopped green chilies to Step
2, for more zest.

Golden Chicken and Noodles

Sue Pennington
Bridgewater, VA

Makes 6 servings

6 boneless, skinless chicken-breast halves
2 10¾-oz. cans broccoli cheese soup
2 cups milk
1 small onion, chopped
½-1 tsp. salt
½-1 tsp. dried basil
⅛ tsp. pepper

1. Place chicken pieces in slow cooker.
2. Combine remaining ingredients. Pour over chicken.
3. Cover. Cook on High 1 hour. Reduce heat to Low. Cook 5-6 hours.
4. Serve over noodles.

Easy Casserole

Ruth Conrad Liechty
Goshen, IN

Makes 6-8 servings

2 10¾-oz. cans chicken gumbo soup
2 10¾-oz. cans cream of mushroom soup
1-2 cups cut up chicken, *or* turkey
1 cup milk
6-oz. can chow mein noodles
1 pint frozen green beans, *or* corn, cooked

1. Combine all ingredients in slow cooker.
2. Cover. Cook on Low 7-8 hours, or High 3-4 hours.

Chicken and Stuffing

Janice Yoskovich
Carmichaels, PA
Jo Ellen Moore, Pendleton, IN

Makes 14-16 servings

2½ cups chicken broth
1 cup butter, *or* margarine, melted
½ cup chopped onions
½ cup chopped celery
4-oz. can mushrooms, stems and pieces, drained
¼ cup dried parsley flakes
1½ tsp. rubbed sage
1 tsp. poultry seasoning
1 tsp. salt
½ tsp. pepper
12 cups day-old bread cubes (½-inch pieces)
2 eggs
10¾-oz. can cream of chicken soup
5-6 cups cubed cooked chicken

1. Combine all ingredients except bread, eggs, soup, and chicken in saucepan. Simmer for 10 minutes.
2. Place bread cubes in large bowl.
3. Combine eggs and soup. Stir into broth mixture until smooth. Pour over bread and toss well.
4. Layer half of stuffing and then half of chicken into very large slow cooker (or two medium-sized cookers). Repeat layers.
5. Cover. Cook on Low 4½-5 hours.

When using fresh herbs you may want to experiment with the amounts to use, because the strength is enhanced in the slow cooker, rather than becoming weaker.
Annabelle Unternahrer
Shipshewana, IN

Chicken Dressing

Mary V. Warye
West Liberty, OH

Makes 25-30 servings

12-13 cups bread cubes
1 tsp. poultry seasoning
1½ tsp. salt
1 tsp. dried thyme
½ tsp. pepper
½ tsp. dried marjoram
¾ cup margarine, *or*
   butter
2 cups chopped onions
2 cups chopped celery
¼ cup chopped fresh
   parsley
8-oz. can mushrooms,
   drained
3½-4½ cups chicken broth
4 cups diced, cooked
   chicken
2 eggs, beaten
1 tsp. baking powder

1. Put bread cubes in large bowl. Add all seasonings and mix well.
2. Melt margarine in skillet. Saute onions, celery, parsley, and mushrooms. Add to bread cubes.
3. Heat broth and pour into bread cubes, stirring until well moistened. Fold in chicken.
4. Add eggs. Toss well. Add baking powder. Toss well.
5. Pack lightly into very large slow cooker, or two medium-sized cookers.
6. Cover. Cook on Low 5-6 hours.

One-Dish Chicken Supper

Louise Stackhouse
Benton, PA

Makes 4 servings

4 boneless, skinless
   chicken-breast halves
10¾-oz. can cream of
   chicken, *or* celery, *or*
   mushroom, soup
⅓ cup milk
1 pkg. Stove Top stuffing
   mix and seasoning
   packet
1⅔ cups water

1. Place chicken in slow cooker.
2. Combine soup and milk. Pour over chicken.
3. Combine stuffing mix, seasoning packet, and water. Spoon over chicken.
4. Cover. Cook on Low 6-8 hours.

Chicken and Dumplings

Elva Ever
North English, IA

Makes 8-10 servings

4 whole chicken breasts, *or*
   1 small chicken
¾ cup sliced carrots
¼ cup chopped onions
¼ cup chopped celery
1½ cups peas
4-6 Tbsp. flour
1 cup water
salt to taste
pepper to taste
buttermilk baking mix
   dumplings
paprika to taste

1. Cook chicken in water in soup pot. Cool, skin, and debone chicken. Return broth to boiling in soup pot.
2. Cook vegetables in microwave on High for 5 minutes.
3. Meanwhile, combine flour and water until smooth. Add to boiling chicken broth. Add enough extra water to make 4 cups broth, making sure gravy is fairly thick. Season with salt and pepper.
4. Combine chicken, vegetables, and gravy in slow cooker.
5. Mix dumplings as directed on baking mix box. Place dumplings on top of chicken in slow cooker. Sprinkle with paprika.
6. Cover. Cook on High 3 hours.

Sloppy Chicken

Marjora Miller
Archbold, OH

Makes 4-6 servings

28-oz. can boneless
chicken
10¾-oz. can cream of
chicken soup
1 stack butter crackers,
crushed
15-oz. can chicken broth
10¾-oz. can cream of
mushroom soup

1. Combine all ingredients in slow cooker.
2. Cover. Cook on Low 5-6 hours, stirring occasionally.

Elizabeth's Hot Chicken Sandwiches

Elizabeth Yutzy
Wauseon, OH

Makes 8 servings

3 cups cubed cooked
chicken
2 cups chicken broth
1 cup crushed soda
crackers
¼-½ tsp. salt
dash pepper
8 sandwich buns

1. Combine chicken, broth, crackers, and seasoning in slow cooker.
2. Cover. Cook on Low 2-3 hours, until mixture thickens and can be spread.
3. Fill sandwich buns and serve while warm.

Loretta's Hot Chicken Sandwiches

Loretta Krahn
Mt. Lake, MN

Makes 12 servings

8 cups cubed cooked
chicken, *or* turkey
1 medium onion, chopped
1 cup chopped celery
2 cups mayonnaise
1 cup cubed American
cheese
buns

1. Combine all ingredients except buns in slow cooker.
2. Cover. Cook on High 2 hours.
3. Serve on buns.

Barbecue Chicken for Buns

Linda Sluiter
Schererville, IN

Makes 16-20 servings

6 cups diced cooked
chicken
2 cups chopped celery
1 cup chopped onions
1 cup chopped green
peppers
4 Tbsp. butter
2 cups ketchup
2 cups water
2 Tbsp. brown sugar
4 Tbsp. vinegar
2 tsp. dry mustard
1 tsp. pepper
1 tsp. salt

1. Combine all ingredients in slow cooker.
2. Cover. Cook on Low 8 hours.
3. Stir chicken until it shreds.
4. Pile into steak rolls and serve.

Chicken Reuben Bake

Gail Bush
Landenberg, PA

Makes 4 servings

4 boneless, skinless chicken-breast halves
2-lb. bag sauerkraut, drained and rinsed
4-5 slices Swiss cheese
1 1/4 cups Thousand Island salad dressing
2 Tbsp. chopped fresh parsley

1. Place chicken in slow cooker. Layer sauerkraut over chicken. Add cheese. Top with salad dressing. Sprinkle with parsley.
2. Cover. Cook on Low 6-8 hours.

No-Fuss Turkey Breast

Dorothy Miller
Gulfport, MI

Makes 3-4 pints cooked meat

1 turkey breast
olive oil
1-2 Tbsp. water

1. Rub turkey breast with oil. Place in slow cooker. Add water.

2. Cover. Cook on High 1 hour, or Low 4-5 hours.
3. Cool. Debone and cut into bite-sized pieces and store in pint-size plastic boxes in freezer. Use when cooked turkey or chicken is called for.

Turkey in a Pot

Dorothy M. Pittman
Pickens, SC

Makes 10-12 servings

4-5 lb. turkey breast (if frozen, it doesn't have to be thawed)
1 medium onion, chopped
1 rib celery, chopped
1/4 cup melted margarine
salt to taste
lemon-pepper seasoning to taste
1 1/2 cups chicken broth

1. Wash turkey breast. Pat dry. Place in greased slow cooker. Put onion and celery in cavity.
2. Pour margarine over turkey. Sprinkle with seasonings. Pour broth around turkey.
3. Cover. Cook on High 6 hours. Let stand 10 minutes before carving.

Turkey Breast

Barbara Katrine Rose
Woodbridge, VA

Makes 6-8 servings

1 large boneless turkey breast
1/4 cup apple cider, *or* juice
1 tsp. salt
1/4 tsp. pepper

1. Put turkey breast in slow cooker. Drizzle apple cider over turkey. Sprinkle on both sides with salt and pepper.
2. Cover. Cook on High 3-4 hours.
3. Remove turkey breast. Let stand for 15 minutes before slicing.

Onion Turkey Breast

Mary Ann Wasick
West Allis, WI

Makes 6-8 servings

4-6-lb. boneless, skinless turkey breast
1 tsp. garlic powder
1 envelope dry onion soup mix

1. Place turkey in slow cooker. Sprinkle garlic powder and onion soup mix over breast.
2. Cover. Cook on Low 8-10 hours.

Note:
Use au jus over rice or pasta.

Easy and Delicious Turkey Breast

Gail Bush
Landenberg, PA

Makes 4-6 servings

1 turkey breast
15-oz. can whole berry cranberry sauce
1 envelope dry onion soup mix
1/2 cup orange juice
1/2 tsp. salt
1/4 tsp. pepper

1. Place turkey in slow cooker.
2. Combine remaining ingredients. Pour over turkey.
3. Cover. Cook on Low 6-8 hours.

Turkey Stew

Ruth S. Weaver
Reinholds, PA

Makes 8 servings

2 lbs. skinless turkey thighs
1 lb., *or* 5 large, carrots, sliced
2 medium onions, chopped
8 medium potatoes, cubed
4 ribs celery, chopped
3 garlic cloves, minced
1 tsp. salt
1/4 tsp. pepper
2 Tbsp. Worcestershire sauce
15-oz. can tomato sauce
2 bay leaves

1. Place turkey in large slow cooker.
2. In separate bowl, mix together carrots, onions, potatoes, celery, garlic, salt, pepper, Worcestershire sauce, tomato sauce, and bay.
3. Pour over turkey. Cover. Cook on Low 8-12 hours, or High 6-8 hours. Remove bay leaves before serving.

Pheasant a la Elizabeth

Elizabeth L. Richards
Rapid City, SD

Makes 4 servings

6 pheasant breasts, deboned and cubed
3/4 cup teriyaki sauce
1/3-1/2 cup flour
1 1/2 tsp. garlic salt
pepper to taste
1/3 cup olive oil
1 large onion, sliced
12-oz. can beer
3/4 cup fresh mushrooms, sliced

1. Marinate pheasant in teriyaki sauce for 2-4 hours.
2. Combine flour, garlic salt, and pepper. Dredge pheasant in flour. Brown in olive oil in skillet. Add onion and saute for 3 minutes, stirring frequently. Transfer to slow cooker.
3. Add beer and mushrooms.
4. Cover. Cook on Low 6-8 hours.

Variation:
Instead of pheasant, use chicken.

Pot-Roasted Rabbit

Donna Treloar
Gaston, IN

Makes 4 servings

2 onions, sliced
4-5-lb. roasting rabbit
salt to taste
pepper to taste
1 garlic clove, sliced
2 bay leaves
1 whole clove
1 cup hot water
2 Tbsp. soy sauce
2 Tbsp. flour
1/2 cup cold water

1. Place onion in bottom of slow cooker.
2. Rub rabbit with salt and pepper. Insert garlic in cavity. Place rabbit in slow cooker.
3. Add bay leaves, clove, hot water, and soy sauce.
4. Cover. Cook on Low 10-12 hours.
5. Remove rabbit and thicken gravy by stirring 2 Tbsp. flour blended into 1/2 cup water into simmering juices in cooker. Continue stirring until gravy thickens. Cut rabbit into serving-size pieces and serve with gravy.

Baked Lamb Shanks

Irma H. Schoen
Windsor, CT

Makes 4-6 servings

1 medium onion, thinly sliced
2 small carrots, cut in thin strips
1 rib celery, chopped
3 lamb shanks, cracked
1-2 cloves garlic, split
1 1/2 tsp. salt
1/4 tsp. pepper
1 tsp. dried oregano
1 tsp. dried thyme
2 bay leaves, crumbled
1/2 cup dry white wine
8-oz. can tomato sauce

1. Place onions, carrots, and celery in slow cooker.
2. Rub lamb with garlic and season with salt and pepper. Add to slow cooker.
3. Mix remaining ingredients together in separate bowl and add to meat and vegetables.
4. Cover. Cook on Low 8-10 hours, or High 4-6 hours.

Herb Potato-Fish Bake

Barbara Sparks
Glen Burnie, MD

Makes 4 servings

10 3/4-oz. can cream of celery soup
1/2 cup water
1-lb. perch fillet, fresh *or* thawed
2 cups cooked, diced potatoes, drained
1/4 cup grated Parmesan cheese
1 Tbsp. chopped parsley
1/2 tsp. salt
1/2 tsp. dried basil
1/4 tsp. dried oregano

1. Combine soup and water. Pour half in slow cooker. Spread fillet on top. Place potatoes on fillet. Pour remaining soup mix over top.
2. Combine cheese and herbs. Sprinkle over ingredients in slow cooker.
3. Cover. Cook on High 1-2 hours, being careful not to overcook fish.

If you have them available, use whole or leaf herbs and spices rather than crushed or ground ones.
Barbara Sparks
Glen Burnie, MD

Shrimp Jambalaya
Karen Ashworth
Duenweg, MO

Makes 6-8 servings

2 Tbsp. margarine
2 medium onions, chopped
2 green bell peppers,
    chopped
3 ribs celery, chopped
1 cup chopped cooked
    ham
2 garlic cloves, chopped
1½ cups minute rice
1½ cups beef broth
28-oz. can chopped
    tomatoes
2 Tbsp. chopped parsley
1 tsp. dried basil
½ tsp. dried thyme
¼ tsp. pepper
⅛ tsp. cayenne pepper
1 lb. shelled, deveined,
    medium-size shrimp
1 Tbsp. chopped parsley
    for garnish

1. Melt margarine in slow
cooker set on High. Add
onions, peppers, celery, ham,
and garlic. Cook 30 minutes.
2. Add rice. Cover and
cook 15 minutes.
3. Add broth, tomatoes, 2
Tbsp. parsley, and remaining
seasonings. Cover and cook
on High 1 hour.
4. Add shrimp. Cook on
High 30 minutes, or until liquid is absorbed.
5. Garnish with 1 Tbsp.
parsley.

Jambalaya
Doris M. Coyle-Zipp
South Ozone Park, NY

Makes 5-6 servings

3½-4-lb. roasting chicken,
    cut up
3 onions, diced
1 carrot, sliced
3-4 garlic cloves, minced
1 tsp. dried oregano
1 tsp. dried basil
1 tsp. salt
⅛ tsp. white pepper
14-oz. can crushed
    tomatoes
1 lb. shelled raw shrimp
2 cups cooked rice

1. Combine all ingredients
except shrimp and rice in
slow cooker.
2. Cover. Cook on Low
2-3½ hours, or until chicken
is tender.
3. Add shrimp and rice.
4. Cover. Cook on High 15-
20 minutes, or until shrimp
are done.

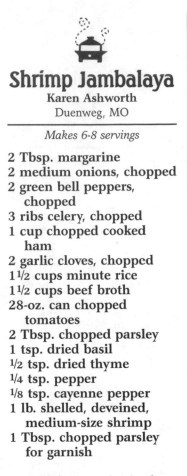

Shrimp Creole
Carol Findling
Princeton, IL

Makes 8-10 servings

½ cup butter
⅓ cup flour
1¾ cups sliced onions
1 cup diced green peppers
1 cup diced celery
1½ large carrots, shredded
2¾-lb. can tomatoes
¾ cup water
½ tsp. dried thyme
1 garlic clove, minced
pinch of rosemary
1 Tbsp. sugar
3 bay leaves
1 Tbsp. Worcestershire
    sauce
1 Tbsp. salt
⅛ tsp. dried oregano
2 lbs. shelled shrimp,
    deveined

1. Melt butter in skillet.
Add flour and brown, stirring
constantly. Add onions, green
peppers, celery, and carrots.
Cook 5-10 minutes. Transfer
to slow cooker.
2. Add remaining ingredi-
ents, except shrimp, and stir
well.
3. Cover. Cook on Low 6-8
hours.
4. Add shrimp during last
hour.
5. Serve over rice.

Seafood Gumbo

Barbara Katrine Rose
Woodbridge, VA

Makes 10 servings

1 lb. okra, sliced
2 Tbsp. butter, melted
1/4 cup butter, melted
1/4 cup flour
1 bunch green onions,
    sliced
1/2 cup chopped celery
2 garlic cloves, minced
16-oz. can tomatoes and
    juice
1 bay leaf
1 Tbsp. chopped fresh
    parsley
1 fresh thyme sprig
1 1/2 tsp. salt
1/2-1 tsp. red pepper
3-5 cups water, depending
    upon the consistency
    you like
1 lb. peeled and deveined
    fresh shrimp
1/2 lb. fresh crabmeat

1. Saute okra in 2 Tbsp.
butter until okra is lightly
browned. Transfer to slow
cooker.
2. Combine remaining but-
ter and flour in skillet. Cook
over medium heat, stirring
constantly until roux is the
color of chocolate, 20-25 minutes. Stir in green onions, celery, and garlic. Cook until
vegetables are tender. Add to
slow cooker. Gently stir in
remaining ingredients.
3. Cover. Cook on High 3-4
hours.
4. Serve over rice.

Seafood Medley

Susan Alexander
Baltimore, MD

Makes 10-12 servings

1 lb. shrimp, peeled and
    deveined
1 lb. crabmeat
1 lb. bay scallops
2 10 3/4-oz. cans cream of
    celery soup
2 soup cans milk
2 Tbsp. butter, melted
1 tsp. Old Bay seasoning
1/4-1/2 tsp. salt
1/4 tsp. pepper

1. Layer shrimp, crab, and
scallops in slow cooker.
2. Combine soup and milk.
Pour over seafood.
3. Mix together butter and
spices and pour over top.
4. Cover. Cook on Low 3-4
hours.
5. Serve over rice or noodles.

Salmon Cheese Casserole

Wanda S. Curtin
Bradenton, FL

Makes 6 servings

14 3/4-oz. can salmon with
    liquid
4-oz. can mushrooms,
    drained
1 1/2 cups bread crumbs
2 eggs, beaten
1 cup grated cheese
1 Tbsp. lemon juice
1 Tbsp. minced onion

1. Flake fish in bowl,
removing bones. Stir in
remaining ingredients. Pour
into lightly greased slow
cooker.
2. Cover. Cook on Low 3-4
hours.

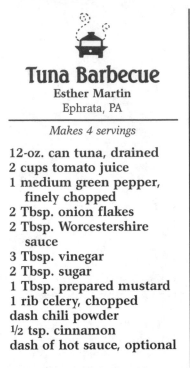

Tuna Barbecue

Esther Martin
Ephrata, PA

Makes 4 servings

12-oz. can tuna, drained
2 cups tomato juice
1 medium green pepper,
  finely chopped
2 Tbsp. onion flakes
2 Tbsp. Worcestershire
  sauce
3 Tbsp. vinegar
2 Tbsp. sugar
1 Tbsp. prepared mustard
1 rib celery, chopped
dash chili powder
1/2 tsp. cinnamon
dash of hot sauce, optional

1. Combine all ingredients
in slow cooker.
2. Cover. Cook on Low 8-
10 hours, or High 4-5 hours.
If mixture becomes too dry
while cooking, add 1/2 cup
tomato juice.
3. Serve on buns.

Tuna Salad Casserole

Charlotte Fry, St. Charles, MO
Esther Becker, Gordonville, PA

Makes 4 servings

2 7-oz. cans tuna
10 3/4-oz. can cream of
  celery soup
3 hard-boiled eggs,
  chopped
1/2 to 1 1/2 cups diced celery
1/2 cup diced onions
1/2 cup mayonnaise
1/4 tsp. ground pepper
1 1/2 cups crushed potato
  chips

1. Combine all ingredients
except 1/4 cup potato chips in
slow cooker. Top with
remaining chips.
2. Cover. Cook on Low 5-8
hours.

Tuna Noodle Casserole

Leona Miller
Millersburg, OH

Makes 6 servings

2 6 1/2-oz. cans water-
  packed tuna, drained
2 10 1/2-oz. cans cream of
  mushroom soup
1 cup milk
2 Tbsp. dried parsley
10-oz. pkg. frozen mixed
  vegetables, thawed
10-oz. pkg. noodles, cooked
  and drained
1/2 cup toasted sliced
  almonds

1. Combine tuna, soup,
milk, parsley, and vegetables.
Fold in noodles. Pour into
greased slow cooker. Top with
almonds.
2. Cover. Cook on Low 7-9
hours, or High 3-4 hours.

If your recipe turns out to have too much liquid, remove
the cover and use the High setting for about 45 minutes.
Esther Porter
Minneapolis, MN

Tempeh-Stuffed Peppers

Sara Harter Fredette
Williamsburg, MA

Makes 4 servings

4 oz. tempeh, cubed
1 garlic clove, minced
28-oz. can crushed
   tomatoes
2 tsp. soy sauce
1/4 cup chopped onions
1 1/2 cups cooked rice
1 1/2 cups shredded cheese
Tabasco sauce, optional
4 green, red, *or* yellow, bell
   peppers, tops removed
   and seeded
1/4 cup shredded cheese

1. Steam tempeh 10 minutes in saucepan. Mash in bowl with the garlic, half the tomatoes, and soy sauce.
2. Stir in onions, rice, 1 1/2 cups cheese, and Tabasco sauce. Stuff into peppers.
3. Place peppers in slow cooker, 3 on the bottom and one on top. Pour remaining half of tomatoes over peppers.
4. Cover. Cook on Low 6-8 hours, or High 3-4 hours. Top with remaining cheese in last 30 minutes.

Tastes-Like-Chili-Rellenos

Roseann Wilson
Albuquerque, NM

Makes 6 servings

2 tsp. butter
2 4-oz. cans whole green
   chilies
1/2 lb. grated cheddar
   cheese
1/2 lb. grated Monterey Jack
   cheese
14 1/2-oz. can stewed
   tomatoes
4 eggs
2 Tbsp. flour
3/4 cup evaporated milk

1. Grease sides and bottom of slow cooker with butter.
2. Cut chilies into strips. Layer chilies and cheeses in slow cooker. Pour in stewed tomatoes.
3. Combine eggs, flour, and milk. Pour into slow cooker.
4. Cover. Cook on High 2-3 hours.

Barbecued Lentils

Sue Hamilton
Minooka, IL

Makes 8 servings

2 cups barbecue sauce
3 1/2 cups water
1 lb. dry lentils
1 pkg. vegetarian hot dogs,
   sliced

1. Combine all ingredients in slow cooker.
2. Cover. Cook on Low 6-8 hours.

Cheryl's Macaroni and Cheese

Cheryl Bartel
Hillsboro, KS

Makes 6 servings

8 oz. dry elbow macaroni, cooked
3-4 cups (about ³/₄-lb.) shredded sharp cheddar cheese, divided
13-oz. can evaporated milk
1¹/₂ cups milk
2 eggs
1 tsp. salt
¹/₄ tsp. black pepper
chopped onion to taste

1. Combine all ingredients, except 1 cup cheese, in greased slow cooker. Sprinkle reserved cup of cheese over top.
2. Cover. Cook on Low 3-4 hours. Do not remove the lid or stir until the mixture has finished cooking.

Variation:
For some extra zest, add ¹/₂ tsp. dry mustard when combining all ingredients. Add thin slices of cheese to top of cooker mixture.
Dorothy M. Pittman
Pickens, SC

Macaroni and Cheese

Martha Hershey, Ronks, PA
Marcia S. Myer, Manheim, PA
LeAnne Nolt, Leola, PA
Ellen Ranck, Gap, PA
Mary Sommerfeld, Lancaster, PA
Kathryn Yoder, Minot, ND

Makes 6 servings

8-oz. pkg. dry macaroni, cooked
2 Tbsp. oil
13-oz. can evaporated milk (fat-free will work)
1¹/₂ cups milk
1 tsp. salt
3 cups (about ¹/₂ lb.) shredded cheese: cheddar, American, Velveeta, *or* a combination
2-4 Tbsp. melted butter
2 Tbsp. onion, chopped fine
4 hot dogs, sliced, optional

1. In slow cooker, toss macaroni in oil. Stir in remaining ingredients except hot dogs.
2. Cover. Cook on Low 2-3 hours. Add hot dogs, if desired, and cook 1 hour longer.

Variations:
1. Use 3 cups evaporated milk, instead of 13-oz. evaporated milk and 1¹/₂ cups milk.
2. Add more onion, up to ¹/₄ cup total.
3. Add ¹/₂ tsp. pepper
Stacy Petersheim
Mechanicsburg, PA
Sara Wilson, Blairstown, MO

When cooking on High, stir occasionally for more even cooking and improved flavor.
Roseann Wilson
Albuquerque, NM

Bean Main Dishes

From-Scratch Baked Beans

Wanda Roth
Napoleon, OH

Makes 6 servings

2½ cups Great Northern
  dried beans
4 cups water
1½ cups tomato sauce
½ cup brown sugar
2 tsp. salt
1 small onion, chopped
½ tsp. chili powder

1. Wash and drain dry
beans. Combine beans and
water in slow cooker. Cook
on Low 8 hours, or overnight.
2. Stir in remaining ingredients. Cook on Low 6 hours.

New England Baked Beans

Mary Wheatley
Mashpee, MA
Jean Butzer
Batavia, NY

Makes 8 servings

1 lb. dried beans—Great
  Northern, pea beans, *or*
  navy beans
¼ lb. salt pork, sliced *or*
  diced
1 qt. water
1 tsp. salt
1-4 Tbsp. brown sugar,
  according to your
  preference
½ cup molasses
½-1 tsp. dry mustard,
  according to your
  preference
½ tsp. baking soda
1 onion, coarsely chopped
5 cups water

1. Wash beans and remove
any stones or shriveled beans.
2. Meanwhile, simmer salt
pork in 1 quart water in
saucepan for 10 minutes.
Drain. Do not reserve liquid.
3. Combine all ingredients
in slow cooker.
4. Cook on High until contents come to boil. Turn to
Low. Cook 14-16 hours, or
until beans are tender.

Variations:
1. Add ½ tsp. pepper to
Step 3.
Rachel Kauffman
Alton, MI

2. Add ¼ cup ketchup to
Step 3.
Cheri Jantzen
Houston, TX

Mom's New England Baked Beans

Debbie Zeida
Mashpee, MA

Makes 6-8 servings

3 cups dried navy beans
9 cups water
1 medium onion, chopped
1 cup ketchup
1 cup brown sugar
1 cup water
2 tsp. dry mustard
2 Tbsp. dark molasses
1 Tbsp. salt
¼ lb. salt pork, ground *or* diced

1. Cook beans in water in soup pot until softened, or bring to boil, cover, and let stand for 1½ hours. Drain. Pour beans into slow cooker.
2. Stir in remaining ingredients. Mix well.
3. Cover. Cook on Low 8 hours, or High 4 hours, stirring occasionally.

Variation:
Use 1 lb. dried Great Northern beans instead of 3 cups navy beans.

Dorothy Miller
Gulfport, MI

Home-Baked Beans

Carolyn Baer
Conrath, WI

Makes 15-25 servings

2 lbs. (4 cups) dried navy, *or* pea, beans
1 lb. salt pork, *or* bacon, chopped
1 lb. (2½ cups), *or* less, brown sugar
1-lb. 3-oz. can tomatoes
2 medium onions, chopped
2 Tbsp. prepared mustard
½ tsp. salt
½ tsp. pepper

1. Wash and pick over beans. Cover generously with water and soak overnight. Simmer in salted water until tender. Drain. Save liquid.
2. Place pork or bacon in bottom of slow cooker.
3. Mix together brown sugar, tomatoes, onions, mustard, salt, and pepper. Alternately layer sauce mixture and beans over pork.
4. Add enough reserved water to cover beans.
5. Cover. Cook on Low 8-10 hours, stirring occasionally.

Note:
These beans freeze well.

Barbecued Lima Beans

Hazel L. Propst
Oxford, PA

Makes 10 servings

1½ lbs. dried lima beans
6 cups water
2¼ cups chopped onions
1¼ cups brown sugar
1½ cups ketchup
13 drops Tabasco sauce
1 cup dark corn syrup
1 Tbsp. salt
½ lb. bacon, diced

1. Soak washed beans in water overnight. Do not drain.
2. Add onion. Bring to boil. Simmer 30-60 minutes, or until beans are tender. Drain beans, reserving liquid.
3. Combine all ingredients except bean liquid in slow cooker. Mix well. Pour in enough liquid so that beans are barely covered.
4. Cover. Cook on Low 10 hours, or High 4-6 hours. Stir occasionally.

Refried Beans with Bacon

Arlene Wengerd
Millersburg, OH

Makes 8 servings

2 cups dried red, *or* pinto, beans
6 cups water
2 garlic cloves, minced
1 large tomato, peeled, seeded, and chopped, *or* 1 pint tomato juice
1 tsp. salt
½ lb. bacon
shredded cheese

1. Combine beans, water, garlic, tomato, and salt in slow cooker.

2. Cover. Cook on High 5 hours, stirring occasionally. When the beans become soft, drain off some liquid.

3. While the beans cook, brown bacon in skillet. Drain, reserving drippings. Crumble bacon. Add half of bacon and 3 Tbsp. drippings to beans. Stir.

4. Mash or puree beans with a food processor. Fry the mashed bean mixture in the remaining bacon drippings. Add more salt to taste.

5. To serve, sprinkle the remaining bacon and shredded cheese on top of beans.

Variations:

1. Instead of draining off liquid, add ⅓ cup dry minute rice and continue cooking about 20 minutes. Add a dash of hot sauce and a dollop of sour cream to individual servings.

2. Instead of frying the mashed bean mixture, place several spoonfuls on flour tortillas, roll up, and serve.
Susan McClure
Dayton, VA

Red Beans and Rice

Margaret A. Moffitt
Bartlett, TN

Makes 8-10 servings

1-lb. pkg. dried red beans
water
salt pork, ham hocks, *or* sausage, cut into small chunks
2 tsp. salt
1 tsp. pepper
3-4 cups water
6-oz. can tomato paste
8-oz. can tomato sauce
4 garlic cloves, minced

1. Soak beans for 8 hours. Drain. Discard soaking water.

2. Mix together all ingredients in slow cooker.

3. Cover. Cook on Low 10-12 hours, or until beans are soft. Serve over rice.

Variation:

Use canned red kidney beans. Cook 1 hour on High and then 3 hours on Low.

Note:

These beans freeze well.

New Mexico Pinto Beans

John D. Allen
Rye, CO

Makes 8-10 servings

2½ cups dried pinto beans
3 qts. water
½ cup ham, *or* salt pork, diced, *or* a small ham shank
2 garlic cloves, crushed
1 tsp. crushed red chili peppers, optional
salt to taste
pepper to taste

1. Sort beans. Discard pebbles, shriveled beans, and floaters. Wash beans under running water. Place in saucepan, cover with 3 quarts water, and soak overnight.

2. Drain beans and discard soaking water. Pour beans into slow cooker. Cover with fresh water.

3. Add meat, garlic, chili, salt, and pepper. Cook on Low 6-10 hours, or until beans are soft.

Scandinavian Beans

Virginia Bender
Dover, DE

Makes 8 servings

1 lb. dried pinto beans
6 cups water
12 ozs. bacon, *or* 1 ham hock
1 onion, chopped
2-3 garlic cloves, minced
1/4 tsp. pepper
1 tsp. salt
1/4 cup molasses
1 cup ketchup
Tabasco to taste
1 tsp. Worcestershire sauce
3/4 cup brown sugar
1/2 cup cider vinegar
1/4 tsp. dry mustard

1. Soak beans in water in soup pot for 8 hours. Bring beans to boil and cook 1 1/2-2 hours, or until soft. Drain, reserving liquid.
2. Combine all ingredients in slow cooker, using just enough bean liquid to cover everything. Cook on Low 5-6 hours. If using ham hock, debone, cut ham into bite-sized pieces, and mix into beans.

New Orleans Red Beans

Cheri Jantzen
Houston, TX

Makes 6 servings

2 cups dried kidney beans
5 cups water
2 Tbsp. bacon drippings
1/2 lb. hot sausage, cut in small pieces
2 onions, chopped
2 cloves garlic, minced
1 tsp. salt

1. Wash and sort beans. In saucepan, combine beans and water. Boil 2 minutes. Remove from heat. Soak 1 hour.
2. Heat bacon drippings in skillet. Add sausage and brown slowly. Add onions and garlic and saute until tender.
3. Combine all ingredients, including the bean water, in slow cooker.
4. Cover. Cook on Low 8-10 hours. During last 20 minutes of cooking, stir frequently and mash lightly with spoon.
5. Serve over hot cooked white rice.

No Meat Baked Beans

Esther Becker
Gordonville, PA

Makes 8-10 servings

1 lb. dried navy beans
6 cups water
1 small onion, chopped
3/4 cup ketchup
3/4 cup brown sugar
3/4 cup water
1 tsp. dry mustard
2 Tbsp. dark molasses
1 tsp. salt

1. Soak beans in water overnight in large soup kettle. Cook beans in water until soft, about 1 1/2 hours. Drain, discarding bean water.
2. Mix together all ingredients in slow cooker. Mix well.
3. Cover. Cook on Low 10-12 hours.

Hot Bean Dish Without Meat

Jeannine Janzen
Elbing, KS

Makes 8-10 servings

16-oz. can kidney beans, drained
15-oz. can lima beans, drained
1/4 cup vinegar
2 Tbsp. molasses
2 heaping Tbsp. brown sugar
2 Tbsp. minced onion
mustard to taste
Tabasco sauce to taste

1. Place beans in slow cooker.
2. Combine remaining ingredients. Pour over beans.
3. Cover. Cook on Low 3-4 hours.

Variation:
Add 1 lb. browned ground beef to make this a meaty main dish.

Barbecued Beans

Jane Steiner
Orrville, OH

Makes 12-15 servings

4 11-oz. cans pork and beans
3/4 cup brown sugar
1 tsp. dry mustard
1/2 cup ketchup
6 slices bacon, diced

1. Pour 2 cans pork and beans into slow cooker.
2. Combine brown sugar and mustard. Sprinkle half of mixture over beans.
3. Cover with remaining cans of pork and beans. Sprinkle with rest of brown sugar and mustard.
4. Layer bacon over top. Spread ketchup over all.
5. Cut through bean mixture a bit before heating.
6. Cover. Cook on Low 4 hours.

Frances' Slow-Cooker Beans

Frances B. Musser
Newmanstown, PA

Makes 6-8 servings

1/2 cup ketchup
1 Tbsp. prepared mustard
1/2 cup brown sugar
1 small onion, chopped
1 tsp. salt
1/4 tsp. ground ginger
1/2 cup molasses
1 lb. turkey bacon, browned and crumbled
2-lb., 8-oz. can Great Northern beans, drained

1. Combine all ingredients in slow cooker.
2. Cover. Cook on Low 4 hours.

If there is too much liquid in your cooker, stick a toothpick under the edge of the lid to tilt it slightly and to allow the steam to escape.

Carol Sherwood
Batavia, NY

Kelly's Baked Beans

Kelly Bailey
Mechanicsburg, PA

Makes 6 servings

40-oz. can Great Northern
beans, juice reserved
15½-oz. can Great
Northern beans, juice
reserved
¾ cup brown sugar
¼ cup white corn syrup
½ cup ketchup
½ tsp. salt
half a medium-sized
onion, chopped
8-9 slices bacon, browned
and crumbled, optional

1. Drain beans overnight
in colander. Save ¼ cup liquid.
2. Mix together brown
sugar, corn syrup, and
ketchup. Mix well. Add salt
and onion.
3. Stir in beans and pour
into greased slow cooker. If
beans appear dry while cooking, add some of the ¼ cup
reserved bean juice.
4. Cover. Cook on Low 6-8
hours.

Four Beans and Sausage

Mary Seielstad
Sparks, NV

Makes 8 servings

15-oz. can Great Northern
beans, drained
15½-oz. can black beans,
rinsed and drained
16-oz. can red kidney
beans, drained
15-oz. can butter beans,
drained
1½ cups ketchup
½ cup chopped onions
1 green pepper, chopped
1 lb. smoked sausage,
cooked and cut into
½-inch slices
¼ cup brown sugar
2 garlic cloves, minced
1 tsp. Worcestershire sauce
½ tsp. dry mustard
½ tsp. Tabasco sauce

1. Combine all ingredients
in slow cooker.
2. Cover. Cook on Low 9-
10 hours, or High 4-5 hours.

Mary Ellen's Three-Bean Dish

Mary Ellen Musser
Reinholds, PA

Makes 10-20 servings

10-oz. pkg. frozen lima
beans, cooked
3 16-oz. cans baked beans
40-oz. can kidney beans,
drained
1 lb. sausage links,
browned and cut into
pieces
½ lb. cooked ham, cubed
1 medium onion, chopped
8-oz. can tomato sauce
½ cup ketchup
¼ cup packed brown sugar
1 tsp. salt
½ tsp. pepper
½ tsp. prepared mustard

1. Combine lima beans,
baked beans, kidney beans,
sausage, and ham in 3½-4-
quart slow cooker.
2. In separate bowl, com-
bine onion, tomato sauce,
ketchup, brown sugar, salt,
pepper, and mustard and
pour into slow cooker. Mix
gently.
3. Cover. Cook on Low 4-6
hours.

Sausage Bean Casserole

Juanita Marner
Shipshewana, IN

Makes 8 servings

1 lb. ground pork sausage
1/2 cup chopped onions
1/2 cup chopped green
   peppers
1 lb. cooked speckled
   butter beans
2 cups diced canned
   tomatoes
1/2 cup tomato sauce
1/4 tsp. salt
1/8 tsp. pepper

1. Brown sausage, onions, and green peppers in saucepan.
2. Combine all ingredients in slow cooker.
3. Cover. Cook on High 2 hours, or Low 4 hours.

Cajun Sausage and Beans

Melanie Thrower
McPherson, KS

Makes 4-6 servings

1 lb. smoked sausage,
   sliced into 1/4-inch pieces
16-oz. can red beans
16-oz. can crushed
   tomatoes with green
   chilies
1 cup chopped celery
half an onion, chopped
2 Tbsp. Italian seasoning
Tabasco sauce to taste

1. Combine all ingredients in slow cooker.
2. Cover. Cook on Low 8 hours.
3. Serve over rice or as a thick zesty soup.

Sausage Bean Quickie

Ellen Ranck
Gap, PA

Makes 4 servings

4-6 cooked brown 'n serve
   sausage links, cut into 1-
   inch pieces
2 tsp. cider vinegar
2 16-oz. cans red kidney *or*
   baked, beans, drained
7-oz. can pineapple
   chunks, undrained
2 tsp. brown sugar
3 Tbsp. flour

1. Combine sausage, vinegar, beans, and pineapple in slow cooker.
2. Combine brown sugar with flour. Add to slow cooker. Stir well.
3. Cover. Cook on Low 5-10 hours, or High 1-2 hours.

Beans with Rice

Miriam Christophel
Battle Creek, MI

Makes 8 servings

3 cups dried small red
  beans
8 cups water
3 garlic cloves, minced
1 large onion, chopped
8 cups fresh water
1-2 ham hocks
½- ¾ cup ketchup
2 tsp. salt
pinch of pepper
1½-2 tsp. ground cumin
1 Tbsp. parsley
1-2 bay leaves

1. Soak beans overnight in
8 cups water. Drain. Place
soaked beans in slow cooker
with garlic, onion, 8 cups
fresh water, and ham hocks.
2. Cover. Cook on High 12-
14 hours.
3. Take ham hocks out of
cooker and allow to cool.
Remove meat from bones.
Cut up and return to slow
cooker. Add remaining ingredients.
4. Cover. Cook on High 2-3
hours.
5. Serve over rice with dollop of sour cream.

Nan's Barbecued Beans

Nan Decker
Albuquerque, NM

Makes 10-12 servings

1 lb. ground beef
1 onion, chopped
5 cups canned baked
  beans
2 Tbsp. cider vinegar
1 Tbsp. Worcestershire
  sauce
2 Tbsp. brown sugar
½ cup ketchup

1. Brown ground beef and
onion in skillet. Drain.
2. Combine all ingredients
in slow cooker.
3. Cover. Cook on Low 4-6
hours.

Betty's Calico Beans

Betty Lahman
Elkton, VA

Makes 6-8 servings

1 lb. ground beef, browned
  and drained
14¾-oz. can lima beans
15½-oz. can pinto beans
15¼-oz. can corn
¼ cup brown sugar
1 cup ketchup
1 Tbsp. vinegar
2 tsp. prepared mustard
1 medium onion, chopped

1. Combine all ingredients
in slow cooker.
2. Cover. Cook on High 3-4
hours.

Three-Bean Barbecue

Ruth Hofstetter
Versailles, MO
Kathryn Yoder
Minot, ND

Makes 6-8 servings

1½-2 lbs. ground beef
¾ lb. bacon
1 cup chopped onions
2 31-oz. cans pork and
  beans
1-lb. can kidney beans,
  drained
1-lb. can lima beans,
  drained
1 cup ketchup
¼ cup brown sugar
1 Tbsp. liquid smoke
3 Tbsp. white vinegar
1 tsp. salt
dash of pepper

1. Brown beef in
saucepan. Drain.
2. Fry bacon and onions in
saucepan. Drain.
3. Combine all ingredients
in slow cooker.
4. Cover. Cook on Low 4-6
hours.

Note:
This is good served with
baked potatoes.

Baked Beans in Slow Cooker

Ruth Hershey
Paradise, PA

Makes 12 servings

1 1/2 lbs. ground beef
1/2-1 cup chopped onions,
   according to your
   preference
3 lbs. pork and beans
1-lb. can kidney beans,
   drained
1 cup ketchup
1/4 cup brown sugar,
   packed
3 Tbsp. cider vinegar

1. Brown ground beef and onion in skillet. Drain.
2. Combine all ingredients in slow cooker. Mix well.
3. Cover. Cook on Low 4-6 hours. Stir occasionally.

Roseann's Baked Beans

Roseann Wilson
Albuquerque, NM

Makes 12 servings

2 42-oz. cans baked beans,
   drained
l lb. ground beef, cooked
   and drained
1/2 cup barbecue sauce
1/4 cup ketchup

1 Tbsp. prepared mustard
3 strips bacon, diced
1/4 cup brown sugar
2 Tbsp. minced onion
3 strips bacon, cut in half

1. Combine all ingredients except half strips of bacon in slow cooker. Place 6 half-strips of bacon over top.
2. Cover. Cook on Low 3 hours.

Carla's Baked Beans

Carla Koslowsky
Hillsboro, KS

Makes 8-10 servings

1/2 lb. ground beef
1/2 lb. bacon, chopped
1 medium onion, minced
1 tsp. salt
1/2 tsp. pepper
16-oz. can red kidney
   beans, drained
16-oz. can pork and beans,
   drained
15-oz. can butter, or green
   lima, beans
1/3 cup brown sugar
1/4 cup sugar
1/4 cup barbecue sauce
1/4 cup ketchup
1 Tbsp. prepared mustard
2 Tbsp. molasses

1. Brown meats and onion in skillet. Drain.
2. Add salt, pepper, and beans. Stir in remaining ingredients. Mix well. Pour into slow cooker.

3. Cover. Cook on High 4-5 hours.

Five-Bean Hot Dish

Dede Peterson
Rapid City, SD

Makes 10 servings

1 lb. ground beef
1 tsp. prepared mustard
2 tsp. vinegar
1/2 lb. bacon, finely diced
3/4 cup brown sugar
15-oz. can lima beans,
   drained
1 tsp. salt
15-oz. can butter beans,
   drained
1 cup ketchup
16-oz. can kidney beans,
   drained
32-oz. can pork & beans,
   undrained
15-oz. can red beans,
   drained

1. Brown ground beef in deep saucepan. Drain.
2. Stir in mustard, vinegar, and bacon.
3. Add remaining ingredients. Mix well. Pour into large cooker.
4. Cover. Cook on Low 3-5 hours.

Note:
These beans freeze well.

Char's Calico Beans

Char Hagner
Montague, MI

Makes 10-12 servings

¼ lb. bacon
1 onion, chopped
1 lb. ground beef
½ cup brown sugar
½ cup ketchup
1 Tbsp. prepared mustard
1 tsp. salt
2 15-oz. cans lima beans, drained
28-oz. can Boston baked beans
2 16-oz. cans kidney beans, drained

1. Cut bacon in pieces. Brown in skillet and drain. Brown onion with beef in skillet. Drain.

2. Combine all ingredients in slow cooker.

3. Cover. Cook on Low 6 hours.

Casey's Beans

Cheryl Bartel
Hillsboro, KS

Makes 10-12 servings

½ lb. ground beef
10 slices bacon, diced
½ cup chopped onions
⅓ cup brown sugar
⅓ cup sugar, optional
¼ cup ketchup
¼ cup barbecue sauce
2 Tbsp. prepared mustard
2 Tbsp. molasses
½ tsp. salt
½ tsp. chili powder
½ tsp. pepper
1-lb. can kidney beans, drained
1-lb. can butter beans, drained
1-lb. can black beans, drained
1-lb. can pork and beans

1. Brown ground beef, bacon, and onion in deep saucepan. Drain.

2. Stir in remaining ingredients, except beans. Mix well. Stir in beans. Pour into slow cooker.

3. Cover. Cook on Low 5-6 hours.

Hearty Slow-Cooker Beans

Kim McEuen
Lincoln University, PA

Makes 10 servings

1 lb. ground beef
½ lb. bacon, diced
1 onion, chopped
16-oz. can red kidney beans, drained
15-oz. can butter beans, drained
15-oz. can pork and beans
15-oz. can hot chili beans
½ cup brown sugar
½ cup sugar
1 Tbsp. prepared mustard
1 Tbsp. cider vinegar
½ cup ketchup

1. Brown beef, bacon, and onion in skillet. Drain.

2. Combine all ingredients in slow cooker. Mix well.

3. Cover. Cook on High 3 hours, or Low 5-6 hours.

Allen's Beans

John D. Allen
Rye, CO

Makes 10-12 servings

1 large onion, chopped
1 lb. ground beef, browned
15-oz. can pork and beans
15-oz. can ranch-style
   beans, drained
16-oz. can kidney beans,
   drained
1 cup ketchup
1 tsp. salt
1 Tbsp. prepared mustard
2 Tbsp. brown sugar
2 Tbsp. hickory-flavored
   barbecue sauce
1/2-1 lb. small smoky link
   sausages, optional

1. Brown ground beef and onion in skillet. Drain. Transfer to slow cooker set on High.
2. Add remaining ingredients. Mix well.
3. Reduce heat to Low and cook 4-6 hours. Use a paper towel to absorb oil that's risen to the top before stirring and serving.

Six-Bean Barbecued Beans

Gladys Longacre
Susquehanna, PA

Makes 15-18 servings

1-lb. can kidney beans,
   drained
1-lb. can pinto beans,
   drained
1-lb. can Great Northern
   beans, drained
1-lb. can butter beans,
   drained
1-lb. can navy beans,
   drained
1-lb. can pork and beans
1/4 cup barbecue sauce
1/4 cup prepared mustard
1/3 cup ketchup
1 small onion, chopped
1 small pepper, chopped
1/4 cup molasses, *or*
   sorghum molasses
1 cup brown sugar

1. Mix together all ingredients in slow cooker.
2. Cook on Low 4-6 hours.

Four-Bean Medley

Sharon Brubaker
Myerstown, PA

Makes 8 servings

8 bacon slices, diced and
   browned until crisp
2 medium onions, chopped
3/4 cup brown sugar
1/2 cup vinegar
1 tsp. salt
1 tsp. dry mustard
1/2 tsp. garlic powder
16-oz. can baked beans,
   undrained
16-oz. can kidney beans,
   drained
15 1/2-oz. can butter beans,
   drained
14 1/2-oz. can green beans,
   drained
2 Tbsp. ketchup

1. Mix together all ingredients. Pour into slow cooker.
2. Cover. Cook on Low 6-8 hours.

Variation:
   Make this a main dish by adding 1 lb. hamburger to the bacon, browning it along with the bacon and chopped onions in skillet, then adding that mixture to the rest of the ingredients before pouring into slow cooker.

I generally spray the inside of my slow cooker with non-stick cooking spray prior to putting my ingredients in. It helps with cleanup.

Barb Yoder
Angola, IN

Lauren's Calico Beans

Lauren Eberhard
Seneca, IL

Makes 12-16 servings

8 slices bacon
1 cup chopped onions
1/2 cup brown sugar
1/2 cup ketchup
2 Tbsp. vinegar
1 tsp. dry mustard
14 1/2-oz. can green beans, drained
16-oz. can kidney beans, drained
15 1/2-oz. can butter beans, drained
15 1/2-oz. can pork and beans

1. Brown bacon in saucepan, reserving drippings. Crumble bacon. Cook onions in bacon drippings. Drain.
2. Combine all ingredients in slow cooker.
3. Cover. Cook on Low 6-8 hours.

Sweet and Sour Beans

Julette Leaman
Harrisonburg, VA

Makes 6-8 servings

10 slices bacon
4 medium onions, cut in rings
1/2-1 cup brown sugar, according to your preference
1 tsp. dry mustard
1 tsp. salt
1/4 cup cider vinegar
1-lb. can green beans, drained
2 1-lb. cans butter beans, drained
1-lb., 11-oz. can pork and beans

1. Brown bacon in skillet and crumble. Drain all but 2 Tbsp. bacon drippings. Stir in onions, brown sugar, mustard, salt, and vinegar. Simmer 20 minutes.
2. Combine all ingredients in slow cooker.
3. Cover. Cook on Low 3 hours.

Mixed Slow-Cooker Beans

Carol Peachey
Lancaster, PA

Makes 6 servings

16-oz. can kidney beans, drained
15 1/2-oz. can baked beans
1 pint home-frozen, *or* 1-lb. pkg. frozen, lima beans
1 pint home-frozen green beans, *or* 1-lb. pkg. frozen green beans
4 slices bacon, browned and crumbled
1/2 cup ketchup
1/2 cup sugar
1/2 cup brown sugar
2 Tbsp. vinegar
salt to taste

1. Combine beans and bacon in slow cooker.
2. Stir together remaining ingredients. Add to beans and mix well.
3. Cover. Cook on Low 8-10 hours.

Lizzie's California Beans

Lizzie Weaver
Ephrata, PA

Makes 12 servings

2 medium onions, cut in
   rings
1 cup brown sugar
1 tsp. dry mustard
1 tsp. salt
1/4 cup vinegar
1/3 cup ketchup
1 lb. bacon, browned and
   crumbled
16-oz. can green beans,
   drained
40-oz. can butter beans,
   drained
2 16-oz. cans baked beans

1. In saucepan, mix
together onions, brown sugar,
dry mustard, salt, vinegar,
and ketchup. Simmer in covered pan for 20 minutes. Add
bacon and beans.
2. Pour into slow cooker.
Cover. Cook on High 2 hours.

Marcia's California Beans

Marcia S. Myer
Manheim, PA

Makes 10-12 servings

16-oz. can barbecue beans,
   or pork and beans
16-oz. can baked beans
16-oz. can kidney beans
14 1/2-oz. can green beans
15-oz. can lima beans
15 1/2-oz. can Great
   Northern beans
1 onion, chopped
1 tsp. prepared mustard
1 cup brown sugar
1 tsp. salt
1/4 cup vinegar
1/2 lb. bacon, browned
   until crisp and
   crumbled

1. Drain juice from beans.
Combine beans in slow
cooker.
2. In saucepan, combine
onion, mustard, brown sugar,
salt, vinegar, and bacon.
Simmer for 10 minutes. Pour
sauce over beans.
3. Cover. Cook on Low 3
hours.

LeAnne's Calico Beans

LeAnne Nolt
Leola, PA

Makes 10 servings

1/4-1/2 lb. bacon
1 lb. ground beef
1 medium onion, chopped
2-lb. can pork and beans
1-lb. can Great Northern
   beans, drained
14 1/2-oz. can French-style
   green beans, drained
1/2 cup brown sugar
1/2 cup ketchup
1/2 tsp. salt
2 Tbsp. cider vinegar
1 Tbsp. prepared mustard

1. Brown bacon, ground
beef, and onion in skillet
until soft. Drain.
2. Combine all ingredients
in slow cooker.
3. Cover. Cook on Low 5-6
hours, or on High 2-3 hours.

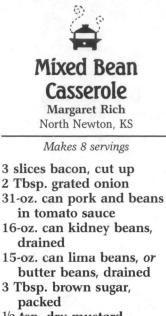

Mixed Bean Casserole

Margaret Rich
North Newton, KS

Makes 8 servings

3 slices bacon, cut up
2 Tbsp. grated onion
31-oz. can pork and beans
  in tomato sauce
16-oz. can kidney beans,
  drained
15-oz. can lima beans, *or*
  butter beans, drained
3 Tbsp. brown sugar,
  packed
1/2 tsp. dry mustard
3 Tbsp. ketchup

1. Combine all ingredients
in slow cooker.
2. Cover. Cook on Low 7-8
hours.

LaVerne's Baked Beans

LaVerne Olson
Willow Street, PA

Makes 16 servings

1/2 lb. bacon
1 medium onion, chopped
1/2 cup molasses
1/2 cup brown sugar
1/2 tsp. dry mustard
40-oz. can butter beans,
  drained

2 16-oz. cans kidney beans,
  drained
40-oz. can Great Northern
  beans, drained

1. Brown bacon and onion
in skillet until bacon is crisp
and crumbly. Drain.
2. Combine all ingredients
in slow cooker.
3. Cover. Cook on Low 1-3
hours.

Joan's Calico Beans

Joan Becker
Dodge City, KS

Makes 10-12 servings

1/4-1/3 lb. bacon, diced
1/2 cup chopped onions
2 16-oz. cans pork and
  beans
15-oz. can butter beans,
  drained
16-oz. can kidney beans,
  drained
1/2 cup packed brown sugar
1/2 cup ketchup
1/2 tsp. salt
1 tsp. dry mustard

1. Brown bacon in skillet
until crisp. Drain, reserving 2
Tbsp. drippings. Cook onion
in drippings until tender. Add
bacon and onion to slow
cooker.
2. Stir in beans, brown
sugar, ketchup, salt, and mustard. Mix well.
3. Cover. Cook on Low

4 1/2-5 1/2 hours, or on High 3-
3 1/2 hours.

Pat's Calico Baked Beans

Pat Bishop
Bedminster, PA

Makes 10-12 servings

2 cups green lima beans
2 cups limas, cooked
2 cups kidney beans
2 cups baked beans
6 slices bacon
1 1/2 cups onion, diced
3/4 cup brown sugar
2 tsp. salt
1 tsp. dry mustard
1 clove garlic, minced
1/2 cup vinegar
1/2 cup ketchup

1. Combine beans in slow
cooker.
2. Brown bacon in skillet
and crumble. Add to beans.
Stir in onion.
3. Mix together brown
sugar, salt, mustard, garlic,
vinegar, and ketchup. Pour
over beans. Mix well.
4. Cover. Cook on High 4
hours, or Low 6 hours.

Variation:
Add a chopped green pep-
per to the mixture in Step 2.
Barbara Tenney
Delta, PA

Barbara's Calico Beans

Barbara Kuhns
Millersburg, OH

Makes 12 servings

1 lb. bacon, diced
1 onion, chopped
1/2 cup ketchup
1/3-1/2 cup brown sugar, according to taste
3 Tbsp. cider vinegar
28-oz. can pork and beans, drained
16-oz. can kidney beans, drained
16-oz. can butter beans, drained

1. Brown bacon in skillet. Drain, reserving 2 Tbsp. drippings. Saute onion in bacon drippings.
2. Mix together ketchup, sugar, and vinegar.
3. Combine all ingredients in slow cooker.
4. Cover Cook on Low 3-4 hours.

Doris' Sweet-Sour Bean Trio

Doris Bachman
Putnam, IL

Makes 6-8 large servings

4 slices bacon
1 onion, chopped
1/4 cup brown sugar
1 tsp. crushed garlic
1 tsp. salt
3 Tbsp. cider vinegar
1 tsp. dry mustard
1-lb. can lima beans, drained
1-lb. can baked beans, drained
1-lb. can kidney beans, drained

1. Cook bacon in skillet. Reserve 2 Tbsp. bacon drippings. Crumble bacon.
2. In slow cooker, combine bacon, bacon drippings, onion, brown sugar, garlic, salt, and vinegar. Add beans. Mix well.
3. Cover. Cook on Low 6-8 hours.

Carol's Calico Beans

Carol Sommers
Millersburg, OH

Makes 10-12 servings

1/2 lb. bacon, *or* ground beef
32-oz. can pork and beans
1-lb. can green limas, drained
16-oz. can kidney beans, drained
1-lb. can whole kernel corn, drained
1 tsp. prepared mustard
2 medium onions, chopped
3/4 cup brown sugar
1 cup ketchup

1. Brown bacon or ground beef in skillct. Drain and crumble.
2. Combine beans and meat in slow cooker.
3. Combine mustard, onions, brown sugar, and ketchup. Pour over beans. Mix well.
4. Cover. Cook on Low 4-6 hours.

Ethel's Calico Beans

Ethel Mumaw
Berlin, OH

Makes 6-8 servings

1/2 lb. ground beef
1 onion, chopped
1/2 lb. bacon, diced
1/2 cup ketchup
2 Tbsp. cider vinegar
1/2 cup brown sugar, packed
16-oz. can red kidney beans, drained
14 1/2-oz. can pork and beans, undrained
15-oz. can butter beans, drained

1. Brown ground beef, onion, and bacon in skillet. Drain.
2. Combine all ingredients in slow cooker.
3. Cover. Cook on Low 8 hours.

Mary Ellen's and Nancy's Calico Beans

Mary Ellen Wilcox
Scotia, NY
Nancy W. Huber
Green Park, PA

Makes 12-15 servings

1/2 lb. bacon
1 lb. ground beef
2 15 1/2-oz. cans pork and beans
2 15 1/2-oz. cans butter beans, drained
2 16-oz. cans kidney beans, drained
1/2 cup sugar
1/2 cup brown sugar
1/4 cup ketchup
1 tsp. prepared mustard
1 tsp. garlic, finely chopped

1. Brown bacon in skillet and then crumble. Drain drippings. Add ground beef and brown. Drain.
2. Combine all ingredients in slow cooker.
3. Cover. Cook on Low 4-6 hours.

Variation:
Add 1 Tbsp. liquid smoke in Step 2.
Jan Pembleton
Arlington, TX

Sara's Bean Casserole

Sara Harter Fredette
Williamsburg, MA

Makes 6 servings

16-oz. can kidney beans, drained
2 1-lb. cans pork and beans
1 cup ketchup
1 Tbsp. Worcestershire sauce
1 tsp. salt
2 cups chopped onions
1 Tbsp. prepared mustard
1 tsp. cider vinegar

1. Combine all ingredients in slow cooker.
2. Cover. Cook on High 2 hours, or Low 4 hours.

Main Dish Baked Beans

Sue Pennington
Bridgewater, VA

*Makes 6-8 main-dish servings, or
12-16 side-dish servings*

1 lb. ground beef
28-oz. can baked beans
8-oz. can pineapple tidbits,
   drained
4 1/2-oz. can sliced
   mushrooms, drained
1 large onion, chopped
1 large green pepper,
   chopped
1/2 cup barbecue sauce
2 Tbsp. soy sauce
1 clove garlic, minced
1/2 tsp. salt
1/4 tsp. pepper

1. Brown ground beef in
skillet. Drain. Place in slow
cooker.
2. Stir in remaining ingredients. Mix well.
3. Cover. Cook on Low 4-8
hours, or until bubbly. Serve
in soup bowls.

Fruity Baked Bean Casserole

Elaine Unruh
Minneapolis, MN

Makes 6-8 servings

1/2 lb. bacon
3 medium onions, chopped
16-oz. can lima beans,
   drained
16-oz. can kidney beans,
   drained
2 16-oz. cans baked beans
15 1/2-oz. can pineapple
   chunks
1/4 cup brown sugar
1/4 cup cider vinegar
1/4 cup molasses
1/2 cup ketchup
2 Tbsp. prepared mustard
1/2 tsp. garlic salt
1 green pepper, chopped

1. Cook bacon in skillet.
Crumble. Reserve 2 Tbsp.
drippings in skillet. Place
bacon in slow cooker.
2. Add onions to drippings
and saute until soft. Drain.
Add to bacon in slow cooker.
3. Add beans and pineap-
ple to cooker. Mix well.
4. Combine brown sugar,
vinegar, molasses, ketchup,
mustard, garlic salt, and
green pepper. Mix well. Stir
into mixture in slow cooker.
5. Cover. Cook on High 2-3
hours.

Apple Bean Bake

Barbara A. Yoder
Goshen, IN

Makes 10-12 servings

4 Tbsp. butter
2 large Granny Smith
   apples, cubed
1/2 cup brown sugar
1/4 cup sugar
1/2 cup ketchup
1 tsp. cinnamon
1 Tbsp. molasses
1 tsp. salt
24-oz. can Great Northern
   beans, undrained
24-oz. can pinto beans,
   undrained
ham chunks, optional

1. Melt butter in skillet.
Add apples and cook until
tender.
2. Stir in brown sugar and
sugar. Cook until they melt.
Stir in ketchup, cinnamon,
molasses, and salt.
3. Add beans and ham
chunks. Mix well. Pour into
slow cooker.
4. Cover. Cook on High 2-4
hours.

Apple-Bean Pot

Charlotte Bull
Cassville, MO

Makes 12 servings

53-oz. can baked beans,
  well drained
1 large onion, chopped
3 tart apples, peeled and
  chopped
½ cup ketchup, *or*
  barbecue sauce
½ cup firmly packed
  brown sugar
1 pkg. smoky cocktail
  sausages, *or* chopped
  hot dogs, *or* chopped
  ham chunks, optional

1. Place beans in slow
cooker.
2. Add onions and apples.
Mix well.
3. Stir in ketchup or barbecue sauce, brown sugar, and
meat. Mix.
4. Cover. Heat on Low 3-4
hours, and then on High 30
minutes.

Linda's Baked Beans

Linda Sluiter
Schererville, IN

Makes 12 servings

16-oz. can red kidney
  beans, drained
15½-oz. can butter beans,
  drained
18-oz. jar B&M beans
¼ lb. Velveeta cheese,
  cubed
½ lb. bacon, diced
½ cup brown sugar
⅓ cup sugar
2 dashes Worcestershire
  sauce

1. Combine all ingredients
in slow cooker.
2. Cover. Cook on Low 6
hours. Do not stir until nearly
finished cooking.

Ann's Boston Baked Beans

Ann Driscoll
Albuquerque, MN

Makes 20 servings

1 cup raisins
2 small onions, diced
2 tart apples, diced
1 cup chili sauce
1 cup chopped ham, *or*
  crumbled bacon
2 1-lb., 15-oz. cans baked
  beans
3 tsp. dry mustard
½ cup sweet pickle relish

1. Mix together all ingredients.
2. Cover. Cook on Low 6-8
hours.

Vegetables

Very Special Spinach

Jeanette Oberholtzer
Manheim, PA

Makes 8 servings

3 10-oz. boxes frozen spinach, thawed and drained
2 cups cottage cheese
1½ cups grated cheddar cheese
3 eggs
¼ cup flour
1 tsp. salt
½ cup butter, *or* margarine, melted

1. Mix together all ingredients.
2. Pour into slow cooker.
3. Cook on High 1 hour. Reduce heat to Low and cook 4 more hours.

Spinach Casserole

Ann Bender
Ft. Defiance, VA

Makes 6 servings

2 10-oz. pkgs. frozen spinach, thawed and drained
2 cups white sauce, *or* cottage cheese
¼ cup butter, cubed
1¼ cups American cheese, cut into squares
2 eggs, beaten
¼ cup flour
1 tsp. salt
1 clove garlic, *or* ¼ tsp. garlic power

1. Combine all ingredients. Mix well. Pour into greased slow cooker.
2. Cover. Cook on High 1 hour. Reduce heat to Low and cook 4-5 hours.

Caramelized Onions

Mrs. J.E. Barthold
Bethlehem, PA

Makes 6-8 servings

6-8 large Vidalia *or* other sweet onions
4 Tbsp. butter, *or* margarine
10-oz. can chicken, *or* vegetable, broth

1. Peel onions. Remove stems and root ends. Place in slow cooker.
2. Pour butter and broth over.
3. Cook on Low 12 hours.

Note:
Serve as a side dish, or use onions and liquid to flavor soups or stews, or as topping for pizza.

Barbecued Green Beans

Arlene Wengerd
Millersburg, OH

Makes 4-6 servings

1 lb. bacon
¼ cup chopped onions
¾ cup ketchup
½ cup brown sugar
3 tsp. Worcestershire sauce
¾ tsp. salt
4 cups green beans

1. Brown bacon in skillet until crisp and then break into pieces. Reserve 2 Tbsp. bacon drippings.
2. Saute onions in bacon drippings.
3. Combine ketchup, brown sugar, Worcestershire sauce, and salt. Stir into bacon and onions.
4. Pour mixture over green beans and mix lightly.
5. Pour into slow cooker and cook on High 3-4 hours, or on Low 6-8 hours.

Dutch Green Beans

Edwina Stoltzfus
Narvon, PA

Makes 4-6 servings

½ lb. bacon, *or* ham chunks
4 medium onions, sliced
2 qts. fresh, frozen, *or* canned, green beans
4 cups canned stewed tomatoes, *or* diced fresh tomatoes
½ -¾ tsp. salt
¼ tsp. pepper

1. Brown bacon until crisp in skillet. Drain, reserving 2 Tbsp. drippings. Crumble bacon into small pieces.
2. Saute onions in bacon drippings.
3. Combine all ingredients in slow cooker.
4. Cover. Cook on Low 4½ hours.

Orange Glazed Carrots

Cyndie Marrara
Port Matilda, PA

Makes 6 servings

32-oz. (2 lbs.) pkg. baby carrots
½ cup packed brown sugar
½ cup orange juice
3 Tbsp. butter, *or* margarine
¾ tsp. cinnamon
¼ tsp. nutmeg
2 Tbsp. cornstarch
¼ cup water

1. Combine all ingredients except cornstarch and water in slow cooker.
2. Cover. Cook on Low 3-4 hours until carrots are tender crisp.
3. Put carrots in serving dish and keep warm, reserving cooking juices. Put reserved juices in small saucepan. Bring to boil.
4. Mix cornstarch and water in small bowl until blended. Add to juices. Boil one minute or until thickened, stirring constantly.
5. Pour over carrots and serve.

Vegetables do not overcook as they do when boiled on your range. Therefore, everything can go into the cooker at one time, with the exception of milk, sour cream, and cream, which should be added during the last hour.

Darlene Raber
Wellman, IA

Glazed Root Vegetable Medley

Teena Wagner
Waterloo, ON

Makes 6 servings

2 medium parsnips
4 medium carrots
1 turnip, about 4½ inches around
½ cup water
1 tsp. salt
½ cup sugar
3 Tbsp. butter
½ tsp. salt

1. Clean and peel vegetables. Cut in 1-inch pieces.
2. Dissolve salt in water in saucepan. Add vegetables and boil for 10 minutes. Drain, reserving ½ cup liquid.
3. Place vegetables in slow cooker. Add liquid.
4. Stir in sugar, butter, and salt.
5. Cover. Cook on Low 3 hours.

Acorn Squash

Valerie Hertzler
Weyers Cave, VA

Makes 2 servings

1 acorn squash
salt
cinnamon
butter

1. Place whole, rinsed squash in slow cooker.
2. Cover. Cook on Low 8-10 hours.
3. Split and remove seeds. Sprinkle each half with salt and cinnamon, dot with butter, and serve.

Zucchini Special

Louise Stackhouse
Benten, PA

Makes 4 servings

1 medium to large zucchini, peeled and sliced
1 medium onion, sliced
1 qt. stewed tomatoes with juice, *or* 2 14½-oz. cans stewed tomatoes with juice
¼ tsp. salt
1 tsp. dried basil
8 oz. mozzarella cheese, shredded

1. Layer zucchini, onion, and tomatoes in slow cooker.
2. Sprinkle with salt, basil, and cheese.
3. Cover. Cook on Low 6-8 hours.

Squash Casserole

Sharon Anders
Alburtis, PA

Makes 4-6 servings

2 lbs. yellow summer squash, *or* zucchini, thinly sliced (about 6 cups)
half a medium onion, chopped
1 cup peeled, shredded carrot
10¾-oz. can condensed cream of chicken soup
1 cup sour cream
¼ cup flour
8-oz. pkg. seasoned stuffing crumbs
½ cup butter, *or* margarine, melted

1. Combine squash, onion, carrots, and soup.
2. Mix together sour cream and flour. Stir into vegetables.
3. Toss stuffing mix with butter. Spread half in bottom of slow cooker. Add vegetable mixture. Top with remaining crumbs.
4. Cover. Cook on Low 7-9 hours.

Doris' Broccoli and Cauliflower with Cheese

Doris G. Herr
Manheim, PA

Makes 8 servings

1 lb. frozen cauliflower
2 10-oz. pkgs. frozen broccoli
1/2 cup water
2 cups shredded cheddar cheese

1. Place cauliflower and broccoli in slow cooker.
2. Add water. Top with cheese.
3. Cook on Low 1½-3 hours, depending upon how crunchy or soft you want the vegetables.

Julia's Broccoli and Cauliflower with Cheese

Julia Lapp
New Holland, PA

Makes 6 servings

5 cups raw broccoli and cauliflower
1/4 cup water
2 Tbsp. butter, *or* margarine
2 Tbsp. flour
1/2 tsp. salt
1 cup milk

1 cup shredded cheddar cheese

1. Cook broccoli and cauliflower in saucepan in water, until just crispy tender. Set aside.
2. Make white sauce by melting the butter in another pan over low heat. Blend in flour and salt. Add milk all at once. Cook quickly, stirring constantly until mixture thickens and bubbles. Add cheese. Stir until melted and smooth.
3. Combine vegetables and sauce in slow cooker. Mix well.
4. Cook on Low 1½ hours.

Variation:
Substitute green beans and carrots or other vegetables for broccoli and cauliflower.

Golden Cauliflower

Carol Peachey
Lancaster, PA

Makes 4-6 servings

2 10-oz. pkgs. frozen cauliflower, thawed
8-oz. jar cheese sauce
4 slices bacon, crisply browned and crumbled

1. Place cauliflower in slow cooker
2. Pour cheese over top. Top with bacon.
3. Cover. Cook on High 1½ hours and then reduce to Low for an additional 2 hours. Or cook only on Low 4-5 hours.

Broccoli Cheese Casserole

Janie Steele
Moore, OK

Makes 8-10 servings

10-oz. pkg. frozen chopped broccoli, thawed
1 cup cooked rice
1/4 cup chopped celery
10 3/4-oz. can cream of chicken soup
4-oz. jar cheese sauce
4-oz. can mushrooms, optional
1/8 tsp. garlic powder
1/8 tsp. pepper
1/4-1/2 tsp. salt

1. Mix together all ingredients in slow cooker.
2. Cook on Low 1½ hours, or until heated through.

Sweet-Sour Cabbage

Irma H. Schoen
Windsor, CT

Makes 6 servings

1 medium-sized head red, *or* green, cabbage, shredded
2 onions, chopped
4 tart apples, pared, quartered
1/2 cup raisins
1/4 cup lemon juice

1/4 cup cider, *or* apple juice
3 Tbsp. honey
1 Tbsp. caraway seeds
1/8 tsp. allspice
1/2 tsp. salt

1. Combine all ingredients in slow cooker.
2. Cook on High 3-5 hours, depending upon how crunchy or soft you want the cabbage and onions.

Bavarian Cabbage

Joyce Shackelford
Green Bay, WI

Makes 4-8 servings, depending upon the size of the cabbage head

1 small head red cabbage, sliced
1 medium onion, chopped
3 tart apples, cored and quartered
2 tsp. salt
1 cup hot water
2 Tbsp. sugar
1/3 cup vinegar
3 Tbsp. bacon drippings

1. Place all ingredients in slow cooker in order listed.
2. Cover. Cook on Low 8 hours, or High 3 hours. Stir well before serving.

Variation:
Add 6 slices bacon, browned until crisp and crumbled.
Jean M. Butzer
Batavia, NY

Cabbage Casserole

Edwina Stoltzfus
Narvon, PA

Makes 6 servings

1 large head cabbage, chopped
2 cups water
1 Tbsp. salt
1/3 cup butter
1/4 cup flour
1/2-1 tsp. salt
1/4 tsp. pepper
1 1/3 cups milk
1 1/3 cups shredded cheddar cheese

1. Cook cabbage in saucepan in boiling water and salt for 5 minutes. Drain. Place in slow cooker.
2. In saucepan, melt butter. Stir in flour, salt, and pepper. Add milk, stirring constantly on low heat for 5 minutes. Remove from heat. Stir in cheese. Pour over cabbage.
3. Cover. Cook on Low 4-5 hours.

Variation:
Replace cabbage with cauliflower.

Vegetable Curry

Sheryl Shenk
Harrisonburg, VA

Makes 8-10 servings

16-oz. pkg. baby carrots
3 medium potatoes, cubed
1 lb. fresh, *or* frozen, green beans, cut in 2-inch pieces
1 green pepper, chopped
1 onion, chopped
1-2 cloves garlic, minced
15-oz. can garbanzo beans, drained
28-oz. can crushed tomatoes
3 Tbsp. minute tapioca
3 tsp. curry powder
2 tsp. salt
1 3/4 cups boiling water
2 tsp. chicken bouillon granules, *or* 2 chicken bouillon cubes

1. Combine carrots, potatoes, green beans, pepper, onion, garlic, garbanzo beans, and crushed tomatoes in large bowl.
2. Stir in tapioca, curry powder, and salt.
3. Dissolve bouillon in boiling water. Pour over vegetables. Mix well. Spoon into large cooker, or two medium-sized ones.
4. Cover. Cook on Low 8-10 hours, or High 3-4 hours. Serve with cooked rice.

Variation:
Substitute canned green beans for fresh beans but add toward the end of the cooking time.

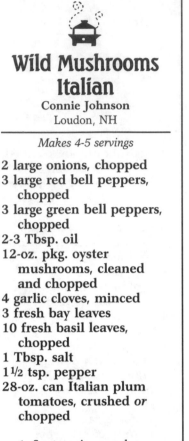

Wild Mushrooms Italian

Connie Johnson
Loudon, NH

Makes 4-5 servings

2 large onions, chopped
3 large red bell peppers, chopped
3 large green bell peppers, chopped
2-3 Tbsp. oil
12-oz. pkg. oyster mushrooms, cleaned and chopped
4 garlic cloves, minced
3 fresh bay leaves
10 fresh basil leaves, chopped
1 Tbsp. salt
1 1/2 tsp. pepper
28-oz. can Italian plum tomatoes, crushed *or* chopped

1. Saute onions and peppers in oil in skillet until soft. Stir in mushrooms and garlic. Saute just until mushrooms begin to turn brown. Pour into slow cooker.
2. Add remaining ingredients. Stir well.
3. Cover. Cook on Low 6-8 hours.

Note:
Good as an appetizer or on pita bread, or serve over rice or pasta for main dish.

Corn Pudding

Barbara A. Yoder
Goshen, IN

Makes 10 plus servings

2 10-oz. cans whole kernel corn with juice
2 1-lb. cans creamed corn
2 boxes corn muffin mix
1 stick (1/4 lb.) margarine
8-oz. box sour cream

1. Combine all ingredients in slow cooker.
2. Cover. Heat on Low 2-3 hours until thickened and set.

Corn on the Cob

Donna Conto
Saylorsburg, PA

Makes 3-4 servings

6-8 ears of corn (in husk)
1/2 cup water

1. Remove silk from corn, as much as possible, but leave husks on.
2. Cut off ends of corn so ears can stand in the cooker.
3. Add water.
4. Cover. Cook on Low 2-3 hours.

Cheesy Corn

Tina Snyder
Manheim, PA
Jeannine Janzen
Elbing, KS
Nadine Martinitz
Salina, KS

Makes 10 servings

3 16-oz. pkgs. frozen corn
8-oz. pkg. cream cheese, cubed
1/4 cup butter, cubed
3 Tbsp. water
3 Tbsp. milk
2 Tbsp. sugar
6 slices American cheese, cut into squares

1. Combine all ingredients in slow cooker. Mix well.
2. Cover. Cook on Low 4 hours, or until heated through and the cheese is melted.

Be careful about adding liquids to food in a slow cooker. Foods have natural juices in them, and unlike oven cooking which is dry, food juices remain in the slow cooker as the food cooks.

Ann Sunday McDowell
Newtown, PA

Slow-Cooker Rice

Dorothy Horst
Tiskilwa, IL

Makes 10 servings

1 Tbsp. butter
4 cups converted long
   grain rice, uncooked
10 cups water
4 tsp. salt

1. Pour rice, water, and salt into greased slow cooker.
2. Cover. Cook on High 2-3 hours, or until rice is tender, but not overcooked. Stir occasionally.

Risi Bisi
(Peas and Rice)

Cyndie Marrara
Port Matilda, PA

Makes 6 servings

1½ cups converted long
   grain white rice,
   uncooked
3/4 cup chopped onions
2 garlic cloves, minced
2 14½-oz. cans reduced-
   sodium chicken broth
1/3 cup water
3/4 tsp. Italian seasoning
1/2 tsp. dried basil leaves
1/2 cup frozen baby peas,
   thawed
1/4 cup grated Parmesan
   cheese

1. Combine rice, onions, and garlic in slow cooker.
2. In saucepan, mix together chicken broth and water. Bring to boil. Add Italian seasoning and basil leaves. Stir into rice mixture.
3. Cover. Cook on Low 2-3 hours, or until liquid is absorbed.
4. Stir in peas. Cover. Cook 30 minutes. Stir in cheese.

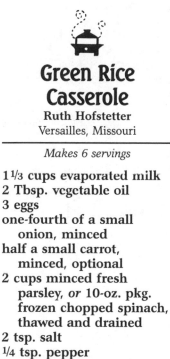

Green Rice
Casserole

Ruth Hofstetter
Versailles, Missouri

Makes 6 servings

1⅓ cups evaporated milk
2 Tbsp. vegetable oil
3 eggs
one-fourth of a small
   onion, minced
half a small carrot,
   minced, optional
2 cups minced fresh
   parsley, *or* 10-oz. pkg.
   frozen chopped spinach,
   thawed and drained
2 tsp. salt
1/4 tsp. pepper
1 cup shredded sharp
   cheese
3 cups cooked long grain
   rice

1. Beat together milk, oil, and eggs until well combined.
2. Stir in remaining ingredients. Mix well. Pour into greased slow cooker.

3. Cover. Cook on High 1 hour. Stir. Reduce heat to Low and cook 4-6 hours.

Wild Rice

Ruth S. Weaver
Reinholds, PA

Makes 4-5 servings

1 cup wild rice, *or* wild
   rice mixture, uncooked
1/2 cup sliced mushrooms
1/2 cup diced onions
1/2 cup diced green, *or* red,
   peppers
1 Tbsp. oil
1/2 tsp. salt
1/4 tsp. pepper
2½ cups chicken broth

1. Layer rice and vegetables in slow cooker. Pour oil, salt, and pepper over vegetables. Stir.
2. Heat chicken broth. Pour over ingredients in slow cooker.
3. Cover. Cook on High 2½-3 hours, or until rice is soft and liquid is absorbed.

Baked Potatoes

Lucille Metzler, Wellsboro, PA
Elizabeth Yutzy, Wauseon, OH
Glenda S. Weaver, Manheim, PA
Mary Jane Musser, Manheim, PA
Esther Becker, Gordonville, PA

Makes 6 servings

**6 medium baking potatoes
butter, *or* margarine**

1. Prick potatoes with fork. Rub each with either butter or margarine. Place in slow cooker.
2. Cover. Cook on High 3-5 hours, or Low 6-10 hours.

Baked Potatoes

Valerie Hertzler
Weyers Cave, VA
Carol Peachey, Lancaster, PA
Janet L. Roggie, Lowville, NY

Potatoes

1. Prick potatoes with fork and wrap in foil.
2. Cover. Do not add water. Cook on High 2½-4 hours, or Low 8-10 hours.

Pizza Potatoes

Margaret Wenger Johnson
Keezletown, VA

Makes 4-6 servings

**6 medium potatoes, sliced
1 large onion, thinly sliced
2 Tbsp. olive oil
2 cups grated mozzarella cheese
2 oz. sliced pepperoni
1 tsp. salt
8-oz. can pizza sauce**

1. Saute potato and onion slices in oil in skillet until onions appear transparent. Drain well.
2. In slow cooker, combine potatoes, onions, cheese, pepperoni, and salt.
3. Pour pizza sauce over top.
4. Cover. Cook on Low 6-10 hours, or until potatoes are soft.

Mustard Potatoes

Frances B. Musser
Newmanstown, PA
Nancy Zimmerman
Loysville, PA

Makes 6 servings

**6 medium potatoes, peeled, cooked, cooled, and grated
½ cup chopped onions
¼ cup butter
1½ tsp. prepared mustard
1 tsp. salt
¼ tsp. pepper
½ cup milk
¼ lb. American, *or* cheddar, cheese**

1. Put potatoes in greased slow cooker.
2. Saute onion in butter in skillet. Add mustard, salt, pepper, milk, and cheese. Pour over potatoes.
3. Cover. Cook on Low 3 hours. Stir or toss lightly when ready to serve.

Cut up vegetables for your slow-cooker dish the night before and place them in ziplock bags in the refrigerator. This cuts down on preparation time in the morning.
Tracy Supcoe
Barclay, MD

Potatoes O'Brien
Rebecca Meyerkorth
Wamego, KS

Makes 6 servings

32-oz. pkg. shredded
  potatoes
1/4 cup chopped onions
1/4 cup chopped green
  peppers
2 Tbsp. chopped pimento,
  optional
1 cup chopped ham,
  optional
3/4 tsp. salt
1/4 tsp. pepper
3 Tbsp. butter
3 Tbsp. flour
1/2 cup milk
10³/4-oz. can cream of
  mushroom soup
1 cup shredded cheddar
  cheese, divided

1. Place potatoes, onions,
green peppers, pimento, and
ham in slow cooker. Sprinkle
with salt and pepper.
2. Melt butter in sauce-
pan. Stir in flour; then add
half of milk. Stir rapidly to
remove all lumps. Stir in
remaining milk. Stir in mushroom soup and 1/2 cup cheese.
Pour over potatoes.
3. Cover. Cook on Low 4-5
hours. Sprinkle remaining
cheese on top about 1/2 hour
before serving.

Potluck Potatoes
Lovina Baer
Conrath, WI

Makes 6-8 servings

4 cups potatoes, cooked,
  peeled, diced
10³/4-oz. can cream of
  chicken soup
1 cup sour cream
1 cup shredded cheddar
  cheese
1/3 cup butter, *or*
  margarine, melted
1/4 cup chopped onions
1/2 tsp. garlic salt
1/2 tsp. salt
1/2 tsp. pepper

1. Combine all ingredients
in slow cooker. Mix well.
2. Cover. Cook on Low 3-4
hours.

Variations:
1. If you prefer soft
onions, saute in skillet in butter or margarine before combining with other ingredients.
Tracey Yohn
Harrisburg, PA

2. Add chopped ham or
dried beef.

German Potato Salad
Lauren Eberhard
Seneca, IL

Makes 8 servings

6 slices bacon
3/4 cup chopped onions
10³/4-oz. can cream of
  chicken soup
1/4 cup water
2 Tbsp. cider vinegar
1/2 tsp. sugar
pepper to taste
4 cups parboiled, cubed
  potatoes
parsley

1. Brown bacon in skillet
and then crumble. Reserve
2 Tbsp. bacon drippings.
Saute onions in drippings.
2. Blend together soup,
water, vinegar, sugar, and
pepper. Add bacon and
onions. Mix well.
3. Add potatoes and pars-
ley. Mix well. Pour into slow
cooker.
4. Cover. Cook on Low 4
hours.
5. Serve warm or at room
temperature.

Slow-Cooker Scalloped Potatoes

Ruth S. Weaver
Reinholds, PA

Makes 10 servings

1/2 tsp. cream of tartar
1 cup water
8-10 medium potatoes,
    thinly sliced
half an onion, chopped
salt to taste
pepper to taste
1 cup grated American, *or*
    cheddar, cheese
10¾-oz. can cream of
    celery, *or* mushroom, *or*
    chicken, soup
1 tsp. paprika

1. Dissolve cream of tartar in water. Add potatoes and toss together. Drain.
2. Place half of potatoes in slow cooker. Sprinkle with onions, salt, pepper, and half of cheese.
3. Repeat with remaining potatoes and cheese.
4. Spoon soup over the top. Sprinkle with paprika.
5. Cover. Cook on Low 8-10 hours, or High 4 hours.

Variations:
1. For thicker scalloped potatoes, sprinkle each layer of potatoes with 2 Tbsp. flour.
    Ruth Hershey
    Paradise, PA

2. Instead of sprinkling the layers of potatoes with grated cheese, place ¼ lb. Velveeta,

or American cheese slices over top during last 30 minutes of cooking.
    Pat Bishop
    Bedminster, PA
    Mary Ellen Musser
    Reinholds, PA
    Annabelle Unternahrer
    Shipshewana, IN

Saucy Scalloped Potatoes

Sue Pennington
Bridgewater, VA

Makes 4-6 servings

4 cups peeled, thinly sliced
    potatoes
10¾-oz. can cream of
    celery, *or* mushroom,
    soup
12-oz. can evaporated milk
1 large onion, sliced
2 Tbsp. butter, *or*
    margarine
1/2 tsp. salt
1/4 tsp. pepper
1½ cups chopped, fully
    cooked ham

1. Combine potatoes, soup, evaporated milk, onion, butter, salt, and pepper in slow cooker. Mix well.
2. Cover. Cook on High 1 hour. Stir in ham. Reduce to

Low. Cook 6-8 hours, or until potatoes are tender.

Creamy Red Potatoes

Mrs. J.E. Barthold
Bethlehem, PA

Makes 4-6 servings

2 lbs. small red potatoes,
    quartered
8-oz. pkg. cream cheese,
    softened
10¾-oz. can cream of
    potato soup
1 envelope dry Ranch
    salad dressing mix

1. Place potatoes in slow cooker.
2. Beat together cream cheese, soup, and salad dressing mix. Stir into potatoes.
3. Cover. Cook on Low 8 hours, or until potatoes are tender.

Be sure vegetables are thinly sliced or chopped because they cook slowly in a slow cooker.
Marilyn Yoder
Archbold, OH

Extra Good Mashed Potatoes

Zona Mae Bontrager
Kokomo, IN
Mary Jane Musser, Manheim, PA
Elsie Schlabach, Millersburg, OH
Carol Sommers, Millersburg, OH
Edwina Stoltzfus, Narvon, PA

Makes 12 servings

5 lbs. potatoes, peeled,
 cooked, and mashed
8-oz. pkg. cream cheese,
 softened
1½ cups sour cream
3 tsp. onion, *or* garlic, salt
1½ tsp. salt
¼-½ tsp. pepper
2 Tbsp. butter, melted

1. Combine all ingredients.
Pour into slow cooker.
2. Cover. Cook on Low 5-6
hours.

Note:
 These potatoes may be
prepared 3-4 days in advance
of serving and kept in the
refrigerator until ready to
use.

Variations:
 1. Add 1½ cups shredded
cheddar cheese to Step 1.
Maricarol Magill
Freehold, NJ

 2. Sprinkle with paprika
before cooking.
Pat Unternahrer
Wayland, IA

Potato Cheese Puff

Mary Sommerfeld
Lancaster, PA

Makes 10 servings

12 medium potatoes,
 boiled and mashed
1 cup milk
6 Tbsp. butter
¾ tsp. salt
2¼ cups Velveeta cheese,
 cubed
2 eggs, beaten

1. Combine all ingredients.
Pour into slow cooker.
2. Cover. Cook on High
2½ hours, or Low 3-4 hours.

Creamy Hash Browns

Judy Buller, Bluffton, OH
Elaine Patton
West Middletown, PA
Melissa Raber, Millersburg, OH

Makes 14 servings

2-lb. pkg. frozen, cubed
 hash brown potatoes
2 cups cubed *or* shredded
 American cheese
1 pint (2 cups) sour cream
10¾-oz. can cream of
 celery soup
10¾-oz. can cream of
 chicken soup
½ lb. sliced bacon, cooked
 and crumbled

1 medium onion, chopped
¼ cup margarine, melted
¼ tsp. pepper

1. Place potatoes in slow
cooker. Combine remaining
ingredients and pour over
potatoes. Mix well.
2. Cover. Cook on Low 4-5
hours, or until potatoes are
tender.

Cheese and Potato Bake

Ann Gouinlock
Alexander, NY

Makes 8 servings

2-lb. bag frozen hash
 browns
10¾-oz. can cheddar
 cheese soup
10¾-oz. can cream of
 chicken soup
1 cup milk
2.8-oz. can French-fried
 onion rings
½ cup grated cheddar
 cheese

1. Combine hash browns,
soups, and milk in slow
cooker. Mix well.
2. Top with half can of
onion rings.
3. Cover. Cook on Low 6-8
hours. Sprinkle with cheddar
cheese and remaining onion
rings about 1 hour before
serving.

Cheesy Hash Brown Potatoes

Clarice Williams
Fairbank, IA

Makes 6-8 servings

2 10¾-oz. cans cheddar
  cheese soup
1⅓ cups buttermilk
2 Tbsp. butter, *or*
  margarine, melted
½ tsp. seasoned salt
¼ tsp. garlic powder
¼ tsp. pepper
2-lb. pkg. frozen, cubed
  hash brown potatoes
¼ cup grated Parmesan
  cheese
1 tsp. paprika

1. Combine soup, butter-
milk, butter, seasoned salt,
garlic powder, and pepper in
slow cooker. Mix well.
2. Stir in hash browns.
Sprinkle with Parmesan
cheese and paprika.
3. Cover. Cook on Low 4-
4½ hours, or until potatoes
are tender.

Slow-Cooker Cheese Potatoes

Bernice M. Wagner
Dodge City, KS
Marilyn Yoder
Archbold, OH

Makes 6 servings

2-lb. pkg. frozen hash
  browns
10¾-oz. can cream of
  potato soup
10¾-oz. can cream of
  mushroom soup
8 oz. (2 cups) shredded
  cheddar cheese
1 cup grated Parmesan
  cheese
1 pint sour cream

1. Mix together all ingredients in slow cooker.
2. Cover. Cook on Low 7
hours.

Scalloped Taters

Sara Wilson
Blairstown, MD

Makes 6-8 servings

½ cup melted margarine
¼ cup dried onions
16-oz. pkg. frozen hash
  brown potatoes
10¾-oz. can cream of
  chicken soup
1½ cups milk
1 cup shredded cheddar
  cheese
⅛ tsp. black pepper
1 cup crushed cornflakes,
  divided

1. Stir together margarine,
onions, potatoes, soup, milk,
cheese, pepper, and ½ cup
cornflakes. Pour into greased
slow cooker. Top with
remaining cornflakes.
2. Cover. Cook on High 3-4
hours.

To prevent potatoes from darkening, slice them, then stir
a mixture of 1 cup water and ½ tsp. cream of tartar into
them. Drain, then place potatoes in cooker and proceed with
the recipe.

Dale Peterson
Rapid City, SD

Slow-Cooker Cottage Potatoes
Marjora Miller
Archbold, OH

Makes 10-12 servings

2 lbs. frozen hash brown
  potatoes
1 pint sour cream
10¾-oz. can cream of
  chicken soup
dash of pepper
2 cups Velveeta cheese,
  cubed
½ cup chopped onions
¾ tsp. salt
¼ tsp. pepper

1. Combine all ingredients
except potatoes in large bowl.
Then fold in potatoes. Spoon
into slow cooker.
2. Cover. Cook on High
1½ hours, and then on Low
2½ hours.

Cheesy Potatoes
Darla Sathre
Baxter, MN

Makes 6 servings

2-lb. pkg. frozen hash
  browns, partly thawed
2 10¾-oz.cans cheddar
  cheese soup
12-oz. can evaporated milk
2.8-oz. can French-fried
  onion rings
salt to taste
pepper to taste

1. Combine all ingredients.
Pour into greased slow
cooker.
2. Cover. Cook on Low 6-8
hours, or on High 3-4 hours.

Slow-Cooker Potatoes
Arlene Wiens
Newton, KS

Makes 8 servings

32-oz. pkg. frozen hash
  brown potatoes
2 10¾-oz. cans cheddar
  cheese soup
2.8-oz. can French-fried
  onion rings

1. Combine all ingredients
in greased slow cooker.
2. Cover. Cook on Low 7-8
hours.

Au Gratin Hash Brown Potatoes
Penny Blosser
Beavercreek, OH

Makes 12 servings

2 lb.-pkg. frozen hash
  brown potatoes, thawed
1 small onion, diced
1 stick butter, melted
16-oz. container French
  onion dip
16-oz. jar Cheez Whiz,
  heated

1. Place hash browns in
slow cooker.
2. Combine onion, butter,
dip, and Cheez Whiz. Pour
over hash browns. Mix well.
3. Cover. Cook on Low 4-6
hours, or High 2-3 hours.
(Use the greater number of
hours if potatoes are frozen.)

Candied Sweet Potatoes

Julie Weaver
Reinholds, PA

Makes 8 servings

6-8 medium sweet potatoes
1/2 tsp. salt
1/4 cup butter, *or*
    margarine, melted
20-oz. can crushed
    pineapples, undrained
1/4 cup brown sugar
1 tsp. nutmeg
1 tsp. cinnamon

1. Cook sweet potatoes until soft. Peel. Slice and place in slow cooker.
2. Combine remaining ingredients. Pour over sweet potatoes.
3. Cover. Cook on High 4 hours.

Potato Filling

Miriam Nolt
New Holland, PA

Makes 16-20 servings

1 cup celery, chopped fine
1 medium onion, minced
1 cup butter
2 15-oz. pkgs. bread cubes
6 eggs, beaten
1 qt. milk
1 qt. mashed potatoes
3 tsp. salt
2 pinches saffron
1 cup boiling water
1 tsp. pepper

1. Saute celery and onion in butter in skillet for about 15 minutes.
2. Combine sauted mixture with bread cubes. Stir in remaining ingredients. Add more milk if mixture isn't very moist.
3. Pour into large, or several medium-sized, slow cookers. Cook on High 3 hours, stirring up from bottom every hour or so to make sure the filling isn't sticking.

Mild Dressing

Jane Steiner
Orrville, OH

Makes 6 servings

16-oz. loaf homemade
    white bread
2 eggs, beaten
1/2 cup celery
1/4 cup diced onions
3/4 tsp. salt
1/2 tsp. pepper
giblets, cooked and cut up
    fine
milk

1. Set bread slices out to dry the day before using. Cut into small cubes.
2. Combine all ingredients except milk.
3. Moisten mixture with enough milk to make bread cubes soft but not soggy.
4. Pour into greased slow cooker. Cook on Low 3½ hours, stirring every hour. When stirring, add a small amount of milk to sides of cooker—if needed—to keep dressing moist and to prevent sticking.

It's quite convenient to use a slow cooker to cook potatoes for salads or for fried potatoes or as baked potatoes. Just fill the slow cooker with cleaned potatoes and cook all day until done.

Darla Sathre
Baxter, MN

Slow Cooker Stuffing with Poultry
Pat Unternahrer
Wayland, IA

Makes 18 servings

1 large loaf dried bread, cubed
1¹/2-2 cups chopped cooked turkey, *or* chicken, meat & giblets
1 large onion, chopped
3 ribs celery with leaves, chopped
¹/2 cup butter, melted
4 cups chicken broth
1 Tbsp. poultry seasoning
1 tsp. salt
4 eggs, beaten
¹/2 tsp. pepper

1. Mix together all ingredients. Pour into slow cooker.
2. Cover and cook on High 1 hour, then reduce to Low 6-8 hours.

Moist Poultry Dressing
Virginia Bender, Dover, DE
Josie Bollman, Maumee, OH
Sharon Brubaker, Myerstown, PA
Joette Droz, Kalona, IA
Jacqueline Stefl, E. Bethany, NY

Makes 14 servings

2 4¹/2-oz. cans sliced mushrooms, drained
4 celery ribs, chopped (about 2 cups)
2 medium onions, chopped
¹/4 cup minced fresh parsley
¹/4-³/4 cup margarine (enough to flavor bread)
13 cups cubed day-old bread
1¹/2 tsp. salt
1¹/2 tsp. sage
1 tsp. poultry seasoning
1 tsp. dried thyme
¹/2 tsp. pepper
2 eggs
1 *or* 2 14¹/2-oz. cans chicken broth (enough to moisten bread)

1. In large skillet, saute mushrooms, celery, onions, and parsley in margarine until vegetables are tender.
2. Toss together bread cubes, salt, sage, poultry seasoning, thyme, and pepper. Add mushroom mixture.
3. Combine eggs and broth and add to bread mixture. Mix well.

4. Pour into greased slow cooker. Cook on Low 5 hours, or until meat thermometer reaches 160°.

Note:
This is a good way to free up the oven when you're making a turkey.

Variations:
1. Use 2 bags bread cubes for stuffing. Make one mixed bread (white and wheat) and the other corn bread cubes.
2. Add ¹/2 tsp. dried marjoram to Step 2.
Arlene Miller
Hutchinson, KS

Fresh Herb Stuffing

Barbara J. Fabel
Wausau, WI

Makes 6-8 servings

½ cup butter
2 onions, chopped
3 celery ribs, chopped
½ cup chopped fresh
    parsley
1 Tbsp. chopped fresh
    rosemary
1 Tbsp. chopped fresh
    thyme
1 Tbsp. chopped fresh
    marjoram
1 Tbsp. chopped fresh sage
1 tsp. salt
½ tsp. freshly ground
    pepper
1 loaf stale sourdough
    bread, cut in 1-inch
    cubes
1½-2 cups chicken broth

1. Saute onions and celery
in butter in skillet for 10 minutes. Remove from heat and
stir in fresh herbs and seasonings.
2. Place bread cubes in
large bowl. Add onion/herb
mixture. Add enough broth to
moisten. Mix well. Turn into
greased slow cooker.
3. Cover. Cook on High 1
hour. Reduce heat to Low
and continue cooking 3-4
hours.

Slow-Cooker Dressing

Helen King
Fairbank, IA

Makes 10-12 servings

14-15 cups bread cubes
3 cups chopped celery
1½ cups chopped onions
1½ tsp. sage
1 tsp. salt
½ tsp. pepper
1½ cups *or* more chicken
    broth (enough to
    moisten the bread)
¼-1 cup melted butter, *or*
    margarine (enough to
    flavor the bread)

1. Combine all ingredients
but butter. Mix well. Toss
with butter.
2. Spoon into slow cooker.
Cook on Low 4-5 hours.

Slow Cooker Stuffing

Dede Peterson
Rapid City, SD

Makes 10 servings

12 cups toasted bread
    crumbs, *or* dressing mix
1 lb. bulk sausage,
    browned and drained
¼-1 cup butter, *or*
    margarine (enough to
    flavor bread)

1 cup *or* more finely
    chopped onions
1 cup *or* more finely
    chopped celery
8-oz. can sliced
    mushrooms, with liquid
¼ cup chopped fresh
    parsley
2 tsp. poultry seasoning
    (omit if using dressing
    mix)
dash of pepper
½ tsp. salt
2 eggs, beaten
4 cups chicken stock

1. Combine bread crumbs
and sausage.
2. Melt butter in skillet.
Add onions and celery and
saute until tender. Stir in
mushrooms and parsley. Add
seasonings. Pour over bread
crumbs and mix well.
3. Stir in eggs and chicken
stock.
4. Pour into slow cooker
and bake on High 1 hour, and
on Low an additional 3 hours.

Variations:
1. For a drier stuffing,
reduce the chicken stock to
1½ cups (or 14½-oz. can
chicken broth) and eliminate
the sausage.
2. For a less spicy stuffing,
reduce the poultry seasoning
to ½ tsp.
Dolores Metzler
Mechanicsburg, PA

3. Substitute 3½-4½ cups
cooked and diced giblets in
place of sausage. Add another
can mushrooms and 2 tsp.
sage in Step 2.
Mrs. Don Martins
Fairbank, IA

Desserts

Bread Pudding

Winifred Ewy, Newton, KS
Helen King, Fairbank, IA
Elaine Patton
West Middletown, PA

Makes 6 servings

8 slices bread (raisin bread
   is especially good),
   cubed
4 eggs
2 cups milk
¼ cup sugar
¼ cup melted butter, *or*
   margarine
½ cup raisins (use only
   ¼ cup if using raisin
   bread)
½ tsp. cinnamon

Sauce:
2 Tbsp. butter, *or*
   margarine
2 Tbsp. flour
1 cup water
¾ cup sugar
1 tsp. vanilla

1. Place bread cubes in greased slow cooker.
2. Beat together eggs and milk. Stir in sugar, butter, raisins, and cinnamon. Pour over bread and stir.
3. Cover and cook on High 1 hour. Reduce heat to Low and cook 3-4 hours, or until thermometer reaches 160°.
4. Make sauce just before pudding is done baking. Begin by melting butter in saucepan. Stir in flour until smooth. Gradually add water, sugar, and vanilla. Bring to boil. Cook, stirring constantly for 2 minutes, or until thickened.
5. Serve sauce over warm bread pudding.

Variations:

1. Use dried cherries instead of raisins. Use cherry flavoring in sauce instead of vanilla.

Char Hagnes
Montague, MI

2. Use ¼ tsp. ground cinnamon and ¼ tsp. ground nutmeg, instead of ½ tsp. ground cinnamon in pudding.
3. Use 8 cups day-old unfrosted cinnamon rolls instead of the bread.

Beatrice Orgist
Richardson, TX

4. Use ½ tsp. vanilla and ¼ tsp. ground nutmeg instead of ½ tsp. cinnamon.

Nanci Keatley
Salem, OR

To achieve the best volume in baked goods, always use large fresh eggs.

Sara Wilson
Blairstown, MO

Old-Fashioned Rice Pudding

Ann Bender, Fort Defiance, VA
Gladys M. High, Ephrata, PA
Mrs. Don Martins, Fairbank, IA

Makes 6 servings

2½ cups cooked rice
1½ cups evaporated milk
  (or scalded milk)
⅔ cup brown, *or* white,
  sugar
3 Tbsp. soft butter
2 tsp. vanilla
½-1 tsp. nutmeg
3 eggs, beaten
½-1 cup raisins

1. Mix together all ingredients. Pour into lightly greased slow cooker.
2. Cover and cook on High 2 hours, or on Low 4-6 hours. Stir after first hour.
3. Serve warm or cold.

Mama's Rice Pudding

Donna Barnitz, Jenks, OK
Shari Jensen, Fountain, CO

Makes 4-6 servings

½ cup white rice,
  uncooked
½ cup sugar
1 tsp. vanilla
1 tsp. lemon extract
1 cup plus 2 Tbsp. milk
1 tsp. butter
2 eggs, beaten
1 tsp. cinnamon
½ cup raisins
1 cup whipping cream,
  whipped
nutmeg

1. Combine all ingredients except whipped cream and nutmeg in slow cooker. Stir well.
2. Cover pot. Cook on Low 6-7 hours, until rice is tender and milk absorbed. Be sure to stir once every 2 hours during cooking.
3. Pour into bowl. Cover with plastic wrap and chill.
4. Before serving, fold in whipped cream and sprinkle with nutmeg.

Ann's Rice Pudding

Ann Sunday McDowell
Newtown, PA

Makes 6-8 servings

1 cup uncooked, long grain
  white rice
3 cups milk
3 Tbsp. butter
½ tsp. salt
¾ cup sugar
3 eggs, beaten
½ tsp. freshly ground
  nutmeg
1 tsp. vanilla

1. Cook rice according to package directions.
2. Mix together all ingredients in greased 1½-qt. casserole dish. Cover with greased foil and set inside slow cooker. Add 1 cup water to slow cooker (around the outside of the casserole).
3. Cover and cook on High 2 hours.

Chopping dried fruit can be difficult. Make it easier by spraying your kitchen scissors with nonstick cooking spray before chopping. Fruits won't stick to the blade.
Cyndie Marrara
Port Matilda, PA

Dolores' Rice Pudding

Dolores Metzler
Mechanicsburg, PA

Makes 8-10 servings

1 cup white uncooked rice
1 cup sugar
8 cups milk
3 eggs
1½ cups milk
2 tsp. vanilla
¼ tsp. salt
nutmeg, *or* cinnamon

1. In slow cooker, mix together rice, sugar, and 8 cups milk.
2. Cook on High 3 hours.
3. Beat together, eggs, 1½ cups milk, vanilla, and salt. Add to slow cooker. Stir.
4. Cook on High 25-30 minutes.
5. Sprinkle with nutmeg *or* cinnamon. Serve warm.

Custard Rice Pudding

Iva Schmidt
Fergus Falls, MN

Makes 4-6 servings

¼ cup rice, uncooked
2 eggs
⅓ cup sugar
¼ tsp. salt

½ tsp. vanilla
1½ cups milk
⅓ cup raisins
nutmeg, *or* cinnamon
2 cups water

1. Cook rice according to package directions.
2. Beat together eggs, sugar, salt, vanilla, and milk. Stir in rice and raisins.
3. Put in 1-quart baking dish that will fit into your slow cooker. Sprinkle with nutmeg or cinnamon.
4. Cover with foil and set on metal trivet or a canning jar ring in bottom of slow cooker. Pour water around casserole.
5. Cover cooker. Cook on High 2-2½ hours, or until set.
6. Serve warm or cold.

Slow-Cooker Tapioca

Nancy W. Huber
Green Park, PA

Makes 10-12 servings

2 quarts milk
1 cup small pearl tapioca
1 to 1½ cups sugar
4 eggs, beaten
1 tsp. vanilla
whipped cream, *or* fruit of choice, optional

1. Combine milk, tapioca, and sugar in slow cooker. Cook on High 3 hours.
2. Mix together eggs,

vanilla, and a little hot milk from slow cooker. Add to slow cooker. Cook on High 20 more minutes. Chill.
3. Serve with whipped cream or fruit.

Tapioca Salad

Karen Ashworth
Duenweg, MO

Makes 10-12 servings

10 Tbsp. large pearl tapioca
½ cup sugar to taste
dash salt
4 cups water
1 cup grapes, cut in half
1 cup crushed pineapple
1 cup whipped cream

1. Mix together tapioca, sugar, salt, and water in slow cooker.
2. Cook on High 3 hours, or until tapioca pearls are almost translucent.
3. Cool thoroughly in refrigerator.
4. Stir in remaining ingredients. Serve cold.

Variation:
Add 1 small can mandarin oranges, drained, when adding rest of fruit.

Blushing Apple Tapioca

Julie Weaver
Reinholds, PA

Makes 8-10 servings

8-10 tart apples
1/2 cup sugar
4 Tbsp. minute tapioca
4 Tbsp. red cinnamon
  candy
1/2 cup water
whipped topping, optional

1. Pare and core apples. Cut into eighths lengthwise and place in slow cooker.
2. Mix together sugar, tapioca, candy, and water. Pour over apples.
3. Cook on High 3- 4 hours.
4. Serve hot or cold. Top with whipped cream.

Baked Apples with Raisins

Vera Schmucker
Goshen, IN
Connie B. Weaver
Bethlehem, PA

Makes 6-8 servings

6-8 medium-sized baking
  apples, cored
2 Tbsp. raisins
1/4 cup sugar
1 tsp. cinnamon
1 Tbsp. butter
1/2 cup water

1. Remove top inch of peel from each apple.
2. Mix together raisins and sugar. Spoon into center of apples.
3. Sprinkle with additional sugar and dot with butter.
4. Place apples in slow cooker. Add water. Cover and cook on Low 7-9 hours, or on High 2 1/2-3 1/2 hours.

Raisin Nut-Stuffed Apples

Margaret Rich
North Newton, KS

Makes 6 servings

6 baking apples, cored
2 Tbsp. butter, *or*
  margarine, melted
1/4 cup packed brown sugar
3/4 cup raisins
3 Tbsp. chopped walnuts
1/2 cup water

1. Peel a strip around apple about one-third of the way below the stem end to prevent splitting.
2. Mix together butter and brown sugar. Stir in raisins and walnuts. Stuff into apple cavities.
3. Place apples in slow cooker. Add water.
4. Cover and cook on Low 6-8 hours.

"Bake" cakes in a cake pan set directly on the bottom of your slow cooker. Cover the top with 4-5 layers of paper towels to help absorb the moisture from the top of the cake. Leave the cooker lid open slightly to let extra moisture escape.

Eleanor J. Ferreira
North Chelmsford, MA

Fruit/Nut Baked Apples

Cyndie Marrara
Port Matilda, PA

Makes 4 servings

4 large firm baking apples
1 Tbsp. lemon juice
1/3 cup chopped dried
    apricots
1/3 cup chopped walnuts,
    or pecans
3 Tbsp. packed brown
    sugar
1/2 tsp. cinnamon
2 Tbsp. melted butter
1/2 cup water, *or* apple
    juice
4 pecan halves, optional

1. Scoop out center of apples creating a cavity 1 1/2 inches wide and stopping 1/2 inch from the bottom of each. Peel top of each apple down about 1 inch. Brush edges with lemon juice.
2. Mix together apricots, nuts, brown sugar, and cinnamon. Stir in butter. Spoon mixture evenly into apples.
3. Put 1/2 cup water or juice in bottom of slow cooker. Put 2 apples in bottom, and 2 apples above, but not squarely on top of other apples. Cover and cook on Low 1 1/2-3 hours, or until tender.
4. Serve warm or at room temperature. Top each apple with a pecan half, if desired.

Nut-Filled Baked Apples

Joyce Cox
Port Angeles, WA

Makes 8 servings

1 cup nuts of your choice,
    ground
1/4 cup (packed) brown
    sugar
1/2 tsp. cinnamon
1 egg, beaten
8 medium baking apples,
    kept whole, but cored
1 cup sugar
1/3 cup water
2 Tbsp. butter
1/2 cup water

1. Mix together nuts, brown sugar, cinnamon, and egg. Place apples on rack in large, rectangular slow cooker. Spoon nut-sugar mixture into apples until they are two-thirds full.
2. In saucepan, combine sugar, 1/3 cup water, and butter. Stir over medium heat until sugar dissolves. Pour syrup over the filling in the apples until their cavities are filled.
3. Add 1/2 cup water to slow cooker around apples.
4. Cover and cook on Low 8-10 hours, or on High 3-4 hours. Serve warm. Top with whipped cream, whipped topping, ice cream, or frozen yogurt, if you wish.

Caramel Apples

Elaine Patton
West Middletown, PA
Rhonda Lee Schmidt
Scranton, PA
Renee Shirk
Mount Joy, PA

Makes 4 servings

4 very large tart apples,
    cored
1/2 cup apple juice
8 Tbsp. brown sugar
12 hot cinnamon candies
4 Tbsp. butter, *or*
    margarine
8 caramel candies
1/4 tsp. ground cinnamon
whipped cream

1. Remove 1/2-inch-wide strip of peel off the top of each apple and place apples in slow cooker.
2. Pour apple juice over apples.
3. Fill the center of each apple with 2 Tbsp. brown sugar, 3 hot cinnamon candies, 1 Tbsp. butter, or margarine, and 2 caramel candies. Sprinkle with cinnamon.
4. Cover and cook on Low 4-6 hours, or until tender.
5. Serve hot with whipped cream.

Golden Fruit Compote

Cindy Krestynick
Glen Lyon, PA
Judi Manos
West Islip, NY

Makes 6-8 servings

1-lb. 13-oz. can peach, *or*
  pear, slices, undrained
1/2 cup dried apricots
1/4 cup golden raisins
1/8 tsp. cinnamon
1/8 tsp. nutmeg
3/4 cup orange juice

1. Combine undrained peach or pear slices, apricots, raisins, cinnamon, and nutmeg in slow cooker. Stir in orange juice. Completely immerse fruit in liquid.

2. Cover and cook on Low 6-8 hours.

3. Serve cold with angel food or pound cake, or ice cream. Serve warm as a side dish in the main meal.

Variation:

If you prefer a thicker compote, mix together 2 Tbsp. cornstarch and 1/4 cup cold water until smooth. Stir into hot fruit 15 minutes before end of cooking time. Stir until absorbed in juice.

Fruit Compote Dessert

Beatrice Orgish
Richardson, TX

Makes 8 servings

2 medium tart apples,
  peeled
2 medium fresh peaches,
  peeled and cubed
2 cups unsweetened
  pineapple chunks
1 1/4 cups unsweetened
  pineapple juice
1/4 cup honey
2 1/4-inch thick lemon
  slices
3 1/2-inch cinnamon stick
1 medium firm banana,
  thinly sliced
whipped cream, optional
sliced almonds, optional
maraschino cherries,
  optional

1. Cut apples into 1/4-inch slices and then in half horizontally. Place in slow cooker.

2. Add peaches, pineapple, pineapple juice, honey, lemon, and cinnamon. Cover and cook on Low 3-4 hours.

3. Stir in banana slices just before serving. Garnish with whipped cream, sliced almonds, and cherries, if you wish.

Hot Curried Fruit Compote

Cathy Boshart
Lebanon, PA

Makes 12 servings

1-lb. can peach halves
1-lb. can pear halves
1-lb. can apricot halves
1-lb. can pineapple chunks
4 medium bananas, sliced
15 maraschino cherries
1/3 cup walnut halves
1/3 cup margarine
2/3 cup brown sugar
1/2 tsp. curry powder (or to
  taste)

1. Drain fruit. Pour canned fruit into slow cooker. Add bananas.

2. Scatter cherries and walnuts on top.

3. In skillet, melt margarine. Mix in sugar and curry powder. Pour over fruit.

4. Cook on Low 2 hours.

5. Serve hot as a side dish to beef, pork, or poultry; serve warm as a dessert; or serve cold as a topping for ice cream.

Scandinavian Fruit Soup

Willard E. Roth
Elkhart, IN

Makes 12 servings

1 cup dried apricots
1 cup dried sliced apples
1 cup dried pitted prunes
1 cup canned pitted red cherries
1/2 cup quick-cooking tapioca
1 cup grape juice, *or* red wine
3 cups water, *or* more
1/2 cup orange juice
1/4 cup lemon juice
1 Tbsp. grated orange peel
1/2 cup brown sugar

1. Combine apricots, apples, prunes, cherries, tapioca, and grape juice in slow cooker. Cover with water.
2. Cook on Low for at least 8 hours.
3. Before serving, stir in remaining ingredients.
4. Serve warm or cold, as a soup or dessert. Delicious served chilled over vanilla ice cream or frozen yogurt.

Hot Fruit Compote

Sue Williams
Gulfport, MS

Makes 4-6 servings

1 lb. dried prunes
1 1/3 cups dried apricots
13 1/2-oz. can pineapple chunks, undrained
1-lb. can pitted dark sweet cherries, undrained
1/4 cup dry white wine
2 cups water
1 cup sugar

1. Mix together all ingredients in slow cooker.
2. Cover and cook on Low 7-8 hours, or High 3-4 hours.
3. Serve warm.

Fruit Medley

Angeline Lang
Greeley, CO

Makes 6-8 servings

1 1/2 lbs. mixed dried fruit
2 1/2 cups water
1 cup sugar
1 Tbsp. honey
peel of half a lemon, cut into thin strips
1/8 tsp. nutmeg
1 cinnamon stick
3 Tbsp. cornstarch
1/4 cup cold water
1/4 cup Cointreau

1. Place dried fruit in slow cooker. Pour in water.
2. Stir in sugar, honey, lemon peel, nutmeg, and cinnamon.
3. Cover and cook on Low 2-3 hours. Turn cooker to High.
4. Mix cornstarch into water until smooth. Stir into fruit mixture. Cook on High 10 minutes, or until thickened.
5. Stir in Cointreau.
6. Serve warm or chilled. Serve as a side dish with the main course, as a dessert on its own, or as a topping for ice cream.

Rhubarb Sauce

Esther Porter
Minneapolis, MN

Makes 4-6 servings

1 1/2 lbs. rhubarb
1/8 tsp. salt
1/2 cup water
1/2-2/3 cup sugar

1. Cut rhubarb into 1/2-inch slices.
2. Combine all ingredients in slow cooker. Cook on Low 4-5 hours.
3. Serve chilled.

Variation:
Add 1 pint sliced strawberries about 30 minutes before removing from heat.

Strawberry Rhubarb Sauce

Tina Snyder
Manheim, PA

Makes 6-8 servings

6 cups chopped rhubarb
1 cup sugar
1 cinnamon stick
½ cup white grape juice
2 cups sliced strawberries

1. Place rhubarb in slow cooker. Pour sugar over rhubarb. Add cinnamon stick and grape juice. Stir well.
2. Cover and cook on Low 5-6 hours, or until rhubarb is tender.
3. Stir in strawberries. Cook 1 hour longer.
4. Remove cinnamon stick. Chill.
5. Serve over cake or ice cream.

Old-Fashioned Rice Pudding

Ann Bender
Fort Defiance, VA

Makes 6 servings

2½ cups cooked rice
1½ cups whole milk
⅔ cup brown sugar
3 eggs, beaten
3 Tbsp. butter, melted
2 tsp. vanilla
½ tsp. ground nutmeg
½ tsp. ground cinnamon
½ cup raisins

1. Mix together all ingredients. Pour into a lightly greased slow cooker.
2. Cover and cook on High 1-2 hours, or on Low 4-6 hours. Stir once during last 30 minutes.
3. Serve warm or cold.

Spiced Applesauce

Judi Manos
West Islip, NY

Makes 6 cups

12 cups pared, cored, thinly sliced, cooking apples
½ cup sugar
½ tsp. cinnamon
1 cup water
1 Tbsp. lemon juice
freshly grated nutmeg, optional

1. Place apples in slow cooker.
2. Combine sugar and cinnamon. Mix with apples. Stir in water and lemon juice, and nutmeg, if desired.
3. Cover. Cook on Low 5-7 hours, or High 2½-3½ hours.
4. Stir for a chunky sauce. Serve hot or cold.

Cook your favorite "Plum Pudding" recipe in a can set inside a slow cooker on a metal rack or trivet. Pour about 2 cups warm water around it. The water helps steam the pudding. Cover the can tightly with foil to keep the cake dry. Cover the cooker with its lid. Cook on High.
Eleanor J. Ferreira
North Chelmsford, MA

Chunky Applesauce

Joan Becker
Dodge City, KS
Rosanne Hankins
Stevensville, MD

Makes 8-10 servings

8 apples, peeled, cored, and cut into chunks *or* slices (6 cups)
1 tsp. cinnamon
1/2 cup water
1/2-1 cup sugar, *or* cinnamon red hot candies

1. Combine all ingredients in slow cooker.
2. Cook on Low 8-10 hours, or High 3-4 hours.

Applesauce

Charmaine Caesar
Lancaster, PA

Makes 4 cups

10 medium Winesap, *or* Golden Delicious, cooking apples
1/2 cup water
3/4 cup sugar
cinnamon, optional

1. Core, peel, and thinly slice apples.
2. Combine all ingredients in slow cooker.

3. Cover. Cook on Low 5 hours.
4. Stir until well blended. If you want a smooth sauce, put through blender or mix with a hand mixer. Cool and serve.

Quick Yummy Peaches

Willard E. Roth
Elkhart, IN

Makes 6 servings

1/3 cup buttermilk baking mix
2/3 cup dry quick oats
1/2 cup brown sugar
1 tsp. cinnamon
4 cups sliced peaches (canned *or* fresh)
1/2 cup peach juice, *or* water

1. Mix together baking mix, oats, brown sugar, and cinnamon in greased slow cooker.
2. Stir in peaches and peach juice.
3. Cook on Low for at least 5 hours. (If you like a drier cobbler, remove lid for last 15-30 minutes of cooking.)
4. Serve with frozen yogurt or ice cream.

Scalloped Pineapples

Shirley Hinh
Wayland, IA

Makes 8 servings

2 cups sugar
3 eggs
3/4 cup butter, melted
3/4 cup milk
1 large can crushed pineapple, drained
8 slices bread (crusts removed), cubed

1. Mix together all ingredients in slow cooker.
2. Cook on High 2 hours. Reduce heat to Low and cook 1 more hour.
3. Delicious served as a side dish to ham or poultry, or as a dessert served warm or cold. Eat hot or chilled with vanilla ice cream or frozen yogurt.

Black and Blue Cobbler

Renee Shirk
Mount Joy, PA

Makes 6 servings

1 cup flour
3/4 cup sugar
1 tsp. baking powder
1/4 tsp. salt
1/4 tsp. ground cinnamon
1/4 tsp. ground nutmeg
2 eggs, beaten
2 Tbsp. milk
2 Tbsp. vegetable oil
2 cups fresh, *or* frozen, blueberries
2 cups fresh, *or* frozen, blackberries
3/4 cup water
1 tsp. grated orange peel
3/4 cup sugar
whipped topping, *or* ice cream, optional

1. Combine flour, 3/4 cup sugar, baking powder, salt, cinnamon, and nutmeg.
2. Combine eggs, milk, and oil. Stir into dry ingredients until moistened.
3. Spread the batter evenly over bottom of greased 5-quart slow cooker.
4. In saucepan, combine berries, water, orange peel, and 3/4 cup sugar. Bring to boil. Remove from heat and pour over batter. Cover.
5. Cook on High 2-2 1/2 hours, or until toothpick inserted into batter comes out clean. Turn off cooker.
6. Uncover and let stand 30 minutes before serving. Spoon from cooker and serve with whipped topping or ice cream, if desired.

Cranberry Pudding

Margaret Wheeler
North Bend, OR

Makes 8-10 servings

Pudding:
1 1/3 cups flour
1/2 tsp. salt
2 tsp. baking soda
1/3 cup boiling water
1/2 cup dark molasses
2 cups whole cranberries
1/2 cup chopped nuts

1/2 cup water

Butter Sauce:
1 cup confectioners sugar
1/2 cup heavy cream, *or* evaporated milk
1/2 cup butter
1 tsp. vanilla

1. Mix together flour and salt.
2. Dissolve soda in boiling water. Add to flour and salt.
3. Stir in molasses. Blend well.
4. Fold in cranberries and nuts.
5. Pour into well greased and floured bread or cake pan that will sit in your cooker. Cover with greased tin foil.
6. Pour 1/2 cup water into cooker. Place foil-covered pan in cooker. Cover with cooker lid and steam on High 3 to 4 hours, or until pudding tests done with a wooden pick.
7. Remove pan and uncover. Let stand 5 minutes, then unmold.
8. To make butter sauce, mix together all ingredients in saucepan. Cook, stirring over medium heat until sugar dissolves.
9. Serve warm butter sauce over warm cranberry pudding.

Slow Cooker Pumpkin Pie Pudding

Joette Droz
Kalona, IA

Makes 4-6 servings

15-oz. can solid pack pumpkin
12-oz. can evaporated milk
3/4 cup sugar
1/2 cup buttermilk baking mix
2 eggs, beaten
2 Tbsp. melted butter, *or* margarine
1 Tbsp. pumpkin pie spice
2 tsp. vanilla
whipped cream

1. Mix together all ingredients except whipped cream. Pour into greased slow cooker.
2. Cover and cook on Low 6-7 hours, or until thermometer reads 160°.
3. Serve in bowls topped with whipped cream.

Lemon Pudding Cake

Jean Butzer
Batavia, NY

Makes 5-6 servings

3 eggs, separated
1 tsp. grated lemon peel
1/4 cup lemon juice
3 Tbsp. melted butter
1 1/2 cups milk
3/4 cup sugar
1/4 cup flour
1/8 tsp. salt

1. Beat eggs whites until stiff peaks form. Set aside.
2. Beat eggs yolks. Blend in lemon peel, lemon juice, butter, and milk.
3. In separate bowl, combine sugar, flour, and salt. Add to egg-lemon mixture, beating until smooth.
4. Fold into beaten egg whites.
5. Spoon into slow cooker.
6. Cover and cook on High 2-3 hours.
7. Serve with spoon from cooker.

Apple Cake

Esther Becker
Gordonville, PA
Wanda S. Curtin
Bradenton, FL

Makes 8-10 servings

2 cups sugar
1 cup oil
2 eggs
1 tsp. vanilla
2 cups chopped apples
2 cups flour
1 tsp. salt
1 tsp. baking soda
1 tsp. nutmeg
1 cup chopped walnuts, *or* pecans

1. Beat together sugar, oil, and eggs. Add vanilla.
2. Add apples. Mix well.
3. Sift together flour, salt, baking soda, and nutmeg. Add dry ingredients and nuts to apple mixture. Stir well.
4. Pour batter into greased and floured bread or cake pan that fits into your slow cooker. Cover with pan's lid, or greased tin foil. Place pan in slow cooker. Cover cooker.
5. Bake on High 3 1/2-4 hours. Let cake stand in pan for 5 minutes after removing from slow cooker.
6. Remove cake from pan, slice, and serve.

Variation:
Instead of a bread or cake pan, pour batter into greased and floured 2-lb. coffee can. Cover top of can with 6 to 8 paper towels. Place can in

slow cooker. Cover cooker, tilting lid slightly to allow release of extra moisture. Continue with Step 5 above.

Apple Peanut Crumble

Phyllis Attig, Reynolds, IL
Joan Becker, Dodge City, KS
Pam Hochstedler, Kalona, IA

Makes 4-5 servings

4-5 cooking apples, peeled and sliced
2/3 cup packed brown sugar
1/2 cup flour
1/2 cup quick-cooking dry oats
1/2 tsp. cinnamon
1/4-1/2 tsp. nutmeg
1/3 cup butter, softened
2 Tbsp. peanut butter
ice cream, *or* whipped cream

1. Place apple slices in slow cooker.
2. Combine brown sugar, flour, oats, cinnamon, and nutmeg.
3. Cut in butter and peanut butter. Sprinkle over apples.
4. Cover cooker and cook on Low 5-6 hours.
5. Serve warm or cold, plain or with ice cream or whipped cream.

Harvey Wallbanger Cake

Roseann Wilson
Albuquerque, NM

Makes 8 servings

Cake:
16-oz. pkg. pound cake mix
1/3 cup vanilla instant pudding (reserve rest of pudding from 3-oz. pkg. for glaze)
1/4 cup salad oil
3 eggs
2 Tbsp. Galliano liqueur
2/3 cup orange juice

Glaze:
remaining pudding mix
2/3 cup orange juice
1 Tbsp. Galliano liqueur

1. Mix together all ingredients for cake. Beat for 3 minutes. Pour batter into greased and floured bread or cake pan that will fit into your slow cooker. Cover pan.
2. Bake in covered slow cooker on High 2 1/2-3 1/2 hours.
3. Invert cake onto serving platter.
4. Mix together glaze ingredients. Spoon over cake.

Cherry Delight

Anna Musser
Manheim, PA
Marianne J. Troyer
Millersburg, OH

Makes 10-12 servings

21-oz. can cherry pie filling
1 pkg. yellow cake mix
1/2 cup butter, melted
1/3 cup walnuts, optional

1. Place pie filling in greased slow cooker.
2. Combine dry cake mix and butter (mixture will be crumbly). Sprinkle over filling. Sprinkle with walnuts.
3. Cover and cook on Low 4 hours, or on High 2 hours.
4. Allow to cool, then serve in bowls with dips of ice cream.

Note:
For a less rich, less sweet dessert, use only half the cake mix and only 1/4 cup butter, melted.

Chocolate Fondue

Eleanor J. Ferriera
North Chelmsford, MA

Makes 6 servings

1 pkg. (8 squares) semisweet chocolate
4-oz. pkg. sweet cooking chocolate
3/4 cup sweetened condensed milk
1/4 cup sugar
2 Tbsp. kirsch
fresh cherries with stems
squares of sponge cake

1. Break both chocolates into pieces and place in cooker. Set cooker to High and stir chocolate constantly until it melts.
2. Turn cooker to Low and stir in milk and sugar. Stir until thoroughly blended.
3. Stir in kirsch. Cover and cook on Low until fondue comes to a very gentle simmer.
4. Bring fondue to table, along with cherries and sponge cake squares to dip into it.

You can use a 2-lb. coffee can, 2 1-lb. coffee cans, 3 16-oz. vegetable cans, a 6-7 cup mold, or a 1 1/2-2-quart baking dish for "baking" cakes in a slow cooker. Leave the cooker lid slightly open to let extra moisture escape.
Eleanor J. Ferreira
North Chelmsford, MA

Hot Fudge Cake
Maricarol Magill
Freehold, NJ

Makes 6-8 servings

1 cup packed brown sugar
1 cup flour
3 Tbsp. unsweetened cocoa
   powder
2 tsp. baking powder
1/2 tsp. salt
1/2 cup milk
2 Tbsp. melted butter
1/2 tsp. vanilla
3/4 cup packed brown sugar
1/4 cup unsweetened cocoa
   powder
13/4 cups boiling water
vanilla ice cream

1. Mix together 1 cup brown sugar, flour, 3 Tbsp. cocoa, baking powder, and salt.
2. Stir in milk, butter, and vanilla. Spread over the bottom of slow cooker.
3. Mix together 3/4 cup brown sugar and 1/4 cup cocoa. Sprinkle over mixture in slow cooker.
4. Pour in boiling water. Do not stir.
5. Cover and cook on High 2-3 hours, or until a toothpick inserted comes out clean.
6. Serve warm with vanilla ice cream.

Self-Frosting Fudge Cake
Mary Puterbaugh
Elwood, IN

Makes 8-10 servings

21/2 cups of 181/2-oz. pkg. chocolate fudge pudding cake mix
2 eggs
3/4 cup water
3 Tbsp. oil
1/3 cup pecan halves
1/4 cup chocolate syrup
1/4 cup warm water
3 Tbsp. sugar

1. Combine cake mix, eggs, 3/4 cup water, and oil in electric mixer bowl. Beat 2 minutes.
2. Pour into greased and floured bread or cake pan that will fit into your slow cooker.
3. Sprinkle nuts over mixture.
4. Blend together chocolate syrup, 1/4 cup water, and sugar. Spoon over batter.
5. Cover. Bake on High 2-3 hours.
6. Serve warm from slow cooker.

Chocolate Pudding Cake
Lee Ann Hazlett
Freeport, IL
Della Yoder
Kalona, IA

Makes 10-12 servings

181/2-oz. pkg. chocolate cake mix
3.9-oz. pkg. instant chocolate pudding mix
2 cups (16 oz.) sour cream
4 eggs
1 cup water
3/4 cup oil
1 cup (6 oz.) semisweet chocolate chips
whipped cream, *or* ice cream, optional

1. Combine cake mix, pudding mix, sour cream, eggs, water, and oil in electric mixer bowl. Beat on medium speed for 2 minutes. Stir in chocolate chips.
2. Pour into greased slow cooker. Cover and cook on Low 6-7 hours, or on High 3-4 hours, or until toothpick inserted near center comes out with moist crumbs.
3. Serve with whipped cream or ice cream.

Peanut Butter and Hot Fudge Pudding Cake

Sara Wilson
Blairstown, MO

Makes 6 servings

1/2 cup flour
1/4 cup sugar
3/4 tsp. baking powder
1/3 cup milk
1 Tbsp. oil
1/2 tsp. vanilla
1/4 cup peanut butter
1/2 cup sugar
3 Tbsp. unsweetened cocoa powder
1 cup boiling water
vanilla ice cream

1. Combine flour, 1/4 cup sugar, and baking powder. Add milk, oil, and vanilla. Mix until smooth. Stir in peanut butter. Pour into slow cooker.
2. Mix together 1/2 cup sugar and cocoa powder. Gradually stir in boiling water. Pour mixture over batter in slow cooker. Do not stir.
3. Cover and cook on High 2-3 hours, or until toothpick inserted comes out clean.
4. Serve warm with ice cream.

Seven Layer Bars

Mary W. Stauffer
Ephrata, PA

Makes 6-8 servings

1/4 cup melted butter
1/2 cup graham cracker crumbs
1/2 cup chocolate chips
1/2 cup butterscotch chips
1/2 cup flaked coconut
1/2 cup chopped nuts
1/2 cup sweetened condensed milk

1. Layer ingredients in a bread or cake pan that fits in your slow cooker, in the order listed. Do not stir.
2. Cover and bake on High 2-3 hours, or until firm. Remove pan and uncover. Let stand 5 minutes.
3. Unmold carefully on plate and cool.

Easy Chocolate Clusters

Marcella Stalter
Flanagan, IL

Makes 3 1/2 dozen clusters

2 lbs. white coating chocolate, broken into small pieces
2 cups (12 oz.) semisweet chocolate chips
4-oz. pkg. sweet German chocolate
24-oz. jar roasted peanuts

1. Combine coating chocolate, chocolate chips, and German chocolate. Cover and cook on High 1 hour. Reduce heat to Low and cook 1 hour longer, or until chocolate is melted, stirring every 15 minutes.
2. Stir in peanuts. Mix well.
3. Drop by teaspoonfuls onto waxed paper. Let stand until set. Store at room temperature.

Beverages

Apple-Honey Tea

Jeanne Allen
Rye, CO

Makes 6 1-cup servings

**12-oz. can frozen apple
  juice/cider concentrate
2 Tbsp. instant tea powder
1 Tbsp. honey
1/2 tsp. ground cinnamon**

1. Reconstitute the apple juice/cider concentrate according to package directions. Pour into slow cooker.

2. Add tea powder, honey, and cinnamon. Stir to blend.

3. Heat on Low 1-2 hours. Stir well before serving since cinnamon tends to settle on bottom.

Hot Mulled Cider

Phyllis Attig, Reynolds, IL
Jean Butzer, Batavia, NY
Doris G. Herr, Manheim, PA
Mary E. Martin, Goshen, IN
Leona Miller, Millersburg, OH
Marjora Miller, Archbold, OH
Janet L. Roggie, Lowville, NY
Shirley Sears, Tiskilwa, IL
Charlotte Shaffer, East Earl, PA
Berenice M. Wagner
Dodge City, KS
Connie B. Weaver
Bethlehem, PA
Maryann Westerberg
Rosamond, CA
Carole Whaling, New Tripoli, PA

Makes 8 1-cup servings

**1/4-1/2 cup brown sugar
2 quarts apple cider
1 tsp. whole allspice
1 1/2 tsp. whole cloves
2 cinnamon sticks
2 oranges sliced, with peels
  on**

1. Combine brown sugar and cider in slow cooker.

2. Put spices in tea strainer or tie in cheesecloth. Add to slow cooker. Stir in orange slices.

3. Cover and simmer on Low 2-8 hours.

Variation:
Add a dash of ground nutmeg and salt.
Marsha Sabus
Fallbrook, CA

Autumn Sipper

Shari Jensen
Fountain, CO

Makes 8 1-cup servings

1 Tbsp. whole allspice
3 3-inch cinnamon sticks
2 whole cloves
1 piece each lemon and orange peel, each about the size of a half dollar
1 piece crystallized ginger, about the size of a quarter
3 cups apricot nectar
5 cups apple juice
cinnamon sticks and orange slices, optional

1. Place spices, citrus peels, and ginger in a cheesecloth or coffee filter. Tie securely. Place in bottom of slow cooker.
2. Pour in apple juice and nectar. Cover.
3. Cook on High 1 hour, then on Low 3 hours.
4. Garnish filled glasses with cinnamon sticks and orange slices.

Hot Mulled Apple Tea

Barbara Tenney
Delta, PA

Makes 16 1-cup servings

1/2 gallon apple cider
1/2 gallon strong tea
1 sliced lemon
1 sliced orange
3 3-inch cinnamon sticks
1 Tbsp. whole cloves
1 Tbsp. allspice
brown sugar to taste

1. Combine all in slow cooker.
2. Heat on Low 2 hours.

Spiced Apple Cider

Janice Muller
Derwood, MD

Makes 18-20 servings

2 sticks cinnamon
1 cup orange juice
1 tsp. cinnamon
1 tsp. ground cloves
1/4 cup lemon juice
2 tsp. whole cloves
1 gallon apple cider
2 tsp. ground nutmeg
1/2 cup pineapple juice
1 tsp. ginger
1 tsp. lemon peel
1 cup sugar

1. Mix all ingredients in 6-quart slow cooker.
2. Simmer on Low 4-6 hours.

Yummy Hot Cider

Char Hagner
Montague, MI

Makes 10-11 1-cup servings

3 3-inch sticks cinnamon
2 tsp. whole cloves
1 tsp. whole nutmeg, *or* 1/2 tsp. ground nutmeg
1/2 gallon apple cider
1 cup sugar
2 cups orange juice
1/2 cup lemon juice

1. Tie spices in cheesecloth or tea strainer and place in slow cooker.
2. Add apple cider and sugar, stirring well.
3. Cover. Simmer on Low 1 hour. Remove spices and stir in orange juice and lemon juice. Continue heating 1 more hour. Serve cider from cooker, set on Low.

Great Mulled Cider

Charlotte Shaffer
East Earl, PA
Barbara Sparks
Glen Burnie, MD

Makes 8-10 1-cup servings

2 qts. apple cider
1/2 cup frozen orange juice
  concentrate
1/2 cup brown sugar
1/2 tsp. ground allspice, *or* 1
  tsp. whole allspice
1 1/2 tsp. whole cloves
2 cinnamon sticks
orange slices

1. Tie all whole spices in
cheesecloth bag, then combine all ingredients in slow
cooker.
2. Cover and simmer on
Low 3 hours.

Hot Spiced Cider

Elva Evers
North English, IA

Makes 6 1-cup servings

12-oz. can frozen apple
  juice
3 3-inch cinnamon sticks
6 whole cloves

1. Combine all ingredients
in slow cooker.
2. Cover and simmer on
Low 4 hours.
3. Remove cinnamon and
cloves before serving.

Variation:
  Omit the cinnamon and
cloves. Use 1/4 cup fresh or
dried mint tea leaves instead.

Spiced Cider

Mary Puterbaugh
Elwood, IN

Makes 12 1-cup servings

12 whole cloves
1/2 gallon apple cider
2/3 cup red hot candies
1/4 cup dry orange drink
  mix
1 qt. water

1. Place cloves in cheesecloth bag or tea ball.
2. Combine all ingredients
in slow cooker.

3. Cover. Cook on Low 3-4
hours.
4. Serve hot from cooker
during fall, or on Halloween.

Hot Wassail Drink

Dale Peterson
Rapid City, SC

Makes 24-27 1-cup servings

12-oz. can frozen orange
  juice
12-oz. can frozen lemonade
2 qts. apple juice
2 cups sugar, *or less*
3 Tbsp. whole cloves
2 tbsp. ground ginger
4 tsp. ground cinnamon
10 cups hot water
6 cups strong tea

1. Mix juices, sugar, and
spices in slow cooker.
2. Add hot water and tea.
3. Heat on High until Hot
(1-2 hours), then on Low
while serving.

Holiday Wassail

Dolores S. Kratz
Souderton, PA

Makes 8 1-cup servings

16-oz. can apricot halves,
    undrained
4 cups unsweetened
    pineapple juice
2 cups apple cider
1 cup orange juice
18 whole cloves
6 3½-inch cinnamon
    sticks, broken

1. In blender or food
processor, blend apricots and
liquid until smooth.
2. Place cloves and cinnamon sticks in cheesecloth
bag.
3. Put all ingredients in
slow cooker. Cook on Low 3-
4 hours. Serve hot.

Hot Cider

Ilene Bontrager
Arlington, KS

Makes 18-20 1-cup servings

1 gallon cider
1 qt. cranberry juice
5-6 cinnamon sticks
2 tsp. whole cloves
½ tsp. ginger
1 whole orange, sliced

1. Combine cider and
cranberry juice in slow
cooker.
2. Place cinnamon sticks
and cloves in cheesecloth bag
and add to slow cooker. Stir
in ginger.
3. Heat on High 5-6 hours.
4. Float orange slices on
top before serving.

Wassail

John D. Allen, Rye, CO
Susan Yoder Graber
Eureka, IL
Jan Pembleton, Arlington, TX

Makes 12 1-cup servings

2 qts. cider
1 pint cranberry juice
⅓-⅔ cup sugar
1 tsp. aromatic bitters
2 sticks cinnamon
1 tsp. whole allspice
1 small orange, studded
    with whole coves
1 cup rum, optional

1. Put all ingredients into
cooker. Cover and cook on
High 1 hour, then on Low 4-8
hours.
2. Serve warm from
cooker.

Note:
If the wassail turns out to
be too sweet for you, add
more cranberry juice until
you find the flavor balance to
be more pleasing.

Holiday Spice Punch

Maryland Massey
Millington, MD

Makes 10 1-cup servings

2 qts. apple cider
2 cups cranberry juice
2 Tbsp. mixed whole
    spices — allspice, cloves,
    coriander, and ginger
2 3-inch cinnamon sticks,
    broken
lemon, *or* orange, slices
    studded with whole
    cloves

1. Pour cider and juice into
slow cooker. Place mixed
spices in muslin bag or tea
ball. Add to juice.
2. Cover and simmer on
Low 2 hours.
3. Float cinnamon sticks
and fruit slices in individual
mugs as you serve.

Hot Cranberry-Apple Punch
Barbara Sparks
Glen Burnie, MD
Shirley Thieszen
Larkin, KS

Makes 10-11 1-cup servings

4½ cups cranberry juice
6 cups apple juice
¼ cup + 1 Tbsp. brown
  sugar
¼ tsp. salt
3 cinnamon sticks
1 tsp. whole cloves

1. Pour juices into slow cooker. Mix in brown sugar and salt. Stir until sugar is dissolved.
2. Tie cinnamon sticks and cloves in cheesecloth and drop into liquid.
3. Cover. Simmer on High 2 hours. Remove spice bag. Keep warm on Low.

Hot Cranberry Tea
Sherrill Bieberly
Salina, KS

Makes 14 1-cup servings

1 cup sugar
2 qts. water
3 cinnamon sticks
1 qt. cranberry juice
6-oz. can frozen orange
  juice

1¼ cups water
3 Tbsp. lemon juice
fresh lemon and/or orange
  slices

1. In saucepan, mix together sugar, 2 quarts water, and cinnamon sticks. Bring to boil.
2. Pour into slow cooker along with remaining ingredients. Cover and cook on High 1 hour. Turn to Low. Serve warm.

Josie's Hot Cranberry Punch
Josie Bollman
Maumee, OH

Makes 6 1-cup servings

32-oz. bottle cranberry
  juice
2 sticks cinnamon
6-oz. can frozen lemonade
12-oz. can frozen orange
  juice

1. Mix together all ingredients in slow cooker.
2. Cook on High 3-4 hours.

Spiced Wassail
Dorothy Horst
Tiskilwa, IL

Makes 10-11 1-cup servings

2 32-oz. jars cranberry
  juice
2 cups water
6-oz. can frozen orange
  juice concentrate
3 3-inch cinnamon sticks
3 whole cloves

1. Combine all ingredients in 5-quart slow cooker.
2. Cover and cook on Low 2-8 hours.

Variation:
Use small candy canes as stir sticks in individual cups during the holiday season.

Note:
This is a refreshing cold drink to serve over ice on a hot day.

Hot Cranberry Punch

Marianne Troyer
Millersburg, OH

Makes 13-14 1-cup servings

2 qts. hot water
1½ cups sugar
1 qt. cranberry juice
¾ cup orange juice
¼ cup lemon juice
12 whole cloves, optional
½ cup red hot candies

1. Combine water, sugar, and juices. Stir until sugar is dissolved.
2. Place cloves in double thickness of cheesecloth and tie with string. Add to slow cooker.
3. Add cinnamon candies.
4. Cover and Cook on Low 2-3 hours, or until heated thoroughly.
5. Remove spice bag before serving.

Hot Spicy Lemonade Punch

Mary E. Herr
The Hermitage
Three Rivers, MI

Makes 9-10 1-cup servings

4 cups cranberry juice
⅓-⅔ cup sugar
12-oz. can lemonade concentrate, thawed
4 cups water
1-2 Tbsp. honey
6 whole cloves
2 cinnamon sticks, broken
1 lemon, sliced

1. Combine juice, sugar, lemonade, water, and honey in slow cooker.
2. Tie cloves and cinnamon in small cheesecloth square. Add spice bag and lemon slices to slow cooker.
3. Cover and cook on Low 3-4 hours. Remove spice bag. Keep hot in slow cooker until ready to serve.

Hot Fruit Punch

Karen Stoltzfus
Alto, MI

Makes 10 1-cup servings

1 qt. cranberry juice
3 cups water
6-oz. can frozen orange juice concentrate, thawed
10-oz. pkg. frozen red raspberries, thawed
2 oranges, sliced
6 sticks cinnamon
12 whole allspice

1. Combine all ingredients in slow cooker.
2. Heat on High 1 hour, or until hot. Turn to Low while serving.

Punch

Kathy Hertzler
Lancaster, PA

Makes 12 1-cup servings

1 tsp. whole cloves
5 cups pineapple juice
5 cups cranberry juice
2¼ cups water
½ cup brown sugar
2 cinnamon sticks
¼ tsp. salt

1. Place cloves in small cheesecloth bag or tea ball.
2. Mix together all ingredients in slow cooker.
3. Cook on Low 6 hours. Remove cloves. Serve hot.

Wine-Cranberry Punch

C. J. Slagle
Roann, IN

Makes 8 1-cup servings

1 pint cranberry juice cocktail
1 cup water
¾ cup sugar
2 sticks cinnamon
6 whole cloves
4/5 qt. burgundy wine
1 lemon, sliced thin

1. Combine ingredients in slow cooker.

2. Heat on Low 1-2 hours. Strain and serve hot.
3. Keep hot and serve from slow cooker set on lowest setting.

Hot Cranberry Punch

Barbara Aston
Ashdown, AR

Makes 10 1-cup servings

2 16-oz. cans jellied cranberry sauce
2 qts. water
2 cups frozen orange juice concentrate
1 qt. pineapple juice, optional
half a stick of butter
¾ cup firmly packed brown sugar
½ tsp. ground cinnamon
½ tsp. ground allspice
¼ tsp. ground cloves
¼ tsp. ground nutmeg
¼ tsp. salt

1. Mix together all ingredients.
2. Heat on High until boiling, then reduce to Low for 4 hours. Serve hot.

Kate's Mulled Cider / Wine

Mitzi McGlynchey
Downingtown, PA

Makes 8-10 1-cup servings

½ tsp. whole cloves
½ tsp. whole allspice
½ gallon apple cider, *or* red burgundy wine
2 3-inch cinnamon sticks
1 tsp. ground nutmeg
orange slices, optional
cinnamon sticks, optional

1. Place cloves and allspice in cheesecloth bag or tea ball.
2. Combine spices, apple cider or wine, 2 cinnamon sticks, and nutmeg in slow cooker.
3. Cook on High 1 hour. Reduce heat, and simmer 2-3 hours.
4. Garnish individual servings with orange slices or cinnamon sticks.

Mulled Wine

Julie McKenzie
Punxsutawney, PA

Makes 8 1-cup servings

1/2 cup sugar
1 1/2 cups boiling water
half a lemon, sliced thin
3 cinnamon sticks
3 whole cloves
1 bottle red dinner wine
   (burgundy *or* claret)

1. Dissolve sugar in boiling water in saucepan.
2. Add remaining ingredients.
3. Pour into slow cooker. Heat on Low for at least 1 hour, until wine is hot. Do not boil.
4. Serve from cooker into mugs.

Almond Tea

Frances Schrag
Newton, KS

Makes 12 1-cup servings

10 cups boiling water
1 Tbsp. instant tea
2/3 cup lemon juice
1 cup sugar
1 tsp. vanilla
1 tsp. almond extract

1. Mix together all ingredients in slow cooker.

2. Turn to High and heat thoroughly (about 1 hour). Turn to Low while serving.

Carolers Hot Chocolate

Pat Unternahrer
Wayland, IA

Makes 12-14 1-cup servings

10 cups milk
3/4 cup sugar
3/4 cup cocoa, *or* hot
   chocolate mix
1/2 tsp. salt
2 cups hot water
marshmallows

1. Measure milk into slow cooker. Turn on High.
2. Mix together sugar, salt, and cocoa in heavy pan. Add hot water. Stir and boil 3 minutes, stirring often.
3. Pour into milk. Cook on High 2-2 1/2 hours.

Home-Style Tomato Juice

Jean Butzer
Batavia, NY

Makes 4-5 1-cup servings

10-12 large tomatoes
1 tsp. salt
1 tsp. seasoned salt
1/4 tsp. pepper
1 Tbsp. sugar

1. Wash and drain tomatoes. Remove cores and blossom ends. Place in slow cooker.
2. Cover and cook on Low 4-6 hours, or until tomatoes are soft.
3. Press through sieve or food mill.
4. Stir in seasonings. Chill.

Index

Index

About the Authors

Dawn J. Ranck has been a convinced slow-cooker user for years. She, along with her many friends, have been lining up their various-sized cookers on their kitchen counters before they set off each morning—and coming home to richly flavored full dinners.

Ranck , who lives in Harrisonburg, Virginia, is the co-author of *A Quilter's Christmas Cookbook* and *Favorite Recipes with Herbs*.

Phyllis Pellman Good has been part of many cookbook projects, authoring *The Best of Amish Cooking* and *The Festival Cookbook*, and co-authoring *Recipes from Central Market, Favorite Recipes with Herbs, The Best of Mennonite Fellowship Meals,* and *From Amish and Mennonite Kitchens.*

Good and her husband, Merle, live in Lancaster, Pennsylvania, and are co-directors of The People's Place, a heritage interpretation center in the Lancaster County village of Intercourse, Pennsylvania.

Dictionary
of Modern
Theological
German

HELMUT W. ZIEFLE

BAKER BOOK HOUSE
Grand Rapids, Michigan 49506

Contents

Preface

This *Dictionary of Modern Theological German* contains approximately ten thousand entries of basic theological vocabulary for reading the Bible and German theological texts. As an additional feature, the general meaning of the vocabulary entries is included as well. Scripture references point out where a particular word is used in Luther's translation of the Bible. The handy and comprehensive format of this dictionary should facilitate the study of theological German.

Two primary sources for the biblical and theological meanings included in this dictionary are the *Wortkonkordanz zur Stuttgarter Konkordanz-Bibel* (Stuttgart: Deutsche Bibelstiftung, 1953) and Walter M. Mosse's *Theological German Vocabulary* (New York: Macmillan, 1955). For the basic modern meanings of words and for the general layout I am especially indebted to *Cassell's German Dictionary* (London: Cassell, 1971). I gratefully acknowledge the kind permission of Cassell & Company, Ltd., to make use of their material.

Helmut W. Ziefle
February, 1982

Advice to the User

NOUNS. The gender of each noun is indicated by the German definite article *der* (m.), *die* (f.), or *das* (n.). For the benefit of the user the plural form of nouns has been included as well. Thus "**der Abend** (-e)" means that the plural of *Abend* is *die Abende.*

VERBS. All verbs are listed with their grammatical function(s). Thus, "**abgehen,** 1. *ir.v.n.* (*aux.* s.) to go off, to depart. 2. *v.a.* to wear out by walking; to measure by steps" means that *abgehen* is first an irregular intransitive verb using the auxiliary verb *sein* in the perfect tenses and second a transitive verb. The different meanings of the verb reflect its various functions.

PARENTHESES. Parentheses are used in various ways. For example, (*acc.*), (*dat.*), or (*gen.*) following a word means that the word governs the case indicated. The use of (*einem etwas*) with a verb like *bescheren* means that German requires the accusative form of the thing granted and the dative form of the person to whom it is granted, with the dative coming first. When the same form of a German noun is used for both the masculine and feminine (or neuter), both articles are given, with the feminine (or neuter) in parentheses. For proper names the definite article is given in parentheses as well. Thus, "**(der) Jakob**" tells the user that it is a masculine noun.

PUNCTUATION. The English translations of German words are separated by a semicolon if a clear demarcation in meaning or usage can be established; otherwise they are separated by a comma.

IRREGULAR VERBS. For easy reference the principal parts of the most common irregular and semi-irregular verbs are listed in the appendix on page 196.

SCRIPTURE REFERENCES. The Scripture references reflect Martin Luther's German Bible (Stuttgart).

Abbreviations

acc.	accusative		neg.	negative
adj.	adjective		num.	numerical
adv.	adverb		orig.	originally
art.	article		part.	particle
aux.	auxiliary verb		pers.	personal
comp.	comparative degree		pl.	plural
conj.	conjunction		poss.	possessive
dat.	dative		p.p.	past participle
dem.	demonstrative		pred.	predicate
f.	feminine		prep.	preposition
fig.	figurative		pres.	present
gen.	genitive		pron.	pronoun
h.	*haben*		pr.p.	present participle
imp.	impersonal		reg.	regular
indec.	indeclinable		rel.	relative
indef.	indefinite		s.	*sein*
inf.	infinitive		sep.	separable
insep.	inseparable		sing.	singular
int.	interjection		sup.	superlative
inter.	interrogative		v.a.	transitive verb
ir.	irregular		v.imp.	impersonal verb
m.	masculine		v.n.	intransitive verb
n.	neuter		v.r.	reflexive verb

Aa

das A und das O, Alpha and Omega. (Rev. 1:8)

das Aas (-e), carcass. (Gen. 15:11)

das Abbild (-er), likeness, image.

abborgen, *v.a.* (*einem etwas*) to borrow from. (Matt. 5:42)

abbrechen, *ir.v.a. & n.* (*aux.* s. & h.) 1. to break off, to snap, to demolish, to dismantle, to pull down. 2. to interrupt, to discontinue, to stop short. (Isa. 38:12)

der Abend (-e), evening, night. (Gen. 1:5)

die Abendandacht (-en), evensong, vesper.

das Abendessen (-), supper. (John 21:20)

das Abendgebet (-e), evening prayer.

das Abendgeläut (-e), vesper bell.

die Abendglocke (-n), vesper bell.

der Abendgottesdienst (-e), vesper.

das Abendland, the Occident, the West.

abendländisch, *adj.* occidental.

das Abendmahl, the Lord's Supper, the Last Supper, Eucharist, holy communion. (Luke 22:20)
das Abendmahl in beiderlei Gestalt, communion with bread and wine; *das Abendmahl nehmen,* to partake of the Lord's Supper; *das Abendmahl reichen,* to administer the sacrament.

das Abendmahlsbrot, Host.

der Abendmahlsgänger (-), communicant.

der Abendmahlsgast (⁀e), communicant.

der Abendmahlskelch, chalice, communion cup.

der Abendmahlstisch, communion table.

das Abendopfer (-), evening sacrifice. (Ps. 141:2)

die Abendzeit, evening. (Gen. 8:11)

der Aberglaube, superstition. (Acts 25:19)

abergläubisch, *adj.* superstitious.

abermals, *adv.* again, once more. (Gen. 8:10)

der Abfall (⁀e), apostasy, secession. (II Thess. 2:3)

abfällig, *adj.* disloyal, rebellious. (Acts 5:37)
vom Glauben abfällig werden, to turn apostate.

abfertigen, *v.a.* to send away, to dispatch. (Acts 17:10)

abführen, *v.a.* to lead away, to mislead. (Matt. 7:13)

die Abgabe (-n), tax, tribute, duty.

abgabepflichtig, *adj.* liable to tax, assessable, taxable.

abgehen, 1. *ir.v.n.* (*aux.* s.) to go off, to depart. 2. *v.a.* to wear out by walking; to measure by steps. (Mark 6:31)

abgeschieden, *p.p. & adj.* 1. separated. 2. solitary, secluded, retired. 3. departed, defunct, dead.
die Abgeschiedene, divorced woman (Matt. 5:32); *der abgeschiedene Geist,* departed spirit; *die abgeschiedene Seele,* departed spirit.

der Abgott (⁀er), idol. (I Thess. 1:9)
einen zu seinem Abgott machen, to idolize a person.

die Abgötterei, idolatry. (Deut. 32:21)
Abgötterei treiben, to practice idolatry.

abgöttisch, *adj.* idolatrous. (Acts 17:16)

der Abgrund (⁀e), abyss, bottomless pit. (Prov. 27:20)

die Abhandlung (-en), tract, tractate.

der Abhang (⁀e), slope. (Mark 5:13)

abhängig, *adj.* 1. sloping, inclined. 2. dependent on, subject to.

die Abhängigkeit, 1. slope, declivity. 2. dependence.

das Abhängigkeitsgefühl (⁻e), emotional dependence.

abhauen, *ir.v.a.* to cut off; to cut down. (Ps. 37:2)

abheben, 1. *ir.v.a.* to lift up or off; to contrast, to bring into relief; to uncover, to remove. 2. *v.r.* to be contrasted, to be brought into relief. (John 11:39)

abirren, *v.n.* (*aux.* s.) to lose one's way; to deviate; to err. (Ps. 119:10)

die Abkehr, act of turning away, withdrawing, renunciation; alienation, estrangement; backsliding.
die Abkehr von Gott, estrangement from God.

abkehren, *v.a.* 1. to turn away, to turn off; to avert; to divert; to distract. 2. to brush away.
sich von einem abkehren, to turn one's back upon a person.

abkürzen, 1. *v.a.* to shorten, to abridge; to abbreviate; to lessen, to curtail, to condense. 2. *v.n.* (& *a.*) to take a short cut. (Job 17:1)

der Ablaß (⁻[ss]e), indulgence.
vollkommener Ablaß, plenary indulgence.

der Ablaßbrief (-e), letter of indulgence; dispensation.

ablassen, 1. *ir.v.a.* to drain, to empty, to let off; to decant; to tap. 2. *v.n.* (*aux.* h.) to leave off, to desist, to cease. (Gen. 11:6)

das Ablaßgeld (-er), shrove-money.

der Ablaßhandel, sale of indulgences.

das Ablaßjahr, jubilee.

der Ablaßkrämer (-), seller of indulgences.

der Ablaßprediger (-), seller of indulgences.

die Ablaßwoche, week of Corpus Christi.

der Ablaßzettel (-), ticket of indulgence.

ablegen, 1. *v.a.* to put away, to take off; to lay off, down, or aside. 2. *v.n.* (*aux.* h.) to put out to sea; to shove off. (John 13:4)

ableiten, *v.a.* to lead away, to divert, to deflect; to mislead; to drain; to trace back; to derive; to deduce; to escape.

die Ablution (-en), washing; ablution.

die Abnahme (-n), diminution, decline; decrease, falling off, shrinkage; decay; taking off or down.
die Abnahme vom Kreuze, the descent from the cross; *die Abnahme der Tage,* the shortening of the days.

abnehmen, 1. *ir.v.a.* to take off or away; to amputate; to remove; to gather (fruit); to buy (goods); to examine. 2. *v.n.* (*aux.* h.) to wane; to decrease, to decline. (John 3:30)

(der) Abraham, Abraham.

abreißen, 1. *ir.v.n.* (*aux.* s.) to break away, to tear off. 2. *v.a.* to tear, to pull off, to pull down; to demolish. (Exod. 32:2)

absagen, 1. *v.a.* to refuse, to decline. 2. *v.n.* (*aux.* h.) to renounce. (Job 1:11)

abscheiden, 1. *ir.v.a.* to separate; to disengage. 2. *v.n.* (*aux.* s.) to depart. (Phil. 1:23)
von der Welt abscheiden, to depart this life; *von der Welt abgeschieden,* secluded from the world.

die Abscheidung, parting, separation; death.

der Abschied (-e), departure; discharge, dismissal; leave. (Luke 9:61)

abschlagen, 1. *ir.v.a.* to knock off; to chip; to strike. 2. *v.n.* (*aux.* s.) to abate, to decline, to fall off. (II Sam. 1:21)

abschneiden, 1. *ir.v.a.* to cut off; to clip; to amputate. 2. *v.n.* (*aux.* h.) to form a contrast, to differ. (I Sam. 24:6)

abschütteln, *v.a.* to shake off; to shake violently. (Luke 9:5)

absetzen, *v.a.* to remove (from office); to depose (a king); to dismiss, to discard. (Dan. 2:21)

die Absicht (-en), intention, design, purpose, end, aim.

die Absolution, absolution.
einem die Absolution erteilen, to give absolution to a person.

absondern, 1. *v.a.* to separate, to isolate. 2. *v.r.* to separate oneself. (Lev. 20:24)

abstehen (von), to desist from, to refrain from, to relinquish. (Ps. 37:8)

absterben, *ir.v.n.* (*aux.* s.) to die away or out, to wither, to perish; to fade away; to mortify. (Rom. 6:2)
der Welt absterben, to withdraw from the world; *allen Vergnügungen abgestorben sein,* to be indifferent to all pleasure.

die Abstinenz, fasting; abstinence.

der Abstinenzler (-), total abstainer.

der Abt (⁻e), abbot.

die Abtei (-en), abbey.

abteilich, *adj.* abbatial.

die Äbtin (-nen), abbess.

die Äbtissin (-nen), abbess.

äbtlich, *adj.* abbatial.

abtöten, *v.a.* to kill, to deaden; to mortify. *das Fleisch abtöten,* to mortify the flesh.

die Abtötung, mortification.

abtreten, 1. *ir.v.a.* to relinquish, to resign, to abandon. 2. *v.n.* (*aux.* s.) to retire; to withdraw; to secede from. (I Tim. 4:1)

der Abtreter (-), resigner, transferrer.

die Abtretung (-en), cession; abdication; surrender.

abtrünnig, *adj.* faithless; disloyal, rebellious. (Jer. 3:12)
abtrünnig werden, to turn apostate; *von der Religion abtrünnig,* apostate.

der Abtrünnige (-n), deserter, renegade; apostate. (Ps. 68:19)

die Abtrünnigkeit, apostasy.

abtun, *ir.v.a.* to take or put off; to abolish; to dispose of. (Ps. 27:9)
sich seines Glaubens abtun, to renounce one's faith.

abwälzen, *v.a.* to roll off or away. (Mark 16:4)

abwaschen, *ir.v.a.* to cleanse by washing. (Acts 22:16)

die Abwaschung (-en), washing; ablution.

abweisen, *ir.v.a.* to reject, to refuse, to send away. (Heb. 12:25)

abwenden, 1. *reg.* & *ir.v.a.* to avert, to prevent. 2. *v.r.* to turn away from; to desert. (I Sam. 15:11)
das wolle Gott abwenden, God forbid!

die Abwendung, alienation.

abwerfen, *ir.v.a.* to throw, to cast. (Rev. 6:13)

abwesend, *adj.* absent. (II Cor. 10:1)

die Abwesenheit, absence.

abwischen, 1. *v.a.* to wipe off, to clean. 2. *v.r.* to wipe oneself clean. (Isa. 25:8)

abziehen, 1. *ir.v.a.* to take off, to remove. 2. *v.n.* (*aux.* s.) to retire, to retreat; to depart. (Num. 14:34)

die Achsel (-n), shoulder.

die Acht, outlawry; attention, heed.
Acht und Bann, excommunication; *in die Acht verfallen,* to be outlawed; *aus der (außer) Acht lassen,* to pay no attention to.

achten, *v.a.* & *n.* to regard, to esteem, to respect. (Deut. 10:17)

ächten, *v.a.* to outlaw, to proscribe.
geächtet und gebannt, outlawed and excommunicated.

achthaben auf, (*acc.*) to pay attention to, to heed. (Job 1:8)

der Acker (¨), field, arable land; soil. (Gen. 3:17)

der Ackerbau, agriculture.

die Ackerleute, (*pl.*) farmers. (Isa. 61:5)

der Ackermann (¨er), farmer. (Gen. 4:2)

ackern, *v.a.* to till, to plow. (Ps. 129:3)

das Ackerwerk, tillage. (Ps. 104:23)

(der) Adam, Adam.

der Adamit (-en), Adamite.

die Ader (-n), vein, artery; streak, grain (in wood). (Job 10:11)

der Adler (-), eagle. (Ps. 103:5)

die Adlerflügel, (*pl.*) eagle's wings. (Exod. 19:4)

(der) Adonai, Adonijah.

der Advent, advent.

der Adventist (-en), Adventist.

die Adventszeit, advent season.

der Affe (-n), ape, monkey. (I Kings 10:22)

äffen, *v.a.* to ape, to mock, to make a fool of. (II Chron. 36:16)

afterreden, *v.n.* & *v.a.* (*dat.*) to slander. (I Peter 2:1)

die Agende (-n), book of liturgy, ritual.

der Agnostiker (-), agnostic.

agnostisch, *adj.* agnostic.

der Agnostizismus, agnosticism.

Ägypten, Egypt. (Exod. 3:7)

der Ägypter (-), Egyptian. (I Kings 5:10)

ägyptisch, *adj.* Egyptian.

der Ahn (-en), ancestor.

die Ahne (-n), ancestress.

ähneln, *v.n.* to bear a likeness to, to look like, to resemble.

ahnen, *v.a.* & *n.* (*aux.* h.) to suspect, to surmise; to have a presentiment of.
es ahnt mir nichts Gutes, I have a foreboding of evil.

ähnlich, *adj.* similar, like, resembling. (Gen. 5:3)

die **Ähnlichkeit,** resemblance, similarity, likeness.

die **Ahnung** (-en), misgiving, presentiment.
keine blasse Ahnung von einer Sache haben, to have not the faintest notion of a thing.

ahnungslos, *adj.* unsuspecting.

ahnungsvoll, *adj.* ominous, full of misgivings.

die **Ähre** (-n), ear (of grain). (Gen. 41:5)

der **Ährenleser** (-), gleaner.

die **Albe** (-n), alb.

die **Albigenser,** (*pl.*) Albigenses.

die **Albigenser-Kreuzzüge,** (*pl.*) crusades against Albigenses.

die **Alchemie,** alchemy.

der **Alchemist** (-en), alchemist.

alchemistisch, *adj.* alchemistic.

die **Alienation,** alienation.

alienieren, *v.a.* to alienate.

all, *adj.* (*used collectively*) all; entire, whole. (Ps. 33:8)
alle Menschen, all men; *alle Welt,* the whole world; *sie alle,* all of them.

all, *adj.* (*used distributively*) every, each, any, all. (I Sam. 16:11)
alle beide, both of them; *alle und jede Hoffnung,* all and every hope; *auf alle Fälle,* in any case; *auf alle Weise,* by all means; *ohne alle Ursache,* without any cause; *ohne allen Zweifel,* undoubtedly.

All-, *in compounds* = universally, all; *prefixed to adverbs it is archaic and hardly affects the meaning.*

allbekannt, *adj.* notorious.

alle, *adv.* all gone, all spent, exhausted.

alle-, (*in compounds*) *bei* or *trotz alledem,* for all that, nevertheless.

allein, 1. *indec. adj. & adv.* alone, sole, single. 2. *adv.* only, merely. 3. *conj.* only, but. (Gen. 2:18)

alleinig, *adj. & adv.* exclusive, sole.
der alleinige Gott, the one God.

alleinseligmachend, *adj.* only saving (faith).
der alleinseligmachende Glaube, the only true faith.

allemal, *adv.* always; yet, still.

allenfalls, *adv.* in any event, at all events; if need be, possibly.

allenthalben, *adv.* everywhere.

aller-, *in compounds with the sup.* = of all; *with titles* = most.

der **Allerbarmer,** the All-merciful.

allerchristlichst, *adj.* most Christian.

allerdings, 1. *adv.* certainly, to be sure, of course, by all means, indeed. 2. *conj.* though. (Deut. 15:4)

allererst, *adj. & adv.* first of all. (Matt. 24:8)

allergeringst, *adj.* the very least. (I Cor. 4:9)

allergewissest, *adv.* most surely. (Rom. 4:21)

allergrößest, *adj.* greatest. (II Peter 1:4)

Allerheiligen, (*pl.*) All Saints' Day.

das **Allerheiligste,** Holy of Holies. (Exod. 26:33)

der **Allerhöchste,** God. (Deut. 32:8)

allerlei, *indec. adj.* all sorts of, all kinds of. (Gen. 1:29)

allerliebst, *adv.* most gladly. (II Cor. 12:9)

allermeist, 1. *adj.* most of all. 2. *adv.* especially, chiefly. (Acts 20:38)

Allerseelen, (*pl.*) All Souls' Day.

allerverachtetst, *adj.* most despised. (Isa. 53:3)

alles, *n.* (*used substantively*) everything; everybody. (Deut. 32:4)

allesamt, *adv.* altogether. (Ps. 19:10)

allewege, *adv.* everywhere and always. (II Chron. 9:7)

allezeit, *adv.* always, at all times. (Eph. 5:20)

der **Allgeber,** God, Giver of all.

die **Allgegenwart,** omnipresence.

allgegenwärtig, *adj.* omnipresent.

allgemein, *adj.* universal, general.

die **Allgötterei,** pantheism.

allgütig, *adj.* all-bountiful, infinitely good.

die **Allmacht,** omnipotence.

allmächtig, *adj.* omnipotent.

allseitig, *adj.* universal.

der **Alltag,** weekday.

die **Alltagswelt,** workaday world.

die **Alltagsworte,** (*pl.*) household words.

allumfassend, *adj.* all-embracing, comprehensive.

allwaltend, *adj.* supreme, sovereign, all-ruling.

die Allweisheit, infinite wisdom.

allwissend, *adj.* omniscient.

die Allwissenheit, omniscience.

allzu, *adv.* too much, far too.

allzumal, *adv.* all at once; altogether.

das Almosen (-), alms. (Matt. 6:1)
um ein Almosen bitten, to ask for a charity.

die Almosenbüchse (-n), poor-box.

der Almosenempfänger (-), beggar, pauper.

die Aloe (-n), aloe. (Ps. 45:9)

alsbald, *adv.* forthwith, immediately; as soon as may be; thereupon. (Matt. 21:19)

alsdann, *adv.* then, thereupon. (Matt. 5:24)

also, 1. *adv.* so, thus. 2. *conj.* therefore, consequently, hence, so. (Gen. 1:9)

alt, *adj.* old, aged, ancient; stale. (Matt. 9:17)
das Alte Testament, the Old Testament.

der Altar (⁻e), altar. (Matt. 5:23)

das Altarbild (-er), altarpiece, altar painting.

der Altardiener (-), acolyte.

der Altarkelch (-e), chalice.

der Altarraum (⁻e), chancel.

das Altartuch (⁻er), altar cloth.

das Alter, age, old age; antiquity; epoch. (Gen. 48:10)

das Altertum, antiquity.

der Älteste (-n), elder. (I Kings 12:6)

das Ältestenamt, eldership.

das Ältestenrecht, right of primogeniture.

die Altweiberfabel (-n), fables fit only for old women. (I Tim. 4:7)

der Ambo, ambo.

ambrosianisch, *adj.* Ambrosian.
die ambrosianische Liturgie, Ambrosian liturgy; *der ambrosianische Lobgesang,* Ambrosian chant.

die Ameise (-n), ant. (Prov. 30:25)

das Amen, Amen. (Matt. 6:13)

die Amme (-n), nurse. (Gen. 35:8)

das Amt (⁻er), ecclesiastical duty, ministry; office. (Exod. 28:30)

das Amtschild, the breastplate of judgment. (Exod. 28:29)

die Amtshandlung (-en), official function; ministration.

der Amtsverlust (-e), loss of official position.

der Anabaptismus, Anabaptism.

der Anabaptist (-en), Anabaptist.

der Anachoret (-en), anchorite.

die Analogie (-ien), analogy.

das Anathem(a), anathema, excommunication.

der Anbeginn, earliest beginning, origin. (Matt. 19:8)

anbeten, *v.a.* to adore, to worship. (Matt. 2:2)

der Anbeter (-), adorer, worshiper. (John 4:23)

die Anbetung, adoration, worship.

anbetungswürdig, *adj.* adorable.

anbieten, *ir.v.a.* to offer, to tender. (Acts 8:18)

anblasen, *ir.v.a.* to blow at or upon; to breathe on. (Ezek. 37:9)

anbrechen, 1. *ir.v.n.* (*aux.* s.) to start; to break; to dawn. 2. *v.a.* to broach; to open; to start on, to break into; to cut (a loaf, etc.). (Gen. 32:25)
der Tag brach an, the day dawned.

der Anbruch (⁻e), opening; beginning. (Rom. 11:16)

die Andacht (-en), devotion; prayers.
seine Andacht verrichten, to say one's prayers.

die Andächtelei (-en), hypocrisy.

andächteln, *v.n.* to affect devotion; to be overpious.

andächtig, *adj. & adv.* devout, pious; attentive. (Acts 13:50)
sie hörte andächtig zu, she listened with close attention.

der Andächtler (-), hypocrite.

die Andächtlerin (-nen), hypocrite.

das Andachtsbuch (⁻er), devotional book.

andachtslos, *adj.* irreverent.

andachtsvoll, *adj.* devout.

das Andenken (-), memory, remembrance.

ander, *adj. & pron.* other, else, different. (Num. 14:24)

ändern, 1. *v.a.* to alter, to change, to rectify, to amend. 2. *v.r.* to alter, to vary, to reform, to change. (Gen. 35:2)

anders, *adv.* otherwise; else; differently. (I Tim. 6:3)

der Andersgläubige (-n), dissenter, heretic.

die Änderung (-en), change, alteration, correction.

andeuten, *v.a.* to point out, to indicate; to hint. (Prov. 16:30)

anempfehlen, *ir.v.a.* to recommend.

anempfinden, *v.n.* to appreciate or to share the feelings of others.

anerkennen, *ir.v.a.* to recognize, to acknowledge; to appreciate; to admit.

anfahren, 1. *ir.v.n.* (*aux.* s.) to drive up to; to drive or strike against. 2. *v.a.* to carry; to address angrily; to put into (port). (Matt. 16:22)

der Anfall (-̈e), share, part (in inheritance); *pl.* yearly returns, yield. (Acts 8:21)

der Anfang (-̈e), beginning, start, onset, outset. (Gen. 1:1)

anfangen, 1. *ir.v.a.* to begin, to commence; to set about. 2. *v.n.* (*aux.* h.) to begin, to originate. (Matt. 4:17)

der Anfänger (-), beginner, novice. (Heb. 12:2)

anfänglich, 1. *adj.* initial, incipient, original. 2. *adv.* at first.

anfassen, *v.a.* to take hold of, to grasp, to seize.

anfechtbar, *adj.* contestable, vulnerable.

anfechten, *ir.v.a.* to combat; to contest; to tempt.

die Anfechtung (-en), temptation. (I Peter 1:6)

anfeinden, *v.a.* to bear ill will, to show enmity.

die Anfeindung (-en), persecution; enmity, hostility, ill will.

anflehen, *v.a.* to implore.

die Anflehung, supplication.

anfordern, *v.a.* to claim, to request.

anführen, *v.a.* to lead on; to lead, to guide.

angeben, *ir.v.a.* to declare, to state; to mention; to pretend.

angeboren, *adj.* inborn, innate; congenital, hereditary.

angehen, 1. *ir.v.a.* to approach, to apply to; to be related to. 2. *v.n.* (*aux.* s.) to begin, to commence; to grow; to catch fire. (Matt. 27:5)

angehören, *v.n.* (*aux.* s.) to belong to, to appertain to. (Exod. 32:26)

die Angel (-n), door-hinge. (Prov. 26:14)

die Angel (-n), fishing tackle. (Matt. 17:27)

angeloben, *v.a.* to vow; to promise solemnly.

das Angelöbnis (-se), vow, solemn protestation.

der Angelus, angel; messenger.

das Angelus läuten, angelus bell.

angenehm, *adj.* (*dat.*) agreeable, pleasant.

der Anger (-), (village) green; meadow, pasture, mead, lawn. (Ps. 65:14)

das Angesicht (-er), face; countenance. (Heb. 9:24)
im Schweiße seines Angesichts, in the sweat of his brow.

der Anglikaner (-), Anglican.

anglikanisch, *adj.* Anglican.
die Anglikanische Kirche, the Anglican Church, the Church of England.

der Anglikanismus, Anglicanism.

angreifen, 1. *ir.v.a.* to handle; to lay hands on; to undertake; to attack, to assail. 2. *v.r.* to exert oneself. (Matt. 18:28)

der Angriff (-e), attack, assault, invasion.

die Angst (-̈e), fear; anxiety; anguish. (Gen. 42:21)
die Todesangst, death agony.

das Angstgeschrei, cry of terror or anguish.

ängstigen, 1. *v.a.* to frighten, to alarm. 2. *v.r.: sich ängstigen vor,* to be afraid of; *sich ängstigen um,* to be anxious about. (I Sam. 28:15)

ängstlich, *adj.* anxious. (Isa. 26:16)

der Angstschweiß, cold sweat.

anhaben, *ir.v.a.* to wear, to have on, to be dressed in. (II Kings 1:8)

anhalten, 1. *ir.v.a.* to stop, to pull up; to spur on, to urge, to encourage. 2. *v.r.: sich anhalten (an einer Sache),* to cling to, to hold on to. 3. *v.n.* (*aux.* h.) to stop, to halt; to continue, to go on. (Acts 6:4)

anhangen, *ir.v.n.* (*aux.* s.) to stick to, to hold by, to remain faithful to. (Gen. 49:10)

anheben, 1. *ir.v.a.* to hoist, to raise; to commence. 2. *v.n.* (*aux.* h.) to begin. (Mark 14:72)

anheften, *v.a.* to fasten to, to affix. (Acts 2:23)

anheimstellen, *v.a.* to suggest, to submit, or to leave to a person.
stelle das Weitere dem Himmel anheim, to leave the rest in the hands of God.

der Anker (-), anchor. (Heb. 6:19)

die Anklage (-n), charge, accusation. (Exod. 23:1)

anklagen, *v.a.* to accuse. (Acts 23:6)
öffentlich anklagen, to impeach, to indict.

der Anklageprozeß (-sse), prosecution.

der Ankläger (-), accuser; plaintiff.

die Anklägerin (-nen), accuser; plaintiff.

anklägerisch, *adj.* prone to accuse.

die Anklageschrift (-en), indictment, accusation, complaint.

ankleben, 1. *v.n.* to stick to, to adhere. 2. *v.a.* to glue or paste on.

anklopfen, *v.n.* to knock (at), to rap. (Matt. 7:7)

der Anknüpfungspunkt, point of contact, point of reference; starting point.

ankommen, 1. *ir.v.n.* (*aux.* s.) to arrive; to approach. 2. *v.a.* to befall, to come upon.

der Ankömmling (-e), newcomer, arrival.

ankünden, ankündigen, *v.a.* to announce; to declare, to proclaim.

die Ankündigung, declaration, proclamation, announcement.

die Ankunft (¨e), arrival, advent.

der Anlaß (¨[ss]e), cause, occasion, motive, inducement.

der Anlauf (¨e), attack, advance. (Eph. 6:11)

anlaufen, *ir.v.n.* (*aux.* s.) to rush against, to run up to.

anlegen, 1. *v.a.* to lay or put on (or against); to apply; to found. 2. *v.r.* to lean against; to adhere to. 3. *v.n.* (*aux.* h.) to land; to lie against. (I Kings 20:11)

anleiten, *v.a.* to guide, to conduct; to train; to introduce. (Acts 8:31)

die Anleitung (-en), guidance; introduction.

anliegen, 1. *ir.v.n.* to lie close to, to be adjacent to, to border on; to entreat (someone). 2. *n.* desire, wish, request; concern. (Luke 23:23)

anlocken, *v.a.* to allure, to attract, to entice.

die Anlockung (-en), enticement.

das Anlockungsmittel (-), lure, decoy, bait.

anlügen, *ir.v.a.* to lie to a person's face, to lie brazenly.

anmaßen, *v.r.* to presume; to claim; to assume; to arrogate.

die Anmaßung (-en), presumption; arrogance.

anmerken, *v.a.* to perceive, to observe, to remark, to notice; to note, to write down.

die Annahme (-n), supposition, assumption; hypothesis.

annehmbar, *adj.* acceptable.

annehmen, *ir.v.a.* 1. to take, to receive; to accept. 2. to suppose, to take for granted; to assume. (Ps. 6:10)
an Kindes Statt annehmen, to adopt.

die Anpassung, adjustment, adaptation, accommodation.

anrichten, *v.a.* 1. to regulate; to produce, to cause. 2. to prepare.

anrufen, *ir.v.a.* to call to, to hail, to challenge; to appeal to. (Gen. 33:20)
zum Zeugen anrufen, to call as a witness.

die Anrufung, invocation.

anrühren, *v.a.* to touch.

ansagen, *v.a.* to announce; to notify. (Job 1:15)

anschauen, 1. *v.a.* to look at; to contemplate. 2. *n.* aspect. (Gen. 3:6)

die Anschauung, perception; conception; mode of viewing; view; observation; contemplation; intuition.
zu der Anschauung kommen, to come to the view or conclusion.

der Anschlag (¨e), assault, attack. (Ps. 146:4)

anschlagen, 1. *ir.v.a.* to strike against, upon, or at; to sound, to ring; to affix, to stick up; to estimate, to value; to splice (a rope). 2. *v.n.* to strike or fall against; take effect; to operate. (Rev. 14:15)

anschreiben, *ir.v.a.* to write down, to note down. (Ps. 69:29)

15

ansehen, 1. *ir.v.a.* to look at; to view. 2. *n.* appearance, aspect; authority. (Gen. 1:31) *man sieht es ihm gleich an, wes Geistes Kind er ist,* you can read his character in his face; *vor Gott gilt kein Ansehen der Person,* God is no respecter of persons.

die Ansicht (-en), sight, view, prospect; opinion, notion; inspection.
nach meiner Ansicht, meiner Ansicht nach, in my opinion.

anspannen, *v.a.* 1. to yoke to, to hitch. 2. to stretch; to bend (sails). 3. to strain; to exert. (I Kings 18:44)

anspeien, *ir.v.a.* to spit at or upon. (Matt. 27:30)

die Ansprache (-n), address, speech.

die Anständigkeit, decency, propriety; respectability.

anstehen, *ir.v.n.* (*aux.* h. & s.) to stand near or next; to be fixed; to suit or fit (a person). (I Cor. 14:35)

anstiften, 1. *v.a.* to cause, to set on foot, to plot; to provoke. 2. *n. see* **Anstiftung.**

die Anstiftung (-en), instigation; contriving.

der Anstoß (⁻[ss]e), offense, scandal. (Isa. 8:14)

anstoßen, 1. *ir.v.a.* to strike, to push against; to give offense. 2. *v.n.* (*aux.* h.) to stumble against.

anstößig, *adj.* offensive.

die Anstößigkeit, offensiveness.

antasten, *v.a.* to touch. (Job 1:11)

der Antichrist, Antichrist.

das Antlitz (-e), face, countenance.

der Antrieb (-e), impulse, motive, inducement; instigation; power.

antun, *ir.v.a.* to put on (clothes); to inflict violence on, to injure, to insult. (II Chron. 6:41)

die Antwort (-en), answer, reply. (I Kings 18:26)

antworten, *v.a. & n.* to answer, to reply. (I Sam. 14:37)

das Anzeichen (-), omen, foreboding. (Phil. 1:28)

anzeigen, *v.a.* to announce, to notify; to point out; to show. (II Kings 4:27)

anziehen, 1. *ir.v.a.* to draw; to put on. 2. *v.n.* (*aux.* h.) to draw; to stick. (Ps. 109:18)

anzünden, *v.a.* to kindle, to light (a fire). (Jer. 7:18)

die Apathie, apathy.

die Apokalypse, Apocalypse.

apokalyptisch, *adj.* apocalyptic.
die apokalyptischen Reiter, the four horsemen of the Apocalypse.

apokryph, apokryphisch, *adj.* apocryphal.

der Apologet (-en), apologist.

die Apologetik, apologetics.

apologetisch, *adj.* apologetic(al).

die Apostasie, apostasy.

der Apostat, apostate.

der Apostel (-), apostle. (Matt. 10:2)

das Apostelamt, das Apostolat, apostleship. (Acts 1:25)

die Apostelgeschichte, Acts of the Apostles.

die Apostellehre, the Didache.

das Apostolikum, the Apostles' Creed.

apostolisch, *adj.* apostolic.
das apostolische Glaubensbekenntnis, the Apostles' Creed.

die Apsis (*pl., Apsen*), apse.

der Araber (-), Arab.

die Arbeit (-en), work, labor. (Gen. 5:29)

arbeiten, 1. *v.a.* to work, to make, to execute. 2. *v.n.* (*aux.* h.) to work, to toil, to labor. (Exod. 20:9)

der Arbeiter (-), worker, laborer. (Matt. 9:37)

archaisch, *adj.* archaic.

die Arche, ark. (Matt. 24:38)

der Archidiakon (-en), archdeacon.

arg, 1. *adj.* bad, wicked, evil; deceitful. 2. *n.* deceit, malice. (Mic. 3:2)
es ist kein Arg an ihm, he is not malicious; *er denkt von jedermann Arges,* he thinks ill of everyone.

der Ärger, anger; irritation.

ärgerlich, *adj.* angry; provoking, annoying. (Matt. 16:23)

sich ärgern, *v.a.* to take offense (at or over). (Isa. 52:14)

das Ärgernis (-se), vexation, anger, annoyance; scandal; offense. (Matt. 18:7)

die Argheit, wickedness, malice.

die Arglist, cunning, deceitfulness.

arglistig, *adj.* cunning, deceitful.

der Argwohn, suspicion, mistrust.

der Arianismus, Arianism.

arm, *adj.* poor, needy. (I Sam. 2:7)
die Armen, the poor; *armer Sünder,* poor wretch.

der Arm (-e), arm. (John 12:38)
der Arm Gottes, the arm of God.

die Armenanstalt (-en), almshouse.

das Armenhaus (¨er), almshouse, workhouse.

der Arme(r)sünder (-e[n]sünder), condemned criminal, condemned man.

das Armesündergesicht (-er), hangdog look.

der Arminianer, Arminian.

armselig, *adj.* poor, miserable; despicable.

die Armseligkeit, wretchedness, misery.

die Armut, poverty. (Prov. 6:11)

die Art (-en), species, type, kind; race. (Gen. 1:11)

artig, *adj.* good; courteous.
gutartig, good-natured; *bösartig,* malicious.

die Arznei (-en), medicine. (Ezek. 47:12)

die Asche (-n), ash. (Gen. 18:27)
zu Asche verbrennen, to burn to ashes.

das Ascherabild (-er), image of the goddess Asherah.

der Aschermittwoch, Ash Wednesday.

die Askese, asceticism.

der Asketiker (-), ascetic.

asketisch, *adj.* ascetic.

das Asyl (-e), asylum, sanctuary.

der Atem, breath.
in einem Atem, in a twinkling.

der Atemzug (¨e), breath.
den letzten Atemzug tun, to breathe one's last.

der Athanasianer, Athanasian.
das Athanasianische Glaubensbekenntnis, Athanasian Creed.

der Atheismus, atheism.

atheistisch, *adj.* atheistic.

atmen, *v.a. & n.* to breathe, to inhale.

die Atmung, breathing, respiration.

die Aue (-n), pasture. (Ps. 23:2)

aufblähen, 1. *v.a.* to puff up; to inflate; to expand. 2. *v.r.* to be puffed up, to boast. (I Cor. 4:18)

aufblasen, *ir.v.a.* to blow up, to inflate; to distend. (I Cor. 8:1)

aufbrechen, 1. *ir.v.a.* to break open, to force open. 2. *v.n.* (*aux.* s.) to burst open; to rise from table; to start, to depart. (Gen. 7:11)

aufbringen, *ir.v.a.* 1. to raise up, to lift up; to bring up. 2. to irritate, to provoke, to enrage. (Acts 25:18)

aufdecken, 1. *v.a.* to uncover; to disclose, to reveal. 2. *v.n.* to lay the cloth or table.

auferstanden, *p.p.* (*of* **auferstehen**) *& adj.* risen.

auferstehen, *ir.v.n.* (*aux.* s.) to rise from the dead. (Matt. 16:21)

die Auferstehung, resurrection. (Matt. 22:30)

die Auferstehungsfeier, Easter.

auferwecken, *v.a.* to raise from the dead, to restore to life; to resuscitate. (John 5:21)

die Auferweckung, resuscitation.

auferziehen, *v.a.* to educate. (Isa. 1:2)

auffahren, *ir.v.n.* (*aux.* s.) to rise, to ascend. (Gen. 17:22)

die Auffassung (-en), comprehension, apprehension; interpretation; conception, view.

auffressen, *ir.v.a.* to eat up (of beasts); to devour; to corrode. (Gen. 41:20)

die Aufgabe, proposition, lesson; surrender (of a town); resignation; abandonment.

der Aufgang (¨e), rising, ascension. (Ps. 113:3)

aufgehen, *ir.v.n.* (*aux.* s.) 1. to rise (of dough, of the sun, etc.); to dawn on one. 2. to evaporate; to dissolve. 3. to come loose or untied. 4. to sprout.

aufheben, 1. *ir.v.a.* to lift, to raise, to hold up; to take up, to pick up, to seize; to keep, to preserve, to store away, to provide for; to abolish, to suspend; to sublate, to mediate (Hegel). 2. *n.* lifting (up). (Josh. 4:3)

die Aufhebung (-en), lifting up; suspension.
die Aufhebung einer Versammlung, dissolution of an assembly.

aufhelfen, *ir.v.a.* to aid; to succor. (Ps. 41:11)
einem aufhelfen, to help someone up.

aufhören, 1. *v.n.* (*aux.* h.) to cease, to stop. 2. *n.* cessation. (Gen. 8:22)

aufklären, 1. *v.a.* to clear up; to enlighten. 2. *v.r.* to clear up (of weather), to brighten (of the countenance, etc.).

der Aufklärer (-), enlightener, apostle of culture.

die Aufklärung, enlightenment.
das Zeitalter der Aufklärung, age of enlightenment.

aufkommen, 1. *ir.v.n.* (*aux.* s.) to rise, to get up. 2. *n.* getting up; recovery (from sickness).

aufladen, *ir.v.a.* to load; to charge. (Acts 28:10)
einem etwas aufladen, to charge or burden someone with; *sich (dat.) aufladen,* to take upon oneself.

die Auflage (-n), edition (of a book).

auflecken, *v.a.* to consume. (I Kings 18:38)

auflegen, *v.a.* to put or lay on; to impose. (I Kings 12:4)

auflehnen, 1. *v.a.* to lean (against or on). 2. *v.r.* to rebel, to revolt. (Gen. 49:9)

auflösen, *v.a.* to untie, to unravel. (Job 38:31)

aufmachen, 1. *v.a.* to open; to untie; to get ready. 2. *v.r.* to rise, to get up; to set out. (Gen. 19:27)

aufmerken, *v.n.* (*aux.* h.) to pay attention, to give heed to. (Deut. 32:1)

aufmerksam, *adj.* attentive, alert.

die Aufmerksamkeit, attention, alertness.

aufnehmen, *ir.v.a.* 1. to take up; to take in, to admit, to receive. 2. to hold, to contain. 3. to raise. (Ps. 27:10)

aufrecht, *adj.* straight; upright. (Acts 14:10)

aufrichten, 1. *v.a.* to set up, to erect. 2. *v.r.* to raise oneself. (Gen. 17:7)

aufrichtig, *adj.* sincere, upright. (Eccles. 7:29)

die Aufrichtigkeit, uprightness, sincerity. (I Chron. 29:17)

der Aufruhr (-e), riot, revolt. (Matt. 26:5)

aufrühren, *v.a.* to stir up, to incite (to rebellion); to mention again. (Prov. 17:9)

der Aufrührer (-), rebel, insurgent. (Prov. 24:21)

die Aufsätze, (*pl.*) tradition. (Mark 7:3)

aufschieben, *ir.v.a.* to postpone. (Ecclesiasticus 5:8)

aufschießen, *ir.v.n.* (*aux.* s.) to spring up. (Isa. 53:2)

aufschreiben, *ir.v.a.* to write down; to take note of. (Judg. 8:14)

der Aufschub (¨e), postponement, delay; adjournment. (Acts 25:17)

aufschürzen, *v.a.* to tuck up; to gird. (Luke 12:37)

aufsehen, 1. *ir.v.n.* (*aux.* h.) to look up or upon. 2. *n.* stir, sensation. (Luke 21:1)
Aufsehen erregen, to attract attention.

der Aufseher (-), warden, keeper.

aufsperren, *v.a.* to unlock; to open wide. (Ps. 22:8)

aufspringen, *ir.v.n.* (*aux.* s.) to leap up, to jump up, to spring up. (Acts 3:8)

aufstehen, *ir.v.n.* (*aux.* s.) to stand up; to rise, to get up. (Gen. 21:14)

aufsteigen, 1. *ir.v.n.* (*aux.* s.) to ascend, to rise, to mount. 2. *n.* ascent. (Gen. 28:12)

auftauen, *v.n.* (*aux.* s.) to thaw. (Ps. 147:18)

der Auftrag (¨e), commission, order, charge, mandate; message, task, mission.
in einem besonderen Auftrag, on a special mission; *einen Auftrag ausführen,* to execute a commission.

auftreten, 1. *ir.v.a.* to kick open. 2. *v.n.* (*aux.* s.) to appear, to come forward. (Ps. 35:11)
als Zeuge auftreten, to appear as witness.

auftun, 1. *ir.v.a.* to open; to disclose. 2. *v.r.* to open; to become visible. (Gen. 7:11)

aufwachen, *v.n.* (*aux.* s.) to awaken, to wake up. (I Kings 18:27)

aufwachsen, *ir.v.n.* (*aux.* s.) to grow up. (Gen. 2:9)

aufwecken, *v.a.* to rouse, to waken. (Matt. 8:25)

aufwerfen, 1. *ir.v.a.* to cast up; to proclaim. 2. *v.r.: sich aufwerfen zu,* to set oneself up (for). (Ps. 20:6)

aufziehen, 1. *ir.v.a.* to raise, to hoist; to bring up (children); to arrange, plan (festival); to wind up (a watch). 2. *v.n.* (*aux.* s.) to march, to mount guard. (Eph. 6:4)

der Augapfel, apple of the eye. (Deut. 32:10)

das Auge (-en), eye. (Gen. 27:1)
Augen aufheben, to lift one's eyes; *die Augen auftun, öffnen,* to open the eyes.

der Augenblick (-e), moment. (Ps. 30:6)

die Augensalbe (-n), ointment, salve for the eyes. (Rev. 3:18)

der Augenzeuge (-n), eyewitness.

die Augsburger Konfession, Augsburg Confession.

der Augsburger Religionsfrieden, Augsburg Confession.

der Augustiner (-), Augustinian.

der Augustinismus, Augustinianism.

ausbeten, *v.a.* to finish praying. (I Kings 8:54)

die Ausbeute, gain. (Jer. 21:9)

die Ausbildung, improvement, development; education; instruction, training; culture.

ausbleiben, *ir.v.n.* (*aux.* s.) to stay away, to fail to appear. (Hab. 2:3)

ausbrechen, 1. *ir.v.a.* to break or force out. 2. *v.n.* (*aux.* s.) to break out (as fire, a disease, etc.).

ausbreiten, 1. *v.a.* to spread, to expand. 2. *v.r.* to go into details, to spread. (Exod. 1:12)

die Ausbreitung, spreading.

ausbrüten, 1. *v.a.* to hatch (out); to brood over, to plot. 2. *n.* hatching; plotting. (Job 39:14)

ausdehnen, *v.a. & r.* to extend, to spread out. (Isa. 40:22)

ausdrücken, *v.a.* to press or squeeze out; to express, to utter. (Judg. 6:38)

auserkoren, *adj.* chosen, elect, selected. (I Sam. 20:30)

auserwählen, *v.a.* to select, to choose; to predestine. (I Thess. 1:4)

auserwählt, chosen. (Matt. 20:16)

der Auserwählte (-n), the chosen one, the elect one.

ausfahren, 1. *ir.v.a.* to take out for a drive. 2. *v.n.* (*aux.* s.) to come out, to drive out; to break out. (Matt. 8:32)

ausfliegen, *ir.v.a. & n.* (*aux.* s.) to send forth; to fly out; to make an excursion. (Gen. 8:7)

ausführen, *v.a.* 1. to put into effect, to execute. 2. to lead out, to take out. (Gen. 15:7)

die Ausgabe (-n), expenses. (Phil. 4:15)

der Ausgang (-e), exit; departure. (Ps. 121:8)

ausgeben (sich), to exalt oneself. (II Thess. 2:4)

ausgehen, *ir.v.n.* (*aux.* s.) to proceed, to emanate; to go out. (Gen. 2:10)

ausgießen, *ir.v.a.* to pour out. (Isa. 19:14)

die Ausgießung, descent or coming.
die Ausgießung des Heiligen Geistes, the descent or coming of the Holy Ghost.

aushacken, *v.a.* to pick out. (Prov. 30:17)

aushauen, *ir.v.a.* to hew out. (Deut. 6:11)

aushelfen, *ir.v.n.* (*aux.* h.) to help out, to assist. (Ps. 22:5)

ausjäten, *v.a.* to weed out. (Matt. 13:28)

auskaufen, *v.a.* to buy up. (Eph. 5:16)
die Zeit auskaufen, to make the most of one's time.

auskundschaften, *v.a.* to explore; to spy out. (Gal. 2:4)

der Ausländer (-), foreigner, alien.

auslassen, 1. *ir.v.a.* to let out, to release. 2. *v.r.* to express oneself. (John 10:4)

auslegen, 1. *v.a.* to lay out (money, etc.), to spend; to explain, to expound, to interpret. 2. *v.r.* to stand on guard. (Dan. 8:27)

der Ausleger (-), interpreter, expositor.

die Auslegung (-en), interpretation. (II Peter 1:20)

auslöschen, *v.a.* to put out, to extinguish, to quench. (Isa. 42:3)

ausraufen, *v.a.* to pluck out. (Matt. 12:1)

ausrecken, *v.a.* to stretch out. (Gen. 22:10)

ausreden, *v.a.* to utter. (Ps. 106:2)

ausreißen, 1. *ir.v.a.* to pluck out. 2. *v.n.* (*aux.* s.) to run away; to desert. (Matt. 5:29)

ausreuten, *v.a.* to root out. (Matt. 15:13)

ausrichten, *v.a.* to level, to make straight; to adjust; to execute, to fulfil. (Ps. 103:20)

ausrotten, *v.a.* to exterminate, to root out, to stamp out, to destroy. (Deut. 7:1)

die Ausrottung, extermination, destruction.

der Ausrottungskrieg (-e), war of extermination.

ausrufen, 1. *ir.v.a.* to proclaim. 2. *v.n. (aux.* h.) to cry out. (Gen. 41:43)

ausrüsten, *v.a.* to equip. (Ps. 51:14)

die Ausrüstung (-en), armament; equipment.

der Aussatz, leprosy.

aussätzig, *adj.* leprous. (Num. 12:10)

der Aussätzige (-n), leper. (Matt. 8:2)

ausschicken, *v.a.* to send out. (Matt. 2:16)

ausschlagen, *v.n. (aux.* h.) to sprout, to bud. (Luke 21:30)

ausschließen, *ir.v.a.* to exclude; to lock out. (Rom. 3:27)

ausschütteln, *v.a.* to shake out, to extract.

ausschütten, *v.a.* to pour out; to shed. (I Sam. 1:15)

aussenden, *ir.v.a.* to send out. (Matt. 22:3)

die Aussendung (-en), mission.

außer, 1. *prep. (dat.)* out of, outside; besides, except. 2. *conj.* except, unless, save, but. 3. *prefix* = external, outer, extra. (I Sam. 2:2)

außerhalb, 1. *prep. (gen.)* outside, beyond. 2. *adv.* on the outside, externally. (Mark 7:15)

äußerlich, *adj.* external, outward. (Luke 17:20)

äußerst, 1. *adv.* extremely, exceedingly. 2. *adj.* extreme, utmost, uttermost. (Ps. 139:9)

aussondern, *v.a.* to single out; to select. (Jer. 1:5)

ausspannen, 1. *v.a.* to spread (out); to stretch; to expand. 2. *v.a. & n.* to relax; to slacken; to unfold. (Isa. 48:13)

ausspeien, *v.a.* to spit at. (Matt. 26:67)

aussprechen, *ir.v.a.* to utter, to say, to pronounce. (Matt. 13:35)

ausstechen, *ir.v.a.* to put out. (Judg. 16:21)

ausstoßen, *ir.v.a.* to thrust out, to knock out; to expel, to drive out.

ausstrecken, 1. *v.a.* to reach out, to hold out, to extend. 2. *v.r.* to stretch oneself, to spread oneself (out). (Gen. 3:22)

ausstreuen, *v.a.* to give freely, to disseminate. (Ps. 112:9)

austeilen, *v.a.* to distribute; to divide, to allot. (Gen. 49:27)

austilgen, *v.a.* to destroy utterly; to erase, to efface. (Rev. 3:5)

austreiben, *ir.v.a.* to drive out, to expel. (Gen. 3:24)

austreten, 1. *ir.v.a.* to tread under foot; to trample. 2. *v.n. (aux.* s.) to step out; to come forth; to set out; to be excused. (John 21:9)
aus der Kirche austreten, to secede from a church.

auswendig, *adj.* outside, outward; by heart. (Gen. 6:14)

auswerfen, *ir.v.a.* to throw out; to knock out; to reject; to cast (anchor). (Luke 5:4)

ausziehen, 1. *ir.v.a.* to pull out, to extract. 2. *v.r.* to undress. 3. *v.n. (aux.* s.) to move; to march off, to set out; to emigrate. (Gen. 12:4)

das Auto-da-Fé, burning of heretics.

die Autokephalie, sovereignty of national churches within the Greek Orthodox Church.

das Ave-Maria, Ave Maria, Hail Mary.

die Axt (-̈e), axe. (Matt. 3:10)

Bb

der **Babylonier** (-), Babylonian.

babylonisch, *adj.* Babylonian.

der **Bach** (⁻e), brook, stream. (I Sam. 17:40)

die **Backe** (-n), cheek. (Matt. 5:39)

backen, *reg. & ir.v.a.* to bake (bread, etc.), to roast, to fry; to burn, to fire (pottery tiles). (Gen. 18:6)

der **Bäcker** (-), baker. (Gen. 40:1)

das **Bad** (⁻er), bath; watering place. (Titus 3:5)

die **Bahn** (-en), path, track, road; course; orbit. (Ps. 27:11)

bald, *adv.* soon, shortly. (Ps. 2:12)

der **Baldachin** (-e), canopy.

der **Balken** (-), beam, rafter, joist; bar. (Matt. 7:3)

der **Balsam** (-e), balsam, balm, salve, ointment. (Ps. 133:2)

(**der**) **Balthasar,** Balthazar.

das **Band** (⁻er), ribbon, tape, band; bond. (Ps. 2:3)

bange, *adj.* afraid, alarmed; timid, anxious. (John 13:22)

der **Bann,** jurisdiction, constraint; ban, proscription; excommunication. (Josh. 7:13)

der **Bannbrief** (-e), interdict.

die **Bannbulle** (-n), papal edict or bull.

bannen, *v.a.* to banish, to expel; to excommunicate; to enchant, to charm; to fix, to confine.

der **Baptist** (-en), Baptist.

die **Baptistengemeinde** (-n), Baptist Church.

das **Baptisterium,** baptistry.

der **Bär** (-en), bear. (I Sam. 17:37)

der **Barfüßer** (-), Franciscan friar.

barmherzig, *adj.* merciful; compassionate; charitable. (Exod. 34:6)

die **Barmherzigkeit,** mercy, compassion, charity. (Gen. 32:11)

der **Bart** (⁻e), beard. (II Sam. 10:5)

der **Basilisk** (-en), basilisk. (Isa. 11:8)

der **Bastard** (-e), bastard; hybrid, mongrel. (Heb. 12:8)

der **Bau,** building, erection, construction; build, frame, form. (Mark 13:1)

der **Bauch** (⁻e), belly; stomach; abdomen. (Matt. 12:40)

bauen, 1. *v.a.* to build, to construct, to erect; to till, to cultivate; to raise (flowers, etc.); to work (a mine); to make (a road). 2. *v.r.* to be founded (*auf,* on), to rest on. 3. *v.n.* (*aux.* h.) to count, to rely (*auf,* on). (Gen. 2:5)

die **Bauleute,** (*pl.*) builders. (Ps. 118:22)

der **Baumeister** (-), master builder. (Isa. 49:17)

beben, 1. *v.n.* (*aux.* h.) to shake, to tremble, to shiver. 2. *n.* trembling; tremor. (Exod. 19:18)

der **Becher** (-), cup, beaker. (Matt. 10:42)

das **Becken** (-), basin. (John 13:5)

bedächtig, *adj.* prudent, cautious; deliberate. (Prov. 15:14)

bedecken, *v.a.* to cover, to shelter, to protect. (Matt. 8:24)

bedenken, 1. *ir.v.a.* to consider, to think (over), to ponder (over). 2. *v.r.* to deliberate, to consider, to weigh, to hesitate. (Ps. 90:12)

bedeuten, *v.a.* to mean, to signify, to imply; to inform. (I Peter 3:21)

die **Bedingung** (-en), condition, proviso, terms, restriction.

bedingungslos, *adj.* unconditional, without conditions.

21

bedrängen, *v.a.* to oppress, to afflict, to grieve. (Exod. 22:21)

bedrohen, *v.a.* to threaten, to menace. (Matt. 8:26)

bedürfen, *ir.v.n.* (*aux.* h.) & *imp.* (*gen.*) to be in want of, to need, to have need of, to require. (Matt. 3:14)

beeidigen, beeiden, *v.a.* to confirm by oath, to swear.

beendigen, beenden, *v.a.* to finish, to end, to terminate, to conclude, to cease.

die Beere (-n), berry. (Rev. 14:18)

der Befehl (-e), order, command, mandate. (Ps. 19:9)

befehlen, 1. *ir.v.a.* (*dat.*) to order, to command, to dictate, to bid. 2. *v.r.: sich Gott befehlen,* to commend oneself to God, to commit oneself to God. (Ps. 10:14)

befestigen, *v.a.* to fasten, to fix, to make fast, to attach; to fortify; to establish; to strengthen. (Luke 16:26) *da wurden die Gemeinden im Glauben befestigt,* so were the churches established in the faith.

beflecken, *v.a.* to spot, to stain, to soil; to defile, to pollute. (Isa. 59:3)

befleißigen, *reg.v.r.* (*gen.*) to apply oneself to, to take great pains with; to devote oneself to. (II Tim. 2:15)

befragen, 1. *reg.* & *ir.v.a.* to interrogate, to question, to examine. 2. *v.r.: sich bei einem befragen* (*um* or *über eine Sache* or *wegen einer Sache*), to consult with someone (about something). (Luke 24:15)

befreien, *v.a.* to free, to set free, to liberate; to rescue; to release. (Gal. 5:1)

befremden, 1. *v.a.* & *imp.* to appear strange, to astonish, to surprise. 2. *n.* consternation, surprise, dislike (of), distaste (for). (I Peter 4:4)

begeben, 1. *ir.v.a.* to negotiate, to transfer; to sell. 2. *v.r.* to go, to proceed (to), to set out (for). 3. *imp. v.r.: es begab sich, daß,* it happened or chanced that; it came to pass that. 4. *v.r. with gen.: sich einer Sache begeben,* to give up, renounce, or forgo something. (Luke 14:31)

begegnen, 1. *v.n.* (*aux.* s.) to meet, to meet with; to happen, to come to pass. 2. *v.r.* to meet; to concur. (John 18:4)

begehen, *ir.v.a.* to traverse; to pace off; to walk on; to celebrate (a festival); to commit (an error, etc.). (Matt. 14:6)

der (or **das**) **Begehr,** desire, wish.

das Begehrungsvermögen, will (Kant).

die Begier, die Begierde (-n), eager desire, inordinate longing; lust; greed. (Ps. 38:10)

begießen, *ir.v.a.* to water (plants, etc.); to sprinkle; to wet, to moisten; to pour over. (I Cor. 3:6)

begraben, *ir.v.a.* to bury, to inter; to entomb. (Gen. 15:15)

das Begräbnis (-se), burial, funeral; grave. (Matt. 27:7)

begreifen, 1. *ir.v.a.* to understand, to comprehend, to conceive. 2. *v.r.: das begreift sich leicht,* that is easily understood. (Ps. 139:6)

der Begriff (-e), idea, notion; conception.

die Begründung, foundation, establishment; argument, proof, reason, motivation.

begrüßen, *v.a.* to greet, to welcome, to salute, to hail. (Acts 25:13)

behaften, *v.a.* to burden, to charge, to load; to infect, to affect.

behaftet, *p.p.* & *adj.* subject to (fainting, fits, etc.); afflicted (with); burdened. (Matt. 4:24)

behalten, 1. *ir.v.a.* to keep, to retain; to maintain; to remember. 2. *p.p.* & *adj.: wohlbehalten,* safe and sound; well preserved. (Gen. 14:21)

das Behältnis (-se), container, case; receptacle; shrine (for relics). (Rev. 18:2)

beharren, 1. *v.n.* (*aux.* h.) to continue, to persist in, to persevere, to remain firm or steadfast. 2. *n.* perseverance, persistence. (Matt. 10:22)

die Behausung (-en), lodging; house, dwelling, home, abode. (Acts 1:20)

behend, *adj.* agile, adroit; quick, smart, handy. (Acts 12:7)

beherbergen, *v.a.* to lodge, to shelter, to put up. (Matt. 25:35)

die Beherbergung, lodging.

behilflich, *adj.* helpful, serviceable, useful. (I Tim. 6:18)

behüten, *v.a.* to guard (*vor,* against), to preserve; to watch over; to defend, to protect. (Num. 6:24)
der Himmel behüte mich vor solchen Gedanken, heaven preserve me from harboring such thoughts; *behüte dich Gott!* God save you! may God protect you!

die Beichte (-n), confession.
die Beichte ablegen, to confess.

beichten, *v.a. & n.* to confess, to go to confession.

der Beichter (-), father confessor; penitent.

das Beichtgeheimnis (-se), seal of confession.

der Beichtiger (-), father confessor.

das Beichtkind (-er), **der Beichtling** (-e), penitent.

das Beichtsiegel (-), seal of confession.

der Beichtstuhl (⁻e), confessional.

der Beichtvater (⁻er), father confessor.

beilegen, 1. *v.a.* to add, to enclose; to confer; to attribute, to ascribe to, to attach (value, importance) to. 2. *v.n.* to heave to; to come round to (someone's opinion). (II Tim. 4:8)

das Bein (-e), leg; bone. (Gen. 2:23)

beisammen, *adv.* together. (I John 5:8)

das Beisammensein, union, association, fellowship.

beiseit, beiseits, *adv.* aside, apart. (II Sam. 6:6)

das Beispiel (-e), example, instance, illustration. (Ps. 44:15)

beißen, *ir.v.a. & n.* (*aux.* h.) to bite; to burn, to itch. (Num. 21:6)

der Beistand (⁻e), help, aid, support, assistance; assistant, helper, supporter. (Ps. 60:13)

beistehen, *ir.v.n.* (*aux.* h.) (*dat.*) to help, to aid, to assist. (Isa. 63:5)
Gott stehe mir bei! God help me!

bekannt, *p.p.* (*of* **bekennen**) *& adj.* known, well-known, renowned; acquainted, familiar. (Ps. 48:4)

der Bekannte (-n), acquaintance, friend. (Luke 2:44)

die Bekanntmachung (-en), publication, notification, announcement; proclamation.

bekehren, 1. *v.a.* to convert. 2. *v.r.* to become converted, to mend one's ways. (I Kings 8:33)

der Bekehrer (-), proselytizer, converter; evangelist.

die Bekehrung (-en), conversion. (Acts 15:3)

der Bekehrungsbote (-n), missionary.

bekennen, 1. *ir.v.a.* to confess, to admit, to acknowledge (sins, a crime, the truth). 2. *v.r.:* *sich zu einer Tat bekennen,* to acknowledge having done something; *sich schuldig bekennen,* to plead guilty; *sich zu einer Religion bekennen,* to profess or embrace a religion. (Lev. 16:21)

der Bekenner (-), one who confesses or professes (a religion); follower.

das Bekenntnis (-se), confession, avowal, acknowledgment; (religious) denomination. (I Tim. 6:12)
das Glaubensbekenntnis (-se), creed.

die Bekenntniskirche (-n), Confessional Church.

die Bekenntnisschriften, (*pl.*) symbolic books.

die Bekenntnisschule (-n), denominational school.

bekleiden, *v.a.* to clothe, to dress; to occupy, to hold. (Matt. 6:29).

bekommen, 1. *v.a.* to get, to receive; to obtain; *etwas wiederbekommen,* to recover (something lost). 2. *v.n.* (*aux.* s.) to agree with someone, to suit someone. (Heb. 11:19)

bekräftigen, *v.a.* to strengthen, to confirm; to affirm, to assert. (Mark 16:20)

bekümmern, 1. *v.a.* to afflict, to trouble, to distress, to grieve. 2. *v.r.* to sorrow, to grieve; to be anxious (about). (Gen. 45:5)

die Bekümmernis (-se), grief, affliction; solicitude. (Ps. 94:19)

bekümmert, *p.p. & adj.* grieved, troubled, afflicted; anxious, concerned. (Jer. 31:25)

beladen, *ir.v.a.* to load, to charge, to burden. (Matt. 11:28)

belagern, *v.a.* to besiege, to lay siege to. (Isa. 29:3)

beleidigen, *v.a.* to offend, to insult, to shock. (Matt. 5:44)

die Beleidigung (-en), offense; insult, affront.

(der) **Belial,** Belial.

belohnen, *v.a.* to reward, to recompense, to remunerate. (Jer. 31:16)

die **Belohnung** (-en), reward, recompense; commendation. (Heb. 11:26)

bemühen, 1. *v.a.* to trouble, to give trouble. 2. *v.r.* to take trouble or pains; to strive, to endeavor. (Prov. 23:4)

benedeien, *v.a.* to bless; to glorify. *die Gebenedeite,* the Blessed Virgin.

die **Benedeiung** (-en), benediction; glorification.

der **Benediktiner,** Benedictine.

die **Benediktiner Ordensregel,** Benedictine rule.

beraten, 1. *ir.v.a.* to advise, to counsel; to furnish. 2. *v.r.* to deliberate, to take counsel together. (James 2:16)

beratschlagen, *v.n. & r.* (*aux.* h.) to deliberate, to consult, to confer with. (Dan. 4:14)

berauben, *v.a.* (*einen einer Sache*) to rob (someone of something); to deprive of; to divest of. (Gen. 42:36)

bereden, 1. *v.a.* to persuade, to talk (someone) over. 2. *v.r.* to confer (with), to talk (something) over. (Acts 18:4)

bereit, *adj.* ready, prepared. (Ps. 57:8)

bereiten, *v.a.* to prepare, to make or get ready; to cause, to give. (Ps. 8:4)

der **Berg** (-e), mountain; hill. (I Kings 18:19)

bergen, *ir.v.a.* to save, to secure; to rescue, to recover; to contain, to shelter.

die **Bergpredigt,** (the) Sermon on the Mount. (see Matt. 5–7; Luke 6:20–49)

der **Bericht** (-e), report, account, statement; information. (II Kings 22:9)

berichten, *v.a.* to report, to inform, to advise, to notify. (Acts 21:21)

der **Bernhardinermönch** (-e), Bernardine monk.

berüchtigt, *p.p. & adj.* infamous, ill-famed, notorious. (Luke 16:1)

der **Beruf** (-e), profession, calling, vocation, occupation; office. (I Cor. 7:20)

berufen, 1. *ir.v.a.* to call, to appoint, to nominate; to call together, to convoke; to blame, to censure. 2. *v.r.: sich auf einen berufen,* to appeal to or refer to someone. 3. *p.p. & adj.* competent, qualified. (Matt. 2:7)

der **Berufer** (-), appellant; one who calls. (Rom. 9:12)

die **Berufung** (-en), call, summons; vocation; appointment; nomination; convocation. (Rom. 11:29)

berühmt, *p.p. & adj.* famous, celebrated, renowned. (Ps. 48:2)

berühren, 1. *v.a.* to touch, to border on; to allude to. 2. *v.a. & n.* to concern, to affect. 3. *v.r.* to touch one another, to be in contact. (II Kings 13:21)

besamen, 1. *v.a.* to sow; to impregnate. 2. *v.r.* to be propagated by seed. (Gen. 1:11)

beschädigen, 1. *v.a.* to injure, to harm, to damage, to impair. 2. *v.r.* to hurt oneself. (Luke 9:25)

die **Beschaffenheit,** nature, state, condition, constitution, quality, character, disposition, accident.

beschauen, 1. *v.a.* to view, to behold; to inspect, to examine; to contemplate. 2. *v.r.* to examine oneself, to look into one's own heart. (Exod. 3:3)

bescheiden, 1. *ir.v.a.* to allot, to assign, to apportion; to inform. 2. *v.r.* to resign oneself (to), to be satisfied (with). (Prov. 30:8)

bescheren, *reg.v.a.* (*einem etwas*) to give (as a share or lot or present); to bestow upon; to present (with). (Prov. 31:10)

die **Bescherung** (-en), distribution of (Christmas) presents; gift, present.

beschicken, *v.a.* to send for or to; to convey; to manage; to attend to, to prepare. (Exod. 20:9)

beschirmen, *v.a.* to screen, to cover; to protect, to shelter, to defend. (Ps. 5:12)

beschließen, *ir.v.a.* to close, to conclude, to end, to finish; to resolve, to determine on, to decide; to enclose, to lock up. (Ps. 41:9)

beschneiden, *ir.v.a.* to cut, to clip; to circumcise; to curtail. (Gen. 17:10)

die **Beschneidung** (-en), clipping; circumcision; curtailment. (Rom. 2:25)

beschreiben, *ir.v.a.* to write upon, to cover with writing; to describe, to depict, to portray. (Rev. 5:1)

beschuldigen, *v.a.* to accuse (*gen.*) of; to charge (with); to impute (to). (Mark 15:3)

die **Beschuldigung** (-en), charge, accusation, impeachment.

beschweren, 1. *v.a.* to load, to charge; to burden. 2. *v.r.* to complain (*bei einem über einen,* to a person of or about someone). (Luke 21:34)

beschwerlich, *adj.* troublesome; painful; difficult, hard. (II Cor. 11:9)

die Beschwerung (-en), charge, burden, trouble. (Acts 15:28)

beschwören, *ir.v.a.* 1. to swear, to affirm or testify on oath. 2. to conjure; to exorcise; to entreat, to implore. (Matt. 26:63)

der Beschwörer (-), conjurer, exorcist, magician.

die Beschwörung (-en), confirmation by oath; exorcism; entreaty, adjuration.

besehen, 1. *ir.v.a.* to look at; to inspect, to examine. 2. *p.p.: bei Lichte besehen,* on closer inspection, viewed in the right light. (Matt. 22:11)

besessen, *p.p.* (*of* **besitzen**) & *adj.* possessed; frenzied. (Mark 1:23)

der Besessene (-n), demoniac, fanatic, madman. (Matt. 4:24)

die Besessenheit, frenzy, madness, demoniacal possession.

die Besetzung, cathexis (in psychoanalysis); occupation; filling (of a vacancy).

besiegeln, *v.a.* to seal, to put one's seal to. (John 3:33)

besinnen, *ir.v.r.: sich (auf eine Sache) besinnen,* to recollect, to remember, to call to mind, to think of. (Acts 12:12)

die Besinnung, reflection, consideration, deliberation; recollection.

besitzen, *ir.v.a.* to possess, to be in possession of, to own, to be endowed with, to hold, to occupy. (Gen. 22:17)

besonder, *adj.* particular, special, specific; peculiar, separate, distinct. (Gen. 1:9)

besonders, *adv.* especially, particularly, in particular; apart, separate; exceptionally; chiefly. (Num. 23:9)

besprechen, 1. *ir.v.a.* to discuss, to talk over, to arrange; to criticize, to review. 2. *v.r.: sich mit einem besprechen,* to confer with someone; *sich mit einem über eine Sache besprechen,* to discuss something with someone. (Gal. 1:16)

die Besprechung (-en), conversation; discussion, conference, consultation; criticism, review.

besprengen, *v.a.* to sprinkle, to spray. (Isa. 52:15)

die Besprengung (-en), sprinkling. (I Peter 1:2)

besser, *adj.* (*comp. of* **gut**) better. (I Sam. 1:8)

bessern, 1. *v.a.* to make better, to better, to improve; to amend, to reform; to mend, to repair. 2. *v.r.* to improve, to get better, to mend one's ways. (II Kings 12:6)

die Besserung (-en), improvement, amendment, betterment; correction, reformation, recovery, convalescence. (Isa. 58:8)

beständig, 1. *adj.* constant, steady, continual, permanent, lasting, steadfast; faithful, firm. 2. *adv.* continually, perpetually, constantly, faithfully. (I Sam. 2:35)

bestätigen, *v.a.* to confirm, to establish, to verify, to ratify; to sanction, to authorize, to make valid. (II Sam. 7:12)

bestatten, *v.a.* to bury, to inter. (Acts 8:2)

die Bestattung (-en), burial, funeral, interment.

bestehen, 1. *ir.v.a.* to undergo, to endure; to go through; to pass through, to overcome; to stand (a test); to pass, to get through (an examination). 2. *v.n.* (*aux.* s. & h.) to stand steadfast, to withstand, to resist; to exist; to last, to continue. 3. *n.* existence, persistence, composition. (Deut. 19.15)

bestellen, *v.a.* to order (goods); to bespeak; to arrange, to dispose, to set in order; to appoint; to execute (a commission); to deliver (a message); to till, to cultivate (land). (Isa. 38:1)

bestimmen, 1. *v.a.* to decide, to determine, to ascertain; to settle; to define, to allot. 2. *v.r.: sich bestimmen (zu einer Sache),* to determine, to resolve on, to choose (something). (Dan. 7:12)

die Bestimmung (-en), determination; destination; destiny; statement.

bestürzt, *p.p.* & *adj.* confounded, dismayed. (Mark 9:6)

besuchen, *v.a.* to visit; to call on or upon; to attend; to resort to, to frequent. (I Sam. 17:18)

besudeln, *v.a.* to dirty, to stain, to soil, to defile. (Rev. 3:4)

betagt, *p.p.* & *adj.* aged, stricken in years. (Luke 1:7)

betasten, *v.a.* to handle, to touch, to finger, to feel. (Gen. 27:12)

die Betätigung, activity; practical proof; participation; manifestation; application.

betäuben, *v.a.* to stun, to deafen, to stupefy; to bewilder, to confuse; to deaden. (Luke 18:5)

der Betbruder (⸚), worshiper.

das Betbuch (⸚er), prayer book.

beten, 1. *v.a.* to say in prayer. 2. *v.n.* (*aux.* h.) to pray, to say one's prayers. (Gen. 24:63)

die Betfahrt (-en), pilgrimage.

die Betglocke (-n), angelus.

(der) Bethania, Bethany.

betrachten, *v.a.* to look at, to view, to consider, to contemplate, to examine, to reflect upon. (Ps. 27:4)

die Betrachtung (-en), view, opinion; meditation, contemplation; reflection, observation; inspection.

betreten, 1. *ir.v.a.* to set foot on or in; to tread (on); to enter upon; to follow; to enter (a house); to mount (a pulpit, etc.); to find, to meet with; to surprise, to catch. 2. *p.p. & adj.* trodden, beaten; startled, surprised, disconcerted. (Luke 9:7)

betrüben, *v.a.* to grieve, to distress, to afflict; to cast down, to depress. (Ps. 42:6)

die Betrübnis (-se), affliction, sorrow, grief, distress, sadness. (Ps. 31:11)

betrübt, *p.p. & adj.* sad, depressed, dejected, distressed, miserable, sorrowful. (Ps. 42:7)
zu Tode betrübt, grieved to death.

der Betrug, fraud, deception, swindle, deceit, trickery. (Isa. 53:9)
frommer Betrug, white lie.

betrügen, *ir.v.a.* to cheat, to deceive, to defraud. (Gen. 3:13)

betrüglich, *adj.* fraudulent; false, deceptive, illusory, fallacious. (Mark 4:19)

der Betsaal, chapel, oratory.

der Betschemel (-), hassock.

die Betstunde (-n), prayer time; prayer meeting.

das Betstundenbuch (⸚er), breviary.

das Bett (-en), bed; channel. (Matt. 9:6)

der Bettag (-e), day of prayer or thanksgiving; fast day; Rogation day.

die Bettelei (-en), begging, mendicancy; trash.

der Bettelmönch (-e), mendicant friar.

betteln, 1. *v.n.* (*aux.* h.) to beg; to solicit, to importune. 2. *n. see* **Bettelei.** (Luke 16:3)

der Bettelorden (-), mendicant order; order of mendicant friars.

betten, 1. *v.a.* to make up a bed; to put to bed; to embed. 2. *v.r.* to make one's bed. (Ps. 139:8)

der Bettler (-), beggar.

die Betwoche (-n), Rogation week.

beugen, 1. *v.a.* to bend, to bow, to flex; to deflect; to humble. 2. *v.r.* to humble oneself, to submit; to bend low, to bow down (before). (Exod. 23:6)

die Beule (-n), bump, lump; tumor, boil, ulcer, swelling; hurt; bruise; dent. (Gen. 4:23)

die Beute (-n), booty, spoil, captured material; loot, plunder; prey. (Gen. 49:27)

der Beutel (-), bag, pouch, purse; sac, cyst; sieve. (Luke 10:4)

bewahren, *v.a.* to keep, to preserve. (Gen. 2:15)
Gott bewahre! God forbid!

bewähren, 1. *v.a.* to establish as true; to prove, to confirm, to verify; to approve. 2. *v.r.* to prove true; to hold good; to stand the test. (Acts 9:22)

bewährt, *adj.* proved, tried, tested, approved, trustworthy. (Isa. 28:16)

die Bewahrung (-en), keeping; preservation; conservation.

bewegen, 1. *v.a.* to move; to stir; to put in motion, to shake. 2. *v.r.: sich bewegen,* to move (about), to stir, to be in motion. 3. *ir.v.a.* to induce, to persuade, to prevail upon. (Matt. 11:7)

beweglich, *adj.* movable. (Heb. 12:27)

die Bewegung (-en), movement, motion; stir, commotion, agitation; motive, stimulus. (Acts 19:23)

beweinen, *v.a.* to mourn, to bewail, to lament; to weep over. (Deut. 34:8)

beweisen, *ir.v.a.* to prove, to show, to manifest. (Ps. 17:7)

bewohnen, *v.a.* to inhabit, to dwell in, to live in, to reside in, to occupy. (Isa. 44:26)

bewußt, *adj.* known; conscious of, aware of. (Acts 15:18)

bezahlen, *v.a.* to pay; to discharge, to repay (a debt); to cash (a bill). (Ps. 22:26)

die Bezahlung (-en), payment, settlement; pay. (Mark 10:45)

bezaubern, *v.a.* to bewitch, to enchant; to fascinate. (Acts 8:9)

bezeugen, *v.a.* to attest, to certify; to declare. (Exod. 25:22)

bezwingen, 1. *ir.v.a.* to overcome, to conquer, to vanquish; to master. 2. *v.r.* to restrain or control oneself. (Heb. 11:33)

die Bibel (-n), the Bible; Holy Scripture; the Scriptures.

der Bibelabschnitt (-e), chapter of the Bible.

der Bibelausdruck (¨e), biblical expression.

der Bibelausleger (-), interpreter of the Bible; exegete.

die Bibelauslegung (-en), exegesis.

der Bibelerklärer (-), exegete.

die Bibelerklärung (-en), exegesis.

der Bibelexeget (-en), Bible exegete.

bibelfest, *adj.* versed in the Scriptures.

der Bibelforscher (-), Bible scholar.

die Bibelforschung, Bible research.

die Bibelgesellschaft (-en), Bible Society.

der Bibelkanon, canon.

das Bibelkapitel (-), chapter of the Bible.

die Bibelkonkordanz (-en), Bible concordance.

die Bibelkritik, biblical criticism.

die Bibelkunde, biblical research.

das Bibellatein, biblical Latin.

die Bibellehre, biblical teaching, scriptural doctrine.

die Bibelsprache, scriptural language.

der Bibelspruch (¨e), Bible sentence; Bible passage.

die Bibelstelle (-n), Bible passage.

die Bibelstunde (-n), Bible class; Sunday school.

die Bibelübersetzung (-en), Bible translation.

biblisch, *adj.* biblical, scriptural.
Biblische Geschichte, scriptural (or sacred) history.

die Biene (-n), bee. (Ps. 118:12)

bieten, *ir.v.a.* to offer, to proffer; to bid; to make a bid (*auf eine Sache*, for something) (at a sale). (Matt. 7:9)

das Bild (-er), picture, image, figure; illustration; portrait; likeness; emblem, symbol. (Gen. 1:26)

bilden, 1. *v.a.* to form, to fashion, to shape, to mold, to model; to be, to constitute, to compose; to educate, to train, to discipline. 2. *v.r.* to form, to arise, to develop; to improve one's mind. (Ps. 139:13)

bilderstürmend, *adj.* iconoclastic.

der Bilderstürmer (-), iconoclast.

die Bilderstürmerei (-en), iconoclastic riots.

das Bildnis (-se), portrait, likeness; image, effigy; parable. (Exod. 20:4)

die Bildursache, formal cause.

(der) Bileam, Balaam.

billig, *adj.* cheap, moderate, inexpensive, reasonable; right, fair, just. (Eph. 6:1)

die Binde (-n), bandage, sling; band; string. (Acts 19:12)

binden, 1. *ir.v.a.* to bind, to tie, to fasten; to tie up; to tie down; to restrain. 2. *v.n.* to unite, to combine, to consolidate; to harden. (Gen. 49:11)

der Bischof (¨e), bishop. (I Tim. 3:2)

das Bischofsamt (¨er), episcopate. (I Tim. 3:1)

der Bischofshof (¨e), episcopal palace.

der Bischofshut (¨e), miter.

die Bischofsmütze (-n), miter.

der Bischofsornat, bishop's robes.

der Bischofssitz (-e), bishop's see.

der Bischofsstab (¨e), crosier.

der Bischofsstuhl (¨e), bishop's seat.

die Bischofswürde, episcopal dignity; episcopate.

bisher, *adv.* hitherto, up to now, till now. (John 5:17)

der Bissen (-), morsel, bite, bit; tidbit; mouthful. (I Kings 17:11)

das Bistum (¨er), bishopric; episcopate; diocese. (Acts 1:20)

die Bitte (-n), request, petition, prayer; supplication. (I John 5:15)
die sieben Bitten des Vaterunsers, the seven petitions of the Lord's Prayer.

bitten, *ir.v.a.* to ask (for), to request; to beg, to implore; to invite; to bid. (I Sam. 7:5)

bitter, *adj.* bitter; sharp, stinging, biting; severe. (Exod. 12:8)

die Bitterkeit, bitterness; sarcasm, acrimony. (Rom. 3:14)

bitterlich, 1. *adj.* bitterish. 2. *adv.* bitterly. (Isa. 33:7)

die Bittfahrt (-en), pilgrimage.

der Bittgang (⁻e), procession of pilgrims.

das Bittgebet (-e), rogation, litany.

der Bittgesang (⁻e), rogation, litany.

blähen, 1. *v.a. & r.* to inflate, to swell out. 2. *v.n.* (*aux.* h.) to cause flatulence; to distend, to swell. (I Cor. 13:4)

blasen, *ir.v.a. & n.* (*aux.* h.) to blow; to sound, to play (trumpets, etc.). (Exod. 15:8)

die Blasphemie, blasphemy.

das Blatt (⁻er), leaf, petal; blade (of shoulder, grass, oar, saw, sword, axe); layer; sheet (of paper). (Lev. 26:36)

das Blei, lead. (Exod. 15:10)

bleiben, 1. *ir.v.n.* (*aux.* s.) to remain, to stay, to continue; to last, to endure. 2. *n.* stay. (Gen. 5:22)

bleibend, *pr.p. & adj.* lasting, permanent, abiding, stable. (I John 3:15)

blenden, *v.a.* to blind (*fig.*), to dazzle; to deceive; to shade; to screen. (Isa. 6:10)

blind, *adj.* blind; false, sham; hidden; tarnished. (Exod. 4:11)

die Blindheit, blindness. (Rom. 11:25)

der Blitz (-e), lightning flash. (Matt. 24:27)

blitzen, *v. imp. & n.* to lighten; to flash, to sparkle. (Luke 17:24)

blöde, *adj.* stupid; bashful, timid, shy; weak (of eyes). (Prov. 10:15)

bloß, 1. *adj.* bare, naked; destitute; mere, sole. 2. *adv.* merely, only. (Rev. 3:17)

die Blöße (-n), bareness, nakedness; clearing, opening. (Rom. 8:35)

blühen, *v.n.* (*aux.* h.) to flower, to bloom, to blossom; to flourish. (Ps. 72:7)

die Blume (-n), flower, blossom. (Ps. 103:15)

das Blut, blood; race; lineage. (Gen. 4:10)

der Blutacker (⁻), the field of blood. (Matt. 27:8)

der Blutbräutigam (-e), bloody husband. (Exod. 4:25)

die Blüte (-n), blossom, flower; bloom; blossoming time. (Num. 17:23)

das Blutgeld (-er), the price of blood. (Matt. 27:6)

der Bluthund (-e), bloodhound. (II Sam. 16:7)

die Blutschuld, murder; capital crime; incest. (Ps. 51:16)

das Blutvergießen, bloodshed, slaughter.

der Bock (⁻e), ram, he-goat, buck. (Lev. 16:7)

das Bocksblut, the blood of goats.

der Boden (- or ⁻), ground, soil; floor, base, bottom (of sea). (Gen. 6:16)

der Bogen (- or ⁻), bow, bend, curve, curvature; arc; arch, vault; sheet (of paper). (Gen. 9:13)

der Bogenschuß (⁻[ss]e), bowshot. (Gen. 21:16)

die Böhmischen Brüder, (*pl.*) Bohemian Brethren.

(der) Bonifatius, Boniface.

borgen, *v.a.* 1. to borrow; to take on credit. 2. to lend; to give on trust. (Deut. 15:6)

der Born (-e), spring, well, fountain. (Jer. 6:7)

bös, böse, 1. *adj. & adv.* bad, ill; evil; wicked; angry; malicious. 2. *n.: das Böse,* evil. (Prov. 1:10)

der Bösewicht (-e), villain, scoundrel. (Matt. 21:41)

boshaft, *adj. & adv.* malicious, spiteful; malignant, wicked. (Isa. 1:4)

die Bosheit, malice, spite, ill nature. (Gen. 6:5)

der Bote (-n), messenger; carrier; apostle. (I Kings 14:6)

die Botschaft (-en), message; news, tidings; legation, embassy. (I John 3:11)

der Botschafter (-), ambassador. (II Cor. 5:20)

der päpstliche Botschafter, nuncio, (papal) legate.

brachen, *v.a.* 1. to plow or break up fallow land; to fallow. 2. to leave uncropped, to let lie fallow. (Isa. 28:24)

der Brahmane (-n), Brahman.

der Brahmanismus, Brahmanism.

der Brand ("-e), burning, combustion, fire; brand; burn. (Amos 4:11)

das Brandmal (-e), scar from burning. (I Tim. 4:2)

das Brandopfer (-), burnt offering. (Gen. 8:20)

braten, 1. *reg. & ir.v.a. & n. (aux.* h.) to roast, to bake. 2. *m. (Braten)* roast (meat). (Luke 24:42)

der Brauch ("-e), use, usage, custom. (Rom. 1:26)

brauchen, *v.a.* to need, to want, to require; to use, to make use of, to employ. (II Cor. 13:10)

bräuchlich, *adj.* useful, in use. (II Tim. 2:21)

bräunlich, *adj.* brownish. (I Sam. 16:12)

brausen, 1. *v.n. (aux.* h.) to storm, to rage, to bluster; to rush, to roar. 2. *v.a.* to water, to sprinkle; to shower. (Ps. 42:8)

die Braut ("-e), fiancée, betrothed; bride. (Isa. 49:18)

der Bräutigam (-e), fiancé; bridegroom. (Ps. 19:6)

brechen, 1. *ir.v.a.* to break, to break up, to break through, to break down; to pluck, to pick, to gather (flowers). 2. *v.r.* to break (as waves); to be interrupted; to vomit, to be sick. 3. *v.n. (aux.* s.) to break, to be broken; to rupture; to break forth, to dawn (as the day). 4. *n.* violation; breach; breaking; crushing; vomiting; dressing (of flax, etc.). (Gen. 3:22)

breit, *adj.* broad, wide; flat. (Matt. 7:13)

die Breite (-n), breadth, width; latitude; verbosity. (Eph. 3:18)

breiten, *v.a.* to make broad, to widen; to spread, to extend; to flatten out. (Exod. 9:33)

brennen, *ir.v.a.* to burn; to brand; to sting (as a nettle); to bite (the tongue, etc.). (Exod. 3:2)

brennend, *pr.p. & adj.* burning; caustic; smarting; ardent, eager, fiery. (Jer. 20:9)

brettern, *adj.* made of boards, boarded. (II Kings 4:10)

der Brief (-e), letter; epistle, document, charter. (II Sam. 11:14)

bringen, *ir.v.a.* to bring, to fetch; to convey; to yield; to lead; to produce. (Gen. 42:38)

der Brocken (-), crumb, morsel, fragment; *(pl.)* scraps. (Matt. 14:20)

der Brosam, die Brosame (-[e]n), crumb, scrap. (Mark 7:28)

das Brot (-e), bread; loaf; *(fig.)* support, livelihood. (Gen. 3:19)

das Brotbrechen, breaking of bread. (Acts 2:42)

der Bruch ("-e), breach, break; breaking, breakage; fracture; crack, flaw. (Ps. 60:4)

der Bruder ("-), brother; friar. (Gen. 4:9)

die Brüder, *see* **Bruder:** *barmherzige Brüder,* order of friars devoted to charity; *böhmische Brüder, Brüder vom Gesetz Christi,* Hussites; *graue Brüder,* Cistercians; *Brüder der heiligen Jungfrau,* Carmelites; *Joseph und seine Brüder,* Joseph and his brethren; *meine lieben Brüder,* my dear brethren (in church); *mährische Brüder,* Moravian Brethren.

die Brüdergemeinde, the Moravian Brethren.

brüderlich, *adj.* brotherly, fraternal. (Rom. 12:10)

die Bruderliebe, brotherly love. (I Peter 1:22) *christliche Bruderliebe,* charity.

der Bruderrat, consistory of the Confessional Church.

die Brüderschaft (-en), brotherhood, fellowship.

brüllen, *v.a. & n. (aux.* h.) to roar, to bellow, to howl, to shout. (I Sam. 15:14)

brummen, *v.a. & n. (aux.* h.) to growl, to grumble; to hum, to rumble; to mutter, to mumble. (Isa. 59:11)

der Brunnen (-), spring, well, fountain; mineral spring, spa. (Gen. 7:11)

die Brunst ("-e), ardor, passion; lust. (I Cor. 7:9)

brünstig, *adj.* burning, ardent; lustful, sensual. (Rom. 12:11)

die Brust ("-e), breast; chest; bosom. (Luke 11:27)

brüsten, *v.r.* to give oneself airs, to boast, to brag (*über,* about). (Ps. 73:7)

brüten, *v.a. & n.* (*aux.* h.) to sit (on eggs); to hatch, to incubate, to brood (*also fig.*). (Isa. 59:5)

der Bube (-n), boy, lad; rogue, scamp. (I Sam. 2:12)

das Bubenstück (-e), boyish trick; piece of villainy. (Ps. 41:9)

das Buch (⁻er), book. (Exod. 24:7) *das Buch des Lebens,* book of life.

der Buchstabe (-n), letter. (Matt. 5:18)

bücken, *v.r.* to stoop, to bend, to bow, to make a bow or obeisance. (Gen. 18:2)

der Buddhismus, Buddhism.

der Buddhist, Buddhist.

buddhistisch, *adj.* Buddhist.

Bund, 1. *n.* (-e), bundle; bunch (of keys, etc.); truss (of hay); knot (of silk); hank (of flax). 2. *m.* (⁻e), band, tie; lashing; league, union, alliance, confederacy, confederation; dispensation, covenant. (Gen. 9:12). *der alte und neue Bund,* the old and the new covenant.

die Bundeslade, ark of the covenant.

bunt, *adj. & adv.* colored, bright, gay; motley, many-colored; mottled, spotted; wild, gay, disorderly. (Gen. 37:3)

die Bürde (-n), burden, load. (Matt. 23:4)

die Burg (-en), castle; citadel, stronghold, fortress; (place of) refuge. (Ps. 18:3)

der Bürger (-), citizen, townsman, burgess, burgher; bourgeois, commoner. (Ps. 39:13)

die Bürgerschaft, citizens, townspeople. (Eph. 2:12)

der Busch (⁻e), bush, shrub; thicket, copse, covert; brushwood; bunch. (Exod. 3:2)

der Busen (-), bosom; breast; heart; gulf, bay. (Exod. 4:6)

die Buße, repentance, penitence; compensation, amends, fine, penalty; penance, atonement. (Jer. 31:19)

büßen, *v.a. & n.* to make amends for, to atone for, to make good; to suffer for, to do penance, to expiate; to repair, to mend.

der Büßer (-), penitent.

die Büßerin (-nen), penitent.

bußfällig, *adj.* liable to punishment, punishable.

bußfertig, *adj.* penitent, repentant, contrite.

die Bußfertigkeit, penitence, repentance, contrition.

das Bußhemd (-en), hair shirt.

die Bußordnung (-en), penitential regulation.

der Bußprediger (-), preacher of repentance, Lenten preacher.

die Bußpredigt (-en), penitential sermon.

der Bußtag (-e), day of humiliation, day of repentance.

die Bußübung (-en), penance.

die Büßung, penance, atonement, expiation.

die Bußzeit, time of penance; Lent.

der Byzantiner (-), Byzantine.

byzantinisch, *adj.* Byzantine.

Cc

der **Calvinismus,** Calvinism.

der **Calvinist** (-en), Calvinist.

calvinistisch, *adj.* Calvinistic.

die **Caritas,** charity.

(der) **Cäsar,** Caesar.

(das) **Chaldäa,** Chaldea.

der **Chaldäer** (-), Chaldean.

chaldäisch, *adj.* Chaldean.

das **Chaos,** chaos.

der **Chassid** (-en), Hasidean.

chassidisch, *adj.* Hasidic.

der **Chassidismus,** Hasidism.

der **Cherub** (-inen & -im), cherub. (Gen. 3:24)

cherubinisch, *adj.* cherubic.

der **Chiliasmus,** chiliasm; millenarianism.

der **Chiliast** (-en), chiliast; millenarian.

chiliastisch, *adj.* chiliastic.

die **Chiromantie,** chiromancy; palmistry.

der **Chor,** 1. *m.* (⸚e), choir; chorus. 2. *n.* & *m.* (-e & ⸚e) choir, chancel. (Ps. 28:2) *der Männerchor,* male chorus; *der gemischte Chor,* mixed or full chorus.

der **Choral** (⸚e), chorale, anthem, hymn.

der **Choraltar** (⸚e), high altar.

das **Choramt** (⸚er), cathedral service.

der **Chorbischof** (⸚e), suffragan bishop.

der **Chordirektor** (-en), conductor of the chorus; choirmaster.

der **Chorführer** (-), first chorister.

die **Chorgalerie** (-n), choir loft.

der **Chorgehilfe** (-n), acolyte.

der **Chorgesang** (⸚e), chorus; choral singing; anthem.
einstimmiger Chorgesang, plain chant, Gregorian chant.

das **Chorhemd** (-en), surplice.

der **Chorherr** (-en), canon, prebendary.

der **Chorist** (-en), member of the chorus.

die **Choristin** (-nen), member of the chorus.

der **Chorknabe** (-n), choirboy, chorister.

der **Chorleiter** (-), leading or first chorister.

die **Chornische** (-n), apse.

die **Chornonne** (-n), officiating nun.

das **Chorpult** (-e), lectern.

der **Chorrock** (⸚e), surplice, cope.

der **Chorsänger** (-), chorister.

das **Chorsingen,** choir; chorus.

der **Chorstuhl** (⸚e), choir stall.

das **Chrisam,** chrism.

der **Christ** (-en), Christian. (Acts 11:26) *Christ werden,* to become Christian; to profess Christianity.

der **Christabend,** Christmas Eve.

der **Christbaum** (⸚e), Christmas tree.

der **Christdorn,** holly.

die **Christengemeinde** (-n), Christian congregation; Christian community.

der **Christenglaube,** Christian faith.

die **Christenheit,** Christendom.

das **Christentum,** Christianity.

die **Christenverfolgung** (-en), persecution of Christians.

das **Christenvolk,** Christendom.

das **Christfest,** Christmas.

die **Christin** (-nen), Christian woman.

christisch, *adj.* of Christ. (I Cor. 1:12)

das **Christkind,** Christ child, baby Jesus.

christlich, *adj.* Christian.

der **Christmonat,** der **Christmond,** December.

die **Christnacht,** night before Christmas.

die **Christolatrie,** adoration of Christ.

die **Christologie,** Christology.

christologisch, *adj.* christological.

Christus, Christ. (Matt. 1:16)

die **Christwoche,** Christmas week.

Dd

das Dach ("-er), roof; shelter, cover; house. (Matt. 8:8)

dahergehen, *v.n.* (*sep.*) (*aux.* s.) to walk along, to come along, to draw near. (John 6:19)

dahin, 1. *adv.* thither; to that place, time, or state. 2. *sep. prefix* = away, along; gone, past, lost.

dahinten, *adv.* behind, at the back. (Phil. 3:13)

dahinter, *adv.* behind (something). (II Peter 2:18)

Damaskus, Damascus. (Acts 9:2)

der Damast (-e), damask. (Amos 3:12)

damasten, *adj.* damask.

der Dämon (-en), demon.

dämonisch, *adj.* demoniac(al); irresistible, overpowering.

der Dampf ("-e), vapor, steam; mist; smoke; (*pl.*) fumes. (Ps. 18:9)

dämpfen, *v.a.* to damp, to smother, to suffocate; to smooth; to quench, to extinguish; to deaden (sound); to suppress, to quell, to depress, to subdue. (Ps. 81:15)

(der) Daniel, Daniel.

der Dank, 1. *m.* thanks or gratitude, reward; recompense. 2. *prep.* (*gen.*) thanks to, owing to. (Ps. 50:14)

dankbar, *adj.* grateful, thankful, obliged (*dat.*, to); profitable, advantageous. (Col. 2:7)

die Dankbarkeit, gratitude.

danken, 1. *v.n.* (*aux.* h.) (*dat.*) to thank, to return thanks. 2. *v.a.* to owe (something to someone), to be indebted (to someone) for; to decline an offer. (Deut. 32:6)

dankenswert, *adj.* deserving of thanks.

das Dankfest (-e), thanksgiving festival.

der Dankgottesdienst (-e), thanksgiving service.

das Danklied (-er), hymn of thanksgiving.

die Dankpredigt (-en), thanksgiving sermon.

die Danksagung (-en), returning or giving thanks, acknowledgment; thanksgiving. (John 6:23)

daran, dran, *adv.* thereon, thereat, thereby.

darben, *v.n.* (*aux.* h.) to starve, to famish; to be in want (*an einer Sache*, of something). (Ps. 34:11)

darbieten, *ir.v.a.* to offer, to present, to hold out, to tender. (Isa. 50:7)

die Darbietung (-en), recital, entertainment, performance.

darlegen, *v.a.* to lay down; to state, to set forth, to explain, to expound, to demonstrate, to display, to exhibit. (Matt. 25:20)

darreichen, *v.a.* to offer, to proffer, to present, to administer (sacrament). (Matt. 22:19)

die Darreichung (-en), offering.

darstellen, *v.a.* to describe; to state; to represent; to display, to exhibit; to present. (Luke 2:22)

dartun, *ir.v.a.* to prove, to verify, to demonstrate; to set forth. (Luke 10:35)

dasein, 1. *v.n.* to exist, to be there. 2. *n.* presence; existence, life. (Rom. 13:11)

dastehen, *v.n.* (*sep.*) to be there, to stand there; to stand forth. (Ps. 33:9)

davon, *adv.* therefrom, thereof, thereby; of, by, or respecting it, that, or them; thence; hence, away, off.

davonbringen, *v.a.* (*sep.*) to save. (Jer. 38:2)

davonfahren, *v.n.* (*sep.*) (*aux.* s.) to perish. (Ps. 49:21)

davonfliegen, *v.n.* (*sep.*) (*aux.* s.) to fly away. (Ps. 90:10)

davongehen, *v.n.* (*sep.*) (*aux.* s.) to go off, to go one's way. (Matt. 13:25)

davonkommen, *v.n.* (*sep.*) (*aux.* s.) to get off, to escape. (Mic. 6:14)

dazu, *adv.* thereto; for that purpose, to that end; moreover, besides, in addition.

dazutun, *v.a.* (*sep.*) to add to; to make haste, to set about. (Deut. 4:2)

die Decke (-n), cover, coverlet, blanket, quilt, rug, covering; ceiling, roof; skin, envelope; pretense, pretext. (Exod. 34:33)

der Deckel (-), lid, cover; cornice. (I Peter 2:16)

decken, 1. *v.a.* to cover, to protect, to guard, to secure, to conceal; to reimburse, to defray; to superpose; to lay (the table). 2. *v.r.* to be identical, to be congruent, to coincide. (Luke 23:30)

dehnen, 1. *v.a.* to stretch, to extend, to lengthen, to expand, to dilate; to drawl (speech). 2. *v.r.* to stretch; to last long. (Isa. 54:2)

dein, 1. *m. & n. poss. adj. & pron.* (*f. & pl.* -e), your, yours; thy, thine. 2. **deiner, deine, deines,** or **der, die, das deinige,** *poss. pron.* yours, thine; your property; your part. (Exod. 23:5)

deinetwillen, *adv.* on your account, for your sake, as far as you are concerned. (Gen. 3:17)

der Deismus, deism.

deistisch, *adj.* deistical.

der Dekalog, Decalogue; the Ten Commandments.

der Dekan (-e), dean.

das Dekanat, deanery; deanship.

die Dekanei, deanery.

das Dekret (-e), decree, edict, ordinance.

das Dekretale (-alien), decretal; papal decree.

dekretieren, *v.a.* to decree, to ordain by decree.

der Demant, diamond. (Ezek. 3:9)

der Demiurg (-en), demiurge.

die Demut, humility, meekness, lowliness. (I Peter 5:5)

demütig, *adj.* humble, submissive, meek. (Matt. 11:29)

demütigen, *v.a.* to humble; to humiliate, to abase, to bring low. (Lev. 26:41)

die Demütigung (-en), humiliation, abasement, mortification.

demutsvoll, *adj.* humble, meek.

denken, *ir.v.a. & n.* (*aux.* h.) to think, to reflect. (Gen. 45:26)

der Denkzettel (-), memorandum, reminder; phylactery; reprimand. (Matt. 23:5)

dennoch, *conj.* yet, still, however, nevertheless, for all that. (Ps. 46:5)

dermaleinst, *adv.* in days to come, hereafter. (Matt. 5:25)

dermaßen, *adv.* to such an extent, so much. (Phil. 1:7)

der Derwisch, dervish.

desto, *adv.* (*used before comparatives*) the, so much. (Rom. 6:1)

der Determinismus, determinism.

der Determinist (-en), determinist.

deterministisch, *adj.* deterministic.

deuten, 1. *v.a.* to explain, to expound, to interpret. 2. *v.n.* (*aux.* h.) to point (*auf,* to or at), to indicate, to signify; to bode, to augur. (Matt. 13:36)

deutlich, *adj.* distinct, clear, plain; intelligible. (I Cor. 14:9)

der Diakon (-e & -en), deacon.

das Diakonat (-e), diaconate.

die Diakonissin (-nen), sister of a Protestant nursing order.

die Diaspora, Diaspora; dispersion (of the Jews).

dichten, 1. *v.a. & n.* (*aux.* h.) to compose (as an author or a poet), to write poetry; to invent, to devise. 2. *n.* meditation, musing; composition of poetry. (Gen. 8:21)

dick, *adj.* thick; fat, stout, corpulent; big, bulky, large; swollen, inflated, voluminous. (Ps. 65:14)

die Didache, Didache; the teaching of the twelve apostles.

die Didaktik, didactics, the art of teaching.

der Didaktiker (-), didactic person, teacher of didactics.

didaktisch, *adj.* didactic, instructional.

der Dieb (-e), thief, burglar. (Jer. 7:9)

die Dieberei, theft, thieving, stealing; larceny. (Matt. 15:19)

dienen, *v.n.* (*aux.* h.) to serve; to be of service to; to assist. (Gen. 25:23)

der Diener (-), (man-)servant, attendant; official; curtsy, bow. (Ps. 101:6)

die Dienerin (-nen), maidservant, maid. (Rom. 13:4)

der Dienst (-e), service; post, employment, office, situation; good turn; duty. (Exod. 1:13)

dienstbar, *adj.* serviceable; liable to serve; subservient, subject. (Rom. 9:12)

die Dienstbarkeit, servitude, bondage, subjection. (Isa. 40:2)

das Diesseits, this life; life here and now.

der Dill (-e), dill. (Matt. 23:23)

das Ding (-e), object, thing, matter. (Gen. 39:6)

das Ding-an-sich, thing-in-itself (Kant).

dingen, 1. *ir.v.a.* to bargain for; to hire, to engage. 2. *v.n.* to bargain, to haggle. (Matt. 20:7)

der Diözesan (-en), diocesan.

die Diözese (-n), diocese.

die Disputation (-en), debate.

disputieren, *v.a. & n.* (*aux.* h.) to dispute; to debate.

der Dissident (-en), dissenter.

die Distel (-n), thistle. (Gen. 3:18)

der Docht (-e), wick. (Isa. 42:3)

das Dogma (-men), dogma.

dogmatisch, *adj.* dogmatic.

dogmatisieren, *v.n.* to dogmatize.

der Dogmatismus, dogmatism.

die Doktrin, doctrine.

der Dolmetscher (-), interpreter. (Gen. 42:23)

der Dom (-e), cathedral; dome, cupola; (*fig.*) vault, canopy.

der Domchor (-e), cathedral choir.

die Domfreiheit, cathedral close.

der Domherr (-en), prebendary, canon.

der Domherrnornat, canonicals.

das Domkapitel (-), (cathedral) chapter; dean and chapter.

die Domkirche (-n), cathedral, minster.

der Domsänger (-), cathedral chorister.

die Domschule (-n), cathedral school; grammar school attached to a cathedral.

das Domstift (-e), cathedral chapter; seminary.

der Donner (-), thunder. (Exod. 20:18)

donnern, *v.n.* (*aux.* h.) to thunder, to roar. (Exod. 19:16)

der Donnerstag, Thursday.
grüner Donnerstag, Gründonnerstag, Maundy Thursday; *der feiste Donnerstag,* Thursday before Lent.

das Dorf (-er), village.

die Dorfgemeinde (-n), rural parish.

der Dorfpfarrer (-), country parson.

der Dorn (-en), thorn, prickle, spine; spike, prong. (Gen. 3:18)
er ist mir ein Dorn im Auge, he is a thorn in my side.

der Dornbusch (-e), brier. (Judg. 9:14)

die Dornenkrone (-n), crown of thorns. (Matt. 27:29)

der Dornstrauch (-er), brier.

drängen, 1. *v.a.* to push, to press, to urge, to hurry; to oppress, to afflict. 2. *v.r.* to crowd. (Ps. 42:10)

draußen, *adv.* outside, out of doors, without; abroad. (Gen. 24:31)

drei, 1. *num. adj.* three. 2. *f.* three. (Deut. 17:6)

die Dreieinheit, triad, trinity.

dreieinig, *adj.* three in one, triune.

die Dreieinigkeit, Trinity.

der Dreieinigkeitsbekenner (-), trinitarian.

das Dreieinigkeitsdogma, doctrine of the Trinity.

die Dreieinigkeitslehre, doctrine of the Trinity.

dreifach, dreifältig, *adj.* threefold; triple, treble. (Eccles. 4:12)

die Dreifaltigkeit, Trinity.

die Dreifaltigkeitskirche (-n), Holy Trinity Church.

dreihundert, *num. adj.* three hundred. (Gen. 5:22)

der Dreikönigsabend, eve of the Epiphany.

das Dreikönigsfest, Epiphany, Twelfth Night.

dreimal, *adv.* three times, threefold; thrice. (Exod. 23:14)

dreißig, *num. adj.* thirty. (Matt. 26:15)

dreist, *adj.* bold, daring; audacious, impudent, pert, cheeky. (II Cor. 10:1)

dreschen, *ir.v.a.* to thresh. (Deut. 25:4)

der Dreschwagen (-), threshing instrument. (Isa. 28:27)

dringen, *ir.v.n.* (*aux.* h. & s.) to urge, to press forward, to press, to rush; to penetrate, to pierce; to force a way. (Luke 2:35)

drinnen, *adv.* within, indoors. (I Cor. 5:12)

dritte, *num. adj.* third. (Matt. 16:21)

droben, *adv.* above, up there. (Gal. 4:26)

drohen, *v.a. & n.* (*einem mit einer Sache*) to threaten, to menace. (Acts 4:29)

drücken, 1. *v.a.* to press, to push, to clasp, to squeeze, to pinch; to oppress, to afflict; to depress, to weigh down. 2. *v.r.* to shirk, to malinger; to sneak away. (Ps. 38:3)

der Druide (-n), druid.

der Dualismus, dualism.

dualistisch, *adj.* dualistic.

die Dualität, duality.

dulden, 1. *v.a.* to suffer, to endure, to bear patiently; to tolerate. 2. *n.* sufferance, patient endurance. (Matt. 17:17)

duldsam, *adj.* patient, tolerant, long-suffering.

die Duldsamkeit, toleration, spirit of toleration.

die Duldung, toleration, patience.

dumm, *adj.* dull, stupid, slow; foolish, silly, ridiculous. (Matt. 5:13)

dunkel, 1. *adj.* dark, obscure, dim, dusky; gloomy; deep, mysterious. 2. *n.* darkness; obscurity, ambiguity. (Gen. 27:1)

die Dunkelheit, darkness; obscurity.

dünken, 1. *ir.v.n.* (*aux.* h.) & *imp.* to seem, to look, to appear. 2. *v.r.* to imagine or fancy oneself. (Gen. 29:20)

dünn, *adj.* thin, fine; flimsy; slender, slim; weak, diluted (fluids); rare (air). (Isa. 38:12)

durchdringen, 1. *ir.v.n.* (*aux.* s.) (*sep.*) to force one's way through; to penetrate, to pierce; to permeate; to prevail, to get the mastery; to accomplish; to succeed. 2. *v.a.* (*insep.*) to penetrate, to pierce; to permeate, to pervade. (Rom. 5:12)

durchgraben, *ir.v.a.* (*insep.*) to dig through; to pierce by digging. (Ps. 22:17)

durchkommen, *ir.v.n.* (*aux.* s.) (*sep.*) to come or get through; to succeed, to pass (examinations). (Luke 19:4)

durchsäuern, *v.a.* (*insep.*) to leaven thoroughly, to acidify. (Matt. 13:33)

durchschauen, 1. *v.n.* (*aux.* h.) (*sep.*) to see through, to look through. 2. *v.a.* (*insep.*) to look through or over (items individually); to see through, to penetrate, to understand, to grasp. (James 1:25)

durchscheinen, *ir.v.n.* (*aux.* h.) (*sep.*) to shine through, to be visible through.

durchscheinend, *pr.p. & adj.* translucent, diaphanous. (Rev. 21:21)

durchsuchen, *v.a.* (*sep. & insep.*) to search through or thoroughly, to search everywhere. (Zeph. 1:12)

durchziehen, 1. *ir.v.a.* (*sep.*) to draw, to drag, or pull through; (*insep.*) to traverse, to penetrate (on foot); to interweave, to interlace. 2. *v.n.* (*aux.* s. & h.) (*sep.*) to go or march through. 3. *v.r.* (*sep.*) to extend all over or through. (Job 1:7)

dürfen, *ir.v.n.* (*aux.* h.) to be permitted, to have permission or authority, to be allowed; may, can, dare. (Matt. 7:4)

dürftig, *adj.* needy, indigent, poor; sorry, insufficient. (Gal. 4:9)

die Dürftigkeit, poverty, indigence, need, want.

dürr, *adj.* arid, parched; lean, thin, skinny, meager. (Ps. 32:4)

die Dürre (-n), dryness, drought; leanness; sterility. (Isa. 58:11)

der Durst, thirst. (I Cor. 4:11)

dürsten, *v.n.* (*aux.* h.) to be thirsty. (John 4:13)

durstig, *adj.* thirsty. (Ps. 107:9)

düster, *adj.* dark, gloomy, dusky; sad, mournful, melancholy, dismal.

die Düsterheit, die Düsterkeit, darkness, dusk, gloom, gloominess.

der Dynast (-en), feudal lord, ruler, prince.

die Dynastie (-n), dynasty.

dynastisch, *adj.* dynastic(al).

Ee

eben, 1. *adj.* even, level, flat, plain, smooth; plane; open (country). 2. *adv. part.* just, even; precisely, exactly, quite, certainly. (Luke 6:38)

das Ebenbild (-er), image, likeness. (Rom. 8:29)

das Ebenbild des Schöpfers, God's image.

(der) Ebräer (-), Hebrew.

die Echtheit, pure quality, genuineness, authenticity; legitimacy, purity.

die Ecke (-n), edge; corner, angle; nook. (Matt. 6:5)

der Eckstein (-e), cornerstone; curbstone. (Ps. 118:22)

edel, *adj.* noble; of noble birth, high-born; lofty, exalted; precious; excellent. (Acts 17:11)

das Edelgestein, precious stone. (Rev. 21:19)

der Edelmann (-leute), nobleman, noble.

Eden, Eden. (Gen. 2:8)

die Egge (-n), harrow; selvage, list, listing.

eggen, *v.a.* to harrow. (Isa. 28:24)

ehe, *conj.* before, until. (I Kings 18:45)

die Ehe (-n), marriage; matrimony, wedlock. (Heb. 13:4)

das Ehebett (-en), nuptial bed.

ehebrechen, *ir.v.n.* to commit adultery. (Exod. 20:14)

der Ehebrecher (-), adulterer. (Heb. 13:4)

die Ehebrecherin (-nen), adulteress.

der Ehebruch, adultery. (Matt. 5:32)

der Ehebund (-e), matrimony.

das Ehebündnis (-se), matrimony.

ehedem, *adv.* before this time, formerly, of old, heretofore.

die Ehefrau (-en), married woman, wife.

die Ehegattin (-nen), wife, (lawful) spouse.

der Ehegemahl (-e), husband.

die Eheleute, (*pl.*) married people.

ehelich, *adj.* matrimonial, conjugal. (Matt. 19:10)

ehelichen, *v.a.* to marry.

ehelos, *adj.* unmarried, single.

die Ehelosigkeit, celibacy.

der Ehemann (-er), married man.

das Ehepaar (-e), married couple.

eher, *adv.* (*comp. of* **ehe**) sooner, rather; formerly, earlier. (John 1:15)

ehern, *adj.* brazen, brass, bronze. (Deut. 28:23)

der Eheschänder (-), adulterer.

die Ehescheidung (-en), divorce.

die Eheschließung (-en), marriage.

der Ehesegen, nuptial blessing.

der Ehestand, married state, wedlock.

ehrbar, *adj.* honorable, of good repute, respectable, honest. (Mark 15:43)

die Ehrbarkeit, respectability; propriety; honorableness, good repute, honesty. (Rom. 12:17)

die Ehre (-n), honor; reputation; respect; rank; glory, praise, credit. (Deut. 32:3)

ehren, *v.a.* to honor, to esteem, to revere. (Exod. 20:12)

ehrenhaft, *adj.* honorable, high-principled.

die Ehrenhaftigkeit, honorableness.

das Ehrenkleid (-er), uniform, ceremonial dress.

ehrerbietig, *adj.* reverential, respectful, deferential.

die Ehrerbietung (-en), deference, respect, veneration.

die Ehrfurcht, respect, reverence, awe.

ehrfürchtig, *adj.* reverential, respectful.

ehrfurchtslos, *adj.* disrespectful, irreverent.

ehrfurchtsvoll, *adj.* respectful, reverential.

der Ehrgeiz, ambition.

ehrgierig, *adj.* highly ambitious.

ehrlich, *adj.* honest, honorable, reliable.

die Ehrlichkeit, honesty.

die Ehrlosigkeit, infamy, dishonesty.

die Ehrwürden, reverence.
Euer Ehrwürden, your Reverence, Reverend Sir.

ehrwürdig, *adj.* venerable; reverend, sacred.

die Ehrwürdigkeit, venerableness.

das Ei (-er), egg. (Luke 11:12)

die Eiche (-n), oak. (II Sam. 18:9)

der Eid (-e), oath; adjuration; execration. (Gen. 24:8)

der Eidam (-e), son-in-law.

der Eidschwur (-̈e), oath.

der Eifer, eagerness, zeal; ardor, fervor, passion. (Deut. 32:16)

der Eiferer (-), zealot.

eifern, *v.n.* (*aux.* h.) to be zealous, to act or advocate with zeal; to be jealous; to endeavor, to take great pains (over or with); to rival. (I Kings 19:10)

die Eifersucht, jealousy.

eifrig, *adj.* eager, keen, zealous; passionate, ardent; jealous. (Exod. 20:5)

die Eifrigkeit, zeal; zealousness, officiousness.

eigen, *adj.* (*dat.*) proper, inherent; own, individual, special; specific, peculiar, characteristic; nice, delicate, particular; odd, strange, curious. (I Sam. 18:1)

das Eigentum (-̈er), property, belongings. (Exod. 19:5)

der Eigentümer (-), owner, proprietor.

die Eile, haste, speed, dispatch. (Isa. 52:12)

eilen, *v.n.* (*aux.* s. & h.) & *r.* to make haste, to hasten, to hurry. (Gen. 18:6)

der Eimer (-), pail, bucket. (Isa. 40:15)

ein, 1. (*eine, ein*) *indef. art.* a, an. 2. *num. adj.* one, the same. 3. *pron.* (*einer, eine, ein[e]s*) one, a person; they, people; a certain portion, some. 4. *adv. & sep. prefix,* in, into. (Gen. 3:22)

einander, *indec. pron.* one another, each other. (Gen. 22:6)

einäugig, *adj.* one-eyed. (Matt. 18:9)

die Einbildung (-en), imagination, fancy, presumption.

die Einbildungskraft, imagination; active understanding (Kant).

einbinden, *ir.v.a.* to bind (a book); to tie up or on. (I Sam. 25:29)

einblasen, *ir.v.a.* to blow or breathe into; to whisper, to suggest, to prompt, to insinuate. (Gen. 2:7)

einbringen, *ir.v.a.* to bring in; to realize (profit). (Hag. 1:6)

eindrängen, 1. *v.a.* to squeeze into, to force into. 2. *v.r.* to crowd in; to intrude oneself into. (Gal. 2:4)

eindringen, *ir.v.n.* (*aux.* s.) to enter by force, to break in, to invade; to penetrate, to pierce; to infiltrate, to soak in; (*fig.*) to fathom, to search into.

der Eindruck (-̈e), impression, mark, sensation.
Eindruck machen, to produce an impression or a sensation.

einerlei, 1. *indec. adj.* of one sort, (one and) the same; immaterial, all the same. 2. *n.* monotony, sameness. (Gen. 11:1)

einernten, *v.a.* to reap, to harvest, to gather in; (*fig.*) to win, to gain, to acquire. (James 5:4)

einfallen, *ir.v.n.* (*aux.* s.) to fall in; to invade, to make an inroad, to attack, to overrun, to raid, to break in, to come in suddenly; to fall down, to collapse. (Ps. 46:4)

die Einfalt, simplicity, artlessness, innocence. (II Cor. 1:12)

einfältig, *adj.* simple, plain; foolish, silly. (Ps. 116:6)

die Einfältigkeit, simplicity, silliness.

einführen, *v.a.* to introduce, to usher in; to set up, to install, to establish; to inaugurate, to induct (to a living, etc.); to bring in, to import. (II Peter 2:1)

der Eingang (-̈e), entering, entry, arrival, entrance, doorway; hall, passage; introduction; importation; access; beginning, preface, preamble, prelude, overture, prologue. (Ps. 121:8)

eingeben, *ir.v.a.* to insert; to suggest, to prompt, to inspire (with); to hand in, to send in, to deliver, to present, to give. (II Tim. 3:16)

eingeboren, *p.p. & adj.* native, indigenous; inborn, innate; only-begotten. (John 1:14)
der eingeborene Sohn, only Son; Christ.

die Eingebung (-en), administration; presentation; inspiration, suggestion.

eingedenk, *prep.* mindful of, remembering.

eingehen, 1. *ir.v.n. (aux.* s.) to go in, to enter, to come in, to arrive; to decay, to perish, to wither (of plants), to die (of game), to come to an end. 2. *v.a.: einen Vergleich eingehen,* to come to terms with; *eine Wette eingehen,* to make a bet. (Gen. 19:8)

die Einheit (-en), unity, oneness, union, uniformity.

der Einheitsgläubige (-n), unitarian.

die Einheitslehre, monotheism.

einhergehen, einherschreiten, *ir.v.n.* to move along, to proceed; to pace about. (Ps. 15:2)

einig, *adj.* at one, united, in agreement, unanimous, agreed. (Deut. 6:4)

die Einigkeit, unity; unanimity. (Eph. 4:3)

einkommen, 1. *ir.v.n. (aux.* s.) to come forward (with a complaint, etc.), to petition, to apply to; to come in; to appear, to arrive. 2. *n.* income, revenue; interest, rent; proceeds. (Heb. 4:1)

einlegen, *v.a.* to lay, to place, or to put in; to enclose, to fold up, to turn inwards; to immerse, to soak, to steep; to preserve; to buy (for future use); to insert, to embed, to inlay. (Exod. 14:4)
ein (gutes) Wort für einen einlegen, to intercede for someone, to speak on someone's behalf, to put in a good word for someone.

die Einleitung, introduction; preamble; prelude; preface.

einmal, *adv. & part.* once, one time; formerly; some (future) time; one day. (Gen. 18:32)

einmütig, *adj.* unanimous, of one mind; with one consent, agreed. (Acts 1:14)

die Einmütigkeit, unanimity.

die Einnahme (-n), receiving; receipt, income, takings, revenue; conquest, occupation. (Phil. 4:15)

einnehmen, *ir.v.a.* to take in, to gather in; to take, to capture; to accept, to receive, to collect (money, etc.); to engage; to charm, to captivate, to fascinate. (Dan. 7:18)

die Einöde (-n), solitude, desert, desolate place, wilderness. (Deut. 32:10)

einpfropfen, *v.a.* to cork in or up; to stuff in, to cram in; to engraft; to implant. (Rom. 11:23)

einreden, *v.a.* to persuade someone to; to talk someone over; to convince someone of, to make someone believe. (Ruth 1:16)

einreißen, 1. *ir.v.a.* to tear down; to pull down, to demolish. 2. *v.n. (aux.* s.) to rend, to tear, to burst, to get torn; to spread, to prevail, to gain ground. (Acts 4:17)

einsam, *adj.* lonely, lonesome; solitary, alone. (Isa. 54:1)

die Einsamkeit, loneliness, solitude.

einsammeln, *v.a.* to collect; to gather. (Exod. 23:10)

die Einsammlung (-en), collection. (Exod. 23:16)

einschärfen, *v.a.* to inculcate, to enjoin; *(einem etwas)* to impress something on someone. (Deut. 6:7)

einschenken, *v.a.* to pour in; to pour out; to fill. (Ps. 23:5)

einschlafen, *ir.v.n. (aux.* s.) to go to sleep, to fall asleep; to die away; to get benumbed. (Matt. 25:5)

einschleichen, *ir.v.r. (aux.* h.) *& n. (aux.* s.) to creep in, to steal in; to insinuate oneself into. (Gal. 2:4)

einschließen, 1. *ir.v.a.* to comprise, to include; to lock in or up; to embed; to encircle, to envelop, to surround. 2. *v.n. (aux.* h.) to catch (of a lock); to fit close. (Exod. 14:3)

einsegnen, *v.a.* to consecrate, to bless, to give benediction (especially at confirmation); to confirm; to ordain.

die Einsegnung (-en), consecration; benediction; (Protestant) confirmation; ordination.

einsenken, *v.a.* to sink in; to bury, to lower into a grave; to set (plants, etc.), to plant. (Prov. 8:25)

einsetzen, 1. *v.a.* to put or set in; to insert; to fix, to fit, to place; to set up; to set; to institute; to nominate, to appoint, to install; to pledge; to employ; to preserve. 2. *v.n.* to set in, to begin. (Ps. 2:6)

der Einsiedel (-), **der Einsiedler** (-), hermit.

die Einsiedelei (-en), hermitage.

einsiedlerisch, *adj.* secluded, solitary.

einst, *adv.* once, one day; some (future) day, some time, in days to come. (Ps. 2:5)

eintauchen, 1. *v.a.* to dip in, to plunge; to steep, to immerse; to imbue. 2. *v.n.* (*aux. s.*) to dive, to duck, to plunge. (John 13:26)

die Einteilung, distribution; division; arrangement, classification.

die Eintracht, concord, union; harmony, agreement. (Zech. 11:7)

einträchtig, *adj.* harmonious, peaceable, united. (Ps. 133:1)

die Einträchtigkeit, unanimity; harmony.

einweihen, *v.a.* to consecrate, to dedicate; to inaugurate, to initiate, to open (ceremonially); to ordain. (Deut. 20:5)

die Einweihung (-en), consecration, dedication, initiation, inauguration, ceremonial opening. (Neh. 12:27)

die Einweihungsfeier (-n), inaugural ceremony.

einwilligen, *v.n.* (*aux. h.*) to consent or agree to, to acquiesce in; to approve of; to subscribe to; to permit. (Acts 18:20)

die Einwilligung (-en), consent in writing, acceptance.

der Einwohner (-), inhabitant, resident. (Exod. 34:12)

die Einwohnerin (-nen), habitant, resident. (Isa. 12:6)

die Einwohnerschaft, population, inhabitants.

die Einwohnerzahl, total population.

die Einwohnerzählung (-en), census.

einwurzeln, *v.n.* (*aux. s.*) to take root. (Ps. 80:10)
tief eingewurzelte Überzeugungen, deep(ly)-rooted convictions.

einzeln, *adj.* single, sole, particular; individual, isolated, detached, separate. (Gen. 29:20)

einziehen, 1. *ir.v.a.* to draw in, to pull in, to get in, to take in; to collect; to absorb; to seize, to arrest. 2. *v.r.* to shrink, to contract; to retire from the world. 3. *v.n.* (*aux. s.*) to enter, to march in, to move into, to take possession (of a house, lodgings, etc.); to soak in, to infiltrate. (Ps. 24:9)

einzig, *adj.* only, single, sole, unique. (Gen. 22:2)

das Eis, ice. (Job 38:29)

das Eisen (-), iron; horseshoe; sword, weapon; iron instrument or tool. (Lev. 26:19)

das Eisenwerk (-e), iron. (Gen. 4:22)

eisern, *adj.* iron; hard, strong, inflexible; indefatigable. (Deut. 4:20)

eitel, *adj.* vain, conceited; frivolous, empty, idle, futile; (*indec.*) nothing but, mere, only. (James 1:26)

die Eitelkeit, vanity; conceit. (Rom. 8:20)

der Eiter, matter, pus. (Prov. 14:30)

die Eiterbeule (-n), abscess, (*fig.*) sink of iniquity. (Isa. 1:6)

der Ekel, loathing, disgust, aversion, nausea. (Job 19:17)
es ist mir zum Ekel, I am sick of it, I am disgusted with it.

ekeln, 1. *v.n.* (*aux. h.*) to arouse disgust, to sicken, to excite loathing. 2. *v.r.: sich ekeln vor einer Sache,* to loathe something, to be disgusted at something. (Exod. 7:18)

das Element (-e), element; rudiment; principle. (II Peter 3:10)

das Elementarbuch (-̈er), primer.

der Elementargeist, elemental or nature spirit.

die Elementargewalt (-en), elemental power.

der Elementarstein, opal.

das Elend, 1. *n.* misery, distress, misfortune; want, need, penury. 2. *adj.* miserable, wretched, pitiful, ill. (Rom. 7:24)

das Elendsviertel (-), slum.

elf, *num. adj.* eleven. (Matt. 28:16)

das Elfenbein, ivory.

elfenbeinern, *adj.* consisting of ivory; made of ivory.

elffach, *adj.* elevenfold.

die **Elle** (-n), ell, yard, yardstick. (Matt. 6:27)

elterlich, *adj.* parental.

die **Eltern,** (*pl.*) parents. (Matt. 10:21)

das **Elternhaus,** house of one's parents, home.

die **Elternliebe,** parental love, filial love.

elternlos, *adj.* orphan, orphaned.

der **Empfang** (⁻e), reception, receipt (of a letter, etc.).

empfangen, 1. *ir.v.a.* to take, to receive; to welcome. 2. *v.n.* (*aux.* h.) to conceive, to become pregnant. (Matt. 7:8)

die **Empfangnahme,** receipt, reception.

die **Empfängnis,** conception. *unbefleckte Empfängnis,* Immaculate Conception.

empfehlen, 1. *ir.v.a.* to commend, to recommend. 2. *v.r.* to take one's leave; to bid farewell.

der **Empfehlungsbrief** (-e), letter of introduction; credentials.

empfinden, *ir.v.a.* to experience; to feel, to perceive, to be sensible of.

empor, *adv. & sep. prefix,* up, upwards, on high, aloft.

empören, 1. *v.a.* to rouse to indignation, to shock; to excite, to stir up. 2. *v.r.* to be enraged or furious; to rebel. (Num. 16:2)

emporhalten, *v.a.* to hold up. (Exod. 17:11)

emporheben, *ir.v.a.* to lift up, to raise, to exalt; to elevate (the Host).

der **Emporkömmling** (-e), upstart, parvenu.

emporragen, *v.n.* to stand out, to project, to tower (*über,* above). (Ps. 48:3)

die **Empörung** (-en), rebellion, revolt; rising; indignation.

das **Ende** (-n), end; conclusion; close, finish; result, issue, purpose. (Gen. 6:13)

endgültig, *adj.* final, definite, conclusive.

endlich, 1. *adj.* finite; final, conclusive, last, ultimate. 2. *adv.* at last, finally, in short, after all; nimbly. (Ps. 73:24)

die **Endursache** (-n), final cause.

der **Endzweck,** goal, ultimate purpose.

eng, *adj.* narrow; tight; close; strict; confined; intimate. (Matt. 7:13)

die **Enge** (-n), narrowness, tightness, constriction; narrow place; crowded or confined state. (Acts 9:22)

der **Engel** (-), angel. (Matt. 4:11)

das **Engelbrot,** manna.

engelgleich, engelhaft, *adj.* angelic.

das **Engelköpfchen,** cherub's head.

die **Engelschar** (-en), angelic host.

die **Engelsgeduld,** patience of Job.

der **Engelsgruß,** Annunciation; Ave Maria.

die **Engelzungen,** (*pl.*) tongues of angels. (I Cor. 13:1)

entäußern, *v.r.* (*sich einer Sache*) to part with, to give up, to dispose of; to deprive oneself of, to divest oneself of. (Phil. 2:7)

die **Entäußerung,** renunciation; parting with; alienation (of property).

entbrennen, *ir.v.n.* (*aux.* s.) to take fire, to be kindled, to become inflamed; to break out; to fly into a passion. (Gen. 43:30) *in Liebe entbrennen,* to fall violently in love.

entdecken, 1. *v.a.* to discover, to detect, to find out. 2. *v.r.* to disclose one's presence.

entfahren, *ir.v.n.* (*aux.* s.) to escape; to slip out from. (Ps. 106:33)

entfallen, *ir.v.n.* (*aux.* s.) to fall out of or from, to escape or slip (the memory); *entfallen auf* (*acc.*), to fall to the share of. (Acts 27:34)

die **Entfaltung,** unfolding, development, expansion.

entfliehen, *ir.v.n.* (*aux.* s.) (*dat.*) to run away or flee from, to escape; to pass quickly, to fly (of time). (Isa. 35:10)

entfremden, *v.a.* (*einem etwas*) to estrange; to alienate (someone from something). (Eph. 4:18)

die **Entfremdung,** estrangement, alienation.

entgegen, 1. *prep.* (*with preceding dat.*) towards, against, in face of; opposed to, contrary to. 2. *adv. & sep. prefix, implying opposition or meeting.* (Lev. 26:21)

entgegnen, *v.a.* (*einem etwas*) to answer, to reply; to retort.

die **Entgegnung** (-en), reply, answer, retort, rejoinder.

entgehen, *ir.v.n.* (*aux.* s.) (*dat.*) to get away from; to escape, to elude; to avoid, to evade. (John 10:39)

enthalten, 1. *ir.v.a.* to hold, to contain, to comprise, to include. 2. *v.r.* to refrain or abstain (from). (Gen. 45:1)

enthaltsam, *adj.* abstinent, sober; temperate; chaste.

die Enthaltsamkeit, abstinence; temperance.

enthaupten, *v.a.* to behead, to decapitate. (Matt. 14:10)

die Enthauptung (-en), beheading, decapitation.

entheiligen, *v.a.* to profane, to desecrate. (Exod. 31:14)

die Entheiligung (-en), desecration, profanation.

entkleiden, *v.a. & r.* to undress, to strip, to unclothe, (*fig.*) to divest. (II Cor. 5:4)

die Entmythologisierung, demythologizing.

entrinnen, *ir.v.n.* (*aux.* s.) (*dat.*) to run away, to escape from; to fly past (of time).

entrücken, *v.a.* to move away, to carry off, to remove; (*fig.*) to enrapture, to entrance, to carry away. (Rev. 12:5)

entrüsten, 1. *v.a.* to provoke, to irritate, to make angry, to enrage. 2. *v.r.* to become angry or indignant; to fly into a passion. (Gal. 5:26)

die Entrüstung, indignation, anger, wrath.

die Entscheidung (-en), decision, sentence, judgment; crisis.

entschlafen, *ir.v.n.* (*aux.* s.) to fall asleep; to die, to pass away. (Acts 7:59)
er ist sanft entschlafen, he has passed away peacefully.

entschlagen, *ir.v.r.* (*gen.*) to get rid of, to give up, to part with, to divest oneself of, to dismiss from one's mind; to decline. (I Tim. 4:7)

entschuldigen, 1. *v.a.* to excuse; to justify, to defend. 2. *v.r.* to apologize (*bei,* to; *wegen,* for). (Luke 14:18)

die Entschuldigung (-en), excuse, apology. (Rom. 1:20)

entsetzen, 1. *v.a.* to displace; to frighten, to terrify. 2. *v.r.* to be horrified, amazed, shocked, or startled (*vor* or *über,* by). 3. *n.* terror, dread, fright, horror. (Matt. 19:25)

entspringen, *ir.v.n.* (*aux.* s.) to escape; to spring up, to rise (of rivers, etc.), to arise, to originate in. (I Tim. 6:4)

entstehen, *ir.v.n.* (*aux.* s.) to begin, to originate (*aus,* in); to arise (*aus,* from); to be formed, produced, or generated; to grow out of; to result (from). (II Cor. 4:6)

die Entstehungsgeschichte, history of the origin and rise (of).

entsühnen, entsündigen, *v.a.* to expiate, to absolve. (Ps. 51:9)

die Entsühnung, die Entsündigung, expiation.

entweichen, *ir.v.n.* (*aux.* s.) to leak, to escape (as gas, etc.); to abscond; to evade (pursuit, etc.); to vanish, to disappear. (Matt. 2:14)

entweihen, *v.a.* to profane, to desecrate, to violate. (Acts 24:6)

die Entweihung, profanation; defilement; desecration; sacrilege.

entwenden, *reg. & ir.v.a.* to steal, to purloin, to pilfer. (Gen. 49:10)

die Entwicklung, evolution, development.

entwöhnen, (*einen einer Sache, einen von einer Sache*) to disaccustom, to break of (a habit); to wean (an infant). (Ps. 131:2)

die Entwöhnung, weaning; disuse.

entziehen, 1. *ir.v.a.* (*einem etwas*) to take away, to remove, to deprive of, to withdraw (from); to extract, to eliminate. 2. *v.r.* to avoid; to evade, to shun, to withdraw from, to forsake. (Isa. 58:7)

entzückt, *p.p. & adj.* charmed, delighted, enraptured, overjoyed. (Acts 10:10)

entzünden, 1. *v.a.* to kindle, to set fire to, to ignite, to light. 2. *v.r.* to catch fire, to flare up, to become inflamed; to break out (as war). (James 3:6)

entzwei, *adv. & sep. prefix,* in two; asunder, apart; torn, broken. (Luke 23:45)

die Enzyklika (-iken), encyclical.

(der) Epheser, Ephesian.

ephesisch, *adj.* Ephesian.

das Epiphaniasfest, Epiphany.

episkopal, Episcopal.

der Episkopale (-n), Episcopalian.

der Episkopalismus, Episcopalianism.

die Episkopalkirche, Protestant Episcopal Church.

das Episkopat, episcopate.

erarbeiten, *v.a. & r.* to gain or get by working, to earn, to achieve by work. (Ps. 144:14)

die Erbanlage (-n), hereditary factor.

erbarmen, 1. *v.a.* to move to pity; *daß Gott erbarme!* God help us!; *imp.* (*with acc. & gen.*) *mich erbarmet des Armen,* I pity the poor man. 2. *v.r.* (*with gen. or* über *with acc.*), to pity, to feel pity, to have or show mercy; *Herr, erbarme dich unser,* Lord, have mercy upon us! 3. *n.* pity, compassion, mercy. (Exod. 33:19)

der Erbarmer, merciful God, God of mercy. (Isa. 49:10)

die Erbarmung, pity.

erbarmungslos, *adj.* pitiless, merciless, remorseless.

erbarmungsvoll, *adj.* full of pity, compassionate.

erbauen, 1. *v.a.* to build up, to raise, to erect, to construct; to edify. 2. *v.r.: sich erbauen an* (*dat.*), to find edification in, to be edified by. (Luke 7:5)

der Erbauer (-), builder; founder.

erbaulich, *adj.* edifying, improving; devotional.

die Erbauung, erection, building, construction; edification.

die Erbauungsschrift (-en), devotional book, religious tract.

die Erbauungsstunde (-n), hour of devotion.

Erbe, 1. *m.* (-en), heir; successor. 2. *n.* (*Erbschaften* or *Erbgüter*) heritage, inheritance. (Deut. 10:9)

erbeben, *v.n.* (*aux.* h. & s.) to tremble, to shudder (*vor,* at), to shake, to quiver, to quake, to vibrate. (Matt. 27:52)

erben, 1. *v.a.* to inherit. 2. *v.n.* (*aux.* s.): *erben auf,* to descend to, to devolve on. (Ps. 37:9)

der Erbfeind (-e), hereditary foe, (*fig.*) sworn enemy, old enemy.

das Erbgut (⁀er), ancestral estate; heirloom.

erbieten, 1. *ir.v.a.* to offer; to volunteer; to deal with, to treat. 2. *n.* offer. (Heb. 12:7)

erbitten, *ir.v.a.* to beg for, to request, to ask for; to prevail upon. (I Sam. 1:20)

erbittern, *v.a.* to embitter, to provoke, to incense, to exasperate. (Isa. 63:10)

erbittert, *adj.* embittered, bitter, incensed.

die Erbitterung, exasperation, animosity.

erbleichen, *ir.v.n.* to grow or turn pale, to fade; to die.

erblich, *adj.* hereditary, inheritable.

die Erblichkeit, heritability, hereditariness; heredity.

erblos, *adj.* disinherited; without an heir.

das Erbrecht, right of succession.

die Erbschaft, inheritance, legacy.

die Erbsünde, original sin.

das Erbteil, portion, inheritance. (Ps. 16:5)

das Erdbeben (-), earthquake.

der Erdboden, earth, ground, soil.

die Erde, earth, ground, soil; the earth, the world. (Gen. 1:1)

der Erdenbürger (-), human being; mortal.

die Erdenfreude (-n), earthly joy; worldly pleasure, transitory happiness.

das Erdengeschöpf (-e), mortal, human being.

erdenken, *ir.v.a.* to think out, to devise, to invent, to conceive, to imagine. (Prov. 16:9)

der Erdenkloß (⁀e), clod of earth. (Gen. 2:7)

das Erdenleben, mortal life.

der Erdenruhm, earthly glory.

das Erdenrund, the earth.

der Erdensohn (⁀e), mortal.

das Erdenwallen, earthly pilgrimage.

erdenwärts, *adv.* earthwards.

die Erderschütterung (-en), earthquake, earth tremor.

das Erdharz, bitumen, asphalt. (Gen. 11:3)

die Erdkugel, terrestrial globe.

das Erdreich, earth, soil, ground; earthly kingdom. (Ps. 46:7)

erdulden, *v.a.* to endure, to suffer; to put up with. (II Tim. 2:10)

die Erduldung, endurance; submission (to); toleration (of).

das Ereignis (-se), event, occurrence, incident.

der Eremit (-en), hermit.

die Eremitage, hermitage.

ererben, *v.a.* to inherit. (Matt. 19:29) *ererbte Krankheit,* hereditary disease.

erfahren, 1. *ir.v.a.* to come to know, to learn, to hear, to be told, to discover; to experience, to suffer, to undergo. 2. *p.p. & adj.* experienced, seasoned, practiced. (Exod. 6:7)

die Erfahrung (-en), (practical) experience, practical knowledge. (Rom. 5:4)

erfinden, *ir.v.a.* to invent, to discover, to find out; to make up (a story). (Acts 5:39)

erfordern, *v.a.* to require, to need; to necessitate, to render necessary, to call for, to demand. (Rom. 8:4)

das Erfordernis (-se), requisite, exigency; (*pl.*) necessaries (of life).

erforschen, *v.a.* to search into, to investigate, to explore, to fathom. (Matt. 2:4)

erfreuen, 1. *v.a.* to gladden, to delight, to give pleasure (to), to cheer, to comfort. 2. *v.r.* to rejoice, to be glad or pleased or delighted (*über eine Sache,* at or over something); to take pleasure, to rejoice (*an einer Sache,* in something), to enjoy (*gen.*). (Matt. 2:10)

erfreut, *adj.* glad, pleased, delighted.

erfrischen, 1. *v.a.* to freshen, to refresh. 2. *v.r.* to take refreshment.

erfüllen, *v.a.* to fill up, to impregnate; to fulfil, to perform, to accomplish; to comply with (a request); to realize (expectations). (Gen. 9:1)

die Erfüllung (-en), fulfilment, accomplishment, performance, realization. (Rom. 13:10)

ergeben, 1. *v.a.* to produce, to yield, to deliver up, to result in, to give as a result, to show; to amount to. 2. *v.r.* to surrender (*with* in & *acc.*), to submit, to yield; to devote oneself to (*dat.*), to become addicted to, to give way to. 3. *p.p. & adj.* devoted, loyal, attached; resigned, submissive, humble.

die Ergebenheit, (*fig.*) resignation, submissiveness; fidelity, loyalty, devotion. *die Ergebenheit in Gott,* humility before God, submissive acquiescence in God's will.

die Ergebung, submission, resignation, surrender.

ergehen, 1. *ir.v.n.* (*aux.* s.) to be issued, published, or promulgated; (*über einen*) to befall, to happen (to someone). 2. *v.r.* to walk, to stroll. 3. *n.* condition, state (health, prosperity, etc.). (James 2:13)

ergötzen, 1. *v.a.* to delight, to please, to amuse. 2. *v.r.* to enjoy oneself. 3. *n.* joy, delight, pleasure, amusement. (Rom. 15:24)

die Ergötzung (-en), joy, delight, pleasure, amusement. (Heb. 11:25)

ergreifen, *ir.v.a.* to lay or take hold of, to seize, to catch; to apprehend; to affect, to touch, to move; to assume (the offensive), to enter on, to take up (a trade, etc.). (Ps. 40:13)

ergrimmen, *v.n.* (*aux.* s.) to get angry or furious. (Exod. 32:10)

ergründen, *v.a.* to fathom, to probe, to investigate, to look into; to ascertain, to discover, to find out, to get to the bottom of. (Jer. 17:9)

erhaben, *adj.* raised, projecting, prominent, elevated; elated; exalted, noble, sublime, stately. (Isa. 2:2)

erhalten, 1. *ir.v.a.* to get, to receive, to obtain, to save, to preserve, to keep, to maintain, to keep up, to support. 2. *p.p. & adj.* preserved; received. (Gen. 50:20) *Gott erhalte den König,* God save the king!

erhängen, *v.a. & r.* to hang (a person). (Matt. 27:5)

erhaschen, *v.a.* to snatch (at); to seize, to catch. (John 10:12)

erheben, 1. *ir.v.a.* to lift or raise up, to elevate; to praise, to exalt, to extol; to set up (a cry); to promote, to advance, to raise in rank; to levy, to gather, to collect (taxes). 2. *v.r.* to raise oneself; to rise, to rise up, to rebel (*gegen,* against); to arise, to spring up. (Gen. 4:8)

erheucheln, *v.a.* to simulate, to feign.

erhitzen, 1. *v.a.* to heat, to warm, to make hot; to excite, to inflame. 2. *v.r.* to grow hot or warm; to become heated; to get angry, to fly into a passion. (Rom. 1:27)

erhöhen, *v.a.* to raise, to elevate, to erect; to heighten, to increase, to enhance (the value, etc.); to extol, to exalt. (Ps. 27:5)

die Erhöhung, elevation; rise, advance, increase; eminence; exaltation.

erhören, *v.a.* to give a favorable hearing; to grant. (Exod. 2:24)

erinnern, 1. *v.a.* (*einen an eine Sache*) to remind, to call to someone's mind, to draw attention to; to mention, to suggest; to admonish. 2. *v.r.* (*gen. or* an *& acc.*) to recall, to remember, to recollect, to call to mind. (II Tim. 1:5)

die Erinnerung (-en), remembrance, memory, recollection, reminiscence; reminder, admonition, suggestion, hint.

erkalten, *v.n.* (*aux.* s.) to grow cold; to cool (down); to cool off (of feelings, etc.). (Matt. 24:12)

erkaufen, *v.a.* to buy, to purchase; to bribe, to corrupt. (Rev. 5:9)

erkennen, *ir.v.a.* to recognize (*an*, by), to perceive, to know, to apprehend, to discern, to distinguish, to understand; to judge, to decide. (Gen. 45:1)

Erkenntnis (-se), 1. *f.* knowledge, cognition; perception, understanding, acknowledgment, recognition, realization. 2. *n.* verdict, finding, sentence, judgment. (Gen. 2:9)
zur Erkenntnis kommen, to repent; *der Baum der Erkenntnis,* the tree of knowledge.

der Erkenntnisgrund, criterion by which something is known.

die Erkenntnistheorie, theory of cognition.

das Erkenntnisvermögen, intellect (Kant).

erkunden, *v.a.* to ascertain, to gain information about; to reconnoiter; to explore. (Luke 1:3)

erkundigen, *v.r.* to inquire, to make inquiries (*bei einem,* of or from someone). (Matt. 10:11)

die Erkundigung (-en), inquiry, search.

erlangen, *v.a.* to reach, to attain, to acquire, to obtain, to procure, to get. (Matt. 5:7)

der Erlaß (-[ss]e), edict, decree, ordinance; deduction, reduction; allowance; pardon, dispensation, exemption, indulgence.

erlassen, *ir.v.a.* to publish, to issue, to proclaim; (*einem etwas*) to remit, to release from; to absolve from, to exempt from, to pardon.

erläßlich, *adj.* remissible, venial, pardonable.

die Erlaßsünde, venial sin.

die Erlassung, remission, release, dispensation.

erlauben, *v.a.* (*einem etwas*) to allow, to permit; to grant or give permission to, to sanction. (Matt. 8:21)

die Erlaubnis, leave, permission, sanction; license, dispensation.

das Erlebnis (-se), experience; occurrence, event.

erleiden, *ir.v.a.* to suffer, to bear, to endure, to undergo, to sustain. (Matt. 27:19)

erleuchten, *v.a.* to illuminate, to light up; (*fig.*) to enlighten. (Rev. 21:23)

die Erleuchtung, illumination, enlightenment, light. (II Cor. 4:6)

erlösen, *v.a.* to redeem; to ransom; to (set) free, to release; to save, to deliver, to rescue; to get (as proceeds from a sale). (Exod. 6:6)

der Erlöser, deliverer; redeemer. (Isa. 41:14)

die Erlösung, release; redemption; deliverance, salvation. (Ps. 130:7)

ermahnen, *v.a.* to admonish, to exhort, to warn. (Luke 3:18)

die Ermahnung (-en), admonition, exhortation. (Heb. 13:22)

ernähren, 1. *v.a.* to nourish, to feed, to support, to maintain. 2. *v.r.* to earn one's livelihood; to live (by); to subsist (*von*, on). (Rev. 12:6)

erneuern, 1. *v.a.* to renew, to renovate, to repair, to replace, to restore, to refresh, to revive; to recommence, to repeat. 2. *v.r.* to become new, to recommence; to be revived. (Heb. 6:6)

die Erneuerung (-en), renewal, renovation, revival; replacement; repetition. (Rom. 12:2)

erniedrigen, *v.a.* to lower, to bring low, to humble, to humiliate, to degrade. (Matt. 18:4)

die Erniedrigung (-en), degradation, abasement, humiliation, reduction, depression, lowering.

der Ernst, 1. earnestness, seriousness, gravity; severity, sternness. 2. *adj.* earnest; serious, grave, stern, severe, solemn. (Ps. 108:2)

ernstlich, *adj.* earnest; in earnest, serious; fervent, ardent, eager, intent, forcible. (James 5:16)

die Ernte (-n), harvest, crop. (Gen. 8:22)

die Erntearbeit, harvesting.

das Erntedankfest, harvest thanksgiving (festival).

das Erntefest, harvest home, harvest thanksgiving.

der Erntemonat, August.

ernten, *v.a.* to harvest, to gather in; to reap. (Matt. 6:26)

der Ernter (-), harvester, reaper. (James 5:4)

erntereif, *adj.* fit for harvesting, ripe for the sickle.

der Erntesegen, rich harvest.

die Erntezeit, harvest time.

erquicken, *v.a.* to revive, to refresh. (Ps. 19:8)

die Erquickung (-en), refreshment, comfort. (Acts 3:20)

erraten, *ir.v.a.* to solve (a riddle), to guess, to divine. (Judg. 14:12)

erregen, *v.a.* to excite, to stir up, to stimulate; to agitate, to irritate; to promote, to provoke, to cause; to inspire (fear, etc.). (Matt. 10:35)

erretten, *v.a.* to save, to rescue, to deliver. (Gen. 19:17)

der Erretter, Savior.

die Errettung, rescue, deliverance. (Gen. 45:7)

ersaufen, *ir.v.n.* (*aux.* s.) to be drowned; to be flooded (as crops, a mine, etc.). (Isa. 28:7)

ersäufen, *v.a.* to drown; to flood. (Isa. 43:2)

erschaffen, *ir.v.a.* to produce, to create. (Jer. 31:22)

der Erschaffer, creator.

die Erschaffung, creation.

erschallen, *reg. & ir.v.n.* (*aux.* s.) to resound, to ring. (Ps. 66:8)
erschallen lassen, to sound or spread abroad; to sound, to let hear.

erscheinen, 1. *ir.v.n.* (*aux.* s.) to appear; to come out (as a book), to be published; to be evident, to seem; *erscheinen lassen,* to bring out, to publish. 2. *n.* appearance, presence. (Gen. 12:7)

die Erscheinung, appearance, figure, apparition, vision (of spirits); manifestation; phenomenon; publication; symptom. (Acts 26:19)
das Fest der Erscheinung Christi, Epiphany.

die Erscheinungswelt, physical world.

erschlagen, 1. *ir.v.a.* to kill, to strike dead, to slay; *vom Blitz erschlagen,* struck by lightning. 2. *p.p.* thunderstruck, dumbfounded. (Gen. 4:15)

erschrecken, 1. *ir.v.n.* (*aux.* s.) to be frightened, scared, alarmed, terrified, or startled (*über eine Sache,* at or by something). 2. *v.a.* to frighten, to scare, to startle, to terrify. 3. *v.r.* to give a start, to be startled, to take fright. (Matt. 2:3)

erschrecklich, *adj.* terrific, terrible, dreadful. (Ps. 47:3)

erschrocken, *p.p. & adj.* frightened, scared, terrified. (Luke 24:38)

ersehen, *ir.v.a.* to see, to perceive; to learn, to note, to observe; to distinguish; *sich* (*dat.*) *etwas ersehen,* to choose, to provide something for oneself. (Gen. 22:8)

ersehnen, *v.a.* to long for, to desire greatly.

erst, 1. *adj.* first, foremost, prime, leading, best, superior; *der, die* or *das erste beste,* the first that comes; *das erste Buch Moses,* Genesis; *bei erster Gelegenheit,* at the first opportunity; *in erster Linie,* in the first place, first of all; *zum ersten, fürs erste,* in the first place, for the present, at first, for some time. 2. *adv.* at first, first of all, at the beginning; for the first time, not till, only, just; some day or time (in the future). (Isa. 41:4)

erstarren, 1. *v.n.* (*aux.* s.) to be benumbed, to grow stiff, to become torpid, to congeal, to solidify, to harden; to be paralyzed (with fear). 2. *n.* torpidity. (Acts 9:7)

erstatten, *v.a.* to refund, to restore, to make good, to return; to replace. (Col. 1:24)

ersterben, *ir.v.n.* (*aux.* s.) to die; to die away, to become extinct; to fade away.
das Wort erstarb auf seinen Lippen, the word died on his lips.

erstgeboren, *adj.* first-born. (Rom. 8:29)

die Erstgeburt, primogeniture; first-born. (Exod. 11:5)
Esau verkaufte sein Erstgeburtsrecht, Esau sold his birthright.

ersticken, 1. *v.a.* to stifle, to suffocate, to choke, to smother; to suppress. 2. *v.n.* (*aux.* s.) to choke, to suffocate, to be choked or suffocated. (Matt. 13:7)

der Erstling (-e), first-born, first production; (*pl.*) first fruits. (Rom. 8:23)

ertöten, *v.a.* to deaden, to smother, to stifle; to mortify (the flesh). (II Cor. 6:9)

ertragen, *ir.v.a.* to bear, to suffer, to tolerate, to endure, to put up with. (Gen. 13:6)

erträglich, *adj.* bearable, tolerable, endurable, passable. (Matt. 10:15)

erwachen, 1. *v.n.* (*aux.* s.) to awake, to awaken, to wake up. 2. *n.* awakening. (Ps. 3:6)

erwählen, *v.a.* to choose, to elect. (Deut. 7:6)

erwarten, *v.a.* to expect, to await, to wait for, to anticipate.

die Erwartung (-en), expectation, anticipation.

erwecken, *v.a.* to rouse, to wake, to waken, to awaken; to arouse, to stir up. (Deut. 18:15)
vom Tode erwecken, to resuscitate, to raise (from the dead); *er erweckte bei ihnen den Glauben,* he caused them to believe or inspired in them the belief; *Hoffnungen erwecken,* to raise hopes.

die Erweckung (-en), awakening; resuscitation; excitation; rousing, revival.

der Erweckungsprediger (-), revivalist.

erweisen, 1. *ir.v.a.* to prove; *einem erweisen,* to show, do, pay, or render (mercy, honor, favor, etc.) to someone. 2. *v.r.* to show or prove oneself (to be), to turn out to be. (Acts 2:22)

erwerben, *ir.v.a.* to gain, to obtain, to acquire; to earn; to win. (Acts 1:18)

erwürgen, 1. *v.a.* to strangle, to choke, to throttle; to slaughter, to put to death. 2. *v.n.* (*aux.* s.) to choke, to be suffocated. (Acts 2:23)

das Erz (-e), ore; metal; brass, bronze. (Lev. 26:19)

Erz-, *in compounds* = principal; arch-, cardinal, chief; excellent, very, extremely, high-.

erzählen, *v.a.* to tell, to relate, to narrate. (Exod. 24:3)

der Erzbetrüger (-), arrant cheat.

der Erzbischof (⁻e), archbishop.

erzbischöflich, *adj.* archiepiscopal.

das Erzbistum (⁻er), archbishopric.

der Erzbösewicht (-e), arrant rogue.

der Erzdekan (-e), archdeacon.

das Erzdiakonat (-e), archdeaconry.

erzeigen, 1. *v.a.* (*einem etwas*) to show, to manifest, to display (feeling, etc.); to render, to do (kindness). 2. *v.r.* to prove to be. (Luke 1:72)

der Erzengel (-), archangel.

der Erzfeind, archenemy, Satan.

erziehen, *ir.v.a.* to bring up, to train; to educate; to rear, to grow, to raise, to tend. (Isa. 49:21)

das Erziehungswesen, educational system.

erzkatholisch, *adj.* ultra-Catholic.

der Erzketzer (-), arch-heretic.

der Erzlügner (-), arch-liar.

das Erzstift (-e), archbishopric.

erzürnen, 1. *v.a.* to irritate, to anger, to enrage, to provoke to anger. 2. *v.r. & n.* (*aux.* s.) to get angry, to quarrel with.

der Erzvater (⁻er), patriarch.

erzväterlich, *adj.* patriarchal.

die Eschatologie, eschatology.

eschatologisch, *adj.* eschatological.

der Esel (-), ass, donkey; fool. (Gen. 49:14)

(der) Esra, Ezra.

essen, 1. *ir.v.a. & n.* (*aux.* h.) to eat; to take one's meals. 2. *n.* food, meal; eating, feeding. (Gen. 2:17)

der Essig (-e), vinegar. (Ps. 69:22)

(die) Esther, Esther.

die Ethik, ethics.

der Ethiker (-), moral philosopher.

ethisch, *adj.* ethical.

etliche, *pl. adj. & pron.* some, several. (Matt. 16:28)

etwa, 1. *adv.* nearly, about; perhaps, by chance, perchance. 2. *part.: er wird doch nicht etwa glauben,* he will not believe, I hope. (Phil. 4:8)

etwas (1 & 2 often abbreviated to *was*), 1. *indef. pron.* (*indec.*) something, some, anything, any. 2. *adv.* somewhat; a little; rather. 3. *n.* entity; *ein gewisses Etwas,* a certain thing, an indefinable something, something unaccountable. (Gen. 18:14)

die Eucharistie, Eucharist.

der Eudämonismus, eudemonism.

eudämonistisch, *adj.* eudemonistic.

euerthalben, eurethalben, *adv.* on your account, for your sake.

euertwillen, euretwillen, *adv.* on your account, for your sake.

der Euhemerismus, euhemerism.

das Evangeliar (-e & ien), Gospel book.

evangelisch, *adj.* evangelical; Protestant, Lutheran.
die evangelische Kirche, the Protestant Church.

die Evangelischen, (*pl.*) Evangelicals; Protestants.

evangelisieren, to evangelize; to preach the gospel.

der Evangelist (-en), Evangelist (Matthew, Mark, Luke, John); evangelist, preacher of the gospel.

das Evangelium (-lien), the gospel.

ewig, *adj.* everlasting, eternal; continual, endless; perpetual. (Exod. 15:18)
die Ewigkeit, eternity; perpetuity; age(s). (Matt. 6:13)

von Ewigkeit zu Ewigkeit, in alle Ewigkeit, world without end, to all eternity.

ewiglich, *adv.* for ever, eternally, perpetually, unceasingly. (Gen. 3:22)

exaltiert, *adj. & p.p.* overexcited, highly strung.

die Exegese, exegesis.

der Exeget (-en), commentator.

die Exegetik, exegetics.

exegetisch, *adj.* exegetic(al).

die Exequien, (*pl.*) obsequies; masses for the dead.

das Exerzitium (-ien), written homework; devotions.

die Existenz (-en), existence; being.

die Existenzberechtigung, right to exist, right to live.

existenzial, *adj.* existentialist.

existieren, *v.n.* (*aux.* h.) to exist, to be, to live, to subsist.

die Exkommunikation, excommunication.

exkommunizieren, *v.a.* to excommunicate.

der Exkommunizierte (-n), excommunicated.

der Exorzismus, exorcism.

die Extase (-n), ecstasy.

der Exzeß (-[ss]e), excess, outrage.

Ff

die Fabel (-n), fable, tale, story; plot (of a drama). (I Tim. 1:4)

die Fackel (-n), torch, flare, flambeau. (John 18:3)

der Faden (⁻), thread; string, twine, cord; fiber, filament; shred, particle. (Isa. 38:12)

fahl, *adj.* pale, faded, sallow, fawn-colored, dun. (Rev. 6:8)

fahren, 1. *ir.v.n.* (*aux.* s.) to go (in any sort of conveyance), to travel, to drive, to ride, to sail; to fare, to get on. 2. *v.a.* to drive; to convey; to take (by vehicle); to sail, to row (a boat). (Gen. 15:15)
fahren lassen, to let go, to abandon, to give up; to let slip. (Deut. 32:15)

der Fakir (-e), fakir.

der Fall (⁻e), fall, tumble, accident; decay, ruin, decline, downfall, failure; waterfall; case, instance, event; condition, situation. (Matt. 7:27)

die Falle (-n), trap, snare; pitfall; catch, latch (of a door). (Ps. 69:23)

fallen, 1. *ir.v.n.* (*aux.* s.) to fall, to tumble; to drop, to sink, to be deposited; to decline, to abate, to subside, to decrease, to diminish; to die, to be killed; to be ruined; to be seduced. 2. *v.r.: sich wundfallen,* to fall and hurt oneself. 3. *n.* subsidence; fall; decay; diminution. (Gen. 33:4)

der Fallstrick (-e), snare, noose; (*fig.*) trick, catch, ruse.

falsch, 1. *adj.* wrong, false, incorrect, untrue; base, artificial, counterfeit, spurious, adulterated; insincere, deceitful, perfidious, treacherous; angry. 2. *m. & n.* dishonesty. (Exod. 20:16)
ohne Falsch wie die Tauben, harmless as doves.

fälschen, *v.a.* to falsify, to forge, to counterfeit (coin); to adulterate (food). (Amos 8:5)

falschgläubig, *adj.* heterodox.

die Falschgläubigkeit, heterodoxy, heresy.

die Falschheit, falsity, falseness; deceit, guile, perfidy; untruth, falsehood, duplicity.

fälschlich, *adj.* false, erroneous. (Lev. 19:11)

der Fanatiker (-), fanatic.

fanatisch, *adj.* fanatic(al).

der Fanatismus, fanaticism.

fangen, 1. *ir.v.a.* to catch, to seize, to capture; to trap, to hook, to snare; to take prisoner. 2. *v.r.* to be caught, to become entangled; to catch, to take hold. 3. *v.n.* (*aux.* h.) to bite; to take hold, to clutch (at), to seize. (Acts 1:16)

der Farre (-n), bullock, young bull, steer. (Ps. 22:13)

fassen, 1. *v.a.* to grasp, to seize, to hold, to lay hold of; to contain, to include; to comprehend, to conceive. 2. *v.r.* to collect oneself, to contain or compose oneself, to pull oneself together. (I Kings 8:27)
sich in Geduld fassen, to possess one's soul in patience.

fast, *adv.* almost, nearly, close upon. (Acts 13:44)

fasten, 1. *v.n.* to fast. 2. *n.* fasting; (*pl.*) fast, time of fasting; Lent. (Matt. 4:2)

der Fastensonntag, Sunday in Lent.

die Fastenspeise, Lenten fare.

die Fastenzeit, Lent.

die Fastnacht, Shrove Tuesday.

der Fasttag (-e), fast day.

fatal, *adj.* disagreeable, annoying, awkward, unfortunate.

der Fatalismus, fatalism.

die Fatalität, fatality; ill luck, misfortune.

faul, *adj.* decayed, rotten, stale, bad; lazy, idle, indolent; worthless; brittle. (Matt. 7:17)

die Faulheit, laziness, idleness, sloth. (Prov. 31:27)

die Faust (⁻e), (clenched) fist. (Matt. 26:67)

fechten, *ir.v.n.* (*aux.* h.) to fight; to fence. (I Cor. 9:26)

die Feder (-n), feather; plume; quill; pen; spring. (III John 13)

fegen, 1. *v.a.* to sweep, to wipe, to clean, to rub off. 2. *v.n.* (*aux.* h. & s.) to scamper; to sweep over, to rush across. (Matt. 3:12)

das Feg(e)feuer, purgatory.

der Fehl (-e), 1. *m.* fault, blemish, failure. 2. *adv.* & *sep. prefix,* wrong, wrongly, amiss; in vain. (Exod. 12:5)

fehlen, 1. *v.a.* to miss. 2. *v.n.* (*aux.* h.) to make a mistake, to be in the wrong, to do wrong, to err, to blunder; to be missing, to be absent, to be wanting, to lack, to ail. (Matt. 19:20)

der Fehler (-), fault, defect, blemish, flaw; mistake, blunder. (Matt. 6:14)

die Feier (-n), celebration, festival, ceremony; recess, holiday.

der Feierabend (-e), time for leaving off work; evening leisure.

der Feiergesang (⁻e), solemn hymn.

das Feierjahr, sabbatical year.

das Feierkleid (-er), festive raiment.

feierlich, *adj.* solemn; festive.

die Feierlichkeit (-en), solemnity; pomp, ceremony.

feiern, 1. *v.n.* (*aux.* h.) to rest, to take a holiday; to stop work, to be idle, to strike. 2. *v.a.* to celebrate, to solemnize; to observe; to extol, to honor. (Lev. 25:2)

die Feierstunde (-n), festive hour; leisure hour.

der Feiertag (-e), holiday; day of rest; festival.

feig, feige, *adj.* cowardly, timid, dastardly, fainthearted. (Deut. 20:8)

die Feige (-n), fig. (Matt. 7:16)

der Feigenbaum (⁻e), fig tree. (Matt. 21:19)

das Feigenblatt (⁻er), fig leaf. (Gen. 3:7)

feil, *adj.* for sale, to be sold; (*fig.*) venal, bribable; mercenary. (Gen. 42:1)

fein, *adj.* fine, delicate, thin; polite, cultivated, refined; elegant, distinguished, fashionable; acute, subtle, sly, artful; beautiful, excellent, capital, fine, grand. (Exod. 2:2)

feind, 1. *adj.* hostile. 2. *m.* (-e), enemy, foe. (Gen. 37:4)

der (*alte*) *böse Feind,* the evil one, the devil.

die Feindschaft, enmity, hatred, hostility. (Gen. 3:15)

die Feindseligkeit, hostility, animosity, war.

die Feindsliebe, love of enemies.

feist, 1. *adj.* fat, stout, plump; *feister Sonntag,* the last Sunday before Lent. 2. *n.* (-es) fat, suet (of deer, etc.). (Amos 5:22)

das Feld (-er), field, open country, plain, ground; area, sphere; battlefield. (Gen. 2:5)

der Feldgeistliche (-n), chaplain to the armed forces, padre.

das Feldgeschrei, war cry. (I Thess. 4:16)

der Feldhauptmann (⁻er), captain. (II Kings 5:1)

der Feldweg (-e), lane, field path.

das Fell (-e), skin, hide, pelt, fur, coat (of animals); film. (Gen. 3:21)

der Fels (-en), rock, crag, cliff. (Num. 20:11)

das Fenster (-), window. (Gen. 6:16)

fern, *adj.* (*dat.*) far, distant, far off, remote. (I Sam. 24:7)

die Ferne (-n), remoteness, distance, distant place or time. (Isa. 57:19)

fernerhin, *adv.* for the future, henceforth, henceforward, furthermore. (Rev. 22:11)

die Ferse (-n), heel; track, footsteps. (Gen. 3:15)

fertig, *adj.* ready, prepared; ready to start, complete, finished, done, ruined; readymade; perfect; skilled; accomplished; fluent. (Isa. 32:4)

fest, 1. *adj., adv., & sep. prefix,* firm, solid, hard, compact; strong, stout, tight, fast, stable; fixed, rigid, permanent, enduring. 2. *suffix* (*in compounds* =) versed in, e.g., *bibelfest,* well-versed in the Scriptures. (Acts 3:7)

das Fest (-e), festival; holiday; feast; banquet. (Exod. 23:14)

das Festessen (-), public banquet.

das Festkleid (-er), ceremonial dress.

festlich, *adj.* festive, solemn, magnificent.

die Festlichkeit (-en), festivity, solemnity.

das Festspiel (-e), festival performance.

die Festzeit, festive season, holidays.

der Festzug (-̈e), festive procession.

der Fetisch (-e), fetish.

die Fetischanbetung, der Fetischdienst, der Fetischismus, fetishism, idolatry.

das Fett, 1. *n.* (-e) fat, grease, lard, dripping; tallow. 2. *adj.* oily, fatty, greasy; fat, plump. (Gen. 41:2)

die Fettigkeit, fatness; fattiness, greasiness. (Gen. 27:28)

feuchten, *v.a. & n.* (*aux.* h.) (usually in compounds with prefix *be-* or *an-*) to wet, to moisten, to dampen. (Gen. 2:6)

das Feuer (-), fire, conflagration; furnace, forge, hearth; firing, bombardment; passion, spirit, vigor. (Gen. 19:24)

der Feueranbeter (-), fire-worshiper.

der Feuereifer, ardent zeal, ardor. (Heb. 10:27)

die Feuerflamme (-n), a flame of fire. (Rev. 1:14)

der Feuerofen, furnace of fire. (Matt. 13:42)

die Feuersäule, pillar of fire. (Exod. 13:21)

die Feuersbrunst, fire, conflagration.

die Feuertaufe, baptism of fire.

feurig, *adj.* fiery, burning; igneous; ardent, passionate, fervid. (Exod. 3:2)
der feurige Busch, the burning bush; *das feurige Schwert,* the flaming sword.

das Fieber (-), fever. (Matt. 8:14)

der Filz (-e), felt.

finden, 1. *ir.v.a.* to find, to discover; to meet with, to light upon; to think, to consider, to deem. 2. *v.r.* to find oneself, to be found; to turn out to be; to occur. (Gen. 2:20)

der Finger (-), finger; digit. (Exod. 8:15)

der Fingerreif (-e), ring. (Luke 15:22)

finster, *adj.* dark, obscure; gloomy, dim; ominous, threatening; morose, sad. (Matt. 6:23)

der Finsterling (-e), obscurantist, bigot; ignoramus.

die Finsternis, darkness; obscurity; gloom; eclipse. (Gen. 1:4)
die Macht der Finsternis, the power of darkness.

firmeln, *v.a.* to confirm.

die Firm(el)ung, confirmation.

der Firmling (-e), candidate for confirmation.

der Fisch (-e), fish. (Gen. 1:26)

fischen, *v.a. & n.* (*aux.* h.) to fish. (John 21:3)

der Fischer (-), fisherman, angler. (Matt. 4:18)

der Fischerring, pope's signet ring.

der Fischhaken (-), fishhook. (Amos 4:2)

der Fischzug, catch, haul, draught (of fish). (Luke 5:9)

der Fittich (-e), wing, pinion. (Deut. 32:11)

der Flachs, flax; *wilder Flachs,* dodder. (Prov. 31:13)

der Fladen, flat cake; cow dung. (Exod. 29:2)

der Flagellant (-en), flagellant.

der Flagellantismus, flagellantism.

die Flamme (-n), flame; blaze, light. (Exod. 3:2)

der Flattergeist (-er), fickle or unstable person. (Ps. 119:113)

flechten, *ir.v.a.* to plait, to braid, to twist; to wreathe, to entwine, to interweave, to interlace; (*fig.*) to interlard. (Matt. 27:29)

der Fleck (-e), **der Flecken** (-), place, spot; plot, piece (of ground); blemish, fault, flaw; blot, stain, mark, speck, spot; patch, shred; tripe. (Jer. 13:23)

der Flecken, (= *Ort*) market town, country town. (Matt. 21:2)

flehen, 1. *v.a. & n.* (*aux.* h.) to implore, to entreat, to beseech, to supplicate. 2. *n.* entreaty, prayers; supplication. (Exod. 32:11)

flehentlich, *adj.* suppliant, imploring, beseeching, fervent.
flehentlich bitten, to beseech; *flehentliche Bitte,* earnest prayer, fervent supplication, entreaty.

das Fleisch, flesh; meat; flesh or pulp (of fruit); cellular tissue (in leaves); fleshy parts; men, humanity, the flesh (physical & sensual part of man). (Gen. 2:23)

fleischern, *adj.* fleshy; meaty. (II Cor. 3:3)

die Fleischeslust, lust, carnal desire.

fleischlich, *adj.* carnal, sensual, fleshly. (Rom. 7:14)

die Fleischlichkeit, sensuality, carnal-mindedness.

der Fleischtopf (⸚e), fleshpot (symbol of good living) (*usually pl.*). (Exod. 16:3)

die Fleischwerdung, incarnation.

der Fleiß, diligence, industry, application, assiduity. (Prov. 2:2)

fleißig, *adj.* industrious, hardworking, diligent, assiduous. (Matt. 2:8)

flicken, 1. *v.a.* to patch, to mend, to repair; to bungle. 2. *m.* (-en) patch. (Matt. 4:21)

die Fliege (-n), fly; imperial (beard). (Isa. 7:18)

fliegen, 1. *ir.v.n.* (*aux.* s. & h.) to fly, to rush, to dash. 2. *v.a.* to fly, to pilot. 3. *n.* flight. (Gen. 7:14)

fliegend, *pr.p. & adj.* flying, flowing. (Rev. 4:7)

fliehen, 1. *ir.v.n.* (*aux.* s.) to flee, to run away, to retreat, to escape. 2. *v.a.* to shun, to avoid, to get out of the way of. (Gen. 19:20)

fließen, *ir.v.n.* (*aux.* h. & s.) to flow, to run, to melt, to trickle down; to pass away, to elapse (of time); to be smooth (of words). (Exod. 3:8)

der Floh (⸚e), flea. (I Sam. 24:15)

der Fluch (⸚e), curse, oath, imprecation, malediction, execration. (Deut. 11:26)

fluchbeladen, *adj.* under a curse, accursed.

fluchen, 1. *v.n.* (*aux.* h.) to curse, to swear; to blaspheme; to use bad language. 2. *v.a.* to utter curses, to curse, to damn, to execrate. (Exod. 21:17)

das Fluchmaul (⸚er), blasphemer, foul-mouthed person.

die Flucht (-en), flight, escape; row, straight line; suite (of rooms). (Ps. 18:41)

flüchtig, *adj.* fugitive, runaway; transient, fleeting, nonpersistent; hasty, hurried. (Gen. 4:12)

der Flügel (-), wing; vane; arm; flank; aisle (of a church). (Exod. 25:20)

flugs, *adv.* quickly, instantly, at once. (Luke 16:6)

der Fluß (⸚[ss]e), river, stream; flow; discharge. (II Cor. 11:26)

flüstern, *v.a. & n.* (*aux.* h.) to whisper. (Isa. 8:19)

die Flut (-en), flood, deluge, inundation; torrent, stream; high tide, high water, flood tide. (Isa. 28:15)

folgen, *v.n.* 1. (*aux.* s.) (*dat.*) to follow (after), to ensue (*aus,* from); to succeed (*auf* [*acc.*], to); to be derived. 2. (*aux.* h.) to obey, to attend to, to listen to, to conform to. (Luke 9:23)

folgerichtig, *adj.* logical, consistent; conclusive.

fordern, *v.a.* to demand, to ask; to claim, to require, to exact. (Isa. 1:12)

fördern, *v.a.* to further, to promote, to advance; to benefit, to encourage, to expedite, to hasten, to accelerate, to dispatch; to raise, to haul, to transport. (Ps. 37:23)

die Förderung, furtherance, help; furthering, advancement, promotion; dispatch; yield, output; hauling. (Phil. 1:12)

die Form (-en), form, figure, shape; make, fashion, mode, usage, method of procedure; model, pattern, cut; mold. (Rom. 2:20)

die Formgeschichte, criticism of literary form (Dibelius).

forschen, 1. *v.a. & n.* (*aux.* h.) to search (*nach,* after or out), to seek, to inquire; to investigate; to do research. 2. *n.* investigation. (Matt. 2:8)

der Forscher (-), investigator; research worker; scholar; scientist; scientific investigator.

der Forschergeist, der Forschersinn, inquiring mind.

fortfahren, 1. *ir.v.n.* (*aux.* s.) to drive off or away; to depart, to set out or off; (*aux.* h.) *mit* or *in einer Sache fortfahren,* to continue, to proceed, to go on with something. 2. *v.a.* to carry away; to remove (in a vehicle); to drive away. (II Cor. 7:1)

fortgehen, *ir.v.n.* (*aux.* s.) to go away, to depart; to go on, to continue, to proceed, to progress. (Isa. 53:10)

fortleben, 1. *v.n.* to live on, to survive. 2. *n.* survival, afterlife. (Ps. 49:10)

der Fortschritt (-e), progress, advance, development, improvement.

die Frage (-n), question, query, inquiry; questionable or uncertain thing, problem. (John 3:25) der **Fragebogen** (- or ⁻), questionnaire.

das **Fragebuch,** catechism.

der **Fragelehrer** (-), catechist.

fragen, *v.a. & n.* (*aux.* h.) to ask, to inquire (*nach,* for), to interrogate, to question; to consult (*um*). (Gen. 32:30)

der **Franziskaner** (-), Franciscan; Gray Friar.

die **Frau** (-en), woman; wife; lady; madam; Mrs. (Isa. 24:2)

die **Frauenkirche,** Church of Our Lady.

das **Frauenkloster** (⁻), nunnery.

die **Frauenstühle,** (*pl.*) women's pews (in church).

das **Frauenwerk,** women's welfare organization.

frech, *adj.* insolent, impudent, shameless, bold, audacious. (Jer. 9:1)

frei, 1. *adj.* free, independent (*von,* of); unconfined, uncontrolled; at liberty; frank, outspoken, candid, open; exonerated. 2. *sep. verbal prefix.* (Exod. 21:2)

der **Freidenker** (-), freethinker.

die **Freidenkerei,** freethinking, latitudinarianism.

die **Freigabe,** release.

freigeben, *ir.v.a.* to set free, to release.

freigebig, *adj.* liberal, generous.

die **Freigebigkeit,** liberality, generosity.

die **Freigebung,** emancipation; release.

der **Freigeist,** freethinker, latitudinarian.

die **Freigeisterei,** freethinking.

der **Freigelassene** (-n), freedman. (I Cor. 7:22)

freigesinnt, *adj.* liberal (in religion, politics).

freigläubig, *adj.* independent in faith.

der **Freigutsbesitzer** (-), freeholder.

die **Freiheit,** freedom, liberty; privilege; immunity; license. (Gal. 5:1)

freiherrschend, *adj.* sovereign.

freiherzig, *adj.* openhearted, frank.

freilassen, *ir.v.a.* to release, to set free, to liberate.

die **Freilassung,** emancipation, release.

die **Freimachung,** freeing, liberation, disengagement, emancipation.

der **Freimaurer** (-), freemason.

die **Freimaurerei,** freemasonry.

freimaurerisch, *adj.* masonic.

die **Freimaurerloge** (-n), masonic lodge.

freimündig, *adj.* free-spoken, uninhibited.

freimütig, *adj.* candid, frank.

die **Freimütigkeit,** ingenuousness.

der **Freisinn,** enlightenment, broad-mindedness.

freisinnig, *adj.* freethinking, broad-minded.

freisprechen, 1. *ir.v.a.* to acquit, to absolve. 2. *n.,* die **Freisprechung,** acquittal; absolution; emancipation.

der **Freistaat** (-en), republic; free state.

die **Freistadt, die Freistätte,** sanctuary, refuge, asylum. (Num. 35:6)

der **Freitod,** suicide.

freiwillig, *adj.* voluntary, spontaneous. (I Chron. 29:9)

die **Freizeit,** spare time, leisure.

fremd, *adj.* strange, foreign; unknown, unfamiliar; unusual, peculiar, exotic. (Gen. 15:13)

die **Fremdherrschaft,** foreign rule.

der **Fremdling** (-e), stranger, foreigner, alien. (Exod. 2:22)

die **Fremdsprache** (-n), foreign language.

fressen, 1. *ir.v.a. & n.* (*aux.* h.) to eat (of beasts); to feed; to devour, to consume, to destroy. 2. *n.* feed, food, fodder (for beasts). (Gen. 41:4)

der **Fresser** (-), glutton; voracious eater. (Matt. 11:19)

die **Freude** (-n), joy, gladness; delight, pleasure, satisfaction; enjoyment, comfort. (Luke 1:14)

freudearm, *adj.* joyless.

die **Freudenbotschaft,** glad tidings.

das **Freudenopfer** (-), thank offering.

freudenreich, *adj.* joyous.

der **Freudentag** (-e), day of rejoicing, red-letter day.

freudestrahlend, *adj.* beaming with joy, radiant.

freudig, *adj.* joyful, joyous, glad, cheerful.

die **Freudigkeit,** joyousness. (Acts 4:13)

freuen, 1. *v.a. & (usually) imp.* to make glad, to gladden, to give pleasure to, to delight. 2. *v.r.* to rejoice, to be glad. (Acts 16:34)

Freund

fügen

der Freund (-e), friend. (Exod. 33:11)

die Freundin (-nen), girl friend, lady friend (when used by men); friend (when used by women). (Luke 15:9)

freundlich, *adj.* friendly, kind, amiable; pleasant, cheerful. (Gen. 31:24)

die Freundlichkeit, kindness, friendliness, pleasantness. (II Cor. 6:6)

die Freundschaft, friendship; intimacy, acquaintance; friends, acquaintances; amity. (Gen. 12:1)

der Frevel (-), outrage, crime, misdeed; sacrilege, violation; wantonness, wickedness; mischief. (Gen. 6:11)

freveln, *v.n.* (*aux.* h.) to commit a crime, offense, or outrage (*gegen* or *wider einen*).

der Friede(n), peace; tranquility; harmony. (Gen. 15:15)

der Friede(ns)fürst, Prince of Peace; Christ. (Isa. 9:5)

friedfertig, *adj.* peaceable, peace-loving. (Matt. 5:9)

der Friedhof (ᵉe), churchyard, cemetery, burial ground.

friedlich, *adj.* peaceable, peaceful, pacific.

die Friedlichkeit, peacefulness, peaceableness.

friedlos, *adj.* quarrelsome; outlawed, outcast, proscribed.

friedsam, *adj.* peaceable, peaceful, pacific. (Heb. 12:11)

frisch, *adj.* fresh, cool, refreshing; new, unused, recent; sharp, brisk, vigorous. (Ps. 23:2)

die Frist (-en), space of time, period, interval; appointed time, term; days of grace. (Gen. 6:3)

frivol, *adj.* frivolous; indecent, obscene.

die Frivolität, frivolity; obscenity.

froh, *adj.* glad, joyful, gay, happy. (Ps. 97:8)

fröhlich, *adj.* cheerful, gay, happy, merry, joyful, gladsome. (Lev. 23:40)

die Fröhlichkeit, cheerfulness, mirth, hilarity, gaiety; gladness, joyfulness.

frohlocken, *v.n.* (*aux.* h.) to rejoice, to exult (at), to triumph (over), to shout for joy. (Ps. 42:5)

frohlocket dem Herrn! rejoice in the Lord!

fromm, *adj.* pious, religious, godly, devout; innocent; harmless; good, gentle; artless. (Gen. 4:7)

die Frömmelei, hypocrisy; bigotry.

frömmeln, *v.n.* (*aux.* h.) to affect piety.

frömmelnd, *pr.p. & adj.* canting, hypocritical.

frömmelnde Sprache, cant.

frommen, *v.n.* (*aux.* h.) (*dat.*) to avail, to profit, to benefit, to be of use. (Prov. 31:18)

die Frömmigkeit, piety, devoutness, godliness, innocence; meekness.

der Frömmling (-e), hypocrite; devotee.

die Fron (-en), compulsory, enforced, or statute labor; (*fig.*) drudgery.

der Fronaltar, high (or holy) altar.

das Fronamt, high mass.

die Fronarbeit (-en), socage, statute labor; drudgery.

der Frondienst (-e), compulsory service, statute labor.

der Fronknecht (-e), serf.

der Fronleichnam, Corpus Christi.

der Fronvogt (ᵉe), taskmaster.

der Frost (ᵉe), frost; cold, chill, coldness; apathy; feverish shivering. (Ps. 147:17)

die Frostigkeit, coolness.

die Frucht (ᵉe), fruit, crop, harvest; produce; corn, grain; result, effect, product, profit. (Gen. 1:11)

fruchtbar, *adj.* fruitful, fertile, prolific, productive. (Gen. 1:22)

früh, frühe, *adj.* early; in the morning; soon, speedy; premature. (Gen. 22:3)

das Frühgebet, morning prayer, matins.

der Frühgottesdienst (-e), morning service.

die Frühmesse (-n), early mass, matins.

der Frühregen (-), the first rain. (Deut. 11:14)

der Fuchs (ᵉe), fox; fox fur. (Judg. 15:4)

die Fuge (-n), joint, seam; gap, space (where bricks, etc., should join). (Col. 2:19)

fügen, 1. *v.a.* to fit together, to join, to unite; to ordain, to direct, to dispose; to add; *wie Gott es fügt,* as God ordains. 2. *v.r.* to accommodate oneself to; to acquiesce in, to submit to; to be fitted, suitable, or proper; to come to pass, to happen; to coincide. (Jer. 50:5)

53

fühlen, 1. *v.a. & n. (aux.* h.) to feel, to perceive, to sense, to be sensitive to; to experience, to be aware of. 2. *v.r.* to feel, to have a feeling, to consider or believe oneself to be, to be conscious of one's worth. (Mark 5:29)

führen, 1. *v.a.* to conduct, to lead, to guide, to direct, to convey, to carry, to bring; to control; to drive. 2. *v.r.* to conduct oneself, to behave. (Gen. 5:24)

die Fülle, abundance; profusion, plenty, fullness, plumpness; intensity, body, depth. (Lev. 26:5)

füllen, *v.a.* to fill, to fill up, to put in, to inflate, to pour in, to charge. (Gen. 1:28)

das Füllen (-), foal; filly (*f.*); colt (*m.*). (Gen. 49:11)

das Fundament (-e), foundation, basis, base.

der Fundamentalismus, fundamentalism.

fundamentalistisch, *adj.* fundamentalistic.

fünf, *num. adj.* five. (Matt. 14:17)

fünfmal, five times. (II Cor. 11:24)

für, 1. *prep. (acc.)* for; instead of, in lieu of; per, in favor of; for the sake of, on behalf of. 2. *adv.* (poetic & archaic instead of *vor;* e.g., *sich herfür drängen, fürnehm, fürtrefflich) für und für,* for ever and ever. (Exod. 3:15)

die Fürbitte, intercession. (II Cor. 1:11)

die Furche (-n), furrow; wrinkle, groove, channel; ridge. (Ps. 65:11)

die Furcht, (*no pl.*) fear, anxiety, terror, dread, fright, awe. (Gen. 9:2)

furchtbar, *adj.* frightful, terrible, awful, dreadful; formidable, fearful.

fürchten, 1. *v.a. & n. (aux.* h.) to fear, to be afraid of; to dread, to stand in awe of. 2. *v.r.* to be afraid, to stand in fear (*vor,* of). (Gen. 15:1)

die Furchtlosigkeit, fearlessness.

furchtsam, *adj.* timid, timorous, nervous, fearful, faint-hearted. (Matt. 8:26)

die Furchtsamkeit, timidity, faint-heartedness; cowardice.

fürder, 1. *adj.* further, onwards. 2. *adv.* henceforward; further. (Heb. 10:26)

das Fürsichsein, independent being (Hegel).

die Fürsorge, precaution; care, solicitude; provision.

die Fürsprache, intercession, defense.

der Fürsprecher, intercessor; advocate.

der Fürst (-en), prince, sovereign. (Gen. 23:6)

das Fürstenhaus (¨er), **der Fürstenstamm** (¨e), royal line, dynasty.

das Fürstentum (¨er), principality. (Rom. 8:38)

die Fürstin (-nen), princess. (Isa. 49:23)

fürstlich, *adj.* princely. (Isa. 32:8)

fürwahr, *adv.* truly, in truth, indeed, verily, forsooth. (Isa. 45:15)

der Fuß (¨e), foot; footing, basis, base; leg (of chair, etc.); pedestal; bottom; pedal; stem (of a glass); foot (measure). (Gen. 8:9)

der Fußfall (¨e), prostration.

fußfällig, *adj.* prostrate, on one's knees.

der Fußschemel (-), footstool.

die Fußsohle (-n), sole of the foot. (Deut. 28:35)

die Fußspur (-en), footprint, footstep, track.

der Fußsteig (-e), footway, footpath; sidewalk. (Ps. 17:5)

die Fuß(s)tapfe (-n), footprint, footstep, track. (Ps. 65:12)

die Fußwaschung (-en), foot washing.

das Futter, food, fodder, feed; provender, forage. (Ps. 147:9)

Gg

die Gabe (-n), gift, present, donation; alms, offering; dose; talent, endowment. (Ps. 68:19)

die Gabel (-n), fork, pitchfork; prong; bracket. (I Sam. 13:21)

der Gabenbringer, der Gabenspender (-), dispenser of gifts, almsgiver.

gaffen, *v.n.* (*aux.* h.) to gape, to stare. (Isa. 8:22)

der Gaffer (-), gaper, idle onlooker or bystander.

(die) Galater, (*pl.*) Galatians.

das Galban, galbanum. (Exod. 30:34)

der Galgen (-), gallows, gibbet.

die Galgenfrist, short delay, respite.

der Galgenhumor, grim humor.

(das) Galiläa, Galilee.

die Galle (-n), gall, bile; bad temper, asperity, rancor, spite, choler. (Acts 8:23)

gallensüchtig, *adj.* choleric; melancholic; bilious.

der Gallikanismus, Gallicanism.

der Ganerbe (-n), joint heir; coproprietor.

der Gang (-e), 1. *m.* motion, movement, action, working, process, procedure; course (of disease). 2. *adj.* only in *gang und gäbe,* customary, usual, traditional. (Matt. 15:17)

gängeln, 1. *v.n.* (*aux.* h.) to toddle. 2. *v.a.* to lead by the hand, to lead someone like a child; to lead someone by the nose.

ganz, 1. *adj.* whole, entire, undivided, complete, intact, full, total. 2. *adv.* quite, wholly, altogether, entirely, thoroughly, all; perfectly, quite. (Deut. 4:29)
ganz andere, wholly other (Otto); *ganz und gar,* totally, wholly, absolutely.

gar, 1. *adj.* (sufficiently) cooked, tender, well done, well roasted or boiled; purified, refined (of metals); tanned, dressed (of skins); finished, all gone. 2. *adv. & part.*

entirely, fully, absolutely; very, quite, even, at all; perhaps, I hope. (Acts 17:16)

die Garbe (-n), sheaf; burst (of fire); beam (of light). (Gen. 37:7)

das Garn (-e), yarn, thread, twine; net, snare; decoy. (Hab. 1:15)

garstig, *adj.* nasty; ugly; horrid; loathsome, detestable; filthy, foul; obscene.

die Garstigkeit, nastiness; vileness; ugliness; filthiness; obscenity.

der Garten (-), garden. (Gen. 2:8)

der Gärtner (-), gardener. (John 20:15)

die Gasse (-n), lane, alley; street. (Matt. 6:2)

der Gassenbettler (-), tramp.

der Gassenbube (-n), urchin, guttersnipe.

der Gassendieb (-e), pickpocket.

das Gassenvolk, scum of the streets, rabble.

der Gast (-e), guest, visitor; customer; client; stranger. (Lev. 25:23)

gastfrei, *adj.* hospitable. (I Peter 4:9)

die Gastfreundschaft, hospitality.

der Gastgeber (-), host, landlord.

die Gastpredigt (-en), sermon by a visiting clergyman.

das Gastrecht, right to hospitality (of a visitor in a foreign country); guest's or innkeeper's rights.

der Gatte (-n), husband, consort, spouse; mate (of animals); (*pl.*) married people.

die Gattung (-en), kind, class, type, sort; species; genus, race, breed; gender.

die Gattungskritik, form- or species-criticism (Gunkel).

das Gaukelbild (-er), illusion, mirage, phantasm.

die Gaukelei (-en), conjuring, juggling, trick, illusion; fraud, imposture.

der Gaumen (-), palate, roof of the mouth; taste.

der Gauner (-), rogue; swindler, cheat, sharper, trickster.

die Gaunerei (-en), swindling, swindle, trickery, imposture.

der Geächtete (-n), outlaw, proscript.

die Gebäranstalt (-en), maternity home.

die Gebärde (-n), air, bearing, appearance, demeanor; gesture, gesticulation. (Gen. 4:5)

gebaren, 1. *v.r.* to behave, to conduct oneself. 2. *n.* conduct, behavior, deportment.

gebären, 1. *ir.v.a.* to bear, to bring forth, to give birth to. 2. *n.* parturition; childbearing. (Matt. 1:21)

die Gebärerin, woman in labor. (Ps. 48:7)

das Gebäude (-), building, structure, edifice. (Matt. 24:1)

das Gebein (-e), bones; frame, skeleton; (*pl.*) corpse, body, remains. (Eph. 5:30)

geben, 1. *ir.v.a.* to give, to present, to confer, to bestow; to yield, to grant, to furnish, to produce, to emit; to render, to play, to act; to show, to express, to evolve, to prove. 2. *v.r.* to acknowledge oneself to be, to behave as if one is; to submit; to relent; to abate. (Gen. 3:6)
Geben ist seliger denn Nehmen, it is more blessed to give than to receive.

der Geber (-), giver, donor, dispenser, sender.

das Gebet (-e), prayer.
das Tischgebet sprechen, to say grace; *das Gebet des Herrn,* the Lord's Prayer; *sein Gebet verrichten,* to say one's prayers; *ein Gebet sprechen,* to offer prayers; *ins Gebet nehmen,* to question closely.

das Gebetbuch (⸚er), prayer book, breviary.

die Gebetformel, form of prayer.

der Gebetgesang, oratorio.

der Gebetriemen, die Gebetschnur, phylactery.

die Gebetsheilung (-en), faith healing, Christian Science.

das Gebettel, importunity, continual begging.

gebieten, 1. *ir.v.a.* (*einem etwas*) to command, to order, to bid. 2. *v.n.* to lay down the law; to govern, to rule. (Matt. 10:5)

der Gebieter (-), master, lord, commander, ruler, governor. (Isa. 3:12)

gebieterisch, *adj.* domineering, dictatorial; imperious, commanding, imperative.

das Gebirge (-), mountain chain or range, mountains, highlands, rock. (Matt. 2:18)

das Gebiß (-[ss]e), set of teeth; bridle bit. (Isa. 37:29)

das Geblüt, blood, blood system; line, lineage, family, descent, race. (John 1:13)

geboren, *p.p. of* **gebären** *& adj.* born; née; by birth, by nature. (Matt. 1:20)

geborgen, *p.p. of* **bergen** *& adj.: geborgen sein,* to be hidden, to be in safety or out of danger.

die Geborgenheit, (place of) safety or security.

das Gebot (-e), command, order; precept; commandment; advance, bid, offer. (Gen. 26:5)
die zehn Gebote, the Ten Commandments.

geboten, *p.p. of* **bieten** *and* **gebieten,** *& adj.* necessary, imperative.

gebrauchen, *v.a.* to use, to employ, to make use of. (I Cor. 7:31)

gebrechen, 1. *ir.v.n. imp.* (*pres. & imperfect tenses only*) (*dat.*) to lack, to be in need of, to be wanting. 2. *n.* infirmity, malady, weakness, defect. (Matt. 25:9)

gebrechlich, *adj.* frail, sickly, weak, feeble, fragile, infirm. (Dan. 1:4)

die Gebrechlichkeit (-en), frailty, feebleness, weakness, infirmity. (Rom. 15:1)

gebühren, 1. *v.n.* (*aux. h.*) to be due, to belong of right to; to appertain to. 2. *v.r. & imp.* to be fitting or proper, to be becoming. (Matt. 3:15)

gebührenpflichtig, *adj.* liable or subject to tax, postage due.

gebunden, *p.p. of* **binden** *& adj.* bound, obliged; metrical; combined (with), linked (to). (John 11:44)

die Gebundenheit, constraint; subjection; affiliation.
die Gebundenheit der Auffassung, narrowness of conception.

die Geburt (-en), birth, labor, delivery, parturition; offspring; origin, family, descent, extraction. (Matt. 1:1)
nach Christi Geburt, A.D.; *vor Christi Geburt,* B.C.

die Geburtenbeschränkung (-en), **die Geburtenregelung** (-en), birth control.

der Geburtenrückgang (ˉe), fall in the birthrate.

die Geburtenziffer (-n), birthrate.

der Geburtsadel, nobility of birth, inherited nobility.

die Geburtsanzeige (-n), announcement of birth.

das Geburtshaus, birthplace.

die Geburtshelferin (-nen), midwife.

das Geburtsland, native land.

das Geburtsmal (-e), birthmark.

das Geburtsrecht, birthright.

die Geburtsschmerzen, (*pl.*) labor pains.

die Geburtsstadt, native town.

der Geburtstag (-e), birthday.

das Gedächtnis (-se), memory, recollection, remembrance; memorial, monument. (Exod. 12:14)

die Gedächtnisfeier (-n), commemoration.
kirchliche Gedächtnisfeier, memorial service.

die Gedächtnisrede (-n), speech in commemoration.

die Gedächtnisschwäche, loss of memory.

die Gedächtnistafel (-n), memorial tablet.

der Gedächtnistag, anniversary, commemoration day.

das Gedächtniszeichen (-), keepsake, souvenir, token of remembrance.

der Gedanke (-n), thought, conception, idea, notion; design, purpose, plan. (Deut. 31:21)

die Gedankenfreiheit, freedom of thought.

der Gedankenkreis, range of ideas.

gedankenleer, *adj.* void of ideas.

das Gedankenlesen, thought reading.

gedankenlos, *adj.* thoughtless.

die Gedankenlosigkeit, thoughtlessness, frivolity.

die Gedankenlyrik, philosophical or contemplative poetry.

der Gedankenraub, plagiarism.

gedankenreich, *adj.* full of good ideas, fertile in ideas.

der Gedankenreichtum, fertility of the mind.

die Gedankensplitter, (*pl.*) aphorisms.

die Gedankenübertragung, thought transference, telepathy.

die Gedankenwelt, world of ideas, ideal world; range of ideas.

gedanklich, *adj.* mental, intellectual.

gedeihen, 1. *ir.v.n.* (*aux.* s.) to increase, to develop, to grow, to thrive, to prosper, to succeed. 2. *n.* growth, development, vitality, vigor, prosperity, success, increase, advantage. (I Cor. 3:6)
Gott gebe sein Gedeihen dazu! may God grant His blessing on it!

gedeihlich, *adj.* thriving, prosperous; salutary, wholesome.

gedenken, 1. *ir.v.a.* (*aux.* h.) (*gen.*) to bear in mind, to think of, to be mindful of, to remember; to make mention of; to mention (particularly in one's will). 2. *v.a.* (*einem etwas*) to remember to the disadvantage of. 3. *n.* memory. (Gen. 8:1)

die Gedenkfeier (-n), commemoration.

der Gedenkgottesdienst (-e), memorial service.

der Gedenkspruch (ˉe), motto, device.

der Gedenkstein (-e), monument, memorial.

die Gedenktafel (-n), memorial tablet.

der Gedenktag (-e), commemoration day; anniversary.

der Gedenkzettel (-), memorandum.

das Gedicht (-e), poem; (*fig.*) gem, dream.

gedichtet, *p.p.* written, composed (as a poem); packed, sealed, made tight.

die Gedichtform: *in Gedichtform,* in verse.

die Gedichtsammlung (-en), anthology.

gediegen, *adj.* solid, compact, massive; unmixed, pure, native; true, genuine, thorough; sterling; superior.

die Gediegenheit, solidity, purity, genuineness; reliability; intrinsic value.

das Gedinge (-), bargain, contract; piecework; haggling, bargaining.

das Gedränge, crowd, press, throng; need, distress, difficulty, dilemma; crowding, pushing, thrusting.

gedruckt, *p.p. & adj.* printed.

gedrückt, *p.p. & adj.* oppressed, depressed.

das Gedruckte, printed matter, printed papers, print.

die Geduld, patience, forbearance, endurance. (Matt. 18:26)

gedulden, *v.r.* to have patience, to wait patiently.

geduldig, *adj.* patient, forbearing. (Exod. 34:6)

die Gefahr (-en), danger, peril, hazard, risk. (Ps. 73:4)

der Gefährte (-n), companion, comrade, associate. (Luke 2:44)

gefahrvoll, *adj.* perilous, dangerous.

gefallen, 1. *ir.v.n.* (*aux.* h.) (*dat.*) to please. 2. *n.* pleasure, liking, preference. (John 8:29)

gefallen, *p.p. & adj.* fallen, killed in action; degraded, separated.
das Los ist gefallen, the die is cast, there is no going back.

die Gefallene, fallen woman.

gefällig, *adj.* pleasing, pleasant, agreeable, helpful, obliging, kind, complaisant. (Luke 1:75)

die Gefälligkeit, kindness, favor; complaisance.

die Gefallsucht, coquetry.

gefallsüchtig, *adj.* coquettish.

gefangen, *p.p. & adj.* captured, caught, captive, imprisoned. (Ps. 14:7)

der Gefangene (-n), captive, prisoner. (Ps. 126:1)

die Gefangene (-n), female prisoner.

das Gefangenenlager (-), prison camp.

die Gefangennahme, arrest, capture.

die Gefangenschaft, captivity, imprisonment, confinement.

das Gefängnis (-se), prison, jail. (Gen. 39:20)

die Gefängnisstrafe (-n), imprisonment.

das Gefäß (-e), vessel, container, receptacle; handle, hilt (of sword). (Matt. 13:48)

gefaßt, *p.p. & adj.* ready, prepared; composed, calm, collected; written; set (of stones).

das Gefecht (-e), fight, fighting, battle, combat, action, engagement.

das Gefilde, fields, open country, tract of land; domain. (Isa. 40:3)
das Gefilde der Seligen, Elysian Fields.

die Geflissenheit, diligence, assiduity.

geflissentlich, 1. *adj.* wilful, intentional, on purpose, premeditated, with malice aforethought. 2. *adv.* assiduously, diligently.

das Gefolge, train, attendants, suite, entourage, retinue; consequences.

die Gefolgschaft, followers, adherents.

das Gefolgschaftsmitglied (-er), subordinate, member of staff, worker.

der Gefolgsmann (-̈er & -leute), follower; vassal, thane.

gefügig, *adj.* pliant, pliable, flexible; adaptable.

die Gefügigkeit, pliancy, flexibility, adaptability, tractability.

das Gefühl (-e), feeling, sentiment, emotion; touch, sense of feeling, consciousness.
das Gefühl schlechthiniger Abhängigkeit, feeling of absolute dependence (Schleiermacher).

gefühllos, *adj.* unfeeling, heartless, apathetic, numb.

die Gefühllosigkeit, heartlessness; apathy; numbness.

die Gefühlsart, disposition.

gefühlsbetont, *adj.* sentimental, sensitive.

der Gefühlsmensch, emotional character; sentimentalist.

der Gefühlssinn, sense of touch.

gefühlvoll, *adj.* feeling, tender; affectionate, sensitive; full of expression; sentimental.

gegen, 1. *prep.* (*acc.*) towards, to, in the direction of; against, opposed to, contrary to, over against, opposite to; compared with; in the presence of; in exchange, in return for. 2. *adv. & as accented prefix,* contrary, opposing, counter, etc.

das Gegenbild, contrast; counterpart; antitype. (Heb. 9:24)

die Gegenforderung (-en), counterclaim, setoff.

der Gegengruß (-̈e), greeting in return.

die Gegenliebe, mutual love.

das Gegenmittel (-), remedy, antidote.

die Gegenpartei (-en), (party in) opposition.

die Gegenrede (-n), contradiction; reply, counterplea, replication.

die Gegenreformation, Counter Reformation.

die Gegenrevolution, counterrevolution.

der Gegensatz, antithesis; contrast; opposition.

gegensätzlich, *adj.* contrary, adverse, opposite.

der Gegenstand (ᵆe), subject; object; matter; affair.

die Gegenstimme (-n), dissentient voice.

der Gegenstrom (ᵆe), **die Gegenströmung** (-en), eddy, countercurrent.

die Gegenstrophe (-n), antistrophe.

das Gegenstück (-e), counterpart; antithesis; companion picture or piece, the other one of a pair.

das Gegenteil, opposite, contrary, reverse, converse.

gegenteilig, *adj.* contrary, to the contrary, opposite.

die Gegenüberstellung (-en), opposition; comparison; contrast; antithesis; confrontation.

das Gegenverhör (-e), cross-examination.

die Gegenwart, presence. (II Cor. 10:10)

die Gegenwirkung (en), reaction, counteraction, countereffect.

das Gegenzeugnis (-se), counterevidence, contradictory evidence.

der Gegner (-), opponent, adversary, enemy, foe.

gegnerisch, *adj.* hostile, antagonistic, opposing, adverse.

das Gehabe, fussy, affected, or pretentious behavior, mannerisms.

gehaben, 1. *ir.v.r.* (*pres. only*) to conduct oneself, to behave; *gehabt euch wohl!* farewell! 2. *n.* behavior.

geharnischt, *p.p. & adj.* armored, violent (of words); fiery, testy, barbed, stinging.

gehässig, *adj.* spiteful, malicious, odious.

die Gehässigkeit, hatefulness, odiousness; spitefulness, animosity, malice.

geheim, *adj.* secret; private, confidential; hidden, concealed.
die geheime Offenbarung, Apocalypse.

der Geheimbund (ᵆe), secret society; underground organization; clandestine alliance.

der Geheimbündler (-), member of a secret society.

die Geheimhaltung, secrecy.

die Geheimlehre (-n), esoteric doctrine.

das Geheimnis (-se), secret, mystery; secrecy; arcanum.

die Geheimschreibekunst, cryptography.

der Geheimschreiber (-), private secretary, confidential clerk.

die Geheimschrift (-en), cipher, code, secret writing.

das Geheimsiegel (-), privy seal.

geheimtuerisch, *adj.* secretive.

gehen, 1. *ir.v.n.* (*aux.* s.) to go, to move, to walk, to proceed, to pass; to leave, to go away; to extend to, to reach; to run; to work (of machinery); to succeed (*imp. with dat.*); to go or fare with, to be (in health, etc.). 2. *n.* walking. (Deut. 18:10)

der Gehenkte (-n), person who is hanged. (Deut. 21:23)

geheuer, *adj.* (*only neg.*): *nicht geheuer,* uncanny, haunted.

das Geheul, howling, lamentation, yelling.

der Gehilfe (-n), assistant, help, helper; aide-de-camp. (Col. 4:11)

die Gehilfin (-nen), assistant, help, helper. (Gen. 2:18)

das Gehirn (-e), brain; brains, sense.

der Gehirnschlag, cerebral apoplexy.

gehorchen, *v.n.* (*aux.* h.) (*dat.*) to obey. (Exod. 19:5)

gehören, 1. *v.n.* (*aux.* h.) (*dat.*) to belong to, to be owned by, to be part of, to appertain to; to be due to. 2. *v.r. & imp.* to be suitable or proper or becoming. (Luke 15:12)

gehörlos, *adj.* deaf.

gehorsam, 1. *adj.* obedient, dutiful; submissive; obsequious. 2. *m.* obedience, dutifulness. (Eph. 6:5)

der Geier (-), vulture, hawk.

geil, *adj.* luxuriant, rank, voluptuous; lustful, lascivious. (Rom. 13:14)

geilen, 1. *v.n.* (*aux.* h.) to lust, to be lascivious; to ask for presents (in an importunate way). 2. *n.* lasciviousness; importunity. (Luke 11:8)

die Geißel (-n), lash, whip; (*fig.*) scourge; cutting reproach or sarcasm. (John 2:15) *Gottes Geißel,* the scourge of God (Attila).

der Geist (-er), spirit, mind, intellect, intelligence, wit, imagination; genius, soul; morale; essence; ghost, spirit, specter. (Gen. 6:3) *der heilige Geist,* the Holy Ghost; *der Geist, der stets verneint,* the spirit of negation; *der Geist Gottes,* the Spirit of God.

geisterähnlich, *adj.* spectral.

der Geisterbann, die Geisterbannung, die Geisterbeschwörung, exorcism.

der Geisterbanner, der Geisterbeschwörer (-), necromancer, exorcist.

das Geisterbild, phantom.

geisterbleich, *adj.* pale as a ghost.

die Geistererscheinung (-en), apparition.

die Geistergeschichte (-n), ghost story.

der Geisterglaube, belief in ghosts.

geisterhaft, *adj.* supernatural; ghostly; ghostlike.

das Geisterreich (-e), spirit world, the realm of spirits.

der Geisterseher (-), visionary, seer.

die Geisterseherei, second sight.

die Geisterstunde, witching hour.

die Geisterwelt, spirit world.

geistesabwesend, *adj.* absent-minded.

die Geistesarbeit, brain work.

geistesarm, *adj.* poor in spirit, stupid.

die Geistesbildung, cultivation of the mind.

der Geistesblitz, brain wave; stroke of genius.

die Geistesfähigkeiten, (*pl.*) intellectual powers.

die Geistesfreiheit, freedom of thought or conscience.

die Geistesfrucht, literary or artistic production.

der Geistesfunke (-n), flash of wit.

die Geistesgegenwart, presence of mind.

die Geistesgeschichte, history of ideas.

geistesgestört, *adj.* deranged, unhinged.

die Geistesgröße, intellectual greatness; intellectual giant; magnanimity.

die Geisteshaltung, mentality, attitude of mind.

der Geistesheld (-en), intellectual, literary, or artistic giant.

die Geisteskraft ("-e), mental power or vigor.

geisteskrank, *adj.* of unsound mind, insane.

die Geisteskrankheit (-en), mental disorder, insanity.

geistesschwach, *adj.* feeble-minded.

die Geistesschwäche (-n), imbecility.

die Geistesstörung (-en), mental derangement; mental disorder.

die Geistesverfassung, state of mind, frame of mind.

geistesverwandt, *adj.* congenial.

die Geistesverwirrung (-en), mental disturbance or unbalance.

die Geisteswissenschaften, (*pl.*) the arts (contrasted with the sciences).

die Geisteszerrüttung (-en), mental disturbance.

der Geisteszustand, mental health or state.

geistig, *adj.* spiritual, mental, intellectual; spirituous, volatile, alcoholic.

die Geistigkeit, spirituality; intellectuality; alcoholic content.

geistlich, *adj.* spiritual, religious, sacred; clerical, ecclesiastical. (Matt. 5:3) *die geistliche Behörde,* the ecclesiastical authorities; *geistliche Güter,* church lands; *geistlicher Herr,* clerical gentleman; *geistliche Kurfürsten,* spiritual electors; *geistliches Lied,* sacred song; *geistliche Musik,* sacred music; *geistliches Recht,* canon law; *in den geistlichen Stand treten,* to take (holy) orders, to enter the church.

der Geistliche (-n), clergyman, minister, priest, pastor, ecclesiastic, divine.

die Geistlichkeit, spirituality; priesthood, clergy, the church; worship. (Col. 2:18)

geistlos, *adj.* dull, lifeless, spiritless; senseless, unintellectual.

die Geistlosigkeit, dullness, mental sluggishness, lifelessness, spiritlessness.

geistreich, geistvoll, *adj.* ingenious, witty, clever, gifted.

geisttötend, *adj.* soul-destroying.

der Geiz, avarice; greediness, covetousness, stinginess; inordinate desire. (Exod. 18:21)

der Geizhals (-̈e), **der Geizhammel** (-), **der Geizkragen** (-), miser, niggard.

geizig, *adj.* avaricious, covetous, stingy, miserly, niggardly. (Gal. 5:26)

der Gekreuzigte, the crucified. (Matt. 28:5)

gelangen, *v.n.* (*aux.* s.) to reach, to arrive (at), to attain (to), to get admitted to. (Phil. 3:11)

gelassen, *p.p. & adj.* calm, cool, composed, collected; passive, patient; deliberate.

gelaunt, *adj.* disposed; *gut gelaunt,* in good humor.

das Geläute, ringing or peal of bells, chime.

das Geld (-er), coin; money; cash. (Gen. 44:1)

gelegen, *p.p. of* **liegen** *& adj.* situated; (*with dat.*) convenient, opportune, fit, proper. (Acts 24:25)

die Gelegenheit, occasion, opportunity; favorable moment. (Matt. 26:16)

die Gelehrsamkeit, learning, erudition, scholarship.

gelehrt, *adj.* learned, scholarly, erudite.

der Gelehrte (-n), man of learning, scholar, savant.

die Gelehrtenkreise, (*pl.*) scholars, the learned world.

der Gelehrtenstand, the learned professions.

der Gelehrtenverein (-e), literary society or club.

die Gelehrtenwelt, the learned world, scholarly circles, literary and scientific world.

die Gelehrtenzeitung (-en), scholarly journal.

geleiten, *v.a.* to accompany, to conduct, to escort, to convoy. (Acts 17:15)
Gott geleite dich! God speed you; God be with you!

das Gelenk (-e), joint, articulation; wrist; link (of a chain); hinge. (Gen. 32:26)

der Geliebte, lover, beloved, sweetheart, love, darling. (Isa. 5:1)
meine Geliebten! dearly beloved brethren!

die Geliebte, sweetheart, darling; mistress.

gelind(-e), *adj.* soft, gentle, light, lenient, mild, tender, smooth. (I Tim. 3:3)

gelingen, 1. *ir.v.n. & imp.* (*aux.* s.) (*dat.*) to succeed (in doing), to manage (to do); to prosper. 2. *n.* success. (Isa. 55:11)

gellen, *v.n.* (*aux.* h.) to sound shrill, to jar, to resound; to sing (of ears). (I Sam. 3:11)

geloben, *v.a.* to promise solemnly, to vow, to pledge. (Deut. 23:24)
mit Hand und Mund or *in die Hand geloben,* to take a solemn oath; *das gelobte Land,* the Promised Land, the Holy Land.

das Gelöbnis (-se), solemn promise, vow.

gelten, *ir.v.n.* (*aux.* h.) to mean, to matter, to carry weight; to be worth, to be of or have value; to be valid, to hold good; to be current, to pass for, to be considered (as); to concern, to apply to, to be intended for, to be aimed at, to be the question of. (Matt. 13:57)
der Prophet gilt nichts in seinem Vaterlande, a prophet is without honor in his own country; *bei Gott gilt kein Ansehen der Person,* God is no respecter of persons.

die Geltung, value, worth, importance; currency; respect, recognition.

das Gelübde (-), vow. (Acts 18:18)

das Gelübdeopfer (-), votive offering.

das Gelüst (-e), desire, longing, appetite; lust. (Rom. 1:24)

gelüsten, *v. imp. n.* (*aux.* h.) to desire, to long for, to hanker after. (Exod. 20:17)

gemach, 1. *adj.* comfortable, convenient, easy. 2. *adv.* softly, quietly, gently; gradually, by degrees, slowly. 3. *n.* (-̈er) room, apartment, chamber. (Acts 12:7)

der Gemahl (-e), husband, consort.

die Gemahlin (-nen), wife, spouse; consort.

das Gemäß, 1. *n.* (-e) measure, moderation; measuring vessel. 2. *adj.* suitable, conformable. 3. *prep.* (*with preceding or following dat.*) according to, conformably to, in conformity with, in consequence of. (I Tim. 6:3)

gemein, *adj.* common, general, ordinary; low, vulgar, mean, base; belonging in common to; kind, friendly, condescending. (Matt. 28:15)

die Gemeinde (-n), community; municipality; corporate body; parish; congregation, parishioners. (Matt. 16:18)
die christliche Gemeinde, Christian communion, the church; *von der Gemeinde ausschließen,* to excommunicate.

die Gemeindeabgabe (-n), local rates.

der Gemeindeanger (-), common, village green.

die Gemeindebehörde (-n), corporation, local council, parish council.

der Gemeindebezirk (-e), parish, borough, municipality, district.

das Gemeindehaus (⁻er), parish or village hall.

das Gemeindemitglied (-er), **das Gemeindeglied** (-er), member of a congregation, parishioner.

der Gemeinderat (⁻e), alderman, town councilor; parish council.

der Gemeindeschreiber (-), town clerk.

die Gemeindeverwaltung (-en), local government.

der Gemeindevorstand, local board, town or borough council.

der Gemeindevorsteher (-), mayor.

die Gemeine (-n), *see* **Gemeinde.**

der Gemeingeist, public spirit.

gemeingültig, *adj.* generally admitted, current.

die Gemeinheit, vulgarity, coarseness, commonness; baseness, mean trick, vileness.

der Gemeinnutz, common good.

die Gemeinnützigkeit, voluntary social work, private charity.

gemeinsam, *adj.* held in common, common, joint, mutual, combined, together.

die Gemeinsamkeit, community, common possession; mutuality.

die Gemeinschaft, community; mutual participation, common possession or interest; communion; partnership, association. (Acts 2:42)

gemeinschaftlich, *adj.* common, mutual; joint, collective, in common.

die Gemeinschaftlichkeit, community of possession; solidarity.

die Gemeinschaftsarbeit, cooperative work.

der Gemeinsinn, public spirit.

der Gemeinspruch (⁻e), common saying.

die Gemse (-n), chamois. (Ps. 104:18)

das Gemurmel, murmuring, muttering, murmur.

das Gemüt (-er), mind, soul, heart, disposition, spirit, feeling, temper; (*fig.*) person, individual, soul. (Matt. 22:37)

die Gemütlichkeit, good-natured, sanguine, or easygoing disposition; good nature, kindliness, geniality; comfort, coziness.
in Geldsachen hört die Gemütlichkeit auf, business is business.

gemütlos, *adj.* devoid of feeling; unfeeling.

die Gemütsanlage, die Gemütsart, die Gemütsbeschaffenheit, character, disposition, turn of mind, temperament.

gemütskrank, *adj.* melancholic.

die Gemütskrankheit, melancholia.

die Gemütslage, frame of mind.

das Gemütsleben, inner life.

die Gemütsregung (-en), emotion.

die Gemütsruhe, composure, calmness, peace of mind.

die Gemütsstimmung, die Gemütsverfassung, der Gemütszustand, frame of mind, humor.

gemütvoll, *adj.* cheerful, kindly, affectionate; agreeable.

geneigt, *p.p. & adj.* (with *zu*) inclined to, disposed to; having a propensity for. (Rom. 1:15)

die Geneigtheit, inclination, propensity, favor; affection; benevolence; slope, incline.

genesen, *ir.v.n.* (*aux.* s.) to get well or better, to recover, to convalesce. (Gen. 32:31)

die Genesung, recovery; convalescence.

das Genie (-s), genius, capacity; man of genius.

genießen, *ir.v.a.* (*aux.* h.) to eat or drink; to take (nourishment); to enjoy, to have the benefit or use of. (Isa. 1:19)

der Genius (*Genien*), spirit, guardian angel.

der Genosse (-en), comrade, companion, colleague, partner, associate. (Gal. 6:10)

genug, *indec. adj.* (*orig. with gen. & still in some idioms*) enough, sufficient, sufficiently. (Gen. 45:28)

die Genüge, enough; a sufficient amount. (John 10:10)

genügen,, *v.a.* (*aux.* h.) to be enough, to suffice, to satisfy; (*with dat.*) *genügen lassen* (*an*), to be satisfied with. (Luke 3:14)

genugsam, *adj.* sufficient, plentiful. (Matt. 3:11)

genügsam, *adj.* easily satisfied; contented; unassuming, modest, moderate; frugal.

die Genügsamkeit, moderation; contentedness.

genugtuend, *adj.* giving satisfaction, satisfying, satisfactory; atoning.

genugtun, *v.n.* to give satisfaction, to satisfy.

die Genugtuung, satisfaction, compensation; amends, atonement, reparation.

der Genuß (¨[ss]e), enjoyment, pleasure, delight, gratification, profit, use; taking, partaking (of food, etc.).

der Genußmensch (-en), epicure, epicurean, voluptuary.

genußreich, *adj.* delightful, enjoyable.

die Genußsucht, craving for pleasure, epicureanism.

genußsüchtig, *adj.* epicurean, sensual.

das Gepränge, pageantry, pomp, splendor, ostentatious display.

gerade, 1. *adj.* straight, direct; erect, upright; straightforward, honest; even (numbers). 2. *adv.* quite, exactly, just, directly. 3. *f.* straightness; straight line. (Acts 9:11)

geradeaus, *adv.* straight ahead or on, right ahead.

die Geradheit, straightness; uprightness (of character); evenness (of a number); rectitude.

das Gerät (-e), implement, tool, instrument; utensil, vessel; effects, chattels; appliances; furniture; equipment, apparatus. (Isa. 52:11)

geraten, 1. *ir.v.n.* (*aux.* s.) to get, fall, or come into, to, or upon; to hit (upon); (*with dat.*) to turn out (well), to prosper, to succeed, to thrive; to prove to be. 2. *p.p. of* **raten** & **geraten,** & *adj.* successful, prosperous; advisable, advised; guessed. (I Cor. 8:9)

der Gerber (-), tanner. (Acts 9:43)

die Gerberei (-en), tannery; tanning.

gerecht, *adj.* just, fair, righteous, upright; legitimate, lawful; fit, right, suitable; skilled. (Deut. 32:4)

der Gerechte (-n), just, righteous, upright. (Gen. 18:23)

die Gerechtigkeit, justice, right; righteousness, fairness, justness; justification. (Gen. 15:6)

das Gerede, talk; report, rumor.

gereichen, *v.n.* (*aux.* h.) to bring about, to cause, to contribute to, to redound to; to turn out to be, to prove to be. (Rom. 7:10)

gereuen, *v.a. imp.* to cause repentance; *es gereut mich,* I repent (of), I am sorry (for). (Matt. 27:3)

das Gericht (-e), court of justice; judgment, jurisdiction, tribunal; dish, course. (Matt. 5:21)
das Jüngste Gericht, the last judgment, doomsday.

die Gerichtsbarkeit, jurisdiction.

der Gerichtsgang, legal procedure.

der Gerichtshandel, lawsuit.

der Gerichtsherr (-en), magistrate, judge.

der Gerichtshof (¨e), law courts, court of justice, tribunal.

die Gerichtsposaune, last trumpet.

der Gerichtsrat (¨e), justice (a title).

der Gerichtssaal (-säle), courtroom.

der Gerichtsvollzieher (-), bailiff, sheriff.

gering, *adj.* small, little, trifling, slight, scanty, petty, unimportant; mean, low, inferior, humble, modest. (Gen. 32:11)

geringfügig, *adj.* insignificant, unimportant, trifling, trivial, petty.

die Geringfügigkeit, insignificance, paltriness; trifle.

geringschätzen, *v.a.* to esteem lightly, to attach little value to, to think little of, to scorn, to despise.

geringschätzig, *adj.* deprecatory, derogatory, disdainful, scornful.

das Gerippe (-), skeleton; framework.

gern(e), *adv.* (comp. *lieber;* sup. *am liebsten*) with pleasure, willingly, gladly, readily; often. (Gen. 46:30)

das Gerstenbrot (-e), barley bread, barley loaf. (John 6:9)

die Gerstenernte, barley harvest. (Ruth 1:23)

der Geruch (⁻e), smell, odor, aroma, scent, fragrance, savor; (*fig.*) reputation; sense of smell. (Gen. 27:27)
im Geruche der Heiligkeit, in the odor of sanctity.

der Geruchssinn (-e), sense of smell.

das Gerücht (-e), rumor, report. (Matt. 4:24)

der Gesalbte, the anointed. (Ps. 2:2)

gesamt, *adj.* whole, entire, complete; united, joint, common; total, collective.

die Gesamtsünde, collective sin.

der Gesamtwille(n), collective will.

der Gesang (⁻e), singing; song; canto. (I Sam. 18:6)
geistliche Gesänge, sacred songs, psalms, hymns.

das Gesangbuch (⁻er), hymnbook, songbook.

der Gesanglehrer (-), singing teacher.

gesanglich, *adj.* vocal, choral.

die Gesangskunst, vocal or choral art.

die Gesangstimme (-n), vocal part.

die Gesangstunde (-n), **der Gesangunterricht,** singing lesson.

der Gesangverein (-e), choral society, glee club.

das Geschaffensein, existence as a created being or thing.

das Geschäft (-e), business, commerce, trade; transaction, deal, dealings, speculation; commercial firm, business house, office, shop; employment, occupation, calling. (Rom. 8:13)

geschehen, 1. *ir.v.n.* (*aux.* s.) to take place, to happen, to come to pass, to occur, to be done. 2. *p.p. & adj.: geschehene Dinge sind nicht zu ändern,* what is done cannot be undone. (Gen. 1:7)

das Geschehnis (-se), happening, event, occurrence.

gescheit, *adj.* clever, intelligent, shrewd, sensible.

die Gescheitheit, discretion; cleverness; common sense.

das Geschenk (-e), present, gift, donation. (Isa. 5:23)
ein Geschenk des Himmels, a heaven-sent blessing.

die Geschichte (-n), history; story; event; affair, business, concern. (Gen. 15:1)

geschichtlich, *adj.* historical, historically true.

die Geschichtlichkeit, authenticity; historical relevance.

das Geschichtsbuch (⁻er), history book; historical work.

die Geschichtsdeutung, interpretation or philosophy of history.

der Geschichtsforscher (-), historian.

die Geschichtsforschung, historical research.

die Geschichtskunde, historical science.

die Geschichtswissenschaft, science of history.

geschickt, *p.p. & adj.* fit, adapted, apt, capable, adept, able, dexterous. (Luke 9:62)

das Geschlecht (-er), sex; genus, kind, species, race, family, stock, generation; gender. (Gen. 12:3)

die Geschlechterkunde, genealogy.

das Geschlechterwesen, aristocracy, patricians.

geschlechtlich, *adj.* sexual; generic.

geschlechtlos, *adj.* asexual; neuter.

der Geschlechtsadel, hereditary nobility, nobility of blood.

der Geschlechtsakt, sexual intercourse, coitus.

das Geschlechtsalter (-), generation.

die Geschlechtsart (-en), genus, kind, species, race; generic character.

der Geschlechtsbaum, pedigree.

die Geschlechtsfolge, lineage.

das Geschlechtsglied (-er), one of a family or generation; sexual organ.

die Geschlechtslinie, lineage, pedigree.

die Geschlechtslust, carnal desire.

das Geschlechtsmerkmal (-e), sex characteristic.

der Geschlechtsname (-n), family name, surname; genus.

das Geschlechtsregister (-), genealogical table, pedigree.

die Geschlechtstafel (-n), genealogical table.

der Geschlechtstrieb, sex instinct or desire.

das Geschluchze, inordinate or prolonged sobbing.

der Geschmack (ˋe), taste, flavor; savor, relish; fancy, liking; good taste.

geschmacklos, *adj.* tasteless, insipid, flat, stale; in bad taste.

die Geschmacklosigkeit, lack of good taste, bad taste.

die Geschmackslehre, esthetics.

das Geschmeide, jewelry, jewels, trinkets. (Isa. 61:10)

der Geschmeidehändler (-), jeweler.

das Geschmeidekästchen (-), jewel case or casket.

geschmeidig, *adj.* soft, supple, pliant, ductile, pliable, flexible; smooth, yielding, versatile.

die Geschmeidigkeit, suppleness, flexibility; softness.

das Geschöpf (-e), creature; production, creation. (Rom. 1:25)

das Geschrei (-e), screams, shrieks, cries, shouting, screaming; outcry, clamor, fuss, ado, stir; disrepute. (Gen. 18:20)

das Geschwätz (-e), idle or empty talk, babble; tittle-tattle, gossiping. (Eph. 4:29)

die Geschwister, (*pl.*) brother(s) and sister(s).

das Geschwisterkind (-er), nephew or niece; first cousin.

gesegnen, *v.a.* (*einem etwas*) to bless. *Gott gesegne es!* God's blessings on His gifts (grace after meal); *gesegneten Leibes,* with child.

der Gesegnete (-n), blessed. (Gen. 24:31)

der Gesell(e) (-en), companion, comrade, partner, mate, fellow, brother member (of a society); journeyman. (Matt. 11:16)

gesellen, *v.a. & r.* to join, to associate, to ally, to associate oneself with; to keep company with. *gleich und gleich gesellt sich gern,* birds of a feather flock together.

gesellig, *adj.* social, sociable; companionable.

die Geselligkeit (-en), sociability, good fellowship, social life.

die Gesellschaft (-en), society, association; fellowship, club; company, partnership; party, social gathering; high society.

der Gesellschafter (-), companion; associate, partner; member of a society or company.

die Gesellschafterin (-nen), lady companion.

gesellschaftlich, *adj.* social, sociable, companionable, gregarious, cooperative.

die Gesellschaftlichkeit, sociable disposition; social life.

der Gesellschaftsgeist, social spirit.

das Gesellschaftsglied (-er), member of a society.

die Gesellschaftslehre, sociology.

die Gesellschaftsschicht (-en), social stratum, group, class.

gesellschaftswidrig, *adj.* antisocial.

die Gesellschaftswissenschaft, sociology.

das Gesetz (-e), law, statute, commandment, decree. (Matt. 5:17) *das göttliche Gesetz,* the divine law.

das Gesetzbuch (ˋer), statute book, book of the law. (II Kings 22:8)

die Gesetzeskraft, force of law, legal power.

gesetzeskundig, *adj.* versed in law.

der Gesetzgeber (-), legislator, lawgiver. (James 4:12)

die Gesetzgebung (-en), legislation.

gesetzkundig, *adj.* versed in law.

gesetzlich, *adj.* legal, statutory, lawful, legitimate.

die Gesetzlichkeit, legality, lawfulness.

gesetzlos, *adj.* lawless, illegal; anarchical.

die Gesetzlosigkeit, lawlessness, illegality; anarchy.

gesetzmäßig, *adj.* lawful, legitimate, legal; according to laws.

gesetzt, *p.p. of* setzen, posited (Hegel).

die Gesetzübertretung (-en), infringement of the law.

der Gesetzvollstrecker (-), executor of the law, sheriff.

gesetzwidrig, *adj.* unlawful, illegal.

das Gesicht, 1. (*no pl.*) sight; eyesight. 2. (-er) face, countenance, visage. 3. (-e) vision. (Acts 10:3)

der Gesichtsausdruck (⁻e), facial expression.

die Gesichtsfarbe (-n), complexion.

der Gesichtskreis, (mental) range, horizon.

der Gesichtspunkt (-e), point of view, viewpoint, aspect.

die Gesichtswahrnehmung (-en), sight, visual perception.

das Gesinde, domestic servants; farmhands. (Matt. 24:45)

das Gesindel, rabble, mob.

der Gesindelohn, servants' wages.

gesinnt, *adj.* minded, disposed, affected. (Phil. 3:15)

die Gesinnung, disposition; sentiment; conviction; intention.

gesinnungslos, *adj.* unprincipled, characterless.

die Gesinnungslosigkeit, lack of character.

gesinnungstreu, *adj.* loyal, truehearted, constant, staunch.

das Gespann (-e), team, horse-drawn vehicle, carriage.

das Gespenst (-er), ghost, specter, phantom. (Matt. 14:26)

gespensterartig, *adj.* spectral.

die Gespenstererscheinung (-en), ghostly apparition, hallucination.

die Gespenstergeschichte (-n), ghost story.

der Gespensterglaube, belief in ghosts.

gespensterhaft, *adj.* ghostly, ghostlike.

das Gespensterreich, spirit world.

das Gespensterschiff (-e), phantom ship.

der Gespensterspuk, witchery.

die Gespensterstunde (-n), witching hour, midnight hour.

gespenstig, gespenstisch, *adj.* ghostly, ghostlike.

das Gespiel, continual playing.

der Gespiele (-n), playmate. (Judg. 11:37)

die Gespielin (-nen), playmate.

das Gespräch (-e), conversation, talk, discussion. (Ps. 19:15)

die Gestalt (-en), form, shape; figure, build, frame, stature. (Luke 3:22)

gestaltet, *p.p. & adj.:* wohl gestalteter Mensch, well-proportioned man.

die Gestaltlehre, morphology.

die Gestaltung (-en), formation, forming, construction, shaping, modeling; form, figure, shape; organization.

die Gestaltungskraft, creative power, power of or gift for organization.

die Gestaltwerdung, emergence, realization, incarnation.

das Gestammel, stammering, stuttering.

gestatten, *v.a.* to permit, to allow, to grant, to consent to. (I Tim. 2:12)

das Gestein (-e), rocks, mineral.

gestern, *adv.* yesterday. (Ps. 90:4)

das Gestirn (-e), star; stars, heavenly body, constellation. (Ps. 74:16)

die Gestirnlehre, astronomy.

gestirnt, *adj.* starry, starred.

gesund, *adj.* healthy, sound, well. (Matt. 10:8)
wieder gesund werden, to get well again, to be restored to health.

der Gesundbeter (-), Christian Scientist.

die Gesundbeterei, faith healing, Christian Science.

die Gesundheit, health; wholesomeness, soundness. (Acts 3:16)

gesundheitlich, *adj.* concerning health; hygienic, sanitary.

gesundheitsschädlich, *adj.* injurious to health, noxious.

das Getränk (-e), drink, beverage. (Luke 1:15)

getrauen, *v.r.* to dare, to venture; to trust, to feel confident.

das Getreide, corn, grain, cereals. (Ps. 72:16)

der Getreidehändler (-), corn merchant.

die Getreidekammer (-n), granary.

getreu, *adj.* faithful, true, trusty, loyal. (Matt. 25:21)

getreulich, *adv.* faithfully, truly, loyally.

getrost, *adj.* confident, hopeful; comforted, of good cheer. (Deut. 31:6)

das Getümmel, tumult; bustle, turmoil. (Matt. 27:24)

das Gewächs (-e), plant, vegetable, herb; vintage, growth; tumor. (II Cor. 9:10)

gewachsen, *p.p. & adj.: einem* or *einer Sache gewachsen sein,* to be a match for someone or equal to something.

die Gewähr, security, surety; warrant, guarantee, bail.

gewähren, *v.a.* (*einem etwas*) to grant, to accord, to concede; to give, to furnish. (Ps. 20:6)

die Gewalt (-en), power, authority, dominion, might; force, violence. (Matt. 20:25)

die Gewaltherrschaft, despotism.

der Gewaltherrscher, despot.

gewaltig, *adj.* powerful, potent, mighty, strong, intense, violent; big, vast, huge, immense. (Ps. 22:13)

das Gewand (-̈er), garment, dress, raiment, robe, vestment. (Rev. 1:13)

das Gewässer (-), waters, flood. (Matt. 7:25)
die Gewässer fallen, the floods subside.

das Gewerbe (-), trade, business, profession, industry, vocation, occupation. (I Tim. 6:5)

das Gewicht (-e), weight, heaviness; gravity, importance, load. (Deut. 25:15)

der Gewinn (-e), gaining, winning; earnings, gain, profit, prize; yield, proceeds, produce. (I Tim. 6:6)

gewinnen, 1. *ir.v.a.* to win, to gain, to obtain, to earn; to prevail over, to conquer; to produce, to reclaim; *Boden gewinnen,* to gain ground. 2. *v.n.* (*aux. h.*) *an Klarheit gewinnen,* to gain in clarity. (Matt. 16:26)

der Gewinst (-e), winnings, takings, gain, profit. (Acts 16:16)

gewiß, 1. *adj.* sure, certain, assured, positive, true, undoubted; stable, steady, fixed. 2. *adv.* certainly, surely, indeed, to be sure, no doubt. (Gen. 28:16)

das Gewissen, conscience. (I Cor. 8:7)

gewissenhaft, *adj.* conscientious; scrupulous.

die Gewissenhaftigkeit, conscientiousness.

gewissenlos, *adj.* unprincipled, unscrupulous.

die Gewissenlosigkeit, lack of principle, unscrupulousness.

die Gewissensangst, qualms of conscience.

der Gewissensbiß, twinge of conscience.

die Gewissensbisse, (*pl.*) pangs of conscience; remorse.

die Gewissensehe, morganatic marriage, cohabitation.

die Gewissensfrage, moral issue, difficult case, question of conscience.

die Gewissensfreiheit, freedom of conscience.

der Gewissensfreund, spiritual father, father confessor.

die Gewissenslehre, casuistry.

die Gewissenspflicht, bounden duty.

die Gewissensprüfung, self-examination.

die Gewissensrüge, remorse.

die Gewissensrührung, compunction.

die Gewissensskrupel, (*pl.*) moral scruples.

der Gewissensvorwurf, self-reproach.

der Gewissenszwang, moral constraint.

der Gewissenszweifel (-), doubt, scruple, qualm.

die Gewißheit, certainty, assurance, proof.

gewißlich, *adv.* certainly, surely, assuredly. (I Tim. 3:1)

das Gewitter (-), thunderstorm, tempest, storm.

gewöhnen, *v.a. & r.* to accustom, to habituate; to inure, to familiarize, to train, to break in; to domesticate. (Prov. 22:6)

die Gewohnheit (-en), habit, custom, usage, fashion. (Matt. 27:15)
zur Gewohnheit werden, to grow into a habit; *aus Gewohnheit,* from habit.

gewohnheitsmäßig, 1. *adj.* customary, habitual, routine. 2. *adv.* as is the (his, their) custom.

der Gewohnheitsmensch (-en), creature or slave of habit.

die Gewohnheitssünde (-n), habitual or besetting sin.

die Gewöhnung, custom, habit; accustoming, habituation.

das Gewölbe (-), vault, arch; cellar.

das Gewürm, worms; reptiles; vermin. (Gen. 1:24)

das Gewürz (-e), spice, condiment, seasoning.

das Gezänke, quarrel, squabble; quarreling, wrangling. (I Tim. 6:20)

das Gezelt (-e), tent, canopy. (Ps. 18:12)

die Gicht, (*no pl.*) gout, arthritis.

gichtbrüchig, *adj.* paralytic, palsied. (Matt. 8:6)
der Gichtbrüchige, the man of the palsy.

die Gichtbrüchigkeit, palsy.

gießen, 1. *ir.v.a.* to pour, to water, to shed, to spill, to sprinkle; to cast, to mold, to found. 2. *v.n.imp.: es gießt,* it is pouring. (Gen. 28:18)

das Gift (-e), poison, toxin, virus, venom. (James 3:8)

giftig, *adj.* poisonous, venomous, virulent, toxic; pernicious; malignant, spiteful; angry, furious. (Rom. 1:29)

girren, *v.n.* (*aux.* h.) to coo.

das Gitter (-), grating, lattice, railing, bars, fence, trellis. (Judg. 5:28)

der Glanz, brightness, luster, gleam, gloss, glossiness, polish, glitter, shine; splendor, glamor, distinction, magnificence. (Isa. 60:3)

glänzen, 1. *v.n.* (*aux.* h.) to shine, to glitter, to glisten, to gleam, to sparkle; to be distinguished or outstanding; *es ist nicht alles Gold, was glänzt,* all is not gold that glitters. 2. *v.a.* to gloss, to glaze; to polish, to burnish. (Exod. 34:29)

glänzend, *pr.p. & adj.* shiny, shining, glossy, glittering, lustrous, brilliant, splendid. (Dan. 2:31)

die Glanzperiode (-n), most brilliant period.

der Glanzpunkt, brightest point, climax.

die Glanzseite (-n), bright side.

das Glas (¨er), glass; drinking glass, tumbler, container; mirror, (*pl.*) eyeglasses. (Matt. 26:7)

gläsern, *adj.* of glass; vitreous, glassy, crystalline. (Rev. 4:6)

glatt, 1. *adj.* smooth, even, flat, flush; polished, slippery, glossy; plain, bare; sleek; (*fig.*) bland, oily, flattering, sweet. 2. *adv.* smoothly; quite, entirely; plainly; unhesitatingly. (Ps. 55:22)

der Glaube(n), (*no pl.*) faith, confidence, trust, belief, credence; religious faith, creed. (Matt. 8:10)
einen Glauben annehmen, to embrace a faith; *einen Glauben bekennen,* to profess a religion; *in gutem Glauben,* in good faith; *etwas in gutem Glauben tun,* to do something with no ulterior motives or without mental reservations; *(einem* or *einer Behauptung) Glauben schenken,* to give credence to (someone or an assertion); *der Glaube macht selig,* faith alone makes happy; *seinen Glauben verleugnen,* to abjure one's faith, to become an apostate.

glauben, *v.a. & n.* (*aux.* h.) to believe, to trust, to have faith in, to give credence to; to think, to suppose, to imagine. (Matt. 8:13)
ich glaubte ihn gerettet, I thought he was saved; *wenn man es ihm glauben soll,* if he is to be believed; *an eine Sache glauben,* to believe in something; *an einen glauben,* to have faith in someone; *einem glauben,* to believe someone; *an Gott glauben,* to believe or trust in God.

der Glaubensabfall, apostasy.

der Glaubensakt, act of faith.

die Glaubensänderung, change of faith.

der Glaubensartikel (-), article of faith.

das Glaubensbekenntnis (-se), confession of faith, creed.
das apostolische Glaubensbekenntnis, the Apostles' Creed.

der Glaubensbote (-n), apostle.

der Glaubensbruder (¨), coreligionist; fellow believer.

der Glaubenseifer, religious zeal.

die Glaubensfreiheit, religious liberty.

der Glaubensgenosse (-n), coreligionist; fellow believer.

die Glaubensgenossenschaft, community of faith.

die Glaubensgerechtigkeit, righteousness of faith.

das Glaubensgericht, inquisition.

die Glaubensheuchelei, hypocrisy.

der Glaubensheuchler, hypocrite.

glaubensheuchlerisch, *adj.* hypocritical.

die Glaubenslehre, religious dogma or doctrine, dogmatic or doctrinal theology.

die **Glaubensmeinung,** religious opinion.

die **Glaubenspartei** (-en), denomination, sect.

der **Glaubensreiniger** (-), reformer; Puritan.

der **Glaubensrichter,** inquisitor.

der **Glaubenssatz,** dogma.

der **Glaubensschwärmer** (-), fanatic.

die **Glaubensschwärmerei,** fanaticism.

die **Glaubensspaltung,** schism.

glaubensstark, *adj.* truthful; deeply religious.

der **Glaubensstreit, die Glaubensstreitigkeit,** religious controversy.

die **Glaubensverbesserung,** reformation.

der **Glaubensverleugner** (-), renegade.

der **Glaubenszeuge** (-n), martyr.

gläubig, *adj.* full of faith, devout; credulous. (Rom. 13:11)

der **Gläubige** (-n), believer. (Ps. 31:24)

der **Gläubiger** (-), creditor.

gleich, 1. *adj.* same, like, equal, equivalent; alike, similar, resembling; adequate, proportionate; even, level, straight. 2. *adv.* alike, equally, exactly, just; immediately, at once, instantly, directly, presently; *gleich als ich ihn sah,* as soon as I saw him. 3. *conj.* although; *wären Sie gleich mein Vater,* even though you were my father.

gleichberechtigt, *adj.* having equal right, equally entitled.

die **Gleichberechtigung,** equality of right(s).

gleichermaßen, gleicherweise, *adv.* in like manner, likewise. (John 5:19)

gleichgesinnt, *adj.* like-minded, congenial, compatible.

die **Gleichheit,** equality, parity, identity, similarity.

das **Gleichnis** (-se), image; simile, comparison; allegory; parable. (Matt. 13:3) *Christi Gleichnisse,* the parables of Christ.

die **Gleichnisrede** (-n), parable, allegory.

gleichnisweise, *adv.* allegorically, symbolically.

das **Gleichniswort** (-e), figurative or symbolic expression or saying.

die **Gleichzeitigkeit,** coexistence, simultaneousness; synchronism.

der **Gleisner** (-), hypocrite, dissembler, pharisee.

die **Gleisnerei,** hypocrisy; shamming; simulation. (I Tim. 4:2)

gleißen, *reg. & ir.v.n.* (*aux.* h.) to glisten. (Jer. 2:22)

gleiten, *reg. & ir.v.n.* (*aux.* s. & h.) to glide, to slide; to slip, to skid. (Ps. 17:5)

das **Glied** (-er), limb, member; rank, file; link (of chains). (Rom. 7:23)

glimmen, *reg. & ir.v.n.* (*aux.* h.) to glimmer, to glow, to smoulder. (Isa. 42:3)

die **Glocke** (-n), bell, gong; any bell-shaped article.

glockenförmig, *adj.* bell-shaped.

das **Glockengeläute** (-), peal of bells.

der **Glockengießer** (-), bell-founder.

glockenklar, *adj.* clear as a bell.

der **Glockenklöppel** (-), clapper of a bell.

der **Glockenläuter** (-), bell ringer.

der **Glockenschlag,** chime, stroke of the hour.

das **Glockenspiel,** chime(s), carillon.

der **Glöckner** (-), sexton, bell ringer.

die **Glorie** (-n), glory; halo. *einen seiner Glorie entkleiden,* to debunk.

der **Glorienschein,** halo.

glorifizieren, *v.a.* to glorify.

die **Gloriole,** halo.

glorios, *adj.* glorious; excellent, capital.

glorreich, *adj.* glorious, illustrious.

das **Glossar** (-e or -ien), glossary.

der **Glossator** (-en), commentator; annotator.

die **Glosse** (-n), gloss, annotation; sarcastic comment.

glossieren, *v.a.* to gloss, to comment on, to supply with marginal notes.

das **Glück,** luck, fortune, good luck; success, prosperity; happiness; fate, chance. (Gen. 39:3) *auf Glück oder Unglück,* for better or worse; *alles auf das Glück ankommen lassen,* to leave everything to chance; *Gott gebe Glück dazu,* may God grant His blessing on it; *Glück und Glas, wie leicht bricht das,* fortune is as brittle as glass; *mancher hat mehr Glück als Verstand,* Fortune favors fools.

glückbringend, *adj.* fortunate, auspicious, propitious.

glücken, *v.n.* (*aux.* h. & s.) *imp.* (*einem*) to prosper, to succeed, to turn out well.

glücklich, *adj.* fortunate, lucky, prosperous, successful; happy. (Ps. 37:7)

die Glücksbotschaft, glad tidings.

glückselig, *adj.* blissful, radiant, very happy, highly blessed. (Ps. 73:12)

die Glückseligkeit, bliss, happiness, rapture.

die Glücksgöttin, Fortune, Fortuna.

das Glückskind (-er), Fortune's favorite, lucky person.

glücksstrahlend, *adj.* radiantly happy.

der Glückwunsch (-̈e), congratulation, good wishes; compliments (of the season).

glühend, *pr.p. & adj.* glowing, ardent, fervent. (Isa. 6:6)

die Glut (-en), heat, embers; glow, ardor, passion; fire; incandescence. (Isa. 33:14)

die Gnade (-n), favor; grace; clemency; mercy; pardon; goodwill, kindness. (Gen. 18:3)
durch Gottes Gnade, by the grace of God; *Wir, von Gottes Gnaden, König von,* we, by the grace of God, king of; *um Gnade rufen,* to cry out for mercy; *einem eine Gnade widerfahren lassen,* to pardon someone.

gnaden, *v.n.* to be gracious, to show grace or mercy; *gnade uns Gott!* God have mercy upon us!

die Gnadenanstalt, institution which dispenses grace (Troeltsch).

die Gnadenbezeichnung (-en), favor.

das Gnadenbild (-er), wonderworking or miraculous image, shrine.

der Gnadenbrief (-e), letter of pardon; warrant, diploma.

das Gnadenbrot, bread of charity, pittance.

die Gnadenfrist, respite.

das Gnadengeschenk (-e), donation.

das Gnadengesuch (-e), appeal for mercy, petition for leniency or reprieve.

das Gnadenmittel (-), means of grace (offered by the church).

die Gnadenordnung, divine ordinance.

der Gnadenort, place of pilgrimage.

der Gnadenplatz, place of pilgrimage; mercy seat.

gnadenreich, *adj.* merciful, gracious.

der Gnadenstuhl, mercy seat; throne of grace. (Exod. 25:17)

der Gnadentisch (-e), altar.

die Gnadenwahl, predestination.

der Gnadenweg, way of mercy, act of grace.

das Gnadenzeichen, token of favor.

gnädig, *adj.* merciful, kind; favorable, gracious, condescending. (Exod. 33:19)
Gott sei uns gnädig! God have mercy upon us!

die Gnosis, der Gnostizismus, Gnosticism.

der Gnostiker (-), Gnostic.

gnostisch, *adj.* Gnostic.

(der) Gog, Gog. (Rev. 20:8)

das Gold, gold. (I Kings 9:28)
es ist nicht alles Gold, was glänzt, all is not gold that glitters.

golden, *adj.* gold, golden, gilt. (Rev. 1:12)
er ist noch golden gegen seinen Bruder, he is an angel compared with his brother; *das goldene Kalb,* molten calf; *die goldene Regel,* golden rule.

das Goldgefäß (-e), gold plate.

die Goldgrube (-n), gold mine; (*fig.*) highly profitable undertaking.

der Goldklumpen (-), nugget, gold ingot. (Job 31:24)

der Goldschmied (-e), goldsmith. (Acts 19:24)

das Goldstück (-e), gold coin.

die Goldwaage, scales for weighing gold, gold balance.

gotisch, *adj.* Gothic.

der Gott, God; the Lord. (Exod. 20:2)
daß sich Gott erbarme! the Lord have mercy upon us! *Gott gebe!* God grant! *so wahr mir Gott helfe!* so help me God! *lieber Gott!* O Lord! (in prayer); *Gott steh' uns bei!* God help us! *Gottes Wege sind wunderbar,* the ways of providence are strange; *will's Gott! so Gott will!* please God!

der Gott (-̈er), heathen god.

gottähnlich, *adj.* godlike.

gottbegnadet, *p.p. & adj.* divinely favored.

die **Gottebenbildlichkeit,** image of God.

das **Götterbild** (-er), image of a god, godlike figure.

die **Götterburg,** Valhalla.

die **Götterdämmerung,** twilight of the gods.

der **Götterdienst,** polytheism.

der **Götterfunken** (-), divine spark.

gottergeben, *adj.* resigned to God's will, devout.

die **Göttergestalt,** divine form.

göttergleich, *adj.* divine, godlike, godly.

götterhaft, *adj.* godlike.

das **Götterhaus** (-er), temple.

das **Götterleben,** life like the gods.

die **Götterlehre,** mythology.

die **Göttersage** (-n), myth.

der **Göttersitz,** abode of the gods, Olympus.

die **Götterspeise,** ambrosia.

der **Götterspruch,** oracle.

die **Götterwelt,** the gods; Olympus; paganism.

das **Götterwesen,** mythology; divine being.

das **Götterwort,** oracle.

die **Götterzeit,** mythological age, golden age.

der **Gottesacker** (-), graveyard, churchyard.

der **Gottesbeweis,** argument for the existence of God.

der **Gottesdienst** (-e), divine service, public worship. (Rom. 9:4)

die **Gottesdienstordnung,** liturgy.

die **Gotteserde,** the earth; consecrated ground.

die **Gottesfahrt,** pilgrimage.

die **Gottesfurcht,** fear of God, piety. (Ps. 36:2)

gottesfürchtig, *adj.* pious; God-fearing. (Acts 2:5)

der **Gottesgedanke,** idea of God.

der **Gottesgelehrte** (-n), divine, theologian.

die **Gottesgelehrtheit, die Gottesgelehrsamkeit,** divinity, theology.

das **Gottesgericht** (-e), das **Gottesurteil,** divine judgment; ordeal.

der **Gottesglaube,** belief in God.

die **Gottesgnade,** grace of God.

das **Gottesgnadentum,** theory of the divine right of kings.

die **Gottesgüte,** goodness of God.

das **Gotteshaus** (-er), place of worship, church, chapel.

die **Gottesidee,** idea of God.

der **Gotteskasten, die Gotteslade,** treasury; alms box. (Matt. 27:6)

das **Gotteskind** (-er), son of God.
er ist ein Gotteskind, he is a child of God.

die **Gotteskindschaft,** sonship of God.

der **Gottesknecht** (-e), servant of God.

das **Gotteslamm,** Lamb of God. (John 1:29)

der **Gotteslästerer** (-), blasphemer.

die **Gotteslästerung** (-en), blasphemy. (Matt. 26:65)

die **Gotteslehre,** theology, divinity.

der **Gottesleugner** (-), atheist.

gottesleugnerisch, *adj.* atheistic.

die **Gottesleugnung,** atheism.

der **Gotteslohn,** God's reward.

der **Gottesmensch,** man of God. (I Tim. 6:11)

der **Gottespfennig,** das **Gottesgeld,** earnest money.

das **Gottesreich,** kingdom of God; theocracy.

der **Gottessohn,** the Son of God.

der **Gottestisch,** the Lord's table, communion table.

der **Gottesverächter** (-), impious person. (Rom. 1:30)

die **Gottesweisheit,** theosophy.

die **Gotteswelt,** God's wide world.

das **Gotteswort,** the Word of God, the Bible.

gottgefällig, *adj.* pleasing to God.

die **Gottgefälligkeit,** piety.

der **Gottgesandte,** the Messiah.

gottgeweiht, *adj.* consecrated to the service of God; Nazirite. (Num. 6:13)

gottgläubig, *adj.* godly; pious.

die **Gottgläubigkeit,** piety; godliness.

gottgleich, *adj.* godlike.

die **Gottgleichheit,** godlikeness.

die Gottheit, deity; divinity; Godhead.

die Göttin (-nen), goddess. (Acts 19:27)

göttlich, *adj.* godlike, divine, godly. (Gen. 5:22)

das Göttliche im Menschen, the divine spark in man.

die Göttlichkeit, divinity, godliness.

gottlos, *adj.* irreligious, ungodly, godless; wicked, impious. (Rom. 1:18)

die Gottlosigkeit, ungodliness.

der Gottmensch, God incarnate, Christ.

der Gott sei bei uns, the devil.

gottselig, *adj.* godly, pious; blessed. (II Tim. 3:12)

die Gottseligkeit, godliness. (II Peter 1:6)

gottsträflich, *adv.* awfully.

Gott-Vater, God the Father.

gottvergessen, *adj.* ungodly.

gottverhaßt, *adj.* abominable, odious.

gottverlassen, *adj.* godforsaken.

das Gottvertrauen, confidence toward God.

die Gottwidrigkeit, opposition or resistance to God.

der Götze (-n), idol, false deity. (Isa. 2:18)

das Götzenbild (-er), graven image, idol.

der Götzendiener (-), idolater. (Eph. 5:5)

der Götzendienst, idolatry. (I Cor. 10:14)

das Götzenopfer (-), idolatrous sacrifice. (Acts 15:29)

der Götzentempel (-), temple of an idol, heathenish temple.

der Götzenzertrümmerer (-), iconoclast.

das Grab (⁻er), grave, tomb, sepulcher; (*fig.*) death, destruction, ruin. (Deut. 34:6) *die Kirche des heiligen Grabes,* Church of the Holy Sepulcher; *treu bis über das Grab hinaus,* faithful unto death.

das Grabdenkmal, tomb.

graben, *ir.v.a.* to dig, to ditch, to trench; to engrave. (Luke 6:48)

der Grabesrand, brink of the grave.

der Grabesschlummer, sleep of death.

die Grabesstille, deathly silence.

die Grabesstimme, sepulchral voice.

das Grabgeläute, knell, tolling of bells.

das Grabgeleite, funeral procession.

der Grabgesang, dirge.

das Grabgewölbe (-), vault, tomb.

der Grabhügel (-), mound, tumulus.

die Grablegung (-en), interment, funeral, burial.

die Grablegung Christi, the burial of Christ.

das Grabmal (⁻er), tomb, monument.

die Grabrede (-n), burial sermon, funeral oration.

die Grabschändung (-en), desecration of graves.

die Grabschrift (-en), epitaph.

die Grabstätte (-n), burial place, sepulcher, tomb, family vault, graveyard, cemetery.

der Grabstein (-e), tombstone, gravestone.

das Grabtuch (⁻er), winding sheet, shroud, pall. (John 11:44)

der Gral, grail.

der Gram, 1. *m.* grief, sorrow, affliction. 2. *adj.* (only used with *sein* or *werden*) *einem gram sein,* to be angry or cross with someone, to bear someone a grudge. (Ps. 119:163)

grämen, 1. *v.a.* to grieve. 2. *v.r.* to grieve (for), to worry or fret (*über eine Sache,* about or at something). (Ps. 119:28)

gramvoll, *adj.* sorrowful, melancholy, gloomy, sad.

das Gras (⁻er), grass. (Gen. 1:11)

grau, 1. *adj.* gray, grizzled, hoary; venerable, ancient. 2. *n.* gray color; dawn. (Gen. 42:38)

grauen, 1. *v.n. & imp.* (*einem*) to have a horror of; to have an aversion to; to dread; to be afraid of; to shudder at. 2. *n.* horror, dread, fear, terror. (Ps. 27:1)

grausam, *adj.* cruel, inhuman, fierce; horrible, terrible, gruesome. (Ps. 40:3)

die Grausamkeit (-en), cruelty, ferocity.

greifen, 1. *ir.v.a. & n.* (*aux.* h.) to seize, to grasp, to catch, to catch hold of, to snatch, to grab. 2. *v.n.* (*aux.* h.) to have effect; to prevail; to feel; to handle. (Matt. 14:3)

das Greisenalter, old age.

greisenhaft, *adj.* senile.

das Gremium (-en), panel, board.

die Grenze (-n), frontier; boundary, limit, border; end, term. (Deut. 32:8)

grenzenlos, *adj.* boundless, unlimited, infinite.

die Grenzenlosigkeit, boundlessness; infinitude.

der Grenzfall ("-e), limiting case, extreme case.

der Grenzstein (-e), landmark; boundary stone.

der Grenzzoll, transit duty, customs.

der Greuel (-), horror, abomination, outrage. (Deut. 7:25)

greulich, *adj.* horrible, abominable, frightful, dreadful. (Rev. 21:8)

der Grieche (-n), Greek. (Acts 6:1)

das Griechenland, Greece. (Dan. 8:21)

das Griechentum, Hellenism.

griechisch, *adj.* Greek. (Acts 17:12)

der Griffel (-), stylus, graver; slate pencil. (Jer. 17:1)

der Grimm, 1. *m.* anger, fury, rage. 2. *adj.* see **grimmig.** (Exod. 15:7)

grimmig, *adj.* enraged, furious, wrathful, violent, fierce, grim.

grob, *adj.* coarse, rude, uncivil, clumsy, rough, gross; big, thick.

der Groschen (-), denarius; penny. (Matt. 18:28)

groß, *adj.* tall, high; large, big, vast, huge, great; important, grand. (Gen. 12:2)

die Größe (-n), size, dimension, bulk, largeness, greatness, bigness; height, tallness; quantity, value, power; magnitude. (Ps. 145:3)

der Größenwahn, megalomania.

großherzig, *adj.* magnanimous.

die Großherzigkeit, magnanimity.

die Großmutter ("-), grandmother. (II Tim. 1:5)

die Großprahlerei, bragging, boasting; boast.

der Großsprecher (-), boaster, swaggerer.

die Großsprecherei, boasting, bragging.

die Großstadt ("-e), large town (over 100,000 inhabitants).

der Großtuer (-), braggart.

der Großvater ("-), grandfather. (Job 12:12)

der Großwürdenträger (-), high dignitary.

großzügig, *adj.* on a generous or large scale; grandiose; noble, grand.

die Grube (-n), mine, pit, hole, cavity; ditch, depression, excavation, quarry. (Gen. 37:20)

grün, *adj.* green, verdant; fresh, young, vigorous; raw, unripe, immature, inexperienced. (Luke 23:31)

der Grund ("-e), ground, earth, soil; land, estate, terrain; sediment, bottoms, dregs, lees; base, foundation, basis, groundwork, rudiments, elements, first principles; reason, cause, motive, argument; background. (Luke 6:49)

der Grundbegriff (-e), fundamental principle, basic idea or concept.

der Grundbestandteil (-e), primary or essential component or constituent.

grundehrlich, *adj.* thoroughly honest.

gründen, 1. *v.a.* to establish, to found, to promote; to sound, to fathom; *gegründete Ansprüche,* established claims. 2. *v.r.* to rest, to be based, to rely. 3. *v.n.* (*aux.* h.) to sound, to feel the bottom; *stille Wasser gründen tief,* still waters run deep. (John 17:24)

der Gründer (-), founder; promoter.

die Grundfeste (-n), (*fig.*) basis, foundation. (Ps. 18:8)

die Grundlegung, laying the foundation.

gründlich, *adj.* thorough, solid, well-founded, profound, radical, fundamental.

die Gründlichkeit, thoroughness, solidity, profundity.

der Gründonnerstag, Maundy Thursday, Holy Thursday.

der Grundsatz ("-e), principle; rule of conduct.

grundsatzlos, *adj.* unprincipled.

der Grundstein (-e), foundation- or cornerstone. (Rev. 21:14)

die Grundsteinlegung, laying of the foundation stone.

der Grundunterschied (-e), basic difference.

die Grundwahrheit, fundamental truth.

der Grundzehnte, land tithe.

der Grundzug ("-e), main feature, characteristic.

grünen, *v.n.* to sprout, to become green; to flourish like grass. (Ps. 72:16)

der Gruß (⁻e), greeting, salutation, salute. (Luke 1:29)

mit bestem Gruß Ihr, yours very truly.

grüßen, *v.a.* to greet; to salute; to present compliments. (Matt. 26:49)

die Gültigkeit, validity, lawfulness.

die Gunst, favor, goodwill, kindness, affection, partiality; credit, advantage. (Acts 24:27)

zu Gunsten von, in favor of, on behalf of.

der Gurt (-e), girth, girdle, belt; strap, webbing. (Isa. 11:5)

der Gürtel (-), belt, girdle, sash; waistband; cordon; zone. (Matt. 3:4)

gürten, 1. *v.a.* to gird, to girdle. 2. *v.r.* to put on one's belt; to make oneself ready, to prepare oneself for. (Exod. 12:11)

gut (comp. *besser,* sup. *best*), 1. *adj.* good, excellent, desirable, beneficial; pleasant, kind, friendly, good-natured; respectable, virtuous; *fröhlich und guter Dinge sein,* to be cheerful and in good spirits. 2. *adv.* well, good; *so gut wie,* as well as; *gut eine Viertelstunde,* fully a quarter of an hour. 3. *n.* (⁻er), good thing, blessing; property, possession; goods, commodity, freight; countryseat, estate, farm. (Gen. 1:31)

das Gute, good quality, goodness. (Ps. 34:15)

die Güte, kindness, goodness; excellence, purity, quality. (Ps. 17:7)

gütig, *adj.* good, kind, gracious; benevolent, charitable; indulgent. (Ps. 145:9)

der Herr ist allen gütig, the Lord is good to all.

die Gütigkeit, goodness, kindness, graciousness; benevolence. (Gal. 5:22)

Hh

das Haar (-e), hair; filament; nap, pile; wool; hairy or wooly side of skins; trifle. (Matt. 5:36)

die Haarflechte (-n), braid of hair. (I Peter 3:3)

die Habe, property, goods, possessions, effects, fortune. (Acts 2:45)

haben, 1. *ir.v.a.* to have; to possess; to hold; to bear. 2. *v.r.* to behave; *sich darum haben,* to grieve for something. (Acts 18:10)

die Habgier, covetousness, avarice, greediness, greed, avidity.

habgierig, *adj.* avaricious, covetous, greedy.

die Habschaft, die Habseligkeit, all that a person has, belongings, property, fortune, effects.

die Habsucht, covetousness, avarice, greediness, greed, avidity.

habsüchtig, avaricious, covetous, greedy.

hacken, *v.a.* to chop, to hash, to mince, to hack; to hoe; to cleave (wood), to pick. (Isa. 5:6)

der Hader, quarrel, brawl, dispute, strife. (Rom. 13:13)

der Haderer (-), grumbler, wrangler, brawler; quarreler, struggler; fang, tusk. (Ps. 35:1)

hadern, *v.n.* (*aux.* h.) to wrangle, to strive, to quarrel, to squabble, to dispute. (Isa. 45:9)

der Hagel, hail. (Rev. 11:19)

hageln, *v.n. imp.* to hail. (Exod. 9:26)

der Hagiograph, hagiographer.

die Hagiographen, (*pl.*) Hagiographa.

die Hagiographie, hagiography; hagiology.

der Hahn (-̈e), cock. (Matt. 26:34)

der Hahnenschrei, cockcrowing, cockcrow. (Mark 13:35)

halb, 1. *adj.* half; *zum halben Preis,* at half the price. 2. *adv.* by halves, half; *halb und halb dazu entschlossen,* half decided on. (Rev. 8:1)

die Hälfte (-n), half, moiety; middle. (Ps. 102:25)

die Halle (-n), hall, great room; public room; market, bazaar, large shop. (John 10:23)

Hallelujah, hallelujah.

das Halljahr, jubilee; *das fünfzigste Jahr ist euer Halljahr,* a jubilee shall that fiftieth year be to you. (Lev. 25:11)

der Halm (-e), blade; stalk, stem, straw. (Gen. 41:5)

der Hals (-̈e), neck; throat. (Luke 15:20)

halsstarrig, *adj.* stiff-necked, stubborn, obstinate, headstrong. (Exod. 32:9)

der Halt, 1. *m.* hold, holding; footing, support; stability, firmness; purchase; stop, halt. 2. *adv. & part.* in my opinion, I think; *er wird halt nicht kommen,* I don't think he will come.

halten, 1. *ir.v.a.* to hold, to keep, to retain; to detain, to keep back, to constrain; to contain, to include; to observe, to perform, to celebrate; to endure, to hold out against; to think, to deem, to consider; *das Abendmahl halten,* to celebrate or administer holy communion; *Frieden halten,* to keep peace. 2. *v.n.* (*aux.* h.) to stop, to halt; to hold out, to stand firm; to insist on; *auf seine Ehre halten,* to be jealous of one's honor; *auf Träume halten,* to believe in dreams. 3. *v.r.* to hold out, to last, to keep good; to behave; *die Festung hält sich,* the fortress holds out. (Ps. 19:12)

der Hammer (-̈), hammer; forge; knocker. (Judg. 4:21)

die Hand (¨e), hand; handwriting; side, direction; source, origin. (Deut. 32:40)

die Handauflegung, laying on of hands. (I Tim. 4:14)

der Handel (¨), trade, traffic, commerce; transaction, business; affair; lawsuit, action; bargain; (*pl.*) difference, quarrel, dispute, fray. (I Cor. 6:1)

handeln, 1. *v.n.* (*aux.* h.) to behave, to act; to treat (*von*, of); to bargain, to negotiate, to haggle (*um*, about or for); to deal, to trade, to traffic (*mit*, in); *mit sich handeln lassen*, to be easy to deal with, to be ready to bargain. 2. *v.r. & imp.: es handelt sich um*, the question is, it is a question of; *um was handelt es sich?* what is the point in question? (Lev. 19:11)

handhaben, *ir.v.a.* (*insep.*) to handle, to manipulate; to manage, to operate; to deal with, to administer; to maintain. (I Chron. 18:14)
gut zu handhaben, handy, easily handled or managed.

die Handleiter (-n), small ladder, stepladder, steps; someone who leads about by the hand. (Acts 13:11)

die Handreichung, charity; help; aid. (Luke 8:3)

die Handschrift (-en), handwriting; signature; manuscript; bond. (Col. 2:14)

das Handwerk, handicraft; trade; calling; guild. (Acts 18:3)

hängen, 1. *v.a.* to cause to hang, to hang (up), to suspend, to attach, to fasten. 2. *v.n.* (*aux.* h.) *aneinander hängen*, to hang or stick together; *sehr am Gelde hängen*, to be very fond of money. 3. *v.r.* to hang oneself; *sich an einen hängen*, to hang round someone's neck, to pursue or pester someone. (Ps. 62:11)

die Hantierung, business, management, handling, manipulation.

die Häresie (-n), heresy.

der Häretiker (-), heretic.

häretisch, *adj.* heretical.

die Harfe (-n), harp. (Ps. 57:9)

der Harfenspieler (-), harpist.

der Harnisch (-e), (suit of) armor. (Eph. 6:11)
in Harnisch geraten, to fly into a passion.

harren, *v.n.* (*aux.* h.) (gen. or *auf* and acc.) to look forward to impatiently; to wait for, to await; to stay, to tarry. (Ps. 25:3)
ich harre des Herrn, I trust confidently in the Lord.

hart, *adj.* (comp. *härter*, sup. *härtest*) hard, difficult; harsh, rough, severe, stern, austere; obstinate; stiff, firm, solid, tough, hardy. (Exod. 7:14)
hart am Feind, in the face of the enemy; *hart anfassen*, to deal with severely, to treat roughly; *hart bedrängt*, hard-pressed, hard beset.

die Härtigkeit, hardness; hardening, tempering. (Matt. 19:8)

der Haß, hate, enmity. (II Sam. 13:15)

hassen, *v.a.* to hate. (Lev. 19:17)

häßlich, *adj.* ugly, hideous, repulsive, ill-favored; nasty, odious, loathsome, offensive. (Gen. 41:3)
häßliche Gesinnung, nasty mind.

hauen, 1. *ir.v.a.* to hew, to cut, to chop, to fell; to carve, to chisel; to whip, to lash; to break (stones); to strike, to beat. 2. *v.r.* to fight. 3. *v.n.* (*aux.* h.) to cut; to strike; *um sich hauen*, to lay about one. (Exod. 20:25)

der Haufe (-n), heap, pile, hoard; large sum, great number, batch, agglomeration; crowd, body, swarm; mass, multitude. (Luke 23:27)
ein Haufen Arbeit, a mass of work.

das Häuflein (-), small group; little band; small body or troop of men. (Ps. 125:3)

das Haupt (¨er), head; leader, chief, principal. (Matt. 6:17)
mit gesenktem Haupt, with bowed head.

das Haupthaar, hair of the head. (Dan. 3:27)

der Hauptmann, 1. (*pl.* -leute) captain; chief priest; magistrate; centurion. 2. (*pl.* -männer) responsible local government official. (Matt. 8:5)

die Hauptsumme (-n), principal sum; sum total. (I Tim. 1:5)

das Haus (¨er), house, residence, dwelling; home; housing, casing, frame, shell; household, family, race; firm. (Deut. 5:6)
das Haus Gottes, the house of God; *das Haus des Herrn*, the house of the Lord; *das Haus Israel*, the house of Israel; *das Haus Juda*, the house of Judah.

der **Hausaltar** (⁻e), domestic altar.

die **Hausandacht** (-en), family prayers.

der **Hausarrest,** confinement to one's own house.

die **Hausarznei** (-en), household remedy.

der **Hausbedarf,** household necessaries.

der **Hausbesitzer** (-), owner, landlord.

der **Hausdiener** (-), house servant (in an inn), manservant.

die **Hausdurchsuchung** (-en), house search (by the police).

die **Hausfrau** (-en), housewife; landlady.

der **Hausfriede,** domestic peace, family concord.

der **Hausfriedensbruch** (⁻e), intrusion, trespass.

der **Hausgenosse** (-n), fellow lodger, member of the same family. (Matt. 10:25)

das **Hausgesinde,** domestic servants. (Mic. 7:6)

der **Hausgottesdienst** (-e), (family) prayers, family worship.

der **Haushalt** (-e), household; housekeeping; household budget.

haushalten, 1. *ir.v.n.* to keep house; to economize. 2. *n.* housekeeping; management. (Luke 16:2)

der **Haushalter** (-), householder, housekeeper; steward. (Luke 12:42)

die **Haushälterin** (-nen), housekeeper.

der **Hausherr** (-en), master of the house, head of the family; landlord. (Luke 12:39)

die **Hauskapelle** (-n), private chapel.

der **Hausknecht** (-e), porter.

der **Hausprediger** (-), family chaplain.

der **Hausrat,** household furniture, utensils, etc. (Matt. 12:29)

der **Haussegen,** children.

die **Haussuchung** (-en), house search (by the police).

die **Haustaufe** (-n), private baptism.

die **Haustrauung** (-en), private wedding.

die **Haustür** (-en), street door, front door. (Judg. 11:31)

der **Hausvater** (⁻), father of a family.

der **Hauswirt** (-e), master of a house; landlord, host. (Luke 13:25)

die **Hauswirtin** (-nen), landlady, hostess.

die **Hauswirtschaft,** housekeeping; domestic economy.

die **Haut** (⁻e), hide; skin; cuticle, dermis; film, flurry, bloom. (Acts 19:12)
treue alte Haut, good old soul; *er kann aus seiner Haut nicht heraus,* he cannot change his nature.

heben, 1. *ir.v.a.* to lift, to raise, to elevate, to heave; to draw up; to exalt; to levy; to make prominent; to remove, to put an end to, to cancel, to settle (disputes). 2. *v.r.* to rise. (Num. 6:26)
die Welt aus den Angeln heben, to put the world out of joint; *in den Himmel heben,* to laud to the skies; *hebe dich weg von mir Satan!* get thee behind me, Satan!

der **Hebräer** (-), Hebrew.

hebräisch, *adj.* Hebrew.

die **Hecke** (-n), 1. hedge, hedgerow, copse, inclosure; brushwood. 2. hatch, brood, breed; breeding time; breeding cage. (Gen. 22:13)

hecken, *v.a. & n. (aux.* h.) to hatch, to breed; to produce. (Ps. 84:4)

der **Hedonismus,** hedonism.

der **Hedonist** (-en), hedonist.

hedonistisch, *adj.* hedonic; hedonistic.

die **Hedschra,** Hegira.

das **Heer** (-e), army, troops; host, multitude. (Gen. 2:1)

das **Heerlager** ( ), camp, encampment; *(fig.)* party, faction, group. (Rev. 20:9)

die **Heerschar** (-en), host, legion. (Ps. 103:21)
die himmlischen Heerscharen, the heavenly host; *der Herr der Heerscharen,* the Lord of Hosts.

die **Hefe** (-n), yeast, barm; leaven; dregs, sediment. (Isa. 25:6)

heftig, *adj.* forcible, violent, severe, vigorous, intense, vehement, fierce, furious, impetuous; passionate, fervent. (Luke 22:44)

das **Hehl,** concealment, secrecy. (Isa. 3:9)
er macht kein Hehl daraus, he makes no secret of it.

hehr, *adj.* exalted, lofty, majestic, sublime; august, sacred. (Ps. 111:9)

der **Heide** (-n), die **Heidin** (-nen), heathen, pagan. (Exod. 34:24)
Juden und Heiden, Jews and Gentiles.

die **Heidenangst,** mortal fright.

der **Heidenapostel,** apostle to the Gentiles.

der **Heidenbekehrer** (-), missionary.

die **Heidenbekehrung,** conversion of heathens, foreign missions, missionary work.

das **Heidenbild** (-er), idol.

der **Heidenchrist** (-en), heathen proselyte (of early Christianity).

das **Heidenchristentum,** Gentile Christianity.

der **Heidengenosse** (-n), fellow pagan.

der **Heidengott** (-̈er), pagan god; heathen god.

die **Heidenmission** (-en), mission in heathen lands.

der **Heidenmissionar** (-e), missionary in heathen lands.

der **Heidentempel** (-), heathen temple.

das **Heidentum,** heathendom; paganism; pagans.

heidnisch, *adj.* heathenish, pagan.
heidnisch machen, heidnisch werden, to paganize.

heil, 1. *adj.* unhurt, safe and sound, whole, intact, unscathed; healed, well, cured, restored. 2. *n.* prosperity, happiness, welfare; salvation, redemption. (Rev. 13:3)

der **Heiland,** Savior. (Acts 5:31)

die **Heilanstalt** (-en), sanatorium, hospital, asylum, convalescent home, nursing home.

das **Heilbad** (-̈er), mineral bath.

heilbar, *adj.* curable; remediable.

die **Heilbehandlung** (-en), treatment, cure.

heilbringend, *adj.* salutary blessing.

der **Heilbringer** (-), bringer of blessings; Savior.

der **Heilbrunnen** (-), mineral springs, spa.

heilen, 1. *v.a.* to heal, to cure, to make well. 2. *v.n.* (*aux.* s.) to grow well, to heal, to be cured. (Deut. 32:39)

heilig, *adj.* holy, sacred, hallowed; solemn, venerable, august. (Gen. 28:17)
der Heilige Abend, Christmas Eve; *das Heilige Abendmahl,* the Lord's Supper, holy communion; *der Heilige Christ,* Christmas; *die Heilige Familie,* the holy family; *der Heilige Geist,* the Holy Spirit;

das Heilige Grab, the holy sepulcher; *den Sonntag heilig halten,* to keep the Sabbath day (holy); *die Heilige Jungfrau,* the blessed virgin (Mary); *heiliger Ort,* holy or sacred place; *heilige Pflicht,* sacred duty; *die Heilige Schrift,* the Scriptures; *die Heilige Sippe,* holy kinship; *der Heilige Stuhl,* Holy See; *der Heilige Vater,* the holy father, the pope; *die Heilige Woche,* Passion Week; *heiliger Zorn,* righteous anger.

der **Heiligabend,** Christmas Eve.

der **Heilige** (-n), die **Heilige** (-n), saint. (Matt. 27:52)

das **Heilige,** holy or sacred thing; Holy Place. (Exod. 26:33)

heiligen, *v.a.* to hallow, to sanctify, to consecrate; to keep holy; to sanction, to justify. (Gen. 2:3)
der Zweck heiligt die Mittel, the end justifies the means; *geheiligt werde Dein Name,* hallowed be thy name.

das **Heiligenbild** (-er), image or picture of a saint.

die **Heiligenblende** (-n), niche for image of a saint.

das **Heiligenbuch** (-̈er), book of legends of saints, martyrology.

der **Heiligendienst,** worship of saints.

die **Heiligengeschichte,** hagiology.

der **Heiligenglanz,** halo.

das **Heiligenhaus** (-̈er), die **Heiligenkapelle** (-n), chapel of a saint; shrine.

der **Heiligenkalender** (-), calendar of saints.

der **Heiligenschein,** halo (of glory), glory.

die **Heilighaltung,** religious observance.

die **Heiligkeit,** holiness, godliness, sanctity, sacredness. (Luke 1:75)
im Geruch der Heiligkeit, in the odor of sanctity; *seine Heiligkeit,* His Holiness.

heiligmachend, *adj.* sanctifying.

die **Heiligsprechung,** canonization.

die **Heiligtuerei,** sanctimoniousness.

das **Heiligtum** (-̈er), holy place, shrine, sanctuary; relic.

der **Heiligtumsraub,** sacrilege.

die **Heiligtumsschändung** (-en), sacrilege.

die **Heiligung,** sanctification.

die **Heilkraft** (-̈e), healing power.

heilkräftig, *adj.* curative; medicinal, therapeutic.

heillos, *adj.* wicked, abandoned, godless; heinous, terrible, disastrous, dreadful; wretched; hopeless; very large, enormous.

die Heillosigkeit, wickedness; wretchedness.

das Heilmittel (-), remedy; medicament.

heilsam, *adj.* healing; wholesome, salutary, beneficial. (II Tim. 1:13)

die Heilsamkeit, wholesomeness, salutariness; recovery.

die Heilsarmee, Salvation Army.

die Heilsbotschaft, gospel, evangel.

die Heilsgeschichte, history of salvation.

die Heilsordnung, way of salvation, *ordo salutis.*

die Heilswahrheit, truth of Christianity or of salvation.

heim, 1. *adv.* home, homeward. 2. *n.* (-e) home; dwelling, abode; domicile.

heimführen, *v.a.* to lead home. (Isa. 37:29)

heimgehen, *v.n.* (*aux.* s.) to go home; to die. (Matt. 9:6)

heimkommen, *ir.v.n.* (*aux.* s.) to return home. (Luke 15:6)

heimlich, *adj.* secret, concealed; stealthy, underhand, secretive, close; private. (Matt. 1:19)

die Heimlichkeit, secrecy; secret; privacy. (Matt. 13:35)

heimsuchen, *v.a.* to visit, to frequent; to haunt; to afflict. (Gen. 21:1)

die Heimsuchung (-en), visitation; affliction. (Isa. 10:3)

heischen, *v.a.* to ask, to demand, to request, to require. (Ps. 2:8)

heiß, *adj.* hot, burning, boiling, torrid; ardent, passionate, fervid, vehement. (Rev. 16:8)

heißen, 1. *ir.v.a.* to command, to enjoin, to bid, to order; to name, to call, to denominate. 2. *v.n.* (*aux.* h.) to be called or named; to mean, to signify. (Gen. 3:20)

der Held (-en), hero; champion; famous person; principal person. (Gen. 49:10)

der Heldentod, death in battle.

das Heldentum, heroism; heroic age.

die Heldenverehrung, hero worship.

helfen, *ir.v.n.* (*aux.* h.) (*dat.*) to help, to aid, to assist, to promote, to support; to avail, to profit; to deliver. (Matt. 8:25)
hilf Gott! Heaven preserve me! *so wahr mir Gott helfe!* so help me God! *was hülfe es dem Menschen, wenn,* what is a man profited if.

hell, *adj.* clear, bright, shining, brilliant, luminous; distinct; light, fair (hair). (Mark 9:3)

der Hellenismus, Hellenism.

hellenistisch, *adj.* Hellenistic.

der Heller (-), small coin; mite. (Matt. 5:26)

der Hellseher (-), clairvoyant.

die Hellseherei, die Hellsehergabe, clairvoyance.

der Helm (-e), helmet, helm, casque; dome, cupola. (Eph. 6:17)

das Hemd (-en), shirt; undervest (man), chemise, vest (woman). (Ps. 109:18)

henken, *v.a.* to hang (someone on the gallows). (Gen. 40:22)

die Henne (-n), hen. (Matt. 23:37)

(der) Henoch, Enoch.

der Henotheismus, henotheism.

her, *adv.* 1. hither, here, this way; *her damit!* out with it! *die Hand her,* give me your hand; *hin und her sprechen,* to debate, to argue. 2. since, ago (of time); *von alters her,* from time immemorial; *von früher her,* from some time earlier, from earlier times. 3. *prefix* (a) *to prepositions (used adverbially), is unaccented; see* **herab, herauf, heraus, herbei,** *etc.: it refers the indicated motion in the direction of the speaker;* (b) *to verbs, it takes the accent and is separable; both as a simple prefix and as a component of the compound prefixes of* (a) *it usually implies the notion of 'hither.'* (Exod. 32:26)

herab, *adv. & sep. prefix (indicates movement downwards as seen by the person below),* down, down here; down from; downward; (*with preceding acc.*) *den Berg herab,* down (from) the mountain.

herabfahren, *v.n.* to come down, to descend. (Exod. 19:11)

herabfließen, *v.n.* to flow or run down. (Ps. 133:2)

herabkommen, *ir.v.n. (aux.* s.) to come down; to be reduced in circumstances, to be brought low. (Rev. 10:1)

herabsteigen, *ir.v.n. (aux.* s.) to descend, to step down; to dismount. (Matt. 27:40)

die Heraldik, heraldry.

heraldisch, *adj.* heraldic.

herauf, *adv. & sep. prefix (indicates movement upwards as seen by the person above),* up, up to(wards), upwards, from below.

heraufbeschwören, *v.a.* to conjure up; to bring on, to cause.

heraufsteigen, 1. *ir.v.a.* to mount (stairs, etc.). 2. *ir.v.n.* to come up (as a storm), to break, to dawn (of day). (I Sam. 28:13)

heraufziehen, 1. *v.a.* to draw up. 2. *v.n. (aux.* s.) to draw near, to approach. (Isa. 37:24)

heraus, *adv. & sep. prefix (indicates movement from inside a place as seen by the person outside),* out, from within, forth, from among.

herausfahren, *ir.v.n. (aux.* s.) to drive or sail out; to rush, fly, or burst out; to slip out (as an unpremeditated remark). (Isa. 59:5)

herausgehen, *v.n.* to go out, to come out, to leave; to lead or open out *(auf,* on to). (Gen. 8:18)

herauskommen, *ir.v.n. (aux.* s.) to come out or forth; to issue; to appear; to be issued; to become known, to be published; to prove correct, to amount to, to be of use, to yield profit. (Matt. 5:26)

herausreden, 1. *v.n. (aux.* h.) to speak freely. 2. *v.r.* to make excuses. (John 16:29)

herausreißen, *ir.v.a.* to pull out, to tear out, to weed out; to free, to deliver. (Ps. 18:20)

heraussagen, *v.a.* to speak one's mind. (John 10:24)

herausziehen, 1. *ir.v.a.* to extract, to remove. 2. *v.n. (aux.* s.) to march out. 3. *v.r.* to extricate oneself (from a scrape). (Matt. 13:48)

herbei, *adv. & sep. prefix (indicates movement from a remoter to a nearer place with reference to the speaker or the point contemplated by him),* hither, here, near, on, this way, into the vicinity of.

herbeikommen, *ir.v.n. (aux.* s.) to be at hand, to draw near.

die Herberge (-n), shelter, lodging, quarters; inn, hostel. (Acts 10:6)

herbergen, *v.a. & n. (aux.* h.) to shelter, to harbor, to lodge; to entertain (wishes, views, etc.). (Acts 10:23)

herbringen, *ir.v.a.* to bring hither, in, or up; to establish; to transmit (from ancestors). (Gen. 27:25)

der Herd (-e), hearth, fireplace, fireside; cooking stove; seat, focus (of rebellion, disease, etc.). (Isa. 31:9)

die Herde (-n), drove, flock, herd; crowd, multitude. (Acts 20:28)
der Herde folgen, to follow the crowd, to be guided by herd instinct.

herein, *adv. & sep. prefix (indicates movement into a place as seen by the person inside)* in, in here; inward.

hereinkommen, *ir.v.n. (aux.* s.) to come in. (Gen. 24:31)

herfahren, *ir.v.n. (aux.* s.) to come, to travel, to approach, to arrive; to move hastily along. (Isa. 5:19)

hergeben, *ir.v.a.* to give up, to deliver; to give away, to hand over. (Matt. 14:8)

hergehen, *ir.v.n. (aux.* s.); *(generally used as v.imp.)* to come to pass, to happen; to go on, to be going on, to be carried on. (Exod. 32:1)

herkommen, *ir.v.n. (aux.* s.) to come hither or near, to approach, to advance; to be caused by, to be the consequence (of), to originate (in), to arise (from), to be derived or descended (from), to be transmitted, to be established as a custom. (Matt. 8:9)

der Herling (-e), unripe grape; wild grape; sour grape. (Isa. 5:2)

die Hermeneutik, hermeneutics.

hermeneutisch, *adj.* hermeneutic.

hernach, *adv.* afterwards, hereafter, after this or that. (Matt. 12:45)

hernieder, *adv. & sep. prefix,* down.

herniederkommen, *ir.v.n. (aux.* s.) to come down. (John 3:13)

der Herr, the Lord. (Gen. 15:7)
der Herr Gott, God our Lord, Lord God; *das Haus des Herrn,* the house of God; *der Herr der Heerscharen,* the Lord of hosts; *der Herr der Schöpfung,* the Lord of creation; *der Tag des Herrn,* the Lord's day; *der Herr Zebaoth,* Lord God of hosts.

der Herrgott, Lord God.

herrlich, *adj.* magnificent, splendid, glorious, capital, excellent, delicious, grand. (Exod. 15:1)

die Herrlichkeit, splendor, magnificence, grandeur, glory, excellence. (Gen. 45:13)

der Herrnhuter (-), Moravian; (*pl.*) Moravian brethren.

das Herrnhutertum, Moravianism.

die Herrschaft, dominion, mastery, control, power, government, sovereign authority, command; manor, estate, domain. (Isa. 9:5)

herrschen, *v.n.* (*aux.* h.) to rule, to reign, to govern, to be lord or master of; to prevail, to be prevalent; to exist. (Gen. 1:26)

der Herrscher (-), ruler, sovereign, lord, monarch, prince, governor. (Gen. 49:10)

hervor, (*archaic* **herfür**) *adv. & sep. prefix (expressing movement forward as seen from out in front)* forth; out.

hervorbrechen, *v.n.* (*aux.* s.) to rush out, to break through; to sally forth, to debouch. (Isa. 58:8)

hervorbringen, *ir.v.a.* to bring forth, to produce, to yield; to generate, to beget; to utter; to elicit. (Gen. 1:24)

die Hervorbringung, production; procreation; utterance.

hervorgehen, *ir.v.n.* (*aux.* s.) to go or come forth, to issue, to proceed, to result, to arise; to come off (victorious, etc.). (John 5:29)

hervorleuchten, *v.n.* (*aux.* h.) to shine forth; to become clear or evident, to be conspicuous or distinguished. (II Cor. 4:6)

das Herz (-en), heart; breast, bosom; feeling, sympathy; mind, spirit; courage; center; vital part. (Gen. 6:5)
aus dem Herzen, sincerely, earnestly; *sein Herz ausschütten,* to open one's heart; *sich das Herz erleichtern,* to unburden oneself; *einem von Herzen gut sein,* to love someone dearly; *ein Herz und eine*

Seele, bosom friends; *wes das Herz voll ist, des gehet der Mund über,* out of the abundance of the heart the mouth speaks.

herzallerliebst, *adj.* dearest, beloved.

das Herzeleid, grief, sorrow, affliction. (Gen. 42:38)

herzen, *v.a.* to press to one's heart, to caress, to embrace. (Mark 9:36)

die Herzensangelegenheit (-en), love affair, affair of the heart.

die Herzensangst (¨e), anguish of mind, deep anxiety.

die Herzensfreude (-n), great joy; heart's delight.

die Herzensgüte, kindheartedness.

der Herzenskündiger, one who knows the heart. (Acts 15:8)

die Herzenslust, great joy.

herzlich, *adj.* hearty, cordial, affectionate, heartfelt, sincere. (Luke 1:78)

die Herzlichkeit, cordiality, affection, sincerity.

der Herzog (¨e), duke; governor. (Matt. 2:6)

herzu, *adv. & sep. prefix (meaning much the same as* **herbei**) up, up to, near, here, towards, hither.

herzutreten, *v.n.* to come, to step up. (Matt. 25:20)

(der) Hesekiel, Ezekiel.

das Heu, hay. (I Cor. 3:12)

die Heuchelei (-en), hypocrisy, dissimulation; cant. (Matt. 23:28)

heucheln, 1. *v.a.* to feign, to affect, to simulate. 2. *v.n.* (*aux.* h.) to dissemble, to sham, to play the hypocrite; to pose (as a saint). (Gal. 2:13)

die Heuchelrede (-n), hypocritical or dissembling speech.

der Heuchelschein, das Heuchelwerk, hypocrisy, sham, false pretense.

der Heuchler (-), hypocrite, dissembler. (Matt. 6:2)

heuchlerisch, *adj.* hypocritical; false, deceitful; dissembling.

heulen, *v.n.* (*aux.* h.) to howl, to yell, to scream, to roar, to cry. (Matt. 8:12)

die Heuschrecke (-n), grasshopper; locust. (Exod. 10:12)

heute, *adv.* today, this day. (Gen. 41:9)

heutig, *adj.* of today, of the present time; present, actual, modern. (Deut. 34:6)

die Hexe (-n), witch, sorceress, enchantress; hag.

der Hexenglaube, belief in witchcraft.

der Hexenprozeß (-sse), witchcraft trial.

der Hexensabbat, witches' Sabbath.

die Hexerei, witchcraft, sorcery, magic.

hier, *adv.* here; present; in this place; at this point. (Gen. 22:1)

die Hierarchie (-n), hierarchy.

hierarchisch, *adj.* hierarchical.

hie(r)her, *adv.* to this time; to this place, this way, hither, here, to me. (Matt. 11:12)

die Hieroglyphenschrift (-en), hieroglyphic or hieratic writing.

(der) Hieronymus, Jerome.

die Hilfe (-n), help, aid, assistance, support; relief; remedy. (Deut. 33:26)

hilfreich, *adj.* helpful, benevolent, charitable.

hilfsbereit, *adj.* helpful; beneficent.

die Hilfsbereitschaft, helpfulness, goodwill; solidarity, collaboration.

der Hilfsbischof (-̈e), suffragan bishop.

der Hilfsprediger (-), deputy clergyman.

der Himmel (-), heaven; heavens, sky, firmament; canopy. (Gen. 1:1)
dem Himmel sei Dank, daß wir …! thank heaven, we …!

himmelab, *adv.* from heaven, from on high.

himmelan, *adv.* heavenwards, to the skies.

himmelangst, *adv.* terribly frightened.

das Himmelbrot, manna. (Ps. 78:24)

die Himmelei, affected piety, canting manner.

die Himmelfahrt, ascension. (see Acts 1:10)
die Himmelfahrt Christi, Ascension Day; *Mariä Himmelfahrt,* Assumption (of the Blessed Virgin).

das Himmelreich, kingdom of heaven; bliss. (Matt. 3:2)

die Himmelskönigin, virgin Mary, mother of God.

die Himmelskost, ambrosia; the sacrament.

die Himmelsleiter, Jacob's ladder.

himmlisch, *adj.* heavenly, celestial, divine; ethereal, beatific; splendid, beautiful, lovely. (Matt. 6:14)
himmlische Fügung, divine ordinance, decree of providence; *die himmlischen Mächte,* the powers above; *himmlische Sehnsucht,* longing for heaven, spiritual yearning.

hinab, *adv. & sep. prefix (movement downwards as seen from the starting place above),* down (there), downward(s).

hinablassen, *ir.v.a.* to let down, to lower. (Matt. 4:6)

hinabsteigen, *ir.v.n.* (*aux.* s.) to descend. (Acts 8:38)

hinabstürzen, 1. *v.n.* (*aux.* s.) to fall down (from a precipice). 2. *v.a.* to throw down, to precipitate. (Luke 4:29)

hinauf, *adv. & sep. prefix (movement upwards as seen from the starting point below),* upward(s), up (to).

hinaufsteigen, *ir.v.n.* (*aux.* s.) to mount, to ascend. (Exod. 19:3)

hinaus, *adv. & sep. prefix (movement outwards as seen from inside),* out, outside, forth.

hinausgehen, *ir.v.n.* (*aux.* s.) to go or walk out. (Gen. 45:1)

hinauswerfen, *ir.v.a.* to throw out, to expel, to eject. (Matt. 22:13)

hinauswollen, *ir.v.n.* to wish to go out; to aim at; to end in. (Matt. 26:58)

die Hinde (-n), hind, doe. (Ps. 22:1)

hindern, *v.a.* to hinder, to impede, to hamper, to prevent, to stop, to obstruct; to embarrass, to cross, to thwart. (Luke 13:7)

das Hindernis (-se), hindrance, impediment, obstacle, bar, check, barrier. (I Cor. 9:12)

der Hinduismus, Hinduism.

hindurch, *adv. & sep. prefix,* through; throughout; across.

hindurchdringen, *v.n.* to penetrate, to permeate. (John 5:24)

hinein, *adv. & sep. prefix (penetration into something, sometimes as seen from the outside, but often figurative),* into, inside, from out here.

hineingehen, *ir.v.n.* (*aux.* s.) to go into, to be contained. (Matt. 22:11)

hineinwollen, *ir.v.n.* (*aux.* h.) to wish or be willing to go in. (Matt. 23:13)

der Hinfall, falling down; fall; decay.

hinfallen, *ir.v.n.* (*aux.* s.) to fall down; to decay. (Isa. 54:10)

hinfort, *adv.* henceforth, in future. (Matt. 5:13)

die Hingabe, giving away; surrender, submission; abandonment, resignation; devotion.

hingehen, *ir.v.n.* (*aux.* s.) to go to that place; to go there, to proceed; to pass, to elapse. (Luke 8:14)

hinken, *v.n.* (*aux.* h. & s.) to limp, to go lame; to be imperfect. (Gen. 32:32)

hinkommen, *ir.v.n.* (*aux.* s.) to come or get there, to arrive at. (John 7:34)

hinlegen, 1. *v.a.* to lay down; to put away. 2. *v.r.* to lie down. (John 11:34)

hinnehmen, *ir.v.a.* to take, to accept; to take upon oneself, to submit to; to bear, to suffer, to put up with. (John 18:31)

hinreißen, *ir.v.a.* to carry along; to overpower, to overcome; to delight, to charm, to transport. (Acts 6:12)

hinscheiden, *ir.v.n.* (*aux.* s.) to depart, to pass away.

hinweg, 1. *adv.* & *sep. prefix*, away, forth, off. 2. *n.* way there or to a place, outward trip.

hinweggehen, *ir.v.n.* (*aux.* s.) to go away; (*über eine Sache*) to pass over, to disregard, to ignore, to regard as unimportant. (Luke 4:30)

hinziehen, 1. *ir.v.a.* to draw along, to extend, to protract; to draw to(wards), to attract. 2. *v.n.* (*aux.* s.) to move off or along; to move to; to pass away, to depart; to draw out. (Gen. 28:15)

hinzu, *adv.* & *sep. prefix (movement into the neighborhood of or as an addition to something)* to, towards, near; in addition, besides, moreover.

hinzukommen, *ir.v.n.* (*aux.* s.) to be added to, to come up to. (Luke 19:37)

hinzutreten, *ir.v.n.* (*aux.* s.) to join (others already there); to supervene. (Luke 7:14)

hinzutun, 1. *ir.v.a.* to add. 2. *n.* addition. (Acts 2:41)

die Hiobsbotschaft (-en), **die Hiobspost** (-en), bad news, ill tidings.

die Hippe (-n), sickle, hedging or pruning knife, scythe. (Rev. 14:17)

der Hirsch (-e), stag, hart; (red) deer. (Gen. 49:21)

der Hirt (-en), **der Hirte** (-n), herdsman, shepherd; pastor. (Matt. 9:36)

das Hirtenamt (⁻er), pastorate.

der Hirtenbrief (-e), pastoral letter.

die Hirtendichtung, pastoral poetry, bucolic poetry.

das Hirtengedicht (-e), pastoral poem, bucolic eclogue.

das Hirtenleben, pastoral life, idyllic existence.

das Hirtenlied (-er), pastoral song.

der Hirtenstab, crosier.

die Hirtentasche (-n), shepherd's purse. (I Sam. 17:40)

(der) Hiskia(s), Hezekiah.

die Hitze, heat; ardor, fervor, passion. (Gen. 8:22)

hoch, 1. *adj.* (when followed by *e* of the inflected cases *ch* becomes *h*, as: *hoher, hohe, hohes,* or *der, die, das Hohe;* comp. *höher;* sup. *höchst*) high; tall, lofty; noble, sublime; proud; expensive, dear; deep; great. 2. *n.* cheer; toast. (Gen. 49:9) *höhere Gewalt,* act of God.

der Hochaltar (⁻e), high altar.

das Hochamt, high mass.

hochbejahrt, hochbetagt, *adj.* aged, advanced in years.

hochdeutsch, *adj.* High German, standard German.

hochgelehrt, *adj.* very learned.

hochgelobt, *adj.* highly praised; magnified, blessed. (Mark 14:61)

der Hochgesang (⁻e), hymn, anthem.

hochheilig, *adj.* most holy. (Exod. 29:37)

die Hochkirche, High Church.

höchlich, *adv.* highly, exceedingly, greatly, mightily; grievously. (Phil. 4:10)

der Hochmut, pride, arrogance, haughtiness. (Isa. 13:11)

hochmütig, *adj.* proud, arrogant, haughty.

die Hochzeit (-en), wedding, marriage. (Matt. 22:2)

hochzeitlich, *adj.* nuptial, bridal. (Matt. 22:11)

der Hof (⁻e), yard, courtyard; place; farm; country house, manor; palace, court; halo, corona. (Matt. 26:36)

die Hoffart, arrogance, pride, haughtiness. (Mark 7:22)

hoffärtig, *adj.* haughty, arrogant. (Rom. 1:30)

hoffen, 1. *v.a. & n.* (*aux.* h.) to hope; to expect, to look for. 2. *n.* hoping, expecting. (Luke 6:35)

die Hoffnung (-en), hope, expectation. (Acts 23:6)

das Hofgesinde, servants of a royal household; servants on a farm or estate; men of war (of a royal household). (Luke 23:11)

die Höhe (-n), height, altitude, elevation, loftiness; summit, top, high place, hill, mountain. (Matt. 21:9)

das Hohelied, Song of Solomon, Song of Songs.

der Hohe(n)priester (-), high priest. (Matt. 16:21)

das Hohepriesteramt, high priest; pontificate.

hohepriesterlich, *adj.* pontifical.

das Hohepriestertum, office of the high priest; pontificate.

hohl, *adj.* hollow, concave; dull, vain, shallow, empty. (Isa. 40:12)

die Höhle (-n), cave, cavern, grotto, den, burrow, cavity, hollow, hole. (Gen. 23:19)

der Hohn, scorn, disdain, derision, mockery; sneer, insult. (Isa. 43:28)

höhnen, *v.a.* to scoff, to sneer or laugh at; to treat with scorn. (Matt. 22:6)

höhnisch, *adj.* scornful, sneering, insulting, sarcastic.

hold, *adj.* gracious, friendly; pleasing, charming, lovely; favorable, propitious.

holdselig, *adj.* most gracious, most lovely, most charming, sweet. (Luke 1:28)

die Holdseligkeit, sweetness, charm, loveliness; graciousness.

holen, *v.a.* to fetch, to go or come for; to get, to catch. (Matt. 24:17)

die Hölle, hell, the infernal regions. (Deut. 32:22)

die Höllenangst, mortal fright or anxiety.

der Höllenbrand, utter scoundrel; insatiable thirst.

die Höllenbrut, scum, wretches, outcasts.

die Höllenfahrt, Christ's descent into hell.

der Höllenfürst, prince of hell, Satan.

der Höllenlärm, infernal noise.

die Höllenmächte, (*pl.*) powers of darkness.

die Höllenpein, die Höllenqual, torments of hell; excruciating pain, agony.

die Höllenpforte (-n), gate of hell.

der Höllenpfuhl, hellish pool, bottomless pit.

der Höllenrachen, der Höllenschlund, mouth of hell; jaws of hell.

der Höllenrand, limbo.

die Höllenwut, fury, satanic rage.

der Höllenzwang, cabalistic incantation, book of black magic.

höllisch, *adj.* hellish, infernal; terrific, abominable. (Matt. 5:22) *das höllische Feuer,* the fires of hell; *höllische Qualen,* torments of hell.

das Holz (⁻er), wood; timber; piece of wood; firewood; thicket, grove; lumber. (Acts 5:30)

hölzern, *adj.* wooden; (*fig.*) stiff, awkward. (Rev. 9:20)

die Homiletik, homiletics.

homiletisch, homiletic(al).

die Homilie, homily; sermon.

der Honig, honey. (Exod. 3:8)

der Honigseim, virgin honey. (Luke 24:42)

hören, *v.a. & n.* (*aux.* h.) to hear; to listen; to listen to; to obey. (Gen. 3:8)

der Hörer (-), hearer; university student. (James 1:22)

das Horn (⁻er), horn; bugle; hard or horny skin; hoof (of horses). (Rev. 5:6)

der Hort (-e), safe retreat, refuge; shield, protection; protector; hoard, treasure. (Ps. 18:3)

Hosianna, hosanna.

die Hostie (-n), consecrated wafer, the host.

das Hostiengefäß (-e), pyx.

das Hostienhäuslein (-), tabernacle.

die **Hostienschändung** (-en), desecration of the host.

der **Hostienteller** (-), paten; tray for the bread in the celebration of the Eucharist.

hübsch, *adj.* pretty, charming, fine, handsome, nice; good, proper; fair, considerable. (Matt. 23:27)

die **Hüfte** (-n), hip, haunch. (Gen. 32:26)

der **Hügel** (-), hill, hillock, knoll. (Exod. 17:9)

der **Hugenotte** (-n), Huguenot.

hugenottisch, *adj.* Huguenot.

die **Huld**, grace, favor, charm, kindness; graciousness.

die **Hülle** (-n), cover, covering, envelope, wrapper, wrapping; pod, husk; jacket, tunic, raiment; veil, cloak, mask. (Isa. 25:7)

hüllen, 1. *v.a.* to wrap (up), to cover, to envelop; to hide. 2. *v.r.* to wrap oneself up, to muffle oneself. (Isa. 37:1)

der **Hund** (-e), dog, hound, (*fig.*) cur, beast, scoundrel. (Matt. 7:6)

hundert, 1. *num. adj.* hundred. 2. *n.* hundred. (Matt. 18:12)

hundertfältig, *adj.* hundredfold. (Matt. 13:8)

der **Hunger**, hunger; appetite; starvation, famine. (Rom. 8:35)

hungrig, *adj.* hungry, starving; poor (of soil). (Matt. 12:1)

die **Hungrigkeit**, hunger, appetite; starvation.

hüpfen, *v.n.* (*aux.* h. & s.) to hop; to frisk about; to jump, to leap, to skip. (Luke 1:41)

die **Hürde** (-n), hurdle; fold, pen. (Luke 2:8)

die **Hure** (-n), prostitute, whore, harlot. (Rev. 17:1)

huren, *v.n.* (*aux.* h.) to whore, to fornicate. (Rev. 17:2)

das **Hurenkind** (-er), bastard. (Hos. 1:2)

der **Hurer** (-), whoremonger, fornicator. (Rev. 21:8)

die **Hurerei**, prostitution, fornication, harlotry. (Matt. 15:19)

der **Hussite** (-n), Hussite.

die **Hussitenkriege**, (*pl.*) the Hussite Wars.

hussitisch, *adj.* Hussite.

der **Hut** (ˉe), hat; cap, cover, lid. (Isa. 62:3)

die **Hut** (-en), keeping, guard, protection, shelter; charge, care. (Acts 12:10)

hüten, 1. *v.a.* to watch, to guard, to take care of, to keep. 2. *v.r.* to be on one's guard, to take care, to beware (of). (Matt. 10:17)

der **Hüter** (-), keeper, guardian; herdsman. (Gen. 4:9)

die **Hütte** (-n), cottage, hut, chalet, cabin, shelter, shed; tent, tabernacle; forge. (Gen. 4:20)

die **Hymne** (-n), hymn.

das **Hymnenbuch** (ˉer), hymnal; hymnbook.

die **Hymnendichtung** (-en), hymnology, hymnody.

der **Hymnengesang** (ˉe), hymnody.

die **Hypnose**, hypnosis.

hypnotisch, *adj.* hypnotic.

hypnotisieren, *v.a.* to hypnotize.

die **Hypnotisierung**, hypnotization.

der **Hypnotismus**, hypnotism.

die **Hypokrisie**, hypocrisy.

der **Hypokrit** (-en), hypocrite.

hypokritisch, *adj.* hypocritical.

die **Hypothese** (-n), hypothesis.

die **Hysterie**, hysteria.

hysterisch, *adj.* hysterical.

Ii

die **Idee** (-n), idea; notion, conception; thought, fancy; purpose, intention.

die **Ideologie,** ideology.

ideologisch, *adj.* ideological.

die **Idiosynkrasie,** fixed aversion, allergy, antipathy.

der **Idiot** (-en), idiot.

das **Idol** (-e), idol.

die **Idolatrie,** idolatry.

das **Ikon** (-e), icon.

der **Ikonoklasmus,** iconoclasm.

der **Ikonoklast** (-en), iconoclast.

ikonoklastisch, *adj.* iconoclastic.

die **Illumination** (-en), illumination.

(der) **Immanuel,** Immanuel.

immer, *adv.* always, ever, every time; perpetually, continually; yet, still, nevertheless; more and more (*with comp.*). (Heb. 12:1)

der **Imperialismus,** imperialism.

das **Imprimatur,** imprimatur.

in, *prep. expressing rest or motion in a place (dat.)* in, at; *implying motion to or towards (acc.)* into, to, within. (John 6:56)

der **Inbegriff** (-e), contents; embodiment, essence; tenor, purport; summary, abstract; sum, total.

die **Inbrunst,** ardor, fervor.

inbrünstig, *adj.* ardent, fervent. (I Peter 1:22)

der **Indeterminismus,** indeterminism; free will.

die **Infallibilität,** infallibility.

die **Inkarnation,** incarnation.

innehaben, *ir.v.a.* to possess; to fill (office, etc.); to hold (title); to occupy (town, etc.). (II Cor. 6:10)

die **innere Mission,** home mission; city mission.

die **Innerlichkeit,** inwardness, subjectivity; cordiality, warmth.

die **innerweltliche Askese,** this-worldly ascetism (Weber).

die **Innigkeit,** cordiality, sincerity, ardor, intimacy; spiritual depth.

(der) **Innozenz,** Innocent.

die **Inquisition,** Inquisition.

der **Inquisitor,** inquisitor.

inquisitorisch, *adj.* inquisitorial.

die **Insel** (-n), island. (Acts 13:6)

die **Inspiration,** inspiration.

inspirieren, *v.a.* to inspire.

das **Intellekt** (-e), intellect.

intellektuell, *adj.* intellectual.

intelligent, *adj.* intelligent.

die **Intelligenz,** intellect; intelligentsia, intellectuals.

das **Interdikt** (-e), interdict.

interkonfessionell, *adj.* interdenominational, undenominational.

der **Interpret** (-en), interpreter.

die **Interpretation** (-en), interpretation; exegesis.

interpretieren, *v.a.* to interpret, to explain, to expound.

intolerant, *adj.* intolerant.

die **Intoleranz,** intolerance.

die **Investitur,** investiture.

der **Investiturstreit,** investiture controversy.

irden, *adj.* earthen, made of earth or clay. (II Cor. 4:7)

irdisch, *adj.* earthly, worldly, terrestrial, mortal, perishable. (John 3:12) *das irdische Dasein,* temporal existence; *die irdische Hülle,* mortal remains.

irr(e), *adj.* in error, wrong; astray, wandering, lost; confused, puzzled. (Acts 2:12)

die Irre, mistaken course, error. (Isa. 53:6)

irreführen, *v.a.* to lead astray, to mislead, to deceive.

die Irrenanstalt (-en), **das Irrenhaus** (-er), lunatic asylum.

der Irrgeist (-er), false spirit, deceptive spirit. (Mic. 2:11)

der Irrglaube, heresy.

irrgläubig, *adj.* heterodox, heretical.

die Irrlehre (-n), false doctrine, heresy.

der Irrlehrer (-), heretic.

der Irrsinn, insanity, madness, delirium.

der Irrtum (-er), error, mistake, false step, fault. (Matt. 24:24)

(der) Ischarioth, Iscariot.

(die) Isebel, Jezebel.

der Islam, Islam.

der Islamit (-en), Islamite.

islamitisch, *adj.* Islamic, Islamitic.

der Israelit (-en), **der Israeliter** (-en), Israelite. (John 1:47)

israelitisch, israelisch, *adj.* Israelite.

das Italien, Italy.

Jj

ja, 1. *adv. & part.* yes; truly, really; indeed, certainly, by all means, of course; even; well; you know. 2. *n.* assent, consent, approval; affirmation. (Gen. 3:1)

jagen, 1. *v.a.* to chase, to pursue, to drive. 2. *v.n.* (*aux.* s. & h.) to hunt, to chase; to rush, to race, to gallop. (Gen. 27:5)

der Jäger (-), hunter, huntsman, sportsman; gamekeeper. (Gen. 10:9)

das Jahr (-e), year. (Rev. 20:2)

das Jahr(es)fest (-e), annual celebration, anniversary. (Isa. 1:14)

der Jahrestag (-e), anniversary; birthday. (Gen. 40:20)

Jahve, Yahweh, Jahveh.

(der) Jakob, Jacob. (Gen. 25:26)

die Jakobsleiter, Jacob's ladder. (see Gen. 28:12)

der Jakobssegen, Jacob's blessing. (see Gen. 49:1–28)

der Jammer, lamentation; misery, distress, wretchedness. (Gen. 44:29)

jämmerlich, *adj.* pitiable, miserable, wretched, deplorable. (Rev. 3:17)

die Jämmerlichkeit, wretchedness; pitiable condition.

jammern, 1. *v.n.* (*aux.* h.) (*über*) to lament, to mourn, to grieve; to moan, to cry, to wail. 2. *v.a.* (*pers. & imp.*) to pity, to feel sorry for; to move to pity. (Matt. 9:36) *meine Seele jammerte der Armen,* my soul was grieved for the poor.

das Jammertal, vale of tears or woe. (Ps. 84:7)

jauchzen, *v.n.* (*aux.* h.) to rejoice, to shout with joy; to exult, to triumph. (Isa. 12:6)

je, 1. *adv.* ever, always, at all times, at any time, at every time; in any case; at a time, each, apiece. 2. *int.* well! ah! why! (Mark 6:7)

jedermann, *pron.* everyone, everybody. (Gen. 16:12)

jeglicher, jegliche, jegliches, *adj. & pron.* every, each; everyone. (Gen. 1:11)

(der) Jehova, Jehovah.

jemals, *adv.* ever, at any time. (I John 4:12)

jemand, *indef. pron.* somebody, someone. (Acts 17:25)

jener, jene, jenes, 1. *dem. adj.* that. 2. *dem. pron.* that one, the former. (Matt. 7:22) *in jenem Leben, in jener Welt,* in the life to come, in the other world.

das Jenseits, the next world, the life to come, the hereafter.

(der) Jeremias, Jeremiah.

(der) Jerobeam, Jeroboam.

Jerusalem, Jerusalem. (Matt. 5:35)

(der) Jesaia(s), Isaiah.

der Jesuit (-en), Jesuit.

der Jesuitenorden, Society of Jesus.

das Jesuitentum, der Jesuitismus, Jesuitism.

jesuitisch, *adj.* Jesuitical.

(der) Jesus, Jesus. (Acts 1:11)

jetzt, 1. *adv.* now, at present, at the present time. 2. *n.* the present, the present time. (Matt. 23:39)

(das) Jiddisch, Yiddish.

das Jobeljahr, jubilee.

das Joch (-e), yoke; crossbeams, transom; (*fig.*) burden, load; saddle (mountains). (Acts 15:10)

(der) Johannes, John. *Johannes der Täufer,* John the Baptist.

der Johanniter (-), knight of St. John.

der Johanniterorden, Order of St. John.

(der) Jona, Jonah.

(der) Josef, Joseph, Joseph.

(der) Josias, Josiah.

(der) Josua, Joshua.

der Jubel, rejoicing, exultation, jubilation.

die Jubelfeier (-n), **das Jubelfest** (-e), jubilee.

der Jubelgesang (-e), song of rejoicing.

das Jubeljahr (-e), jubilee.

jubeln, *v.n.* (*aux.* h.) to rejoice, to shout with joy, to exult.

der Jubeltag (-e), day of rejoicing.

der Jubilar (-e), person celebrating his jubilee.

das Jubiläum (-äen), jubilee, anniversary.

jubilieren, *v.n.* (*aux.* h.) to exult; to shout with joy.

(der) Juda, Judah.

(das) Judäa, Judea.

der Judaismus, Judaism.

der Jude (-n), Jew.

der Judenchrist (-en), Jewish Christian, Christian Jew.

das Judenchristentum, Jewish Christianity.

der Judengenosse (-n), convert to Judaism; proselyte. (Acts 13:43)

der Judenkönig, King of the Jews. (John 19:3)

das Judentum, Judaism, Jewry.

die Jüdin (-nen), Jewess.

jüdisch, *adj.* Jewish.

die Jugend, youth, adolescence; early period; young people. (Gen. 8:21)

die Jugendbewegung (-en), youth movement.

die Jugendblüte, bloom of youth.

die Jugenderziehung, education of youth, early education.

die Jugendfürsorge, young people's welfare.

das Jugendgericht (-e), juvenile court.

die Jugendherberge (-n), youth hostel.

jugendlich, *adj.* youthful, juvenile.

jung, *adj.* (comp. *jünger,* sup. *jüngst*) young, youthful; new, fresh; recent; early. (I Tim. 5:11)

das Junge (-n), young, offspring (of animals), cub, puppy, calf, whelp, etc. (Deut. 32:11)

jünger, 1. *adj.* (*comp. of* **jung**) younger; later; junior. 2. *m.* disciple; follower; adherent. (Matt. 5:1)
die zwölf Jünger, the twelve apostles.

die Jüngerschaft, discipleship.

die Jungfrau (-en), virgin; maid, maiden.
die heilige Jungfrau, the Blessed Virgin; *von der Jungfrau Maria geboren,* born of the Virgin Mary.

jungfräulich, *adj.* maidenly, modest, coy, chaste, pure, virginal.

die Jungfräulichkeit, maidenliness, virginal purity, coyness.

die Jungfrauschaft, virginity.

der Jüngling (-e), young man, youth; adolescent. (Gen. 4:23)

jüngst, 1. *adj.* (*sup. of* **jung**) youngest; latest, last; recent; *zu jüngst,* finally, in the end. 2. *adv.* lately, recently, the other day. (John 12:48)
das jüngste Gericht, der jüngste Tag, judgment day, doomsday.

die Justiz, administration of the law.

das Justizamt, court of law.

der Justizbeamte (-n), officer of justice.

die Justizkammer (-n), court or chamber of justice.

der Justizmord (-e), judicial murder, execution of an innocent person.

Kk

der **Käfer** (-), beetle, bug. (Joel 1:4)

kahl, *adj.* bare, naked; unfledged (of birds); callow; sterile, barren; poor; empty. (Isa. 3:17)

der **Kahlkopf** (⁻e), bald head. (II Kings 2:23)

(der) Kain, Cain. (Gen. 4:2)

das **Kainszeichen,** mark of Cain.

der **Kaiser** (-), emperor. (Matt. 22:17)

das **Kalb** (⁻er), calf; fawn. (Gen. 18:7) *das goldene Kalb anbeten,* to worship the golden calf.

der **Kalk** (-e), lime, limestone, chalk, calcium. (Gen. 11:3)

kalt, *adj.* cold, cool, chill, chilly; frigid, indifferent, calm. (Matt. 10:42)

kaltblütig, *adj.* cold-blooded; calm, composed.

die **Kälte,** cold, coldness, chill, chilliness; coolness, frigidity, indifference. (Acts 28:2)

der **Kalvarienberg,** Calvary.

(der) Kalvin, Calvin.

der **Kalvinismus,** Calvinism.

der **Kalvinist,** Calvinist.

kalvin(ist)isch, *adj.* Calvinist(ic).

das **Kamel** (-e), camel. (Matt. 19:24) *Mücken zu Kamelen machen,* to make mountains out of molehills.

das **Kamelhaar,** camel's hair.

der **Kamerad** (-en), comrade, mate, companion, colleague, fellow (worker, etc.).

die **Kammer** (-n), small unheated room; cavity, hollow, ventricle (of the heart). (Gen. 6:14)

der **Kämmerer** (-), chamberlain; (city) treasurer. (Gen. 37:36)

das **Kämmerlein** (-), cozy little room, closet. (Matt. 6:6)

der **Kampf** (⁻e), combat, fight, contest, engagement, battle, conflict, action; struggle, strife. (Phil. 1:30)

kämpfen, 1. *v.n.* (*aux.* h.) to fight, to combat; to strive, to struggle, to contend with, to do battle. 2. *v.a.* to fight (a battle). (Gen. 32:29)

(das) Kanaan, Canaan.

der **Kanaaniter,** Canaanite.

kanaanitisch, kan(a)anäisch, *adj.* Canaanite. (Matt. 15:22)

der **Kandidat** (-en), candidate, applicant.

die **Kandidatur** (-en), candidature, application.

kandidieren, *v.n.* to be a candidate (for), to stand or apply (for a post).

das **Kaninchen** (-), rabbit. (Ps. 104:18)

die **Kanne** (-n), can, tankard, mug, jug, pot, canister. (I Kings 19:6)

der **Kanon** (-s), canon (of Holy Scriptures).

das **Kanonikat** (-e), prebend, canonry.

der **Kanoniker** (-), der **Kanonikus** (-iki), prebendary, canon.

kanonisch, *adj.* canonical.

kanonisieren, *v.a.* to canonize.

die **Kanonissin** (-nen), canoness.

die **Kantate** (-n), cantata.

der **Kantor** (-en), precentor; choirmaster; organist; cantor.

das **Kantorat** (-e), precento. ⸱⸱ ip; organist's house.

die **Kanzel** (-n), pulpit; turret; chair (university).

die **Kanzelrede** (-n), sermon.

der **Kanzelredner** (-), preacher.

die **Kanzlei** (-en), chancellery, government office.

die **Kanzleisprache, der Kanzleistil,** chancery language, legal language.

die **Kapelle** (-n), chapel; chamber; band, orchestra; church choir. (Jer. 35:2)

das **Kapitel** (-), chapter; topic.

der **Kaplan** (⁻e), chaplain, assistant priest.

die **Kapuze** (-n), cowl; cape, hood.

die **Kapuzinade** (-n), popular sermon, tirade, severe lecture.

der **Kapuziner** (-), Capuchin monk.

der **Kardinal** (⁻e), cardinal.

das **Kardinalat,** cardinalate.

der **Kardinalbischof** (⁻e), bishop cardinal.

der **Kardinalshut,** cardinal's hat.

das **Kardinalskollegium,** college of cardinals.

die **Kardinalstugend,** cardinal virtue.

die **Kardinalswürde,** cardinalship.

der **Karfreitag,** Good Friday.

die **Karfreitagwoche,** Holy Week, Passion Week.

karg, *adj.* scanty, poor, meager; miserly, stingy.

kargen, *v.n.* (*aux.* h.) to be stingy, to be very economical. (Prov. 11:24)

kärglich, *adj.* scanty, poor, paltry, wretched. (II Cor. 9:6)

der **Karmeliter** (-), Carmelite; White Friar.

die **Karmeliterin** (-nen), Carmelite nun.

der **Karneval** (-e), carnival, Shrovetide festivities.

die **Kartause** (-n), Carthusian friar.

die **Karte** (-n), card, postcard, visiting or playing card; map; ticket of admission; menu, bill of fare.

die **Karwoche,** Holy Week.

kasteien, *v.a. & r.* to castigate or mortify (oneself). (Lev. 16:29)

der **Kasten** (-), box, chest, case, housing, crate, coffer; locker, press, cupboard; hutch; setting (of jewels, etc.); body, frame. (Gen. 6:14)

das **Kästlein,** little box or chest. (Exod. 2:3)

der **Kasuist** (-en), casuist.

die **Kasuistik,** casuistry.

kasuistisch, *adj.* casuistic(al).

die **Katakombe** (-n), catacomb.

katastrophal, *adj.* catastrophic.

die **Katechese,** catechizing.

der **Katechet** (-en), catechist, religious instructor.

katechetisch, *adj.* catechetic(al), Socratic.

katechisieren, *v.a.* to catechize.

der **Katechismus,** catechism.

der **Katechumene** (-n), catechumen; neophyte.

die **Kategorie** (-n), category.

kategorisch, *adj.* categorical, positive, unconditional.

kathartisch, *adj.* cathartic, purgative, cleansing, purifying.

der **Katheder** (-), rostrum, desk (for lectures); (*fig.*) chair (university).

der **Kathedersozialismus,** academic socialism.

die **Kathederweisheit,** theoretical knowledge, unpractical views.

die **Kathedrale** (-n), cathedral.

der **Katholik** (-en), (Roman) Catholic.

katholisch, *adj.* catholic; all-embracing. *katholisch werden,* to turn (Roman) Catholic.

der **Katholizismus,** Roman Catholicism.

der **Kauf** (⁻e), buying, purchase; bargain.

der **Kaufbrief** (-e), bill of sale. (Jer. 32:11)

kaufen, *v.a. & n.* (*aux.* h.) to buy, to purchase. (Gen. 42:2)

der **Käufer** (-), purchaser, buyer. (Matt. 21:12)

das **Kaufhaus** (⁻er), warehouse, stores.

der **Kaufmann** (-leute), merchant; tradesman, shopkeeper. (Matt. 13:45)

kaum, *adv.* hardly, scarcely, barely, with difficulty; no sooner…than; only just, just now. (Rom. 5:7)

die **Kehle** (-n), throat, gullet, throttle; fluting, channel, gutter. (Prov. 5:3)

kehren, 1. *v.a.* to turn; *das Schwert in die Scheide kehren,* to put the sword into the scabbard. 2. *v.r.* to turn; *sich kehren an (acc.)* to regard, to heed, to mind, to pay attention to, to follow. (Exod. 32:12) *sich zur Buße kehren,* to become penitent.

der **Keim** (-e), germ; bud, spore, sprout, shoot, nucleus; embryo; origin.

kein, *adj.* no, not a, not one, not any. (II Kings 1:3)

keiner, keine, keines, *pron.* no one, not anyone, none. (Rev. 2:10)

keinerlei, *indec. adj.* of no sort, not any. (Phil. 1:20)

der Kelch (-e), cup, goblet, chalice. (Matt. 20:22)

der Kelchdeckel (-), **der Kelchteller** (-), paten, patin, patine.

die Kelchweihe, consecration of the communion cup.

die Kelter (-n), winepress. (Rev. 14:19)

keltern, *v.a.* to tread or press (grapes). (Amos 9:13)

kennen, *ir.v.a.* to know, to be acquainted with; to have cognizance of. (Exod. 33:12)

der Kenner (-), connoisseur, judge, expert, specialist.

kephisch, *adj.* of Cephas. (I Cor. 1:12)

der Kerker (-), prison, dungeon. (Ps. 142:8)

der Kerkermeister (-), jailer. (Acts 16:23)

der Kerl (-e), fellow.

der Kerub (-inen & -im), cherub.

die Kerze (-n), candle, taper.

der Kessel (-), kettle; cauldron, copper, boiler; valley, depression. (Zech. 14:20)

die Kette (-n), chain; necklace; series; chain, range (of mountains); (*pl.*) bondage, slavery. (Gen. 41:42)

die Kettenfeier: *Petri Kettenfeier,* Peter's chains.

der Ketzer (-), heretic.

die Ketzerei, heresy.

das Ketzergericht, (court of) inquisition.

ketzerhaft, ketzerisch, *adj.* heretical, heterodox. (Titus 3:10)

die Ketzermacherei, intolerance of dissenters.

der Ketzermeister, grand inquisitor.

die Ketzerverbrennung (-en), burning of heretics.

die Ketzerverfolgung (-en), burning of heretics; auto-da-fé.

keusch, *adj.* chaste, pure, virgin, maidenly. (James 3:17)

die Keuschheit, chastity, purity, virginity, continence. (Acts 24:25)

das Keuschheitsgelübde (-), vow of chastity.

der Kieselstein (-e), pebble, flint. (Isa. 50:7)

das Kind (-er), child; offspring. (Gen. 3:16) *wes Geistes Kind ist er?* what sort of a person is he? *Kinder Gottes,* the pious, sons (children) of God.

die Kinderfürsorge, child welfare.

die Kinderlehre, instruction in the catechism; Sunday-school (teaching).

die Kinderlieder, (*pl.*) nursery rhymes.

der Kindermord, infanticide.

die Kinderstube, nursery; early education.

die Kinderzucht, bringing up children.

das Kindeskind, grandchild.

kindhaft, *adj.* childlike, childish.

die Kindheit, childhood, infancy.

kindlich, *adj.* relating to sonship; childlike; filial. (Rom. 8:15)

die Kindschaft, relation of a child to its parents; filiation; adoption. (Rom. 8:23) *die Kindschaft Gottes,* sonship of God.

die Kindtaufe, christening, baptism.

die Kirche (-n), church. *streitende Kirche,* church militant; *herrschende Kirche,* established church.

der Kirchenablaß ('-e), indulgence.

der Kirchenälteste (-n), churchwarden, elder, vestryman.

das Kirchenamt ('-er), church office, ecclesiastical function; eldership.

der Kirchenaustritt, secession from a church; withdrawal from church membership.

der Kirchenbann, excommunication; interdict. *in den Kirchenbann tun,* to excommunicate, to interdict.

die Kirchenbekleidung, pulpit hangings.

der Kirchenbesuch, attendance at church.

der Kirchenbesucher (-), churchgoer.

das Kirchenbuch ('-er), parish register.

die Kirchenbuße, penance imposed by the church.

der Kirchenchor ('-e), choir.

der Kirchendiener (-), church officer; sexton; sacristan, verger.

kirchendienstlich, *adj.* pertaining to the church service.

die Kirchendisziplin, church discipline; ecclesiastical discipline.

die Kircheneinkünfte, (*pl.*) church revenue.

die Kirchenfahne (-n), banner used in church ceremonies.

der Kirchenfluch, anathema.

die Kirchenfreiheit, ecclesiastical immunity.

der Kirchenfrevel (-), sacrilege.

der Kirchenfriede, union of the members of the church; security of church property.

der Kirchenfürst (-en), ecclesiastical prince, high dignitary of the church; prelate.

das Kirchengebet, common prayer.

das Kirchengebetbuch (¨er), book of common prayer, prayer book.

das Kirchengebiet (-e), diocese.

der Kirchengebrauch (¨e), church rite or observance.

das Kirchengefäß (-e), church vessel; (*pl.*) church plate.

das Kirchengeld (-er), church fund; (*pl.*) church property.

die Kirchengemeinde (-n), parish; congregation.

die Kirchengemeinschaft, church membership.

der Kirchengenosse (-n), parishioner.

das Kirchengerät (-e), sacred vessels or garments.

das Kirchengericht, ecclesiastical court, consistory.

der Kirchengesang, hymn; chorale.
liturgischer Kirchengesang, psalmody; *Gregorianischer Kirchengesang,* Gregorian chant.

die Kirchengeschichte, ecclesiastical history.

der Kirchengeschichtler (-), **der Kirchenhistoriker** (-), church historian.

das Kirchengesetz (-e), canon; (*pl.*) decretals.

kirchengesetzlich, kirchengesetzmäßig, *adj.* canonical.

der Kirchenglaube, creed, dogma.

der Kirchengrund, glebe.

das Kirchenjahr (-e), ecclesiastical year.

der Kirchenkonvent (-e), convocation.

das Kirchenkonzert (-e), recital of sacred music.

das Kirchenlehen (-e), ecclesiastical fief.

die Kirchenlehre, church doctrine.

der Kirchenlehrer (-), father of the church; one of the early fathers.

das Kirchenlied (-er), hymn.

die Kirchenmusik, sacred music.

die Kirchenordnung, liturgy, ritual.

das Kirchenornat, canonicals.

der Kirchenrat, consistory, church committee, ecclesiastical court.

der Kirchenraub, sacrilege.

das Kirchenrecht, canon law.

kirchenrechtlich, *adj.* canonical.

das Kirchenregiment, die Kirchenregierung, church government; hierarchy.

die Kirchensache, ecclesiastical affair.

der Kirchensänger (-), chorister.

der Kirchensatz, ecclesiastical tenet.

die Kirchensatzung, rule of the church.

der Kirchenschänder (-), sacrilegious person.

das Kirchenschiff (-e), nave.

der Kirchensitz (-e), pew.

die Kirchenspaltung, schism.

der Kirchenstaat, papal territory, pontifical state.

die Kirchensteuer (-n), church rate.

der Kirchenstreit, die Kirchenstreitigkeit, religious controversy; dissension in the church.

der Kirchenstuhl (¨e), pew.

die Kirchentrennung, schism.

die Kirchentür (-en), church door.

der Kirchenvater (¨er), father of the church.
die Kirchenväter, the early fathers.

die Kirchenverfassung, church constitution.

die Kirchenversammlung (-en), synod; convocation; vestry.

die Kirchenvorschrift (-en), church law; ordinance of the church; liturgy.

der Kirchenvorstand, vestry board.

der Kirchenvorsteher (-), churchwarden.
Versammlung der Kirchenvorsteher, vestry meeting.

das **Kirchenwesen,** church matters.

der **Kirchgang,** procession to church, churchgoing.

der **Kirchgänger** (-), churchgoer.

die **Kirchhalle,** church porch.

der **Kirchhof** (⸚e), churchyard; cemetery, graveyard.

kirchlich, *adj.* ecclesiastical. *kirchliches Begräbnis,* Christian burial.

der **Kirchner** (-), sexton, verger, sacristan.

das **Kirchspiel** (-), parish.

der **Kirchsprengel** (-), diocese.

der **Kirchturm** (⸚e), church tower or steeple.

die **Kirchturmspitze** (-n), steeple, spire.

die **Kirchturmspolitik,** parochialism, local-parish politics.

die **Kirchweihe** (-n), consecration or dedication of a church; church festival. (John 10:22)

das **Kissen** (-), cushion, pillow, bolster, pad, padding. (Mark 4:38)

der **Kittel** (-), smock, overall; frock, blouse; jacket (of a suit).

die **Klafter** (-n), fathom, cord (of wood), span (with outstretched arms).

die **Klage** (-n), complaint; lament, lamentation; grievance, ground of complaint; suit, accusation, impeachment. (John 18:29)

das **Klagegeschrei,** wailing, lamentation.

das **Klagehaus** (⸚er), the house of mourning. (Eccles. 7:2)

die **Klageleute,** (*pl.*) mourners. (Eccles. 12:5)

das **Klagelied** (-er), dirge, lamentation, elegy. *die Klagelieder des Jeremia,* Lamentations (of Jeremiah).

die **Klagemauer,** Wailing Wall.

klagen, 1. *v.a.* to bewail, to complain about, to bemoan. 2. *v.n.* (*aux.* h.) to complain, to lament (*über, um,* for); to sue, to go to law. (Matt. 2:18)

der **Kläger** (-), plaintiff, complainant, accuser.

die **Klageschrift** (-en), writ, written complaint.

die **Klagestimme** (-en), plaintive voice.

das **Klageweib** (-er), (hired) mourner. (Jer. 9:16)

kläglich, *adj.* lamentable, deplorable, pitiable; plaintive; miserable, wretched, pitiful. (Isa. 33:9)

der **Klang** (⸚e), sound, tone, ringing, clang; ring. (Isa. 14:11)

klar, *adj.* clear, limpid, transparent; bright; pure, serene; distinct, plain, lucid, evident. (Rev. 22:1)

die **Klarheit,** clearness, lucidity, clarity; brightness, transparency, purity; fineness. (Acts 22:11)

der **Klassenkampf,** class warfare, class conflict.

die **Klaue** (-n), claw, talon, fang; hoof, paw, clutch. (Dan. 7:19)

die **Klause** (-n), closet; cell, hermitage, den; mountain pass, defile.

der **Klausner** (-), hermit, recluse.

kleben, 1. *v.a.* to paste, to glue, to stick. 2. *v.n.* (*aux.* h.) to stick, to adhere (*an,* to). (Ps. 22:16)

das **Kleid** (-er), frock, dress, gown; garb, (*pl.*) clothes, garments. (Gen. 49:11)

kleiden, 1. *v.a.* to clothe, to dress; to deck, to adorn, to cover; to fit, to suit, to become. 2. *v.r.* to get dressed, to dress oneself. (Matt. 6:30)

die **Kleidung,** clothing, clothes, dress; costume, garb; drapery. (Matt. 6:25)

klein, *adj.* little, small, tiny, minute, diminutive; petty; mean, narrow-minded; exact; scanty; neat, nice. (Matt. 2:6)

(das) **Kleinasien,** Asia Minor.

der **Kleinbürger** (-), petty bourgeois, little man; philistine.

kleingeistig, *adj.* small- or narrow-minded.

kleingläubig, *adj.* of little faith, faint-hearted. (Matt. 6:30)

kleinherzig, *adj.* faint-hearted; narrow-minded.

die **Kleinlichkeit,** meanness, pettiness, paltriness.

der **Kleinmut, die Kleinmütigkeit,** faint-heartedness, despondency.

kleinmütig, *adj.* faint-hearted; dejected, despondent. (I Thess. 5:14)

das **Kleinod** (-ien), jewel, gem; treasure. (Gen. 24:53)

klerikal, *adj.* clerical.

der Klerikalismus, clericalism.

der Kleriker (-), cleric, priest, clergyman.

die Klerisei, clerical set, clergy.

der Klerus, clergy.

klingen, *ir.v.n.* (*aux.* h.) (*usually 3rd person only*) to ring, to sound, to tinkle. (Jer. 19:3)

die Klinik (-en), clinical hospital, nursing home.

klopfen, 1. *v.a. & n.* (*aux.* h.) to beat, to pound, to break (stones); to knock, to tap, to rap; to pulsate, to throb. 2. *n.* knocking, beating, throbbing, palpitation. (Luke 13:25)

das Kloster (⁻), monastery, nunnery, convent, cloister.
ins Kloster gehen, to take the veil (of women), to turn monk.

der Klosterbogen (⁻), Gothic arch.

der Klosterbruder (⁻er), friar.

die Klosterfrau (-en), **das Klosterfräulein** (-), nun.

der Klostergang (⁻e), cloister(s).

das Klostergelübde (-), monastic vow.

die Klostergemeinde (-n), fraternity, sisterhood.

das Klostergut (⁻er), estate belonging to a convent.

das Klosterleben, monastic life.

die Klosterleute, (*pl.*) conventuals, monks, nuns.

klösterlich, *adj.* monastic, conventual.

die Klosterordnung (-en), monastic discipline.

die Klosterschule (-n), monastery school.

die Klosterschwester (-n), lay sister; nun.

der Klostervorsteher (-), superior of a monastery.

das Klosterwesen, monasticism, monastic affairs.

die Klosterzucht, monastic discipline.

die Kluft (⁻e), cleft, fissure, gap, cleavage; chasm, gulf, ravine, abyss, gorge; log of wood. (Luke 16:26)

klug, *adj.* (comp. *klüger,* sup. *klügst*) intelligent, clever, smart, cunning, shrewd, clear-sighted, wise, sensible, prudent. (Gen. 3:6)

die Klugheit, prudence, discretion, good sense. (Eph. 1:8)

der Kluniazenser (-), Cluniac monk.

der Knecht (-e), servant, farmhand, menial. (Gen. 26:24)
Knecht Ruprecht, Santa Claus, St. Nicholas.

knechtisch, *adj.* menial; slavish; servile, crawling. (Rom. 8:15)

die Knechtschaft, servitude, slavery.

kneten, 1. *v.a.* to knead, to mill. 2. *n.* kneading, molding. (Gen. 18:6)

das Knie (- or -e), knee; bend, salient; elbow; bent, angle, joint. (Eph. 3:14)

knieen, *v.n.* (*aux.* h.) to be on one's knees, to be kneeling, to kneel; (*aux.* s.) to go down on one's knees. (Mark 1:40)

der Knöchel (-), knuckle; ankle(bone); (*pl.*) dice, bones. (Acts 3:7)

der Knorpel (-), cartilage, gristle. (Lev. 8:23)

der Kobold (-e), goblin, hobgoblin, elf, sprite.

kochen, 1. *v.a. & n.* (*aux.* h.) to cook; to boil; to stew. 2. *n.* cooking, boiling. (Exod. 23:19)

der Köcher (-), quiver. (Ps. 127:5)

der Kodex (-e & -ices), codex, old manuscript; code (of laws).

kodifizieren, *v.a.* to codify, to systematize (laws, etc.).

das Kodizill (-e), codicil.

der Kohl (-e), cabbage, kale, cole; plant. (Matt. 13:32)

die Kohle (-n), charcoal; coal; carbon. (John 21:9)
feurige Kohlen auf jemandes Haupt sammeln, to heap coals of fire on someone's head.

das Kohlenfeuer (-), a fire of coals. (John 18:18)

der Köhlerglaube, blind faith.

der Köhlerirrtum, belief founded on ignorance.

der Koitus, coitus, copulation.

Kolosser, (*pl.*) the Colossians.

kommen, 1. *ir.v.n.* (*aux.* s.) to come, to arrive; to approach, to get to, to draw near, to reach; to arise, to proceed from; to come about, to result, to fall out, to happen, to take place, to occur. 2. *n.* coming, arrival. (Gen. 9:11)
in den Himmel kommen, to go to heaven.

der Kommentar (-e), commentary.

kommunal, *adj.* communal, municipal.

der Kommunikant (-en), communicant.

die Kommunion, (holy) communion.

der Kommunismus, communism.

der Kommunist (-en), communist.

kommunistisch, *adj.* communist.

kommunizieren, *v.n.* to communicate.

die Kondolenz (-en), condolence.

der Kondolenzbesuch (-e), visit of condolence.

der Kondolenzbrief (-e), letter of condolence.

kondolieren, *v.n.* to condole (with), to express one's sympathy (with).

die Konferenz (-en), conference.

konferieren, *v.n.* (*aux.* h.) to confer together, to meet for or go into conference, to discuss.

die Konfession (-en), confession (of faith), creed; denomination.

konfessionell, *adj.* confessional.

konfessionslos, *adj.* atheistic, free-thinking.

der Konfessionswechsel (-), change of faith.

der Konfirmand (-en), **die Konfirmandin** (-nen), candidate for confirmation.

der Konfirmandenunterricht, confirmation classes.

die Konfirmation, confirmation.

konfirmieren, *v.a.* to confirm.

die Kongregation (-en), congregation; community.

der Kongregationalismus, congregationalism.

der König (-e), king. (Matt. 5:35)
die heilige drei Könige, the three Magi; *das erste Buch der Könige,* the First Book of Kings.

die Königin (-nen), queen. (Rev. 18:7)

königlich, *adj.* royal, kingly or queenly, regal, sovereign. (Luke 7:25)

das Königreich (-e), kingdom, realm. (Exod. 19:6)
das Königreich Gottes, the kingdom of God.

die Königswürde, royal dignity; kingship.

das Königtum, kingship, royalty; monarchial principle.
Königtum von Gottes Gnaden, kingship by divine right or by divine grace.

die Konkordanz (-en), concordance; agreement.

das Konkordat (-e), concordat, treaty between church and state.

das Konkordienbuch, Book of Concord, containing the basic Lutheran confessional formularies (1580).

die Konkordienformel, Formula of Concord (1577).

können, 1. *ir.v.a.* to know, to understand (how to do something); to have skill in; to have power, to be able to. 2. *v.n.* (*aux.* h.) to be able, to be capable of, to be permitted (to), to be in a position (to). 3. *n.* ability, faculty, knowledge, power. (Gen. 15:5)

der Konsens (-e), consent, assent, approval.

das Konsilium (-ien), consultation (of experts); expert opinion.

das Konsistorium (-ien), consistory; (Lutheran) church council.

konstant, *adj.* constant, permanent, stable, invariable, persistent, stationary.

(der) Konstantin, Constantine.

die Konstantinische Schenkung, Donation of Constantine.

die Konstitution (-en), constitution.

der Kontakt (-e), contact.

die Kontemplation, contemplation; meditation.

der Konvent (-e), convention, assembly.

die Konvention (-en), convention, usage; arrangement, agreement.

konventionell, *adj.* conventional, traditional; formal, ceremonious.

die Konvertierung (-en), conversion.

der Konvertit (-en), convert.

das Konzentrationslager (-), concentration camp.

das **Konzept** (-e), rough copy, first draft, notes (of a speech, etc.).

das **Konzil** (-e), council; church council. *das Konzil von Trient*, Council of Trent.

das **Konzilium** (-ien), (church) council.

der **Kopf** (-̈e), head; top, crown; title, heading; talented person, thinker; brains, abilities. (Gen. 3:15)

der **Kopte** (-n), Coptic.

koptisch, *adj.* Coptic.

der **Korb** (-̈e), basket, hamper, crate, pannier; (*fig.*) refusal, dismissal; rejection. (Matt. 14:20)

(der) Korinther, Corinthian.

korinthisch, *adj.* Corinthian.

das **Korn** (-̈er), grain, corn, cereal; seed, kernel; rye. (Gen. 27:28)

der **Körper** (-), body; bulk, matter, compound, substance; carcass, corpse. (I Cor. 15:40)

der (das) **Korpus** (-ora), body, totality, entirety, mass.

die **Kosmogonie,** cosmogony.

der **Kosmos,** universe.

kosten, 1. *pl.* cost(s), expense(s), expenditure, charge(s). 2. *v.a.* to cost; to require. (Ps. 49:9)
auf Kosten seiner Ehre, at the expense of his honor; *es kostet mich* or *mir einen schweren Kampf,* it costs me a hard struggle.

köstlich, *adj.* costly, precious, valuable; exquisite, excellent, delicious, tasty, dainty. (Matt. 13:46)

der **Kot,** dirt, filth; mire, mud; muck, manure, dung; excrement. (II Peter 2:22)

krachen, 1. *v.n.* (*aux.* h. & s.) to crack, to burst, to crash; to fail, to be ruined. 2. *v.a.* to crack (nuts, etc.). 3. *n.* crack, crash, roar. (Isa. 24:19)

die **Kraft** (-̈e), strength; power, force, vigor, energy; validity. (Exod. 32:11)

kräftig, *adj.* strong, powerful, energetic, vigorous, robust; pithy, forceful; effective; valid. (Acts 9:22)

kräftigen, *v.a.* to strengthen, to invigorate; to enforce; to harden. (I Peter 5:10)

krähen, *v.n.* (*aux.* h.) to screech, to squawk; to crow. (Matt. 26:34)

der **Krämer** (-), shopkeeper, retailer, tradesman, grocer. (Matt. 25:9)

der **Kranich** (-e), crane. (Isa. 38:14)

krank, *adj.* ill, sick, ailing, diseased. (Matt. 4:24)

die **Krankheit** (-en), illness, sickness, disease, malady, complaint. (Matt. 4:23)

der **Kranz** (-̈e), garland, wreath, triumphal wreath or crown, corona; (*fig.*) virginity, innocence. (Acts 14:13)

das **Kraut** (-̈er), herb, plant, vegetable, weed, leaves or tops of a plant; cabbage. (Gen. 1:11)

die **Kreatur** (-en), creature, created man, all living creatures; vassal. (Mark 10:6)

der **Krebs** (-e), crab, crayfish; cancer. (II Tim. 2:17)

der **Kreis** (-e), circle, ring, orbit; circuit, district; sphere, range, zone (of action, etc.). (Acts 17:31)

das **Kreuz** (-e), cross, crucifix, crosier; crossbar; loins, rump; (*fig.*) burden, affliction. (Matt. 10:38)
ans Kreuz schlagen, to fix or nail to the cross; *zu Kreuze kriechen,* to humble oneself, to repent.

die **Kreuzabnahme,** descent or deposition from the cross.

der **Kreuzberg,** Calvary. (see Luke 23:33)

das **Kreuzbild,** effigy of the cross.

kreuzbrav, *adj.* thoroughly honest or good.

die **Kreuzerhöhung,** elevation of the cross.

der **Kreuzesstamm,** holy rood.

der **Kreuzfahrer** (-), crusader.

die **Kreuzfahrt** (-en), crusade.

der **Kreuzgang** (-̈e), cloisters.

das **Kreuzgewölbe** (-), cruciform vault.

das **Kreuzheer** (-e), army of the cross or of crusaders.

kreuzigen, *v.a.* to crucify. (Matt. 20:19)

die **Kreuzigung** (-en), crucifixion.

die **Kreuzkirche,** church on cruciform plan; church of the holy cross.

die **Kreuzpredigt** (-en), crusading sermon.

der **Kreuzritter** (-), crusader.

das **Kreuzschiff** (-e), transept.

die **Kreuztragung,** bearing of the cross.

das **Kreuzverhör** (-e), cross-examination.

der Kreuzweg (-e), crossing, crossroads; way or stations of the cross.

die Kreuzwoche, Rogation week.

das Kreuz(es)zeichen, sign of the cross.

der Kreuzzug (⁻e), crusade.

der Krieg (-e), war, warfare; strife. (Matt. 24:6)

kriegen, v.n. (aux. h.) to wage war. (Rev. 2:16)

der Krieger (-), warrior, soldier. (Isa. 5:22)

das Kriegsgeschrei, rumor of war; battle cry. (Mark 13:7)

der Kriegsknecht (-e), mercenary. (Matt. 8:9)

kriminal, adj. criminal, penal.

kriminell, adj. criminal, culpable.

die Krippe (-n), crib, manger, feeding trough; fence. (Luke 2:7)

die Krise (-n), crisis, turning point; depression.

der Kristall (-e), crystal. (Rev. 4:6)

das Kriterium (-ien), criterion.

die Krone (-n), crown; coronet; (fig.) diadem, king, kingdom; (fig.) head. (Rev. 2:10)

krönen, v.a. to crown; to honor, to exalt, to put the finishing touch (to); to surmount. (Ps. 5:13)

der Krug (⁻e), pitcher, jug; mug, pot, jar, urn; public house, tavern. (Gen. 24:14)

krumm, adj. crooked, bent, curved, wry, twisted, bowed, arched; indirect; dishonest. (Ps. 125:5)

der Krummstab (⁻e), crosier; (fig.) episcopal authority.

der Krüppel (-), cripple. (Matt. 18:8)

das Kruzifix (-e), crucifix.

die Krypta (-en), crypt.

der Kuchen (-), cake; tart; pastry. (Gen. 18:6)

das Küchlein (-), chicken, chick. (Matt. 23:37)

die Kuh (⁻e), cow; female of deer, elephant, etc. (Isa. 11:7)
fette or magere Kühe, fat or lean kine.

kühl, adj. cool; fresh; (fig.) lukewarm, unconcerned, indifferent, unmoved. (Gen. 3:8)

kühn, adj. bold, brave, daring, audacious. (II Cor. 11:21)

die Kultur (-en), cultivation, forest plantation; culture, civilization.

die Kulturgeschichte, history of civilization.

kulturgeschichtlich, adj. relating to the history of civilization.

das Kulturgut, cultural value.

der Kulturkampf, Bismarck's struggle with Catholicism.

der Kümmel (-), caraway or cumin(-seed). (Matt. 23:23)

der Kummer, grief, sorrow, sadness, trouble, worry, care. (Gen. 3:17)

kümmerlich, 1. adj. miserable, wretched, pitiful; poor, stunted, scanty, needy. 2. adv. scarcely, barely, with great trouble.

kund, indec. pred. adj. known, public. (Deut. 8:2)

der Kundschafter (-), spy, scout, explorer. (Gen. 42:9)

kundtun, 1. v.a. to notify, to inform; to announce, to proclaim, to set forth. 2. v.r. to declare oneself (to be). (Ps. 143:8)

künftig, adj. future; coming, to come, next. (Matt. 3:7)

die Kunst (⁻e), art, skill, dexterity, ingenuity, trick, artifice. (Acts 17:29)

die Kunstgeschichte, history of art.

das Kunstmittel (-), artificial means.

der Kürbis (-se), pumpkin, gourd.

küren, v.a. to choose, to elect.

die Kurie, curia; papal court.

kurz, 1. adj. short, brief; abrupt; summary, concise, concentrated. 2. adv. in short, in a word, briefly. (Rom. 16:20)

die Kürze, shortness, brevity, conciseness; short space of time; short syllable. (Luke 18:8)

der Kuß (⁻[ss]e), kiss. (Luke 7:45)

küssen, v.a. & n. (aux. h.) & v.r. to kiss. (Gen. 33:4)

die Kutte (-n), cowl.

Ll

laben, 1. *v.a.* to refresh, to revive, to restore; to comfort, to delight. 2. *v.r.: sich mit Speisen laben,* to take some refreshment; *sich an einer Speise laben,* to enjoy a dish thoroughly. (Acts 27:34)

lachen, 1. *v.n.* (*aux.* h.) to laugh; *über einen* or *eine Sache lachen,* to laugh at someone or something. 2. *n.* laughter, laugh. (Gen. 17:17)

lächerlich, *adj.* laughable; ridiculous; droll, comical.

die Lade (-n), box, chest, case; drawer; ark.

laden, *ir.v.a.* to load, to lade; *auf sich (acc.) laden,* to bring down upon oneself, to incur. (Lev. 22:9)
ein Verbrechen auf sich laden, to commit a crime.

die Lage (-n), situation, position, site, location, posture; state, condition, circumstances.

das Lager (-), storehouse, depot, store; camp, encampment; (*fig.*) party, side; stratum; bed; lair, den, hole, cover. (Exod. 19:17)
ins feindliche Lager übergehen, to go over to the enemy; *vom Lager aufstehen,* to rise from a bed of sickness.

lagern, 1. *v.n.* (*aux.* h. & s.) & *v.r.* to lie down, to rest; to camp; to be encamped; to be in store. 2. *v.a.* to lay down; to deposit, to pile, to place; to encamp (troops). (Gen. 3:24)

lahm, *adj.* lame, crippled; paralyzed; weak, impotent, paltry. (Matt. 11:5)

die Lahmheit, lameness.

die Lähmung, lameness, paralysis, palsy.

das Laiblein (-), small loaf (of bread). (Jer. 37:21)

der Laie (-n), layman; novice; (*pl.*) the laity. (Acts 4:13)

der Laienbruder (-̈), lay brother.

die Laiengüter, (*n. pl.*) temporalities.

laienhaft, *adj.* lay, belonging to the laity; uninitiated, amateur.

der Laienpriester (-), lay reader.

der Laienstand, die Laienwelt, laity, laymen.

lallen, *v.a. & n.* (*aux.* h.) to stammer; to babble, to speak indistinctly.

das Lamm (-̈er), lamb. (Isa. 11:6)
das Lamm Gottes, Lamb of God.

die Lamm(e)sgeduld, patience of Job.

lammfromm, lammherzig, *adj.* gentle as a lamb.

die Lampe (-n), lamp. (Matt. 25:1)

das Land, 1. *n.* land (as opposed to water); country (as opposed to town); soil, earth, ground, arable land. 2. *n.* (-̈er) country, region, realm, territory, province, state. (Gen. 12:1)

das Landesarchiv (-e), national archives.

der Landesbrauch (-̈e), national custom.

der Landesfürst (-en), reigning prince, sovereign.

der Landesherr (-en), ruler, sovereign.

die Landesherrschaft, sovereignty, the crown.

die Landeskirche (-n), established church.

die Landesregierung (-en), central government.

die Landessitte (-n), national custom.

der Landesvater (-̈er), sovereign.

der Landesverrat, high treason.

das Landeswohl, national welfare.

der Landfriede(n), public peace.

der Landgeistliche (-n), country clergyman.

die Landgemeinde (-n), village community; country parish.

die Landgemeindeordnung (-en), local government regulations.

die Landleute, (*pl.*) country people, peasant farmers.

der Landpastor (-en), **der Landpfarrer** (-), country parson.

die Landpfarre (-n), country living or parsonage.

der Landpfleger (-), governor, prefect. (Matt. 27:2)

die Landplage (-n), scourge, calamity.

das Landrecht, provincial law or jurisdiction.

die Landschaft (-en), landscape, scenery; district, region.

die Landschule (-n), village school.

der Landsmann (*pl.* -leute), compatriot, fellow countryman.

die Landstraße (-n), highroad, main road, highway. (Luke 14:23)

der Landvogt ("e), provincial governor.

das Landvolk, country people; peasantry.

der Landwirt (-e), farmer.

lang, 1. *adj.* (comp. *länger,* sup. *längst*) long; tall; high, lofty; prolonged, protracted, lengthy. 2. *adv. & prep.* (*preceded by acc.*) long; for, during. 3. **lang(e),** *adv.* (comp. *länger,* sup. *am längsten, längst*) a long while, long; by far. (Matt. 17:17)

die Länge (-n), length; size; longitude; duration, quantity; (*fig.*) tedious passage (in a book, etc.). (Matt. 6:27)

langen, *v.n.* (*aux.* h.) to be sufficient, to suffice; to reach. (Gen. 47:9)

die Langeweile, tediousness, tedium, boredom, ennui.

die Langmut, die Langmütigkeit, forbearance, patience, long-suffering. (Rom. 2:4)

langmütig, *adj.* long-suffering, forbearing, patient. (I Cor. 13:4)

langsam, *adj.* slow, tardy. (James 1:19)

die Langsamkeit, slowness, tardiness; dullness.

das Langschiff (-e), nave.

längst, *adv.* long ago, long since. (Luke 23:8)

langwierig, *adj.* lengthy, protracted, tedious; chronic.

der Lappen (-), rag, cloth, duster; patch. (Matt. 9:16)

die Lärche (-n), larch.

der Lärm, noise, din, uproar, row; bustle; alarm; fuss.

lärmen, *v.a.* (*aux.* h.) to make a noise or an uproar. (Luke 22:6)

laß, *adj.* lax, slack; weary; spiritless; slothful. (Luke 18:1)

lassen, 1. *ir.v.a.* to let; to leave alone, to desist or refrain from; to leave, to relinquish, to part with, to let go; to abandon. 2. *v.n.* (*aux.* h.) to look, to appear, to become, to suit. 3. *n.:* *unser Tun und Lassen,* our commissions and omissions, our behavior or conduct. (Gen. 24:56)

lässig, *adj.* inactive, indolent, sluggish, lazy, idle; careless, negligent. (Jer. 48:10)

die läßliche Sünde, venial sin.

die Laßsünde (-n), venial sin.

die Last (-en), load, burden, weight; cargo, freight, tonnage; charge, tax; trouble. (Exod. 2:11)

lastbar, *adj.* capable of bearing a burden. (Matt. 21:5)

lastbare Tiere, beasts of burden.

der Lästerer (-), slanderer, calumniator; blasphemer. (Eph. 4:27)

lästerlich, *adj.* blasphemous, slanderous; scandalous, shameful, disgraceful, abominable.

lästern, *v.a. & n.* to slander, to defame (*auf* or *über*); to revile (*wider* or *gegen*); to blaspheme. (Isa. 1:4)

die Lästerung (-en), slander, calumny, blasphemy. (Matt. 12:31)

das Lästerwort (-e), blasphemous word. (Acts 6:11)

lästig, *adj.* burdensome, troublesome, annoying, tedious.

die Lästigkeit, irksomeness, inconvenience, annoyance.

der Lastträger (-), porter.

(das) Latein, Latin.

lateinisch, *adj.* Latin.

der Latitudinarier (-), latitudinarian.

lau, *adj.* lukewarm, tepid; mild (of weather); indifferent, halfhearted. (Rev. 3:16)

die Laubhütte (-n), bower, tabernacle. (Ps. 81:4)

das Laubhüttenfest, Feast of Tabernacles.

lauern, *v.n.* (*aux.* h.) to watch, to observe keenly, to be on the lookout; to lie in ambush, to lurk, to lie in wait for. (Acts 23:21)

der Lauf (⁻e), course, career, way; current, circulation, flow; track, path, orbit; progress, movement, running, action, pace. (Acts 20:24)

laufen, 1. *ir.v.n.* (*aux.* h. & s.) to run; to go; to walk, to move; to flow, to ooze, to leak, to run out, to run down; to extend, to stretch; to be in circulation; to pass. 2. *v.a.* to contract by running; to run. (John 20:4)

der Läufer (-), runner, courser, racer; footman; messenger. (Job 9:25)

die Lauge (-n), leach, lye. (Jer. 2:22)

die Laune (-n), mood, humor, temper, frame of mind; whim, caprice.

launenhaft, *adj.* moody, capricious, changeable.

die Launenhaftigkeit, moodiness, capriciousness; waywardness.

laut, 1. *adj.* loud, noisy, audible; open, public. 2. *adv.* aloud; *laut werden,* to become known, to get about or abroad; to become noisy. (Exod. 2:14)

die Laute (-n), lute.

lauten, *v.n.* (*aux.* h.) to sound, to run, to read. (Mark 14:70)
wie lautet das dritte Gebot? what does the third commandment say?

läuten, 1. *v.a. & n.* (*aux.* h.) to ring, to peal, to toll, to sound. 2. *n.* ringing, tolling.
zur Kirche läuten, to ring the bells for church.

der Lautenschläger (-), **der Lautenspieler** (-), lute player, lutenist.

lauter, 1. *adj.* clear; pure, unmixed, unalloyed, undefiled; genuine, true, candid, unvarnished, honest. 2. *adv.* (*used as indec. adj.*) only, nothing but, pure and simple, downright, mere, sheer, rank. (Rev. 21:18)

das Läuterfeuer, purifying fire; purgatory fire.

die Lauterkeit, purity, clearness; uprightness, integrity, sincerity. (I Cor. 5:8)

läutern, *v.a.* to purify, to refine, to clear, to clarify, to strain, to rectify (spirits); to purge; (*fig.*) to ennoble. (Isa. 48:10)

die Läuterung, purification; refining, clarification.

lax, *adj.* lax, loose.
laxe Moral, easy morals; *laxe Sitten,* loose living.

die Laxheit, laxity, looseness.

leben, 1. *v.n.* (*aux.* h.) to live, to be alive, to exist, to pass one's life; to dwell. 2. *v.r.: sich satt leben* or *sich satt gelebt haben,* to be weary of life. 3. *n.* (-) life, existence; activity, vivacity, liveliness, stir; living flesh, the quick; biography. (Gen. 3:22)
der Gerechte wird seines Glaubens leben, the just shall live by faith; *so wahr Gott lebt,* as sure as there is a God; *auf Leben und Tod,* a matter of life and death.

lebendig, *adj.* living, live, alive; active, lively, vivacious. (Gen. 2:7)

lebendigmachend, *adj.* vivifying, enlivening.
lebendigmachende Gnade, quickening grace.

der Lebensabend, decline of life, old age.

das Lebensalter, age.

die Lebensaufgabe, lifework.

der Lebensbaum, tree of life.

die Lebensbedingung (-en), condition essential for life; condition of vital importance.

lebensbejahend, *adj.* optimistic, virile.

die Lebensbeschreibung (-cn), biography.

das Lebensbild (-er), sketch of a person's life, short biography.

das Lebensbuch, book of life. (Rev. 21:27)

das Lebensende, end of life.
bis an mein Lebensende, to the end of my days.

der Lebenserhaltungstrieb (-e), instinct of self-preservation.

die Lebensfrage (-n), vital question.

lebensfreudig, lebensfroh, *adj.* lighthearted, vivacious.

die Lebensführung, manner of living, conduct.

die Lebensgefahr (-en), danger to life.

lebensgefährlich, *adj.* perilous, highly dangerous.

der Lebensgefährte (-n), **die Lebensgefährtin** (-nen), life's companion, partner for life; husband, wife.

die Lebensgeschichte, biography.

die Lebensgewohnheiten, (*pl.*) lifelong habits.

die Lebenshaltung, standard of living or life.

der Lebenshauch, breath of life.

der Lebenskreis, surroundings.

die Lebenslage, position of life.

lebenslang, *adj.* lifelong; for life.

der Lebenslauf (⁻e), curriculum vitae, personal record.

die Lebenslehre, biology; precept, rule of life.

die Lebenslust, vivacity, exhilaration, high spirits.

lebenslustig, *adj.* cheerful, gay; high-spirited.

lebensmüde, *adj.* dispirited, dejected, disconsolate, despondent, depressed.

der Lebensmut, high spirits, exhilaration, energy.

die Lebensnotdurft, (bare) necessities of life.

der Lebensraum, environment, milieu, living space.

die Lebensregel (-n), rule of conduct, maxim, precept.

der Lebensretter (-), lifesaver.

lebenssatt, *adj.* full of years. (Gen. 25:8)

die Lebensstrafe, capital punishment.

der Lebensunterhalt, livelihood, living, subsistence.

lebenswahr, *adj.* true to life, lifelike.

der Lebensweg, path through life.

die Lebensweise (-n), mode of life, way of living, habits.

die Lebensweisheit, practical wisdom.

das Lebenswerk, lifework.

lebenswichtig, *adj.* vital, essential.

die Lebenszeit, age; lifetime.

das Lebensziel (-e), **der Lebenszweck** (-e), aim in life.

das Lebewesen (-), living being or creature, organism.

lebhaft, *adj.* lively, vivacious, spirited, active, gay; bright, vivid, brilliant.

die Lebhaftigkeit, liveliness, vivacity, gaiety.

der Lebtag: (*all*) *mein Lebtag,* in all my life.

die Lebzeiten, (*pl.*) life, lifetime.

lecken, *v.n.* (*archaic*) *wider den Stachel lecken,* to kick against the pricks. (Acts 9:5)

lecken, *v.a.* to lick. (Luke 16:21)

das Leder (-), leather; skin; leather apron.

ledern, *adj.* leather, leathery; dull, tedious. (Matt. 3:4)

ledig, *adj.* unmarried, single; empty, devoid (of), free; exempt (from); vacant. (Luke 4:18)

leer, *adj.* empty, vacant, void, unoccupied, blank; idle, unfounded; hollow, vain. (Gen. 1:2)

legen, 1. *v.a.* to lay, to put, to place; to deposit; to set, to sow, to plant. 2. *v.r.* to lie down; to cease, to die down; to subside, to abate, to settle, to slacken, to be quiet. (Exod. 4:15)

die Legende (-n), legend, myth; inscription, caption, legend.

legendenhaft, *adj.* legendary, mythical.

die Legion (-en), legion. (Matt. 26:53)

die Legislative, legislature.

legitim, *adj.* legitimate, lawful.

die Legitimation, authority (to act); acknowledgment of legitimacy.

legitimieren, 1. *v.a.* to prove the identity of; to authorize; to legitimize; to make lawful. 2. *v.r.* to prove one's identity.

das Lehen (-), fief, feudal tenure.

der Lehensherr (-en), feudal lord, liege lord.

der Lehensmann (⁻er), vassal.

das Lehen(s)recht (-e), feudal law.

der Lehm (-e), loam, clay; mud.

das Lehmhaus (⁻er), house of clay. (Job 4:19)

lehnen, *v.a. & n.* (*aux.* h. & s.) to lean (against), to recline, to rest (upon). (Gen. 18:4)

das Lehramt (⁻er), teacher's post, professorship; teaching profession.

die Lehranstalt (-en), educational establishment.

die Lehraufgabe, program of work.

das Lehrbuch (⁻er), textbook.

die Lehre (-n), instruction, lesson, precept, teaching, warning; moral, doctrine, dogma, tenet, theory, science; apprenticeship. (Deut. 32:2)
die Lehre Christi, Christ's teaching.

lehren, *v.a.* (*einem etwas*) to teach, to instruct; to inform; to show, to prove. (Exod. 24:12)

der Lehrer (-), teacher, schoolmaster, instructor, tutor. (John 3:2)

die Lehrerwelt, scholastic world.

das Lehrfach (¨er), subject, branch of study.

der Lehrgegenstand, subject taught, branch of study.

lehrhaft, *adj.* didactic; schoolmasterly; instructive. (I Tim. 3:2)

die Lehrmeinung (-en), dogma; hypothesis.

lehrreich, *adj.* instructive.

der Lehrsatz (¨e), thesis, dogma, doctrine, proposition, theorem, precept.

der Lehrspruch (¨e), maxim, adage.

das Lehrsystem, doctrinal system.

die Lehrtätigkeit, educational work, teaching.

der Leib (-er), body; abdomen, belly; womb; waist, trunk. (Matt. 5:29)
der Leib des Herrn, the consecrated wafer or bread, the host; *mit Leib und Seele,* with heart and soul.

leibeigen, *adj.* in bondage. (Jer. 34:9)

die Leibesfrucht, fetus, embryo, offspring. (Ps. 127:3)

leibhaftig, *adj.* embodied, real, true, incarnate. (Col. 2:9)

leiblich, *adj.* bodily, material, corporeal, somatic; temporal. (Luke 3:22)
leibliche Güter, carnal things; *leiblicher Tod,* natural death.

die Leiblichkeit, corporeality.

der Leibrock (¨e), frock coat, dress coat. (Exod. 28:4)

der Leibspruch (¨e), favorite saying or maxim.

die Leiche (-n), dead body, corpse, cadaver; funeral.

der Leichenacker (¨), churchyard, burying ground, cemetery, necropolis.

das Leichenbegängnis (-se), funeral.

der Leichenbegleiter (-), mourner.

die Leichenbegleitung, funeral procession.

der Leichenbeschauer (-), coroner.

der Leichenbesorger (-), **der Leichenbestatter** (-), undertaker.

leichenblaß, *adj.* pale as death.

der Leichenchor, funeral dirge, requiem.

der Leichendienst, burial service.

die Leichenfarbe, pallor of death.

die Leichenfeier (-n), obsequies, funeral service.

das Leichenfeld (-er), field strewed with corpses, battlefield.

die Leichengebräuche, (*pl.*) funeral rites.

der Leichengeruch, cadaverous smell.

der Leichengesang, dirge.

das Leichengewölbe (-), **die Leichengruft** (¨e), burial vault, catacombs.

leichenhaft, *adj.* corpselike, cadaverous.

die Leichenhalle (-n), mortuary, morgue.

das Leichenhemd (-en), shroud, winding sheet.

das Leichenmahl (-e), funeral banquet.

die Leichenmusik, funeral music.

die Leichenpredigt (-en), funeral sermon.

die Leichenrede (-n), funeral oration.

die Leichenschädigung (-en), desecration of corpses.

die Leichenschau, coroner's inquest, postmortem examination.

der Leichenschauer (-), coroner.

der Leichenschleier (-), shroud.

der Leichenstein (-e), tombstone.

der Leichenträger (-), bearer.

das Leichentuch (¨er), winding sheet, shroud, pall.

die Leichenverbrennung, cremation.

der Leichenwagen (-), hearse.

der Leichenzug, funeral procession.

der Leichnam (-e), dead body, corpse, remains. (Mark 15:43)

leicht, *adj.* light, easy, free, facile, nimble; mild; slight, moderate, gentle; fickle, frivolous, careless; weak, feeble, faint. (Matt. 9:5)

die Leichtfertigkeit, frivolity, thoughtlessness, wantonness.

leichtgläubig, *adj.* credulous.

die Leichtgläubigkeit, credulity.

leichtherzig, *adj.* cheerful.

leichtsinnig, *adj.* thoughtless, careless, rash, frivolous.

die Leichtsinnigkeit, thoughtlessness, rashness, indiscretion.

leid, 1. *adj.* painful, disagreeable (only predicatively with *sein, tun, werden,* and dat.). 2. *n.* harm, hurt, injury, wrong; pain, sorrow, grief, mourning. (II Sam. 1:26)

leiden, 1. *ir.v.a.* to suffer, to bear, to endure, to undergo, to put up with, to tolerate; to allow, to permit, to admit. 2. *v.n.* (*aux.* h.) to suffer, to be in pain. 3. *n.* suffering, pain, torment; affliction, malady, ailment, chronic complaint, disease. (Matt. 11:12) *das Leiden Christi,* the passion of our Lord.

der Leidensbecher, cup of sorrow.

leidenschaftlich, *adj.* passionate, vehement; enthusiastic.

leidenschaftsfrei, leidenschaftslos, *adj.* apathetic, dispassionate; calm.

die Leidenschaftslosigkeit, apathy.

der Leidensgefährte (-n), **der Leidensgenosse** (-n), fellow sufferer, companion in misfortune.

die Leidensgeschichte, tale of woe; Christ's passion.

der Leidenskelch, cup of sorrow.

die Leidensstationen, (*pl.*) the stations of the cross.

der Leidensweg, way of the cross; life of suffering.

die Leidenswoche, Passion Week.

leidtragend, *adj.* mourning.

der Leidtragende (-n), mourner.

leidvoll, *adj.* full of grief, sorrowful.

das Leidwesen: *zu unserem Leidwesen,* to our sorrow.

die Leier (-n), lyre.

leihen, *ir.v.a.* to lend; to loan; to borrow, to hire. (Luke 6:35)

leinen, 1. *adj.* linen. 2. *n.* linen; linen goods. (John 19:40)

die Leinwand, linen, linen cloth; canvas. (Matt. 27:59)

leis(e), *adj.* low, soft, gentle; slight, faint; fine, delicate.

leisten, *v.a.* to do, to fulfil, to carry out, to perform, to accomplish; to effect, to realize; to afford, to give; to produce. (Rom. 6:12) *Buße leisten,* to do penance.

die Leistung (-en), performance, execution; achievement, work; production, output, result, effect.

der Leitartikel (-), leading article, leader.

leiten, *v.a.* to lead, to guide, to conduct; to train, to direct; to manage, to oversee, to preside over, to govern. (Exod. 33:14)

der Leiter (-), leader, guide, conductor; director, manager, governor, principal, head. (Matt. 23:16)

der Leitgedanke (-n), main idea, keynote.

die Lektion (-en), lesson; rebuke.

die Lektüre (-n), reading; reading matter, books, literature.

die Lende (-n), loin, loins; haunch, hip; thigh. (Exod. 12:11)

lenkbar, *adj.* tractable, manageable, docile.

lenken, *v.a.* to turn, to guide, to direct; to navigate, to pilot; to lead, to control, to manage; to steer, to drive. (Ps. 33:15) *der Mensch denkt, Gott lenkt,* man proposes, God disposes.

der Lenz (-e), spring; prime, bloom (of life); (*pl.*) years (of age).

die Lepra, leprosy.

der Leprakranke (-n), leper.

die Lerche (-n), lark.

lernen, 1. *v.a.* to learn; to study; to teach. 2. *v.r.: die Verse lernen sich leicht,* the verses are easy to learn; *gelernt,* trained, expert, skilled. 3. *n.* learning, study.

lesen, 1. *ir.v.a.* (*also v.n. aux.* h.) to read; to lecture (*über einen Gegenstand,* on a subject). 2. *n.* reading. (Exod. 24:7) *die Messe lesen,* to say mass.

der Leserkreis (-e), readers; public (for newspapers and periodicals).

der Lesestoff, reading matter.

die Lesewelt, reading public.

letzt, 1. *adj.* last, latest, ultimate, final; extreme. 2. *adv.* lately, of late, in the last place. (Matt. 5:26) *die letzte Ölung,* extreme unction.

der Letztere, die Letztere, das Letztere, the latter.

die Leuchte (-n), luminary, light, lamp. (Rev. 21:23)

leuchten, 1. *v.n.* (*aux.* h.) to shine, to light, to illuminate, to radiate, to emit or give light; to beam, to glow, to burn, to glare, to glimmer. 2. *n.* shining, burning; glare, glow, illumination. (Num. 6:25)

der Leuchter (-), candlestick. (Exod. 25:31)

leugnen, *v.a.* to deny; to disavow, to recant, to retract. (Matt. 26:70)

die Leugnung, disavowal.

der Leumund, reputation; character; *guter Leumund,* good name.

die Leute, (*pl.*) people, persons, folk, crowd, public, the world; servants, hands, rank and file, men. (Matt. 5:16)

die Leutseligkeit, kindness; affability, geniality, good nature; popularity.

der Levit (-en), Levite. (Deut. 10:9)

die Lexikalien, (*pl.*) things connected with a dictionary.

(der) Libanon, Mount Lebanon.

licht, 1. *adj.* light, luminous, shining, bright; lucid, clear; pale; thin, sparse. 2. *n.* (-er) light, illumination; lighting. (Gen. 1:3) *sein Licht unter den Scheffel stellen,* to hide one's light under a bushel; *es werde Licht,* let there be light!

der Lichterbaum (-̈e), Christmas tree.

der Lichterglanz, brightness, brilliancy (of light).

der Lichtkreis, luminous circle, halo.

lieb, *adj.* dear, beloved; valued, esteemed; attractive, charming, agreeable, delightful. (Ps. 106:24) *der liebe Gott,* God (Almighty).

die Liebe, love, affection, fondness; kindness, favor, charity; beloved, love. (Matt. 24:12) *Lieb und Leid, in Liebe und Leid,* in joy and grief, for better or for worse; *christliche Liebe, Nächstenliebe,* love for others.

liebeleer, *adj.* loveless, lacking in love.

lieben, *v.a.* to love, to be fond of; to like; to fancy, to cherish (an idea, etc.). (I John 2:10)

das Liebesband (-e), bond of love.

das Liebesmahl (-e), love feast, agape; banquet.

das Liebespaar (-e), lovers, couple.

die Liebespflicht, Christian duty.

die Liebestreue, constancy.

das Liebeswerk, work of charity, Christian act.

die Liebesworte, (*pl.*) loving words.

liebevoll, *adj.* loving, kind, affectionate.

die Liebfrauenkirche, Church of Our Lady.

liebgewinnen, *v.a.* (*sep.*) to take a fancy to, to grow fond of. (I Sam. 18:1)

liebhaben, *v.a.* (*sep.*) to be fond of, to like, to love. (John 3:35)

der Liebhaber (-), lover, admirer, gallant; dilettante, amateur; fancier. (Luke 6:32)

lieblich, *adj.* lovely; charming, delightful, pleasing, sweet. (Gen. 3:6)

der Lieblingssohn (-̈e), favorite son.

lieblos, *adj.* loveless; unloving, unkind, hardhearted.

die Lieblosigkeit, uncharitableness, unkindness.

liebreich, *adj.* loving, kind.

das Lied (-er), song; lay, ballad; air, tune. (Exod. 15:1) *geistliches Lied,* hymn, psalm; *das Hohe Lied (Salomonis),* Song of Solomon, Song of Songs.

das Liederbuch (-̈er), songbook; hymnbook.

der Liederdichter (-), lyric poet; song writer.

der Liederkranz, choral society; collection of song.

liederlich, *adj.* slovenly, disorderly; lewd, immoral, loose.

die Liederlichkeit, slovenliness, disorderliness; debauchery, loose living, immoral conduct.

die Liedertafel, glee club.

liedhaft, *adj.* lyrical, tuneful.

liegen, *ir.v.n.* (*aux.* h. & s.) to lie, to rest, to repose; to be situated, to be; to lodge. (Gen. 47:30)

die Lilie (-n), lily. (Matt. 6:28)

lind, *adj.* soft, gentle, mild; smooth, scoured. (Prov. 15:1)

lindern, *v.a.* to mitigate, to alleviate, to soften, to ease; to soothe, to relieve, to moderate. (Isa. 1:6)

die Lindigkeit, moderation. (Phil. 4:5)

link, *adj.* left; left-hand; clumsy, awkward; left-handed. (Matt. 6:3)

die Linke, left hand, left; left wing, the left (politics). (Deut. 5:29)

das Linsengericht (-e), pea soup, mess of pottage, pottage of lentils. (Gen. 25:34)

die Lippe (-n), lip; labium; edge, border. (Matt. 15:8)

das Lippenbekenntnis, lip service.

die List (-en), cunning, craftiness, artfulness; artifice, device, trick. (Gen. 27:35)

listig, *adj.* crafty, cunning, deceitful, sly. (Gen. 3:1)

die Litanei (-en), litany.

der Literat (-en), man of letters, literary man, writer.

die Literaturangaben, (*pl.*) bibliographical data.

der Literaturnachweis, reading list, books consulted.

die Literaturzeitung (-en), literary journal, (literary and critical) review.

die Liturgie (-n), liturgy; responses.

liturgisch, *adj.* liturgical.

das Lob, praise, commendation, eulogy, applause; fame, reputation. (Matt. 21:16)

loben, *v.a.* to praise, to commend, to laud; to glorify, to extol; to value, to estimate. (Acts 2:47)
gelobt sei Gott! God be praised!

lobenswert, lobenswürdig, *adj.* praiseworthy, laudable, commendable.

der Lobgesang (-e), song of praise, hymn of praise, panegyric. (Exod. 15:2)

löblich, *adj.* praiseworthy, laudable, commendable. (Ps. 96:6)

das Loblied, *see* **Lobgesang.**

lobpreisen, *v.a.* (*insep.*) to praise, to extol.

die Lobpreisung (-en), praise, glorification.

die Lobrede (-n), eulogy, panegyric.

lobsingen, *ir.v.n.* (*aux.* h.) (*sep.*) (*einem*) to sing praises to. (Ps. 18:50)

der Lobspruch (-e), eulogy.

das Loch (-er), hole, opening, cavity, orifice, aperture; gap, breach; slot; pore, eye; perforation, leak. (Isa. 11:8)

löch(e)rig, *adj.* full of holes; porous; perforated; (*fig.*) untenable, shaky (of arguments). (Jer. 2:13)

locken, *v.a. & n.* (*aux.* h.) to attract, to entice, to coax, to allure, to tempt, to bait. (James 1:14)

die Lockung (-en), attraction, enticement, allurement.

lodern, *v.n.* (*aux.* h.) to blaze, to flame or flare up; (*fig.*) to glow, to burn.

die Loge (-n), Freemason's lodge.

der Logenbruder (-), (brother) mason.

der Logenmeister (-), master of a lodge.

die Logik, logic.

der Logiker (-), logician.

logisch, *adj.* logical.

der Lohn (-e), reward, recompense, compensation; payment, salary, wages. (Gen. 15:1)

lohnen, *v.a. & n.* (*aux.* h.) to remunerate, to reward, to recompense, to compensate; to pay, to repay.
Gott lohn' es dir! may God reward you for it!

die Lokalverhältnisse, (*pl.*) local conditions.

der Lorbeerbaum (-e), laurel, bay tree. (Ps. 37:35)

los, *pred. adj. & adv.* loose, slack; flowing; free, released. (Ps. 124:7)

das Los (-e), lot, share, allotment, portion; fate, destiny; chance, fortune, hazard. (Matt. 27:35)

löschen, 1. *ir.v.n.* (*aux.* s.) to go out, to be extinguished. 2. *v.a.* to extinguish, to quench, to put out; to discharge. (Jer. 4:4)

lose, *adj.* loose, slack, movable, unsteady; vagrant; wanton, frivolous, irresponsible, naughty. (I Sam. 1:16)

das Lösegeld (-er), ransom.

losen, *v.n.* (*aux.* h.) to draw lots (*um,* for). (John 19:24)

lösen, *v.a.* to loosen, to slacken, to untie, to unbind, to relax; to detach, to dissociate, to break off, to give up. (Matt. 16:19)

losgeben, *ir.v.a.* to set free, to liberate. (Matt. 27:15)

loskaufen, *v.a.* to redeem, to ransom.

loslassen, *ir.v.a.* to let loose, to let go, to release, to set free; to break out into. (Matt. 18:27)

losmachen, 1. *v.a.* to loosen, to make loose; to undo, to cast off. 2. *v.r.* to get away; to disengage or extricate oneself (from); to get free (from).

lossagen, *v.r.* (*von*) to renounce, to give up.

die Lossagung (-en), renunciation, withdrawal.

die Lossprechung (-en), acquittal; absolution; release.

die Losung (-en), watchword, sign, countersign, signal.

das Losungswort (-e), watchword.

der Lotterbube (-n), rascal, good-for-nothing. (Acts 17:18)

der Löwe (-n), lion. (Gen. 49:9)

die Löwengrube (-n), lions' den.

die Löwenstärke, stubborn, invincible strength.

der Löwenzahn, lion's tooth; dandelion. (Ecclesiasticus 21:2)

die Löwin (-nen), lioness.

loyal, *adj.* loyal.

die Loyalität, loyalty.

die Lücke (-n), gap, break, breach, opening, space, cavity, hole; blank, omission, deficiency. (Isa. 58:12)

das Luder (-), carrion; bait, lure, decoy; low scoundrel, wretch, rascal.

das Luderleben, dissolute life.

die Luft (-̈e), air, atmosphere; breeze, breath; relief. (Eph. 2:2)

das Luftgespinst (-e), airy nothing, chimera.

der Lug: *Lug und Trug,* falsehood and deceit.

die Lüge (-n), lie, falsehood, untruth. (John 8:44)

lügen, 1. *ir.v.a. & n.* (*aux.* h.) to lie, to tell a lie, to deceive, to be false. 2. *n.* lying, deceitfulness. (Matt. 5:11)

der Lügenbold (-e), habitual liar.

der Lügenfürst, der Lügengeist, Satan.

lügenhaft(ig), *adj.* lying, false, untrue; deceitful, mendacious. (II Thess. 2:9)

die Lügenhaftigkeit, mendacity; falseness.

das Lügenmaul (-̈er), brazen or barefaced liar.

der Lügenprophet (-en), false prophet.

der Lügner (-), liar. (Rev. 21:8)

(der) Lukas, Luke.

der Lump (-en), scamp, rascal, scoundrel.

das Lumpengesindel, riffraff, rabble.

die Lumperei (-en), rascality; shabby trick, meanness, trifle.

die Lust (-̈e), pleasure, joy, delight; fancy, inclination, desire, wish, longing; lust, carnal pleasure; fun. (John 8:44)

die Lustbarkeit (-en), amusement, entertainment, diversion, pleasure; sport.

lüsten, *v.a. imp.: es lüstet mich sehr danach,* I covet it, I would fain have or do it.

lüstern, *adj.* greedy (for); desirous, covetous (of); lustful, lewd.

die Lüsternheit, lasciviousness; lust, greed.

das Lustgefühl (-e), pleasurable sensation.

lustig, *adj.* merry, gay, joyous, jovial; amusing, funny, comical. (Gen. 2:9)

die Lustigkeit, gaiety, mirth, merriment, fun, jollity.

die Lustlosigkeit, dullness, flatness.

der Lutheraner (-), Lutheran.

lutheranisch, lutherisch, *adj.* Lutheran. *die lutheranische Kirche,* Lutheran Church.

das Luthertum, Lutheranism.

der Luxus, luxury, extravagance.

(der) Luzifer, Lucifer.

die Lyra (-en), lyre, harp.

die Lyrik, lyric poetry.

der Lyriker (-), lyric poet.

lyrisch, *adj.* lyric(al).

Mm

machen, 1. *v.a.* to make, to do; to manufacture, to fabricate, to create; to cause, to effect, to produce; to constitute. 2. *v.r.* to do well, to get on; to come right, to happen. (Gen. 1:26)

die Macht (-e), might, strength, authority, influence, power, potency; forces. (Exod. 15:4)

mächtig, 1. *adj.* mighty, strong, powerful; vast, huge, immense, thick. 2. *adv.* extremely. (Exod. 13:3)

machtlos, *adj.* powerless, weak, impotent.

die Machtlosigkeit, impotence, powerlessness, weakness.

das Mädchen (-), girl; servant (girl); maiden, maid; sweetheart.

die Made (-n), maggot, mite; worm. (Isa. 14:11)

das Madonnenbild (-er), image of the Virgin Mary.

madonnenhaft, *adj.* Madonnalike.

der Madonnenkultus, die Madonnenverehrung, worship of the virgin.

die Magd (-e), maid, maidservant, general servant; handmaid; maiden, virgin. (Gen. 21:10)

(die) Magdalena, Magdalene.

das Mägdlein (-), little girl. (Matt. 9:24)

der Magen (- & -), stomach. (I Tim. 5:23)

mager, *adj.* thin, lean, spare; poor, meager, scanty; sterile. (Gen. 41:3)

die Magie, magic.

der Magier (-), magician; (*pl.*) Magi.

der Magiker (-), magician.

magisch, *adj.* magic(al).

der Magister (-), schoolmaster; tutor.

der Magistrat, borough or municipal council, local authority.

das Mahl (-e & -er), meal, repast, banquet. (John 21:12)

mahlen, *reg. & ir.v.a. & n.* (*aux.* h.) to grind, to mill, to pound, to crush, to bray, to beat, to powder, to pulverize. (Matt. 24:41)

die Mahlzeit, mealtime, meal.

die Mähne (-n), mane. (Job 39:19)

mahnen, *v.a.* to remind; to warn, to admonish; to exhort.

der Mahnruf (-e), warning cry.

die Mahnung (-en), reminder; warning, admonition; dunning.

die Mährischen Brüder, (*pl.*) Bohemian Brethren.

der Mai (-), May.

der Maibaum (-e), maypole.

die Maifeier (-n), Mayday celebration.

die Majestät (-en), majesty.

majestätisch, *adj.* majestic.

die Makkabäer, (*pl.*) Maccabees.

makkabäisch, *adj.* Maccabean.

der Makrokosmus, macrocosm.

der Malter (-), corn measure (about 150 liters); cord (of wood). (Luke 16:7)

das Malzeichen (-), mark, sign; memorial. (Rev. 13:17)

der Mammon, mammon, lucre, worldly riches. (Matt. 6:24)

der Mammonsdiener (-), **der Mammonsknecht** (-e), mammon-worshiper, worldling.

das Man, *see* **das Manna.** (Exod. 16:15)

manch, (-er, -e, -es) *indef. adj. & pron.* many a, many a one. (Jer. 2:28)

mancherlei, *indec. adj.* various, sundry, divers. (Matt. 4:24)

manchmal, *adv.* sometimes, now and again, from time to time. (Heb. 1:1)

das Mandat (-e), mandate; authorization, brief.

der **Mandelbaum** (¨e), almond tree. (Eccles. 12:5)

der **Mangel** (¨), want, need, lack, scarcity, deficiency; absence, defect, blemish, fault, shortcoming. (Luke 22:35)

mangeln, *v.n.* (*aux.* h.) & *imp.* to want, to be wanting or deficient, to lack. (Rom. 3:23)

die **Manier** (-en), manner, way; deportment; fashion, habit; mode, style; mannerism.

der **Mann,** 1. (¨er) man; husband. 2. (-en) retainer, vassal. (Gen. 1:27)

das **Manna,** manna. (Rev. 2:17)

das **Männchen** (-), little man, manikin; male (of beasts, birds, etc.).

der **Männerchor** (¨e), male chorus.

die **Männerstimme** (-n), man's voice, male part.

das **Manneswort** (¨e), honest man's word.

mannhaft, *adj.* manly, brave, valiant; resolute.

mannigfach, mannigfaltig, *adj.* various, manifold, diverse. (James 3:2)

die **Männin,** virago; woman. (Gen. 2:23)

männlich, *adj.* male, manly; masculine; bold, valiant. (Gen. 17:10)

die **Männlichkeit,** manhood, virility; masculinity, maleness; manliness, bravery.

der **Mantel** (¨), overcoat, topcoat; cloak, gown, robe; mantle; envelope, sheathing, case, shell. (Matt. 5:40)

die **Mantik,** divination.

mantisch, *adj.* mantic.

das **Manuskript** (-e), manuscript; copy.

die **Mär** (-en), das **Märlein** (-), news, tidings, rumor, report, story. (Luke 24:11)

(die) Maria, Marie, Mary.

das **Marienbild** (-er), image of the Virgin Mary.

der **Marinegeistliche** (-n), navy chaplain.

das **Mark,** marrow; pith; pulp; core, heart, medulla, essence; strength, vigor. (Gen. 45:18)

der **Markt** (¨e), market, marketplace; market town; bargain, business, trade. (Matt. 9:35)

die **Markthalle** (-n), covered market; market hall.

(der) Markus, Mark.

die **Marter** (-n), torture; torment, agony, pang.

das **Martergerät** (-e), instruments of torture.

die **Martergeschichte,** martyrology.

das **Marterholz,** the cross.

die **Marterkammer** (-n), torture chamber.

martern, *v.a.* to torment; to torture, to inflict torture on. (Isa. 53:4)

der **Marterpfahl,** the stake.

der **Martertod,** death by torture, painful death.

martervoll, *adj.* excruciating.

der **Martinstag, das Martinsfest, Martini,** Martinmas, St. Martin's Day.

der **Märtyrer** (-), die **Märtyrerin** (-nen), martyr.

die **Märtyrergeschichte,** martyrology.

der **Märtyrertod,** martyrdom.

das **Märtyrertum, das Märtyrium** (-ien), martyrdom.

die **Maske** (-n), mask; disguise; pretense, pretext; camouflage, screen; fancy dress or costume.

maskieren, *v.a.* to mask, to camouflage; to put on a mask, to disguise.

das **Maß** (-e), measure, measurement, size, dimension, gauge; index, extent, degree, criterion, standard, rate; moderation; (*pl.*) limits, bounds, height. (Matt. 7:2)

das **Massaker** (-), massacre.

massakrieren, *v.a.* to massacre.

die **Masse** (-n), mass, heap, quantity, number; multitude, the masses, the people; lump, block, bulk; substance, paste, dough; pulp.

die **Massenbeeinflussung,** propaganda.

der **Massenmord,** general massacre, wholesale murder.

mäßig, 1. *adj.* moderate; frugal, modest, reasonable, temperate, middling. 2. *adv.* fairly, moderately. (Rom. 12:3)

die **Mäßigkeit,** moderation, temperance, frugality; mediocrity. (II Peter 1:6)

maßlos, *adj.* boundless, immoderate, extravagant, exorbitant.

die **Maßlosigkeit,** want of moderation, extravagance, vehemence.

die Maßnahme (-n), measure; precaution, preventive measure; mode of acting.

der Mast (-en), mast, pole, tower.

der Mastbaum ("e), mast. (Prov. 23:34)

mästen, *v.a.* to feed, to fatten, to cram. (Isa. 1:11)
das gemästete Kalb schlachten, to kill the fatted calf.

die Mästung, fattening.

der Materialismus, materialism.

der Materialist (-en), materialist, sensualist, worldling.

materialistisch, *adj.* materialistic.

die Materie (-n), matter, stuff, substance; subject, cause.

materiell, *adj.* material, real; materialistic. *materieller Mensch,* matter-of-fact person; materialist.

matt, *adj.* faint, weak, dim, feeble, languid; flat, stale, exhausted, insipid, tasteless; dull, dead, lifeless. (Isa. 1:5)

(der) Matthäus, Matthew.

die Mattheit, dullness, faintness.

mattherzig, *adj.* faint-hearted, spiritless.

die Mattigkeit, feebleness, weakness, lassitude.

die Mauer (-n), wall; battlement. (Exod. 14:22)

das Maul ("er), mouth, jaws, muzzle (of animals); (*fig.*) tongue. (Gen. 4:11)
kein Blatt vors Maul nehmen, to speak one's mind, not mince one's words.

der Maulbeerbaum ("e), mulberry tree. (Luke 17:6)

das Maultier (-e), mule. (Isa. 66:20)

der Maurer (-), mason, bricklayer, builder; *(Frei)maurer,* (Free)mason.

die Maurerei, masonry; freemasonry.

maurerisch, *adj.* masonic.

die Meditation, meditation; contemplation.

meditieren, *v.n.* to meditate.

das Meer (-e), sea; ocean. (Gen. 1:10)

die Meereswoge (-n), billow. (James 1:6)

das Meerwunder, sea monster, (*fig.*) miracle. (James 3:7)

das Mehl (-e), flour, meal; dust, powder. (Matt. 13:33)

mehr, 1. *indec. num. adj. & adv.* more. 2. *n.* (-e) majority; increase; surplus, excess. (Matt. 6:25)
es ist nicht mehr als billig, it is only fair.

mehren, *v.a. & r.* to increase, to augment; to multiply, to grow, to propagate. (Gen. 1:22)

die Mehrheit, majority, plurality.

mehrstimmig, *adj.* arranged for several voices; part (song).

meiden, *ir.v.a.* to avoid, to shun, to flee from. (I Thess. 4:3)

mein, 1. *poss. adj.* my, mine. 2. *poss. pron.* mine. 3. *n.* my own, my property. (Exod. 19:5)

der Meineid, perjury.
einen Meineid leisten or *schwören,* to perjure oneself, to commit perjury.

meineidig, *adj.* perjured. (Jer. 7:9)
meineidig werden, to commit perjury, to perjure oneself; *der Meineidige,* perjurer.

meinen, *v.a. & n.* (*aux.* h.) 1. to be of the opinion, to believe, to think, to suppose; to mean, to intend, to purpose. 2. to love; *Freiheit, die ich meine,* Freedom that I love. (Matt. 16:23)

meiner, meine, meines; meinige (der, die, das -ige), *poss. pron.* mine.
nicht dein Bruder, sondern meiner or *der meinige,* not your brother but mine.

meinesgleichen, *indec. adj. or pron.* my equals, such as I, people like me. (Gal. 1:14)

meinetwillen, *adv.* for my sake; so far as I am concerned, for all I care; by all means. (Matt. 5:11)

die Meinung (-en), opinion, view, belief; idea, notion, thought; meaning, significance; intention. (Rom. 14:5)

die Meinungsäußerung (-en), expression of opinion.

der Meinungsaustausch, interchange of ideas; comparing notes.

die Meinungsverschiedenheit (-en), difference of opinion.

der Meinungswechsel (-), change of opinion or mind.

der Meister (-), master, chief, leader. (Gen. 4:22)

meistern, *v.a.* to master; to rule, to control; to censure, to find fault with; to correct, to put right. (Ps. 78:41)

die Melancholie, melancholy, melancholia.

der Melancholiker (-), person of melancholy disposition.

melancholisch, *adj.* melancholy.

die Melodie (-n), melody, tune, air.

die Menge (-n), quantity, number, amount, a great many or deal; mass; multitude, crowd. (Gen. 32:12)

mengen, 1. *v.a.* to mix, to mingle, to blend. 2. *v.r.* to mix, to mingle; to meddle with, to interfere in. (Dan. 2:43)

der Mensch (-en), human being, man, person; (*pl.*) people, mankind. (Gen. 1:26) *der Mensch gewordene Gott,* God incarnate; *der Mensch denkt, Gott lenkt,* man proposes, God disposes.

das Menschenalter (-), generation, age.

die Menschenart, race of men, kind or species of man.

das Menschenblut, human blood. (Gen. 9:6)

die Menschenfamilie, human race.

der Menschenfeind (-e), misanthrope.

die Menschenfischer, (*pl.*) fishers of men. (Matt. 4:19)

der Menschenfreund (-e), philanthropist.

die Menschengattung, human species.

das Menschengeschlecht, human race, mankind.

die Menschengestalt, human shape or form.

die Menschenkenntnis, knowledge of human nature.

das Menschen(s)kind (-er), human being. (Num. 23:19)

die Menschenlehre, anthropology.

die Menschenliebe, philanthropy, charity; love of one's fellow man.

das Menschenopfer (-), human sacrifice.

das Menschenrecht (-e), rights of man, human rights; natural law, human law.

menschenreich, *adj.* populous.

die Menschenseele (-n): *es war keine Menschenseele zu erblicken,* not a living soul was to be seen.

der Menschensohn, Son of man. (Matt. 24:30)

der Menschenverstand, human understanding.

das Menschenwerk, (fugitive or transitory) works of man.

die Menschenwürde, human dignity.

die Menschheit, human race, humanity, mankind.

menschlich, *adj.* human; humane. (Gen. 8:21)

die Menschlichkeit, human nature; humanity, humaneness; (*also pl.*) human weakness, human frailties.

die Menschwerdung, incarnation, anthropogenesis.

die Mentalität (-en), mentality, way of thinking.

merken, 1. *v.a. & n.* (*aux. h. with* auf) to mark, to note, to observe, to notice, to perceive. 2. *v.a.* (*dat. & acc.*) to bear in mind, to make a note of. (Matt. 15:17)

der Mesner (-), sacristan, sexton.

das Meßamt, celebration of mass.

das Meßbuch (-̈er), missal.

der Meßdiener (-), acolyte.

die Messe (-n), mass; fair, market.

messen, *ir.v.a. & n.* (*aux.* h.) to measure, to gauge, to survey; to be a certain size. (Matt. 7:2)

das Messer (-), knife. (Gen. 22:10)

das Meßgerät (-e), ornaments and utensils used in celebrating mass.

das Meßgewand (-̈er), vestment, chasuble.

das Meßglöckchen (-), mass bell.

das Meßhemd (-en), alb.

messianisch, *adj.* messianic.

der Messias, Messiah.

das Messing (-e), brass. (Rev. 1:15)

der Meßkelch (-e), chalice.

das Meßopfer (-), (sacrifice of the) mass; host.

das Meßtuch (-̈er), corporal, communion cloth.

der Meßwein, consecrated wine.

die Metamorphose (-n), metamorphosis.

metaphysisch, *adj.* metaphysical.

die Metempsychose, metempsychosis; reincarnation; transmigration.

der Methodismus, Methodism.

der Methodist (-en), Methodist.

methodistisch, *adj.* Methodist.

(der) Methusalem, Methuselah.

der Metropolit (-en), archbishop.

die Metropolitankirche (-n), cathedral.

der Meuchelmord (-e), assassination.

der Meuchelmörder (-), assassin. (Acts 21:38)

meuchelmörderisch, *adj.* assassinlike; dastardly.

die Meuchelrotte (-n), band of assassins.

meuchlerisch, meuchlings, *adv.* treacherous(ly), dastardly.

der Michaelistag, Michaelmas (day), St. Michael's Day.

mieten, *v.a.* to hire, to rent, to lease; to engage. (Matt. 20:1)

der Mietling (-e), hireling, mercenary. (John 10:12)

der Mikrokosmus, der Mikrokosmos, microcosm.

die Milch, milk; emulsion. (Exod. 3:8)

mild(e), *adj.* mild, soft, mellow, tender; gentle, kind; liberal, generous, charitable. (Luke 5:39)

das Milieu (-s), surroundings, background, environment.

der Milieueinfluß (-[ss]e), influence of environment.

das Millenium, millennium.

der Ministrant (-en), acolyte.

ministrieren, *v.n.* to minister, to officiate.

die Minze, mint. (Matt. 23:23)

die Mischehe (-n), mixed marriage.

mischen, 1. *v.a.* to mix, to mingle; to blend, to combine; to adulterate, to alloy. 2. *v.r.* to mix (with people), to join in; to blend, to combine; to interfere or meddle with. (Ps. 102:10)

mißbrauchen, *v.a.* to misuse, to abuse. (I Cor. 7:31)

den Namen des Herrn mißbrauchen, to take the Lord's name in vain.

die Missetat (-en), sin, misdeed, crime. (Gen. 44:16)

der Missetäter (-), criminal, offender, evildoer, sinner.

die Mission (-en), mission.
die Innere Mission, home mission.

der Missionar (-e), **die Missionarin** (-nen), missionary.

die Missionsanstalt (-en), mission house.

die Missionsgesellschaft (-en), **der Missionsverein** (-e), missionary society.

mißraten, 1. *ir.v.n.* (*aux.* s.) (*dat.*) to turn out badly, to miscarry, to fail; to cross. 2. *v.a.* (*einem etwas*) to dissuade someone from something. 3. *adj.* naughty, badly brought up. (Jer. 18:4)

der Mist (-e), dung, manure, muck; haze. (Jer. 9:21)

mit, 1. *prep.* (*dat.*) with; along with, in company with, at the same time with; by; at; to. 2. *adv.* along with, together or in company with; jointly, likewise; also; simultaneously. 3. *prefix with nouns and some adjs.* = fellow-, joint-, co-; *sep. prefix with practically any verb* = in company with, in common with, simultaneously.

der Mitarbeiter (-), assistant, colleague, collaborator, coworker, contributor (to a journal). (I Cor. 3:9)

der Miterbe (-n), coheir, joint heir. (Eph. 3:6)

der Mitgenoß (-[ss]en), **der Mitgenosse** (-n), copartner; consort; companion. (Rev. 1:9)

der Mithelfer (-), assistant; accomplice. (II Cor. 6:1)

das Mitleid, pity, compassion; sympathy.

mitleiden, 1. *ir.v.n.* (*aux.* h.) to suffer at the same time; to feel for, to pity, to suffer with; to sympathize. 2. *n.* compassion, pity. (Heb. 10:34)

mitleidig, *adj.* sympathetic, compassionate. (I Peter 3:8)

mitnichten, *adv.* by no means. (Gen. 3:4)

der Mittag, 1. (-e) midday, noon; meridian; south. 2. *n.* dinner, lunch. (Acts 22:6)

das Mittagsmahl, midday meal. (Luke 11:37)

die Mitte (-n), middle, center; midst; mean, medium. (Job 30:5)

mitteilen, 1. *v.a.* (*einem etwas*) to communicate, to impart, to pass on (something to someone); to inform, to notify (someone of something); to tell (someone something). 2. *v.r.* to communicate one's thoughts; to spread, to communicate itself, to be contagious. (Rom. 1:11)

die Mitteilung (-en), announcement, communication, information, news.

das Mittel (-), remedy, medicine; expedient, way, measure, means; middle; average; (*pl.*) means, wealth, property, resources. (Isa. 59:16)

das Mittelalter, Middle Ages.

mittelalterlich, *adj.* medieval.

das Mittelglied, middle term (logic).

das Mittelschiff (-e), middle aisle.

mitten, *adv.* (*used with a prep. following*) midway; *mitten am Tage*, in broad daylight; *mitten auf*, in the midst or middle of; *mitten aus*, from amidst or among; *mittendrein*, into the center; *mittendrin*, in the center; *mittendrunter*, in their midst; *mittendurch*, through the middle, right through; *mitten unter*, amongst, amidst, in the midst of. (Rev. 1:13)

die Mitternacht, midnight; north. (Matt. 25:6)

der Mittler (-), mediator, intercessor; third party. (Gal. 3:19)
unser Mittler, Christ.

mitwirken, *v.n.* (*aux.* h.) to cooperate, to concur, to assist, to collaborate, to take part.

der Moder, dry rot, mold, moldering, decay, rottenness; damp, close air. (Job 13:28)

modern, *adj.* modern; fashionable, up-to-date.

der Modernismus, modernism.

der Modernist (-en), modernist.

modernistisch, modernist(ic).

mögen, *ir.v.a. & n.* (*aux.* h.) to want, to wish, to like, to desire, to have a mind to, to be inclined; to be able, to be permitted or at liberty. (Isa. 1:13)

möglich, *adj.* possible; practicable, feasible. (Matt. 19:26)

der Mohammedaner (-), Mohammedan.

der Mohammedanismus, Mohammedanism.

der Mohr (-en), Moor; Negro. (Jer. 13:23)

die Monade (-n), monad, atom, radical element, ultimate unit.

die Monadenlehre (-n), theory of monads, monadism.

der Monarch (-en), monarch.

der Monat (-e), month. (Exod. 2:2)

der Mönch (-e), monk, friar.

mönchisch, *adj.* monastic, monkish.

das Mönchskloster (-), monastery.

die Mönchskutte (-n), cowl, capuche.

der Mönchsorden (-), monastic order.

die Mönchsplatte (-n), (monastic) tonsure.

das Mönchswesen, monachism, monasticism, monastic life.

die Mönchszucht, monastic discipline.

das Mönchtum, monasticism.

der Mond (-e), moon; satellite; month. (Gen. 37:9)

mondsüchtig, *adj.* given to sleepwalking, somnambulistic; (*fig.*) moonstruck, afflicted with insanity. (Matt. 17:15)

die Monogamie, monogamy.

monogam(isch), *adj.* monogamous.

der Monotheismus, monotheism.

der Monotheist (-en), monotheist.

monotheistisch, *adj.* monotheistic.

die Monstranz (-en), monstrance, pyx.

das Monument (-e), monument.

die Moral, morals, morality, ethics, moral philosophy; moral lesson.

moralisch, *adj.* moral.

moralisieren, *v.n.* (*aux.* h.) to moralize.

der Moralist (-en), moral philosopher, moralist.

die Moralität, morality; morality play.

die Moralphilosophie, moral philosophy, ethics.

der Mord (-e), murder, assassination, homicide. (Matt. 15:19)

morden, *v.a.* to murder; to slay, to kill. (Acts 9:1)

der Mörder (-), murderer, (*fig.*) destroyer. (Matt. 26:55)

die Mördergrube (-n), den of thieves or cutthroats. (Matt. 21:13)

mörderisch, *adj.* murderous, bloody.

mordgierig, *adj.* bloodthirsty.

der Morgen (-), 1. morning, daybreak, dawn; east. 2. *n.* (-) the next day, the morrow. 3. measure of land (*local variations from 0.6 to 0.9 acres*). 4. *adv.* tomorrow; *morgen früh*, tomorrow morning. (Gen. 1:5)

die Morgenandacht (-en), morning prayers, matins.

das Morgenland, East; Orient, Levant. (Matt. 2:1)

morgenländisch, *adj.* eastern, oriental.

das Morgenrot, die Morgenröte, dawn, sunrise, aurora; (*fig.*) youthful bloom, prime. (Gen. 19:15)

der Morgenstern, morning star. (Rev. 2:28)

die Morgenwache, morning watch. (Ps. 130:6)

der Mormone (-n), Mormon.

das Mormonentum, Mormonism.

mosaisch, *adj.* Mosaic.

die Moschee (-n), mosque.

(der) Moses, Moses.

der Most (-e), fruit juice, new wine, must; cider. (Matt. 9:17)

die Motte (-n), moth. (Matt. 6:19)

mottenfräßig, *adj.* moth-eaten. (James 5:2)

die Mücke, Mucke (-n), gnat, midge; fly. (Matt. 23:24)

mucken, *v.n.* (*aux.* h.) to utter a low sound; to grumble, to mutter, to be up in arms; to budge, to move, to stir, to flinch; to sulk. (Exod. 11:7)

müde, *adj.* weary, tired, exhausted, fatigued, worn out. (Rev. 2:3)

die Mühe (-n), trouble, pains, toil, labor, effort. (Gen. 5:29)

mühen, *v.r.* (*mit einer Sache*) to take pains or trouble (about something). (Prov. 30:1)

die Mühle (-n), mill; crusher, grinder. (Matt. 24:41)

der Mühlstein (-e), millstone. (Matt. 18:6)

die Mühsal (-e), toil, difficulty, trouble, hardship, affliction, distress. (Job 15:35)

mühselig, *adj.* difficult, hard, laborious, toilsome; weary. (Matt. 11:28)

der Müller (-), miller. (Eccles. 12:3)

die Mumie (-n), mummy.

mumifizieren, *v.a.* to mummify, to embalm.

der Mund (-e & ̈er), mouth; muzzle, orifice, opening, aperture, vent. (Exod. 4:12)

mündlich, *adj.* oral, verbal, by word of mouth. (Gen. 45:12)

der Mundschenk (-e), cupbearer.

das Münster (-), cathedral, minster.

murmeln, *v.a. & n.* (*aux.* h.) to murmur, to mutter. (Acts 6:1)

murren, 1. *v.n.* (*aux.* h.) to murmur, to grouse, to grumble (*über,* at). 2. *n.* grudging, murmuring, grumbling. (I Peter 4:9)

mürrisch, *adj.* surly, sullen, disgruntled, bad-tempered.

die Muse (-n), muse.

die Musik, music; band.

musikalisch, *adj.* musical, musically gifted.

das Musikinstrument (-e), musical instrument.

musisch, *adj.* poetic, musical, artistic.

musizieren, *v.n.* (*aux.* h.) to play or have music.

müssen, *ir.v.n. aux. of mood,* to be obliged to, to have to, must. (Acts 3:21)

müßig, *adj.* idle, lazy; unemployed, at leisure. (Matt. 20:3)

der Müßigang, idleness, sloth, indolence.

der Mut, courage, pluck, fortitude, boldness, mettle, spirit; state of mind, mood, humor. (James 5:13)

die Mutter (-), mother. (Gen. 2:24)

die Muttergottes, Blessed Virgin.

das Mutterland, mother country.

der Mutterleib, womb, uterus. (Luke 1:15) *vom Mutterleibe an,* from birth.

mütterlich, *adj.* motherly, maternal.

die Mutterliebe, mother love.

die Muttersprache, mother tongue, native tongue.

der Mutwille, wantonness, mischievousness.

mutwillig, *adj.* wanton, mischievous, petulant.

die Myrrhe (-n), myrrh. (Matt. 2:11)
die Myrte (-n), myrtle. (Isa. 41:19)
mysterifizieren, *v.a.* to mystify.
das Mysterium (-erien), mystery.
die Mystik, mystics, mysticism.
der Mystiker (-), mystic.
mystisch, *adj.* mystic(al).

die Mythe (-n), myth, fable.
die Mythenforschung, die Mythenkunde, mythology.
mythenhaft, mythisch, *adj.* mythical.
die Mythologie, mythology.
mythologisch, *adj.* mythological.
der Mythos, der Mythus, myth.

Nn

nach, 1. *prep.* (*dat.*) (*precedes the word it governs*) after, behind, following; towards, to; (*sometimes follows the word it governs*) in conformity with, according to, as regards, after the manner of; on the authority of; by; at; in; for, considering. 2. *adv. & sep. prefix,* after, behind; afterwards; *nach und nach,* little by little, by and by, gradually.
im Jahre . . . nach Christi Geburt, in the year . . . of our Lord; *die Flucht nach Ägypten,* the flight into Egypt.

die Nachahmung, imitation (as of Christ).

der Nachbar (-n), **die Nachbarin** (-nen), neighbor. (Luke 14:12)

nachbarlich, *adj.* neighboring; adjoining; adjacent; friendly.

die Nachbarschaft, neighborhood, vicinity; neighbors.

nachbeten, *v.a. & n.* (*aux.* h.) (*dat.*) (*fig.*) to repeat mechanically, to echo.

der Nachbeter (-), blind adherent.

nachbilden, *v.a.* to copy, to imitate, to reproduce; to liken; to counterfeit. (Isa. 40:18)

nachdenken, 1. *ir.v.n.* (*aux.* h.): *über* (*eine Sache*) *nachdenken,* to think, to reflect, to consider, to ponder or muse (on), to meditate (on). 2. *n.* reflection, meditation, consideration. (Phil. 4:8)

nachdenklich, *adj.* reflective, thoughtful, pensive, meditative.

nacheilen, *v.n.* (*aux.* s.) to hasten after, to pursue. (Ps. 16:4)

nachempfinden, *ir.v.a.* to enter into or appreciate, to feel for, to sympathize with.

die Nachempfindung, appreciation, sensitivity, receptivity, sympathy.

die Nachfolge, succession (in office, etc.); reversion; sequence, following.
Nachfolge Christi, imitation of Christ.

nachfolgen, *v.n.* (*aux.* s.) (*dat.*) to follow, to pursue; to succeed; to imitate. (Deut. 6:14)

der Nachfolger (-), successor, follower, imitator. (Eph. 5:1)

die Nachfolgerschaft, successors.

nachforschen, *v.n.* (*aux.* h.) to inquire or search after; to trace; to investigate.

die Nachforschung (-en), quest, search, investigation; research.

nachfragen, *reg. & ir.v.* (*aux.* h.) (*dat.*) to inquire about or after.

der Nachgesang, epode.

nachgiebig, *adj.* flexible, pliable, yielding, supple, soft; compliant, indulgent, easygoing.

die Nachgiebigkeit, yielding or weak disposition; softness, indulgence; subservience.

nachjagen, 1. *v.n.* (*aux.* s.) (*dat.*) to pursue, to hunt or chase (after). 2. *v.a.* to send after. (Heb. 12:14)

nachkommen, *ir.v.n.* (*aux.* s.) (*dat.*) to come after, to follow on, to come later, to (re)join, to overtake; to fulfil, to perform, to observe, to comply with, to accede to. (I Peter 3:13)

die Nachkommenschaft, posterity, descendants, offspring, progeny.

nachlässig, *adj.* negligent, careless.

die Nachlässigkeit, negligence, carelessness.

nachlesen, *ir.v.a. & n.* (*aux.* h.) to glean; to read after, to reread; to look up (in a book). (Isa. 24:13)

der Nachname (-n), surname.

nachprüfen, *v.a.* to check, to verify, to test.

die Nachprüfung (-en), verification, testing, checking.

nachreden, *v.a. & n.* (*aux.* h.) to repeat (what another has said).

die Nachricht (-en), news, communication, account, information, report, advice, notice.

der Nachruf (-e), posthumous fame, memory; memorial address, obituary notice, in memoriam.

der Nachruhm, fame after death.

nachschlagen, *ir.v.a. & n.* (*aux.* h.) to consult (a book), to look up (a word), to refer to.

das Nachschlagewerk (-e), work of reference, reference book.

die Nachschrift (-en), postscript; transcript, copy.

nachsehen, 1. *ir.v.n.* (*aux.* h.) to look after, to follow with one's eyes. 2. *v.a.* to look into, to examine, to investigate, to attend to; to inspect, to check, to revise, to overhaul. (Acts 1:10)

die Nachsicht, indulgence, forbearance, leniency, clemency, pity; respite.

nachsichtig, *adj.* considerate, forbearing, indulgent, lenient.

die Nachsichtigkeit, good nature, indulgence.

der Nächste (-n), fellow man or creature, neighbor. (Exod. 20:16)

nachstellen, 1. *v.n.* (*aux.* h.) (*dat.*) to lie in wait for; to waylay. 2. *v.a.* to place after; to put back (clocks), to adjust. (Acts 9:24)

die Nächstenliebe, Christian charity, love for one's fellow men.

nachstreben, *v.n.* (*aux.* h.) (*dat.*) to strive after, to aspire to, to emulate. (Rom. 14:19)

die Nacht (-̈e), night; darkness. (Gen. 1:5)

das Nachtgebet (-e), evening prayer.

das Nachtgesicht (-e), a vision of the night. (Job 33:15)

die Nachtigall (-en), nightingale.

das Nachtmahl, supper.

die Nachtmette, nocturn.

nachtragen, *ir.v.a.* (*einem etwas*) to carry after; to add, to append; (*fig.*) to bear a grudge (against), to be resentful (of). (Luke 23:26)

die Nachtseite, dark or seamy side.

die Nachtwache, night watch; vigil. (Matt. 14:25)

der Nachtwächter (-), night watchman; stupid person.

nachtwandeln, 1. *v.n.* (*aux.* h.) (*insep.*) to walk in one's sleep. 2. *n.* sleepwalking, somnambulism.

der Nachtwandler (-), sleepwalker, somnambulist.

nachweinen, *v.a. & n.* (*aux.* h.) (*dat.*) to bewail, to mourn, to lament.

nachweisbar, *adj.* authenticated, demonstrable, manifest, evident, detectable.

die Nachwelt, posterity, future generations.

die Nachwirkung (-en), aftereffect, secondary effect.

das Nachwort, epilogue, concluding remarks.

der Nacken (-), nape of the neck, neck. (Isa. 48:4)

nackt, *adj.* naked, bare, nude. (Gen. 2:25)

die Nadel (-n), needle, pin; point; pinnacle.

das Nadelöhr (-e), eye of a needle. (Matt. 19:24)

der Nagel (-̈), nail, stud; spike, peg. (Isa. 22:23)

das Nägelmal (-e), the print of the nails. (John 20:25)

nahe, *adj.* (*with dat.*) & *adv.* (comp. *näher,* sup. *nächst*) near, close, neighboring, adjoining, adjacent; approaching, impending, imminent. (Rev. 1:3)

die Nähe, nearness, proximity; neighborhood, vicinity, surroundings. (Isa. 57:19)

nahen, *v.r. & n.* (*aux.* s.) (*dat.*) to approach, to come up, to draw near. (Exod. 24:2)

nähren, 1. *v.a.* to feed, to provide or supply with nourishment; to nurse, to suckle; to keep, to support; to nourish; (*fig.*) to cherish; to entertain (hope, etc.). 2. *v.r.* to gain a livelihood; to maintain or keep oneself (by), to live (on), to feed on. 3. *v.n.* (*aux.* h.) to be nourishing. (Gen. 3:17)

die Nahrung, nourishment, nutriment, food; support, sustenance, livelihood. (Mark 12:44)

der Name (-n), name, title, denomination; noun; character, reputation, good name. (Exod. 3:15)
in Gottes Namen, in the name of God.

der Namenchrist (-en), nominal Christian.

das Namenregister (-), index of names, list of names, roll.

der Namenstag, saint's day, name day; birthday.

namhaft, *adj.* well-known, noted, renowned, worth mentioning, noteworthy, considerable. (Acts 21:39)

die Narde (-n), nard, spikenard. (John 12:3)

der Narr (-en), fool, clown, jester, buffoon. (Matt. 5:22)

die Narrheit, foolishness, folly, craziness, madness. (Prov. 12:23)

närrisch, *adj.* foolish, crazy, silly, mad; strange, eccentric, ridiculous. (Job 2:10)

der Narziß (-[ss]e), one lost in self-admiration.

der Narzißmus, narcissism, self-worship.

die Nase (-n), nose, snout; scent (dog, etc.); nozzle, spout; beak (of a ship); nostrils. (Gen. 2:7)

naseweis, *adj.* pert, saucy, impertinent.

die Nation (-en), nation.

der Nationalcharakter, national character.

der Nationalfeiertag (-e), national holiday.

die Nationalsachen, (*pl.*) domestic or home affairs.

der Nationalsozialismus, National Socialism.

nationalsozialistisch, *adj.* National Socialist.

die Natur (-en), nature, disposition, constitution, essence; temperament, temper, frame of mind; (natural) scenery. (Eph. 2:3)

es liegt in der Natur der Sache, it is in the nature of things.

der Naturalismus, naturalism; natural religion.

naturalistisch, *adj.* naturalistic.

der Naturdienst, natural religion, worship of nature.

die Naturerscheinung (-en), natural phenomenon.

das Naturgefühl, feeling for nature.

das Naturgesetz (-e), law of nature, natural law.

der Naturglaube, natural religion.

das Naturkind, child of nature.

die Naturkunde, natural history.

die Naturlehre, natural philosophy, physics.

natürlich, *adj.* natural, native, innate; normal, genuine, uninhibited, artless. (Matt. 15:17)

der Naturmensch (-en), primitive man, uncivilized man; nature worshiper.

die Naturnotwendigkeit, physical necessity.

das Naturrecht (-e), natural right, natural law, law of nature.

das Naturreich, kingdom of nature; nature.

die Naturreligion, natural religion.

der Naturtrieb (-e), instinct.

die Naturverehrung, worship of nature.

naturwidrig, *adj.* unnatural; abnormal.

die Naturwissenschaft (-en), (natural or physical) science.

der Naturwissenschaftler (-), scientist.

naturwissenschaftlich, *adj.* scientific.

das Naturwunder (-), prodigy.

der Naturzustand, natural or primitive state.

der Nazarener (-), Nazarene.

nazarenisch, *adj.* Nazarene.

der Nebel (-), mist, fog, haze. (Gen. 2:6)

nebelig, *adj.* (*also* **neblig**) foggy, misty, hazy. (Joel 2:2)

neben, *adv. & prep.* (*with acc. when expressing motion absolutely; with dat. when expressing rest or limited motion*) beside, near, next to, by the side of, close to; with, in addition to, besides. (Exod. 20:3)

der Nebenbuhler (-), rival, competitor.

die Nebenbuhlerschaft (-en), rivalry.

die Nebensache (-n), matter of secondary importance; nonessential, accessory.

nebensächlich, *adj.* unimportant, immaterial; accidental, incidental, accessory, subsidiary.

(der) Nebuchadnezar, Nebuchadnezzar.

der Neffe (-n), nephew. (Col. 4:10)

der Neger (-), Negro, black.

die Negerin (-nen), Negro, black (woman, girl, etc.).

nehmen, *ir.v.a.* to take; to seize, to appropriate, to capture, to lay hold of; to receive, to accept. (Gen. 3:19)
einen ins Gebet nehmen, to speak seriously to a person; to take someone to task; to pray for someone; *etwas zu Herzen nehmen,* to take something to heart.

der Neid, envy; grudge; jealousy. (Matt. 27:18)

neiden, *v.a. & n. (aux.* h.) to envy. (Acts 7:9)
einem etwas neiden, to envy or begrudge a person something.

neidisch, *adj.* envious, jealous (*auf einen,* of someone).

neidlos, *adj.* not envious, ungrudging.

neigen, 1. *v.a.* to tilt, to bend (over); to incline, to bow, to lower. 2. *v.r. & n.* (*aux.* h.) to bend over, to bow, to dip, to lean; to slope, to incline; to decline, to draw to a close; to be inclined to, to tend. (Gen. 37:7)

die Neigungsehe (-n), **die Neigungsheirat** (-en), love match.

nein, *adv.* no. (Matt. 5:37)

der Nekrolog (-e), obituary (notice), necrology.

der Nekromant (-en), necromancer.

die Nekromantie, necromancy.

die Nekrose, necrosis, gangrene, mortification.

nennen, *ir.v.a.* to name, to call, to term, to style, to denominate; to mention by name, to quote, to speak of. (Gen. 1:5)

der Neophyt (-en), neophyte, convert, novice.

der Nervenzusammenbruch (⁒e), nervous breakdown.

das Nest (-er), nest; aerie; (*fig.*) home, haunt, den; (*fig.*) small country town, village; hole. (Matt. 8:20)

das Nestküchlein, nestling; (*fig.*) pet.

das Netz (-e), net, netting, mesh, gauze; lattice, network; (*pl.*) toils. (Matt. 4:18)

netzen, *v.a.* to wet, to moisten, to sprinkle, to soak, to humidify. (Luke 7:38)

neu, *adj.* new, fresh; recent, modern, novel, latest. (Matt. 9:16)
in neuerer Zeit, in neuester Zeit, in recent times, of late years; *das Neue Testament,* New Testament.

neugeboren, *adj.* newborn. (Matt. 2:2)

neugierig, *adj.* curious, inquisitive.

die Neuheit (-en), novelty, newness.

das Neujahr, der Neujahrstag, New Year's Day.

der Neujahrsabend, New Year's Eve.

das Neujahrsfest, New Year festival.

neulateinisch, *adj.* Neo-Latin.

der Neuling (-e), novice, beginner, neophyte; stranger. (I Tim. 3:6)

der Neumond, new moon.

neun, 1. *num. adj.* nine. 2. *f.* (-en) number nine. (Luke 17:17)

neunt, *adj.* ninth. (Matt. 20:5)

neunzig, *num. adj.* ninety. (Gen. 17:17)

der Neuphilolog(e), modern-language specialist.

der Neuplatoniker (-), Neoplatonist.

neutral, *adj.* neutral, impartial.

die Neutralität, neutrality.

die Neuzeit, modern times.

neuzeitlich, *adj.* modern.

nicht, *adv.* not; *nicht mehr,* not any longer, no longer. (Gen. 6:3)

die Nichtduldung, intolerance.

das Nicht-Ich, nonego, world of objective reality (philosophy).

nichtig, *adj.* null, void; invalid; futile, idle, empty; transitory; perishable. (Isa. 40:17)

die Nichtigkeit, nullity, invalidity, nothingness; futility, vanity.

nichts, 1. *indec. pron.* nothing, naught. 2. *n.* nothingness, emptiness, void, nothing, chaos; insignificance, trifle. (Matt. 17:20)

das Nichtvorhandensein, absence, lack; nonexistence (philosophy).

nichtwesentlich, *adj.* nonessential.

nie, niemals, *adv.* never, at no time. (Matt. 7:23)

nieder, 1. *adj.* low, inferior, mean, base, vulgar. 2. *adv. & sep. prefix* down; low.

niederbücken, *v.a. & r.* to bow down, to stoop, to grovel. (John 8:6)

die Niederfahrt, descent.

niederfallen, *ir.v.n.* (*aux.* s.) to fall down; to settle. (Gen. 37:10)
vor einem niederfallen, to fall at a person's feet.

der Niedergang, downfall, decline; setting (of the sun); west. (Matt. 24:27)

niedergeschlagen, *p.p. & adj.* dejected, depressed, low-spirited, cast-down.

die Niedergeschlagenheit, depression, dejection, low spirits.

niederkommen, *ir.v.n.* (*aux.* s.) to be confined, to lie in (of women).

die Niederkunft (-en & ⁺e), delivery, confinement.

niederlassen, 1. *ir.v.a.* to let down, to lower. 2. *v.r.* to sit down; to settle, to establish oneself; to alight. (Gen. 8:4)

niederlegen, 1. *v.a.* to lay or put down, to deposit, to store; to resign, to abdicate. 2. *v.r.* to lie down, to go to bed. (Deut. 6:7)

niederschlagen, *ir.v.a.* to strike or knock down, to cast down (eyes); to prostrate; to deposit; to pacify; to fell; to put down, to quell. (Isa. 64:11)

die Niederschrift (-en), written copy, notes.

niedersetzen, 1. *v.a.* to set or put down; to deposit. 2. *v.r.* to sit down. (Luke 22:14)

niedersteigen, *ir.v.n.* (*aux.* s.) to descend, to step down. (Gen. 28:12)

die Niedertracht, meanness, baseness.

niederträchtig, *adj.* low, base, mean, vile.

die Niederträchtigkeit, base act, vile action.

niederwerfen, 1. *v.a.* to throw down; to put down, to suppress, to overcome, to crush (a rising). 2. *v.r.* to prostrate oneself.

die Niederwerfung, suppression.

niedrig, *adj.* low; lowly, inferior, humble, obscure; base, abject, vile, vulgar; mean. (James 1:9)

die Niedrigkeit, lowness; lowliness; baseness. (Acts 8:33)

niemand, *indef. pron.* nobody, no one. (Matt. 6:24)

die Niere (-n), kidney; (*pl.*) loins. (Ps. 7:10)

der Nimbus, nimbus cloud; nimbus, halo, aura; prestige, respect, solemnity.

nimmer, *adv.* never, nevermore, at no time; no more, no longer. (Luke 2:37)

nimmermehr, *adv.* nevermore; never, not at all. (Matt. 21:19)

das Ninive, Nineveh.

nisten, *v.n.* (*aux.* h.), to nest, to build a nest. (Ps. 104:17)

das Niveau (-s), level; standard.

das Nizäa, Nicea.

nizäisch, nizänisch, *adj.* Nicene. *nizäisches* or *nizänisches Glaubensbekenntnis,* Nicene Creed.

noch, *adv. & part.* still, yet; in addition, besides, further. (Gen. 18:30)

der Nomade (-n), nomad.

nomadenhaft, nomadisch, *adj.* nomadic.

die Nonne (-n), nun.

das Nonnenkloster (-), nunnery, convent.

der Nonnenschleier (-), veil.

die Nonnenweihe, taking the veil.

der Nordost, tempestuous wind, Euroclydon. (Acts 27:14)

die Norm (-en), rule, standard, model, norm, criterion.

die Not (⁺e), 1. need, want, distress, misery; necessity, emergency, trouble, urgency, difficulty, peril, danger. 2. *pred. adj.* needful, necessary. (Matt. 14:24) *wenn die Not am größten, ist Gottes Hilfe am nächsten,* man's extremity is God's opportunity.

die Notdurft, necessaries, necessity, pressing need. (Acts 20:34)

notdürftig, *adj.* scanty; needy, indigent; makeshift.

die Notdürftigkeit, indigence, want.

das Notgesetz (-e), provisional or emergency decree.

der Nothelfer (-), helper in need, one of fourteen catholic saints; holy helper.

nötig, *adj.* needful, necessary, required. (Acts 15:28)

nötigen, *v.a.* to necessitate; to oblige, to force, to coerce, to compel, to urge, to press. (Matt. 5:41)

das Notjahr (-e), year of scarcity.

der Novize (-n), novice, probationer, acolyte.

das Noviziat (-e), novitiate.

nüchtern, *adj.* (on an) empty (stomach); sober, temperate, moderate, calm, reasonable, sensible; flat, dry, dull, prosaic, Philistine. (I Peter 1:13)

nutz(e), (nütze), *adj.* useful, of use, profitable. (Matt. 5:13)

nützen, 1. *v.n.* to be of use; to be profitable, to serve for. 2. *v.a.* to use, to make use of, to utilize. (Gal. 5:2)

nützlich, *adj.* useful, of use, serviceable, profitable, advantageous, conducive. (Acts 20:20)

die Nützlichkeit, utility, usefulness, advantage, profitableness.

das Nützlichkeitsprinzip (-e), **das Nützlichkeitssystem** (-e), utilitarianism.

die Nützlichkeitsrücksichten, (*pl.*) considerations of utility, practical considerations.

Oo

ob, *prep.* (*dat.*) over, above, on, upon; (*gen.* or *dat.*) on account of.

(der) Obadja, Obadiah.

die Obedienz, obedience.

oben, *adv.* above, aloft, overhead, on high; upstairs; at the top; on the surface. (Exod. 20:4)

obenan, *adv.* at the top, at the head; in the first place. (Matt. 23:6)

ober, 1. *prep.* (*dat.*) over, above, beyond. 2. *adj.* situated above, upper, higher, superior; supreme, chief, principal, leading. (Acts 19:1)

die Obergewalt, supreme power or authority; supremacy, sovereignty.

die Oberhand, back of the hand; wrist; (*fig.*) upper hand, ascendancy. (Lam. 1:16)

der Oberhauptmann (⁼er), captain. (John 18:12)

der Oberherr (-en), supreme lord, sovereign, prince of the Gentiles. (Matt. 20:25)

oberherrlich, *adj.* sovereign.

die Oberherrschaft, sovereignty, supremacy.

die Oberin (-nen), Mother Superior; hospital matron.

der Oberkirchenrat, high consistory (Protestant); member of a high consistory.

die Oberklasse (-n), upper class (of society).

das Oberkleid (-er), outer garment.

die Obermacht, superiority, ascendancy; supreme authority.

der Oberpfarrer (-), rector.

der Oberpriester (-), high priest.

oberpriesterlich, *adj.* pontifical.

das Oberpriestertum, pontificate.

der Obersatz, major term (logic).

oberst, *adj.* (*sup. of* **ober**) top, topmost, uppermost, highest; chief, head, first, principal, supreme. (Gen. 40:9)

die Oblate (-n), consecrated wafer, host.

obliegen, *ir.v.n.* (*sep.*) 1. (*aux.* h.) (*dat.*) to be incumbent on, to be one's duty (to), to have the task of; to apply oneself to, to be devoted to. 2. (*aux.* s.) (*dat.*) to prevail over. (Gen. 32:29)

die Obrigkeit (-en), ruling body, government, authorities; magistrate. (Matt. 8:9)

die Observanz (-en), observance, conformance; usage, convention, custom.

obskur, *adj.* obscure.

das Obst (-arten), fruit. (Amos 8:1)

obszön, *adj.* obscene.

die Obszönität, obscenity.

der Ochse (-n), ox, bull, bullock. (Exod. 20:17)

das Ochsenfleisch, beef. (Ps. 50:13)

der Ochsenstecken, ox goad. (Judg. 3:31)

öd(e), *adj.* waste, empty, bare, bleak, desolate, deserted; tedious, dull, dreary. (Isa. 5:9)

die Öde (-n), desert, solitude, waste. (Jer. 44:6)

der Odem, *poetic for* **Atem.**

der Ofen (⁻), stove, oven, furnace, kiln. (Gen. 15:17)

offen, *adj.* open; frank, outspoken, candid, clear, sincere; public, free, bare. (Gen. 13:9)

offenbar, *adj.* manifest, evident, plain, obvious, palpable. (Matt. 10:26)

offenbaren, *v.a.* to disclose, to reveal, to manifest, to discover; to proclaim, to publish. (Matt. 11:25)
geoffenbarte Religion, revealed religion.

die Offenbarung, manifestation; disclosure; revelation. (Rev. 1:1) der **Offenbarungseid,** oath of manifestation, pauper's oath.

der **Offenbarungsglaube,** belief in revealed religion.

die **Offenheit,** frankness, candor.

öffentlich, *adj.* public, open. (Matt. 6:4)

die **Öffentlichkeit,** publicity; public.

öffnen, *v.a. & r.* to open; to unlock, to unseal; to reveal, to disclose; to dissect (a body). (Luke 24:32)

oft, *adv.* (comp. *öfter,* sup. *öftest*) often, frequently. (Luke 22:35)

öfter, 1. *adj.* (*comp. of* **oft**) repeated. 2. *adv.* more frequently; oftener. (II Cor. 11:23)

oftmals, *adv.* often, frequently, repeatedly. (Heb. 10:11)

ohne, *prep.* (*acc.*) without, apart from; but for, not to speak of; but that, except, save; besides. (Matt. 10:29)

die **Ohnmacht** (-en), faint, fainting fit, unconsciousness; impotency, impotence, powerlessness, weakness.

ohnmächtig, *adj.* swooning, unconscious; faint, weak, helpless, powerless, feeble. (Ps. 77:5)

das **Ohr** (-en), ear; auricle; hearing; handle. (Exod. 32:2)

die **Ohrenbeichte** (-n), auricular confession.

der **Ohrenbläser** (-), talebearer, scandalmonger, slanderer.

der **Okkultismus,** occultism.

die **Okkupation** (-en), occupation, seizure.

ökumenisch, *adj.* ecumenical.
die ökumenische Bewegung, ecumenical movement.

der **Okzident,** occident.

das **Öl** (-e), oil; petroleum; olive oil. (Matt. 25:3)

der **Ölbaum** (⁻e), olive tree. (Rom. 11:17)

der **Ölberg,** Mount of Olives.

das **Ölblatt** (⁻er), olive leaf. (Gen. 8:11)

ölen, *v.a.* to oil, to lubricate; to anoint.

das **Ölglas** (⁻er), vial of oil. (I Sam. 10:1)

das **Ölhorn** (⁻er), horn of oil. (I Sam. 16:13)

die **Olive** (-n), olive.

das **Olivenöl,** olive oil.

der **Ölkrug** (⁻e), cruse of oil. (I Kings 17:14)

die **Ölung,** oiling, lubrication; anointing.

der **Ölzweig** (-e), olive branch (symbol of goodwill and peace). (Ps. 128:3)

das **Opfer** (-), offering, sacrifice; victim, martyr. (Gen. 4:3)

der **Opferaltar** (⁻e), sacrificial altar.

opferbereit, *adj.* unselfish, self-forgetful.

das **Opferbrot,** consecrated bread or wafer; showbread (of Mosaic ritual).

der **Opferdienst,** worship by sacrifices.

opferfreudig, *adj.* self-sacrificing.

die **Opfergabe** (-n), offering.

das **Opfergebet** (-e), offertory.

der **Opfergebrauch** (⁻e), sacrificial rite.

der **Opfergeist,** readiness to make sacrifices.

das **Opfergeld** (-er), money offering.

das **Opferlamm,** sacrificial lamb; the Lamb (Jesus); (*fig.*) innocent victim.

opfern, *v.a. & n.* (*aux.* h.) to sacrifice, to offer as a sacrifice, to offer up, to immolate. (Gen. 8:20)

der **Opferpriester** (-), sacrificer.

die **Opferschale** (-n), dish for receiving the blood of the victim.

die **Opferstätte** (-n), place for sacrifices.

der **Opferstock** (⁻e), poor box, collection box.

der **Opferteller** (-), collection plate, offertory.

das **Opfertier** (-e), victim.

der **Opfertod,** sacrifice of one's life; expiatory death (of Christ).

die **Opferung** (-en), offering, sacrifice.

der **Opferwein** (-e), oblation drink; libation.

die **Opferwilligkeit,** readiness to make sacrifices, self-sacrificing devotion.

der **Opponent** (-en), objector (in disputations).

das **Orakel** (-), oracle.

orakelhaft, *adj.* oracular.

der **Orakelspruch** (⁻e), oracle, oracular decree.

das **Oratorium** (-ien), oratorio; oratory.

das **Ordal** (-ien), (*usually pl.*) (judgment by) ordeal.

der **Orden** (-), order; decoration, distinction, medal.

das **Ordensband** (⁻er), ribbon of an order.

der **Ordensbruder** (⁻), friar.

das **Ordensgelübde** (-), vow, profession. *das Ordensgelübde ablegen,* to take the (monastic) vows.

das **Ordenshaus** (⁻er), religious house.

das **Ordenskleid** (-er), monastic garb or habit.

das **Ordenskloster** (⁻), monastery of an order.

die **Ordensregel** (-n), statute(s) of an order.

der **Ordensritter** (-), knight of an order.

die **Ordensschwester** (-n), sister, nun.

das **Ordenszeichen** (-), badge, order.

ordentlich, *adj.* orderly, neat, tidy; regular, steady; ordinary, proper, usual; respectable, decent; downright, out-and-out, really, seriously.

die **Ordentlichkeit,** orderliness; respectability.

die **Ordination,** ordination, investment.

ordnen, *v.a.* to arrange, to (set or put in) order, to classify, to sift, to sort; to regulate, to settle, to organize. (Acts 14:23)

die **Ordnung,** arrangement, regulation; classification, order; tidiness, orderliness; class, rank, succession, series. (Luke 1:3)

die **Organisation** (-en), organization.

der **Organist** (-en), organist.

die **Orgel** (-n), organ (music).

der **Orgelbauer** (-), organ builder.

das **Orgelchor,** organ loft.

das **Orgelkonzert** (-e), organ recital.

das **Orgelspiel,** organ playing.

der **Orgelspieler** (-), organist.

der **Orient,** orient.

orientalisch, *adj.* oriental, eastern.

original, 1. *adj.* original, initial; genuine, innate, inherent. 2. *n.* (-e) original, oddity, eccentric.

die **Originalausgabe** (-n), first edition.

die **Originalität,** originality; peculiarity.

die **Original(hand)schrift** (-en), autograph, author's own hand.

der **Ornat** (-e), official robes, gown, vestments.

der **Ort,** 1. (-e) place, spot, point, site. 2. (⁻er) region, locality. (Gen. 28:16)

orthodox, *adj.* orthodox.

die **Orthodoxie,** orthodoxy.

der **Ost,** der **Osten,** east.

der **Osterabend,** Easter Eve.

das **Osterei** (-er), Easter egg.

die **Osterferien,** (*pl.*) Easter vacation.

das **Osterfest,** Easter; *das Osterfest der Juden,* Passover. (Mark 15:6)

der **Osterfladen** (-), Passover bread.

das **Osterlamm,** paschal lamb.

österlich, *adj.* of Easter, paschal.

der **Ostermonat,** der **Ostermond,** April.

der **Ostermontag,** Easter Monday.

die **Ostern,** (*pl.*) (*but used as a sing.*) Easter; Passover. (Matt. 26:2)

der **Ostersonntag,** Easter Sunday.

die **Osterwoche,** Holy Week.

die **Otter** (-n), viper, adder. (Acts 28:3)

das **Otterngezüchte** (-), generation of vipers. (Matt. 3:7)

das **Otterngift,** adder's poison. (Ps. 140:4)

Pp

das **Paar** (-e), 1. pair, couple, brace. 2. *adj.* like, matching. 3. *num. adj.* (*indec.*) some, a few. (Gen. 6:19)

der **Palast** (⁻e), palace. (Luke 11:21)

palastartig, *adj.* palatial.

Palästina, Palestine.

der **Palästiner** (-), Palestinian.

palästinisch, Palestinian.

das **Pallium** (-lien), pallium.

der **Palmbaum** (⁻e), palm tree. (Ps. 92:13)

die **Palme** (-n), palm (tree). (Rev. 7:9)

der **Palmenzweig** (-e), palm branch. (John 12:13)

der **Palmsonntag,** Palm Sunday.

der **Palmwedel** (-), palm branch (symbol of victory).

die **Palmwoche,** Holy Week.

das **Panier** (-e), banner, standard. (Exod. 17:15)

die **Panik,** panic.

der **Panzer** (-), armor, cuirass, coat of mail; breastplate. (Rev. 9:9)

der **Papismus,** popery.

papistisch, *adj.* popish.

der **Papst** (⁻e), pope, pontiff; Holy Father.

päpstisch, *adj.* popish.

die **Papstkrone,** tiara.

der **Päpstler** (-), papist.

päpstlich, *adj.* papal, pontifical. *päpstlicher Stuhl,* Holy See.

das **Papsttum,** papacy.

die **Papstwürde,** papal dignity, papacy, pontificate.

die **Parabel** (-n), parable, simile.

das **Paradies** (-e), paradise. (Rev. 2:7)

paradiesisch, *adj.* heavenly, delightful.

der **Paraklet,** Paraclete, Holy Spirit, Comforter.

die **Paränese,** exhortations (in *Formgeschichte*).

der **Parder** (-), leopard. (Dan. 7:6)

die **Parodie** (-n), parody, travesty.

die **Partei** (-en), faction, party following; part, side; plaintiff or defendant; tenant.

das **Parteiwesen,** party system.

die **Parthenogenesis,** parthenogenesis, virgin birth.

der **Partner** (-), die **Partnerin** (-nen), partner.

die **Partnerschaft,** partnership.

das **Passah** (-s), Passover. (Exod. 12:11)

die **Passion** (-en), passion, passionate devotion.

passioniert, *p.p. & adj.* impassioned.

die **Passionsbetrachtung,** Lenten meditation.

die **Passionspredigt,** Good Friday sermon.

das **Passionsspiel,** Passion play.

die **Passionswoche,** Holy Week.

der **Passus** (-), passage (in a book), paragraph; case, instance.

der **Pastor** (-en), pastor, clergyman, minister.

pastoral, *adj.* pastoral.

das **Pastorale,** idyll, eclogue, pastoral.

das **Pastoralschreiben,** pastoral (letter).

das **Pastorat** (-e), parsonage, vicarage; incumbency.

die **Pastorin** (-nen), (female) pastor, minister; minister's wife.

das **Patchen** (-), godchild.

die **Patene,** paten; tray for the bread in the celebration of the Eucharist.

das **Patenkind** (-er), godchild.

die **Patenschaft** (-en), sponsorship.

das **Paternoster** (-), paternoster.

der **Patriarch** (-en), patriarch.

patriarchalisch, *adj.* patriarchal.

das Patrimonium (-nien), patrimony.

der Patriot (-en), patriot.

patriotisch, *adj.* patriotic.

der Patriotismus, patriotism.

die Patristik, patristics.

patristisch, *adj.* patristic.

der Patrizier (-), patrician.

das Patriziertum, patricians, the upper class.

patrizisch, *adj.* patrician.

der Patron (-e), patron; patron saint.

das Patronat (-e), patronage.

der Patronatsherr (-en), patron of a living.

das Patronatsrecht, patronage.

die Pauke (-n), kettledrum. (Exod. 15:20) *mit Pauken und Trompeten,* with drums beating and trumpets sounding.

pauken, *v.n.* (*aux.* h.) to beat the kettledrum. (Jer. 31:4)

paulisch, paulinisch, *adj.* of Paul. (I Cor. 1:12)

(der) Paulus, Paul. (I Cor. 1:13)

der Pazifismus, pacifism.

der Pazifist (-en), pacifist.

pazifizieren, *v.n.* (*mit einem*) to come to an agreement.

das Pech, pitch; cobbler's wax; hard or bad luck. (Ecclesiasticus 13:1)

die Pein, pain, agony, torture, torment. (Matt. 25:46)

peinigen, *v.a.* to torture; to torment, to harass. (Acts 12:1)

der Peiniger (-), torturer, tormentor.

die Peinigung (-en), torture; torment.

peinlich, *adj.* painful, distressing, embarrassing; precise, exact, minute.

die Peitsche (-n), whip, lash, scourge. (I Kings 12:11)

peitschen, 1. *v.a.* to whip, to flog, to scourge, to lash; to sweep or drive along. 2. *v.n.* to flap (of sails); to pelt (of rain).

das Pensum (-a & -en), task, lesson; curriculum.

perfid(e), *adj.* perfidious, insidious.

die Perfidie, die Perfidität, perfidy, perfidiousness; insidiousness.

das Pergament (-e), parchment, vellum. (II Tim. 4:13)

das Pergamentpapier, thick vellum.

die Pergamentrolle (-n), parchment scroll.

die Perle (-n), pearl; bead; (*fig.*) gem, jewel. (Matt. 13:45) *Perlen vor die Säue werfen,* to cast pearls before swine.

permanent, *adj.* permanent, lasting, enduring, durable.

die Permanenz, permanency, permanence, durability.

der Perser (-), Persian.

Persien, Persia.

persisch, *adj.* Persian.

die Person (-en), person, personage. (Acts 10:34)

personell, *adj.* personal.

der Personenname (-n), proper name or noun.

persönlich, 1. *adj.* personal. 2. *adv.* in person, personally.

die Persönlichkeit, personality, individuality; personage.

der Pessimismus, pessimism.

der Pessimist (-en), pessimist.

pessimistisch, *adj.* pessimistic.

die Pestilenz, pestilence.

die Peterskirche, St. Peter's (Rome).

der Peterspfennig, Peter's pence.

die Petrikirche, St. Peter's (Rome).

(der) Petrus, Peter.

der Petschaftring (-e), signet ring.

der Pfad (-e), path, lane. (Ps. 77:20)

der Pfaffe (-n), priest; cleric, parson.

die Pfaffenherrschaft, clerical rule.

der Pfaffenknecht (-e), slavish adherent of the clergy.

das Pfaffentum, clericalism; priests.

die Pfaffenwirtschaft, clerical control.

pfäffisch, *adj.* priestlike; clerical; priestridden.

der Pfahl (⁻e), stake, stick, post, pole, pile, picket; thorn; pillory. (II Cor. 12:7)

das Pfand (⁻er), pledge, security, forfeit, pawn; mortgage; deposit. (II Cor. 1:22)

die Pfanne (-n), pan, bowl, boiler. (I Sam. 2:14)

der **Pfarracker,** glebe land.

das **Pfarramt,** incumbency, parsonage, pastorate.

das **Pfarrbesetzungsrecht,** patronage.

der **Pfarrbezirk** (-e), parish.

das **Pfarrbuch** (ˉer), parish register.

die **Pfarre** (-n), die **Pfarrei** (-en), (church) living; parsonage, vicarage; parish.

der **Pfarrer** (-), clergyman, parson; rector, vicar; minister; priest.

die **Pfarrerin** (-nen), parson's wife.

die **Pfarrgemeinde** (-n), parish.

das **Pfarrgut** (ˉer), glebe land.

das **Pfarrhaus** (ˉer), parsonage; rectory, vicarage.

der **Pfarrherr** (-en), parson.

das **Pfarrkind** (-er), parishioner.

die **Pfarrkirche** (-n), parish church.

die **Pfarrschule** (-n), church school.

der **Pfarrzehnte** (-n), parochial tithe.

der **Pfau** (-e & -en), peacock. (I Kings 10:22)

die **Pfeife** (-n), pipe; organ pipe; whistle. (Isa. 5:12)

pfeifen, ir.v.a. & n. (aux. h.) to whistle, to squeal, to hiss; to sing, to howl, to squeak. (Matt. 11:17)

der **Pfeifer** (-), piper; whistler. (Matt. 9:23)

der **Pfeil** (-e), arrow, dart; bolt, shaft. (Eph. 6:16)

der **Pfeiler** (-), pillar; prop; upright; doorpost; pier. (Rev. 3:12)

der **Pfennig** (-e), one-hundredth part of a mark; penny; farthing. (Matt. 10:29)

das **Pferd** (-e), horse. (Rev. 6:2)

der **Pfingstabend,** Whit-Saturday.

das **Pfingsten,** das **Pfingstfest,** Whitsuntide, Pentecost. (Acts 2:1)

die **Pfingstferien,** (pl.) Whitsun holidays, Whitsuntide recess.

pfingstlich, adj. Pentecostal; Whitsun-.

der **Pfingstmontag,** Whit-Monday.

der **Pfingstsonntag,** Whit-Sunday.

die **Pfingsttage,** (pl.) Whitsun holidays.

die **Pfingstwoche,** Whitsun week.

die **Pflanze** (-n), plant. (Matt. 15:13)

pflanzen, v.a. to plant; (fig.) to implant. (Gen. 2:8)

die **Pflanzung** (-en), planting; plantation; settlement, colony.

das **Pflaster** (-), plaster, poultice; patch; pavement, paving; (fig.) amends, sop. (II Kings 20:7)

die **Pflege** (-n), care, attention; rearing, tending, nursing; bringing up, fostering, cultivation, culture; guardianship.

pflegen, 1. v.a. (reg.) (with gen., archaic except in stock phrases) to tend, to nurse, to cherish, to care for, to attend to, to take care of; to cultivate, to foster. 2. v.n. (with inf.) (reg. only) to be used to, to be accustomed to, to be in the habit of, to be given to. (Acts 17:25)

der **Pfleger** (-), die **Pflegerin** (-nen), nurse; guardian, curator. (Isa. 49:23)

die **Pflicht** (-en), duty, obligation. (Rom. 4:4)

die **Pflichtenlehre,** ethics, moral philosophy.

das **Pflichtgesetz,** moral law.

pflichttreu, adj. conscientious, dutiful.

der **Pflug** (ˉe), plow. (Luke 9:62)

pflügen, v.a. & n. (aux. h.) to plow; to till. (Judg. 14:18)

der **Pflüger** (-), plowman. (Ps. 129:3)

die **Pflugschar** (-en), plowshare. (Isa. 2:4)

die **Pforte** (-n), gate, door, opening, entrance. (Gen. 28:17)

die **Pfoste** (-n), der **Pfosten** (-), post, pale; stake; jamb (of doors). (Exod. 12:7)

pfropfen, v.a. to cram into, to stuff full of; to cork, to plug; to graft. (Rom. 11:17)

der **Pfuhl** (-e), pool; puddle, slough; Sündenpfuhl, sink of corruption; Höllenpfuhl, bottomless pit. (Rev. 19:20)

der **Pfühl** (-e), bolster, pillow, cushion; couch. (Ezek. 13:18)

das **Pfund** (-e), pound (weight); pound (sterling); talent. (Matt. 18:24)

die **Phantasie** (-n), imagination, fancy; fantastic vision; reverie.

(der) Pharao, Pharaoh.

der **Pharisäer** (-), Pharisee, hypocrite. (Matt. 5:20)

das **Pharisäertum,** pharisaism.

pharisäisch, adj. pharisaic.

der **Philanthrop** (-en), philanthropist.

philanthropisch, adj. philanthropic.

(der) Philipp, Philip.

der Philister (-), Philistine; unimaginative person; vulgarian.

die Philisterei, Philistinism; lack of imagination, pedantry.

philisterhaft, *adj.* philistine, pedantic, uncultured.

das Philistertum, humdrum existence, everyday routine.

der Philologe (-n), philologist, linguist.

die Philologie, philology, language studies.

philologisch, *adj.* philological, linguistic.

der Philosoph (-en), philosopher. (Acts 17:18)

die Philosophie (-n), philosophy. (Col. 2:8)

philosophieren, *v.n.* (*aux.* h.) to philosophize.

philosophisch, *adj.* philosophical.

die Phylakterien, (*pl.*) phylacteries. (see Deut. 6:8)

die Pietät, reverence, devotion, attachment; piety.

pietätlos, *adj.* irreverent, disrespectful.

die Pietätlosigkeit, irreverence.

pietätvoll, *adj.* reverent, devout.

der Pietismus, form of evangelical devotional piety.

der Pietist (-en), Pietist.

pietistisch, *adj.* pietistic.

der Pilger (-), **der Pilgrim** (-e), pilgrim.

die Pilgerfahrt (-en), pilgrimage.

pilgern, *v.n.* (*aux.* h. & s.) to go on a pilgrimage.

die Pilgerväter, (*pl.*) Pilgrim Fathers.

die Plage (-n), vexation; misery; drudgery; trouble, bother; plague, pest, calamity, torment. (Exod. 9:14)
die zehn Plagen Ägyptens, the ten plagues of Egypt.

plagen, 1. *v.a.* to plague, to torment; to annoy; to worry, to bother, to harass. 2. *v.r.* to toil, to drudge; to be troubled. (Gen. 15:13)

plappern, *v.a. & n.* (*aux.* h.) to babble, to chatter, to jabber; to rattle off. (Matt. 6:7)

der Platoniker (-), Platonist.

platonisch, *adj.* Platonic, unworldly, spiritual.

der Platzregen (-), rain. (Matt. 7:25)

der Plebejer (-), plebeian.

plebejisch, *adj.* plebeian, low, vulgar.

plötzlich, 1. *adj.* sudden, abrupt. 2. *adv.* all at once. (Acts 9:3)

die Plymouthbrüder, (*pl.*) Plymouth Brethren; Darbyites.

der Pöbel, mob, populace, people, rabble. (Ps. 73:10)

pöbelhaft, *adj.* vulgar, low, plebeian.

das Pöbelvolk, mixed multitude. (Exod. 12:38)

der Poet (-en), poet.

die Polemik (-en), polemics, controversy.

der Polemiker (-), controversialist.

polemisch, *adj.* polemic.

polemisieren, *v.n.* to carry on a controversy.

die Politik, politics; policy.

der Politiker (-), politician.

politisch, *adj.* political; politic.

das Polster (-), cushion, pillow, bolster; stuffing, pad, padding. (Mark 14:15)

die Polygamie, polygamy.

polygam(isch), *adj.* polygamous.

der Polytheismus, polytheism.

der Polytheist (-en), polytheist.

polytheistisch, *adj.* polytheistic.

das Pontifikalbuch, pontifical book; *Pontificale Romanum.*

der Pope (-n), priest of the Greek church.

populär, *adj.* popular.

die Popularität, popularity.

das Portal (-e), portal, main entrance.

die Posaune (-n), trombone; (*fig.*) trumpet. (Exod. 19:16)
letzte Posaune, last trump(et), trump of doom.

posaunen, *v.a. & n.* (*aux.* h.) to play the trombone; to trumpet, to sound, to proclaim aloud. (Matt. 6:2)

der Posaunenbläser (-), trumpet player.

der Posaunist (-en), trombonist.

die Postille, book of homilies.

die Pracht, pomp, display, state; splendor, magnificence; luxury. (Ps. 45:9)

prächtig, *adj.* magnificent, splendid; gorgeous, brilliant, superb, glorious, lovely, excellent, fine. (Rom. 16:18)

die Prädestination, predestination.

die Prädestinationslehre, dogma of predestination.

prädestinieren, *v.a.* to predestinate; to foreordain.

der Prädikant (-en), preacher.

die Präexistenz, preexistence.

der Präfekt (-en), prefect, governor.

pragmatisch, *adj.* pragmatic.

prahlen, *v.n.* (*aux.* h.) to boast, to brag, to swagger, to show off, to be loud (of colors). (Ps. 94:3)

der Prahler (-), boaster, braggart, swaggerer.

die Prahlerei, boast(ing), bragging; ostentation.

prahlerisch, *adj.* boastful, bragging, swaggering.

der Prälat (-en), prelate.

prangen, *v.n.* (*aux.* h.) to make a show, to look fine; to glitter, to shine, to sparkle; to be displayed; to boast. (Jer. 22:15)

die Präsenz, presence.

der Präsident (-en), president.

prassen, *v.n.* (*aux.* h.) to feast, to revel, to carouse; to live in debauchery. (Luke 15:13)

der Prasser (-), glutton, reveler; rake.

die Prasserei, feasting, revelry; debauchery, dissipation.

predigen, *v.a. & n.* (*aux.* h.) to preach; to rant, to discourse, to sermonize. (Gen. 4:26)

der Prediger (-), preacher, clergyman, minister. (Matt. 3:3)

der Prediger in der Wüste, a voice crying in the wilderness.

der Predigerorden, Dominican Order.

das Predigerseminar (-e), theological college.

die Predigt (-en), sermon; lecture. (Matt. 12:41)

eine Predigt halten, to preach a sermon.

das Predigtamt, holy orders; dispensation. (Col. 1:25)

der Preis (-e), price, cost, charge; fee, fare, rate, terms; reward, prize; praise, glory. (Rev. 4:9)

Preis und Ehre sei Gott! praise and glory be to God.

preisen, *ir. & reg. v.r.* to praise, to commend, to extol, to exalt, to laud, to glorify. (Exod. 15:2)

Gott sei gepriesen! glory be to God!

der Presbyter (-), presbyter.

die Presbyterialverfassung, the Presbyterian system.

der Presbyterianer (-), Presbyterian.

presbyterianisch, *adj.* Presbyterian.

der Presbyterianismus, Presbyterianism.

das Presbyterium (-rien), presbytery.

der Priester (-), priest. (Gen. 14:18)

das Priesteramt, priesthood, priest's office. (Luke 1:8)

das Priesterbeffchen, clergyman's bands.

die Priesterbinde (-n), fillet.

das Priestergewand (¨er), vestment.

das Priesterhemd (-en), alb, surplice.

die Priesterherrschaft, hierarchy.

die Priesterin (-nen), priestess.

priesterlich, *adj.* priestly, sacerdotal. (Exod. 19:6)

die Priesterschaft, das Priestertum, priesthood, clergy. (Heb. 7:24)

die Priesterweihe, ordination; holy orders.

der Primas (-aten), primate.

der (das) Primat, primacy.

primitiv, *adj.* primitive, original; simple.

der Prior (-en), prior.

die Priorin (-nen), prioress.

die Priorität (-en), priority.

der Probabilismus, probabilism.

das Problem (-e), problem.

die Problematik, uncertainty, ambiguity, difficulty (in arriving at a solution).

problematisch, *adj.* problematic.

profan, *adj.* profane, secular.

profanieren, *v.a.* to profane.

die Profanierung (-en), **die Profanation** (-en), profanation; desecration.

prominent, *adj.* prominent, outstanding.

promovieren, 1. *v.a.* to confer a degree. 2. *v.n.* (*aux.* h.) to graduate, to take a degree.

die Propaganda, propaganda, publicity.

propagieren, *v.a.* to propagate, to publicize.

der Prophet (-en), prophet. (Exod. 7:1)
die großen Propheten, Major Prophets;
die kleinen Propheten, Minor Prophets.

die Prophetengabe (-n), prophetic gift.

die Prophetenschaft, prophethood; the prophets.

das Prophetentum, prophethood.

die Prophetin (-nen), prophetess. (Exod. 15:20)

prophetisch, *adj.* prophetic. (II Peter 1:19)

prophezeien, *v.a.* to prophesy.

die Prophezeiung (-en), prophecy.

der Proselyt (-en), proselyte; neophyte; convert.
Proselyten machen, to proselytize.

der Proselytenmacher (-), proselytizer.

die Proselytenmacherei, der Proselytismus, proselytism.

der Protestant (-en), Protestant.

protestantisch, *adj.* Protestant; evangelical.
die Protestantische Reformation, the Reformation.

der Protestantismus, Protestantism.

protestieren, 1. *v.n.* (*aux.* h.) to protest (*gegen etwas,* against something). 2. *v.a.* to protest (a bill, etc.).

die Provinz (-en), province, provinces.

prüfen, *v.a.* to try, to test, to examine; to inspect, to investigate; to check (an account). (Rom. 12:2)

die Prüfung (-en), examination, investigation; check, test, trial; affliction; temptation.

der Psalm (-en), psalm.
die Psalmen, Book of Psalms, Psalter.

der Psalmist, der Psalmendichter, psalmist.

die Psalmodie, der Psalmengesang, psalmody.

der Psalter, Psalter, Book of Psalms; psaltery (musical instrument).

die Pseudepigraphen, (*pl.*) pseudepigrapha.

pseudepigraphisch, *adj.* pseudepigraphic.

das Pseudonym (-e), 1. pseudonym, assumed name. 2. *adj.* pseudonymous, fictitious.

die Pubertät, puberty.

das Purgatorium, purgatory.

der Puritaner (-), Puritan.

das Puritanertum, der Puritanismus, Puritanism.

puritanisch, *adj.* puritan(ical).

der Purpur, purple; crimson, deep red; purple or scarlet robe. (Rev. 17:4)

das Purpurkleid (-er), purple robe. (John 19:2)

die Purpurkrämerin (-nen), seller of purple. (Acts 16:14)

der Purpurmantel (-̈), scarlet robe. (Matt. 27:28)

purpurn, *adj.* purple, crimson, scarlet, deep red.

die Pyramide (-n), pyramid.

der **Quäker** (-), Quaker.

der **Quäkerbund,** Society of Friends.

quäkerisch, *adj.* Quakerish.

die **Quäkerspeisung,** Friends Relief Organization.

das **Quäkertum,** Quakerism.

die **Qual** (-en), torment, torture, agony, pangs, pain; affliction. (Matt. 8:6)

quälen, 1. *v.a.* to torture, to torment; to agonize, to afflict, to distress, to cause pain; to pester, to molest, to harass, to annoy, to worry. 2. *v.r.* to toil, to slave, to drudge. (Matt. 8:29)

der **Quäler** (-), tormentor, torturer; bore.

die **Quälerei,** tormenting; torments, torture; vexation; persecution; drudgery.

der **Quälgeist** (-er), tormentor, bore, nuisance, plague, pest.

der **Quell** (-e), die **Quelle** (-n), spring, source, fountain, well; fountainhead, origin; authority. (Ps. 36:10)

quellen, 1. *ir.v.n.* (*aux.* s. & h.) to gush, to well (up); to issue, to flow or arise from, to originate or spring from; to swell, to expand. 2. *reg. & ir.v.a.* to cause to swell; to soak, to steep. (James 3:11)

die **Quellenforschung,** critical study of sources; original research.

das **Querschiff** (-e), transept.

der **Quietismus,** quietism.

der **Quietist** (-en), quietist.

Rr

der **Rabbi** (-nen & -s), der **Rabbiner** (-), rabbi. (Matt. 23:8)

das **Rabbineramt, die Rabbinerwürde,** rabbinate.

rabbinisch, *adj.* rabbinic(al).

der **Rabe** (-n), raven, crow. (Gen. 8:7)

die **Rache,** vengeance, revenge. (Deut. 32:35)

der **Rachen** (-), jaws (of beasts); throat, mouth; yawning abyss. (Ps. 22:22)

rächen, 1. *ir.v.a.* to avenge, to revenge. 2. *v.r.* to take revenge (*an*, on). (Gen. 4:15)

der **Rächer** (-), avenger. (I Thess. 4:6)

die **Rächerin** (-nen), avenger. (Rom. 13:4)

rachsüchtig, *adj.* vindictive; (re)vengeful, resentful.

das **Rad** (¨er), wheel. (Ezek. 1:15)

rasen, *v.n.* (*aux.* h.) to rave, to rage; to be mad or delirious. (Acts 26:24)

die **Räson,** reason, common sense.

der **Rat,** 1. (*pl.* -schläge) counsel, advice, suggestion. 2. (*pl.* Beratungen) deliberation, consultation; remedy, means, expedient, ways and means. 3. (*pl.* -sversammlungen) senate, assembly, board, council. 4. (*pl.* ¨e) councilor. 5. (*pl.* -sherrn) alderman, senator. (Matt. 12:14)

raten, *ir.v.a. & n.* (*aux.* h.) (*dat.*) to advise, to counsel; to guess, to conjecture, to solve.

der **Ratgeber** (-), adviser, counselor; counsel. (Isa. 40:13)

das **Rathaus** (¨er), town hall, guild hall, synagogue. (Matt. 10:17)

rational, *adj.* rational, sensible.

die **Rationalisierung,** rationalization, simplification.

der **Rationalismus,** rationalism.

rationalistisch, *adj.* rationalistic.

rationell, *adj.* expedient.

der **Ratschlag** (¨e), advice, counsel, suggestion. (Isa. 7:5)

ratschlagen, *v.n.* (*aux.* h.) (*insep.*) to deliberate, to consult (together). (Ps. 2:2)

der **Ratschluß** (¨[ss]e), resolution, decision; decree. (Isa. 25:1)

das **Rätsel** (-), riddle, puzzle, problem, mystery, enigma. (Judg. 14:12)

der **Raub** (-e), robbery; plundering, pillaging; rape; piracy; prey, loot, booty. (Heb. 10:34)

rauben, 1. *v.a.* to steal, to plunder, to abduct, to ravish; to take away, to deprive of. 2. *v.n.* (*aux.* h.) to rob; to pillage. (Matt. 12:29)

der **Räuber** (-), robber, thief; pirate. (Luke 18:11)

der **Rauch,** smoke; fume, vapor, steam; haze. (Gen. 19:28)

der **Rauchaltar** (¨e), der **Räucheraltar** (¨e), altar for incense. (Exod. 40:5)

rauchen, 1. *v.n.* (*aux.* h.) to smoke, to fume, to reek. 2. *v.a.* to smoke. (Gen. 15:17)

räuchern, 1. *v.a.* to fumigate, to smoke; to cure. 2. *v.n.* (*aux.* h.) to burn incense. (I Kings 22:44)

das **Räuch(er)werk,** perfumes, scents, perfumery; frankincense. (Rev. 5:8)

das **Rauchfaß** (¨[ss]er), das **Räuch(er)faß** (¨[ss]er), censer. (Rev. 8:3)

das **Rauchopfer** (-), incense offering. (Ps. 141:2)

raufen, 1. *v.a.* to pluck, to pull out. 2. *v.r.* to fight, to scuffle, to tussle. (Isa. 50:6)

der **Raum** (¨e), room, space; place; area; expanse; capacity, volume. (Mark 3:20)

räumen, *v.a.* to clear away, to remove; to sell off (cheap), to clear, to clean up; to quit, to leave, to evacuate. (Isa. 57:14)

die **Raupe** (-n), caterpillar; grub, maggot. (Joel 1:4)

rauschen, *v.n.* (*aux.* h.) to rush; to rustle, to murmur, to roar, to thunder; (*aux.* s.) to move with a rustle, to swish. (Lev. 26:36)

die Rebe (-n), vine, grape tendril. (John 15:2)

(die) Rebekka, Rebekah.

das Rebhuhn (¨er), partridge. (I Sam. 26:20).

der Rebstock (¨e), vine.

die Rechenschaft, account. (Matt. 12:36) *Rechenschaft ablegen* or *geben,* to answer or account for, to give an account of.

rechnen, 1. *v.a.* & *n.* (*aux.* h.) to count, to calculate, to reckon, to compute, to figure, to estimate, to do sums; to esteem, to consider; to rank, to class. 2. *n.* arithmetic. (Gen. 15:6)

die Rechnung (-en), calculation, computation; sum; account, bill, reckoning. (Luke 16:2)

recht, 1. *adj.* right, right-hand; proper, correct, fitting, agreeable, suitable; true, real, genuine; just, lawful, legitimate. 2. *adv.* well, right; greatly, remarkably, very; quite, exactly, really. 3. *n.* (-e) right, privilege; claim; title; law; justice; administration of justice. (Gen. 18:19)

das Rechte, the proper, appropriate, or real thing.

der Rechte (-n), the right person, the very man.

die Rechte, right hand; right side. (Gen. 13:9)

rechten, *v.n.* (*aux.* h.) to go to law, to litigate; to contest, to dispute, to remonstrate, to demand one's right. (Matt. 5:40)

rechtfertigen, *v.a.* & *r.* (*insep.*) to justify, to vindicate. (Matt. 11:19)

die Rechtfertigung, justification, vindication. (Rom. 5:18) *die Rechtfertigung durch den Glauben,* justification by faith.

rechtgläubig, *adj.* orthodox.

die Rechtgläubigkeit, orthodoxy.

rechtschaffen, *adj.* righteous, upright, just, honest; mighty, mightily. (Deut. 18:13)

die Rechtschaffenheit, integrity, honesty, uprightness.

die Rede (-n), words, talk, discourse, conversation; speech, address, oration; utterance, report, rumor. (Deut. 32:2)

der Redemptorist (-en), Redemptorist.

reden, 1. *v.a.* & *n.* (*aux.* h.) to speak; to talk; to converse; to discourse. 2. *n.* talking, speaking; speech. (Exod. 6:28)

redlich, *adj.* honest; sincere, upright, candid, just.

die Redlichkeit, honesty; sincerity.

das Referat (-e), lecture, talk, report.

die Reform (-en), reform.

die Reformation, Reformation.

das Reformationsfest, Reformation Day.

der Reformator, reformer.

reformatorisch, *adj.* pertaining to the Reformation.

der Reformierte (-n), member of the Reformed Church. *die Reformierte Kirche,* Reformed Church.

die Regalien, (*pl.*) regalia.

die Regel (-n), rule, standard; regulation, law. *die goldene Regel,* golden rule.

der Regen, shower, downpour; precipitation. (Acts 14:17)

der Regenbogen, rainbow. (Rev. 4:3)

der Regent (-en), regent; sovereign, reigning prince. (Gen. 42:6)

regieren, 1. *v.a.* to regulate, to conduct, to manage; to rule, to govern. 2. *v.n.* (*aux.* h.) to reign, to rule. (Ps. 147:5)

das Regiment, 1. (-e) power, authority; *das Regiment haben* or *führen,* to rule, to command, to have control. 2. (-er) regiment (of soldiers).

regnen, *v.a.* & *n.* (*aux.* h.) & *imp.* to rain. (Exod. 16:4)

das Reh (-e), roe (deer). (Isa. 13:14)

(der) Rehabeam, Rehoboam.

reich, *adj.* rich, wealthy; abundant, copious; opulent, ample, plentiful, fertile. (Gen. 13:2)

das Reich (-e), state, realm, empire, kingdom; reign. (Matt. 4:8) *das Reich Gottes,* the kingdom of God; *das Heilige Römische Reich Deutscher Nation,* the Holy Roman Empire of the German Nation (843–1806).

Reicharabien, Sheba. (I Kings 10:1)

reichen, 1. *v.a.* to reach; (*einem etwas*) *reichen,* to give, to present, to pass, to hand. 2. *v.n.* (*aux.* h.) to reach, to extend to; to last, to hold out. (Gen. 11:4) *das Abendmahl reichen,* to administer the sacrament; *Almosen reichen,* to bestow alms.

reichlich, *adj.* ample, profuse, plentiful, abundant. (Ps. 59:11)

der Reichtum (⁻er), riches, wealth; abundance; richness. (Rev. 5:12)

reif, *adj.* ripe, mature, mellow; fully developed, ready. (Rev. 14:18)

der Reif (-e), hoarfrost; bloom (on fruit). (Exod. 16:14)

die Reife, maturity, puberty; ripeness. (Job 29:4)

der Reigen (-), round dance. (Luke 15:25)

der Reiher (-), heron. (Ps. 104:17)

rein, *adj.* clean, clear, neat; genuine, pure, chaste; quite, mere. (Rev. 15:6)

die Reinheit, purity, pureness, chastity; cleanness, cleanliness.

reinigen, *v.a.* to clean, to cleanse; to purify; to purge; to refine, to rectify. (Matt. 8:3)

die Reinkarnation, reincarnation.

reinlich, *adj.* clean, neat, tidy, distinct. (Matt. 23:25)

die Reinlichkeit, cleanliness, neatness, tidiness.

das Reis (-er), twig, sprig; shoot. (Isa. 53:2)

die Reise (-n), journey, tour, trip. (Gen. 24:21)

reisen, *v.n.* (*aux.* h. & s.) to travel, to journey; to set out (for). (Gen. 28:20)

reißen, 1. *ir.v.a.* to tear, to rip, to rend; to pull; to seize, to grasp; to sketch, to scribe. 2. *v.n.* (*aux.* h. & s.) to tear, to split, to break; to break loose. (Gen. 37:33)

reiten, 1. *ir.v.n.* (*aux.* s.) to ride, to go on horseback. 2. *v.a.* to ride (a horse). (John 12:14)

der Reiter (-), rider, horseman, cavalryman. (Exod. 14:23)

reizen, *v.a.* to excite, to stimulate, to provoke, to stir up, to irritate; to charm, to attract, to entice. (Deut. 32:21)

die Religion (-en), religion.

das Religionsbekenntnis (-se), religious profession.

das Religionsbuch (⁻er), religious textbook.

die Religionsduldung, religious toleration.

die Religionsfreiheit (-en), religious liberty.

der Religions(ge)brauch (⁻e), rite.

die Religionsgemeinschaft (-en), sect.

der Religionskrieg (-e), religious war.

die Religionslehre (-n), doctrine.

der Religionslehrer (-), Scripture teacher; divine.

religionslos, *adj.* irreligious.

die Religionsphilosophie (-n), philosophy of religion.

der Religionssatz (⁻e), dogma.

der Religionsschwärmer (-), fanatic.

die Religionssoziologie, sociology of religion.

der Religionsstifter (-), founder of a religion.

der Religionsstreit, dispute, disputation.

die Religionsstunde (-n), religious instruction.

die Religionstrennung (-en), schism.

der Religionsunterricht, Scripture (teaching or lessons).

die Religionsverfolgung (-en), religious persecution.

die Religionswissenschaft, theology, divinity.

der Religionszwang, intolerance, religious compulsion.

religiös, *adj.* religious. *religiöse Handlungen,* religious acts; *eine religiöse Schwärmerin,* a religious fanatic; *religiöse Zweifel haben,* to have religious doubts.

die Religiosität, religiosity, religiousness.

die Reliquie (-n), relic.

der Reliquiendienst, worship of relics.

das Reliquienkästchen (-), **der Reliquienschrein** (-e), reliquary.

der Renegat (-en), renegade.

das Requiem (-ien), requiem (mass).

retten, 1. *v.a.* to save, to rescue, to recover; to deliver; to free, to preserve. 2. *v.r.* to escape, to save oneself. (Gen. 19:17)

der Retter (-), rescuer, deliverer; Savior, Redeemer.

die Rettung (-en), saving, preservation; salvation, deliverance, redemption, rescue; escape.

die Reue, repentance; regret, remorse. (II Cor. 7:10)

das Reu(e)gefühl, remorse.

reuen, *v.a. & n. (aux.* h.) *& imp.* to regret, to be sorry (for); to repent (of). (Gen. 6:6)

reuevoll, *adj.* repentant.

reuig, reumütig, *adj.* penitent, contrite.

die Reumütigkeit, contrition.

die Reverenz (-en), reverence; courtesy; respect; bow, curtsy.

richten, 1. *v.a.* to set right, to adjust, to arrange, to put in order, to straighten; to prepare (a meal, etc.), to settle (a dispute, etc.). 2. *v.r.* to rise, to stand erect. 3. *v.a. & n. (aux.* h.) to judge, to try, to pass sentence on, to condemn; to execute (a criminal). (Deut. 32:36)

der Richter (-), judge; justice; umpire. (Gen. 16:5)

der Richterspruch, sentence.

das Richthaus, palace, praetorium. (Phil. 1:13)

richtig, 1. *adj.* right, accurate, correct, true; fair, just, genuine, real; in order. 2. *adv.* quite right; certainly, just so, sure enough. (Matt. 3:3)

der Richtplatz (¨e), **die Richtstätte** (-n), place of execution.

der Richtstuhl, der Richterstuhl, judgment seat. (Matt. 27:19)

riechen, *ir.v.a. & n. (aux.* h.) to smell, to scent; to foresee, to perceive, to find out. (Gen. 8:21)

der Riegel (-), bolt; rail, bar, crossbar, tie. (Isa. 45:2)

der Riemen (-), strap, sling; belt; thong, shoelace. (Mark 1:7)

der Riese (-n), giant. (Isa. 49:24)

das Rind (-er), ox, cow; (*pl.*) (horned) cattle. (I Kings 7:25)

der Ring (-e), ring; circle; cycle; arena. (Gen. 41:42)

ringen, 1. *ir.v.n. (aux.* h.) to struggle; to wrestle. 2. *v.a.* to wring, to wrench, to wrest. (Gen. 32:25)

rinnen, *ir.v.n. (aux.* s.) to run, to flow; to trickle, to drip; (*aux.* h.) to leak. (Jer. 9:17)

die Rippe (-n), rib; vein (of a leaf). (Gen. 2:22)

der Riß (-[ss]e), tear, rent, laceration; cleft, fissure, gap; crack, flaw; elevation, design, outline; schism, breach. (Matt. 9:16)

der Ritter (-), knight; cavalier.
der Tempelritter, Templar; *der Johanniterritter,* Knight of St. John, Knight Hospitaler.

ritterlich, *adj.* knightly; valiant, gallant.

die Ritterlichkeit, gallantry, chivalry.

die Ritterschaft, knighthood, body of knights, chivalry. (II Cor. 10:4)

das Ritual (-e), ritual.

ritual, rituell, *adj.* ritual.

der Ritualismus, ritualism.

der Ritus (-en), rite.

der Rizinus, gourd. (Jonah 4:6)

die Robe (-n), robe.

der Rock (¨e), coat (for men), skirt (for women), garment, robe. (Gen. 3:21)

das Rohr (-e), reed, cane; tube, pipe; flue. (Matt. 11:7)

der Rohrstab (¨e), staff. (II Kings 18:21)

Rom, Rome.

der Römer (-), Roman.

römisch, *adj.* Roman.

römisch-katholisch, *adj.* Roman Catholic.

die Rose (-n), rose. (Hos. 14:6).

der Rosenkranz (¨e), garland of roses; rosary.

der Rosenkreuzer (-), Rosicrucian.

das Roß (-[ss]e), steed, charger; (*pl.* ¨er) horse. (Exod. 15:1)

der Rost, rust; blight, mildew, smut (on corn). (Matt. 6:19)

rösten, *v.a.* to roast, to grill, to broil; to toast. (I Kings 19:6)

rot, 1. *adj.* red; ruddy. 2. *n.* red; redness; rouge. (Gen. 25:30)

rötlich, *adj.* reddish. (Isa. 63:1)

die Rotte (-n), file (military); band, gang, horde, rabble. (Gal. 5:20)

(der) Ruben, Reuben.

der Rubin (-e), ruby. (Isa. 54:12)

ruchbar, *adj.* notorious; known, public. (Matt. 9:31)

ruchlos, *adj.* wicked, infamous, impious, vicious, malicious. (Prov. 1:7)

der Rücken, 1. *m.* (-) back, rear; ridge. 2. *v.a.* to jerk, to pull; to move, to push along, to bring nearer. 3. *v.n.* (*aux.* h. & s.) to move; to proceed, to advance; *ins Feld rücken,* to take the field, to go to war, to go into action; *in ein Land rücken,* to invade a country. (Isa. 50:6)

das Ruder (-), oar; rudder, helm. (James 3:4)

rudern, *v.a. & n.* (*aux.* h. & s.) to row, to paddle. (Mark 6:48)

der Ruf (-e), call, shout, cry, calling; repute, reputation, name, fame. (Prov. 22:1)

rufen, *ir.v.a. & n.* (*aux.* h.) to call; to cry out, to shout, to exclaim. (Gen. 3:9)

die Ruhe, rest, repose, sleep; peace, quiet, calm, silence. (Matt. 11:29)

das Ruhebett (-en), couch, sofa. (Amos 6:4)

ruhen, *v.n.* (*aux.* h.) to rest, to repose, to sleep; to pause; to be idle. (Gen. 2:2)

ruhig, 1. *adj.* quiet, silent, tranquil; still, at rest; serene, peaceful, composed. 2. *adv.* safely, unhesitatingly. (Gen. 25:8)

der Ruhm, glory, honor; fame, reputation, praise. (Rom. 3:23)

rühmen, 1. *v.a.* to praise, to extol, to glorify, to celebrate, to mention with praise. 2. *v.r.* (*gen.*) to boast (of), to brag (about). (James 1:9)

ruhmredig, *adj.* vainglorious, boastful. (Ps. 73:3)

die Ruhr, dysentery. (Acts 28:8)

rühren, 1. *v.n.: an etwas rühren,* to finger or touch a thing; to make reference to a thing. 2. *v.a.* to stir, to move; to touch, to strike; to affect, to make an impression on. 3. *v.r.* to stir; to be active, to make a move. (Mark 7:33)

der Ruin, ruin, downfall, decay.

rund, 1. *adj.* round; circular; plain; fat, plump. 2. *n.* globe, sphere, circle. (Exod. 16:14)

die Runzel (-n), wrinkle, fold. (Eph. 5:27)

rüsten, 1. *v.a.* to prepare, to equip, to arm, to mobilize, to prepare for war. 2. *v.n. & r.* (*aux.* h.) to make preparations, to get ready. (Rev. 8:6)

die Rüstung (-en), armaments, arms; armor; (*fig.*) mobilization. (Isa. 9:4)

das Rüstzeug, tool, implement; (*fig.*) knowledge, capacity, (mental) equipment. (Acts 9:15)

die Rute (-n), rod, twig, switch; (*archaic land measure;* rod, pole, or perch). (Isa. 9:3)

rütteln, *v.a. & n.* (*aux.* h.) to shake; to jog, to jolt, to vibrate; to undermine. (Luke 6:38)

Ss

der Saal (Säle), hall, assembly room, large room; ward. (Mark 14:15)

die Saat (-en), sowing; seed; standing corn; green crops. (Gen. 8:22)

das Saba, Sheba.

der Sabbat (-e), Sabbath; Sunday. (Exod. 16:23)
den Sabbat heiligen, to keep the Sabbath; *den Sabbat entheiligen,* to break the Sabbath.

die Sabbatruhe, Sabbath rest; Sunday rest.

der Sabbatschänder (-), Sabbath-breaker.

(der) Sacharja, Zechariah.

die Sache (-n), thing, object, article; cause, action, case; subject; affair, business, event; fact, circumstance; (*pl.*) goods, clothes, etc. (Matt. 12:10)

die Sachlichkeit, reality, objectivity; impartiality.

der Sack (-̈e), sack, bag; sac, pouch; purse, pocket. (Rev. 6:12)

(der) Sadduzäer, Sadducee.

säen, *v.a. & n.* (*aux.* h.) to sow. (Matt. 6:26)

der Saft (-̈e), juice; sap; syrup; liquor, fluid, moisture. (Rom. 11:17)

saftig, *adj.* juicy, luscious, succulent. (Matt. 24:32)

die Säge (-n), saw. (Isa. 10:15)

sagen, *v.a.* to say, to tell; to speak; to declare, to testify, to mean. (Gen. 3:1)

das Saitenspiel, string music; lyre. (I Sam. 16:17)

das Sakrament (-e), sacrament; consecrated host.

sakramental, sakramentlich, *adj.* sacramental.

der Sakramentierer (-), sacramentarian (e.g., Zwingli).

der Sakramentsstreit, controversy about the Lord's Supper.

das Sakrileg, sacrilege.

der Sakristan (-e), sacristan, sexton.

die Sakristei (-en), vestry, sacristy.

sakrosankt, *adj.* sacrosanct.

die Sakrosanktheit, sacrosanctity.

säkular, *adj.* secular.

die Säkularfeier (-n), centenary.

die Säkularisation, secularization.

säkularisieren, *v.a.* to secularize.

der Säkularismus, secularism.

die Salbe (-n), ointment, salve; scented oil, pomade. (John 11:2)

salben, *v.a.* to apply ointment, to anoint; to embalm. (Gen. 50:2)

die Salbung, anointing; unction. (I John 2:20)

(der) Salomo, Solomon.

das Salz (-e), salt. (Matt. 5:13)

salzen, *ir. & reg. v.a.* to salt; to pickle; to season. (Mark 9:49)

salzig, *adj.* salt; saline. (James 3:12)

die Salzsäule, pillar of salt. (Gen. 19:26)

der Sämann (-̈er), sower. (Matt. 13:3)

der Samariter (-), Samaritan. (Matt. 10:5)
der barmherzige Samariter, the Good Samaritan.

der Same (-n), seed, grain; sperm, semen; (*fig.*) germ, source; descendants. (Gen. 1:11)

sammeln, 1. *v.a.* to gather, to collect; to accumulate; to assemble, to concentrate (troops, etc.). 2. *v.r.* to collect, to assemble, to flock together, to concentrate, to collect one's thoughts. (Gen. 1:9)

die Sammlung (-en), collection. (Gen. 1:10)

samt, *adv. & prep.* (*dat.*) with, together with, along with. (Rom. 6:5)

(der) Samuel, Samuel. (Acts 3:24)

der Sand, sand, grit. (Gen. 22:17)

sanft, *adj.* gentle, easy; smooth, soft; placid, tender, mild; slight. (Gen. 25:27)

die Sänfte (-n), sedan chair, litter. (Isa. 66:20)

die Sanftmut, gentleness, meekness, good temper. (James 1:21)

sanftmütig, *adj.* gentle, mild, meek. (Matt. 11:29)
selig sind die Sanftmütigen, blessed are the meek.

(der) Sanherib, Sennacherib.

der Saphir (-e), sapphire. (Exod. 24:10)

(die) Sara, Sarah. (Isa. 51:2)

der Sarg (⸚e), coffin. (Luke 7:14)

(der) Satan (-e), **Satanas,** Satan, devil. (Matt. 4:10)

satanisch, *adj.* satanic, diabolical.

der Satanismus, Satanism.

satt, *adj.* satisfied, full, satiated; saturated; dark, intensive, rich (of color). (Gen. 35:29)

sättigen, 1. *v.a.* to fill, to sate, to satisfy, to appease, to satiate; to saturate, to impregnate. 2. *v.r.* to satisfy one's hunger. (Luke 16:21)

die Satzung, statute, charter; law, fixed rule, ordinance, precept, dogma. (Gal. 4:3)

die Sau, 1. (⸚e) sow. 2. (-en) wild sow. (Matt. 7:6)

säuberlich, *adj.* clean; careful, cautious, wary. (II Sam. 18:5)

sauer, 1. *adj.* (comp. *saurer,* sup. *sauerst*) (*when inflected generally* **saur**) sour, acid; acetous. 2. *n.* giblets prepared with vinegar; vinegar; yeast. (Matt. 6:16)

der Sauerteig, leaven, yeast. (Exod. 12:15)

saufen, 1. *ir.v.a. & n.* (*aux.* h.) to drink (of beasts). 2. *n.* drinking. (Luke 21:34)

die Säugamme (-n), wet-nurse. (Isa. 49:23)

saugen, *ir.v.a. & n.* (*aux.* h.) to suck; to absorb. (Luke 11:27)

säugen, *v.a.* to suckle, to nurse. (Luke 23:29)

der Säugling (-e), infant, suckling. (Ps. 8:3)

(der) Saul, Saul. (I Sam. 10:11)

die Säule (-n), column (*also military*), pillar (*also fig.*), post, jamb, upright, support. (I Kings 7:6)

der Säulenheilige, stylite.

der Saum (⸚e), hem, seam, margin, border, edge; fillet; brink. (Matt. 9:20)

säumen, 1. *v.n.* (*aux.* h.) to delay, to linger, to tarry; to defer, to put off, to hesitate. 2. *n.* delay, tarrying. (Isa. 46:13)

sausen, *v.n.* (*aux.* h. & s.) to bluster, to blow hard, to howl (as wind); to whistle; to rush, to dash. (John 3:8)

schaben, *v.a.* to scrape, to grate, to scratch, to rub; to pare, to shave. (Job 2:8)

der Schächer (-), thief, robber, malefactor, felon.

der Schade (⸚n), **der Schaden** (⸚), damage, injury, defect, hurt, harm, wrong, mischief; prejudice, disadvantage, loss. (Matt. 16:26)

die Schädelstätte, Golgotha, Calvary. (Matt. 27:33)

schaden, *v.n.* (*aux.* h.) (*dat.*) to harm, to hurt, to injure, to damage; to prejudice. (Acts 18:10)

die Schadenfreude, malicious pleasure, gloating.

schädlich, *adj.* (*dat.*) detrimental, prejudicial, disadvantageous, harmful, destructive, dangerous. (Rom. 1:30)

das Schaf (-e), sheep. (Acts 8:32)

schaffen, 1. *ir.v.a. & n.* (*aux.* h.) to create; to produce. 2. *reg. v.a.* to do, to make, to accomplish; to procure, to provide, to let have; to bring, to transport. (Gen. 1:1)

die Schaffung, production, creation; establishing.

die Schafhürde (-n), sheep-pen or fold. (II Sam. 7:8)

die Schafmutter (⸚), ewe. (Isa. 40:11)

das Schafott (-e), scaffold.

der Schafstall (⸚e), sheepfold. (John 10:1)

der Schakal (-e), jackal. (Jer. 9:10)

die Schale (-n), skin, peel, rind, bark, crust, shell; dish, vial, bowl, basin, vessel; cup. (Rev. 5:8)
die Schale seines Zorns über einen ausgießen, to pour out the vials of one's wrath on a person.

der Schalk (-e), scoundrel, scamp, rogue, knave; wag. (Matt. 6:23)

die Schalkheit, roguishness, mischief; roguery, villainy. (Acts 13:10)

der Schalksknecht (-e), unfaithful servant. (Matt. 18:32)

der Schall (-e), sound, ring, resonance, noise. (Rom. 10:18)

schallen, v.n. (aux. h.) to sound, to resound, to ring, to peal. (Isa. 30:30)

die Scham, shame, bashfulness, modesty, chastity; genitals; nakedness. (Luke 14:9)

schämen, v.r. to be ashamed (*über eine Sache, wegen einer Sache, also with gen.,* of something). (Gen. 2:25)

schamlos, adj. devoid of shame, shameless.

die Schamlosigkeit, shamelessness.

schandbar, adj. infamous, disgraceful; abominable. (Eph. 5:4)

die Schande (-n), shame, disgrace, dishonor; infamy, ignominy. (Rev. 3:18)

schänden, v.a. to violate, to rape, to ravish; to profane, to defame, to desecrate, to revile; to spoil, to deface. (Rom. 1:24)

schändlich, adj. shameful, disgraceful, infamous, dishonorable, scandalous, abominable, vile, base. (Rom. 1:26)

die Schändung (-en), disfiguring, spoiling, profanation, desecration; violation, rape.

die Schar (-en), troop, band, platoon; herd, flock; host, multitude, crowd. (Matt. 27:27)

der Schatten (-), shadow, shade; phantom, spirit. (Matt. 4:16)

der Schatz (¨e), treasure, wealth; store, stock; sweetheart, love, darling. (Matt. 2:11)

schätzen, v.a. to value, to appraise, to estimate, to assess, to consider (to be); to esteem, to respect, to prize. (Luke 2:1)

die Schatzkammer (-n), treasury. (Acts 8:27)

der Schatzmeister (-), treasurer; chancellor. (Isa. 22:15)

die Schätzung, estimation, valuation, evaluation, estimate, assessment; tax, taxation.

die Schau (-en), show, sight, view; inspection, review; exhibition, display.
zur Schau tragen, to make display of. (Col. 2:15)

das Schaubrot (-e), showbread; bread of the presence. (Exod. 25:30)

schauen, v.a. & n. to behold, to see; to look (at), to gaze (upon), to view. (Exod. 24:11)

der Schaum (¨e), foam, froth; scum; flurry, lather, bubbles; dross. (Isa. 1:22)

schäumen, 1. v.n. (aux. h.) to foam, to froth, to lather; to sparkle. 2. v.a. to skim; to pour out. (Prov. 15:28)

der Schauplatz (¨e), theater, scene, arena, stage, seat (of war). (Acts 19:29)

das Schauspiel (-e), spectacle, sight, scene; play, drama. (I Cor. 4:9)

scheel, adj. envious; cross-eyed, squinting; evil. (Matt. 20:15)

der Scheffel (-), bushel. (Matt. 5:15)

die Scheide (-n), boundary, border, limit, divide; case, sheath. (John 18:11)

der Scheidebrief, farewell letter; bill of divorce. (Deut. 24:1)

scheiden, 1. ir.v.r. & n. (aux. s.) to separate, to part; to depart, to go away, to leave. 2. v.a. to separate, to divide, to pick, to sort, to sift; to part, to divorce; to analyze, to refine, to clarify; to decompose. (Gen. 1:4)

der Schein (-e), shine, light, brilliance, gleam, luster, bloom, sheen; appearance, air, look; pretense, pretext, illusion; bank note, receipt, bond, document, bill, license; (*fig.*) glory, halo, blaze. (Matt. 24:29)

der Scheinchrist (-en), pretended or lip-Christian.

scheinen, ir.v.n. (aux. h.) to shine; (*with dat.*) to seem, to appear, to look. (Gen. 1:15)

scheinheilig, adj. hypocritical, sanctimonious.

der Scheinheilige (-n), hypocrite.

die Scheinheiligkeit, hypocrisy.

der Scheitel (-), top, vertex, apex, summit; crown (of the head); parting (of the hair). (Isa. 3:17)
vom Scheitel bis zur Sohle, from head to foot, from top to toe.

der Scheiterhaufen (-), stake.

die Schelle (-n), cymbal, (little) bell. (I Cor. 13:1)

schelten, ir.v.a. & n. (aux. h.) to reproach, to scold, to chide, to reprimand, to abuse; to call, to nickname. (Matt. 11:20)

das Scheltwort, invective. (I Peter 3:9)

der Schemel (-), (foot)stool. (Matt. 5:35)

der Schemen (-), phantom, shadow, delusion.

der Schenk(e) (-en), cupbearer. (Gen. 40:1)

der Schenkel (-), thigh, shank; side (of angles); hinged leg, arm, limb, foot. (Acts 3:7)

schenken, *v.a.* to give, to present, to bestow, to grant; to remit, to forgive, to acquit; to pour out, to fill. (Luke 7:42) *wenn Gott mir das Leben schenkt,* if God grants me life.

die Schenkung (-en), donation, gift.

die Scherbe (-n), fragment (of glass, etc.); earthenware vessel; flowerpot. (Job 2:8)

scheren, 1. *reg. & ir.v.a.* to shear, to clip, to cut, to trim, to mow, to shave. 2. *v.n.* to sheer. 3. *v.r.* to go away, to clear off. (Gen. 31:19)

der Scherer (-), shearer; barber. (Isa. 53:7)

der Scherge (-n), beadle, constable; executor.

das Schermesser (-), razor. (Num. 6:5)

der Scherz (-e), jest, joke, fun, pleasantry. (Eph. 5:4)

die Scherzeit, shearing time.

scherzen, *v.n.* (*aux.* h.) to jest, to joke, to have fun (with), to make fun (of). (Ecclesiasticus 47:3)

scheu, 1. *adj.* shy, timid; bashful. 2. *f.* shyness, timidity; awe, aversion. (Ps. 27:12)

scheuen, 1. *v.a.* to fear, to dread, to shun, to avoid, to shrink from. 2. *v.r.* (*vor*), to be afraid (of); to hesitate (at); to be shy. 3. *v.n.* (*aux.* h.) to be frightened, to take fright. (Matt. 21:37)

die Scheuer (-n), barn, shed, granary. (Matt. 13:30)

die Scheune (-n), barn, granary, hayloft, shed. (Matt. 3:12)

das Scheusal (-e), horrible creature, monster. (Deut. 28:37)

die Schicht (-en), layer, course, bed; level, class, rank (in society, etc.).

schicken, 1. *v.a.* to send, to dispatch, to remit (money). 2. *v.r.* to come to pass, to happen; to suit, to be proper. (Rom. 12:11)

das Schicksal (-e), destiny; fate, fortune, lot.

die Schickung, providence, fate, dispensation.
Gottes Schickung, divine ordinance, the finger of God.

schier, *adv.* almost, nearly, barely, simply. (Isa. 21:11)

schießen, 1. *ir.v.n.* (*aux.* s.) to shoot (as stars), to dart; to spring up, to burst forth. 2. *v.n.* (*aux.* h.) to shoot, to fire; to burst, to blast. (Rev. 12:15)

das Schiff (-e), ship, vessel; nave (of a church); shuttle (weaving). (Acts 28:11)

die Schiffahrt, navigation; shipping; voyage. (Acts 27:10)

der Schiffbruch (⁻e), shipwreck. (II Cor. 11:25)

schiffen, 1. *v.a.* to ship (goods, etc.). 2. *v.n.* (*aux.* s.) to navigate, to sail (on), to go by water. (Acts 13:4)

die Schiffsleute, (*pl.*) crew, sailors. (Rev. 18:17)

der Schild (-e), shield, buckler; coat of arms; shell. (Gen. 15:1)

die Schildwacht, sentry. (I Sam. 13:3)

das Schilf (-e), reed, rush; sedge. (Exod. 2:3)

das Schilfmeer, Red Sea. (Exod. 13:18)

schinden, 1. *ir.v.a. & n.* (*aux.* h.) to skin, to flay; to exploit. 2. *v.r.* to work oneself to death, to drudge, to slave. (Exod. 22:20)

der Schinder (-), slave driver; oppressor. (Isa. 49:26)

die Schinderei, oppression; extortion, ill treatment; grind, drudgery. (Isa. 5:7)

der Schirm (-), umbrella; screen, shelter, protective cover, protection, hiding place. (Ps. 119:114)

das Schisma (-men), schism.

schismatisch, *adj.* schismatic.

die Schlacht (-en), battle, engagement, fight. (Gen. 14:17)

die Schlachtbank, shambles, slaughterhouse, slaughter. (Isa. 53:7)
das Opfer zur Schlachtbank führen, to lead the lamb to the slaughter.

schlachten, 1. *v.a.* to slaughter; to butcher, to slay, to immolate (a sacrifice). 2. *v.n.* (*aux.* h.) to massacre, to butcher. (Gen. 22:10)

der Schlachtenlenker, God of hosts.

der Schlachtgesang (⁻e), battle song.

das Schlachtgeschrei, war cry.

der Schlachttag, slaughter day; day of battle. (James 5:5)

der Schlaf, sleep, slumber. (Gen. 2:21)

schlafen, *ir.v.n.* (*aux.* h.) to sleep, to be asleep; to slumber, to rest, to repose; to be or lie dormant. (Deut. 31:16)

schläfrig, *adj.* sleepy, drowsy; (*fig.*) slow, indolent. (Matt. 25:5)

der Schlag (⁀e), blow, knock, bang, rap, slap, punch, kick; movement; concussion, shock; stroke, fit; stamp, kind, sort. (II Sam. 7:14)

schlagen, *ir.v.a.* to beat, to strike, to hit, to clap, to dash; to defeat, to rout (an enemy); to toll (a bell). (Gen. 8:21)

der Schlamm, mud, slime, mire, sludge, silt. (Ps. 40:3)

die Schlange (-n), snake, serpent. (Gen. 3:1)

der Schlauch (⁀e), tube, pipe, hose; leather bottle or skin, wineskins. (Matt. 9:17)

schlecht, *adj.* bad, wicked, base; poor, inferior, wretched.

die Schlechtigkeit, badness, baseness, wickedness.

schleichen, *ir.v.r. & n.* (*aux.* s.) to crawl, to creep; to sneak, to steal, to prowl. (Ps. 91:6)

der Schleier (-), veil; pretense, cloak, screen; haze, film. (Jer. 2:32)

schleifen, 1. *v.n.* (*aux.* h. & s.) to slide; to glide, to skid, to slip along. 2. *v.a.* to drag, to trail; to raze, to demolish (a fortress); to knot, to tie in a bow. (Acts 14:19)

schlemmen, *v.n.* (*aux.* h.) to revel, to carouse. (Amos 2:8)

schlenkern, 1. *v.n.* (*aux.* h.) to dangle; to shamble (in walking). 2. *v.a.* to dangle, to swing; to shake off, to jerk, to sling, to fling. (Acts 28:5)

die Schleuder (-n), sling, catapult. (I Sam. 17:50)

schlicht, *adj.* plain, homely, simple, modest, straightforward; smooth. (Isa. 40:4)

das Schloß (⁀[ss]er), castle, palace; lock (of doors, etc.); bolt, clasp, snap (of bracelets, etc.). (Prov. 18:10)

schlummern, *v.n.* (*aux.* h.) to slumber, to sleep, to doze, to nap; to lie dormant. (Matt. 13:15)

der Schlund (⁀e), pharynx, throat, gullet; gorge, gulf, abyss, crater. (Isa. 5:14)

der Schluß, deduction, inference, conclusion; syllogism.

der Schlüssel (-), key; ratio; code. (Matt. 16:19)

der Schlußsatz, conclusion, final proposition (logic).

die Schmach, insult, outrage, offense; disgrace, humiliation. (Acts 5:41)

schmähen, *v.a. & n.* (*aux.* h.) to abuse, to revile, to despise, to insult, to slander. (Matt. 5:11)

die Schmähschrift (-en), libel; lampoon.

die Schmähung (-en), abuse, invective, slander, defamation. (Ps. 69:10)

schmal, *adj.* narrow, thin, slim, slender; poor, meager. (Matt. 7:14)

schmecken, 1. *v.a.* to taste; to try by tasting; (*fig.*) to experience. 2. *v.n.* (*aux.* h.) to taste (bitter, sweet); to taste good; to smell. (Matt. 16:28)

schmeicheln, *v.n.* (*aux.* h.) (*dat.*) to flatter, to compliment; to fawn upon; to caress, to fondle, to pet.

das Schmeichelwort (-e), flattering word or speech. (I Thess. 2:5)

schmelzen, 1. *ir.v.n.* (*aux.* s.) to melt, to fuse; to diminish, to melt away; to soften (of heart). 2. *reg. & ir.v.a.* to melt, to smelt; to fuse, to blend. (II Peter 3:10)

das Schmer, fat, grease, suet. (Ps. 119:70)

der Schmerz (-en), pain, ache; (*fig.*) grief, suffering, sorrow. (Gen. 3:16)

der Schmerzensmann, Man of sorrows.

der Schmetterling (-e), butterfly.

der Schmied (-e), (black)smith. (I Sam. 13:19)

schmieren, 1. *v.a.* to grease, to oil; to smear, to spread; to tip heavily. 2. *v.n.* (*aux.* h.) to smear, to rub off; to scribble, to scrawl. (John 9:6)

schminken, *v.a. & r.* to paint one's face, to make up, to use makeup. (Isa. 3:16)

der Schmuck (-e), 1. *m.* ornament, decoration; jewels, jewelry, ornaments, adornment. 2. *adj.* spruce, tidy, pretty, nice, handsome. (I Peter 3:3)

schmücken, 1. *v.a.* to decorate; to trim, to ornament. 2. *v.r.* to deck oneself out. (Rev. 21:2)

schnauben, *reg. & ir.v.a. & n. (aux.* h. & s.) to pant, to puff, to blow, to breathe heavily, to snort. (Acts 9:1)
(vor) Wut schnauben, to foam or fume with rage; *Rache schnauben,* to breathe vengeance.

der Schnee, snow. (Num. 12:10)

schneeweiß, *adj. & n.* snow-white. (Dan. 7:9)

die Schneide (-n), edge (of a knife, etc.), cutting edge; sharpness, keenness, cut. (I Sam. 13:21)

schneiden, 1. *ir.v.a. & n. (aux.* h.) to cut, to mow, to trim, to carve, to engrave. 2. *v.r.* to intersect, to meet; *(fig.)* to make a mistake, to be mistaken, to be disappointed. (Matt. 25:24)

schnell, *adj.* rapid, swift, fast, quick, speedy; prompt, sudden, hasty, brisk. (Mark 13:36)

der Schnitter (-), harvester, reaper, mower. (Matt. 13:30)

die Schnur (⁻e & -en), string, cord, twine; string of beads; braid. (Exod. 28:28)

der Scholar (-en), scholar, medieval student.

die Scholastik, scholastic; *(pl.)* the Schoolmen.

scholastisch, *adj.* scholastical.

der Scholastizismus, scholasticism.

der Scholiast (-en), scholiast.

schon, *adv. & part.* already, as yet, by this time, so far; certainly, surely, indeed, no doubt, after all. (John 3:18)

schön, 1. *adj.* beautiful, lovely, fair, handsome; fine, nice. 2. *adv.* very, exceedingly, nicely. (Gen. 6:2)

die Schöne (-n), beauty, beautiful woman. (Isa. 33:17)

schonen, 1. *v.a. & v.n. (aux.* h.) *(gen.)* to treat with consideration or indulgence; to be sparing of, to save, to spare, to conserve; to protect, to care for. 2. *v.r.* to take care of or look after oneself. (Amos 1:3)

die Schönheit, beauty, fineness, beauty, belle; *(pl.)* compliments.

schöpfen, *v.a.* to draw (water); to dip, to scoop out; to derive, to obtain (information). (I Sam. 7:6)
Atem schöpfen, to take or draw a breath.

der Schöpfer, drawer (of water); maker, creator, author, originator. (Rom. 1:25)

die Schöpferhand, hand of the creator.

die Schöpfung, creation; the universe, created things. (Rom. 1:20)

die Schöpfungsgeschichte, history of creation, genesis.

der Schöpfungstag, day of creation.

der Schoß (-[ss]e[n] & ⁻[ss]e[r]), sprig, sprout; tax, impost. (Rom. 13:6)

der Schoß (⁻e), lap; womb; *(fig.)* bosom; coattail. (II Sam. 12:3)

die Schranke (-n), barrier; crossing gate, fence; limit, boundary, bound; arena, enclosure. (I Cor. 9:24)

schrecken, 1. *v.a.* to frighten, to startle, to alarm, to terrify; to frighten away; to chill; to crack. 2. *ir.v.n. (aux.* s.) to be afraid, to become frightened; to be chilled suddenly; to crack. 3. *m.* (-) fright, scare, terror, fear, horror, dread. (Ps. 2:5)

schrecklich, *adj.* frightful, terrible, dreadful, awful, horrible. (Dan. 2:31)

das Schrecknis (-se), *see* **der Schrecken.** (Job 6:4)

schreiben, 1. *ir.v.a. & n. (aux.* h.) to write; to write down, to record. 2. *n.* writing; letter; note. (Exod. 17:14)

schreien, *ir.v.a. & n. (aux.* h.) to cry, to shout, to shriek, to scream; to screech (owl).

die Schrift (-en), writing, handwriting, hand; letters, script, text, type; book, publication, paper, review, periodical, pamphlet, composition, work; Scripture. (Exod. 32:16)

der Schriftgelehrte (-n), scribe; authority on the Scriptures. (Matt. 5:20)

der Schritt (-e), step, stride, pace; walk, gait. (I Sam. 20:3)

der Schuh (-e), shoe, boot; foot (as measure); shoeing. (Exod. 3:5)

der Schuhriemen (-), shoelace; latchet. (John 1:27)

die Schuld (-en), debt, indebtedness, obligation; fault, cause, blame; offense, sin, guilt; *(pl.)* debts, liabilities. (Matt. 6:12)

das Schuldbekenntnis (-se), acknowledgment of liabilities, confession of sin.

schulden, *v.a.* to owe; to be indebted to (someone for something).

schuldig, *adj.* due, owing; indebted, obliged; guilty, at fault, to blame. (Matt. 5:22)

der Schuldiger (-), **der Schuldner** (-), debtor; culprit. (Matt. 6:12)
wie wir vergeben unseren Schuldigern, as we forgive them that trespass against us.

das Schuldopfer (-), guilt offering. (Lev. 7:1)

die Schule (-n), school, college, academy; school of thought; synagogue. (Matt. 4:23)

die Schulter (-n), shoulder. (Isa. 9:3)

die Schuppe (-n), scale; scurf; flake. (Acts 9:18)

der Schurz (-e & -̈e), apron, loincloth. (Gen. 3:7)

schürzen, 1. *v.a.* to tie (a knot, etc.); to tuck or fasten up (one's skirt); to purse (one's lips). 2. *v.r.* to tuck up one's dress, to pick up one's skirts. (Luke 17:8)

die Schüssel (-n), dish, basin, bowl; dish (of food), course (of a meal). (Matt. 14:8)

schütteln, 1. *v.a.* to shake, to agitate; to jolt; to churn. 2. *v.r.* to tremble, to shiver, to shudder (*vor,* with). (Matt. 10:14)

schütten, 1. *v.a.* to pour (out), to cast, to shed, to throw, to shoot. 2. *v.n.* to yield in abundance; to shed leaves (of trees); to litter; (*imp.*) to pour (with rain). (Ezek. 7:8)

der Schutz, shelter, refuge, cover, screen, defense, protection, safeguard, care, keeping. (Rom. 13:6)

der Schütze (-n), marksman, sharpshooter, rifleman; archer. (Gen. 21:20)

schützen, *v.a.* to protect, to guard, to defend; to shelter. (Isa. 31:5)

der Schutzengel (-), guardian angel.

der Schutzheilige (-n), **der Schutzpatron** (-e), **die Schutzpatronin** (-nen), patron saint.

schwach, *adj.* weak, feeble, infirm, frail, delicate; mild, poor, meager, sparse; faint, dim, dull. (Num. 13:18)

schwächen, *v.a.* to weaken, to debilitate; to impair, to diminish; to seduce, to ravish. (Rom. 8:3)

schwachgläubig, *adj.* weak in faith.

die Schwachheit (-en), weakness, feebleness, frailty, debility; weak will. (Matt. 8:17)

die Schwalbe (-n), swallow, martin. (Ps. 84:4)

der Schwamm (-̈e), sponge; mushroom, toadstool. (Matt. 27:48)

der Schwang, (*only in*) *im Schwange, in Schwange,* in motion, in full swing; in vogue. (Ps. 85:14)

schwanger, *adj.* pregnant, with child. (Gen. 3:16)

der Schwanz (-̈e), tail; end; string (of people). (Rev. 9:10)

schwänzeln, *v.n.* (*aux.* h.) to wag the tail; to strut; to fawn upon, to flatter.

der Schwären (-), abscess, ulcer. (Job 2:7)

der Schwärmer (-), enthusiast, dreamer, visionary, fanatic.

die Schwärmerei (-en), enthusiasm, rapture, fanaticism; ecstasy.

schwärmerisch, *adj.* fanciful, visionary, rapturous, wild, fanatical, enthusiastic.

schwarz, 1. *adj.* black; dark; gloomy, dismal. 2. *n. indec.* black, blackness. (Rev. 6:5)
die schwarze Kunst, black art, witchcraft.

der Schwätzer (-), babbler, chatterer, gossip. (Prov. 2:12)

schweben, *v.n.* (*aux.* h.) to soar; to hover, to float in the air; to hang; to be undecided; to move. (Gen. 1:2)

der Schwefel, sulfur; brimstone. (Gen. 19:24)

schweigen, 1. *ir.v.n.* (*aux.* h.) to be silent, to keep silence, to say nothing, to be quiet. 2. *n.* silence. (Ps. 22:3)

das Schwein (-e), hog, pig; swine. (Lev. 11:7)

das Schweinefleisch, pork. (Isa. 65:4)

der Schweiß, sweat, perspiration; moisture; yolk; (*fig.*) sweat of one's brow. (Gen. 3:19)

das Schweißtuch (-̈er), sweat rag, sudarium. (John 11:44)

schwelgen, *v.n.* (*aux.* h.) to feast, to carouse; to riot, to revel, to indulge. (Mic. 2:11)

die Schwelle (-n), threshold, doorstep, sill; ledge, joist; (*fig.*) brink, door. (I Sam. 5:5)

schwellen, 1. *ir.v.n.* (*aux.* s.) to swell, to rise, to increase, to grow (fat), to grow bigger. 2. *v.a.* to swell, to inflate, to bloat. (Acts 28:6)

die Schwemme (-n), watering place (for cattle). (II Peter 2:22)

schwer, *adj.* heavy, weighty, ponderous, clumsy; difficult, hard, severe; grave, serious, grievous. (Gen. 18:20)

schwergläubig, *adj.* incredulous.

die Schwermut, melancholy, sadness, depression.

schwermütig, *adj.* dejected, sad, melancholy, mournful.

das Schwert (-er), sword; (*fig.*) force of arms, military force. (Gen. 3:24)

die Schwester (-n), sister; hospital nurse; nun. (Gen. 12:13)
barmherzige Schwester, sister of mercy, hospital nurse.

die Schwiegermutter (-), mother-in-law. (Matt. 8:14)

der Schwiegersohn (-e), son-in-law.

die Schwiegertochter (-), daughter-in-law. (Ruth 1:22)

der Schwiegervater (-), father-in-law. (John 18:13)

der Schwindelgeist, perverse spirit. (Isa. 19:14)

schwören, *ir.v.a. & n.* (*aux.* h.) to swear (on oath); to take an oath; to swear, to curse. (Gen. 22:16)

der Schwur (-e), oath, vow; curse.

sechs, *num. adj.* six. (Exod. 20:9)

sechsfältig, *adj.* sixfold.

sechst, *num. adj.* (*der, die, das -te*) the sixth. (Matt. 27:45)

die Sedisvakanz, vacancy of the papal see.

der See, 1. (-n) lake. 2. *f.* (-n) sea; ocean. (Luke 5:1)

die Seele (-n), soul; mind, spirit, heart; human being. (Gen. 2:7)
ein Herz und eine Seele sein, to be of one heart and mind.

der Seelenadel, nobility of soul.

das Seelenamt, office for the dead, requiem.

die Seelenangst (-e), anguish of soul, mental agony.

die Seelenbraut, mystical bride of Christ, the church.

der Seelenbräutigam, Christ.

die Seelenforschung, psychology.

der Seelenfriede(n), peace of mind.

das Seelenheil, salvation, spiritual welfare.

die Seelenheilkunde, psychotherapy.

der Seelenhirt (-en), pastor.

die Seelenkunde, psychology.

das Seelenleben, inner life, spiritual existence, psyche.

seelenlos, *adj.* heartless, soulless.

die Seelenmesse (-n), mass for the dead, requiem.

die Seelennot, die Seelenpein, die Seelenqual, anguish of mind, spiritual torment.

die Seelenruhe, peace of mind, tranquility.

seelenverwandt, *adj.* in harmony or unison with, congenial, sympathetic.

die Seelenverwandtschaft, congeniality, amity, understanding, harmony.

die Seelenwanderung, transmigration of souls, metempsychosis, reincarnation.

die Seelsorge, care of souls; ministerial work, pastoral duties.

seelsorgerisch, *adj.* pastoral, ministerial.

der Segen (-), blessing, benediction; grace (at mealtimes); prosperity, abundance. (Gen. 12:2)
den Segen geben or *erteilen,* to pronounce the benediction; *Gott gebe seinen Segen dazu!* God's blessing on it!

segnen, *v.a.* to bless, to give benediction, to consecrate. (Gen. 1:22)

sehen, 1. *ir.v.n.* (*aux.* h.), *a. & r.* to see, to perceive, to behold, to observe, to notice, to realize; to look, to appear. 2. *n.* seeing, vision. (John 1:14)

der Seher (-), seer, prophet. (I Sam. 9:9)

die Sehergabe, prophetic vision, gift of prophecy.

seherisch, *adj.* prophetic(al).

sehnen, *v.r.* to long, to yearn (*nach,* for), to desire ardently. (Rom. 8:22)

sehnlich, *adj.* ardent, passionate, longing. (Phil. 1:20)

die Seide (-n), silk. (Rev. 18:12)

die Seife (-n), soap. (Jer. 2:22)

seihen, *v.a.* to filter, to strain, to sieve. (Matt. 23:24)
Mücken seihen und Kamele verschlucken, to strain at a gnat and swallow a camel.

sein (-), 1. *poss. adj. m., f., & n. sing. & pl., referring to 3rd person sing. m. & n. antecedents (declined as definite article)* his, its, her; one's. 2. *personal pron. standing alone when antecedent is m. or n. nom. or n. acc.: das Haus ist sein,* the house is his. (Rom. 2:22)

das Sein, being, existence.

seinetwegen, *adv.* on his account or behalf, for his sake, so far as he is concerned. (Matt. 27:19)

die Seite (-n), side; page; flank (military); party; aspect (of a problem). (John 19:18)

das Seitenschiff (-e), aisle.

die Sekte (-n), sect.

der Sektierer (-), sectarian.

sektiererisch, *adj.* sectarian.

selbdritt, *adv.* with two others, three together. (Isa. 19:24)

selber, selbst, *indec. adj. & pron.* self; myself, himself, yourself, etc. (Mark 15:30)

selbständig, *adj.* independent.

die Selbstaufopferung, self-sacrifice.

die Selbstbestimmung, self-determination.

das Selbstbewußtsein, self-consciousness.

die Selbstentsagung, self-denial.

die Selbstkritik, self-criticism.

die Selbstliebe, self-love, self-esteem.

der Selbstmord, suicide.

die Selbstsucht, egoism, selfishness.

die Selbsttäuschung, self-deception.

die Selbstüberwindung, self-conquest.

die Selbstverblendung, self-deception.

die Selbstvergötterung, self-adulation.

die Selbstverleugnung, self-abnegation.

der Selbstwille, obstinacy, self-will.

die Selbstzucht, self-discipline.

selig, *adj.* blessed, happy, blissful, blest; deceased, late.
eines seligen Todes sterben, to go to one's rest; *selig machen,* to save. (Matt. 1:21)

der Seliggesprochene (-n), beatified person, canonized saint.

die Seligkeit, happiness, bliss, blessedness; salvation. (I Thess. 5:9)
ewige Seligkeit, everlasting bliss, salvation.

seligmachen, *v.a.* to save. (Matt. 1:21)

seligmachend, *adj.* beatific.

die Seligmachung, salvation; sanctification.

seligpreisen, *v.a.* to glorify, to beatify.

die Seligpreisung, Beatitude.

seligsprechen, *v.a.* to beatify.

die Seligsprechung, beatification.

seltsam, *adj.* strange, peculiar, unusual; odd, curious. (I Peter 4:12)

der Semit (-en), Semite.

semitisch, *adj.* Semitic.

der Semitismus, Semitism.

der Semmel (-n), roll, wafer. (Exod. 16:31)

das Semmelmehl, white or wheat flour. (II Kings 7:1)

senden, *ir. & reg. v.a.* to send, to dispatch. (Gen. 24:7)

das Sendgericht, synod.

die Sendung (-en), sending; mission; shipment.

das Senfkorn (-er), grain of mustard seed. (Matt. 13:31)

der Seraph (-phim), seraph, angel. (Isa. 6:2)

seraphisch, *adj.* seraphic, angelic, ecstatic.

setzen, 1. *v.a.* to place, to set, to put; to plant, to erect; to stake (money); to assume, to suppose; to breed. 2. *v.r.* to seat oneself, to sit down, to take a seat; to subside, to settle; to clarify; to calm down. 3. *v.n.* (*aux.* h. & s.) to run, to spring, to leap; to attack. (Gen. 1:17)

die Seuche (-n), contagious disease, epidemic; pestilence. (Matt. 4:23)

seufzen, 1. *v.n.* (*aux.* h.) to sigh. 2. *n.* sighing, groaning. (Mark 7:34)

die Sichel (-n), sickle; crescent. (Rev. 14:15)

sicher, *adj.* secure, safe; sure, certain, assured; trusty, trustworthy, reliable, steady. (Isa. 12:2)

die Sicherheit, certainty; trustworthiness; guarantee; security, safety. (Isa. 32:17)

sichtbar, *adj.* visible, perceptible, evident. (Col. 1:16)

das Sieb (-e), sieve, filter, riddle, strainer; screen. (Amos 9:9)

sieben, *num. adj.* seven.

siebenfältig, *adj.* sevenfold. (Gen. 4:15)

siebenmal, *adv.* seven times. (Gen. 4:24)

siebent, (*der, die, das -te*) *num. adj.* seventh. (Gen. 2:2)

siebzig, *num. adj.* seventy. (Luke 10:1)

das Siechbett (-en), sickbed. (Ps. 41:4)

sieden, 1. *reg. & ir.v.n.* (*aux.* h.) to boil; to simmer. 2. *v.a.* to boil, to refine (sugar); to make (soap). (Jer. 1:13)

der Sieg (-e), victory, conquest, triumph. (I John 5:4)

das Siegel (-), seal. (Rev. 5:2)

der Siegelring (-e), signet ring. (Jer. 22:24)

siegen, *v.n.* (*aux.* h.) to be victorious, to triumph, to conquer, to gain a victory; to win. (Rev. 6:2)

das Silber, silver; silver plate. (Acts 3:6)

der Silvesterabend (-e), New Year's Eve.

die Simonie, simony.

simonisch, *adj.* simoniacal.

(der) Simson, Samson.

die Sindflut, flood, deluge.

die Sinekure, sinecure.

singen, *ir.v.a. & n.* (*aux.* h.) to sing, to chant, to carol (of birds). (Rev. 5:9)

sinken, 1. *ir.v.a.* to sink (a shaft). 2. *v.n.* (*aux.* s.) to sink, to subside, to give way; to descend, to drop, to fall; to go down, to decrease, to diminish, to decline. (Matt. 14:30)

der Sinn (-e), sense, faculty, organ of perception; intellect, mind, wit, intelligence; consciousness, memory; taste, disposition, direction; wish, opinion, temper; interpretation, meaning. (Rev. 17:9)

sinnen, 1. *ir.v.n.* (*aux.* h. & s.) to think, to think over, to meditate, to reflect, to speculate about or upon (*über,* acc.). 2. *v.a.* to think out, to plot, to invent. 3. *n.* thinking, planning; thoughts, aspirations. (Ps. 119:148)

sinnlich, *adj.* sensuous; physical; sentient; material.

die Sintflut, die Sündflut, die Sindflut, flood, deluge. (Gen. 6:17)

(der) Sirach, Ecclesiasticus.

die Sitte (-n), custom, habit, usage; mode, practice, fashion; (*pl.*) manners, morals. (Lev. 3:17)

das Sittengesetz, moral law or code.

sittig, *adj.* modest, chaste; polite, well-bred. (I Tim. 3:2)

sittlich, *adj.* moral, ethical.

die Sittlichkeit, morality, morals.

der Sitz (-e), seat, chair; perch; residence, domicile. (I Kings 8:13)

sitzen, *ir.v.n.* (*aux.* h. & s.) to sit; to perch (of bird); to stay, to be situated, to remain; to adhere. (Matt. 4:16)

der Skorpion (-e), scorpion. (Rev. 9:5)

der Skribent (-en), writer; scribbler, literary hack.

der Smaragd (-e), emerald. (Rev. 21:19)

der Sohn (⁻e), son. (I Kings 17:23) *der Sohn Gottes,* the Son of God (Matt. 4:3); *der Sohn des Menschen, des Menschen Sohn,* Son of man (Matt. 8:20); *der verlorene Sohn,* the prodigal son.

solch, 1. *adj. & dem. pron.* (-er, -e, es) such; *ein solcher Mensch, solch ein Mensch,* a man like him, such a man. 2. *adv.:* in *solch schlechter Lage,* in such a bad position or state.

solcherlei, *indec. adj.* of such a kind, such.

das Sold, (soldier's) pay. (Rom. 6:23)

der Söldner, hired soldier, mercenary.

sollen, 1. *ir.v.n.* (*aux.* h.) to be obliged or bound to; to have to, must; to be in debt. 2. *n.* one's duty, obligations, responsibilities. *du sollst nicht töten,* thou shalt not kill.

der Söller (-), balcony; loft.

der Sommer (-), summer.

sondern, 1. *v.a.* to separate, to segregate, to part, to sever. 2. *v.r.* to separate. *gesonderter Haushalt,* separate (domestic) establishment.

die Sonne (-n), sun, sunshine. (Gen. 37:9)

der Sonntag (-e), Sunday; Lord's day.

der Sonntagabend, Sunday evening.

sonntägig, *adj.* Sunday, on Sunday.

sonntäglich, *adj.* every Sunday.

der Sonntagsentheiliger (-), Sabbath-breaker.

die Sonntagsfeier, day of rest.

die Sonntagsheiligung, keeping the Sabbath.

die Sonntagsruhe, Sabbath rest, observance of the Sabbath.

die Sonntagsschule, Sunday school.

sonst, *adv.* else, otherwise; besides, more-over; in other respects, at other times; as a rule, usually, formerly. (Luke 17:18)

die Sorge (-en), grief, sorrow; worry, apprehension, anxiety, care, trouble, un-easiness, concern. (Ps. 127:2)

sorgen, 1. *v.r.* to be anxious, apprehensive, concerned, solicitous or troubled, to worry (*um,* about). 2. *v.n.:* *sorgen für etwas* or *dafür, daß...* to attend to or look after something, to care for or take care of something, to provide for something. (Matt. 6:25)

sorgfältig, *adj.* careful, attentive; pain-staking, scrupulous, precise, accurate. (Rom. 12:8)

die Soutane (-n), priest's cassock, soutane.

spalten, (p.p. *gespalten* and *gespaltet*) 1. *v.a.* to split, to cleave, to slit, to cut open; to crack; to decompose (a ray of light). 2. *v.r. & n.* (*aux.* s.) to split off, to crack; to open, to divide, to branch off; to dissociate. (Lev. 11:3)

die Spaltung, fissure, split, crack, cleav-age; splitting, cleaving, division, fission; (*fig.*) dissension, rupture, quarrel, schism. (I Cor. 1:10)

die Spannader, sinew.

die Spanne (-n), span; stretch; short space of time; margin (between prices).

sparen, *v.a. & n.* (*aux.* h.) to economize, to cut down expenses; to save, to lay by, to put by, to be thrifty; to spare, to use spar-ingly. (II Peter 3:7)

der Spätregen, latter rain. (Deut. 11:14)

der Speer (-e), spear, lance, javelin. (II Sam. 21:16)

der Speichel (-), spittle, saliva. (John 9:6)

speien, *ir.v.a. & n.* (*aux.* h.) to spit; to spew, to vomit; to belch forth (fire); to discharge (water). (Isa. 19:14)

die Speise (-n), food, nourishment, meal, dish. (Ps. 111:5)

der Speisemeister (-), governor of the feast. (John 2:8)

speisen, 1. *v.a.* to give to eat, to feed; to board, to entertain. 2. *v.n.* (*aux.* h.) to eat, to take food, to take one's meals, to board, to dine. (Ps. 146:7)

das Speiseopfer (-), oblation. (Isa. 1:13)

die Speisung, feeding, issue of food supply.
Speisung der Fünftausend, feeding of the five thousand.

der Sperling (-e), sparrow. (Matt. 10:31)

die Spezerei (*usually pl.* -en), spices; groceries.

die Sphäre (-n), sphere, range, domain, province; globe.

der Spiegel (-), looking glass, mirror; reflector, reflecting surface. (I Cor. 13:12)

spiegeln, 1. *v.n.* (*aux.* h.) to sparkle, to glitter, to shine. 2. *v.a.* to reflect. 3. *v.r.* to be reflected, to be revealed. (II Cor. 3:18)

spielen, *v.a. & n.* (*aux.* h.) to play; to sport; to gamble; to act, to perform, to play or take the part of. (Ps. 144:9)

der Spielmann (-leute), bandsman; trouba-dour, minstrel. (II Kings 3:15)

der Spieß (-e), spear, lance, pike, javelin, harpoon; spit. (Isa. 2:4)

die Spinne (-n), spider. (Prov. 30:28)

spinnen, *ir.v.a. & n.* (*aux.* h.) to spin, to twist, to twirl; to purr (as a cat). (Matt. 6:28)

der Spiritismus, spiritualism.

der Spiritist (-en), spiritualist.

spiritistisch, *adj.* spiritualist(ic).

spiritual, *adj.* spiritual.

der Spiritualismus, spiritualism.

spirituell, *adj.* intellectual, mental.

spitzbübisch, *adj.* rascally, roguish.

die Spitze (-n), point, spike; extremity, tip (of tongue); top, summit, peak, vertex, apex; sarcastic remark; (*pl.*) lace. (Gen. 11:4)

der Splitter (-), splinter, chip, fragment; mote. (Matt. 7:3)

der Spott, mockery, ridicule, scorn. (Heb. 6:6)

spotten, *v.a. & n.* (*aux.* h.) (*über* with acc.) to mock, to scoff at, to ridicule. (Matt. 27:41)

der Spötter (-), mocker, scoffer, jeerer. (Prov. 1:22)

die Spottschrift (-en), libel; lampoon.

die Sprache (-n), speech, diction; lan-guage, tongue, idiom, vernacular; voice, accent, style; discussion. (Gen. 11:1)
die Sprache der Bibel, biblical language.

die **Sprachenverwirrung,** confusion of language. (see Gen. 11:7–9)

sprachlos, *adj.* speechless, dumb, mute; dumbfounded. (Mark 7:37)

sprechen, 1. *ir.v.a. & n.* (*aux.* h.) to speak, to talk, to converse; to discuss, to talk over; (*only v.a.*) to say, to pronounce, to declare, to utter. 2. *n.* speaking, talking. (Rev. 14:13)

sprengen, 1. *v.a.* to cause to spring, to make jump; to sprinkle, to spray, to water; to spring, to burst, to explode, to blow up; to burst open, to rupture (a blood vessel). 2. *v.n.* (*aux.* s.) to gallop, to ride at full speed. (Exod. 24:6)

die **Spreu,** chaff. (Matt. 3:12)

das **Sprichwort,** saying, proverb, maxim, adage. (John 16:25)

sprichwörtlich, *adj.* proverbial.

springen, *ir.v.n.* (*aux.* h. & s.) to leap, to spring, to jump, to hop, to skip, to bounce; to run; to gush; to crack, to burst, to split, to break, to explode. (Acts 3:8)

der **Sproß** (-[ss]e), shoot, sprout, spray, sprig; descendant, offspring.

der **Spruch** (–e), sentence, decree, judgment; verdict; saying, motto, dictum, epigram; passage, text. (John 4:37)

sprühen, 1. *v.a.* to spray, to sprinkle, to scatter, to spit, to emit (sparks, etc.). 2. *v.n.* (*aux.* h.) to spark, to sparkle; (*fig.*) to flash (with intellect, etc.). (Ps. 29:7)

spüren, 1. *v.a. & n.* (*aux.* h.) (*nach*) to trace, to track (down), to trail, to follow. 2. *v.a.* to perceive, to notice, to discover, to feel, to experience, to be conscious of. (Dan. 6:24)

der **Staat** (-en), state, country, government.

die **Staatskirche** (-n), established church. *Englische Staatskirche,* Church of England, Anglican Church.

der **Stab** (–e), staff, stick, rod; crosier, (shepherd's) crook; the staff, headquarters (military). (Gen. 32:11)

der **Stachel** (-n), thorn, prickle, prick, sting; spike; (*fig.*) spur, stimulus. (I Cor. 15:55)
wider den Stachel lecken, to kick against the pricks.

die **Stadt** (–e), town, city. (Gen. 4:17)
die Ewige Stadt, the Eternal City (Rome); *die Heilige Stadt,* the Holy City (Jerusalem).

die **Stadtmauer** (-n), town wall. (Josh. 2:15)

das **Stadttor** (-e), town gate. (Luke 7:12)

der **Stall** (–e), stall, stable, kennel. (John 10:16)

der **Stamm** (–e), stem, trunk; family, clan, tribe, race, stock, breed, strain; stem, root (of words); main body (of an army, customers, etc.). (Gen. 49:28)

stammeln, *v.a. & n.* (*aux.* h.) to stammer, to stutter.

stammelnd, *adj.* stammering, stuttering. (Isa. 32:4)

der **Stammvater** (–), progenitor, ancestor.

der **Stand** (–e), standing or upright position, situation, position; standing, state, condition; strength (of army, etc.); class, rank (in society); footing; stand, stall, booth. (Isa. 56:11)

standhalten, *v.n.* (*dat.*) to withstand, to resist, to stand firm, to be steadfast, to hold out.

stark, *adj.* (comp. *stärker,* sup. *stärkst*) strong, robust, vigorous; numerous, considerable; thick, stout; intense, violent, severe, heavy (hail, etc.). (Gen. 48:2)
der starke Gott, the mighty God.

die **Stärke,** strength, vigor; intensity, violence, stress, energy, force, power; greatness, magnitude; (*fig.*) strong point. (Rev. 5:12)

stärken, 1. *v.a.* to strengthen, to fortify, to brace, to invigorate; to confirm. 2. *v.r.* to take refreshment. (Rev. 3:2)

starkgläubig, *adj.* staunch in faith.

die **Statt** (–e), 1. place, stead, lieu. 2. *prep.* (*gen.*) (*also* **anstatt**) instead of, in lieu of, in the place of. (Gen. 22:13)

die **Stätte** (-n), place, abode. (Gen. 22:14)

der **Statthalter** (-), representative, governor.
der Statthalter Christi, vicar of Christ; the pope.

der **Staub,** dust; powder; pollen. (Gen. 13:16)

stäupen, *v.a.* to flog, to scourge. (Matt. 21:35)

stechen, 1. *ir.v.a. & n.* (*aux.* h.) to prick, to pierce; to sting, to bite; to stab, to puncture; to joust; to burn, to scorch (as the sun); to cut (peat, turf, etc.). 2. *n.* jousting; casting lots; shooting pains. (John 19:37)

stecken, 1. *reg.* (*& ir.*) *v.a.* to put, to place; to set, to plant; to stick, to fix. 2. *v.r.: sich hinter eine Sache stecken,* to get behind something; to work something secretly. 3. *reg.* (*& ir.*) *v.n.* (*aux.* h.) to stay, to remain; to stick fast, to be fixed or stuck; to be involved in; to hide, to lie hidden. 4. *m.* stick, staff, rod. (Matt. 26:52)
dein Stecken und dein Stab, thy rod and thy staff.

stehen, *ir.v.n.* (*aux.* h. & s.) to stand, to be upright; to be situated; to be; to stand still, to stop. (Gen. 7:24)

stehlen, 1. *ir.v.a. & n.* (*aux.* h.) to steal, to rob, to pilfer. 2. *v.r.* to steal or slink away. 3. *n.* stealing, robbery, larceny. (Gen. 31:19)

der Steig (-e), path, footpath; mountain track. (Matt. 3:3)

steigen, 1. *ir.v.n.* (*aux.* s.) to climb, to mount, to ascend, to go up; to increase, to rise; to rear; to soar; to take place, to come off. 2. *n.* rising; rise, advance, increase. (Gen. 41:2)

steigern, 1. *v.a.* to raise, to increase, to heighten, to augment, to enhance, to advance; to intensify, to strengthen. 2. *v.r.* to become greater or intensified, to increase, to rise, to mount. (Amos 8:5)

der Stein (-e), stone, rock, flint; precious stone, gem; monument, gravestone; kernel. (Gen. 28:11)
der Stein des Anstoßes, stumbling block.

steinern, *adj.* of stone, stony. (Exod. 24:12)

der Steinhaufe (-n), heap, heap of stones. (Isa. 25:2)

steinig, *adj.* stony; full of stones, rocky. (Matt. 13:5)

steinigen, *v.a.* to stone. (Matt. 23:37)

die Steinigung, death by stoning.

der Steinwurf, stone's throw. (Luke 22:41)

stellen, 1. *v.a.* to put, to place, to set, to lay, to arrange; to put right, to set in order, to adjust, to regulate; to post, to station; to supply, to provide, to furnish. 2. *v.r.* to place, to post or station oneself; to take one's stand; to give oneself up; to appear, to prove to be; to pretend, to affect. (I Peter 1:14)
sein Licht unter den Scheffel stellen, to hide one's light under a bushel.

stellvertretend, *adj.* vicarious, representative, delegated.

sterben, 1. *ir.v.n.* (*aux.* s.) *& a.* to die (*an* with dat., of); to die or fade away, to perish, to become extinct, to pass away, to depart. 2. *n.* dying; death. (John 8:21)

sterblich, *adj.* mortal. (Rom. 6:12)

der Stern (-e), star. (Gen. 15:5)

der Sterndeuter (-), **der Sternseher** (-), astrologer. (Dan. 1:20)

die Sterndeuterei, astrology.

die Steuer (-n), tax, duty, (local) rate; redress, aid, contribution. (Rom. 15:26)

steuern, 1. *v.a. & n.* (*aux.* h.) to pay (taxes); to contribute (to). 2. *v.n.* (*with dat.*) to put a check on, to put a stop to, to make something cease. (Ps. 46:10)

stiefeln, 1. *v.n.* to provide with boots. 2. *v.n.* (*aux.* s.) to walk, to march, to stride along. (Eph. 6:15)

der Stier (-e), bull. (Ps. 22:13)

das Stift (-e & -er), foundation; charitable institution, home (for old people); religious establishment or meeting place, seminary, training college (for clergymen); convent, monastery; bishopric. (Exod. 33:7)

stiften, *v.a.* to found, to establish, to institute; to give, to donate, to make a present of; to bring about, to originate, to cause, to make. (Exod. 20:24)

der Stifter (-), founder, donor; author, originator.

der Stiftler (-), member of a seminary, inmate of an institution.

die Stiftsgemeinde (-n), congregation of a cathedral.

das Stiftsgut (⁻er), chapter property; ecclesiastical endowment.

der Stiftsherr (-en), canon.

die Stiftshütte, Jewish tabernacle.

die Stiftskirche (-n), collegiate church.

die Stiftsschule (-n), school attached to the chapters of collegiate churches.

die Stiftsversammlung (-en), meeting of a chapter.

die Stiftung (-en), founding, establishment; foundation, institution; endowment.

die Stiftungsurkunde (-n), deed of foundation.

das Stigma (-mata & -men), mark, stigma; scar (of plants).

die Stigmatisation, stigmatization.

stigmatisieren, *v.a.* to stigmatize, to brand.

still, *adj.* silent, quiet, soft; still, motionless, calm, peaceful, tacit, secret. (Exod. 14:14)
stiller Freitag, Good Friday; *stilles Gebet,* silent prayer.

stillen, *v.a.* to quiet, to hush, to silence; to appease, to calm, to soothe; to quench (thirst, etc.); to gratify, to satisfy (desires); to nurse (a child). (Prov. 15:1)

die Stimme (-n), voice; vote; opinion. (Gen. 3:10)
die Stimme Gottes, voice of the Lord.

stimmen, 1. *v.a.* to tune; to dispose, to incline. 2. *v.n.* (*aux.* h.) to agree (with), to tally (with), to correspond (to); to be correct, to be all right; to harmonize; to vote.

stinken, *ir.v.n.* (*aux.* h.) to stink, to smell foul. (John 11:39)

der Stipendiat (-en), scholarship holder.

die Stirn (-en), **die Stirne** (-n), forehead, brow. (Rev. 13:16)

die Stoa, der Stoizismus, Stoicism.

der Stock (¨e), stick, staff, rod, pole, wand, baton, cane, walking stick; stocks; stem (of a plant), trunk, stump (of a tree). (Ps. 105:18)

der Stockmeister (-), jailer. (Luke 12:58)

der Stoff (-e), stuff, matter, substance, subject.

die Stoffursache, material cause.

der Stoiker (-), Stoic.

stoisch, Stoic(al).

die Stola, die Stole (-en), stole, surplice.

die Stolgebühren, (*pl.*) surplice fees.

stolz, 1. *adj.* proud, haughty, arrogant; splendid, superb, stately. 2. *m.* pride, vanity, haughtiness, arrogance; glory, boast.

stopfen, 1. *v.a.* to fill, to cram; to darn, to mend (stockings); to plug, to close. 2. *v.n.* (*aux.* h.) to be filling, to bind. 3. *v.r.* to stuff oneself, to gorge; to become blocked or jammed. 4. *n.* stuffing, cramming.

die Stoppel (-n), stubble; bristles (of beard). (Exod. 5:12)

der Storch (¨e), stork. (Jer. 8:7)

stoßen, 1. *ir.v.a.* to push, to shove, to strike, to knock, to hit, to punch; to kick; to drive out, to expel. 2. *v.r.* to knock (*an,* against); to take offense at or exception to something. 3. *v.n.* (*aux.* h.) to adjoin, to border on (*an*); to push, to knock, to strike (*an* or *gegen,* against); to bump; (*aux.* s.) to come across, to meet with, to encounter; to join up (*zu,* with). 4. *n.* pushing, thrusting; jolting; kick. (Ps. 91:12)

das Stoßgebet (-e), short fervent prayer.

die Strafe (-n), punishment, penalty, fine; judgment, sentence. (Rom. 13:4)

strafen, *v.a.* to punish, to fine; to chastise; to blame, to reprove, to rebuke. (Gen. 6:3)

der Strahl (-en), ray, beam; jet (of water, etc.); fiery stream, flash. (Dan. 7:10)

die Straße (-n), street, road, thoroughfare, highway; strait(s), waterway; route. (Ps. 23:3)

straucheln, *v.n.* (*aux.* h. & s.) to stumble, to slip; to fail, to (make a) blunder. (Ps. 73:2)

der Strauß (-e), ostrich. (Lam. 4:3)

strecken, 1. *v.a.* to stretch, to extend; to spread, to flatten, to draw, roll, or beat out; to make something last or go a long way; to dilute, to reduce, to thin. 2. *v.r.* to stretch oneself.

der Streich (-e), stroke, blow, stripe, lash; trick, prank, joke.

streichen, 1. *ir.v.n.* (*aux.* h. & s.) to move or rush quickly past; to run, fly, or sweep over; to cut or plow (through waves). 2. *v.a.* to stroke, to touch gently; to spread (bread). 3. *n.* passing, moving, roving; grazing, touching.

der Streit (-e & -igkeiten), dispute, quarrel, squabble, strife, struggle, lawsuit; combat, fight, conflict.

streitbar, *adj.* warlike, valiant; quarrelsome, disputatious. (I Sam. 16:18)

streiten, 1. *ir.v.n.* (*aux.* h.) to quarrel, to squabble, to dispute, to wrangle, to disagree; to fight, to struggle. 2. *v.r.* to dispute, to quarrel.

die Streitfrage (-n), controversial question, issue.

die Streitschrift (-en), polemic; (*pl.*) controversial writings.

streng(e), *adj.* severe, stern, strict; austere, harsh, rough, stiff, rigorous. (Acts 26:5)

die Strenge, severity, sternness, strictness, austerity, harshness, bitterness. (Lev. 25:43)

strenggläubig, *adj.* orthodox.

die Strenggläubigkeit, orthodoxy.

streuen, *v.a.* to strew, to spread; to spray, to sprinkle. (Matt. 21:8)

der Strick (-e), cord, rope, line, string. (Ps. 91:3)

die Strieme (-n), weal. (Acts 16:33)

das Stroh, straw; thatch. (Exod. 5:7)

der Strom (ᐨe), large or broad river, stream, current; flow, flood (of words, etc.); crowd. (Ps. 80:12)

das Stück (-e), piece, bit, part, fragment, lump. (Luke 24:42)

stückweise, *adv.* piece by piece, piecemeal. (I Cor. 13:12)

das Stückwerk, imperfect, patchy, or bungled work. (I Cor. 13:9)

studieren, *v.a.* & *n.* (*aux.* h.) to study; to be at college.

die Stufe (-n), step, stair, rung (of ladder); gradation, shade, nuance; degree, rank, grade, stage. (I Tim. 3:13)

der Stuhl (ᐨe), chair; stool; seat; pew. (Rev. 7:15)
Gottes Stuhl, God's judgment seat; *Heiliger Stuhl,* holy see; *päpstlicher Stuhl,* holy see.

stumm, *adj.* dumb, mute; silent, speechless. (I Cor. 12:2)

stumpf, *adj.* blunt, obtuse; (*fig.*) dull, dead, flat; insensible, indifferent, apathetic. (Jer. 31:29)

der Stumpf (ᐨe), stump, stub. (Isa. 9:13)

die Stunde (-n), hour; period, lesson. (Matt. 24:42)

das Stündlein, short hour.
wenn sein Stündlein kommt, when his last hour draws nigh.

der Sturm (ᐨe), storm, gale; strong gale; rush, onset, attack. (Rev. 18:21)

stürmen, 1. *v.a.* to storm, to take by storm, to force. 2. *v.n.* (*aux.* h.) to be stormy, to be violent; to advance to the attack; to storm about, to rage; (*aux.* s.) to dash, to rush along. (Acts 7:56)
den Himmel stürmen, to reach for the stars.

stürzen, 1. *v.a.* to hurl, to throw (down), to plunge, to precipitate; to overturn, to overthrow, to ruin; to dump. 2. *v.r.* & *n.* (*aux.* s.) to sink; to be precipitous, to rush, to dash, to hurry, to plunge; to crash, to smash, to fall. (Ps. 73:18)

das Stürzen, collapse; overthrow; breaking up (of ground).

suchen, *v.a.* & *n.* (*aux.* h.) to seek, to want, to desire; to trace, to search (for); to look for, to try to find. (Matt. 7:7)

der Suffraganbischof (ᐨe), suffragan bishop.

die Sühne, atonement, expiation; reconciliation; propitiation.

sühnen, *v.a.* to expiate, to atone for.

das Sühnopfer (-), propitiatory sacrifice, atonement.

der Sumer(i)er (-), Sumerian.

sumerisch, *adj.* Sumerian.

die Summe, sum, total, amount. (Ps. 139:17)

die Sünde (-n), transgression, trespass, offense.
der Tod ist der Sünde Sold, the wages of sin is death. (Rom. 6:23)

das Sündenbekenntnis, confession (of sin).

der Sündenbock (ᐨe), scapegoat.

der Sündenerlaß, remission of sins, absolution.

der Sündenfall, the fall (of man).

sündenfrei, *adj.* guiltless; sinless; free from sin.

das Sündenleben, sinful or wicked life, life of sin.

der Sündenlohn, wages of sin; starvation wages.

sündenlos, *adj.* guiltless, sinless; free from sin.

die Sünd(en)losigkeit, innocence, sinlessness, righteousness.

der **Sündenpfuhl,** pool of sin.

das **Sündenregister** (-), list of sins committed.

sündenrein, *adj.* guiltless.

die **Sündenschuld,** guilt.

die **Sündentilgung,** remission of sin; absolution.

die **Sündenvergebung,** forgiveness of sins; absolution.

der **Sünder** (-), sinner; culprit; delinquent. (Matt. 9:13)
Gott sei mir Sünder gnädig! God forgive me, sinner that I am!

die **Sündflut,** the flood.

sündhaft, *adj.* sinful, erring, wicked.

sündig, *adj.* sinful, iniquitous, wicked. (Luke 5:8)

sündigen, *v.a. & n.* (*aux.* h.) to (commit a) sin, to trespass, to transgress. (John 5:14)

sündlich, *adj.* sinful, unlawful, impious. (Rom. 8:3)

die **Sündlichkeit,** sinfulness.

sündlos, *adj.* sinless, free from sin, guiltless.

die **Sündlosigkeit,** sinlessness.

das **Sündopfer** (-), sin offering. (Lev. 7:37)

das **Sündwasser,** water of purification.

das **Supremat,** supremacy.

(die) Susanna, Susannah.

süß, *adj.* sweet, sweetened, fresh; (*fig.*) charming, dear, delightful. (Matt. 26:17)

die **Süßigkeit** (-en), sweetness; (*pl.*) sweets. (Judg. 9:11)

der **Sylvesterabend** (-e), New Year's Eve.

das **Symbol** (-e), symbol.

die **Symbolik, der Symbolismus,** symbolism.

symbolisch, *adj.* symbolic(al).

symbolisieren, *v.a.* to symbolize.

synagogal, *adj.* synagogal, synagogical.

die **Synagoge** (-n), synagogue.

der **Synkretismus,** syncretism.

synkretistisch, *adj.* syncretistic.

synodal, *adj.* synodal.

die **Synode** (-n), synod.

synodisch, *adj.* synodal; synodic(al).

die **Synopse,** synopsis.

der **Synoptiker** (-), Synoptic.

synoptisch, *adj.* synoptic(al).
die synoptischen Evangelien, the Synoptic Gospels.

die **Synthese,** synthesis.

synthesieren, *v.a.* to synthesize.

(das) Syrien, Syria.

der **Syr(i)er** (-), Syrian.

syrisch, *adj.* Syrian.

das **System** (-e), system, plan; doctrine, school.

das **Szepter** (-), scepter, mace. (Gen. 49:10)

der **Szythe** (-n), Scythian.

szythisch, *adj.* Scythian.

Tt

das (der) **Tabernakel** (-), tabernacle.

der **Tadel,** blame, censure, reproof, rebuke, reprimand; fault, shortcoming. (Gen. 6:9)

tadelfrei, tadellos, *adj.* irreproachable, flawless, faultless, excellent, splendid, perfect.

die **Tafel** (-n), board, blackboard; tablet, slab; plaque, panel; index, register; table, meal, banquet. (Exod. 31:18)

täfeln, *v.a.* to floor, to inlay (a floor); to panel (a wall). (Jer. 22:14)

der **Tag** (-e), day, daylight, broad daylight; open air; life, lifetime. (Gen. 1:5)
der jüngste Tag, doomsday; *Tag und Nacht,* day and night.

der **Tag(e)löhner** (-), day-laborer. (Luke 15:17)

die **Tagereise** (-n), day's journey. (I Kings 19:4)

täglich, *adj.* daily, per diem; ordinary, everyday. (Gen. 39:10)

die **Tagung** (-en), meeting, convention, session, conference.

das **Tal** (-er), valley, vale, dale. (Gen. 14:3)

der **Talar** (-e), robe; gown.

das **Talent** (-e), talent, (natural) gift, ability, faculty, aptitude, capacity; accomplishments, attainments.

der **Taler** (-), thaler (coin).

der **Talismann** (-er), talisman.

die **Tanne** (-n), fir, fir tree. (II Kings 19:23)

der **Tannenbaum** (-e), fir tree.

der **Tanz** (-e), dance, dancing, ball. (Jer. 31:4)

tanzen, *v.a. & n.* (*aux.* h. & s.) to dance. (Matt. 11:17)

tappen, *v.n.* (*aux.* h. & s.) to grope, to fumble. (Deut. 28:29)
im Dunkeln tappen, to grope in the dark.

die **Tasche** (-n), pocket; purse, bag, handbag, satchel, wallet, pouch. (Matt. 10:10)

das **Taschenbuch** (-er), pocketbook, notebook.

die **Tat** (-en), deed, act, action; fact, feat, achievement. (Exod. 15:1)

der **Täter** (-), wrongdoer, culprit; author, perpetrator. (James 1:22)

tätig, *adj.* active, busy, engaged, employed; energetic; effective. (Gal. 5:6)

die **Tätigkeit,** activity, action, function; occupation, profession.

die **Tatsache** (-n), fact; (*pl*) data.

der **Tau,** dew. (Gen. 27:28)

taub, *adj.* deaf; oblivious, unfeeling, callous; numb; empty, hollow; dead, sterile, barren. (Exod. 4:11)

die **Taube** (-n), pigeon; dove. (Gen. 8:8)

tauchen, 1. *v.r. & n.* (*aux.* h. & s.) to dip or plunge (into water), to dive; to remain under water, to submerge. 2. *v.a.* to dip, to immerse, to steep, to soak. (Matt. 26:23)

der **Taufakt** (-e), christening ceremony, baptism.

das **Taufbecken** (-), (christening) font.

das **Taufbuch** (-er), baptismal, church, or parish register.

die **Taufe** (-n), baptism, christening; naming ceremony (ships, etc.). (Matt. 20:22)

taufen, *v.a.* to baptize, to christen, to name. (Matt. 3:6)

der **Täufer** (-), baptizer.
Johannes der Täufer, John the Baptist. (Matt. 3:1)

die **Taufgebühr** (-en), christening fee.

das **Taufgeschenk** (-e), christening present.

der **Taufgesinnte** (-n), (Ana)baptist, Mennonite.

der **Täufling** (-e), infant to be baptized; neophyte, candidate for baptism (of grownup persons).

der **Taufname** (-n), Christian name.

der **Taufpate,** godfather.

die **Taufpatin,** godmother.

der **Taufschein** (-e), certificate of baptism.

der **Taufstein** (-e), (baptismal) font.

das **Taufwasser,** baptismal water.

der **Taufzeuge** (-n), sponsor, godparent.

taugen, v.n. (aux. h.) to be of use or of value, to be worth; to answer, to do, to serve, to be good or fit for. (Matt. 27:6)

täuschen, 1. v.a. to deceive, to delude, to mislead, to cheat, to impose upon; to disappoint. 2. v.r. to deceive oneself, to be mistaken. (Gen. 31:7)

die **Täuscherei,** cunning craftiness. (Eph. 4:14)

die **Täuschung** (-en), deception, fraud; feint; illusion.

tausend, 1. num. adj. thousand. 2. n. (-e) thousand. (Gen. 24:60)

tausendjährig, adj. 1,000 years old; millennial. (see Rev. 20:4)
das *Tausendjährige Reich Christi,* the millennium.

tausendmal, adv. 1,000 times. (Dan. 7:10)

das **Tedeum,** Te Deum.

der **Teich** (-e), pond, pool. (John 5:2)

der **Teig** (-e), dough, paste; pulp. (Rom. 11:16)

der **Teil** (-e), part, portion, piece, element, section; (also n.) share, division; party. (Rev. 21:8)

teilen, 1. v.a. to divide; to share (out), to deal out; to separate, to sever, to distribute, to graduate. 2. v.r. (mit einem in eine Sache) to participate or share in; to branch off, to diverge, to divide. (Gen. 2:10)

teilhaben, v.n. to have a share (an, in), to participate (in), to partake (of). (Rev. 20:6)

teilhaft(ig), adj. partaking of, sharing or participating in. (Matt. 23:30)

der **Tempel** (-), temple, place of worship; synagogue. (Matt. 4:5)

der **Tempeldiener** (-), officer of the temple, priest.

der **Tempelherr** (-en), der **Templer** (-), Templar.

der **Tempelorden,** Order of Knights Templar.

der **Tempelraub,** sacrilege.

tempelräuberisch, adj. sacrilegious.

der **Tempelschänder** (-), desecrator of a temple.

die **Tempelschändung,** sacrilege.

die **Tempelweihe:** *Fest der Tempelweihe,* (Jewish) Feast of Dedication.

die **Tenne** (-n), threshing floor, floor of a barn. (Matt. 3:12)

das **Testament** (-e), one of the two covenants of God called the Old (*das Alte*) and the New (*das Neue*) Testament; will; last will and testament. (Heb. 9:16)

teuer, adj. dear, costly, expensive; (fig.) dear, beloved, cherished. (Matt. 26:9)
die sieben mageren Ähren sind sieben Jahre teure Zeit, and the seven empty ears shall be seven years of famine.

die **Teuerung,** dearth, famine; dearness, high cost of living. (Gen. 12:10)

der **Teufel** (-), devil, demon, fiend. (Matt. 4:1)

die **Teufelei,** devilry, devilment; devilishness, inhumanity.

die **Teufelsaustreibung, der Teufelsbann, die Teufelsbeschwörung,** exorcism.

die **Teufelsbraut,** witch.

die **Teufelsbrut,** hellish crew, bad lot.

das **Teufelskind,** hardened sinner.

die **Teufelslist,** diabolical cunning.

das **Teufelswerk,** piece of devilry.

teuflisch, adj. devilish, diabolical, satanic, fiendish; infernal. (James 3:15)

der **Text** (-e), text, wording; words (of a song).

die **Textkritik,** textual criticism.

der **Theismus,** theism.

theistisch, adj. theistic(al).

die **Theodizee,** theodicy (Leibniz).

die **Theokratie,** theocracy.

der Theolog(e) (-n), **die Theologin** (-nen), theologian.

die Theologie, theology, divinity.
Professor der Theologie, professor of divinity.

theologisch, *adj.* theologic(al).

die Theophanie, theophany.

der Theosoph (-en), theosophist.

die Theosophie, theosophy.

theosophisch, *adj.* theosophic(al).

die These (-n), thesis, postulate, assertion, proposition.

(der) Thessalonicher (-), Thessalonian.

Thessaloniki, Thessalonica.

der Thron (-e), throne. (Jer. 3:17)

die Thronbesteigung, accession (to the throne).

die Tiara, tiara.

tief, *adj.* deep, profound, low, dark; far; *(fig.)* innermost, utmost, extreme, utter. (Ps. 86:13)

die Tiefe (-n), the face of the deep, depth.

das Tier (-e), animal, beast, brute; doe, hind. (Gen. 1:20)

die Tiergattung (-en), genus of animal.

die Tierwelt, animal kingdom, animals.

tilgen, *v.a.* to extinguish, to blot out, to abolish, to eradicate, to obliterate, to efface, to erase, to destroy, to exterminate; to cancel, to annul; to redeem, to pay off. (Exod. 32:32)

(der) Timotheus, Timothy.

die Tinte (-n), ink. (Jer. 36:18)

der Tisch (-e), table, board; meal. (Mark 16:14)
vor (nach) Tisch beten, to say grace; *zum Tische des Herrn gehen,* to partake of the Lord's Supper.

das Tischgebet, grace.
das Tischgebet sprechen, to say grace.

das Tischgespräch (-e), table talk.

die Tischreden, die Tischgespräche, (*pl.*) (Luther's) *Table Talk.*

der Titel (-), title; heading; claim.

toben, *v.n. (aux.* h.) to fume, to storm, to rage, to rave, to bluster, to roar; to romp, to be wild. (II Kings 19:27)

(der) Tobias, Tobit.

die Tochter (-̈), daughter. (Gen. 6:2)

die Tochterkirche (-n), branch church.

der Tod (-e or -esfälle), death; decease. (John 5:24)

todblaß, todbleich, *adj.* deathly pale, pale as death.

die Todesangst (-̈e), mortal terror.

der Todesengel, angel of death.

der Todesfall (-̈e), (case of) death; casualty (in war).

die Todesfurcht, fear of death.

die Todesgefahr (-en), deadly peril, peril of one's life.

der Todeskampf, death agony, throes of death.

todesmutig, *adj.* resolute unto or in the face of death.

die Todesnot (-̈e), peril of death, deadly peril. (II Cor. 11:23)

die Todespein, pangs of death.

die Todespforte, death's door.

der Todesschlaf, sleep of the dead.

der Todesschrecken (-), fear of death; deadly fright.

der Todesschweiß, cold sweat of death.

das Todesurteil (-e), death sentence, sentence of death.

der Todfeind (-e), deadly or mortal enemy.

todkrank, *adj.* sick unto death. (Luke 7:2)

tödlich, *adj.* fatal, deadly, lethal, mortal; murderous. (Rev. 13:3)

der Todschlag, manslaughter.

die Todsünde (-n), mortal sin.

todwund, *adj.* mortally wounded.

tolerant, *adj.* tolerant (*gegen,* of).

die Tolerenz, toleration, tolerance.

tolerieren, *v.a.* to tolerate.

toll, *adj.* mad, raving, insane; frantic, furious, foolish, absurd, comical; wild, excessive. (Deut. 32:6)

der Ton (-e & -sorten), clay; *feuerfester Ton,* fire clay. (Isa. 45:9)

der Ton (-̈e), sound; note; tone; tint, shade, color; fashion, manners; stress, emphasis. (Exod. 19:16)

tönen, 1. *v.n. (aux.* h.) to sound, to resound; to ring. 2. *v.a.* to shade (off). (Exod. 19:13)

die Tonne (-n), cask, barrel; measure. (Luke 16:6)

die Tonsur (-en), tonsure.

der Topf (¨e), pot, jar. (Jer. 1:13)

der Töpfer (-), potter. (Rev. 2:27)

das Tor (-e), gate, gateway. (Gen. 22:17)

der Tor (-en), fool. (Luke 24:25)

der Torflügel (-), wing of a gate.

die Torheit, folly, foolishness, silliness. (I Cor. 1:18)

töricht, *adj.* foolish, silly. (I Peter 2:15)

die Tortur (-en), torture.

tot, *adj.* dead, lifeless, inanimate; stagnant, dull; idle; exhausted. (Matt. 9:24) *die tote Hand,* mortmain.

der Tote (-n), dead person, deceased, corpse. (Luke 7:12)

töten, 1. *v.a.* to kill, to slay, to put to death; to destroy; to deaden; to mortify (the body). 2. *v.r.* to commit suicide.

der Totenacker, burying ground, graveyard.

die Totenbestattung (-en), burial.

das Totenbett, deathbed.

totenblaß, *adj.* pale as death, deathly pale.

die Totenblässe, deathly pallor.

die Totenfeier, funeral rites, exequies.

die Totengebeine, (*pl.*) bones of the dead. (Matt. 23:27)

das Totengerippe (-), skeleton.

der Totengeruch, cadaverous smell.

die Totenglocke, passing bell, knell.

der Totengottesdienst (-e), funeral service.

der Totengräber (-), gravedigger.

die Totengruft (¨e), vault, sepulcher.

die Totenklage, dirge, wake. (Ezek. 24:17)

der Totenkranz (¨e), **die Totenkrone** (-n), funeral wreath.

das Totenlied (-er), funeral chant, dirge.

das Totenmahl, funeral feast, wake.

die Totenmesse (-n), mass for the dead, requiem.

das Totenopfer (-), sacrifices to or for the dead.

das Totenreich, Hades, the underworld.

der Totenschlaf, der Totenschlummer, trance, sleep of death, last sleep.

der Totentag, der Totensonntag, All Souls' Day.

der Totentanz (¨e), dance of death.

der Totschlag (¨e), homicide, manslaughter.

totschlagen, *v.a.* to kill. (Gen. 4:14)

der Totschläger (-), murderer. (Num. 35:16)

die Tötung, homicide.

trachten, 1. *v.n.* (*aux.* h.): *nach einer Sache trachten,* to strive for, to endeavor or try to get something, to aspire to something. 2. *n.* endeavor, aim, aspiration. (Gen. 6:5)

die Tradition, tradition.

traditionell, *adj.* traditional.

die Tragbahre (-n), stretcher, litter.

träge, *adj.* slow, sluggish, dull; idle, indolent, inactive, inert. (Rom. 12:11)

tragen, 1. *ir.v.a.* to bear, to carry, to convey; to wear, to have on (clothes, etc.); to support, to uphold, to sustain; to endure, to suffer; to yield, to produce. 2. *v.r.: sich gut tragen,* to carry oneself well, to wear well (of clothes); *sich mit etwas (herum)-tragen,* to be occupied with, to brood over. 3. *v.n.* (*aux.* h.) to carry, to reach. (Gen. 1:11)

der Träger (-), carrier, porter; stretcher-bearer; supporter; wearer; support bracket; beam, base, post, pillar; bearer. (Luke 7:14)

das Traktat (-e), tract, treatise; treaty; (*pl.*) negotiations.

die Träne (-n), tear, teardrop. (Rev. 7:17)

tränen, *v.n.* (*aux.* h.) to be filled with tears, to water (of eyes); to weep. (Job 16:20)

der Trank (¨e), potion, drink, beverage, draft. (John 6:55)

tränken, *v.a.* to give to drink; to water (cattle, the ground); to soak, to saturate, to impregnate. (Gen. 24:14)

die Transsubstantiation, transubstantiation.

die Transsubstantiationslehre, dogma of transubstantiation.

transsubstantiieren, *v.a.* to transubstantiate.

transzendent, *adj.* transcendental.

die Transzendenz, transcendence.

der Traualtar (¨e), marriage altar.

die Traube (-n), grape; bunch of grapes; cluster. (Rev. 14:18)

der Traubensaft (¨e), juice of the grape; wine.

der Traubenstock ("-e), vine.

trauen, 1. *v.n.* (*aux.* h.): *einem trauen,* to trust (in), to believe in, to have confidence in or rely on someone. 2. *v.r.* to venture, to dare, to be so bold as. 3. *v.a.* to marry, to give in marriage, to join in wedlock. (Ps. 2:12)

die Trauer, das Trauern, mourning, grief, sorrow (*um* or *über,* for).

die Trauerbotschaft (-en), sad news, mournful tidings; news of a death.

das Trauergeleit (-e), funeral procession, mourners.

der Trauergesang ("-e), funeral hymn, dirge.

der Trauergottesdienst (-e), funeral service.

das Trauerhaus ("-er), house of mourning.

das Trauerjahr, year of mourning.

trauern, *v.n.* (*aux.* h.) to mourn, to lament, to grieve for. (Prov. 14:13)

die Trauerrede (-n), funeral oration or sermon.

die Trauerzeit, time of mourning.

der Trauerzug ("-e), funeral procession.

träufeln, *v.a.* to let fall in drops, to drop, to drip. (Isa. 45:8)

der Traum ("-e), dream; vision, fancy, illusion; daze. (Matt. 2:12)

träumen, *v.a. & n.* (*aux.* h.) & *imp.* to dream, to be lost in thought; to believe, to imagine. (Isa. 29:8)

der Träumer (-), dreamer, visionary. (Gen. 37:19)

das Traumgebilde (-), **das Traumgesicht** (-e), **die Traumgestalt** (-en), vision.

traurig, *adj.* sad, melancholy, mournful, sorrowful, grieved; depressed, dismal, wretched. (John 16:20)

die Traurigkeit, sadness, sorrow; depression, melancholy. (James 4:9)

traut, *adj.* dear, beloved; cozy, comfortable, intimate. (Jer. 31:20)

die Trauung (-en), marriage ceremony, wedding.

die Treber, (*pl.*) husks or skins (of grapes). (Luke 15:16)

treffen, 1. *v.a. & n.* (*aux.* h.) to hit, to strike; to affect, to touch, to concern; to befall, to fall in with, to come upon, to meet (with), to encounter, to find; to guess, to hit upon. 2. *v.r.* to happen. 3. *n.* engagement, action, combat, battle; meeting, encounter, gathering; line of battle. (Ps. 46:2)

trefflich, *adj.* excellent, choice, exquisite, admirable. (II Kings 5:1)

treiben, 1. *ir.v.a.* to drive, to push, to force; to set in motion, to propel, to urge on, to stimulate, to promote; to refine; to chase; to work at, to carry on, to practice. 2. *v.n.* (*aux.* h. & s.) to drift, to float; to sprout, to blossom; to ferment. 3. *n.* driving, drifting; urge, germination; doings, bustle, life, activity. (II Kings 9:20)

der Treiber (-), driver; oppressor; instigator; refiner. (Isa. 9:3)

trennen, 1. *v.a.* to separate, to divide, to part, to sever, to disconnect; to resolve; to disunite, to divorce; to break up, to dissolve (partnership, a marriage). 2. *v.r.* to part, to separate (*von,* from), to be(come) divorced; to dissociate, to disintegrate; to branch off (as roads).

die Trennung (-en), separation, division, segregation, parting, severing, dissociation, dissolution; disintegration; divorce. (Jude 19)
die Trennung von Kirche und Staat, separation of church and state.

treten, 1. *ir.v.n.* (*aux.* h. & s.) to tread, to walk, to step; to go, to pass over. 2. *v.a.* to tread, to walk upon; to trample, to kick, to treat with contempt. (Rev. 19:15)

treu, *adv.* (*with dat.*) faithful, loyal, constant; conscientious, staunch, upright, sincere; accurate, true; generous. (Num. 12:7)
Du treuer Gott, Lord God of Truth.

die Treue, fidelity, faithfulness, constancy, loyalty; sincerity, honesty; accuracy. (Gen. 32:11)

treulich, *adv.* truly, faithfully, loyally, conscientiously, reliably. (Ps. 101:2)

das tridentinische Konzil, Council of Trent.

der Trieb (-e), sprout, young shoot; driving force, motive power; impetus, urge, spur; instinct, impulse, inclination, desire, liking.

triefen, *ir.v.n.* (*aux.* h. & s.) to drop, to drip, to trickle, to water, to run. (Joel 4:18)

der Trinitarier (-), Trinitarian.

(der) Trinitas-Sonntag, Trinity Sunday.

die Trinität, Trinity, the Holy Trinity.

trinken, *ir.v.a.* & *n.* (*aux.* h.) to drink; to absorb. (Matt. 6:25)

der Triumph (-e), triumph, victory.

triumphieren, *v.n.* (*aux.* h.) to triumph (*über,* over), to vanquish, to conquer; to exult (in), to boast.

trocken, *adj.* dry, dried up, arid, parched, barren; (*fig.*) dull, tedious, boring. (Gen. 1:10)

trocknen, 1. *v.n.* (*aux.* s.) to dry, to dry up, to become dry. 2. *v.a.* to dry; to air; to drain. (John 12:3)

der Tropfen (-), drop, spot, tear, bead (of perspiration). (Isa. 40:15)

der Trost, comfort, consolation, solace. (Heb. 6:18)

trösten, 1. *v.a.* to comfort, to console, to solace; *jemanden über eine Sache* or *wegen einer Sache trösten,* to console someone concerning something. 2. *v.r.: sich mit . . . trösten,* to take comfort or find consolation in. (Gen. 5:29)

der Tröster (-), comforter, consoler; the Comforter. (John 14:16)

tröstlich, *adj.* consoling, comforting; pleasant, cheering; cheerful, merry. (Ps. 69:17)

trostlos, *adj.* hopeless, cheerless, bleak, desolate, desperate. (Isa. 54:11)

die Tröstung (-en), consolation, comfort. (Ps. 94:19)
die letzten Tröstungen, the last unction.

der Trotz, defiance, insolence, stubbornness, obstinacy, intrepidity; strength. (Prov. 10:29)

trotzen, *v.n.* (*aux.* h.) (*dat.*) to bid defiance to, to defy; to oppose. (I Peter 3:14)

trotzig, *adj.* defiant, obstinate. (Jer. 17:9)

trübe, *adj.* muddy, cloudy, opaque, thick; (*fig.*) gloomy, dreary, cheerless, sad, melancholy; dull, dead, flat, overcast. (Matt. 16:3)

die Trübsal (-e), affliction, distress, misery, sorrow, woe. (Rev. 1:9)

der Trübsinn, melancholy, depression, gloom.

der Trug, deceit, imposture, deception, fraud; delusion, illusion. (Prov. 14:8)

trügen, *ir.v.a.* & *n.* (*aux.* h.) to deceive, to delude, to be deceitful, to mislead, to be deceptive. (I Peter 3:10)
Gottes Wort kann nicht trügen, the word of God cannot fail.

trügerisch, trüglich, *adj.* deceptive, misleading, deceitful, delusive; treacherous. (II Cor. 11:13)

trunken, *adj.* drunk, intoxicated. (Rev. 17:2)

der Trunkenbold (-e), drunkard. (I Cor. 5:11)

die Trunksucht, drunkenness, dipsomania.

das Tuch, 1. (-e) cloth, fabric, stuff, material. 2. (⁻er) kerchief, shawl, scarf. (Matt. 9:16)

tüchtig, *adj.* fit, able, capable, qualified; sound, good, excellent, thorough; clever, skilful, proficient, efficient. (II Cor. 2:16)

die Tücke (-n), prank, trick; malice, malignity, knavery. (Acts 8:22)

die Tugend (-en), virtue; chastity, purity. (I Peter 2:9)

tugendsam, *adj.* virtuous, chaste. (Prov. 12:4)

tun, 1. *ir.v.a.* to do, to perform, to execute; to make; to put. 2. *v.n.* (*aux.* h.) to act, to do; to pretend, to affect. 3. *v.r.: sich dicke tun mit etwas,* to brag or boast of. 4. *n.* doings, proceeding(s); conduct; dealings, action. (Gen. 3:13)
Buße tun, to do penance.

tünchen, *v.a.* to whitewash, to distemper, to whiten. (Acts 23:3)

die Tür(e) (-n), door. (Gen. 4:7)

der Türhüter (-), doorkeeper, porter. (John 10:3)

der Turm (⁻e), tower, spire, steeple, belfry; dungeon, prison; castle. (Gen. 11:4)

die Turteltaube (-n), turtledove. (Luke 2:24)

der Tüttel (-), **das Tüttelchen** (-), dot; tittle, jot. (Matt. 5:18)

der Tyrann (-en), tyrant, despot. (Isa. 25:4)

die Tyrannei, tyranny, despotism.

tyrannisch, *adj.* tyrannical, despotic.

tyrannisieren, *v.a.* to tyrannize over, to oppress, to enslave.

der Tyrier (-), Tyrian.

tyrisch, *adj.* Tyrian.

Tyrus, Tyre.

Uu

übel, 1. *adj. & adv.* evil, bad, wrong; sick, ill. 2. *n.* (-) evil; wound, injury; complaint, ailment, malady; misfortune. (Gen. 39:9)

die Übeltat (-en), misdeed, misdemeanor. (I Peter 3:17)

der Übeltäter (-), wrongdoer, evildoer. (John 18:30)

üben, 1. *v.a. & n.* to exercise, to drill, to train; to practice; to use, to exert; to do military training. 2. *v.r.* (*in* with dat.) to practice, to do exercise. (Rom. 12:8) *Barmherzigkeit an einem üben,* to show someone mercy.

über, 1. *prep.* (a) *with dat. when implying rest or limited motion;* (b) *with acc. when implying transfer or motion across, to, past, or over, and in figurative uses without reference to motion:* over, above, on top of, higher than, superior to, more than; in the process of, during, while; across, beyond, on the other side of; upon, on, about, concerning, with regard to. 2. *with expressions of time or quantity: heute über acht Tage,* a week from today; *heute übers Jahr,* a year from today. 3. *adv.* over, above, too much, in excess; *über und über,* through and through, out and out, entirely.

überantworten, *v.a.* (*insep.*) to deliver up, to surrender, to consign. (Matt. 4:12)

überaus, *adv.* exceedingly, extremely, excessively. (Rom. 7:13)

überbleiben, *ir.v.n.* (*aux.* s.) (sep. p.p. *übergeblieben*) to remain (over), to be left over; (*insep.*) (*only in p.p.*) *überblieben,* surviving.

überdrüssig, *adj.* (*acc. or gen.*) sick, tired or weary of; satiated, disgusted with. (Isa. 1:14)

übereilen, (*insep.*) 1. *v.a.* to hurry (too much), to press forward; to precipitate (a decision, etc.). 2. *v.r.* to be in too much or

too great a hurry, to act rashly or inconsiderately. (Prov. 6:11)

übereinstimmen, *v.n.* (*aux.* h.) to agree, to concur, to be in agreement; to coincide, to correspond (to). (Mark 14:56)

überfallen, *ir.v.a.* (*insep.*) to fall upon suddenly, to attack, to surprise; to invade; to overtake (as illness, etc.). (John 12:35)

der Überfluß, plenty, abundance, surplus, exuberance. (Mark 12:44)

überflüssig, *adj.* superfluous, in excess, surplus, running over. (Luke 6:38)

überführen, *ir.v.a* (*sep.*) to conduct across, to transfer, to transport, to convey, to ferry across; to convert; (*insep.*) to convince; to convict (*gen.,* of a crime, etc.); to transport (a corpse) in state. (John 8:9)

der Übergang (̈-e), passage; change of tactics; transition, conversion; desertion.

übergeben, 1. *ir.v.a.* (*sep.*): *einem eins übergeben,* to beat someone; (*insep.*) (*einem etwas*) to deliver up (to), to hand over (to); to give up (to); to leave or commit to; to surrender. 2. *v.r.* (*insep.*) to vomit, to be sick. 3. *n.* vomiting. (Jer. 20:4)

überheben, 1. *ir.v.a.* (*sep.*) to lift over; (*insep.*) *jemanden einer Sache* (*gen.*) *überheben,* to exempt or excuse from, to relieve from, to spare, to save. 2. *v.r.* (*insep.*) to strain oneself (by lifting); (*fig.*) to be overbearing, to boast (of). (Acts 27:21)

überkommen, (*insep.*) *ir.v.a. & n.* (*aux.* s.) (*dat.*) to get, to receive; to have handed down; to seize, to befall; to overcome. (Acts 1:17)

überlaufen, 1. *ir.v.a.* (*insep.*) to run all over, to run down, to spread over, to overrun; (*fig.*) to overwhelm, to deluge or besiege with, to importune. 2. *v.n.* (*sep.*) (*aux.* s.) to run or flow over, to overflow, to boil over; to desert. (Amos 8:8)

160

überlegen, (*sep.*) 1. *v.a.* (*über* with acc.) to lay over or upon, to cover. 2. *v.r.* to lean or bend over, to heel over (of a ship); (*insep.*) *v.a.* to reflect on, to ponder over, to weigh, to consider. (Rev. 13:18)

überliefern, *v.a.* (*insep.*) (*einem etwas*) to deliver up, to hand over; (to transmit, to hand down, to pass on.

die Überlieferung (-en), delivery, surrender; tradition.

die Übermacht, majesty; superiority, predominance.

der Übermut, high spirits; wantonness; arrogance, presumption. (II Kings 19:28)

übermütig, *adj.* high-spirited, wanton; arrogant, presumptuous. (Deut. 32:15)

überreden, *v.a.* (*insep.*) to persuade; *einen überreden, etwas zu tun* or *einen zu einer Sache überreden,* to persuade someone to do something; *sich durch Gründe überreden lassen,* to allow oneself to be persuaded or convinced by reasons. (Acts 21:14)

der Überrest (-e), rest, remains, remnant; residue, remainder; (*pl.*) ruins, relics. (Rom. 9:27)
sterbliche Überreste, mortal remains, ashes.

überschatten, *v.a.* to overshadow. (Matt. 17:5)

überschlagen, *ir.v.a.* (*sep.*) to fold over; to omit, to leave out; to estimate, to make a rough calculation; to drown (a sound). (Luke 14:28)

überschreiten, *ir.v.a.* (*insep.*) to step or stride over, to pass over, to cross; (*fig.*) to overstep, to go beyond, to exceed; to transgress, to infringe. (Job 14:5)

die Überschrift (-en), inscription, heading, title. (Matt. 22:20)

überschwemmen, *v.a.* (*insep.*) to inundate, to flood, to submerge; (*fig.*) to deluge. (Amos 8:8)

überschwenglich, *adj.* boundless, excessive; exuberant, extravagant. (Eph. 1:19)

übersehen, *ir.v.a.* (*insep.*) to take in at a glance, to perceive, to survey, to glance over; to overlook, to omit, to miss, to wink at, to connive at (a fault), to make allowances for. (Amos 7:8)

übersetzen, 1. *v.n.* (*aux.* s.) & *a.* (*sep.*) to leap or jump over, to cross, to pass over, to transport. 2. *v.a.* (*insep.*) to translate, to adapt (for the stage, etc.); to crowd, to overload.

die Übersetzung (-en), translation (*aus,* from; *in,* into); version.

übertreffen, 1. *ir.v.a.* (*insep.*) to surpass, to exceed, to excel, to outdo. 2. *v.r.* (*insep.*) to do better than usual. (Eph. 3:19)

übertreten, 1. *ir.v.a.* (*insep.*) to overstep, to trespass, to transgress, to violate, to infringe, to break (the law). 2. *v.n.* (*sep.*) (*aux.* s.) to step or pass over, to run over, to overflow (of rivers); to go over, to change over to, to join (a party, etc.). (Matt. 15:2)
zur christlichen Kirche übertreten, to become Christian.

der Übertreter (-), trespasser, transgressor. (Isa. 48:8)

die Übertretung (-en), transgression, trespass; breach, violation (of a law). (Rom. 2:23)

der Übertritt (-e), passage, joining (a party); change (of religion), conversion; stile.

übertünchen, *v.a.* (*insep.*) to whitewash; (*fig.*) to gloss over.
die Wahrheit übertünchen, to veil the truth.

übervorteilen, *v.a.* (*insep.*) to take advantage of, to cheat, to take in. (I Thess. 4:6)

überwältigen, *v.a.* (*insep.*) to overcome, to subdue, to vanquish, to conquer, to overpower, to overwhelm. (Matt. 16:18)

überwinden, *ir.v.a.* (*insep.*) to overcome, to prevail, to conquer, to subdue, to vanquish. (Rev. 2:7)

die Überzeugung, conviction, belief; persuasion.

die Ubiquität, ubiquity, omnipresence.

übrig, *adj.* (left) over, remaining, to spare, residual; *die Übrigen,* the others, the rest. (Isa. 1:8)

übrigbleiben, *v.n.* to remain over. (Matt. 14:20)

das Ufer (-), bank (of river); beach, shore; brink. (Gen. 22:17)

um, 1. *prep.* (*with acc.*) about, round, around; approximately, round about, near, toward(s); for; because of; (in exchange) for; by (so much); at; alternately with, after. 2. *conj.:* um zu (*with inf.*) so as to, in order to, to. 3. *adv.* past, out, ended, over; upset; around, enclosing, surrounding; round about; um und um, round about, everywhere, from or on all sides. 4. *prefix, either sep. or insep.,* implying (a) round, round about; (b) over again, repeatedly; (c) in another way; (d) to the ground, down, over. (Ezek. 1:18)

umbringen, 1. *ir.v.a.* (*sep.*) to kill, to murder, to destroy, to slay. 2. *v.r.* to commit suicide. (John 18:14)

umfangen, *ir.v.a.* (*insep.*) to enclose, to embrace, to surround, to encircle, to encompass. (Ps. 18:5)

umgeben, *ir.v.a.* (*sep.*) to put on (a cloak); (*insep.*) to surround, to encircle. (Jer. 31:22)

umgehen, 1. *ir.v.n.* (*aux.* s.) (*sep.*) to go round, to revolve, to circulate; to make a circuit or detour; (*mit*) to associate (with), to deal (with); to manage, to handle. 2. *v.a.* (*insep.*) to walk around; to elude, to evade, to dodge; to outflank. (Isa. 29:14)

umgürten, *v.a.* (*sep.*) to gird, to gird oneself with; to buckle on (a sword); (*insep.*): seine Lenden umgürten, to gird up one's loins. (John 13:4)

umhauen, *ir.v.a.* (*sep.*) to hew or cut down, to fell (trees, etc.). (Isa. 10:34)

umherführen, *v.a.* to lead or conduct round (a building, etc.). (I Cor. 9:5)

umkehren, (*sep.*) 1. *v.n.* (*aux.* s.) to turn back, to turn round, to return, (*fig.*) to reform, to turn over a new leaf. 2. *v.a.* to turn (round, about, back, over, up, inside out, upside down, etc.); to overturn, to reverse, to convert, to throw into disorder. (Gen. 19:25)

umkommen, *ir.v.n.* (*sep.*) (*aux.* s.) to perish, to die; to fall (in battle); to spoil; to be lost or wasted. (John 6:12)

umlaufen, (*sep.*) 1. *ir.v.a.* to run over, to run or knock down. 2. *v.n.* (*aux.* s.) to rotate, to revolve. (Ps. 19:7)

umleuchten, *v.a.* (*insep.*) (*aux.* h.) to bathe in light, to throw or shed light on, to shine round about. (Acts 9:3)

umreißen, *ir.v.a.* (*sep.*) to pull, to tear or throw down; to blow down (trees, etc.); to demolish; (*insep.*) to outline, to sketch (*usually fig.*). (Ps. 11:3)

umringen, *reg.* & *ir.v.a.* (*insep.*) to encircle, to enclose, to close in on, to encompass, to surround, to beset. (Acts 14:20)

umsehen, *ir.v.r.* (*sep.*) to look back, to look around; to look about one. (Exod. 18:21)

umsonst, *adv.* for nothing, without pay, gratuitously, free of charge; to no purpose, in vain. (Rev. 21:6)

umstoßen, *ir.v.a.* (*sep.*) to overturn, to upset, to overthrow, to knock down; to subvert, to abolish, to cancel, to revoke, to annul, to void. (Matt. 21:12)

der Umsturz (¨e), fall, downfall, ruin, overthrow; revolution; subversion.

umtreiben, *ir.v.a.* (*sep.*) to drive round, to rotate, to revolve, to turn, to spin. (Luke 6:18)

die Umwelt, world around us, (social) surroundings, milieu, environment.

die Umwelteinflüsse, (*pl.*) environmental factors.

umwenden, (*sep.*) 1. *reg.* & *ir.v.a.* & *r.* to turn, to turn round or over; to reverse, to invert. 2. *ir.v.n.* (*aux.* h. & s.) *see* **umkehren.**

unanstößig, *adj.* inoffensive, harmless, unobjectionable. (Phil. 1:10)

unaufrichtig, *adj.* insincere, deceitful, double-faced, shady, shifty.

unbarmherzig, *adj.* unmerciful, merciless, hardhearted, ruthless, cruel, inhuman. (James 2:13)

die Unbarmherzigkeit, harshness, cruelty. (Exod. 1:13)

unbedingt, 1. *adj.* unconditional, unquestioning, absolute; implicit. 2. *adv.* whatever happens, without fail.

unbefleckt, *adj.* spotless, undefiled, unblemished, unspotted, blameless, pure, virgin; immaculate. (James 1:27) *unbefleckte Empfängnis,* immaculate conception.

unbegreiflich, *adj.* inconceivable, incredible, incomprehensible; inexplicable. (Rom. 11:33)

unbekannt, 1. *adj.* unknown, unheard of, obscure; ignorant, unaware (*mit,* of); unacquainted, a stranger (to). 2. *n.* person or persons unknown. (Acts 17:23)

unbekehrbar, *adj.* inconvertible, confirmed.

unberührt, *adj.* untouched, unused, intact; innocent, chaste; virgin (forest, soil); unmoved (by), proof (against); unnoticed.

unbeschnitten, *adj.* uncircumcised; unshorn. (I Sam. 17:26)

unbescholten, *adj.* blameless; of good reputation.

unbeseelt, *adj.* soulless, spiritless, lifeless, inanimate.

unbeständig, *adj.* unstable, unsteady, erratic, changeable. (James 1:8)

unbeweglich, *adj.* immovable, fixed, motionless; apathetic, impassive, unresponsive; resolved; uncompromising. (Col. 1:23)
die unbeweglichen Feste, (*pl.*) set festivals.

unbußfertig, *adj.* impenitent, unrepentant. (Rom. 2:5)

unchristlich, *adj.* unchristian, uncharitable.

undankbar, *adj.* ungrateful, thankless (task). (Luke 6:35)

undeutlich, *adj.* indistinct, blurred, hazy; obscure, vague, confused, unintelligible; inarticulate. (I Cor. 14:8)

unduldsam, *adj.* intolerant, impatient.

die Unduldsamkeit, intolerance.

uneben, *adj.* uneven, rough, rugged; *nicht uneben,* not bad, rather good. (Luke 3:5)

unedel, *adj.* ignoble, vulgar, base; inert. (I Cor. 1:28)

unehelich, *adj.* illegitimate. (John 8:41)

die Unehre, dishonor. (Rom. 9:21)

unehrlich, *adj.* dishonest, insincere, false; shady, double-faced. (I Tim. 3:3)

uneins, *adv.:* *uneins sein,* to disagree (with), to be at odds (with), to join issue (with). (Matt. 12:25)

unempfänglich, *adj.* unreceptive.

unendlich, *adj.* infinite, endless, unlimited, immense. (Heb. 7:16)

unerfahren, *adj.* inexperienced; unskilled. (Heb. 5:13)

unerforschlich, *adj.* inscrutable, impenetrable, inexplicable. (Rom. 11:33)

die Unerforschlichkeit, inscrutability.

unerlaubt, *adj.* unlawful, illicit, forbidden. (Acts 10:28)

unerträglich, *adj.* intolerable, unbearable, insufferable, overpowering (heat, etc.). (Matt. 23:4)

die Unfähigkeit, incapacity, impotence, weakness.

unfehlbar, 1. *adj.* inevitable, unavoidable, unfailing, infallible, unerring. 2. *adv.* certainly, surely.

die Unfehlbarkeit, infallibility.

der Unflat, filth, dirt; riffraff. (Matt. 23:27)

der Unfriede(n), discord, dissension, strife, enmity, friction. (Heb. 12:15)

unfruchtbar, *adj.* unfruitful, unprofitable, unproductive; barren, sterile. (Gen. 11:30)

die Unfruchtbarkeit, barrenness, sterility. (Isa. 49:20)

ungebärdig, *adj.* wild, unruly, boisterous, rowdy. (I Cor. 13:5)

die Ungeduld, impatience.

ungeduldig, *adj.* impatient. (Prov. 3:11)

ungeheuer, 1. *adj.* huge, colossal, enormous, monstrous; atrocious, frightful. 2. *adv.* exceedingly; mighty, mightily. 3. *n.* (-) monster. (Acts 28:6)

ungehorsam, *adj.* disobedient; insubordinate, rebellious. (Isa. 50:5)

der Ungehorsam, disobedience, insubordination, noncompliance. (Rom. 5:19)

das Ungemach, discomfort, hardship, trouble, toil. (Heb. 11:25)

ungerecht, *adj.* unjust, unfair, unrighteous. (Rom. 3:5)

die Ungerechtigkeit, injustice, unfairness. (Matt. 24:12)

ungern, *adv.* unwillingly, reluctantly, regretfully, grudgingly; against the grain. (I Cor. 9:17)

ungesäuert, *adj.* unleavened. (I Cor. 5:7)
das ungesäuerte Brot, unleavened bread.

ungestraft, 1. *adj.* unpunished, absolved. 2. *adv.* with impunity. (Exod. 20:7)

ungestüm, 1. *adj.* stormy, turbulent, blustering, raging, fierce, furious, violent, vehement, boisterous, impetuous. 2. *m. & n.* violence, vehemence, turbulence. (Exod. 14:25)

ungewaschen, *adj.* unwashed, unclean, soiled, dirty. (Matt. 15:20)

ungewiß, *adj.* uncertain, doubtful, dubious, indecisive; hazardous, precarious, problematic; contingent, undecided, indeterminate. (I Cor. 9:26)

das Ungewitter (-), storm, thunderstorm, cloudburst. (Isa. 25:4)

ungezogen, *adj.* ill-bred, ill-mannered, rude, uncivil, impudent. (I Thess. 5:14)

der Unglaube, incredulity, unbelief, disbelief, skepticism. (Matt. 13:58)

ungläubig, *adj.* incredulous, skeptical, doubting; dubious, suspicious, unbelieving, irreligious, undevout, freethinking, lacking faith. (Matt. 17:17)

der Ungläubige (-n), unbeliever, infidel. (I Cor. 10:27)

unglaublich, *adj.* incredible, unbelievable, unheard of, staggering.

ungleich, *adj.* unequal, unlike, different, varying, diverse, diversified; uneven, odd; disproportionate. (Isa. 40:4)

das Unglück, misfortune, ill or bad luck; distress, misery, woe. (Deut. 32:23)

die Ungnade, disgrace, displeasure. (Rom. 2:8)
in Ungnade fallen, to fall out of favor.

der Ungrund, abyss.

das Unheil, harm, mischief, trouble; disaster, calamity.

unheilbar, *adj.* incurable, irreparable. (Jer. 30:12)

unheilig, *adj.* unholy, unhallowed, profane. (I Tim. 1:9)

die Unierte, (*pl.*) United Protestants; Greek Catholics.

der Unitarianismus, Unitarianism.

der Unitarier (-), Unitarian.

unitarisch, *adj.* Unitarian.

das Universum, universe.

unkeusch, *adj.* unchaste, impure, immodest. (II Tim. 3:3)

die Unkeuschheit, unchastity, impurity, immodesty. (I Cor. 7:5)

das Unkraut (ˉer), weed, weeds. (Matt. 13:25)

unmittelbar, *adj.* immediate, direct.

unmöglich, *adj.* impossible. (Gen. 18:14)

unmündig, *adj.* under age, not of age. (Matt. 11:25)

unnahbar, *adj.* inaccessible, unapproachable.

die Unnahbarkeit, inaccessibility.

unnatürlich, *adj.* unnatural, abnormal; outlandish, grotesque, monstrous; forced. (Rom. 1:26)

unnütz, *adj.* useless, unprofitable, vain, idle, superfluous; naughty. (Luke 17:10)

unordentlich, *adj.* disorderly; irregular, confused; untidy; dissolute. (Eph. 5:18)

die Unordnung, disorder, confusion; litter, untidiness. (I Cor. 14:33)

unparteiisch, unparteilich, *adj.* impartial, disinterested, unprejudiced, unbiased, neutral. (James 3:17)

unrecht, 1. *adj.* wrong, false, incorrect, not right; unsuitable. 2. *n.* wrong, injustice; error, fault. (I John 3:4)

unrein, *adj.* unclean, dirty, impure, obscene. (Lev. 10:10)

die Unreinheit, uncleanness; impurity, foulness, pollution.

die Unreinigkeit, uncleanness. (Eph. 4:19)

die Unruhe (-n), unrest, commotion, disturbance, restlessness; disquiet, anxiety, alarm; (*pl*) disturbances, tumult, riot. (Acts 15:19)

unruhig, *adj.* unsettled, uneasy, restless, agitated, excited, troubled, turbulent. (James 3:8)

unsauber, *adj.* unclean, dirty, filthy; unfair. (Matt. 10:1)

die Unsauberkeit, uncleanliness, dirtiness. (Rev. 17:4)

die Unschuld, innocence; purity, chastity. (Job 31:6)
ich wasche meine Hände in Unschuld, I wash my hands of it.

unschuldig, *adj.* innocent, guiltless, guileless; pure, chaste (girl); harmless (remark). (Exod. 34:7)

unselig, *adj.* unhappy, unlucky, unfortunate, accursed, wretched.

die Unseligkeit, misery, wretchedness.

unsichtbar, *adj.* invisible, imperceptible. (Rom. 1:20)

die Unsichtbarkeit, invisibility.

unsinnig, *adj.* absurd, crazy, senseless, foolish; mad, insane. (John 10:20)

die Unsitte, bad habit; abuse.

unsittlich, *adj.* immoral; immodest, indecent.

die Unsittlichkeit, immorality; indecency, immoral act.

unsterblich, *adj.* immortal. (Ecclesiasticus 1:15)

die Unsterblichkeit, immortality. (I Cor. 15:53)

unstet, *adj.* changeable; unsteady; restless, wandering, not fixed. (Gen. 4:12)

unstrafbar, unsträflich, *adj.* irreproachable, blameless, impeccable. (Rev. 14:5)

untadelhaft, untadelig, *adj.* irreproachable, blameless, unexceptionable. (Luke 1:6)

unten, *adv.* below, beneath, under(neath); at the bottom or foot; downstairs. (John 8:23)

untenan, *adv.* at the foot or bottom. (Luke 14:9)

unter, 1. *prep.* (*with acc. or dat.*) (*with dat. in answer to* **wo?** where? in which place? *with acc. in answer to* **wohin?** whither? to which place?) under, below, beneath, underneath, among, amongst; (*with dat. only*) during, by. 2. *adj.* under, underneath; lower, inferior. 3. *adv. & sep. & insep. prefix* below, beneath, under; among; amid.

unterdrücken, *v.a.* (*insep.*) to suppress, to oppress, to crush, to quell, to repress, to stifle, to restrain. (II Cor. 4:9)

untergehen, *ir.v.n.* (*sep.*) (*aux.* s.) to set (of sun, etc.), to sink, to be wrecked; to perish, to be lost or annihilated, to become extinct. (Gen. 7:21)

der Unterlaß, (*only in*) *ohne Unterlaß*, without intermission, unceasingly, incessantly, continuously. (Dan. 6:17)

unterlassen, *ir.v.a.* (*insep.*) to leave off, to discontinue; to fail (to do), to omit (to do), to neglect (doing), to forbear, to abstain (from doing). (Acts 6:2)

die Unterlassungssünde (-n), sin of omission.

unterliegen, *ir.v.n.* (*insep.*) (*aux.* s.) (*with dat.*) to succumb, to be overcome, overthrown, or defeated. (Ps. 116:6)

unterrichten, 1. *v.a.* (*insep.*) to teach, to instruct, to educate, to train; (*von* or *in* with dat., *über* with acc.) to inform of, to acquaint with. 2. *v.r.: sich von einer*

Sache or *über eine Sache unterrichten*, to obtain information about something. (Gal. 6:6)

der Untersatz, minor premise (logic).

unterscheiden, 1. *ir.v.a.* (*insep.*) to distinguish, to discern, to discriminate, to separate, to differentiate. 2. *v.r.* to differ (from). (I Cor. 11:29)

der Unterschied (-e), distinction, difference, discrimination, variation, dissimilarity. (Gen. 1:6)

unterschieden, *p.p. & adj.* different, distinct; several, sundry. (I Cor. 14:7)

die Unterschrift (-en), signature; inscription, caption (under a picture, etc.). (Job 31:35)

unterstehen, 1. *ir.v.n.* (*sep.*) (*aux.* h. & s.) to be or stand under; to shelter under. 2. *v.r.* (*insep.*) to dare, to presume, to venture. 3. *v.n.* (*insep.*) (*with dat.*) to be (placed) under, to be subordinate to. (Acts 18:10)

untertan, 1. *p.p. & adj.* (*dat.*) subject (to); dependent (on); *sich* (*dat.*) (*einen* or *etwas*) *untertan machen*, to subdue (someone or something), to get (someone or something) into one's power. 2. *m.* (-en) subject, vassal. (Gen. 1:28)

untertänig, *adj.* submissive, obedient, humble; subject. (James 4:7)

untertreten, (*sep.*) *ir.v.n.* (*aux.* s.) to step under; to take shelter under; to step on, to oppress. (Amos 4:1)

unterwegs, *adv.* on the way, en route. (Luke 24:17)

unterweisen, *ir.v.a.* (*insep.*) (*in* with dat.) to instruct, to teach. (Acts 18:25)

die Unterwelt, underworld; lower regions, Hades.

unterwerfen, 1. *ir.v.a.* (*insep.*) (*einen jemandem* or *einer Sache*) to subjugate, to subject (to); *einer Sache unterworfen sein*, to be subject or exposed to something. 2. *v.r.* to submit, to yield, to resign oneself to. (Rom. 8:20)

unterwinden, *ir.v.r.* to venture (to), to dare (to), to presume (to). (Gen. 18:27)

untüchtig, *adj.* incapable, unfit, incompetent, inefficient. (II Tim. 3:8)

die Untugend, vice, bad habit. (Isa. 10:25)

unveränderlich, *adj.* unchangeable, constant, immutable.

unverdient, *adj.* unmerited, undeserved; unjust. (Prov. 26:2)

unverfälscht, *adj.* unadulterated, pure; real, genuine. (Titus 2:7)

unvergänglich, *adj.* imperishable, everlasting, ageless, immortal. (Dan. 6:27)

die Unvergänglichkeit, imperishableness, persistence, permanence, immortality.

unverletzlich, *adj.* invulnerable; sacred, sacrosanct.

die Unverletzlichkeit, invulnerability, sanctity.

unverletzt, *adj.* unhurt, uninjured, safe; intact. (Acts 24:16)

unverlierbar, *adj.* safe, secure; immortal.

unvermögend, *adj.* unable, incapable, incompetent, inept, feeble, impotent; penniless. (Isa. 40:29)

unvernünftig, *adj.* irrational, unreasonable, senseless, foolish; ridiculous, absurd; *unvernünftige Tiere,* dumb animals. (II Peter 2:12)

unverrückt, 1. *adj.* unmoved, in its place; steady, fixed. 2. *adv.* fixedly, immovably; steadily. (Eph. 6:24)

unverschämt, *adj.* shameless, impudent, brazen.

unversehens, *adv.* unexpectedly, suddenly; casually, by chance. (Isa. 5:13)

unversehrt, *adj.* undamaged, uninjured, intact, safe. (Dan. 3:25)

unversöhnlich, *adj.* irreconcilable; implacable, intransigent. (Rom. 1:31)

der Unverstand, lack of understanding or judgment, irrationality, imprudence, folly. (Rom. 10:2)

unverständig, *adj.* unwise, foolish, silly, stupid, imprudent. (Matt. 15:16)

unverständlich, *adj.* unintelligible, incomprehensible, inconceivable; obscure, indistinct. (Isa. 28:11)

unverweslich, *adj.* incorruptible. (Num. 18:19)

unverzagt, *adj.* undaunted, undismayed, unabashed; fearless, bold, resolute. (Acts 27:22)

unwert, 1. *adj.* unworthy; worthless. 2. *m.* unworthiness, worthlessness. (Isa. 53:3)

der Unwille(n) (-n), resentment, displeasure, animosity; indignation, anger, annoyance, bitterness; reluctance. (II Cor. 9:7)

unwillig, *adj.* indignant, resentful, angry (*über,* about); reluctant, unwilling. (Matt. 20:24)

unwissend, *adj.* ignorant (of), unacquainted (with), unaware (of), ill informed (about); uninformed, ignorant, stupid. (Acts 17:23)

die Unwissenheit, ignorance, inexperience. (Acts 3:17)

unwürdig, *adj.* unworthy, disgraceful; shameful, mean, base. (I Cor. 11:27)

unzählig, *adj.* innumerable, countless, numberless. (Mic. 6:7)

die Unzeit, wrong time; (*only in*) *zur Unzeit,* unseasonably, inopportunely; prematurely. (II Tim. 4:2)

unzeitig, *adj.* untimely; out of season, inopportune. (I Cor. 15:8)

die Unzucht, unchastity, lechery, lewdness, fornication. (Mark 7:22) *gewerbsmäßige Unzucht,* prostitution.

das Urbild (-er), original; archetype, prototype.

der Urchrist (-en), early Christian.

das Urchristentum, the early church.

die Urkirche, early church.

die Urreligion, original religion.

die Ursache (-n), cause, reason, origin, motive, ground, occasion; charge, accusation. (Acts 25:18)

die Urschrift (-en), original text, original.

der Ursprung, source, origin, inception, provenance, beginning, cause.

die Ursünde, original sin.

das Urteil (-e), judgment, decision; sentence, verdict; view, opinion. (Rom. 2:3)

urteilen, *v.n.* (*aux.* h.) to judge, to pass sentence, to give one's opinion, to form an opinion. (Matt. 16:3)

die Urteilskraft, function of judgment (Kant).

der Urvater, first parent, forefather.

der Urzustand, primitive state, original condition.

die Utopie (-n), utopia, utopian scheme.

der Utraquist (-en), Hussite.

Vv

der **Vasall** (-en), vassal, retainer.

der **Vater** (ˉ), father; (male) parent; the Father (God). (Matt. 5:16)

das **Vaterland,** native country or land, mother country, fatherland. (Gen. 12:1)

väterlich, adj. paternal, fatherly; of one's father(s). (Acts 22:3)

die **Vaterstadt,** native town. (Matt. 13:54)

das **Vaterunser** (-), the Lord's Prayer; paternoster. (see Luke 11:2–4)

der **Vatikan,** Vatican.

vatikanisch, adj. papal, curial.

die **Vatikanstadt,** Vatican City.

der **Veitstanz,** St. Vitus's dance.

verachten, v.a. to despise, to scorn, to disdain, to look down upon. (Gen. 25:34)

der **Verächter** (-), scorner, despiser. (Acts 13:41)

die **Verachtung,** disdain, contempt, scorn. (Ps. 22:7)

veralten, v.n. (aux. s.) to grow old or stale; to go out of use, to become obsolete. (Luke 12:33)

verändern, 1. v.a. to change, to alter, to vary, to transform, to modify. 2. v.r. to change, to alter, to vary, to take another situation (of servants). (Gen. 31:7)

die **Veränderung** (-en), change, alteration, transformation, variation, modification. (James 1:17)

verantworten, 1. v.a. to answer for, to account for, to be responsible for; to defend, to vindicate. 2. v.r. to justify oneself, to vindicate oneself; sich vor einem für etwas or wegen einer Sache verantworten, to justify one's action with someone. (Phil. 1:7)

die **Verantwortung,** responsibility; justification, vindication, excuse. (Phil. 1:17)

verarmen, v.n. (aux. s.) to become poor or impoverished, to be reduced to poverty. (Prov. 23:21)

verbannen, v.a. to banish, to exile; (fig.) to dispel. (Rom. 9:3)

der **Verbannte** (-n), exile.

die **Verbannung,** banishment, exile.

der **Verbannungsort** (-e), place of exile.

verbergen, 1. ir.v.a. to hide, to conceal; etwas einem (or vor einem) verbergen, to hide something from someone. 2. v.r. to hide. (Gen. 4:14)

die **Verbergung,** concealment; covert, shelter. (Isa. 4:6)

der **Verbesserer** (-), improver; reformer.

verbieten, ir.v.a. (einem etwas) to forbid, to prohibit. (Matt. 16:20)

verbinden, ir.v.a. to bind, to unite, to join, to connect, to link, to combine; to dress (wounds), to tie, to bind up; to pledge, to engage. (Luke 10:34)

die **Verbitterung,** embitterment, bitterness (of heart). (Heb. 3:8)

verblenden, v.a. to blind, to dazzle; to delude, to beguile, to infatuate; to mask, to screen (a light). (John 12:40)

die **Verblendung,** delusion.

verborgen, p.p. (of **verbergen**) & adj. hidden, concealed, secret, clandestine; obscure; occult. (Matt. 5:14)
im Verborgenen, in secret, unnoticed; in wait.

das **Verbot** (-e), prohibition; suppression (of a book, etc.); veto.

verbreiten, v.a. & r. to spread, to disseminate, to disperse; to circulate, to spread abroad, to propagate.

verbrennen, 1. ir.v.a. to burn, to scorch, to singe; to cremate (the dead). 2. v.r. & n. (aux. s.) to burn, to be scorched, to be burnt up. (I Kings 13:2)

verdammen, *v.a.* to condemn, to curse. (Job 34:17)

die Verdammnis, damnation, perdition, condemnation. (II Peter 3:7)

die Verdammung, condemnation, damnation; *ewige Verdammung,* eternal damnation.

verdecken, *v.a.* to cover, to hide, to conceal; to camouflage, to mask, to veil, to screen. (II Cor. 4:3)

der Verderb, ruin, destruction; decay.

verderben, 1. *reg. & ir.v.a.* (*einem etwas*) to spoil, to damage, to ruin; to corrupt, to demoralize. 2. *ir.v.n.* (*aux.* s.) to be spoilt, to decay, to perish; to fail. 3. *n.* corruption, destruction, ruin, perdition. (Gen. 6:11)

verderblich, *adj.* corruptible, perishable; ruinous, destructive, injurious; fatal. (II Peter 2:1)

die Verderbnis, corruption, decay; destruction; depravity, perversion.

die Verderbtheit, corruption, depravity, vice.

verdienen, *v.a.* to earn; to gain, to get, to win; to deserve, to merit. (Mic. 3:4)

der Verdienst (-e), gain, profit; earnings, wages. (Rom. 11:6)
nicht aus Verdienst, no more of works.

verdorren, *v.n.* (*aux.* s.) to dry up, to wither. (I Kings 13:4)

die Verdrängung, removal; dispossession; suppression; repression, inhibition (psychology).

verdrießen, *ir.v.a.* to grieve, to vex, to annoy, to displease. (Phil. 3:1)
sich etwas verdrießen lassen, to shrink from, to be discouraged by, to be put off by.

verdrossen, *p.p. & adj.* cross, vexed, annoyed; sulky, sullen. (II Thess. 3:13)

der Verdruß, ill humor, irritation, displeasure, dismay, discontent, annoyance. (Ezek. 8:3)

verdunkeln, 1. *v.a.* to darken, to black out, to obscure, to cloud; to eclipse. 2. *v.r.* to grow dim. (Job 38:2)

verehren, *v.a.* to revere, to worship, to venerate, to reverence; to admire, to respect, to honor, to adore.

die Verehrung, respect, veneration, reverence, devotion, worship, adoration.

der Verein (-e), association, society, club, union, alliance, syndicate.

die Vererbung, inheritance, hereditary transmission.

der Verfall, decay, deterioration; decadence, decline, fall, downfall, ruin; foreclosure.

verfallen, *ir.v.n.* (*aux.* s.) to decay, to decline, to go to ruin; to expire, to fall due; (*with dat.*) to fall to, to come into the power or possession of; (*auf etwas*) to hit or chance upon; (*in etwas*) to fall, sink, or slip back into. (Deut. 34:7)

verfälschen, *v.a.* to adulterate; to falsify, to counterfeit, to debase (coin). (II Cor. 2:17)

die Verfassung (-en), composition; condition, disposition, state; frame of mind; system of government, constitution.

verfaulen, *v.n.* (*aux.* s.) to rot, to decay, to decompose. (James 5:2)

verfinstern, 1. *v.a.* to darken, to obscure, to eclipse. 2. *v.r.* to grow dark. (Rev. 9:2)

verfluchen, *v.a.* to curse, to damn, to execrate. (Gen. 3:14)

die Verfluchung, curse, malediction; anathema.

verfolgen, *v.a.* to pursue, to follow (up); to trail; to persecute, to prosecute. (Rev. 12:13)

der Verfolger (-), pursuer; persecutor. (Phil. 3:6)

die Verfolgung, pursuit, chase; persecution, prosecution; pursuance, continuation. (Matt. 13:21)

verführen, *v.a.* to lead astray, to entice, to tempt, to seduce; to induce, to prevail upon, to suborn (witnesses). (I John 1:8)

der Verführer (-), tempter, seducer. (Matt. 27:63)

verführerisch, *adj.* tempting, seductive, fascinating, alluring. (II Tim. 3:13)

die Verführung, temptation, seduction; subornation. (II Thess. 2:10)

die Verführungskünste, *pl.* art of deception, wiles, artifice.

vergangen, *p.p.* (*of* vergehen) *& adj.* past, gone, bygone; last. (I Peter 4:3)

die Vergangenheit, past.

vergänglich, *adj.* fleeting, passing, transient, transitory; perishable. (Rom. 1:23)

die Vergänglichkeit, perishableness, instability, transitoriness.

vergeben, 1. *ir.v.a.* (*etwas an einen*) to give away or dispose of (to), to confer or bestow (on). 2. (*einem etwas*) to forgive, to pardon. 3. (*also v.r.*) *ein Amt an einen vergeben,* to appoint someone to an office, to bestow an office on someone. (Gen. 4:13)

vergeblich, *adj.* vain, idle, fruitless, futile; *sich* (*dat.*) *vergebliche Mühe machen,* to go to a lot of trouble for nothing. (Matt. 15:9)

die Vergebung, forgiveness, pardon, remission. (Ps. 130:4)

vergehen, 1. *ir.v.n.* (*aux.* s.) to pass, to cease, to elapse, to subside, to vanish, to disappear; to waste away, to perish, to die (*vor*, of). 2. *v.r.* to go astray, to go wrong, to err, to offend, to transgress, to trespass. 3. *n.* disappearance; offense, fault, transgression, sin. (Matt. 24:34) *meine Tage sind vergangen wie ein Rauch,* my days are consumed like smoke.

vergeistigen, *v.a.* to spiritualize.

die Vergeistigung, spiritualization.

vergelten, *v.a.* (*einem etwas*) to requite, to return, to repay, to pay back, to reward, to recompense; to retaliate. (Rom. 12:17) *Böses mit Gutem vergelten,* to return good for evil.

der Vergelter (-), recompenser, remunerator; revenger. (Jer. 51:6)

die Vergeltung, requital, return, reward; retaliation, reprisal. (Isa. 40:10)

der Vergeltungstag, day of retribution, day of judgment.

vergessen, *ir.v.a.* to forget; to neglect. (Ps. 103:2)

vergeßlich, *adj.* forgetful, oblivious; easily forgotten. (James 1:25)

die Vergeßlichkeit, forgetfulness, negligence.

die Vergeudung, squandering, waste, wastefulness, extravagance. (Matt. 26:8)

die Vergewaltigung, assault, violation, rape.

vergießen, 1. *ir.v.a.* to spill, to shed, to pour out. 2. *n.*, **die Vergießung,** spilling, shedding (of blood, etc.). (Gen. 9:6)

vergleichen, 1. *ir.v.a.* to compare, to check, to make a comparison (between things or with a thing); to adjust, to settle (disputes), to reconcile (enemies), to compensate. 2. *v.r.* to come to an arrangement, agreement, or terms; to become reconciled. (Matt. 7:24)

vergotten, 1. *v.n.* to be deified, to become godlike. 2. *v.a., see* **vergöttern.**

vergöttern, *v.a.* to deify; (*fig.*) to idolize, to worship, to adore.

die Vergötterung, deification; adoration, worship, idolatry.

die Vergottung, apotheosis.

vergraben, 1. *ir.v.a.* to bury, to hide. 2. *v.r.* to burrow (of animals); (*fig.*) to hide oneself, to bury oneself (in books). (Amos 9:2)

verhalten, 1. *ir.v.a.* to keep or hold back; to stop, to check; to hold (one's breath); to repress, to suppress, to restrain. 2. *v.r.* to be, to be the case; to act, to behave, to conduct, comport, or demean oneself. 3. *n.* conduct, behavior; procedure; attitude, approach (to a problem). (Acts 17:11)

das Verhältnis (-se), relation, proportion, ratio; (*generally pl.*) (economic) situation, condition, circumstances.

das Verhängnis (-se), fate, destiny; doom, misfortune.

verhärten, 1. *v.a.* to harden, to make hard. 2. *v.n.* (*aux.* s.) to harden, to grow hard; to become obdurate. (Exod. 7:3)

verheeren, *v.a.* to ravage, to devastate, to lay waste. (Isa. 1:7)

verhehlen, *v.a.* (*einem etwas*) to hide, to conceal (from someone). (Ps. 32:5)

verheiraten, 1. *v.a.* to marry, to give in marriage; to perform the marriage ceremony. 2. *v.r.* to marry, to get married.

die Verheiratung, marriage.

verheißen, *ir.v.a.* (*einem etwas*) to promise. (I Kings 8:25) *das verheißene Land,* the Promised Land.

die Verheißung, promise. (Luke 24:49)

verherrlichen, *v.a.* to glorify, to extol, to exalt.

die Verherrlichung, glorification.

verhindern, *v.a.* to hinder, to prevent, to impede. (Rom. 1:13)

verhören, 1. *v.a.* to hear, to try, to question, to interrogate, to examine (an accused person). 2. *v.r.* to hear wrongly, to misunderstand someone's words.

verhüllen, *v.a.* to cover, to veil; to disguise. (Exod. 3:6)

verirren, *v.r. & n.* (*aux.* s.) to go astray, to lose one's way, to err. (Matt. 18:12)

verkaufen, 1. *v.a.* (*einem etwas* or *etwas an einen*) to sell, to dispose of. 2. *v.r.* to sell, to sell oneself. (Gen. 25:31)

der Verkäufer (-), seller, vendor, salesman. (Matt. 21:12)

verkehren, 1. *v.a.* to turn the wrong way, to invert; to turn or change (into), to transform, to convert into; to reverse, to pervert. 2. *v.r.* to change into its opposite, to become reversed. 3. *v.n.* (*aux.* h.) to visit, to come and go. (James 4:9)

verkehrt, *p.p. & adj.* turned the wrong way, reversed, inverted; wrong, perverted, perverse, absurd. (Rom. 1:28)

die Verkehrtheit, perversity, absurdity, folly.

verketzern, *v.a.* to accuse of heresy; (*fig.*) to slander.

die Verketzerung, charge of heresy; slander, abuse.

verkirchlichen, *v.a.* to bring under ecclesiastical control.

verklagen, *v.a.* to sue, to accuse, to inform against. (Matt. 27:13)

verklären, *v.a.* to make radiant; to transfigure; to glorify. (Matt. 17:2)

die Verklärung, transfiguration, glorification, radiance, ecstasy. (see Luke 9:28–36)

verknüpfen, *v.a.* to knot, to tie, to bind, to join, to link, to connect, to combine, to unite; to attach to; to involve. (Acts 8:23)

verkörpern, *v.a.* to embody, to personify, to incarnate, to materialize.

die Verkörperung, embodiment, personification, incarnation.

verkriechen, *ir.v.r.* to crawl away, to sneak off, to hide oneself. (I Sam. 13:6)

verkünden, verkündigen, *v.a.* (*einem etwas*) to announce, to make known, to publish, to proclaim; to preach (the gospel); to pronounce (a judgment). (Gen. 41:25)

die Verkündigung, announcement, publication, proclamation; preaching (of the gospel); prophecy, prediction; pronouncement (of a sentence). (I John 1:5)
Mariä Verkündigung, the Annunciation.

verkürzen, *v.a.* to shorten, to abridge, to curtail, to cut; to lessen, to diminish. (Prov. 10:27)

verlachen, *v.a.* to laugh at, to deride. (Matt. 9:24)

verlangen, 1. *v.a.* to demand, to claim, to ask for, to require, to desire. 2. *v.n.* (*aux.* h.) (with *nach*) to desire, to wish for, to long for, to crave. 3. *n.* request, demand, desire, wish, longing. (Gen. 3:16)

verlassen, 1. *ir.v.a.* to leave, to quit; to relinquish, to give up; to leave behind, to forsake, to abandon, to desert. 2. *v.r.* (*auf etwas*) to rely on, to trust to, to depend upon. 3. *p.p. & adj.* deserted, forsaken, abandoned, lonely. (Gen. 2:24)

verlästern, *v.a.* to slander, to defame, to malign. (Rom. 14:16)

verleugnen, 1. *v.a.* to deny, to disown, to renounce; to act against. 2. *v.r.* (with *nicht*) to reveal itself, to become clear. (Matt. 10:33)
seinen Glauben verleugnen, to renounce one's belief.

verleumden, *v.a.* to slander, to defame, to accuse wrongfully. (Ps. 15:3)

der Verleumder (-), slanderer, backbiter. (Rom. 1:30)

verlieren, 1. *ir.v.a.* to lose, to forfeit, to let slip. 2. *v.n.* (*an*) to fall off, to decline (in value), to suffer loss (of). 3. *v.r.* to get lost, to lose oneself, to lose one's way, to go astray. (Matt. 10:39)

verloben, 1. *v.a.* to betroth (to); *verlobt sein mit . . .* , to be engaged to. . . . 2. *v.r.: sich verloben (mit),* to become engaged (to). (Hos. 2:21)

verlocken, *v.a.* to entice, to mislead, to tempt, to seduce. (Hos. 7:11)

verlogen, *adj.* untruthful. (Isa. 30:9)

verloren, *p.p.* (*of* **verlieren**) *& adj.* lost, forlorn. (John 3:15)

verlöschen, 1. *v.a.* to extinguish; to obliterate, to efface. 2. *ir.v.n.* (*aux.* s.) to be extinguished; to go out, to become extinct, to expire, to die out. (Matt. 25:8)

das Vermächtnis (-se), will, testament; legacy, bequest.

vermahnen, *v.a.* to admonish, to warn, to exhort. (Acts 20:31)

die Vermahnung, admonition, exhortation. (Eph. 6:4)

vermauern, *v.a.* to wall in or up. (Lam. 3:7)

vermengen, 1. *v.a.* to mingle, to mix, to blend; to mix up, to confuse. 2. *v.r.* to meddle (*mit*, with), to be or get mixed up (with) a matter. (Matt. 13:33)

vermessen, 1. *ir.v.a.* to measure; to survey. 2. *v.r.* to make a mistake in measuring; (with gen. or inf. with *zu*) to presume, to venture, to dare. 3. *p.p. & adj.* daring, bold, rash, arrogant. (Rom. 2:19)

die Vermessenheit, boldness, daring, audacity, arrogance. (Deut. 18:22)

vermischen, 1. *v.a.* to mix, to mingle, to blend; to cross; to adulterate. 2. *v.r.* to mix, to mingle, to blend with, to breed, to interbreed. (Luke 13:1)

vermittelt, *p.p. & adj.* mediated.

die Vermittlungstheologie, mediating theology.

vermögen, 1. *ir.v.a.* to be able (to do) or capable (of doing), to have the power or capacity (to do); to have influence (over), to induce, to prevail (upon). 2. *n.* ability, power, capacity; means, fortune, wealth, riches, property. (James 5:16)

vernehmen, 1. *ir.v.a.* to perceive, to become aware of; to understand, to learn, to hear; to examine. 2. *v.r.: sich mit einem vernehmen,* to come to an understanding with someone. 3. *n.: dem Vernehmen nach,* according to report, from what one hears. (Matt. 16:9)

vernichten, *v.a.* to annihilate, to destroy, to demolish, to exterminate, to overthrow; to disappoint (hopes); to annul, to cancel, to nullify, to revoke, to abolish.

die Vernichtung, destruction, annihilation, extermination; abolition.

die Vernunft, reason, intellect, intelligence; understanding, judgment, discernment, common sense.

die Vernunfterkenntnis, conceptual knowledge (Kant).

der Vernunftglaube, rationalism.

vernünftig, *adj.* reasonable, sensible, rational, logical; wise, judicious. (Acts 26:25)

die Vernünftigkeit, reasonableness, rationality; good sense.

der Vernünftler (-), sophist, casuist.

das Vernunftwesen, rational being.

die Veröffentlichung (-en), publication; public announcement.

verordnen, *v.a.* to order, to prescribe; to decree, to enact; to ordain, to establish, to institute. (Acts 10:42)

der Verrat, treason; treachery; betrayal (of).
Verrat an einem begehen, to betray someone.

verraten, 1. *ir.v.a.* to betray, to disclose, to reveal; to manifest. 2. *v.r.* to betray or commit oneself. (Matt. 10:4)

der Verräter (-), traitor, betrayer, informer. (Matt. 26:48)

verringern, 1. *v.a.* to diminish, to lessen, to reduce. 2. *v.r.* to diminish, to decrease. (Amos 8:5)

verrostet, *p.p. & adj.* rusty, rusted. (James 5:3)

verrücken, *v.a.* to displace, to shift, to remove; to confuse, to unsettle, to disturb, to disarrange. (Prov. 22:28)

der Vers (-e), verse, poetry; verse (of the Bible).

versammeln, 1. *v.a.* to assemble, to bring together, to gather, to collect; to convoke, to convene. 2. *v.r.* to meet, to assemble, to come together. (Rev. 19:17)

die Versammlung (-en), assembly, gathering, meeting, congress, convention; company, congregation. (James 2:2)

versäuern, *v.a.* to spoil, to embitter; to sour. (I Cor. 5:6)

versäumen, *v.a.* to neglect, to omit, to miss, to let slip. (Heb. 4:1)

verschaffen, *v.a.* (*einem etwas*) to get, to obtain, to secure; to supply, to provide (someone with something). (Jonah 2:1)

verscheiden, 1. *ir.v.n.* (*aux. s.*) to pass away, to die, to expire. 2. *n.* death, decease. (Matt. 27:50)

verschließen, *ir.v.a.* to close, to shut, to lock; to block, to obstruct. (Rev. 20:3)

verschlingen, *ir.v.a.* to swallow (down or up), to gulp down, to devour. (Rev. 10:9)

verschlucken, 1. *v.a.* to swallow. 2. *v.r.* to swallow the wrong way, to choke. (Matt. 23:24)

verschmachten, *v.n.* (*aux.* s.) to languish, to faint, to die (*vor*, of). (Gen. 31:40)

verschmähen, *v.a.* to disdain, to scorn, to despise, to reject. (Ps. 22:25)

verschnitten, *p.p. & adj.* castrated; badly cut. (Matt. 19:12)

der Verschnittene (-n), eunuch.

verschonen, *v.a.* to spare, to exempt (from). (Gen. 22:12)

verschulden, 1. *v.a.* to be guilty of, to be the cause of. 2. *v.r.* (*an einem* or *wider einen*) to act wrongly (towards someone). 3. *n.* fault, blame. (Gen. 42:21)

verschütten, *v.a.* to fill or choke up with earth or rubble; to spill; to bury (alive), to overwhelm. (Matt. 9:17)

verschweigen, *ir.v.a.* (*einem etwas*) to keep secret, to conceal (from); to suppress. (I Sam. 3:17)

verschwinden, 1. *ir.v.n.* (*aux.* s.) to vanish, to disappear; to be lost, to pass away. 2. *n.* disappearance. (James 4:14)

verschwören, 1. *ir.v.a.* to forswear, to renounce. 2. *v.r.* to plot; to swear, to protest on oath, to bind oneself by an oath. (Acts 23:12)

versehen, 1. *ir.v.a.* to provide, to furnish, to supply with; to discharge or perform (a duty); to administer the sacrament; to do wrong. 2. *v.r.* to equip, to supply or furnish oneself (with); to be mistaken, to be in error, to go wrong (*in* with dat., about); to expect, to look for. 3. *n.* error, mistake. (Matt. 24:50)

versengen, *v.a.* to singe, to scorch, to parch. (Dan. 3:27)

versenken, *v.r.* to meditate, to contemplate.

die Versenkung, contemplation, meditation; sinking, depression.

versetzen, 1. *v.a.* to transfer, to remove, to transplant, to move up, to advance, to promote; to obstruct, to block; to pledge, to pawn; (with *mit*) to treat, to mix, to temper. 2. *v.r.* to change its place, to shift; to curdle. 3. *v.a. & n.* (*aux.* h.) to answer, to reply, to rejoin. (Luke 17:6)

versiegeln, *v.a.* to seal (up), to affix one's seal to. (Dan. 12:9)

versiegen, *v.n.* (*aux.* s.) to dry up; to be exhausted. (Ps. 107:33)

versinken, 1. *ir.v.n.* (*aux.* s.) to sink, to be swallowed up; to founder, to go down (of ships). 2. *n.* sinking; foundering; immersion, submersion. (Exod. 15:4)

versinnbildlichen, *v.a.* to symbolize, to represent.

die Versinnbildlichung, symbolization.

versöhnen, 1. *v.a.* to reconcile, to conciliate, to appease, to atone. 2. *v.r.* to become reconciled, to make one's peace (with). (Rom. 5:10)

die Versöhnung, reconciliation, appeasement, atonement. (Rom. 5:11)

der Versöhnungsbund, covenant of grace.

der Versöhnungstag, Day of Atonement, Yom Kippur.

versorgen, *v.a.* (*einem etwas* or *einen mit etwas*) to provide, to supply, to furnish (with); to provide for, to establish, to settle (in life); to take care of, to look after, to care for, to nurse, to maintain. (I Kings 17:4)

verspotten, *v.a.* to scoff, to mock or jeer at, to ridicule. (Matt. 20:19)

versprechen, 1. *ir.v.a.* (*einem etwas*) to promise (someone something or something to someone); to give one's word; to give promise of (something). 2. *v.r.* to make a slip of the tongue; to be or become engaged. 3. *n.* slip of the tongue. (Luke 22:6)

der Verstand, understanding, mind, intellect, intelligence; comprehension, judgment; sense, meaning. (Rev. 13:18)

der Verstandesbegriff, category (Kant).

verständig, *adj.* intelligent; sensible, reasonable, rational; wise, prudent, cautious, judicious. (Gen. 41:33)

das Verständnis, comprehension, understanding, intelligence; sympathy. (Luke 24:45)

das Versteck (-e), hiding place; ambush.

verstecken, 1. *v.a.* to hide, to conceal, to secrete. 2. *v.r.* to hide, to get hidden. (Gen. 3:8)

verstehen, 1. *v.a.* to understand, to comprehend, to grasp, to know well, to know (how). 2. *v.r.* to understand one another, to agree. (Gen. 11:7)

verstocken, *v.n.* (*aux.* s.) to grow hard, obdurate, or impenitent. (Rom. 2:5)

verstopfen, *v.a.* to plug up, to choke, to clog, to obstruct, to block. (Gen. 8:2)

verstorben, *p.p. & adj.* dead, deceased, late.

der Verstorbene (-n), the deceased.

verstören, *v.a.* to disturb, to interfere (with), to trouble, to confuse, to upset. (Acts 8:3)

verstoßen, 1. *ir.v.n.* (*aux.* h.) (*gegen*) to give offense to, to offend against, to transgress. 2. *v.a.* to push away, to cast off; to repel, to repulse, to reject; to divorce (a wife); to disown, to disinherit (a son, etc.); to expel. (Rom. 11:1)

verstreuen, *v.a.* to scatter, to disperse, to strew about. (Deut. 30:3)

verstricken, 1. *v.a.* to entangle; *in einer Sache verstrickt sein,* to be involved in an affair; *in eine Sache verstrickt werden,* to get mixed up or entangled in something. 2. *v.r.* to get entangled, to be caught. (Ps. 9:17)

verstummen, *v.n.* (*aux.* s.) to grow dumb; to become silent. (Matt. 22:12)

der Versuch (-e), attempt, trial, test, experiment; proof.

versuchen, 1. *v.a.* to attempt; to test; to tempt, to entice; to taste. 2. *v.r.: sich in etwas versuchen,* to have experience of something. (Matt. 4:1)

der Versucher (-), tempter; seducer; the devil. (Matt. 4:3)

die Versuchung (-en), temptation. (Matt. 6:13)
in Versuchung führen, to lead into temptation; *in Versuchung fallen,* to fall into temptation.

versündigen, *v.r.* to sin (*an,* with dat., against), to do wrong. (Dan. 9:8)

die Versündigung, sin, offense.
Versündigung an Gott, sin against God.

verteidigen, 1. *v.a.* to defend; to justify, to vindicate, to uphold, to support. 2. *v.r.* to stand up for one's rights, to defend, justify, or vindicate oneself. (Job 13:7)

vertilgen, *v.a.* to destroy, to annihilate, to exterminate, to blot out, to extinguish; to consume. (Acts 3:19)

die Vertilgung, extermination, destruction.

der Vertrag (¨-e), treaty, contract, agreement, covenant, settlement, accord. (Isa. 28:15)

vertragen, 1. *ir.v.a.* to bear, to stand, to endure, to suffer, to tolerate; to displace. 2. *v.r.* to agree, to harmonize, to be consistent. (I Cor. 13:7)

vertrauen, 1. *v.n.* (*aux.* h.) (dat. or *auf* with acc.) to trust or confide (in), to have confidence (in), to put one's trust (in), to rely upon. 2. *v.a.* (*einem etwas*) to confide, to entrust. 3. *v.r.* (*with dat.*) to confide (in), to open one's heart (to). 4. *n.* confidence, trust; reliance. (Matt. 27:43)

die Vertrauensseligkeit, blind faith, gullibility.

vertreiben, *ir.v.a.* to drive away, to expel, to banish; to disperse, to scatter; to distribute, to sell, to retail (goods). (Mark 16:18)

vertreten, *ir.v.a.* to replace, to represent, to act as substitute; to plead or intercede for (someone); to defend, to advocate; to obstruct, to block. (Rom. 8:26)

der Vertreter (-), representative, substitute; intercessor, advocate, champion.

die Vertretung, representation, substitution; intercession, advocacy, defense.

vertrocknen, 1. *v.n.* (*aux.* s.) to dry up, to wither. 2. *v.a.* to desiccate. (Gen. 8:7)

verunreinigen, *v.a.* to dirty, to contaminate, to defile, to pollute. (Matt. 15:11)

die Verursachung, causation, cause.

verurteilen, *v.a.* to condemn, to convict, to sentence. (Rom. 2:12)
einen zum Tode verurteilen, to sentence a person to death.

verwahren, 1. *v.a.* to keep, to secure; *vor* or *gegen etwas verwahren,* to preserve from, to secure against something. 2. *v.r.* (*gegen*) to take precautions (against), to resist. (Matt. 27:64)

verwandeln, 1. *v.a.* to change, to convert, to transform, to transfigure, to metamorphose; to commute (penalties, etc.). 2. *v.r.* to change, to alter, to be converted, to be transformed, to be transfigured. (Exod. 14:5)

die Verwandlung, alteration, change; transfiguration; conversion, transformation, glorification, metamorphosis, transubstantiation; commutation (of a punishment).

verwandt, *adj.* related, kindred; like, similar; congenial.

der (die) Verwandte (-n), relative, relation. (Ps. 55:14)

die Verwandtschaft, relationship, kinship; sympathy, congeniality.

verwandtschaftlich, *adj.* kindred, allied; congenial.

verwehen, 1. *v.a.* to blow away or about, to scatter. 2. *v.n.* (*aux.* s.) to blow about or away, to drift, to be scattered. (Isa. 41:16)

verwelken, *v.n.* (*aux.* s.) to fade, to wither, to wilt. (Matt. 13:6)

verweltlichen, 1. *v.a.* to secularize. 2. *v.n.* (*aux.* s.) to become worldly.

die Verweltlichung, secularization.

verwerfen, 1. *ir.v.a.* to throw away, to discard; (*usually fig.*) to reject, to refuse, to disavow, to condemn, to repudiate. 2. *v.r.* to throw badly, to miss (the mark); to warp. 3. *v.n.* to bear (young) prematurely. (Ps. 66:20)

verwerflich, *adj.* objectionable, reprehensible, thoroughly bad. (I Cor. 9:27)

die Verwerfung, rejection, refusal; censure, condemnation. (Rom. 11:15)

verwesen, 1. *v.a.* to administer, to manage, to deal with on someone's behalf. 2. *v.n.* (*aux.* s.) to putrefy, to decompose, to decay, to rot. (Ps. 16:10)

verweslich, *adj.* perishable, corruptible, liable to decay. (I Cor. 15:42)

die Verwesung, decay, decomposition, putrefaction; management, administration. (Acts 2:27)

verwirren, *ir.v.a.* to tangle, to entangle, to disarrange; to complicate; to confuse, to embarrass, to bewilder, to perplex. (Gen. 11:7)

verwöhnen, 1. *v.a.* to spoil, to pamper. 2. *v.r.* to (over)indulge oneself, to allow oneself to be pampered. (Ecclesiasticus 30:8)

verwunden, *v.a.* to wound, to injure, to hurt. (Isa. 51:9)

verwundern, 1. *v.a.* to surprise, to astonish. 2. *v.r.* to be astonished, to be surprised, to wonder (*über* with acc., at). 3. *v.imp.: es verwundert mich,* it surprises me, I wonder. (Rev. 13:3)

die Verwünschung, curse, malediction.

verwüsten, *v.a.* to lay waste, to devastate, to ruin, to destroy. (Isa. 5:5)

die Verwüstung, devastation, destruction. (Matt. 24:15)

verzagen, *v.n.* (*aux.* s.) to despair (*an einer Sache,* of something), to lose heart or courage, to be despondent. (Deut. 1:28)

verzehnten, *v.a.* to pay tithe on. (Matt. 23:23)

verzehren, 1. *v.a.* to consume, to eat up; to use up, to waste, to spend, to expend (money). 2. *v.r.* to be consumed (*vor,* with); to fret, to waste away. (Rev. 20:9)

verzehrend, *pr.p. & adj.* (all-)consuming, burning (passion). (Exod. 24:17)

verzeihen, *ir.v.a.* (*einem etwas*) to forgive, to pardon, to excuse; to remit (sins); to pass over (a fault). (Ps. 19:13)

die Verzeihung, pardon, forgiveness, remission (of sins).

verziehen, 1. *ir.v.a.* to distort, to drag, to pull, to contract; to train badly, to spoil (children); to delay. 2. *v.r.* to draw away, to withdraw, to disperse, to be dispersed, to vanish, to pass away, to disappear; to be twisted. 3. *v.n.* (*aux.* s.) to move, to remove, to go away. 4. *v.n.* (*aux.* h.) & *r.* to delay, to go slow, to hesitate. (Exod. 32:1)

der Verzug (-̈e), delay, postponement; darling, pet, spoiled child. (II Peter 3:9)

verzweifeln, *v.n.* (*aux.* s. & h.) to despair; to give up hope, to be despondent.

verzweifelt, *adj.* despairing, desperate.

die Vesper (-n), vesper(s), evensong.

das Vesperbild, Pietà, the virgin with the dead body of Christ.

der Vespergesang, evensong.

die Vesperglocke, vesper bell.

die Vesperstunde, die Vesperzeit, evening time, afternoon; vespers.

das Vestibül (-e), vestibule, hall.

das Vieh, cattle, beast, livestock. (Gen. 1:24)

viehisch, *adj.* brutal, bestial. (Dan. 4:13)

viel, *adj.* (comp. *mehr,* sup. *meist*) much, a great deal, a lot; *pl.* many. (Exod. 1:7)

viele, *pl. adj.* many. (John 6:9)

die Vielgötterei, polytheism.

vielmehr, 1. *adv.* rather, much more. 2. *conj.* rather, on the contrary. (Heb. 12:9)

vier, *num. adj.* four. (Gen. 2:10)

vierfältig, *adj.* fourfold, four, quadruple. (Luke 19:8)

der Vierfürst, tetrarch. (Matt. 14:1)

vierfüßig, *adj.* four-footed. (Rom. 1:23)

vierte, *num. adj.* fourth. (Exod. 20:5) *das vierte Gebot,* the fourth commandment.

vierzehn, 1. *num. adj.* fourteen. 2. *f.* the number fourteen. (II Cor. 12:2)

vierzehnt, *adj.* fourteenth. (Acts 27:33)

vierzig, 1. *num. adj.* forty. 2. *f.* the number forty. (Gen. 7:4)

die Vigilie, vigil; eve (of a feast).

der Vikar (-e), curate; substitute.

die Vision, dream, vision.

visionär, *m. & adj.* visionary.

der Vogel (⁻), bird. (Gen. 1:26)

die Vogeldeuterei, augury.

der Vogler (-), fowler, bird catcher. (Ps. 124:7)

das Vokabular (-e), vocabulary.

das Volk (⁻er), people, nation, tribe, race; troops, men; the common people, the crowd. (Gen. 11:6)

das Volksbuch (⁻er), popular prose romance; chapbook.

der Volksglaube, popular belief.

die Volksmeinung, public opinion.

der Volksmund, vernacular.

die Volksstimme, public opinion.

voll, *adj.* (*comp.* -er, *sup.* -st) (with gen. or *von*) full, filled; complete, whole, entire; rounded. (Matt. 12:34)

vollbringen, *ir.v.a.* (*insep.*) to accomplish, to achieve, to execute, to fulfil, to carry out, to complete, to consummate; to perpetrate. (Rom. 7:18) *es ist vollbracht,* it is finished.

vollenden, 1. *v.a.* (*insep.*) (*aux.* h.) to bring to a close, to finish, to terminate; to achieve, to accomplish, to complete, to consummate, to perfect. 2. *v.r. & n.* (*aux.* h.) to die. (Gen. 2:1)

der Vollender, perfecter (King James: finisher). (Heb. 12:2)

die Völlerei, intemperance, gluttony. (Isa. 5:22)

vollführen, *v.a.* (*insep.*) to carry out, to execute. (Phil. 1:6)

völlig, 1. *adj.* full, total, entire, complete, thorough. 2. *adv.* quite, utterly. (Rom. 15:13)

vollkommen, *adj.* perfect, consummate, full, complete, entire, finished. (Matt. 5:48)

die Vollkommenheit, perfection, completeness. (Col. 3:14)

von, *prep.* (*dat.*) of; from; by; in; on, upon; about; concerning. *von dannen,* from there (Matt. 5:26); *von hinnen,* hence, from here (Matt. 17:20); *von nun an,* henceforth (Matt. 26:29).

vor, 1. *prep.* (*with dat. when it indicates condition or rest; with acc. when it indicates movement or change of condition*) before, previous or prior to (time); before, in front of, ahead of (place); in presence of; for, on account of, through, because of, with (joy, etc.); from or against (with verbs of protection, warning, etc.); in preference to, more than, above. 2. *adv.* only in *nach wie vor,* as always, as ever, still, now as before. 3. *sep. prefix* before, ahead of, formerly, front. *vor Christi Geburt,* B(efore) C(hrist); *vor Gott,* in the presence of God, in the eyes of God.

vorangehen, *ir.v.n.* (*aux.* s.) to go before, to precede; to take the lead, to lead the way. (Exod. 33:14)

vorausbestimmen, *v.a.* to predestine.

die Vorausbestimmung, predetermination, predestination.

die Voraussetzung (-en), hypothesis, presupposition.

vorbehalten, *ir.v.a.* (*einem etwas*) to hold or keep in reserve, to withhold, to reserve (to), to make reservations. (Gen. 27:36)

vorbeigehen, 1. *ir.v.n.* (*aux.* s.) (*an einem*) to go or pass by, to go past, to pass (someone); *daran vorbeigehen,* to overlook or ignore it, to pass over it in silence. 2. *n.: im Vorbeigehen,* in passing. (Luke 11:42)

vorbeten, *v.a. & n.* (*aux.* h.) to repeat or recite (a prayer), to lead in prayer.

der Vorbeter (-), cantor, prayer leader.

das Vorbild (-er), model, example, pattern, standard, original. (Exod. 25:9)

vorbilden, *v.a.* to prepare, to train (*zu,* for), to represent, to typify, to compare. (Mark 4:30)

vorbringen, *ir.v.a.* to bring forward or up, to produce, to propose, to allege; to state, to utter, to express, to make (excuses). (Jer. 7:16)

vorchristlich, *adj.* pre-Christian.

vorehelich, *adj.* prenuptial, premarital.

die Voreltern, (*pl.*) ancestors, forefathers. (Gen. 49:26)

vorenthalten, *ir.v.a. sep. & insep.* (*but inf. only sep. & p.p. only insep.*) (*einem etwas*) to withhold, to keep back (from someone); to detain. (Deut. 24:14)

der Vorfahr (-en), ancestor, forefather, progenitor.

der Vorgang ($\ddot{}$e), event.

der Vorgänger (-), forerunner, predecessor.

vorgehen, 1. *ir.v.n.* (*aux.* s.) to go too fast (of watches, etc.); to go before, to precede, to lead, to go first, to take the lead; to advance, to march (*auf,* upon); to proceed, to act; to take steps or measures; (*with dat.*) to take precedence (over), to excel, to transcend; to happen, to occur, to go on, to take place. 2. *n.* advance; procedure, proceedings. (Matt. 21:9)

vorhaben, 1. *ir.v.a.* to have before one; to have on, to wear; to have in mind or in view, to design, to propose; to be occupied with, to be busy; to rebuke, to chide, to reprimand. 2. *n.* intention, design, plan, project, purpose, intent. (Gen. 41:25)

vorhalten, 1. *ir.v.a.* (*einem etwas*) to hold (something) up to, out to, out for, before, or in front of (someone); to charge or reproach (someone) with (something). 2. *v.n.* (*aux.* h.) to hold out, to endure, to stand, to last. (Acts 17:31)

vorhanden, *adj.* on hand, in stock; present, existing, existent. (II Thess. 2:2)

der Vorhang ($\ddot{}$e), curtain. (Exod. 26:31)

die Vorhaut, foreskin. (Jer. 4:4)

vorher, *adv. & sep. prefix* beforehand, in front, in advance; before, previously.

vorherbestimmen, *v.a.* to determine beforehand; to preordain; to predestine.

die Vorherbestimmung, predestination, predetermination.

der Vorhof ($\ddot{}$e), outer court, forecourt, vestibule, porch. (Mark 14:68)

vorig, *adj.* former, preceding, previous, last. (Deut. 4:32)

vorkommen, 1. *ir.v.n.* (*aux.* s.) to come forth; (*bei*) to visit, to call (on), to drop in (on); (*with dat.*) to seem, to appear, to happen, to occur, to take place; to surpass. 2. *n.* presence, existence. (Matt. 18:24)

vorlängst, *adv.* long ago, long since. (Isa. 44:8)

der Vorläufer (-), forerunner, precursor. (Heb. 6:20)

vorlegen, 1. *v.a.* to put or lay before, to serve (food), to put on, to apply; (*einem etwas*) to display, to show, to exhibit, to produce, to offer, to submit. 2. *v.n.* (*aux.* h.) to eat heartily. (Exod. 19:7)

vormals, *adv.* formerly, once upon a time. (Ps. 85:2)

der Vormund ($\ddot{}$er), guardian, trustee. (Gal. 4:2)

vorn, 1. *adv.* in front; in the front; at the beginning, before; *vorn und hinten,* before and behind. 2. *n.: das Vorn und Hinten,* the front and the back. (Phil. 3:13)

der Vorname (-n), first name, Christian name.

vornehm, *adj.* of high rank, aristocratic, noble, grand, elegant, fashionable, refined; distinguished, eminent, principal, chief. (Matt. 22:36)

vornehmlich, *adv.* particularly, especially, mainly, chiefly, above all. (Rom. 1:16)

der Vorrang, preeminence, superiority, precedence, priority. (Col. 1:18)

der Vorrat ($\ddot{}$e), store, stock, provision, supply, reserve. (Gen. 41:35)

vorrücken, 1. *v.a.* to put, move, or push forward; (*einem etwas*) to reproach or charge (someone with something). 2. *v.n.* (*aux.* s.) to advance, to move forward, to progress, to move or push on. (Rom. 13:12)

der Vorsatz (ˉe), design, project, purpose, resolution, plan, intention; premeditation. (Rom. 8:28)

vorsehen, 1. *ir.v.a.* to consider, to provide for. 2. *v.r.* to take care, to be cautious or careful, to be mindful of, to be on one's guard, to mind, to beware (of). (Matt. 7:15)

die Vorsehung, providence. (Acts 2:23)

vorsetzen, *v.a.* to set, place, or put before; (*einem etwas*) to serve (food); to offer; to set over (someone else). (Rom. 1:13)
sich (dat.) *einen Zweck vorsetzen,* to resolve to do a thing, to determine upon something; *jemanden einem andern vorsetzen,* to set a person over another, to prefer a person to another.

vorsichtig, *adj.* cautious, careful, prudent, guarded, discreet. (Eph. 5:15)

vorstehen, *ir.v.n.* (*aux.* h.) to project, to protrude, to overhang; (*with dat.*) to preside over, to oversee, to manage, to direct, to administer. (I Tim. 3:4)

der Vorsteher (-), principal, chief, administrator, director, manager, superintendent, supervisor; headmaster; superior (of a convent); warden. (I Sam. 19:20)

vorstellen, 1. *v.a.* to place before, to put in front of; to put forward, to advance; (*einem etwas*) to present, to introduce; to demonstrate, to represent; to mean, to signify; to explain; to protest; (with dat.

sich) to imagine, to suppose, to conceive. 2. *v.r.* to go or come forward; to introduce oneself, to make oneself known. (Acts 12:4)

die Vorstellung, introduction; performance; complaint; imagination, idea, notion, conception.

der Vorteil (-e), advantage, benefit, interest, profit, gain. (Rom. 3:1)

vortragen, *ir.v.a.* to carry or bring forward; to carry before or in front of; to explain, to expound; to propose, to speak (of); to recite, to perform, to execute, to express (one's opinion); to give or deliver (a speech). (Luke 10:8)

vorübergehen, 1. *ir.v.n.* (*aux.* s.) to pass, to pass by, to go past or by; to pass over, to neglect; to pass away, to be over. 2. *n.: im Vorübergehen,* in passing (*also fig.*); by the way, incidentally. (Exod. 33:19)

vorüberziehen, *ir.v.n.* (*aux.* s.) to pass (by). (Job 30:15)

der Vorwand (ˉe), pretext, pretense, excuse, plea. (Phil. 1:18)

der Vorwitz, curiosity, inquisitiveness; forwardness, impertinence, pertness. (II Thess. 3:11)

vorwitzig, *adj.* inquisitive, prying; forward, pert, impertinent. (Acts 19:19)

vorzeiten, *adv.* formerly, in time past. (Heb. 1:1)

die Votivmesse, votive mass.

vulgär, *adj.* vulgar, common, base, coarse.

die Vulgata, Vulgate.

Ww

die Waage (-n), scales, balance, weighing machine.

wach, *adj.* awake; on the alert, wide awake, brisk; (*fig.*) alive. (Rev. 3:2)

die Wache (-n), guard, watch, watchman, sentinel, sentry; guardhouse; police station. (Mark 6:48)

wachen, *v.n.* (*aux.* h.) to sit up; to be awake, to be on guard, to keep watch. (Matt. 24:42)

der Wacholder (-), juniper. (I Kings 19:4)

das Wachs (-e), wax. (Ps. 22:15)

wachsen, 1. *ir.v.n.* (*aux.* s.) to grow, to sprout, to come up (of plants); to extend, to increase, to thrive. 2. *n.* growing, growth, increase, development. (Gen. 24:60)

die Wachtel (-n), quail. (Exod. 16:13)

der Wächter (-), watchman, guard, caretaker, attendant, keeper. (II Kings 9:17)

wacker, 1. *adj.* valiant, brave, gallant. 2. *adv.* bravely; well, soundly, thoroughly; heartily, lustily. (Phil. 4:10)

die Waffe (-n), weapon, arm. (I Sam. 17:54)

die Waffenrüstung (-en), armor; armament; warlike preparation.

der Waffenträger (-), armorbearer. (I Sam. 14:1)

die Wage (-n), *former spelling of* **die Waage,** scales, balance, weighing machine. (Rev. 6:5)

wagen, 1. *v.a. & n.* to venture, to risk, to dare, to presume, to attempt. 2. *v.r.: sich an eine Sache wagen,* to venture upon something. (Matt. 22:46)

der Wagen (-), vehicle; van, truck, car; wagon, cart, carriage, coach, chariot. (Gen. 41:43)

wägen, *ir.v.a.* to weigh; to poise, to balance, (*fig.*) to ponder, to consider. (Dan. 5:27)

die Wagenburg (-en), barricade of wagons, laager. (Luke 19:43)

die Wahl (-en), choice, selection; option; alternative. (Rom. 9:11)

wählen, *v.a.* to choose, to select, to pick out; to elect, to vote. (Acts 15:40)

der Wahn, illusion, hallucination; delusion, error, fancy; madness, folly. (Luke 3:15)

das Wahnbild, hallucination, delusion, vision, phantom.

wähnen, *v.a. & n.* (*aux.* h.) to think, to believe, to imagine, to fancy, to suppose, to presume. (Matt. 5:17)

der Wahnglaube, superstition, false belief.

wahnhaft, *adj.* illusory.

der Wahnsinn, madness, insanity, craziness, frenzy.

wahnsinnig, *adj.* mad, insane, crazy, frantic.

der Wahnsinnige (-n), madman, lunatic.

wahr, *adj.* true, real, genuine, sincere, correct, veritable, proper. (John 5:31) *so wahr mir Gott helfe!* so help me God!

währen, *v.n.* (*aux.* h.) to last, to continue, to endure, to hold out. (Deut. 4:40)

wahrhaftig, 1. *adj.* true, actual, genuine, real, truthful, sincere, veracious. 2. *adv.* truly, really, surely, actually, indeed. (Rev. 3:14)

die Wahrheit, truth; reality, fact. (Rom. 1:18)

der Wahrheitsbeweis, factual evidence.

der Wahrheitseifer, zeal for truth.

wahrheitsgemäß, wahrheitsgetreu, *adj.* faithful, true, truthful, in accordance with the truth.

die Wahrheitsliebe, love of truth.

wahrheitsliebend, *adj.* truthful, veracious.

der **Wahrheitssucher** (-), seeker after truth.

wahrlich, *adv.* truly, surely, verily, indeed. (Matt. 6:2)

die **Wahrmachung,** verification, fulfilment.

wahrnehmbar, *adj.* perceptible.

wahrnehmen, *ir.v.a.* (*sep.*) to notice, to observe, to perceive; to look after, to protect, to give attention to; to profit by or from, to make use of, to avail oneself of. (Luke 12:24)

die **Wahrnehmung,** perception, observation; maintenance; protection.

die **Wahrnehmungskraft, das Wahrnehmungsvermögen,** power of perception or observation; perceptive faculty.

wahrsagen, *v.a. & n.* (*aux.* h.) (*sep. & insep.*) (*with dat.*) to prophesy, to predict, to foretell; to tell fortunes. (Acts 16:16)

der **Wahrsager** (-), soothsayer, fortuneteller, prophet. (Gen. 41:8)

die **Wahrsagerei,** soothsaying, divination; fortunetelling.

der **Wahrsagergeist,** spirit of divination. (Acts 16:16)

die **Wahrsagung,** prophecy, prediction.

die **Wahrscheinlichkeit,** probability, likelihood, plausibility.

der **Wahrtraum,** prophetic dream, dream destined to come true.

das **Wahrzeichen,** distinctive mark, token, sign; landmark.

der **Waise** (-n), orphan. (Exod. 22:21)

das **Waisenhaus** (⁼er), orphanage.

der **Waisenknabe** (-n), orphan boy.

die **Waisenmutter,** matron of an orphanage.

der **Waisenvater,** superintendent of an orphanage.

der **Wald** (⁼er), wood, forest, woodland. (James 3:5)

der **Walfisch** (-e), whale. (Gen. 1:21)

der **Walkmüller** (-), fuller. (II Kings 18:17)

der **Wall** (⁼e), rampart, mound, bank, embankment, dam, dike. (II Kings 19:32)

wallen, *v.n.* (*aux.* s.) to travel, to wander; to go on a pilgrimage. (I Peter 1:17)

der **Waller** (-), pilgrim; wanderer.

der **Wallfahrer** (-), pilgrim.

die **Wallfahrt** (-en), pilgrimage. (Gen. 47:9)

wallfahr(t)en, *v.n.* (*insep.*) (*aux.* s.) to go on or make a pilgrimage.

der **Wallfahrtsort** (-e), place of pilgrimage.

die **Walpurgisnacht,** Walpurgis Night.

walten, 1. *v.n.* (*aux.* h.) to rule, to govern, to hold the reins of government; (*with gen.*) to carry out, to execute; (*über* with dat. or acc.) to control, to manage; *schalten und walten,* to have complete authority, to rule, to command. 2. *n.* rule, government. (Ps. 103:11) *das walte Gott!* God grant it! amen! *das Walten Gottes,* God's ruling, God's ordinances.

wälzen, 1. *v.a.* to roll, to turn about, to rotate. 2. *v.r.* to roll, to wallow, to welter; to revolve. 3. *n.* rolling. (Matt. 27:60)

die **Wand** (⁼e), wall (of a room), partition, screen; side, cheek, coat, (rock) face. (I Sam. 18:11)

der **Wandel,** change, alteration, mutation; mode of life, conduct, behavior, habits; trade, commerce. (I Peter 1:15) *Gottes Wege sind ohne Wandel,* God's way is perfect.

die **Wandelbarkeit,** changeability, fickleness.

wandeln, 1. *v.a. & v.r.* to change, to convert, to turn (*in,* into). 2. *v.n.* (*aux.* h. & s.) to go, to walk, to wander, to travel; to live. (Mark 6:48)

der **Wanderer** (-), wanderer, traveler, hiker, pedestrian. (Prov. 24:34)

wandern, *v.n.* (*aux.* s.) to travel (on foot), to go, to walk, to wander. (Ps. 23:4)

der **Wanderprediger** (-), evangelist, itinerant preacher.

die **Wanderschaft,** traveling; travels, journey, trip.

die **Wandlung,** change, alteration, metamorphosis; transubstantiation.

die **Wandlungslehre,** dogma of transubstantiation.

die **Wange** (-n), cheek. (Isa. 50:6)

wankelmütig, *adj.* fickle, changeable, inconsistent. (James 4:8)

wanken, *v.n.* (*aux.* h. & s.) to stagger, to reel, to totter; to waver, to hesitate. (Isa. 28:7)

179

wann, 1. *adv.* when; *seit wann?* since when? how long? 2. *conj.* when. (Matt. 24:3)

der Wanst (ˉe), belly, paunch. (Job 15:27)

das Wappen (-), coat of arms.

wappnen, *v.a.* to arm. (Luke 11:21)

die Ware (-n), article, commodity; (*pl.*) goods, wares, merchandise. (Rev. 18:11)

warm, *adj.* (comp. *wärmer,* sup. *wärmst*) warm; hot. (Rev. 3:15)

wärmen, 1. *v.a.* to warm, to heat; to make warm or hot. 2. *v.r.* to warm oneself, to bask. (Mark 14:54)

warnen, *v.a.* (*vor* with dat.) to warn, to caution (against). (Ezek. 3:17)

der Warnruf (-e), warning cry.

die Warnung (-en), warning; caution, admonition. (I Cor. 10:11)

warum, *adv. & conj.* why, for what reason? wherefore. (Gen. 3:13)

waschen, *ir.v.a. & n.* (*aux.* h.) to wash, to launder. (Gen. 49:11)

die Waschung (-en), washing, ablution; wash, lotion.

das Wasser (-), water. (Gen. 1:2)

der Wasserbach (ˉe), river of water. (Ps. 1:3)

das Wasserbad, washing of water. (Eph. 5:26)

der Wasserbecher (-), cruse of water. (I Sam. 26:11)

der Wasserbrunnen (-), fountain of water. (Rev. 7:17)

die Wasserflut (-en), flood of great water. (Ps. 32:6)

der Wasserkrug (ˉe), waterpot. (John 2:6)

die Wasserleitung (-en), aqueduct, canal; water main, water supply. (II Kings 18:17)

wässern, 1. *v.a.* to water, to irrigate; to soak; to dilute. 2. *v.n.* (*aux.* h.) to water. (Gen. 2:10)

wasserreich, *adj.* well watered; of high humidity. (Gen. 13:10)

der Wasserschlauch (ˉe), water hose. (Job 38:37)

wassersüchtig, *adj.* dropsical, having dropsy. (Luke 14:2)

weben, 1. *reg. & ir.v.a. & n.* to weave. 2. *reg. v.n.* (*aux.* h.) to move, to be active; to wave, to float. (Acts 17:28)

in Ihm leben, weben und sind wir, in Him we live and move and have our being.

der Weber (-), weaver. (Isa. 38:12)

der Weberbaum, weaver's beam, warp beam, yarn roller. (I Sam. 17:7)

der Wechsel (-), change, alteration; succession, turn, alternation; variation, fluctuation; exchange. (James 1:17)

die Wechselbank (-en), bank. (Luke 19:23)

der Wechsler (-), moneychanger. (Matt. 21:12)

wecken, 1. *v.a.* to wake, to waken, to awaken, to rouse. 2. *n.* waking; awakening. (Acts 12:7)

der Weg (-e), way, road, path, course, route, passage; process, manner, means; walk, business. (Gen. 18:19)

weg, 1. *adv., part., & sep. prefix* away, gone, lost, far off, off. 2. *int.: weg da!* be off! get out! (John 19:15)

der Wegbereiter (-), pioneer, forerunner.

wegführen, *v.a.* to lead away, to carry off. (Exod. 7:5)

weggehen, *ir.v.n.* (*aux.* s.) to go away, to leave, to depart. (John 6:67)

wegheben, *ir.v.a.* to lift off, to carry away. *hebe dich weg!* begone! (Matt. 4:10)

das Wegkreuz (-e), wayside crucifix.

wegnehmen, *ir.v.a.* to take away, to remove, to take out; to carry off, to seize, to confiscate; to occupy (space, etc.). (I John 3:5)

wegraffen, *v.a.* to carry off (someone by disease). (Isa. 57:1)

wegreißen, *ir.v.a.* to tear down, to demolish, to pull down; to snatch away. (Isa. 53:8)

wegstoßen, *ir.v.a.* to push away; to knock off, to repel. (Rev. 2:5)

wegtun, *ir.v.a.* to put away, to set or lay aside; to remove, to cast aside. (Amos 5:23)

der Wegweiser (-), signpost, road sign; guide (book).

wegwerfen, 1. *ir.v.a.* to throw away, to cast off, to reject; to throw down. 2. *v.r.* to throw oneself away, to degrade oneself. (Matt. 13:48)

die Wegzehrung, food for the journey; viaticum.

weh(e), 1. *int.* alas! oh dear! 2. *adj.* painful, sore, aching; sad, woeful. 3. *n.* pain, ache; misery, misfortune, woe, grief. (Rev. 8:13)

die Wehklage (-n), lamentation, wail. (Exod. 2:24)

wehklagen, *v.a. & n.* (*insep.*) (*aux.* h.) to lament (*über,* about), to bewail. (Amos 8:10)

die Wehmut, sadness, melancholy.

wehmütig, wehmutsvoll, *adj.* sad, melancholy.

die Wehmutter (-̈), midwife. (Exod. 1:17)

wehren, 1. *v.n.* (*aux.* h.) (*dat.*) to restrain, to arrest, to check. 2. *v.a.* (*einem etwas*) to hinder, to prevent (someone from doing something); to forbid. 3. *v.r.* to defend oneself; to resist. (Matt. 3:14)

wehrlos, *adj.* unarmed, defenseless, weak.

das Weib (-er), woman; wife. (Gen. 1:27)

die Weiberkleider, (*pl.*) woman's garment. (Deut. 22:5)

die Weiblein, (*pl.*) silly women. (II Tim. 3:6)

weiblich, *adj.* womanly, feminine; female. (I Peter 3:7)

weich, *adj.* soft, smooth, mellow; gentle, mild, tender, delicate; weak; sensitive, soft(hearted); supple. (Matt. 11:8)

weichen, 1. *v.a.* to make soft, to soften, to steep, to soak. 2. *v.n.* (*aux.* h. & s.) to become soft, to grow tender or mellow.

weichen, 1. *ir.v.n.* (*aux.* s.) (dat. or *von*) to yield, to give in; to give way; to fall back, to withdraw, to retreat. 2. *n.:* zum Weichen bringen, to push back, to repel. (Exod. 23:2)

die Weichlichkeit, softness, weakness, delicacy, effeminacy.

der Weichling (-e), weakling. (I Cor. 6:9)

die Weide (-n), pasture, meadow. (John 10:9)

die Weide (-n), willow. (Ps. 137:2)

weiden, 1. *v.a.* to lead or drive to pasture; to tend, to feed (a flock). 2. *v.n.* to graze. 3. *v.a. & r.* (*an* with dat.) to feast one's eyes (on), to delight (in). (Rev. 2:27)

weigern, 1. *v.a.* (*einem etwas*) to refuse, to deny (someone something). 2. *v.r.* (*with inf.*) to refuse, to decline (to do). (Acts 25:11)

der Weihaltar (-̈e), holy or consecrated altar.

der Weihbischof (-̈e), suffragan (bishop).

das Weihbrot (-e), consecrated bread, host.

die Weihe (-n), consecration, dedication, ordination; inauguration, initiation; solemn festivity.

der Weiheakt, solemn dedication, ceremony of ordination or consecration.

die Weihegabe, das Weihegeschenk, votive offering, oblation.

weihelos, *adj.* profane.

weihen, *v.a.* to consecrate, to dedicate, to ordain; to sanctify, to bless. (Exod. 28:41)

die Weihestunde, hour of commemoration.

weihevoll, *adj.* solemn, hallowed, holy.

die Weihnacht, die (das) Weihnachten, Christmas.
Fröhliche Weihnachten! Merry Christmas!

weihnachtlich, *adj.* characteristic of Christmas.

der Weihnachtsabend, Christmas Eve.

der Weihnachtsbaum (-̈e), Christmas tree.

das Weihnachtsfest, festival of Christmas; Christmas festivities.

das Weihnachtsgeschenk (-e), Christmas present or gift.

das Weihnachtskind, the child Jesus.

das Weihnachtslied (-er), Christmas carol.

die Weihnachtsrose, Christmas rose.

das Weihnachtsspiel, nativity play.

der Weihnachtstag, Christmas Day.

die Weihnachtszeit, Christmastide, Yuletide.

der Weihrauch, incense, frankincense. (Matt. 2:11)

weihräuchern, *v.n.* (*aux.* h.) (*einem*) to extol, to flatter.

das Weihrauchfaß, censer.

die Weihung, consecration, dedication, ordination; inauguration, initiation; solemn festivity.

das Weihwasser, holy water.

das Weihwasserbecken (-), font.

weiland, *adv.* formerly, of old; late, deceased. (Rom. 7:9)

die Weile, a while, a (space of) time. (John 5:35)

der Wein (-e), wine. (Gen. 9:21)

das Weinbeerblut, blood of grapes. (Gen. 49:11)

der Weinberg (-e), vineyard. (Gen. 9:20)

weinen, 1. *v.a. & n.* (*aux.* h.) to weep, to cry. 2. *n.* weeping. (John 16:20)

der Weingärtner (-), vinedresser. (Matt. 21:33)

der Weinstock (⁻e), grape vine. (Gen. 49:11)

die Weintraube (-n), grape, bunch of grapes.

die Weintreber, die Weintrester, (*pl.*) skins or husks of pressed grapes.

der Weintreter (-), a person who is treading the grapes. (Jer. 25:30)

weise, *adj.* wise; prudent, judicious. (Gen. 41:33)

der Weise (-n), wise man, sage, philosopher. (Prov. 12:18)
die Weisen aus dem Morgenlande, the three kings from the Orient, the three wise men from the East.

die Weise (-n), manner, way, method; style, fashion, mode, habit, custom. (Gen. 26:5)

weisen, 1. *v.a.* (*einem etwas* [*usually direction or place*]) to show, to direct, to indicate, to point out; to send (someone to or from a place). 2. *v.n.* to point (*nach,* at or towards). (II Sam. 22:33)

die Weisheit, wisdom, knowledge; prudence. (Prov. 1:2)
die Weisheit Salomos, Wisdom of Solomon.

die Weisheitslehre, philosophy.

weislich, *adv.* wisely, prudently, well-considered. (Isa. 52:13)

weiß, *adj.* white, clean, blank.

weissagen, *v.a. & n.* (*insep.*) to foretell, to predict, to prophesy. (Isa. 28:7)

der Weissager (-), prophet, fortuneteller, soothsayer. (I Cor. 14:29)

die Weissagung (-en), prophecy, prediction. (Rev. 1:3)

weit, 1. *adj.* wide, broad; large, vast, spacious, ample; far, long, distant, remote. 2. *adv.* off, far, far off, much, greatly, by far, additional, further, moreover. (Rom. 8:37)

weiter, 1. *comp. adj.* farther, further, wider; additional. 2. *adv.* farther, furthermore; on, forward; else. (Matt. 26:65)

der Weizen, wheat; corn. (Matt. 3:12)

das Weizenkorn (⁻er), grain of wheat. (John 12:24)

welk, *adj.* withered, faded; wrinkled, parched; limp. (Ps. 90:5)

die Welle (-n), wave, billow, surge. (Matt. 8:24)

die Welt (-en), world, earth; people, society, humanity; universe. (Gen. 11:1)

das Weltall, universe, cosmos.

weltanschaulich, *adj.* ideological.

die Weltanschauung, philosophy of life, world outlook, views, creed, ideology.

der Weltbau, cosmic system, the universe; the globe.

weltberühmt, *adj.* world-renowned, of worldwide fame.

das Weltbild, view of life; theory of life.

das Weltei, world egg.

der Weltenbaum, world tree.

das Weltende, end of the world.

die Weltenlehre, cosmology.

weltentrückt, *adj.* isolated, secluded.

die Weltflucht, withdrawal from life, seclusion; escapism.

der Weltgeist, spirit of the age.

der Weltgeistliche (-n), secular priest.

die Weltgeistlichkeit, secular clergy.

das Weltgericht, last judgment.

die Weltgeschichte, universal history.

die Weltherrschaft, universal empire, world dominion.

die Weltkenntnis, knowledge of the world.

das Weltkind (-er), worldling, opportunist, hedonist.

die Weltklugheit, worldly wisdom.

der Weltkrieg (-e), world war.

die Weltkugel, globe.

weltlich, *adj.* worldly, mundane; lay, civil, secular, temporal, profane. (Matt. 20:25)

die Weltlichkeit, secular state; civil power; worldliness.

die Weltlichmachung, secularization.

der Weltling (-e), worldling.

die Weltmacht (-̈e), world power.

der Weltmann, man of the world.

weltmüde, *adj.* tired of life.

die Weltoffenheit, cosmopolitanism.

die Weltpolitik, world policy, global politics.

der Weltpriester (-), secular priest.

der Weltraum, space; universe.

das Weltreich (-e), empire.

der Weltschmerz, weariness of life, pessimistic outlook, romantic discontent.

der Weltschöpfer, Creator, God.

die Weltsprache, international or world language.

der Weltstaat, world state, great power.

die Weltstellung, position of great importance in the world.

weltumfassend, *adj.* worldwide, universal.

der Weltuntergang, end of the world.

weltverlassen, weltverloren, *adj.* solitary, lonely, isolated.

der Weltweise (-n), philosopher.

die Weltweisheit, worldly wisdom.

das Weltwunder (-), wonder of the world; prodigy.

wenden, *reg. & ir.v.a. & v.n.* (*aux.* h.) to turn, to turn round, to turn over (hay); to turn up (earth); to change; to turn away. (Acts 13:46)

wenig, *adj.* little, not much; slightly; (*pl.*) few, a few; *ein wenig,* a little, some. (Gen. 47:9)

werden, 1. *ir.v.n.* (*aux.* s.) (imperfect *wurde* or *ward*) (p.p. *geworden* or *worden*) to become; to come to be, to grow, to get, to turn out, to prove; to come into existence. 2. *as auxiliary* (a) (*forming the future and conditional tenses*) shall, will; should, would; (b) (*forming the passive voice,* p.p. *worden*) be, is, are, etc.; *ich werde geliebt,* I am loved. (Matt. 18:3)

werfen, 1. *ir.v.a. & n.* (*aux.* h.) to throw, to cast, to toss, to pitch, to hurl, to project; to bring forth young. 2. *v.r.* to warp, to get warped, to become distorted; to throw oneself (into), to apply oneself (to). (Exod. 15:4)

das Werg, tow. (Isa. 1:31)

das Werk (-e), work, labor; action, act, deed, performance; job, undertaking, enterprise; production, workmanship, composition; mechanism, works; workshops, factory; publication, book, opus; (*pl.*) forts, fortifications. (Gen. 2:2) *groß sind die Werke des Herrn,* great are the works of the Lord.

werkheilig, *adj.* sanctimonious; hypocritical.

der Werkheilige (-n), sanctimonious person, hypocrite.

die Werkheiligkeit, sanctimoniousness, outward piety; hypocrisy.

der Werkmeister (-), overseer, foreman. (Prov. 8:30)

das Werkstück (-e), worked article; hewn stone. (Isa. 9:9)

das Werkzeug (-e), tool, implement; vessel; (*fig.*) instrument, organ. (I Peter 3:7)

der Wermut, wormwood; (*fig.*) bitterness, gall. (Jer. 9:14)

wert, 1. *adj.* (*with dat.*) dear, valued, honored, esteemed, estimable; (*with gen.*) worth, valuable; worthy. 2. *m.* worth, use, value; price, rate; appreciation, merit, importance, stress; standard (of coin); (*pl.*) data. (Matt. 8:8)

das Werturteil, value judgment (Ritschl).

wertvoll, *adj.* valuable, precious.

das Wesen (-), reality, substance, essence; being, creature, living thing, organism; state; intrinsic virtue; conduct; living. (John 3:22)

wesenhaft, *adj.* real, substantial; characteristic.

die Wesenheit, spirit, essence, substance, decisive factors.

die Wesenlosigkeit, unreality.

die Wesenseinheit, consubstantiality.

wesensgleich, *adj.* homogeneous, identical, consubstantial.

die Wesensgleichheit, identity.

die Wesenslehre, ontology.

die Wesensschau, phenomenology.

der Wesenszug (-̈e), characteristic feature.

wesentlich, *adj.* essential, real, substantial, material, important, vital, significant, fundamental, intrinsic, principal.

der West, west; (*pl.* -e) west wind.

wetteifern, *v.n.* (*insep.*) (*aux.* h.) to emulate, to vie (with), to contend (with); *mit einem um etwas wetteifern,* to compete with someone for something.

das Wetter (-), weather; bad weather, storm; air, atmosphere. (Isa. 4:6)

wetterwendisch, *adj.* fickle, capricious, changeable. (Matt. 13:21)

der Wettkampf (⁼e), contest.

der Wettkämpfer (-), champion, athlete; rival.

der Wettlauf (⁼e), race.

wettlaufen, *ir.v.n.* (*sep.*) (*aux.* s.) to run a race, to race.

der Wettläufer (-), runner.

wetzen, 1. *v.a.* to whet, to grind, to sharpen. 2. *v.n.* (*aux.* h.) to brush (against). (Prov. 27:17)

wichtig, *adj.* weighty; important, significant, momentous, serious. (II Cor. 4:17)

wickeln, *v.a.* to roll, to roll up, to coil, to wind; to wrap (up). (Matt. 27:59)

der Widder (-), ram; battering ram. (Dan. 8:4)

wider, 1. *prep.* (*acc.*) against, contrary to, in opposition to, versus. 2. *insep. or sep. prefix,* counter-, contra-, anti-, re-, with-.

der Widerchrist, Antichrist.

widerfahren, *ir.v.n.* (*insep.*) (*3rd person only, with dat.*) (*aux.* s.) to happen, to occur, to befall, to fall (to someone). (Acts 20:19)

die Widerlegung (-en), refutation.

der Widerruf, recantation, revocation, disavowal, disclaimer.

widerruflich, *adj.* revocable; uncertain (tenure of office, etc.).

der Widersacher (-), adversary, opponent. (Matt. 5:25)

widerspenstig, *adj.* refractory, rebellious, unruly, stubborn, obstinate. (II Tim. 2:25)

widersprechen, *ir.v.a. & n.* (*insep.*) (*aux.* h.) (*dat.*) to contradict; to be at variance with, to conflict with, to gainsay, to oppose. (Luke 2:34)

der Widerstand, opposition, resistance. (Eph. 6:13)

widerstehen, *ir.v.n.* (*insep.*) (*aux.* h.) (*dat.*) to oppose, to resist, to withstand; to be repugnant to; to go against the grain. (James 4:7)

widerstreben, 1. *v.n.* (*insep.*) (*aux.* h.) (*dat.*) to resist, to oppose, to struggle against, to be repugnant to (someone). 2. *n.* opposition, resistance, reluctance, repugnance. (Matt. 5:39)

der Widerstreit, opposition, conflict.

widerstreiten, *ir.v.n.* (*insep.*) (*aux.* h.) (*dat.*) to conflict (with), to clash (with), to be antagonistic (to), to be contrary (to). (Rom. 7:23)

wieder, 1. *adv.* again, anew, once more, afresh. 2. *prefix* (*sep. except when stated, when the accent is on the root*) = re-, back (again), in return (for).

die Wiederaufrichtung, reerection; reestablishment.

wiederbringen, *ir.v.a.* to bring back; to restore, to return to. (I Kings 8:34)

wiedergeben, *ir.v.a.* to give back, to return, to restore; to reproduce; to render. (Luke 19:8)

wiedergeboren, *adj.* reborn, born anew, regenerated. (I Peter 1:23)

die Wiedergeburt, rebirth, regeneration. (Matt. 19:28)

die Wiederherstellung, restoration, recovery, reinstatement.

die Wiederkehr, return, reappearance, recurrence, repetition.

wiederkehren, wiederkommen, *v.n.* (*aux.* s.) to come back, to return, to recur, to reappear, to repeat. (Luke 10:35)

die Wiederkunft, return.

wiedersehen, 1. *ir.v.a.* to see again. 2. *n.* reunion. (John 16:22)

der Wiedertäufer (-), anabaptist.

die Wiedervereinigung, reunion, reconciliation; recombination.

wiedervergelten, *v.a.* to retaliate.

die Wiedervergeltung, retaliation.

wiegen, 1. *ir.v.a. & n.* (*aux.* h.) to weigh. 2. *reg. v.a.* to rock (a cradle); to move gently; to shake; to mince. (Eph. 4:14)

wild, 1. *adj.* wild; rough; savage, ferocious, fierce; unruly, noisy, furious; angry. 2. *n.* game; deer, venison. (Gen. 16:12)

das Wildbret, game, venison. (Gen. 27:3)

der Wille (-n), will, volition, determination; design, purpose, intent, intention, wish, inclination. (Matt. 6:10)

die Willensfreiheit, free will, freedom of will.

die Willenskraft, will power, strength of will or mind.

willfahren, *v.n.* (*aux.* h.) (p.p. *willfahrt &* *gewillfahrt*) (*dat.*) to accede to, to comply with, to gratify, to grant (a wish); to please (someone).

willfährig, *adj.* (*dat.*) obliging, accommodating, compliant. (Matt. 5:25)

willig, *adj.* willing, voluntary; ready; docile. (Matt. 26:41)

willkommen, 1. *n.* welcome, reception. 2. *adj.* (*with dat.*) welcome, acceptable, opportune, gratifying.

die Willkür, free will, option, choice; discretion; arbitrary action; despotism. (II Cor. 9:7)

die Willkürherrschaft, despotism; tyranny.

der Wind (-e), wind, breeze; blast; scent. (I Kings 19:11)

die Windel (-n), swaddling cloth, baby's napkin. (Luke 2:7)

die Windsbraut, Euroclydon, tempestuous wind. (Acts 27:14)

der Windwirbel (-), whirlwind. (Isa. 40:24)

der Winkel (-), angle, corner, nook. (Acts 26:26)

winken, *v.a.* & *n.* (*aux.* h.) (*dat.*) to wave, to make signs, to nod, to wink, to signal. (Luke 5:7)

der Winter (-), winter. (Gen. 8:22)

das Winterhaus, winter house. (Jer. 36:22)

wirken, 1. *v.a.* to effect, to do, to work, to operate; to bring about, to produce; to weave; to knead (dough). 2. *v.n.* (*aux.* h.) to work, to operate, to act, to have an effect. (Mark 16:20)

wirklich, 1. *adj.* actual, real; substantial, true, genuine; effective, effectual. 2. *adv.* exactly, quite, indeed, really.

die Wirklichkeit, reality, actuality, actual fact, truth.

die Wirksamkeit, efficiency, virtue; effect.

die Wirkung, working, operation, action, reaction; force; result, consequence, effect, influence. (Eph. 1:19)

der Wirkungskreis, sphere of action or activity; province, domain.

die Wirkungsursache, die Wirkursache, efficient cause.

der Wirt (-e), host; landlord; innkeeper, lodging-house keeper. (Luke 10:35)

wissen, 1. *ir.v.a.* to know, to have knowledge of, to be aware or informed of, to be acquainted with; to understand, to know how to, to be able to. 2. *n.* knowledge, learning, scholarship, erudition. (Gen. 3:5)

die Wissenschaft (-en), learning, knowledge, scholarship, science.

der Wissenschaftler (-), learned man, scholar, scientist, man of science.

die Witwe (-n), widow. (Exod. 22:21)

die Witwenschaft, widowhood. (Isa. 54:4)

wo, 1. *inter. adv.* where, in which. 2. *indef. pronominal adv.* somewhere. 3. *conj.* when. 4. *n.:* es kommt auf das Wo an, it depends on where it is or on its whereabouts. (Gen. 3:9)

die Woche (-n), week. (Luke 18:12)

das Wochenfest, Feast of Weeks, Pentecost.

woher, *inter.* & *rel. adv.* whence, from where, from which or what place; how. (Matt. 13:27)

wohin, *inter.* & *rel. adv.* whither, where, which way, to what or which place. (John 3:8)

wohin gehen Sie? where are you going?

wohl, 1. *adv.* well; *wohl dem, der . . .* happy he, who. 2. *part.* (*unaccented*) indeed, to be sure, no doubt; perhaps, probably, I shouldn't wonder. 3. *n.* welfare, well-being, prosperity; good health. (Matt. 5:12)

wohlan, 1. *adv.* boldly. 2. *int.* come on! well! now then! (Matt. 23:32)

wohlauf, 1. *adv.* well, in good health. 2. *int.* cheer up! come on! now then! (Gen. 11:4)

die Wohlfahrt, welfare, weal. (Ps. 106:5)

das Wohlgefallen, liking, pleasure, satisfaction, goodwill. (Matt. 3:17)

wohlgefällig, *adj.* pleasant, agreeable, satisfactory, complacent. (Matt. 11:26)

der Wohlgeruch (⁀e), pleasant odor, scent, aroma, fragrance, perfume. (Isa. 11:3)

wohlhabend, *adj.* wealthy, well-off, well-to-do. (Ruth 2:1)

das Wohlleben, life of pleasure; luxury, good living. (Isa. 5:12)

die Wohltat (-en), benefit, blessing; kindness, favor; good deed, charity. (Mark 5:19)

der Wohltäter (-), benefactor. (Luke 6:33)

die Wohltäterin (-nen), benefactress.

wohltätig, *adj.* beneficent; charitable.

wohltun, *ir.v.n.* (*sep.*) (*aux.* h.) to do good, to give pleasure, to be comforting, to be pleasing; to dispense charity. (Matt. 5:44)

wohnen, *v.n.* (*aux.* h.) to dwell, to live, to reside, to stay. (Rev. 2:13)

die Wohnung (-en), dwelling, residence, habitation; house, flat. (Exod. 15:13)

die Wölbung (-en), arch, dome, vault; curvature.

der Wolf (⁀e), wolf. (Matt. 7:15)
Wolf im Schafspeltz, wolf in sheep's clothing.

die Wolke (-n), cloud; swarm. (Gen. 9:13)

die Wolkensäule, pillar of a cloud. (Exod. 13:21)

die Wolle (-arten or -n), wool; down; hair (of rabbits, goats, camels, etc.). (Dan. 7:9)

wollen, 1. *ir.v.a.* will, to be willing; to wish, to want, to desire, to like, to choose; to ordain, to intend. 2. *n.* will, volition, intention, inclination. (Matt. 7:12)

die Wollust (⁀e), sensual pleasure, voluptuousness; lust, debauchery; delight, bliss. (James 4:1)

der Wollüstling (-e), sensualist; libertine.

die Wonne (-n), joy, delight, rapture, ecstasy, bliss. (Jer. 7:34)

wonnereich, *adj.* blissful.

wonneselig, *adj.* in ecstasy.

wonnetrunken, *adj.* enraptured.

wonniglich, *adj.* delightful, delicious, blissful.

worfeln, *v.a.* to fan, to winnow, to beat off. (Isa. 27:12)

das Wort (⁀er = *unconnected words, vocables; in all other cases* -e), word, vocable, term, expression, saying; promise, pledge, word of honor. (Exod. 4:15)
das Wort Gottes, Word of God.

das Wörterbuch (⁀er), dictionary; vocabulary; glossary.

das Wörterverzeichnis (-se), list of words, vocabulary.

wortgetreu, *adj.* word for word, literal.

der Wortkrieg (-e), dispute of words. (I Tim. 6:4)

wörtlich, *adj.* literal, verbal, word for word, verbatim.

der Wortschatz, vocabulary, words in use.

die Worttreue, fidelity to the text.

wortwörtlich, *adv.* literally, word for word, exactly.

der Wucher (-), usury; profiteering, gain, profit; interest. (Prov. 28:8)

wuchern, *v.n.* (*aux.* h.) to grow rapidly, to proliferate, to produce abundantly; to give a good return; to practice usury, to profiteer; to make the most of it.

wund, *adj.* sore, chafed, chapped; wounded, injured. (Rev. 13:3)

das Wunder (-), marvel; miracle; wonder, surprise, astonishment. (Exod. 3:20)

wunderbar, *adj.* amazing, surprising, strange, wondrous, miraculous; wonderful, splendid, great. (I Peter 2:9)

der Wunderglaube, belief in miracles.

die Wunderkraft, magic or miraculous power.

die Wunderkur, faith healing.

wunderlich, *adj.* strange, odd, singular, peculiar, curious, eccentric. (I Peter 2:18)

das Wundermittel (-), panacea.

wundern, 1. *v.a. & imp.* to surprise, to astonish. 2. *v.r.* (*aux.* h.) to be surprised (*über,* at). (Luke 2:18)

wundersam, *adj.* amazing, surprising, strange, wondrous, miraculous; wonderful, splendid, great. (Rev. 15:3)

der Wundertäter (-), miracle worker, worker of miracles, thaumaturge. (I Cor. 12:28)

wundertätig, *adj.* wonderworking, doing wonders, miraculous. (Exod. 15:11) das **Wunderwerk,** phenomenal achievement, wonder.

das **Wunderzeichen** (-), miraculous sign, portent. (Ezek. 12:6)

der **Wunsch** (¨e), wish, desire; (*pl.*) good wishes, congratulations. (Rom. 10:1)

wünschen, *v.a.* to wish, to desire (*einem etwas,* something for someone); *sich wünschen* (*dat.*) to long for, to wish for. (Rom. 9:3)

die **Würde** (-n), dignity, majesty; propriety; (*pl.*) post (of honor), rank, office, honor, title, (academic) degree.

der **Würdenträger** (-), dignitary.

würdevoll, *adj.* dignified.

würdig, *adj.* worthy, deserving (*gen.*, of); respectable, dignified. (Luke 20:35)

würdigen, *v.a.* (*acc. of person & gen. of thing*) to deem worthy, to deign; to value, to appreciate, to rate, to estimate.

würfeln, 1. *v.n.* (*aux.* h.) to play at dice, to throw dice. 2. *v.a.* to throw or toss about, to winnow (grain).

das **Würfelspiel,** game of dice.

die **Wurfschaufel** (-n), winnowing shovel or fan. (Matt. 3:12)

würgen, 1. *v.n.* (*aux.* h.) & *r.* to choke, to gulp; to wreak havoc. 2. *v.a.* to choke, to strangle; to take by the throat; to slaughter, to slay, to massacre. (Matt. 18:28)

der **Würgengel,** angel of destruction or death.

der **Wurm** (¨er), worm, grub; (*pl. also* ¨e), serpent, snake, dragon, reptile; fancy, whim. (Acts 12:23)

das **Würmlein** (-), (little) worm. (Isa. 41:14)

die **Wurzel** (-n), root. (Rom. 11:16)

wurzeln, 1. *v.n.* (*aux.* h. & s.) to take or strike root, to become rooted, to send out roots. 2. *v.r.: sich fest wurzeln,* to become firmly established. (Isa. 27:6)

wüst, *adj.* desert, waste, desolate, deserted, confused, wild, disorderly; dissolute; filthy, ugly, vulgar, rude. (Gen. 1:2)

die **Wüste** (-n), desert, wilderness. (Exod. 3:1)

die **Wüstung,** derelict area or site, (abandoned) site. (Isa. 5:17)

wüten, *v.n.* (*aux.* h.) to rage, to rave, to be furious. (Ps. 46:4)

187

Yy

der Ysop (-e), hyssop. (John 19:29)

Zz

(der) Zacharias, Zachariah.

(der) Zachäus, Zacchaeus.

zagen, *v.n.* (*aux.* h.) to be afraid, to be faint-hearted, to hesitate. (Matt. 26:37)

die Zahl (-en), number, numeral, figure, digit, cipher. (Acts 4:4)

zählen, *v.a.* & *n.* (*aux.* h.) to count, to reckon, to number, to compute; (with *zu*) to belong to, to be classed with, to be among. (Gen. 15:5)

zähmen, *v.a.* to tame, to domesticate, to break in (a horse); to subdue, to check, to control, to master, to restrain. (James 3:7)

der Zahn (¨e), tooth, fang, tusk; prong. (Gen. 49:12)

das Zähneklappe(r)n, chattering of teeth. (Matt. 8:12)

die Zange (-n), pliers, pincers, tongs; tweezers, forceps. (Isa. 6:6)

der Zank (¨e), quarrel, wrangle, brawl. (Gen. 13:8)

zanken, 1. *v.r.* & *n.* (*aux.* h.) to quarrel, to wrangle, to fall out, to have words (with). 2. *v.a.* to scold. (Gen. 45:24)

zänkisch, *adj.* quarrelsome. (Rom. 2:8)

zart, *adj.* delicate, fragile, frail; slender, slight; tender, soft, fine, sensitive; subdued, pale (of colors). (Isa. 47:1)

zärteln, *v.n.* to fondle, to caress; to flirt. (Ecclesiasticus 30:9)

der Zauber (-), spell, charm; magic, enchantment, glamor, fascination.

die Zauberei, magic, sorcery, witchcraft; spell, enchantment. (Rev. 9:21)

die Zaubereisünde (-n), sin of witchcraft. (I Sam. 15:23)

der Zauberer (-), magician, sorcerer, wizard, conjurer, juggler. (Rev. 21:8)

zaubern, 1. *v.a.* to conjure up, to charm, to cast a spell on or over. 2. *v.n.* (*aux.* h.) to practice magic or witchcraft, to do magic; to conjure.

der Zauberspruch (¨e), incantation, charm, spell.

der Zauderer (-), irresolute person; procrastinator.

der Zaun (¨e), fence, railing; hedge. (Matt. 21:33)

Zebaoth, *Gott Zebaoth, Herr Gott Zebaoth,* Lord of hosts, God of hosts; the Lord. (Ps. 80:5).

(der) Zebedäus, Zebedee.

die Zeder (-n), cedar. (I Kings 5:13)

das Zedernholz, cedar wood. (I Kings 5:22)

zehn, *num. adj.* ten. (Gen. 18:32)
die Zehn Gebote, Ten Commandments, Decalogue.

zehnt, *num. adj.* (der, die, das -te) tenth. (John 1:39)

der Zehnte (-n), tithe. (Gen. 14:20)

das Zeichen (-), sign, symbol, mark, token; indication, proof, testimony, evidence, symptom; brand; signal; omen. (Gen. 1:14)

der Zeichendeuter (-), astrologer, wizard, augur, prophet. (Lev. 20:27)

zeichnen, 1. *v.a.* & *n.* (*aux.* h.) to draw, to sketch, to design, to mark, to brand; to sign, to subscribe. 2. *n.* drawing, sketching, designing, graphic art. (Isa. 49:16)

zeigen, 1. *v.a.* (*einem etwas*) & *n.* (*aux.* h.) to show, to point at or out, to exhibit, to display, to indicate; to manifest, to demonstrate, to prove. 2. *v.r.* to appear, to be found, to emerge, to become evident, to turn out, to prove to be. (Rev. 1:1)

der Zeiger (-), dial, finger, hand (of clocks, watches). (II Kings 20:11)

189

zeihen, *ir.v.a.: einen zeihen einer Sache,* to accuse someone of something, to charge someone with something. (John 8:46)

die Zeit (-en), time; epoch; period, age, era; season, term, duration; (*pl.*) tides. (Mark 1:15)

der Zeitgenosse (-n), contemporary.

die Zeitlang, while; *eine Zeitlang,* a while, for some time. (Luke 4:13)

zeitlich, *adj.* temporal, secular, earthly; passing, temporary, transient, periodic, momentary. (II Cor. 4:17)

die Zeitrechnung, chronology; era.

die Zeitschrift (-en), periodical, journal, magazine.

der Zelebrant (-en), officiating priest (at mass); celebrant.

zelebrieren, *v.a.* to celebrate, to officiate at.

der Zelot (-en), zealot; fanatic.

das Zelotentum, der Zelotismus, fanaticism.

zelotisch, *adj.* fanatical.

zensieren, *v.a.* to censor; to criticize, to censure.

der Zensor (-en), censor (of films, press).

die Zensur (-en), censorship; marks (at school), certificate.

der Zentner (-), hundredweight, fifty kilograms; talent. (Matt. 25:15)

das (der) Zepter (-), scepter, mace. (Gen. 49:10)

zerarbeiten, *v.a. & v.r.* to destroy by working; *sich zerarbeiten,* to overwork. (Isa. 57:10)

zerbeißen, *ir.v.a.* to crunch, to bite through, to break with the teeth or beak. (Rev. 16:10)

zerbrechen, *ir.v.a. & n.* (*aux.* s.) to break in or to pieces, to shatter, to smash. (Exod. 12:46)
sich (dat.) *den Kopf zerbrechen,* to rack one's brains.

die Zeremonie (-n), ceremony, formality.

der Zerfall, ruin, decay, decomposition, disintegration, destruction; (*fig.*) decadence.

zerfallen, *ir.v.n.* (*aux.* s.) to fall apart or to pieces, to crumble away, to decay, to decompose; to disintegrate; to break down, to come to grief. (Amos 9:11)

zerfließen, *ir.v.n.* (*aux.* s.) to melt, to dissolve, to run (out); to disperse. (Isa. 64:1)
in Tränen zerfließen, to melt into tears.

zergehen, *ir.v.n.* (*aux.* s.) to melt, to dissolve; to dwindle away, to vanish, to pass (away). (Matt. 5:18)

die Zergliederung, analysis.

zerhauen, *ir.v.a.* to cut in pieces; to chop or cut up. (Ps. 118:10)

zermalmen, 1. *v.a.* to bruise, to crush; to grind, to crunch, to pulverize; (*fig.*) to cast down, to depress. 2. *n.,* **die Zermalmung,** bruising, crushing, crunching; pulverization. (Matt. 21:44)

zerpulvern, *v.a.* to pulverize. (Hos. 8:6)

zerreißen, 1. *ir.v.a.* to tear or rip up, to tear to pieces, to rend; to break up, to dismember; to split, to rupture; to lacerate, to mutilate; to worry; to break (an alliance, someone's heart, etc.). 2. *v.n.* (*aux.* s.) to break, to tear, to split, to wear out. (Gen. 37:33)

zerrinnen, *ir.v.n.* (*aux.* s.) to melt, to dissolve; to disappear, to come to nothing. (Mal. 3:9)

zerrütten, *v.a.* to disarrange, to derange, to unsettle, to disturb, to throw into confusion; to ruin, to destroy. (I Tim. 6:5)

zerschellen, 1. *v.a.* to dash in pieces, to smash, to shatter, to shiver. 2. *v.n.* (*aux.* s.) to go to pieces, to be dashed to pieces, to be shattered or smashed. (Matt. 21:44)

zerschlagen, 1. *ir.v.a.* to dash to pieces; to batter, to bruise; to destroy. 2. *p.p. & adj.* broken, battered, shattered. 3. *v.r.* to break off, to break up, to be dispersed; to come to nothing, to be disappointed (hopes, etc.). (Luke 4:18)

zerschmettern, 1. *v.a.* to shatter, to smash, to crush, to destroy, to overwhelm, to confound. 2. *v.n.* (*aux.* s.) to be shattered or smashed. (Ps. 110:5)

zerschneiden, *ir.v.a.* to cut in pieces, to cut into shreds, to cut up, to carve, to dissect. (Jer. 36:23)

die Zerschneidung, concision. (Phil. 3:2)

zerspalten

zerspalten, *v.a. & n. (aux.* s.) to cleave, to split (up), to slit. (Acts 23:7)

zerstören, *v.a.* to destroy, to demolish, to ruin, to devastate, to ravage, to disrupt, to overthrow. (Acts 6:14)

die Zerstörung, destruction, demolition; disorganization, overthrow, ruin.

zerstücke(l)n, *v.a.* to cut into little pieces, to chop up, to cut up, to mangle, to dismember; to divide, to parcel out, to partition. (I Sam. 11:7)

zerteilen, *v.a.* to divide, to separate; to cut, to split or break up, to disintegrate, to dissolve; to disperse; to resolve. (Dan. 2:41)

zertreten, *v.a.* to trample under foot, to trample down, to bruise. (Gen. 3:15)

der Zeuge (-n), **die Zeugin** (-nen), witness. (John 1:7)

zeugen, *v.n.* to bear witness, to testify, to depose, to give evidence (of); (*von*) to show, to prove, to be evidence of. (James 1:18)

die Zeugenvernehmung, hearing of witnesses.

das Zeugnis (-se), testimony, witness, evidence, proof; certificate, testimonial, character. (Exod. 20:16)
Zeugnis ablegen, to bear witness (to), to give testimony.

das Ziborium, ciborium.

der Ziegel (-), brick; tile. (Gen. 11:3)

der Ziegelstein (-e), brick; tile. (Isa. 9:9)

der Ziegenbock (-̈e), he-goat, billy goat. (Dan. 8:5)

das Ziegenfell (-e), goatskin. (I Sam. 19:13)

ziehen, 1. *ir.v.a.* to draw, to pull, to drag, to haul; to pull out; to bring up, to rear, to grow, to train, to educate. 2. *v.r.* to move, to draw (toward), to march (toward); to stretch, to extend; to distort; to penetrate, to soak in. 3. *v.n. (aux.* h.) to prove attractive, to make an impression, to have a strong appeal, to attract; (*aux.* s.) to move, to stroll, to wander; to grow (of flowers, plants); to march, to go, to advance; to move (to). 4. *n.* drawing, pulling; cultivation, rearing; draught; removal, migration; attraction, appeal. (Acts 8:28)

das Ziel (-e), goal, end, objective, destination; target, aim; limit, boundary, scope. (Col. 2:18)

zielen, *v.n. (aux.* h.) (with *nach*) to aim (at); *auf eine Sache zielen,* (*fig.*) to aim at, to drive at, to refer to something. (Ps. 7:13)

die Zielstrebigkeit, teleology.

ziemen, *v.r. & n. (aux.* h.) (*imp. with dat.*) to be seemly, to become, to suit, to be suitable, to be fitting or proper. (Matt. 12:2)

die Zierde, ornament, decoration. (Ps. 93:5)

zieren, 1. *v.a.* to adorn, to grace, to be an ornament to; to decorate, to embellish, to set off; to garnish. 2. *v.r.* to be affected, to behave affectedly; to mince (one's words). (Isa. 60:7)

zierlich, *adj.* graceful, neat, elegant, pretty, nice, fine, smart; decorative, ornamental. (I Tim. 2:9)

die Zimbel (-n), cymbal. (Ps. 150:5)

der Zimmermann (-̈er & -leute), carpenter. (II Sam. 5:11)

zimmern, *v.a. & n. (aux.* h.) to frame, to build; to carpenter; to make, to fabricate. (Isa. 44:13)

die Zinne (-n), pinnacle; battlement, rocky crag. (Matt. 4:5)

der Zins (-e), tax, duty, rent, tribute; (*pl.* -en) interest. (Matt. 17:25)

der Zionismus, Zionism.

der Zionist (-en), Zionist.

zionistisch, *adj.* Zionist.

der Zipfel (-), tip, point, end; lobe, tongue; corner (of a piece of cloth, kerchief, etc.). (Acts 10:11)

zischen, 1. *v.a. & n. (aux.* h. & s.) to hiss, to sizzle, to fizz, to fizzle, to whiz. 2. *n.* hiss(ing), whiz(zing), hisses (in theater, etc.). (Isa. 7:18)

der Zisterzienser (-), Cistercian.

das Zitat (-e), quotation, citation.

zittern, *v.n. (aux.* h.) to tremble, to shiver, to shudder, to shake, to quiver, to flutter, to quake, to waver, to vibrate.
mit Zittern und Zagen, with fear and trembling, shaking with fear. (Acts 9:6)

die Zivilehe (-n), civil marriage.

der Zögling (-e), pupil.

der (das) Zölibat. celibacy; bachelordom.

der Zoll (-̈e), tariff, customs, duty, toll; dues; (*fig.*) tribute. (Matt. 9:9)

191

der **Zollbeamte** (-n), customs officer; revenue officer.

der **Zöllner** (-), tax collector; publican. (Matt. 5:46)

das **Zönakel** (-), monastery refectory.

der **Zopf** (ᵬe), pigtail, plait, tress; tuft; red tape. (I Tim. 2:9)

der **Zorn,** anger, wrath, rage; passion, temper. (Rev. 6:17)

zornig, *adj.* angry, irate, in a temper, rage, or passion. (Luke 14:21)

zu, 1. *prep.* (*dat.*) to, towards, up to, unto; in addition to, along with; at, on, in, by; for, in order to. 2. *part.* (*with inf.*) *ich habe zu arbeiten,* I have to work, I have work to do. 3. *adv. & sep. prefix* to, towards; closed, shut.

zubereiten, *v.a.* to prepare, to get ready, to dress, to finish; to cook. (Heb. 11:16)

zubinden, *ir.v.a.* to bind or tie up, to bandage. (Isa. 8:16)
einem die Augen zubinden, to blindfold someone.

zubringen, *ir.v.a.* (*einem etwas*) to bring, to carry, to convey or take to; to pass or spend (time). (I Peter 4:3)

die **Zucht** (-en), breeding, rearing (cattle, etc.); cultivation; breed, stock, race; education, training; discipline; propriety, decorum, good manners, modesty. (II Tim. 1:7)

züchtig, *adj.* chaste, modest, bashful, coy; proper, discreet. (Titus 2:4)

züchtigen, *v.a.* to chastise, to punish; to discipline, to correct. (Rev. 3:19)

der **Züchtiger** (-), instructor. (Rom. 2:20)

die **Züchtigung** (-en), punishment, chastisement, correction. (II Tim. 3:16)

zuchtlos, *adj.* insubordinate; undisciplined; dissolute, licentious. (Exod. 32:25)

der **Zuchtmeister** (-), taskmaster; disciplinarian.

zudecken, *v.a.* to cover up; to put a lid on; to cloak, to conceal. (Isa. 25:7)

zuerst, *adv.* first, firstly, in the first place, at first, first of all; above all, especially. (Acts 13:46)

zufahren, *ir.v.n.* (*aux.* h. & s.) to drive or go on; to approach, to drive towards; to rush at. (Gal. 1:16)

der **Zufall** (ᵬe), contingency, spontaneity.

zufallen, *ir.v.n.* (*aux.* s.) to close, to fall to; (*with dat.*) to fall to one's lot, to devolve (up)on. (Matt. 6:33)

die **Zuflucht** (-en), refuge, shelter; recourse. (Isa. 4:6)
zu einem or *einer Sache Zuflucht nehmen,* to have recourse to or take refuge with someone or in something.

der **Zufluchtsort** (-e & ᵬer), die **Zufluchtsstätte** (-n), place of refuge, retreat, asylum.

zufrieden, *adj.* content, pleased, satisfied. (Ps. 116:7)
sich zufrieden geben (mit), to rest content (with), to acquiesce (in).

der **Zug** (ᵬe), drawing, pulling; pull, tension; tug; train; march, passage, progress, procession, migration; flight, flock, herd; drift (of clouds); range (of mountains); band, troop; feature, characteristic; inclination, impulse; gulp.
in den letzten Zügen liegen, to be at one's last gasp, to be dying. (Mark 5:23)

der **Zugang** (ᵬe), admittance, access, entry, entrance, approach; increase. (Rom. 5:2)

zugänglich, *adj.* (*with dat.*) accessible, approachable, open (to), susceptible (to).

zugeben, *ir.v.a.* to add; to give into the bargain, (*einem etwas*) to grant, to concede, to admit, to allow; to agree to, to acknowledge, to own, to confess. (Rom. 7:16)

zugehen, *ir.v.n.* (*aux.* s.) to close, to shut, to meet, to fasten; (with *auf*) to go up to, to move towards; to come to pass, to take place, to happen. (I Cor. 14:40)

zugehören, *v.a.* (*aux.* h.) (*with dat.*) to belong or appertain to. (Eccles. 12:13)

zugesellen, *v.a. & r.* to associate with, to join. (Gen. 3:12)

zugleich, *adv.* at the same time, together, along (with), also. (Matt. 13:29)

zugut(e), *adv.* to the benefit or advantage of. (Rom. 13:4)

zuhalten, 1. *ir.v.a.* to keep shut; to close (one's eyes, etc.); to clench (one's fist). 2. *v.n.* (*aux.* h.) (*auf* with acc.) to make for, to proceed towards, to go straight for. 3. *v.r.* to hurry, to make haste. (Acts 7:56)

zuhören, *v.n.* (*aux.* h.) (*dat.*) to listen (to); to attend (to). (Acts 4:4)

zukehren *v.a.* (*einem etwas*) to turn to(wards), to face.
einem den Rücken zukehren, to turn one's back on someone. (Jer. 2:27)

zukommen, *ir.v.n.* (*aux.* s.) (with *auf*) to come up to, to approach; (*with dat.*) to arrive, to reach; to belong to, to be due to, to befit, to fall to (one's share or lot). (I Tim. 6:16)

die Zukunft, future, life hereafter. (Matt. 24:3)

zukünftig, *adj.* future, what is to come. (I Tim. 4:8)

zulaufen, *ir.v.n.* (*aux.* s.) (*auf* with acc.) to run to, to run towards or up to; to run faster; (*with dat.*) to crowd or flock to. (Ps. 73:10)

zulegen, 1. *v.a.* to add (to), to put more (to), to increase (a salary); to attribute, to assign; to cover up. 2. *v.n.* (*aux.* h.) to continue adding to; to get fatter, to put on weight or flesh. (Isa. 38:5)

zuletzt, *adv.* finally, at last, ultimately, eventually, after all, in the end; last, for the last time. (Eph. 6:10)

die Zunahme (-n), increase, advance, rise, growth; augmentation, advancement, improvement, progress.

der Zuname(n) (-n), family name; surname.

zunehmen, 1. *ir.v.a.* to take in addition, to take more; to increase. 2. *v.n.* (*aux.* h.) to increase, to augment, to grow (larger or heavier); to rise, to swell; to improve, to advance, to thrive, to prosper; to grow worse (of an evil); to get stouter, to put on weight. (I Peter 2:2)

die Zunge (-n), tongue; language. (Gen. 11:1)

das Zungenreden, speaking in tongues.

zunichte, *adv.* ruined, destroyed.
zunichte machen, to ruin, to destroy, to frustrate; *zunichte werden,* to come to nothing. (I Cor. 1:17)

zuordnen, *v.a.* to adjoin, to coordinate, to associate with, to attach or appoint to. (Acts 1:26)

zurechnen, *v.a.* (*einem etwas*) to add in or to; to put to (someone's account); to ascribe, to attribute to, to impute. (Rom. 4:4)

zurecht, *adv. & sep. prefix* right, in (good) order, rightly, with reason; in the right place; as it ought to be.

zurechtbringen, *ir.v.a.* to restore. (Matt. 17:11)

zurechthelfen, *ir.v.n.* (*aux.* h.) (*dat.*) to restore. (Gal. 6:1)

zurichten, *v.a.* to prepare, to make or get ready, to finish; to dress (leather, cloth, etc.); to leaven (dough), to convert, to shape, to trim. (Matt. 21:16)

zürnen, *v.n.* (*aux.* h.): *auf eine Sache* or *wegen einer Sache zürnen,* to be annoyed or angry about something; (*mit*) *einem* or *auf einen zürnen,* to be angry with someone. (Gen. 18:30)

zurück, 1. *int.* stand back! back there! 2. *adv. & sep. prefix* back, backward(s), behind, in the rear, late.

zurückkehren, *v.n.* (*aux.* s.) to return, to go or come back, to revert. (Ps. 6:11)

zurücklaufen, *ir.v.n.* (*aux.* s.) to run back; to ebb, to flow back; to retrograde. (Isa. 38:8)

zurücksehen, *ir.v.n.* (*aux.* h.) to look back, to look behind; to reflect on, to review (the past, etc.). (Luke 9:62)

zurücktreten, *ir.v.n.* (*aux.* s.) to step back; (with *von*) to resign, to withdraw (from); to return (to), to recede; to subside (of a river); to diminish. (Ps. 38:12)

zurückweichen, 1. *ir.v.n.* (*aux.* s.) (with *vor*) to give way, to fall back, to give ground, to recede (before); to retreat, to withdraw, to shrink back (from); to yield, to give in. 2. *n.* withdrawal, recession, retreat. (John 18:6)

zurückwerfen, *ir.v.a.* to throw back; to reflect (rays); to repel, to repulse (an enemy). (Isa. 38:17)

zurüsten, *v.a.* to fit out, to equip; to prepare or get ready. (I Peter 3:20)

die Zusage (-n), assent, acceptance, promise, pledge. (Isa. 26:3)

zusagen, 1. *v.a.* (*einem etwas*) to promise. 2. *v.n.* (*aux.* h.) (*with dat.*) to accept (an invitation); to suit someone; to agree with someone (of food). (Ps. 33:4)

zusammenbeißen, *v.a.* to clench, to set (one's teeth). (Acts 7:54)

zusammenbringen, *ir.v.a.* to bring together, to join, to unite; to collect, to gather together, to amass (a fortune), to rally (troops). (John 11:52)

zusammenfassen, *v.a.* to embrace, to include, to combine, to comprise, to comprehend, to unite, to collect (one's thoughts, etc.); to summarize, to condense, to sum up. (Eph. 1:10)

zusammenfügen, *v.a.* to join (together), to unite, to combine; to fit into one another, to articulate; to pair, to match. (Matt. 19:6)

zusammenhalten, 1. *ir.v.a.* to hold together; to compare; to maintain, to keep going, to support. 2. *v.n.* (*aux.* h.) to hold or stick together; to be firm friends; to cohere. (Col. 2:19)

der Zusammenhang ("-e), connection, association; relationship, relation, correlation; cohesion, continuity, coherence; context.

zusammenkommen, *ir.v.n.* (*aux.* h.) to come together; to assemble; to meet. (Acts 2:6)
scharf mit einem zusammenkommen, to quarrel.

zusammenlegen, *v.a.* to place, lay, or put together; to pile up; to fold up; to collect, to contribute; to combine, to consolidate, to unite, to merge. (Rom. 15:26)

zusammenlesen, *ir.v.a.* to gather together, to collect. (Matt. 13:48)

zusammenreimen, 1. *v.a.* to understand, to make out. 2. *v.n.* to rhyme (with each other). 3. *v.r.* to make sense (of), to fit in. (Jer. 23:28)

zusammenrollen, *v.a.* to roll together. (Rev. 6:14)

zusammensammeln, *v.a.* to gather together. (Luke 15:13)

die Zusammensetzung, synthesis.

zuschicken, *v.a.* (*einem etwas*) to send on, to forward, to transmit, to remit (money), to consign (goods). (Matt. 26:53)

zuschließen, *ir.v.a.* to lock (up). (Gen. 2:21)

zusehen, 1. *ir.v.n.* (*aux.* h.) (*with dat.*) to look on, to watch, to witness; to wait and see, to stand by, to tolerate, to overlook; to look out for, to take care, to see to (it), to look after or to. 2. *n.* view; the role of spectator. (Matt. 3:8)

zusehends, *adv.* visibly, obviously, noticeably. (Acts 1:9)

zusetzen, 1. *v.a.* to add to, to replenish; to contribute; to mix up with; to lose, to sacrifice (money, etc.); to close, to obstruct. 2. *v.n.* (*aux.* h.) (*with dat.*) to press, to importune, to pester; to pursue closely, to attack vigorously. (Matt. 6:27)

zustehen, *ir.v.n.* (*aux.* h.) (*with dat.*) to belong to, to pertain, to be due to; to become, to suit. (Matt. 20:23)

zutragen, 1. *ir.v.a.* to carry or bring to; to tell, to repeat, to report. 2. *v.r.* to happen, to take place, to come to pass. (Acts 16:16)

der Zutritt (-e), access, entrance, admission, admittance.

zutun, 1. *ir.v.a.* to add to; to close, to shut. 2. *n.* assistance, help, cooperation. (Acts 11:24)

die Zuversicht, confidence, trust, faith (*auf,* in), reliance, hope; certainty, conviction. (Acts 28:15)
Zuversicht zu Gott, trust in God.

zuversichtlich, *adj.* confident, assured, positive, certain, undoubting, hopeful.

die Zuversichtlichkeit, trust, confidence; certainty, assurance, self-assurance.

zuvor, *adv.* before, previously, beforehand, first, formerly. (Matt. 5:24)

zuvörderst, *adv.* in the front rank, foremost; first of all, in the first place, first and foremost, to begin with. (Acts 3:26)

zuvorkommen, *ir.v.n.* (*aux.* s.) (*sep.*) (*with dat.*) to come first, to get in front of, to forestall, to anticipate; to prevent. (Rom. 12:10)

zuvorsagen, *v.a.* to tell before. (Matt. 24:25)

zuwege, *adv.: zuwege bringen,* to bring about, to effect, to bring to pass, to accomplish. (Acts 22:28)

zuwenden, 1. *reg. & ir.v.a.* (*einem etwas*) to turn to(wards), to give, to bestow (upon), to make a present (of), to let have, to devote (to). 2. *v.r.* (*with dat.*) to devote oneself (to), to apply oneself (to). (Acts 19:24)

der Zwang, force, coercion, compulsion, constraint, control, restraint; (moral) obligation, pressure; constriction. (Ps. 107:10)

der Zweck (-e), purpose, end, aim, goal.

zwei, 1. *num. adj.* two. 2. *f.* (-en) two. (Gen. 1:16)

zweierlei, *indec. adj.* of two kinds; twofold, different. (Deut. 25:13)

zweifach, *adj.* double, twofold.

der Zweifel (-), doubt, uncertainty, hesitation, misgiving, suspicion. (Phil. 2:14)

der Zweifelgeist, skepticism.

zweifeln, *v.n.* (*aux.* h.) to doubt, to question, to suspect, to be in doubt (about), to waver. (Matt. 14:31)

der Zweifler (-), doubter, skeptic. (James 1:8)

der Zweig (-e), branch, bough, twig; scion; department, section. (Ps. 104:12)

zweijährig, *adj.* of two years, two years old; biennial. (Matt. 2:16)

zweimal, *adv.* twice; double. (Mark 14:30)

zweischneidig, *adj.* two-edged. (Rev. 1:16)

zweizüngig, *adj.* double-tongued; double-faced, two-faced, shifty, insincere, hypocritical. (I Tim. 3:8)

zwiefach, zwiefältig, *adj.* twofold, double. (I Tim. 5:17; Matt. 23:15)

die Zwietracht, discord, dissension. (Luke 12:51)

der Zwilling (-e), twin; sign of Castor and Pollux. (Acts 28:11)

zwingen, 1. *ir.v.a.* to force, to compel, to constrain; to master, to overcome, to get the better of; to finish, to complete, to bring to an end, to cope with. 2. *v.r.* (with *zu*) to force oneself to (do, etc.). (Exod. 1:13)

zwölf, 1. *num. adj.* twelve. 2. *f.* the number twelve; a dozen. (Gen. 35:22)

zwölfmal, *adv.* twelve times; every month of the year. (Rev. 22:2)

Appendixes
Irregular and Semi-irregular Verbs

Infinitive	3rd-Person Present Indicative	Imperfect	Past Participle	English
backen	bäckt	buk	gebacken	bake
beginnen	beginnt	begann	begonnen	begin
beißen	beißt	biß	gebissen	bite
binden	bindet	band	gebunden	bind
bitten	bittet	bat	gebeten	ask
blasen	bläst	blies	geblasen	blow
bleiben	bleibt	blieb	geblieben	stay
brechen	bricht	brach	gebrochen	break
brennen	brennt	brannte	gebrannt	burn
bringen	bringt	brachte	gebracht	bring
denken	denkt	dachte	gedacht	think
dürfen	darf	durfte	gedurft	be allowed
essen	ißt	aß	gegessen	eat
fahren	fährt	fuhr	gefahren	go, drive
fallen	fällt	fiel	gefallen	fall
fangen	fängt	fing	gefangen	catch
finden	findet	fand	gefunden	find
fliegen	fliegt	flog	geflogen	fly
fliehen	flieht	floh	geflohen	flee
fließen	fließt	floß	geflossen	flow
fressen	frißt	fraß	gefressen	eat
frieren	friert	fror	gefroren	freeze
geben	gibt	gab	gegeben	give
gehen	geht	ging	gegangen	go
gewinnen	gewinnt	gewann	gewonnen	win
graben	gräbt	grub	gegraben	dig
haben	hat	hatte	gehabt	have
halten	hält	hielt	gehalten	hold, stop
helfen	hilft	half	geholfen	help
kennen	kennt	kannte	gekannt	know
kommen	kommt	kam	gekommen	come
können	kann	konnte	gekonnt	can, be able
lassen	läßt	ließ	gelassen	let, leave
laufen	läuft	lief	gelaufen	run
leiden	leidet	litt	gelitten	suffer
leihen	leiht	lieh	geliehen	loan
lesen	liest	las	gelesen	read
liegen	liegt	lag	gelegen	lie
messen	mißt	maß	gemessen	measure
mögen	mag	mochte	gemocht	like

Infinitive	3rd-Person Present Indicative	Imperfect	Past Participle	English
müssen	muß	mußtc	gcmußt	must
nehmen	nimmt	nahm	genommen	take
nennen	nennt	nannte	genannt	name, call
reiten	reitet	ritt	geritten	ride
rennen	rennt	rannte	gerannt	run
riechen	riecht	roch	gerochen	smell
saufen	säuft	soff	gesoffen	drink
scheinen	scheint	schien	geschienen	shine, seem
schießen	schießt	schoß	geschossen	shoot
schlafen	schläft	schlief	geschlafen	sleep
schlagen	schlägt	schlug	geschlagen	hit
schließen	schließt	schloß	geschlossen	close
schneiden	schneidet	schnitt	geschnitten	cut
schreiben	schreibt	schrieb	geschrieben	write
schreien	schreit	schrie	geschrie(e)n	scream
schweigen	schweigt	schwieg	geschwiegen	be silent
schwimmen	schwimmt	schwamm	geschwommen	swim
sehen	sieht	sah	gesehen	see
sein	ist	war	gewesen	be
senden	sendet	sandte	gesandt	send
singen	singt	sang	gesungen	sing
sinken	sinkt	sank	gesunken	sink
sitzen	sitzt	saß	gesessen	sit
sollen	soll	sollte	gesollt	ought
sprechen	spricht	sprach	gesprochen	talk, speak
springen	springt	sprang	gesprungen	jump
stehen	steht	stand	gestanden	stand
stehlen	stiehlt	stahl	gestohlen	steal
steigen	steigt	stieg	gestiegen	climb
sterben	stirbt	starb	gestorben	die
stinken	stinkt	stank	gestunken	stink
tragen	trägt	trug	getragcn	wcar, carry
treffen	trifft	traf	getroffen	meet
treten	tritt	trat	getreten	step
trinken	trinkt	trank	getrunken	drink
tun	tut	tat	getan	do
verlieren	verliert	verlor	verloren	lose
wachsen	wächst	wuchs	gewachsen	grow
waschen	wäscht	wusch	gewaschen	wash
wenden	wendet	wandte	gewandt	turn
werden	wird	wurde	geworden	become
werfen	wirft	warf	geworfen	throw
wiegen	wiegt	wog	gewogen	weigh
wissen	weiß	wußte	gewußt	know
wollen	will	wollte	gewollt	want
ziehen	zieht	zog	gezogen	pull

Books of the Bible

1. Old Testament (Das Alte Testament) (A.T.)

Das erste Buch Mose	(1.Mose)	Genesis
Das zweite Buch Mose	(2.Mose)	Exodus
Das dritte Buch Mose	(3.Mose)	Leviticus
Das vierte Buch Mose	(4.Mose)	Numbers
Das fünfte Buch Mose	(5.Mose)	Deuteronomy
Das Buch Josua	(Jos.)	Joshua
Das Buch der Richter	(Richt.)	Judges
Das Buch Ruth	(Ruth)	Ruth
Das erste Buch Samuel	(1.Sam.)	I Samuel
Das zweite Buch Samuel	(2.Sam.)	II Samuel
Das erste Buch von den Königen	(1.Kön.)	I Kings
Das zweite Buch von den Königen	(2.Kön.)	II Kings
Das erste Buch der Chronik	(1.Chron.)	I Chronicles
Das zweite Buch der Chronik	(2.Chron.)	II Chronicles
Das Buch Esra	(Esr.)	Ezra
Das Buch Nehemia	(Neh.)	Nehemiah
Das Buch Esther	(Esth.)	Esther
Das Buch Hiob	(Hiob)	Job
Der Psalter (Die Psalmen)	(Ps.)	Psalms
Die Sprüche Salomos	(Spr.)	Proverbs
Der Prediger Salomo	(Pred.)	Ecclesiastes
Das Hohelied Salomos	(Hohel.)	Song of Solomon
Jesaja	(Jes.)	Isaiah
Jeremia	(Jer.)	Jeremiah
Klagelieder Jeremia's	(Klagl.)	Lamentations
Hesekiel	(Hesek.)	Ezekiel
Daniel	(Dan.)	Daniel
Hosea	(Hos.)	Hosea
Joel	(Joel)	Joel
Amos	(Amos)	Amos
Obadja	(Obad.)	Obadiah
Jona	(Jon.)	Jonah
Micha	(Mich.)	Micah
Nahum	(Nah.)	Nahum
Habakuk	(Hab.)	Habakkuk
Zephanja	(Zeph.)	Zephaniah
Haggai	(Hagg.)	Haggai
Sacharja	(Sach.)	Zechariah
Maleachi	(Mal.)	Malachi

2. Apocrypha (Die Apokryphen)

Das Buch Judith	Judith
Die Weisheit Salomos	Wisdom
Das Buch Tobit	Tobit
Sprüche Jesus', des Sohnes Sirachs	Ecclesiasticus
Die Sprüche Baruch	Baruch
Das erste Buch der Makkabäer	I Maccabees
Das zweite Buch der Makkabäer	II Maccabees
Zusätze zum Buch Esther	The Rest of Esther
Zusätze zum Buch Daniel	The Rest of Daniel

3. New Testament (Das Neue Testament) (N.T.)

Das Evangelium des Matthäus	(Matth.)	Matthew
Das Evangelium des Markus	(Mark)	Mark
Das Evangelium des Lukas	(Luk.)	Luke
Das Evangelium des Johannes	(Joh.)	John
Die Apostelgeschichte des Lukas	(Apg.)	Acts
Der Brief des Paulus an die Römer		
(Der Römerbrief)	(Röm.)	Romans
Der erste Brief des Paulus an die Korinther		
(Der erste Korintherbrief)	(1.Kor.)	I Corinthians
Der zweite Brief des Paulus an die Korinther		
(Der zweite Korintherbrief)	(2.Kor.)	II Corinthians
Der Brief des Paulus an die Galater		
(Der Galaterbrief)	(Gal.)	Galatians
Der Epheserbrief*	(Eph.)	Ephesians
Der Philipperbrief	(Phil.)	Philippians
Der Kolosserbrief	(Kol.)	Colossians
Der erste Thessalonicherbrief	(1.Thess.)	I Thessalonians
Der zweite Thessalonicherbrief	(2.Thess.)	II Thessalonians
Der erste Timotheusbrief	(1.Tim.)	I Timothy
Der zweite Timotheusbrief	(2.Tim.)	II Timothy
Der Titusbrief	(Tit.)	Titus
Der Philemonbrief	(Philm.)	Philemon
Der erste Brief des Petrus	(1.Petr.)	I Peter
Der zweite Brief des Petrus	(2.Petr.)	II Peter
Der erste Brief des Johannes	(1.Joh.)	I John
Der zweite Brief des Johannes	(2.Joh.)	II John
Der dritte Brief des Johannes	(3.Joh.)	III John
Der Brief an die Hebräer		
(Der Hebräerbrief)	(Hebr.)	Hebrews
Der Brief des Jakobus	(Jak.)	James
Der Brief des Judas	(Judas)	Jude
Die Offenbarung des Johannes	(Offenb.)	Revelation

---

*Only the short form is indicated for the remaining Pauline Epistles.